Whomever He Wills

A Surprising Display of Sovereign Mercy

Whomever He Wills

A Surprising Display of Sovereign Mercy

Edited by
Matthew M. Barrett
and
Thomas J. Nettles

 Founders Press

Committed to historic Baptist principles
Cape Coral, Florida

Published by

Founders Press

Committed to historic Baptist principles

P.O. Box 150931 • Cape Coral, FL 33915
Phone (239) 772–1400 • Fax: (239) 772–1140
Electronic Mail: founders@founders.org or
Website: http://www.founders.org

©2012 Founders Press

Printed in the United States of America

ISBN: 978–0–9849498–0–9

Cover Design by Elizabeth Barrett

Dedication

To the Apostle Paul,

the single greatest literary influence on our lives and whose question, "For now am I seeking the favor of men, or of God?" has weighed heavy on the conscience as motivation for both of our ministries.

Contents

Contributors

Thomas K. Ascol (PhD, Southwestern Baptist Theological Seminary) has for twenty-five years been Senior Pastor of Grace Baptist Church in Cape Coral, Florida. As Executive Director of the Founders Ministries, he also edits the *Founders Journal*. He projected a vision for doctrinal and spiritual reformation in churches and in the personal lives of pastors through editing and contributing to *Dear Timothy: Letters on Pastoral Ministry*. He regularly contributes to other publications.

Matthew Barrett (PhD, The Southern Baptist Theological Seminary) is Assistant Professor of Christian Studies at California Baptist University. He is also the founder and executive editor of *Credo Magazine*, an evangelical publication focusing on the foundational doctrines of the Christian faith. He has contributed articles and reviews to a variety of theological journals and is the author of several forthcoming books, including *Reclaiming Monergism: The Case for Sovereign Grace in Effectual Calling and Regeneration; 40 Questions on Salvation* (co-authored with Gregg Allison); *John Owen on the Christian Life* (co-authored with Michael A.G. Haykin), and *The Grace of Godliness: An Introduction to Doctrine and Piety in the Canons of Dort*.

Andrew Davis (PhD, The Southern Baptist Theological Seminary) has been the Senior Pastor of First Baptist Church in Durham, North Carolina since 1998. Previously he followed the call of the Lord to Tokushima, Japan, where he was involved in church planting through the International Mission Board. Davis has contributed to the 9Marks journal and his sermons are featured on The Gospel Coalition website.

Mark DeVine (PhD, The Southern Baptist Theological Seminary) is Associate Professor of Divinity, History and Doctrine at Beeson Divinity School in Birmingham, Alabama. He is a contributor to many theological journals and books, and speaks regularly on the emerging church. DeVine is the author of *Bonhoeffer Speaks Today: Following Jesus at All Costs*. He has served as pastor of several churches and from 1998 to 2000 was an SBC missionary in Bangkok, Thailand. DeVine serves as pastor at First Baptist Church of Helena, Alabama.

Timothy George (ThD, Harvard University) taught historical theology at The Southern Baptist Theological Seminary from 1978-88 when he became founding Dean of Beeson Divinity School where he continues to maintain a consistent teaching load. He serves as executive editor for *Christianity Today*, and on the editorial advisory boards of *The Harvard Theological Review, Christian History and Books & Culture*. In addition to his contributions to both scholarly and popular journals, George has written more than 20 books including his internationally-used *Theology of the Reformers* and *Amazing Grace*. An ordained minister, he has been pastor of churches in Tennessee, Alabama and Massachusetts.

Tom Hicks (PhD, The Southern Baptist Theological Seminary) is Pastor of Discipleship at Morningview Baptist Church in Montgomery, Alabama, a place that knows him well since he had been nurtured in his Christian faith there as a young person. He has contributed articles and reviews to a variety of theological journals.

Steven Lawson (DMin, Reformed Theological Seminary) is Senior Pastor of Christ Fellowship Baptist Church in Mobile, Alabama. He is the author of several books including *Foundations of Grace, The Unwavering Resolve of Jonathan Edwards, The Expository Genius of John Calvin*, and *The Gospel Focus of Charles Spurgeon*. Lawson's pulpit ministry takes him around the world, preaching the gospel in many countries as well as sustaining a busy conference schedule in the United States.

Thomas J. Nettles (PhD, Southwestern Baptist Theological Seminary) is Professor of Historical Theology at The Southern Baptist Theological Seminary in Louisville, Kentucky. Nettles has published frequently on issues in Baptist history including *By His Grace and For His Glory, Baptists and the Bible* (co-authored with L. Russ Bush), and a three-volume work on Baptist identity entitled *The Baptists*.

Jeff Robinson (PhD, The Southern Baptist Theological Seminary) is Senior Pastor of Philadelphia Baptist Church in Birmingham, Alabama, where his ministry calling was immediately put to use by the greatest outbreak of tornadoes in Alabama history. Having already achieved distinction in the field of journalism in his home state, Jeff served as Director of News and Information for *Towers*, a publication of The Southern Baptist Theological Seminary. He is co-authoring with Michael A.G. Haykin, *The Great Commission Vision of John Calvin*.

Ben Rogers is a PhD candidate in historical theology at The Southern Baptist Theological Seminary in Louisville, Kentucky. He has served as pastor of churches in Mississippi and Indiana and contributed articles to a variety of theological journals on historical figures such as John Bunyan.

Thomas R. Schreiner (PhD, Fuller Theological Seminary) is James Buchanan Harrison Professor of New Testament Interpretation, and Associate Dean of Scripture and Interpretation at The Southern Baptist Theological Seminary. Schreiner is also Pastor of Preaching at Clifton Baptist Church. He is the author of numerous books, including *Still Sovereign: Contemporary Perspectives on Election, Foreknowledge, and Grace* (with Bruce A. Ware), *New Testament Theology, Paul, Apostle of God's Glory in Christ, The Race Set Before Us*, and commentaries on Galatians, Romans, and 1 Peter.

David Schrock is a PhD candidate in systematic theology at The Southern Baptist Theological Seminary and Pastor of Calvary Baptist Church in Seymour, Indiana. He has contributed articles and reviews to a variety of theological journals, and contributes often to The Gospel Coalition blog.

Bruce A. Ware (PhD, Fuller Theological Seminary) is Professor of Christian Theology at The Southern Baptist Theological Seminary in Louisville, Kentucky. Ware has served as President of The Evangelical Theological Society and is the author of *Still Sovereign: Contemporary Perspectives on Election, Foreknowledge, and Grace* (with Thomas R. Schreiner); *God's Lesser Glory: The Diminished God of Open Theism, God's Greater Glory: The Exalted God of Scripture and the Christian Faith*, and *Father, Son and Holy Spirit*. He has published an important theology for children entitled *Big Truths for Young Hearts: Teaching and Learning the Greatness of God*.

Stephen J. Wellum (PhD, Trinity Evangelical Divinity School) is Professor of Christian Theology at The Southern Baptist Theological Seminary in Louisville, Kentucky. Wellum is Editor for the *Southern Baptist Journal of Theology*. He is also the author of *Kingdom through Covenant: A Biblical-Theological Understanding of the Covenants* (co-authored with Peter J. Gentry), and has contributed chapters to books such as *The Deity of Christ, Reclaiming the Center*, and *Believer's Baptism*. Currently Wellum is working on a volume on Christology in the Foundations of Evangelical Theology series (Crossway).

viii   Whomever He Wills

Fred Zaspel (PhD, Free University of Amsterdam) is currently a pastor at the Reformed Baptist Church of Franconia, Pennsylvania, while serving as interim Senior Pastor at New Hyde Park Baptist Church on Long Island. He combines these ministries with an adjunct professorship of Systematic Theology at Calvary Baptist Seminary in Lansdale, Pennsylvania. He is the author of *The Continuing Relevance of Divine Law; The Theology of Fulfillment; Jews, Gentiles, & the Goal of Redemptive History; New Covenant Theology* (with Tom Wells); *The Theology of B.B. Warfield: A Systematic Summary*, and *Warfield on the Christian Life.*

Foreword

I am a Calvinist, but I was not born that way. Like everyone else I know, I came into this world as a pureblooded Pelagian, a sinner of the most original sort, *incurvatus in se*, as Martin Luther described the fallen human condition. In school, my teachers told me that I was bright, articulate, had a way with words, and that if I worked really hard, I could make it on my own. I believed them. During one of my junior high school years, I decided to read all of Ralph Waldo Emerson's essays. My favorite was the one titled "Self Reliance." Entering young adulthood, my philosophy of life was similar to the sentiment expressed on a package of Ginseng-flavored tea I received as a present not long ago.

> Gifts count for nothing; will alone is great; all things give way before it, soon or late.... Each well-born soul must win what it deserves....The fortunate is he whose earnest purpose never swerves. Whose slightest action or inaction serves the one great aim. Why, even death stands still, and waits an hour sometimes for such a will.[1]

"Amazing Grace, how sweet the sound," was the favorite hymn in the Baptist church where I grew up. But there was nothing really very "amazing" about it as I understood it. I believed the Bible, I loved Jesus, I had been saved and baptized, and even called to preach the Gospel which I did fervently as a teenage youth evangelist. But even so, I had a transcendence-starved view of God. I knew and thought little about God's infinite greatness, his aseity, his sovereignty, his eternal purpose of grace, his providence or his awesome love that burns with holy fire. I never heard a sermon on Hebrews 12:29.

---

[1] Ella Wheeler Wilcox, "Will," in *Maurine and Other Poems* (Chicago, IL: W. B. Conkey Co., 1888), 144.

Luther once wrote that "I did not learn my theology all at once, but I had to search deeper for it where my temptations (*Anfechtungen*) took me… not understanding, reading, or speculation, but living, nay, rather dying and being damned make a theologian."[2] Thus it was with me.

On my way to becoming a Reformed theologian, life happened to me. My mother suffered severely from polio and my father, who died in prison when I was twelve years of age, was an alcoholic. How could I make sense of any of that? Then there was the first funeral I ever preached when as a young pastor I tried to say some words of comfort over the fallen body of my friend Steve. He was exactly my age but had been shot and killed in Vietnam trying to help a buddy back into the helicopter. As I stood over that flag-draped casket in the cemetery, I could not help but think, "Why him? Why not me?" How much does God have to do with a human life? What is it all about?

Through these and many other "troubles, toils, and snares," I was forced to my knees. I realized that I had not, and could not, make it on my own. I began to study the Bible with a new intensity. The Gospel of John—my favorite—and Paul's letters to the Romans and Galatians provoked new questions and led to deeper insight. The three questions Paul asked in 1 Corinthians 4:7 (which I later discovered were so important to Augustine in his struggles with the Pelagians) seared themselves into my soul: "For who makes you different from anyone else? What do you have that you did not receive? And if you did receive it, why do you boast as though you did not?" I also remember pondering the meaning of Proverbs 16:33, a verse brought to my attention by Harriett Bond, a godly Bible teacher: "The lot is cast into the lap, but its every decision is from the Lord."

As a theological student at Harvard Divinity School, I was plunged into the close reading of Reformation texts. I devoured the writings of Luther, Calvin, Cranmer, Bucer, Zwingli, as well as the Anabaptists and the Separatists and Puritans of England. While they did not all speak with the same voice, the reformers shared a common passion for a full-sized God—His grandeur, glory, and grace.

I also became a student of Baptist history and read seriously for the first time the sturdy, God-saturated works of John Bunyan, Benjamin Keach, John Gill, Andrew Fuller, Roger Williams, Isaac Backus, and the incomparable Charles Haddon Spurgeon. This was mountain air. No one had ever told me that such theology and spirituality constituted the central stream (though not the only current, to be sure) of my own Baptist heritage. When I was called to the Southern Baptist Theological Seminary to teach church history and theology in 1978, one of the members of the

[2] WA TR 1, 146.

search committee said to me, "Timothy, no one here at Southern has held such views for the past 100 years!" That was perhaps an exaggeration, but in the first edition of my *Theology of the Reformers*, I paid tribute to my colleagues for their toleration of "one who has argued, somewhat against the prevailing consensus, that Reformed and Baptist are not mutually exclusive terms."

The essays in this volume introduce the reader to a centuries-long conversation, one that goes back at least to Paul's response to his unnamed interlocutor in Romans 6. The issue of divine sovereignty and human responsibility in the process of salvation is perennial in Christian theology. Like a bubbling underground spring, it can flow along sometimes for centuries without an eruption, and then suddenly it shoots forth like a geyser for all to see. In the early church, Augustine's debates with Pelagius (and the Pelagians who may have been worse than their master) raised questions that are with us still. What is the relationship of predestination and foreknowledge? Are human beings merely wounded or completely debilitated by the effects of the fall? Is human perfection a possibility in this life? If not, why not? Would Adam have died had he never sinned? What is grace and how does it function in the life of faith?

These questions were taken up once again in the Middle Ages, notably by Thomas Aquinas who almost invariably came down on the Augustinian side of things. They were also debated at Oxford and Paris in the centuries leading up to the Reformation where they were hammered out again in the controversy over the bondage of the will between Luther and Erasmus, a debate that resounded through later discussions between Calvinists and Socinians, between Remonstrants and the Dutch Reformed party that triumphed at the Synod of Dort (1618–1619). To say that such debates were all concerned with a similar problematic does not mean that they were the same in content or focus. In the English-speaking world, disputes about election, grace, and full human participation in God's salvific mission took many twists and turns. Entire libraries are filled with learned discussions of the theology of grace in figures as disparate as William Perkins, Lancelot Andrewes, Benjamin Keach, Thomas Grantham, Charles Chauncy, Jonathan Edwards, John Wesley, George Whitefield, Andrew Fuller, Abraham Booth, and on and on.

I point this out to alert the reader to the fact that this volume represents just the latest sounding on the theological Doppler radar. It is not the first word, nor the last word, nor (I believe the contributors would agree) the definitive word. But the essays here do represent a serious engagement by a team of thoughtful Baptist pastors and theologians to come to grips with a major tension inherent in the Christian Gospel itself. As such, it deserves to be read, discussed, and responded to. It is worth pointing out that this book itself is offered as a response to another recently published volume which attempts to do the same thing from a somewhat different perspective.

Frankly, I commend the contributors of both of these books for tackling this issue with conviction and charity toward one another. Dr. Frank Page, President and CEO of the Executive Committee of the Southern Baptist Convention, has observed that our differing opinions over the details of Calvinism is a family discussion and should not become a source of division and acrimony among us. Where that has happened already, we (both sides) need to repent and learn better how to speak the truth to one another in love. If Wesley and Whitefield, the two greatest awakeners of the 18th century revival, could disagree strongly about such matters and yet work together to bring the saving Gospel of Christ to lost men and women, how can we do any less?

For more than twenty years now, I have been told that the Calvinism debate would cause the next great split within the Southern Baptist Convention. I don't believe it. In the year 2000 I was asked to write the SBC doctrine study on the brewing controversy over Calvinism within our denomination. (A second edition of this book was released in 2011 by Crossway, *Amazing Grace: God's Pursuit, Our Response*.) In that study I quoted these words by Paige Patterson:

> Southern Baptists are a people who believe the Bible to be the Word of God as their final authority, that salvation is by grace through faith alone and that adult-like faith witnessed by believer's baptism provides a testimony to a watching world. If we believe those things all fall within the purview of the Baptist faith, then there's plenty of room for all of us in these various emphases that we bring. There's plenty of room under the umbrella for anyone who is anything from a one- to five-point Calvinist.[3]

That was true in the year 2000 and it is still true now a dozen years later. The SBC should be capacious enough for Paige Patterson and Al Mohler, for Steve Lemke and Mark Dever.

I would like to repeat here what I said at a conference on Baptist identity several years ago.

> Let us confess freely and humbly that none of us understands completely how divine sovereignty and human responsibility coalesce in the grace-wrought acts of repentance and faith. Let us talk about these matters and, let us seek to persuade one another, but let this be done with gentleness

---

[3] n.a., "SBC president Patterson expands on various points of Calvinism," *Alabama Baptist* (2 December 1999), 11.

and respect as we are admonished in 1 Peter 3:15. Let us speak the truth
to one another in love for truth without love is not really truth. It is rather
a perverted form of puffed up pride, just as love without truth is not really love, but mere mushy sentimentality. Above all, let this discussion
not hinder our joining hands and hearts to work together as evangelists
and as Baptists across our theological differences. Let us join together
with Charles Haddon Spurgeon, perhaps the greatest Baptist preacher
who ever lived, in his open, unfettered appeal to the lost, as seen in his
wonderful sermon on John 6:37, "Him that cometh to me I will in no-
wise cast out."[4]

That is the tone we need whether you lean in one way or another on the
decrees of God and how they are ordered from all eternity. Let us get this
right and then when we get to heaven we can spend a few thousand years
in the theology seminar room up there sorting through the details, and we
will understand it by and by.

But this side of glory, we still see through a glass darkly. We are not
there yet. Because of that, the kind of discussion represented by this book
is worth pursuing with candor, integrity, and goodwill. It is important because we stand on common ground in affirming without reservation the
total truthfulness of God's written Word, the Holy Scriptures. It is important because truth matters. To sweep seminal issues of the faith under the
rug will not lead to true lasting unity in the faith. It is important, surely, because in all that we do as believers, churches, denominations, no less than
as theologians, scholars, and pastors, it must be the sincere desire of our
hearts that the triune God of holiness and love, the God who spared not
his Son but gave him up for us all, our sovereign King and dear heavenly
Father be glorified in ever increasing measure.

> Timothy George
> Founding Dean of Beeson Divinity School
> General Editor of the *Reformation Commentary on Scripture*

---

[4] David S. Dockery and Timothy George, *Building Bridges* (Nashville, TN:
Convention Press, 2007), 51.

Preface

A century ago in his *Plan of Salvation* B.B. Warfield argued powerfully that if a Theist allows the necessary implications of the Theism he has already embraced, he must be a Calvinist. That is to say, soteriological Calvinism is but the implicate, the necessary consequence of Theism. It is simply God being God.

Moreover, soteriological Calvinism is the embodiment of the prophet Jonah's declaration, "Salvation is of the Lord!" (Jonah 2:9). It is the outworking of the proposition that salvation is God's doing, that it is His gracious gift to undeserving sinners, and that He saves in such a way that only He receives the glory for it (1 Corinthians 1:26-31; Ephesians 2:8-10). If we adhere to these propositions we are Calvinists.

Compelling as such reasoning is, of course, we are not left to ground our theology in deductions and logical arguments merely. We embrace soteriological Calvinism, ultimately, because we find it to be taught us in the Scriptures. We fully expect God's redemptive plan to be in perfect keeping with Himself, and such logical consistency is therefore inevitable. But whatever the logical necessities and implications—and for that matter, whatever questions may remain unresolved in our minds and whatever tensions we may feel—at the end of the day we hold these doctrines because we believe them to be biblical.

But this discussion is important on another level. A right understanding of these issues is not a matter of exegetical faithfulness only. It is a question of gospel faithfulness also. Please understand. I want very much to affirm that my brothers and sisters in Christ who differ with me on these questions are, in fact, my brothers and sisters. We are joined together in the gospel of Christ, and I rejoice in that. And surely we must keep this unity in plain view whenever we pursue this discussion. Yet if our unity is a unity in the gospel, then the closer we come to gospel issues the more important doctrinal accuracy becomes—and the more important it is for us to discuss our differences frankly in attempt to clear them away. And although I am not prepared to say that "the five points" *are* the gospel, I heartily agree with Charles Spurgeon who described them as the five bright lights that illumine the gospel. And certainly all sides must agree at least that the issues taken up in this book do, in fact, bear immediately on the gospel we all embrace. If this is the case, then each new generation of Christians must feel compelled to seek ever-increasing clarity concerning them.

Further, these doctrines are worship-shaping doctrines. It is important to God that we know that He saves only in such a way that only he receives the glory for it. We sing "Thank you, Lord, for saving my soul!" And well we should. And we should sing it out of a deep, felt sense of rescue. Indeed, we are concerned that it is just this notion of salvation as *rescue* that is absent in so much of contemporary worship. And so, aware of this deficiency, we want to affirm with all our souls that *God saves sinners* in every sense that Scripture reveals, that it is *His* salvation from first to last. Recognizing the great truth that God has not only saved us but also that for our joy He has revealed that salvation to us in the sweeping grandeur of His eternal purpose, we want to explore that saving revelation in all its glorious implications. We want to understand the gospel in light of this divine mission of rescue so that our worship of the Triune God may be brought to its full height and that our own joy may be correspondingly deepened. We want to sense the thrill of soteriological particularism that exultingly sings with understanding, "Thank you, Lord, for saving *my* soul!" Or, better, we want with rapturous joy to sing with the apostle John, "See what kind of love the Father has given to *us* that *we* should be called the children of God! And *we* are!" To worship God in a way that he is deserving, and for the joy of basking in the full sunlight of his saving love, we want not only to discover and believe but also to sing and to proclaim that we who are saved are the objects of a love that was set on us before the world began—indeed, a love that in time overcame our resistance, conquered our enmity, and wooed us to our Redeemer in faith. In short, a love that did for us all that was required of us.

This, in turn, is why (odd as it may seem) we love the doctrine of total depravity and human inability. It is essential to a worship that is worthy of God that we recognize the depths of our lostness. A right understanding of this great divine rescue hinges on it. Similarly, our ability to sing "To the praise of His glorious grace!" turns on our grasp of the divine initiative in salvation and the efficacy of God's saving grace. The song of the redeemed— "Worthy are you... for you were slain, and by your blood you ransomed people for God *out of* every tribe and language and people and nation" —is likewise a song grounded in the notion of substitutional particularism. And for eternity our song of praise to God will be nothing less than one of praise for the triumphant success of His grace that not only taught our hearts to fear and then relieved those fears in Christ, but a grace that infallibly brought us home to glory, according to His purpose. These truths are not mere incidentals. This is the stuff of worship.

These are the reasons for this discussion. And these are the motivations behind the contributors to this book. It is not party spirit but worship. Not personal prejudice but jealousy for God that has grown out of a deep and humbling sense of rescue. They do not mean to say that those who disagree are not Christians. But neither do they mean to say that these issues are therefore unimportant. These issues are essential to a consistent Theism. They are essential to any confession of divine rescue. They are an essential part of the very fabric of the biblical revelation of divine salvation. They are essential to a right understanding of the gospel. They are essential to a worship that would rightly acknowledge God as the savior of sinners. And they are basic to a realized joy in God's salvation.

> Lost was I and helpless, damnation deserved,
> Yet in my proud mind, thought 'twould never be served.
> No cares for my God, no concerns for my pride,
> My sin I would keep—knew no reason to hide.
>
> But God, rich in mercy and grace all divine
> Had chosen to save me, despite my designs.
> He said he would love me and make me His son,
> For reasons unknown—explanations I've none.
>
> To save me He paid such an infinite cost –
> His dear Son from glory He sent to my cross!
> Laid all my sin on Him and punished Him there,
> For me, who for Him would not ever have cared.
>
> Then to me He came, and with o'erwhelming grace
> He drew me to Him Who had taken my place.
> I saw then in Him the great Savior alone,
> Went running to take Him and make Him my own.
>
> He took me, and oh, with what gladness I find –
> He loves me and leads me with gentleness kind!
> What mercy, what love, and what grace, oh so free!
> My God unto thee shall my praise ever be!
>   (Fred G. Zaspel, 1995)

Fred G. Zaspel
Author of *The Theology of B.B. Warfield: A Systematic Summary*
Pastor at Reformed Baptist Church of Franconia, PA.

Postscript

The editors submit this book and its several arguments with a commitment of heart to these truths. God, through them, has transformed our lives and given us a deep complacency in submission to the will of God, trust in his infinite wisdom, and a hunger to see his glory manifest in all things. We want to send the reader forward with the words of Luther Rice (1783-1837), that great soul that was responsible largely for the formation of the General Missionary Convention in 1814, the first nationwide foreign mission organization among Baptists in the United States.

> This you are aware is not only an item in my creed, but enters into the very ground-work of the hope of immortality and glory, that has become established in my bosom; and constitutes the basis of the submission and joyfulness found in my religious experience. Unless it were possible, which it is not, for God to make some mistake as to what it is best should be developed in the system adopted and pursued by him! Why should it not be the very joy of our bosoms, that he has "foreordained whatsoever comes to pass?" What can real benevolence desire, but that every thing should "come to pass" in the wisest and best manner? To the wisest and best ultimate end? Could not an infinitely wise and good God ordain every thing to come to pass in this very way, and to this very end? Such, too, being the fact, is it not evidently the duty and happiness of every one to give up himself in absolute submission to the will of God; and to be pleased that all things are at the disposal and under the control of this infinitely wise and good Being.[1]

Matthew Barrett
Tom J. Nettles

---

[1] Luther Rice in J. B. Taylor, ed. *Memoir of the Rev. Luther Rice* (Baltimore, MD: Armstrong and Berry, 1840), 327

Introduction

Paul warns against provoking one another (Galatians 5:26). Among the works of the flesh are "rivalries, dissensions, divisions" (Galatians 5:20). Neither the editors nor the authors of this book have any desire to violate the principles of biblical godliness and brotherhood in extending this theological discussion. Polemical discussion offers too much opportunity for all the evils mentioned above. We hope, therefore, to approach this book in a way to avoid creating fertile ground for the growth of enmity, envy, slander, provocation to evil of any kind. This is not to be a work of the flesh, but one consistent with the fruit of the Spirit. The purpose of this kind of engagement is that all who engage the discussion will become more knowledgeable of Bible truth and thus have a way cleared for themselves and others for greater conformity to Christ in personal life and a purer enunciation of the gospel in public ministry. In principle we affirm and appreciate the stated intention of the authors of *Whosoever Will* in their introductory comments entitled "Differing Views, United Spirit."[1]

It All Comes Down to Soteriology

While the specific topics selected for treatment in this volume parallel those that the writers of *Whosoever Will* chose to address, the justification for their inclusion in another discussion goes much further back in theological history and far transcends in significance this particular denominational engagement. The question as to how God saves sinners has been the subject of enquiry since God told Satan that the woman's seed would crush his head (Genesis 3:15). That promise in itself provides matter for grasping

---

[1] David L Allen and Steve W. Lemke, "Introduction," in *Whosoever Will: A Biblical-Theological Critique of Five-Point Calvinism*, ed. David L. Allen and Steve W. Lemke (Nashville, TN: B&H, 2010), 8, 9.

the inter-relationship between divine promise and determination and all the historical events and human decisions that eventually and certainly in the fullness of time brought it to pass. The promise of a redeemer, which absorbed the minds of the prophets (who in themselves were marvels of providence and direct divine intervention) with wonder and challenged even the intellect of angels (Isaiah 52:3–53; 1 Peter 1:10–12), was immediately trampled on by false teachers and defended with amazing ardor by apostles (Galatians). The promise created greater mysteries even as its revelation clarified other mysteries (Romans 9–11), and will be the source of eternal adoration and exclamation of all the redeemed (Revelation 5; 22:1–5).

Every theological discussion in the history of the church eventually dissolves into soteriological implications. Christology is a worthy subject of study simply from the staggering claim that the eternally generated Son of God took on a temporally generated human frame, the uncreated became one in person with the created, the intrinsically impeccable was indivisibly united in person with a nature that must be tempted and proven, the One whose very person constitutes the reality of righteousness achieved by dint of travail of soul, a life-course of obedience to the will of the Father, and constant vigilance in the face of evil powers a righteousness to be imputed to all those that would trust Him. The terms of Christology, however, finally find their most coherent framework in the context of soteriology, since it was "for us men and for our salvation" that the Word was made flesh and dwelt among us. Our understanding of the inter-personal relations of the Triune God depends largely on inferences drawn from the economy of salvation, that which each person of the Trinity does to save sinful man. So the same could be noted in discussions about the church, the meaning of the ordinances and the historical perversion of the ordinances into sacraments, the presence of evil in the world and in humanity, the purpose of this present world, and the issue of eternal consignment of persons to joy or woe. Addressing the subjects of this book is not mere doctrinal jangling but unfolds the concern with truth that should be at dead-center in the affections of every creature and most assuredly the most vital concern of every person that claims to be saved by divine grace. What view of our salvation gives one the clearest channel for the pure knowledge that he exists for the glory of God (Ephesians 1:11–14)? Indeed, we want the spirit of wisdom and revelation in the knowledge of God that shows the unfading hope of His calling us, some unalloyed understanding of the riches of His glorious inheritance in the saints, and some way to adore the immeasurable greatness of His power toward us who believe. We want confidence that the gospel is indeed the power of God unto salvation.

Whomever He Wills and Whosoever Wills

The title for this book is taken from a biblical text. The ESV translation of Romans 9:18 states, "So then he has mercy on whomever he wills, and he hardens whomever he wills." It is a startling, but eminently clear, truth of divine revelation. It is as much a biblical idea as is the title "Whosoever Will," and conceptually precedes and determines the latter. As the subtitle indicates, we believe that the mercy of God should never cease to surprise us and its sovereign distribution gives no cause for resistance or the histrionics of righteous indignation. How surprised must Zacchaeus have been when Jesus invited Himself to eat at his home, resulting in salvation coming to that house. He hurried down from the tree and received Jesus joyfully, while the crowd grumbled at this surprising display of sovereign mercy (Luke 19:6, 7). Jesus was undisturbed by this disapproval for He had come "to seek and to save the lost" (Luke 19:10). Amazing! Surprising! And just how surprised was that Samaritan woman when a Jewish man dared to speak to her and ask a favor—and then led her to think about what it really means to be satisfied, to know and worship God even after blowing her moral cover. To her He revealed His omniscience and His trans-national, trans-ethnic purpose of gathering a people to be God-worshippers (John 4:7–42). She, as well as the rest of that Samaritan town, was joyfully surprised at this sovereign intervention of mercy in the visitation of the Messiah Himself to their village. Oh, how marvelous, that God would seek and save rebels and sinners and the most unlikely, the non-wise, the poor, the un-eugenic, and the nothings, "so that all flesh would be prohibited from boasting before the eyes of God" (1 Corinthians 1:29).

Jesus had announced that such would be the case when He went public with His ministry. Immediately after garnering popular approval in His hometown, He reminded them that in the Old Testament though there were lepers aplenty in Israel, only Naaman, a hated Syrian was cleansed; and though there was a multitude of hungry widows in Israel, Elijah was sent to give sustenance to one in Zarephath in the land of Sidon. The synagogue crowd did not respond well to this but postured themselves as righteously indignant and sought immediately to rid the world of this imposter that did not respect their position as first-in-line for Messianic goodies. He had dared show that the mercy of God, because it was indeed mercy, had no obligations to any based on a prior fitness to be its beneficiaries. He had dared to demonstrate even from their Scriptures, that in the most extreme of conditions and executed by two of their most celebrated prophets, the relative moral positions of God and man rendered utter sovereignty the only appropriate way to envision any merciful intervention of the Great I Am. Jesus' words certainly took them by surprise, so shocked their contrived moral sensibilities that murderous rage seemed an entirely defensible response.

Mercy still outrages because we do not want to be surprised by it; its intrinsic sovereignty is the very thing we try to suck out of it. Oh sure, God is powerful and is sovereign; to say less would be to have no God at all. But we can redefine sovereignty so that He relinquishes His own wisdom, changes the character of His mercy, and puts just a bit of human merit as a warrant for His display of grace by our contention that none of these will operate apart from human consent clearing the path. But the Bible still insists that mercy is an absolutely sovereign display of the divine goodness in glorifying His righteousness by saving a group of His own selection in spite of their unrighteousness. "But God having resident within his very being a richness in mercy, and specifically on account of the great electing love with which He loved us, us, the very ones dead in trespasses, made us alive together with Christ—our state of salvation arising completely from grace" (Ephesians 2:4, 5). While we live in malice, and envy, and in captivity to pride and passion and pleasure, hating others and in turn being hated, God appears in goodness and lovingkindness, and, ignoring the fact that we have no works of righteousness (nor do we intend to do any) and only works that invite His righteous unspeakable wrath, out of sheer mercy he saved us. Regeneration, justification, the hope of eternity, all the gifts of His grace, have their source in a surprising display of sovereign mercy (Titus 3:3–7). None should think it harsh, or in any sense unjust, or find any personal warrant for revolt when we see that God shows mercy on whomever He wills.

In the end all the doctrines of soteriology funnel into this great over-arching proposition cementing the reality of God-centeredness in all the issues of Creation, Providence, Revelation and Redemption. All the individual truths with which we deal are birthed from this august and all-consuming matrix of the divine sovereignty. All these truths we discuss, and all others beside, are manifestations of the wisdom by which God reveals all the propensities and intrinsic potentialities of his infinitely glorious and unchallengeable character (Romans 9:19–24). "Consequently, therefore, He is merciful toward whomever He wills, and on the other hand He hardens whomever He wills."

We are trying to provide an expanded viewpoint to be considered alongside, and frankly in many places as a corrective to, the volume entitled *Whosoever Will.* That title is taken from Revelation 22:17. The word "whosoever" from the KJV is used 70 times in the Old Testament and 109 times in the New Testament. In the New Testament it often translates a definite article or a relative pronoun (he who, she who, those who, the one who, etc.) and is defined in terms of a finite verb such as "breaks," "kills," "shall humble," "shall put away," "shall give," "shall call," "shall confess." The results of the action for "the one who" or "whosoever" commits the action is then normally stated such as, "Whosoever shall offend one of these little ones that believe in me, it is better for him that a millstone were hanged about his neck, and he were cast into the sea" (Mark 9:42). Again the relative pronoun defined by the verb in Matthew 12:32 gives parameters that are applied to specific cases: "Whosoever might say a word against the son of man, it will be forgiven him; but on the other hand, whosoever might say [a word] against the Holy Spirit, it will be forgiven him neither in this world nor in the world to come."

At other times, and the greatest percentage of times by the apostle John, "Whosoever" translates the word for "all" and is usually combined with the relative pronoun and has the same effect of the relative pronoun used alone when given definition by the verb. "Whosoever is born of God [All those having been begotten of God] doth not commit [continually commit] sin" (1 John 3:9). So John 3:16, "Whosoever believeth in him [All which are believing into him] shall not perish." We find the same form in John 6:37, the word "all" with a relative pronoun and a verb clause translated "All that the Father giveth me shall come to me." It could just as easily be translated "Whosoever the Father gives to me, will come to me." These "whosoevers" pile up in a variety of situations and express a wide spectrum of responses and actions that people of different characters have to the commands they receive and the options that are placed before them.

The phrase "whosoever will" is the combination of the definite article *ho* in the Greek, meaning *he who* or *the one who*, or simply *the*, and is combined with an absolute participle from a word that means "the will of desire or affection" [*thelo*]. The translation would be "He who is the willing one," or "The willing one" or to make the absolute participle into a verb, "he who wills," or "whosoever wills." The infinitive absolute of this word [*thelein*] is used in Philippians 2:13 translated simply "to will" and is in the phrase, "It is God who works in you both *to will* and to work for his good pleasure." The definite article with the participle is used also in Romans 9:16, "Consequently, therefore, not of the willing one nor of the exerting one but of the showing-mercy God." The willing, therefore, does not arise from the breast of the man left in his naturally depraved condition, but arises from the mercy of God that he distributes according to his good pleasure. All of the authors of this book gladly affirm "Whosoever Will" and each sees that will-of-desire as a manifestation of the prevenient and effectual operation of the grace of a merciful God, so that according to His good pleasure He gives birth to a will that delights in His will.

Calvinism: The Consistent Baptist Expression

The doctrinal concepts under discussion are important and, for the edification of believers and the glory of God, should be a part of ongoing dialogue until we reach unity in the faith and in the knowledge of the Son of God; but the discussion is fraternal and not evangelistic or even ecumenical. The participants are fellow-Christians who are Baptists. Other denominations may join the exchange because the issues are not peculiarly baptistic, and—contrary to Richard Muller's rather flabbergasting and possessive analysis—they are in no sense contrary to the Baptist vision of the church in the world. The originally identifiable Baptists of modern times, those seventeenth-century covenantal pilgrims of English Separatism, believed that their ecclesiology of believers' baptism was a purer and more consistent expression of the doctrines of grace than the infant baptism of their fellow Calvinists. Even John Smyth at the time he embraced believers' baptism was still a Calvinist and viewed his newly-found key to ecclesiology as fully consistent with the purpose of God, the death of Christ, and the operations of the Spirit of God in the New Covenant. The Particular Baptists produced many volumes expressing their full satisfaction that their fervent quest for an ecclesiology that expressed the Reformation doctrines of justification by faith, the bondage of the will, and the effectual operations of the triune God for the salvation of a peculiar people was fulfilled with the adoption of the New Testament practice of the baptism of believers only. This discussion, therefore, is a fully fraternal discussion, and also, while not exclusively baptistic, is most assuredly truly baptistic.

The participants in this discussion agree on the nature of biblical authority. Every proposition constructed out of the words of Scripture is inspired and thus an unfolding of mysteries now revealed. Its history is true, its worldview is true, its literary images are beautiful and precisely instructive for their original intention of communication. Both alignments accept the tri-personed eternality of the divine nature, the orthodox understanding of the divine/human person of the redeemer, our Lord Jesus Christ, the reality of a time-space fall of humanity in the person of Adam, and the consequent necessity of redemption from the culpability of this fallen state. All of us believe that Christ alone is our redemption through His substitutionary death on the cross in which He endured, as a propitiation, the wrath of God for our sins, both original and individually committed. We believe in the necessity of the work of the Spirit in bringing sinners to a saving belief in the gospel, and that He causes them to persevere in faith and increase in holiness and conformity to their Redeemer/elder brother, the Lord Jesus Christ. That same Spirit endows the church by means of

Christ's purchase with sufficient gifts for its proper functioning as a worshiping and witnessing body in this fallen world. Only those that are thus believers in the gospel constitute the church on earth and only those are to be baptized, for they alone have within them the qualifications of discipleship.

Areas in which we are seeking clearer and more precise agreement constitute the subject matter of this volume. How does a Christian witness get closest to the truth in his construction of the biblical teaching on election, predestination, Christ's death for sinners, the effects of the fall on the human affections and will, the way in which the Spirit calls a sinner into fellowship with Christ, how the called sinner progresses through this world safely and faithfully in the hope and assurance of eternal life, how the present darkness and evil of a fallen world relate to divine sovereignty and purpose, and how closely tied are the ideas thus expressed to a purer and more faithful proclamation of revealed truth? This volume is an attempt to take a step forward, not backward, in providing clarity and moving toward unity on these matters.

While these two volumes represent a clear difference in the ways these ideas in general are perceived, the writers of neither volume are absolutely aligned with each other on all issues we discuss. One would discover places in which contributors to this volume might achieve closer unity in nuances of the relation between Law and Gospel in Scripture, places of continuity between the Old Covenant and the New Covenant, the manner in which the Bible describes and engenders perseverance, how the atoning work of Christ relates to the elect and the non-elect and consequently the effectual calling of the Holy Spirit, the importance of certain historical and theological precedents for contemporary ministry, and even the best manner in which this discussion should be continued. What we do not disagree on, however, is the overall commitment to *divine sovereignty* as a necessary expression of *divine glory* in the grace through which sinners participate in the reconciling work of Christ.

What is at Stake in the Calvinism Debate?

It is this common commitment to divine sovereignty and divine glory that is at stake in the Calvinism-Arminianism debate. If God must condition His sovereignty and salvific plan on the will of man, then man in some way, even if it be small, contributes to his salvation and consequently God cannot receive *all* of the glory in redemption. In other words, should God seek to save but His success be dependent not upon His own will but upon the will of man, then inevitably God is at the mercy of man. God's will can be thwarted by man's will. God's success is only fulfilled should man give the final approval. Ultimately, salvation, though initiated by God, depends upon the contributing will of man for its consummation. It is impossible to see how God, in such a paradigm as this, can retain all of the credit in planning, accomplishing, and applying salvation to sinners. In essence, God is robbed of His glory at the expense of demanding libertarian freedom. There can be no way around it; these are the consequences of the Arminian view. Consequently, John R. de Witt can rightly conclude, "Arminianism essentially represents an attack upon the majesty of God and puts in place of it the exaltation of man. It is a danger which constantly recurs, and must be faced, and must be opposed."[2]

Be not mistaken, opposing Arminianism is an aspect of this present volume. And for good reason too for as J. I. Packer states, Arminianism involves a "partial denial of the biblical faith in the God of all grace." But we cannot stop there. It is not enough to oppose those views contrary to Scripture. Rather, we oppose them in order to help others see better what Scripture teaches. As Packer explains, Calvinists should "approach professed Arminians as brother evangelicals trapped in weakening theological mistakes, and seek to help them to a better mind."[3] In part, that is our aim in this volume. We desire to see "the children of God returning in increasing numbers from the dry places of Arminianism to the 'old paths, wherein is the good way,' where they will find rest for their souls and power for their lives."[4]

But opposing Arminianism is only one aspect of our goal in this volume. The main purpose in what follows is to provide a biblical affirmation of the doctrines of grace, one that pulls back the curtain of Scripture to reveal the majesty, supremacy, and glory of our sovereign God. To deny the doctrines of grace is to leave the church with a small, very small, view of God. It is to reduce God so that he is made to fit into our man-centered paradigm. As Boice and Ryken have stated, Arminianism results in a theology "that is not exclusively God-centered but is distorted in the direction of the self."[5] Therefore, we love the doctrines of grace because they turn us away from our human-centered views of salvation and instead open our eyes to a God-centered view of redemption. We love the doctrines of grace because they serve as the foundation on which the gospel itself is built. Behind the life, death, and resurrection of Jesus Christ is a God who has

---

[2] John R. de Witt, "The Arminian Conflict and the Synod of Dort," in vol. 5 of *Puritan Papers, 1968–1969*, ed. J. I. Packer (Phillipsburg, NJ: P&R, 2005), 23.

[3] J. I. Packer, "Arminianisms," in vol. 5 of *Puritan Papers, 1968–1969*, 40.

[4] Ibid., 41.

[5] James Montgomery Boice and Philip Graham Ryken, *The Doctrines of Grace: Rediscovering the Evangelical Gospel* (Wheaton, IL: Crossway, 2002), 28.

already determined the end from the beginning, including the destination of every living soul, not on the basis of anything we will do but purely because of His good pleasure. He is a God who sends His Son to die for those whom He has predestined. He is a God who sends His Spirit to effectually call and monergistically regenerate those whom He has elected and sent His Son to die for. And He is a God who will not be defeated, but rather will preserve His elect children to the very end. It is this *big* God that we can rest assured will triumph in the end. His purpose will stand and He will indeed do all that He pleases (Isaiah 46:9–10; 45:7; Lamentations 3:37–38). As Nebuchadnezzar learned (the hard way!), "all the inhabitants of the earth are accounted as nothing and he does according to his will among the host of heaven and among the inhabitants of the earth; and none can stay his hand or say to him, 'What have you done?'" (Daniel 4:34–35). Because God is sovereign over all things, rather than having His sovereignty limited by libertarian freedom, He can guarantee that His gospel will go forth to the nations, actually having the power to accomplish His saving purpose. His gospel will not fail to save those for whom it is intended. Therefore, His meticulous sovereignty does not squelch missions and evangelism but provides the very impetus for it.

No wonder the great London Baptist preacher, Charles Spurgeon (1834–1892), could say, "I have my own private opinion that there is no such thing as preaching Christ and Him crucified, unless we preach what nowadays is called Calvinism." "It is a nickname to call it Calvinism; Calvinism is the gospel, and nothing else."[6] Such a statement may sound shocking, especially to those *against* Calvinism. But Spurgeon, understood correctly, was not saying that only those who are Calvinists believe in the gospel or that only Calvinists are Christians. Rather, Spurgeon was arguing that Calvinism is simply biblical Christianity. It tells us who God is, what Christ has accomplished, and how exactly God has saved sinners. And what could be more relevant to the gospel than how sinners are saved? Therefore, since the doctrines of grace have everything to do with how a person is saved, Spurgeon finds it appropriate then to say: Calvinism is simply the gospel, nothing else. Consequently, if we are truly to be consistent, it is not an exaggeration to say that the evangelical gospel stands or falls with Calvinism. As Boice and Ryken put the matter, "The doctrines of grace preserve the gospel of grace."[7] And as R. Albert Mohler, Jr., has said, "The 'doctrines of grace' are nothing less than a statement of the gospel itself." It is only when we "return to a more Calvinistic understanding of the

---

[6] Charlies Spurgeon, *The Autobiography of Charles H. Spurgeon* (Cincinnati, OH: Curts & Jennings, 1898), 1:172.

[7] Boice and Ryken, *The Doctrines of Grace*, 24.

gospel and a recognition of the absolute sovereignty of God" that we will "recover our theological inheritance and the essence of biblical Christianity."[8] The purest biblical presentation of the gospel glides upon the waters of the doctrines of grace.[9]

Therefore, what is at stake in this debate is obvious: the glory of our sovereign God. At the nucleus of Calvinism is a passion, zeal, and commitment to see God's glory lifted up. Calvinism is simply another way of saying: *Soli Deo Gloria!* The editors and writers present this testimony to what we feel and believe is the true grace of God and we pray that those who walk the path to which we point "will walk on [their] way securely, and [their] foot will not stumble" (Proverbs 3:23).

---

[8] Thomas J. Nettles, *By His Grace and For His Glory* (Cape Coral, FL: Founders Press, 2004), 261; quoting Mohler in the *Western Recorder*, April 29, 1997.

[9] Ibid., xxiii.

Part One

I

Our Sovereign Savior
SERMON ON REVELATION 5:1–14

Steven J. Lawson

I saw in the right hand of Him who sat on the throne a book written inside and on the back, sealed up with seven seals. And I saw a strong angel
proclaiming with a loud voice, "Who is worthy to open the book and to
break its seals?" And no one in heaven or on the earth or under the earth
was able to open the book or to look into it. Then I began to weep greatly
because no one was found worthy to open the book or to look into it;
and one of the elders said to me, "Stop weeping; behold, the Lion that is
from the tribe of Judah, the Root of David, has overcome so as to open
the book and its seven seals." And I saw between the throne (with the
four living creatures) and the elders a Lamb standing, as if slain, having
seven horns and seven eyes, which are the seven Spirits of God, sent out
into all the earth. And He came and took the book out of the right hand
of Him who sat on the throne. When He had taken the book, the four
living creatures and the twenty-four elders fell down before the Lamb,
each one holding a harp and golden bowls full of incense, which are the
prayers of the saints. And they sang a new song, saying, "Worthy are You
to take the book and to break its seals; for You were slain, and purchased
for God with Your blood men from every tribe and tongue and people
and nation. You have made them to be a kingdom and priests to our God;
and they will reign upon the earth." Then I looked, and I heard the voice
of many angels around the throne and the living creatures and the elders; and the number of them was myriads of myriads, and thousands of
thousands, saying with a loud voice, "Worthy is the Lamb that was slain
to receive power and riches and wisdom and might and honor and glory
and blessing." And every created thing which is in heaven and on the
earth and under the earth and on the sea, and all things in them, I heard

saying, "To Him who sits on the throne, and to the Lamb, be blessing
and honor and glory and dominion forever and ever." And the four living
creatures kept saying, "Amen." And the elders fell down and worshiped
(Revelation 5:1–14).

The greatest vision ever set before human eyes is beholding the glory of
our sovereign Savior, the Lord Jesus Christ. This being true, there is
perhaps no greater display of the dazzling majesty of Christ than what we
find in this heavenly scene in Revelation 5. Here is the dramatic presentation of Christ, not as He once was in the lowly humility of His incarnation,
not as a babe laying in a manger, not as the Teacher in the Temple, not as
the sin-bearing Savior hanging on the cross, nor as the dead Messiah laying in the tomb. Instead, what we see here is Jesus as He now is, in His
present state of glorification. Here is the risen and ascended Christ, exalted
and enthroned in the heavens, ruling and reigning in glory.

This is the towering vision that the church at the end of the first century desperately needed to recapture. From a human perspective, it appeared as though Caesar and the Roman Empire were dominant over the
church and in control of human history. At that time, the apostle John was
suffering political exile on the remote island of Patmos in the Aegean Sea.
Throughout the Empire, the early believers were suffering much tribulation under the heavy hand of Roman oppression. Then, unexpectedly, the
aged apostle was caught up into heaven in order to receive the revelation
of the glorified Christ and witness the world stage from God's eternal
perspective. These early believers needed to be reminded that it was not
Caesar who was sovereign over history, but Jesus Christ.

Nothing has changed over the last twenty centuries. Once again, the
church in this present hour must recapture her once lofty, grand vision of
her risen Lord. And He is no longer as He once was, the lowly Messiah
walking the dusty streets of Judea. He is no longer the humble Galilean,
mocked and maligned. He is no longer the gentle Carpenter, turning the
other cheek. Jesus no longer stands before Pilate, but Pilate must now
stand before Him. The fact is this, we worship Jesus as He now is, the exalted Lord of heaven and earth—the One seated at the right hand of God
the Father, presiding over all of human history, the object of worship of all
the saints and the angels.

Perhaps no other passage in all of Scripture reveals such a comprehensive view of Jesus Christ as that found in Revelation 5. As we consider
this passage, I trust that it will be as though we, too, are caught up into the
heights of heaven so that we might grasp a renewed vision of Jesus Christ
as He towers over this world scene, our lives, and eternal destinies. To be
sure, Jesus is the sole Controller of the affairs of this world, the supreme

Judge of every king and kingdom, and the sovereign Determiner of every destiny. *Every* life is in the hands of this sovereign Savior.

God's Immutable Plan

In verse one, we read, "I saw in the right hand of Him who sat on the throne a book." It is as though the veil of heaven is pulled back to allow the apostle John to behold God the Father seated upon the throne (cf. 4:1–11). But this is no ordinary throne. This is the very throne room of Almighty God. As such, this throne represents the authority that belongs to God alone. Every person, nation, and event is subject to this throne. And notice that this throne is occupied. In other words, God is not an absentee Landlord as many erroneously believe. God Himself is presently and eternally seated upon His throne in heaven.

Even in this tumultuous time in the first century, God is enthroned, presiding over the affairs of this world. Though the Roman Empire is persecuting the church, human history is not left abandoned to run its own course. Despite the imperial might of Rome, with all its godless influences, evil has not seized control from the hand of God. Rather, John sees God seated upon this throne, possessing and exercising all power and dominion over heaven and earth.

Moreover, note that God is holding a "book" in His right hand. This book is not a bound collection of pages as we might think of today, but is best understood as being a scroll that would have been rolled-up and sealed. In ancient times, documents would be written only on the inside and then sealed shut. But this scroll is written on both the inside and the outside, indicating that its contents are so comprehensive that they cannot be limited to one side. The lengthy inscriptions spill over from the inside to the outside. Whatever is written in this book, it is extensive, precise, and exhaustive. No detail is left unaddressed.

Further, this book is held in "the right hand" of God, indicating that He alone is its sole Author. Thus, its contents—its decrees, its judgments—are perfect. What is more, because the writings of this book are "sealed up with seven seals," they are unalterable, immutable, fixed, and settled. This is to say, no creature can alter what God has written in it. In addition, the fact that this book is sealed indicates that its contents are concealed from human eyes. It is impossible for any man to peer inside of it and read its contents. It is a closed book.

Thus, the question begs to be asked: What is this book? And what is recorded in it? One possibility is that it is the Lamb's Book of Life (Revelation 13:8; 17:8). Another possibility is that this sealed scroll contains the detailed record of every human life, with every thought and motive documented (cf. Revelation 20:12). But I would submit to you that neither option reveals the true identity of this book. We read beginning in Revelation 6:1, "Then I saw when the Lamb broke one of the seven seals, and I heard one of the four living creatures saying as with the voice of thunder, 'Come.' And I looked, and behold, a white horse." What is written in this book is unleashed upon the earth in divine wrath. Verse 3 addresses this book again, "He broke the second seal, and I heard a second living creature saying, 'Come.'" Then, verse 5 records a yet further opening of this book, "He broke the third seal." Again, we read in verse 7 of another breaking of the seals and a further opening of the book, immediately followed by the execution of another divine judgment upon the earth. Here is the progressive breaking of these seven seals, allowing this book to be further unrolled and opened.

At the very least, this book contains the record of God's plan for the end of the age as recorded by John in the rest of Revelation. At most, this book records all that God has planned and is accomplishing in human history between the two appearings of Christ. In this book is the pre-written plan by which God will govern human history and bring the world to its divinely-appointed end, culminating with the return of our Lord Jesus Christ to this earth in blazing glory.

In this book, God has recorded His smoldering vengeance that is to be poured out upon this Christ-rejecting world in the last days. But this divine plan is not what God merely foresees will occur. Rather, it is what He has eternally foreordained to come to pass. We even read that God will put it into the hearts of unconverted kings to carry out what He has predetermined (Revelation 17:17). Contained in this book is the end of human history and the taking back of this planet by Christ. All this and more is contained in this scroll.

What a comfort this must have been to the early church as they heard these words trumpeted in their ears. What a glorious thought this must have been, even amid widespread persecution, to hear that human history has already been pre-written by God and that He, not Caesar, is in control. There will be no deviation from this divine plan. This sovereign purpose is unalterable and irrevocable. This course has been determinedly fixed by God and will conclude with the entire world bowing its knee to the King of kings and Lord of lords.

Who Is Worthy?

Then, the voice of a strong angel interrupts John's focus and asks an inescapable question, "Who is worthy to open the book and to break its seals" (verse 2). In other words, who is competent to bring human history to its appointed end? Who is capable of overturning all evil? Who is able to resist the beast in the last day? Who is capable of ushering in the kingdom of God upon the earth on such a grand scale? Who is worthy to take the reins of history and bring it to its God-appointed climax and crescendo?

Verse 3 provides the answer, "And no one in heaven or on the earth or under the earth was able to open the book or to look inside of it." A large-scale search was conducted in heaven, on earth, and under the earth to discover one who could take this book, open it, and execute its contents. But this desperate search proved to be futile. No angel was found worthy. No glorified saint was competent. No earthly ruler, pastor, church, or denomination was capable. Here is the utter bankruptcy of man to solve his own problems. Here is the total inability of man to bring history to its proper end.

In verse 4, John records, "Then I began to weep greatly" because from a human vantage point, this futile search meant that there will be no final triumph of God's plan. To John it appears that history would be like an ever-flowing river, easily diverted by evil, going its own way. The apostle feared there would be no final punishment of sin, no reward of good. John saw the earth under the dominion of the Roman Empire with no solutions in sight. As he is taken up into heaven, he sees that there is no one in glory who can grab the reigns of history and bring it to its proper end. Consequently, John began to cry profusely because, as verse 4 says, "no one was found worthy to open the book or to look into it." The hope of mankind is contained in this book. But who can execute it?

Then, one of the elders around God's throne suddenly interrupts John's weeping. This glorified leader issues this gentle rebuke, "Stop weeping" (verse 5). There is no need for this kind of despair. Crying is totally an inappropriate response. This reproof is intended to jolt John into a more proper estimate of the hour in which the church finds itself. The apostle must regain the divine perspective of the world. He needs to refocus and see God's perspective of history. He needs to see with a distinctly Christian worldview.

The Kingly Lion

This glorified elder then points to a Lion, "Behold, the Lion that is from the tribe of Judah, the root of David, has overcome so as to open the book and its seven seals" (verse 5). By saying "behold," this elder is commanding John to gaze upon this victorious Lion from the tribe of Judah. The apostle needs to see the world in light of this Lion. Here is the lens through which he must view reality. This lion imagery echoes the messianic prophecy in Genesis 49:9–10, where Judah is promised the right to rule over the other tribes. This Lion from the tribe of Judah is the dominant world force over all other earthly powers. The apostle will not understand world events and the state of the church apart from beholding this Lion.

This Lion is none other than the Lord Jesus Christ—ferocious, kingly, aggressive, dominant, domineering, conquering, stalking, and devouring. Christ is "King of kings and Lord of lords" (Revelation 17:14; 19:16), dominating even the strongest world rulers. He is the King of the earth, the King of heaven, and the King of hell. He is the King over events in the affairs of providence. He is King over the nations that rise up against Him. He is King over the church. He is King over Satan and all the forces of darkness. He is King over the hearts and wills of men. There is no place but that Jesus is King.

Further, the lineage of this Lion is according to promise. He is from "the tribe of Judah," which is the kingly line of Israel. And He is "the root of David," meaning He grew out of the Davidic line as prophesied by Scripture. Simply put, Jesus came onto the scene of human history of the proper descent, perfectly possessing all the messianic credentials.

Finally, this elder states that this Lion has "overcome." This kingly beast has devoured all His foes. Note the use of the past tense. This Lion has already won a great and decisive victory. He has already triumphed over all who would oppose Him. He alone possesses sovereign rights and supreme authority to take this book, break open its seals, and execute what is written in it. He alone is worthy to bring human history to its appointed end. No one else, except this Lion, can usher in what God ordained for human history.

The Sovereign Lamb

But as John turns to behold the Lion, he is not prepared for what he sees. "And I saw between the throne (with the four living creatures) and the elders a Lamb standing, as if slain, having seven horns and seven eyes, which are the seven Spirits of God, sent out into all the earth" (verse 6). Instead of seeing a ferocious Lion, John witnesses a totally different figure—a gentle Lamb. We know who this Lamb is. He is the same One who is the Lion—the Lord Jesus Christ. He is represented here as a lamb because He is the fulfillment of the entire sacrificial system in the Old Testament. This Lamb became the perfect atonement by which sinful man could find acceptance with holy God. Jesus is "the Lamb of God who takes away the sin of the world" (John 1:29). Without this Lamb, there is no access to God. "Without shedding of blood, there is no remission of sin" (Hebrews 9:22).

Without this Lamb, there is no redemption, no forgiveness, no propitiation, and no reconciliation.

What an apparent contradiction! John is looking for a kingly Lion, and instead sees a submissive Lamb. Here he beholds the Lord Jesus Christ, "standing, as if slain." The word *slain* means "to cut up and mutilate," as an animal sacrifice would be butchered for priestly sacrifice. When John sees the Lamb, he beheld Him as One that had been slaughtered. He sees Him as still bearing the marks of His brutal crucifixion. He must have seen the nail-pierced hands and the wounded side, the marks of that violent, vicious death that Jesus suffered. But take note, this Lamb is "standing," clearly indicating that He has been raised from the dead. In other words, this slain Lamb is alive.

In fact, this Lion-Lamb is on the prowl, stalking human history, taking it by the nape of the neck, and subjecting it to the crushing power of His jaws. Here is the living, resurrected Christ, standing in triumph over both time and eternity. He is standing in dominance. He is standing in victory. He is standing in authority. Jesus has *already* been raised from the dead, ascended to heaven, and is presently enthroned at the right hand of God the Father. He is now the dominant force over the entire universe and human history.

Furthermore, this Lamb has "seven horns" (verse 6) by which to inflict wounds. Seven is the number of completeness and perfection, indicating full dominance over all opposition to His will. Seven horns denotes that He possesses unrivaled, irresistible dominance to inflict defeat upon those who would try to butt heads with Him. He has seven horns, meaning that He is omnipotent, both possessing and exercising all power. There is no power, in the ultimate sense, but that it is His power. Any lesser power that the creature would possess is a delegated power, granted by Christ. No king can resist His overruling power. No individual or nation can successfully rise up against this sovereign Lamb.

In addition, this reigning Lamb has "seven eyes" (verse 6), meaning He sees everything with perfect, penetrating insight. Nothing can catch Him off guard. No one can prevail against Him with some unforeseen attack. No one can unexpectedly alter the flow of human history. He has "seven eyes, which are the seven Spirits of God, sent out into all the earth." That is to say, Christ is all-seeing throughout the world. He possesses all insight, all wisdom, and all discernment. There is nothing that He does not see and know. Nothing escapes His gaze. He sizes up every situation for what it truly is before it occurs. He sees with eyes of fire, peering and penetrating into the crevices of every heart and mind. And as He sees all, He never looks down the proverbial tunnel of time into the future, and learns anything that He does not already know. The reason this Lamb foresees all is because He has foreordained all.

Assuming The Reign Of History

In verse 7, we read, "And He came and took the book out of the right hand of Him who sat on the throne." The sheer drama of this scene defies human imagination. By approaching God the Father and taking the scroll out of His right hand, this bold act signifies a transfer of authority to the Lion-Lamb. This bestows upon the Lord Jesus Christ the sovereign right to execute the contents of this book that has been written by God. By this, Christ now assumes the reign of human history.

Several summers ago, I was in Europe and went to the Louvre in Paris, that extraordinary art museum, virtually un-paralleled in the world, with its collection of great art. There I saw the most extraordinary painting I have ever seen in my life. It was painted by the official portrait artist of Napoleon, Jacque Louis David. The painting was titled *The Coronation of Josephine*. On the right side of this large-scale painting was Napoleon, with all of his military, kingly, and regal splendor. The French emperor—dressed in gold and blue and red, with sashes and medals and all of the emblems of nobility and sovereignty—is arising from his throne. On the left side, approaching the throne, is Josephine, with all of her attendants surrounding her. Every eye in the entire painting is focused upon Josephine as she proceeds to the throne, where the crown is to be placed upon her head by Napoleon. This coronation scene is an epic portrayal of regal splendor and majesty.

But this earthly coronation is nothing in comparison to the full transfer of supreme authority in this heavenly scene. Here is the coronation of Jesus Christ as the King of kings and the Lord of lords. As He proceeds to the throne of God, the Father hands this book to His Son. As Jesus takes the book, this Lion-Lamb assumes the full right of unrivaled sovereignty as the King of heaven and earth. This is the very fulfillment of the words of Christ, "All authority in heaven and earth have been given unto me" (Matthew 28:18; cf. Ephesians 1:20–22). By virtue of His obedience unto death, Jesus now receives this unlimited authority. He assumes His place at the right hand of the Father, that place of highest power in the universe. In His glorified state, Jesus Christ has all authority to build His church (Matthew 16:18), convert His enemies (Acts 9:1–5), overturn circumstances (Acts 12:3–11), grant repentance (Acts 11:19), give saving faith (Acts 3:16), cause His work to triumph (Acts 9:31), raise up workers for the harvest (Matthew 9:36–38), send out missionaries (Acts 13:1–5), open human hearts (Acts 16:14), control hearts (Proverbs 21:1), remove rulers (Luke 1:52), and open a door which no man can close (Revelation 3:7).

Such unilateral authority the Lord Jesus Christ now possesses, enthroned at the right hand of God the Father. Jesus is certainly not represented here as a frustrated Savior, pacing back and forth in heaven, wringing His hands, anxious for someone to accept Him. There is no panic in heaven, only plans—and the power to carry out His purposes. As history unfolds, He remains completely in control of the world scene, not only in the macro sense, but in the micro. Here is Christ, ready to break open these seals and execute all that God has purposed upon the earth.

All Praise To Christ

What kind of response was there to Christ in this magnificent scene? When the Lamb takes the scroll, we read, "the four living creatures and the twenty-four elders fell down before Him, each holding a harp and golden bowls full of incense, which are the prayers of the saints" (verse 8). These four angels with the closest proximity to the throne of God are guardian angels. The twenty-four elders represent all Old and New Testament saints around the throne of God. They are so in awe, being in the immediate presence of the Lamb, that they keep falling down before Him. They cannot remain standing in the presence of Him who possesses such infinite worth and value.

Each elder has a harp, an instrument of joy and gladness. What adoration explodes in heaven, in the hearts of those around the throne. They are overwhelmed with exuberant praise because they now understand that human history has *not* been hijacked by evil forces. The world will not be randomly moving forward into an uncharted future. Instead, all world events will be perfectly governed by the sovereign hand of the Lord Jesus Christ. These worshipers have golden bowls full of incense, which are the prayers of the saints. These prayers are intercessions for God's ultimate triumph over the forces of darkness in the world. They have been long praying, "Your kingdom come. Your will be done on earth as it is in heaven" (Matthew 6:10). They now see, at last, their prayers will be answered. Their petitions will not be like random stars floating in outer space, never hitting their mark, never being answered. To the contrary, these prayers are made effectual by Christ Himself, who will make right every wrong and cause His kingdom to triumph. No wonder heaven is filled with such dynamic, reverential praise.

In response to Christ's possession of sovereignty, the four living creatures and the twenty-four elders sang a new song, "Worthy are You to take the scroll and to open its seals, for You were slain, and by Your blood You ransomed people for God from every tribe and language and people and nation" (verse 9). All of heaven erupts in jubilant praise, singing this new song. It is this new awareness of Christ's supreme authority that ignites such a heart-felt response.

When I first came to understand the sovereignty of God, there was this kind of extraordinary joy in my own heart which continues to this day. As I have studied the Word of God, my eyes have been opened to this amazing truth of His kingship over all. When I came to realize that Jesus Christ is sovereign in bestowing salvation and governing the affairs of this world, my heart was flooded with praise. When eyes are opened to the unrivaled supremacy of Christ, worship ascends yet even higher.

In this "new song," the unique emphasis is principally upon the sovereignty of Christ. These glorified worshipers are so overwhelmed by the uncontested right of Christ to rule over history that they *must* sing this new song. High theology always produces such high doxology. Before the throne, there is this heightened awareness that the entire universe is run by the absolute theocracy of Christ. There are no maverick molecules in the universe, but all things exist to do His bidding. Here, specifically, is why Christ is worthy to be praised: "For You were slain and purchased for God with Your blood men from every tribe and tongue and people and nation" (verse 9). There is this increased awareness that salvation is—start to finish and everything in between—of the Lord (Psalm 3:8; Jonah 2:9). With glorified eyes, these worshipers see more clearly that saving grace is entirely the sovereign work of God *alone*.

Purchased By His Blood

What does this new song mean, that Christ has purchased with His blood a people for Himself? This word *purchased* is a word drawn from the marketplace. It is a term taken from the business world, indicating that a finished financial transaction has taken place. It means that a purchase price has been paid, and the purchased object is given to the rightful buyer. Notice, there is no ransom to Satan theory of the atonement in this text. Jesus is not paying the gold and silver of His blood to Satan in order to free sinners from his bondage. To the contrary, when He died upon the cross, Jesus did business directly and exclusively with the Father. This was an inter-Trinitarian transaction between the Father and the Son by which the Son paid the definite price to secure the salvation of all who would believe upon Him. Jesus Christ bought His people with His shed blood (Acts 20:28). This Lamb gave His life for His sheep (John 10:11, 15).

Do not miss the *particularity* of Christ's atoning work on the cross. Heaven is rejoicing that He bought us "from every tribe and tongue and people and nation" (verse 9). This text does not say He redeemed everyone in every tribe, tongue, people, and nation. If that were so, the whole world would be saved. The fact is, a perfectly just God cannot require a double payment for the same sin. If Jesus has already paid the ransom for everyone's sin at the cross, then no one would go to hell. If purchased sinners did go to hell, God would cease to be righteous, something that is clearly impossible (1 John 1:9).

But to the contrary, Jesus actually purchased a specific people *out of*, or *out from among*, every people group. "Tongue" here speaks of language groups, "people" of ethnic races, "nations" of national identities, and "tribe" of genealogical descents. Out of fallen, ruined humanity, Jesus purchased all who had been given to Him by the Father from before the foundation of the world (John 6:37–39; 10:26–30; 17:2, 6, 9, 24). Not a drop of His blood was shed in vain. It is all victory at the cross.

Simply put, Jesus possesses everything He paid for at the cross. Jesus was not jilted, nor shortchanged. Jesus did not pay an infinite price for the salvation of sinners and receive less than what He bought. He did not purchase the entire world, but only received believers in return. He did not merely make the world *savable*, contingent upon man exercising faith and, thus, in part, saving himself. Instead, He *actually* saved a definite group of people out of the world. He did not simply make us *redeemable*. Rather, Jesus *actually* redeemed us by His death upon Calvary's cross. It was a finished transaction upon that cursed tree. Jesus did not procure a hypothetical salvation for all sinners, if only they would have the good sense to believe on Him and close the deal. Instead, at the cross, Jesus *actually* purchased out of these groups a specific people for whom He intentionally died and *actually* secured their redemption. Only by this understanding of the cross can one truly sing "Jesus *saves*."

Moreover, all whom Jesus purchased will one day find themselves around the throne of God. He did not die for an anonymous mob of people, some of whom will never make it to heaven. He did not die for a nameless, faceless human race. Rather, upon the cross, He died for each individual sheep. He gave Himself up for the church (Ephesians 5:25). All for whom He died, He saves. It is impossible to exhaust the significance of this redeeming work of Christ upon the cross. We can never get our arms around it completely. We can never ascend to the heights of it, nor plumb the depths of it. It is too high, too deep, and too broad. It is too wonderful to comprehend that Jesus Christ redeemed a vast number of hell-bound rebels in His sin-bearing death.

Dominion Forever

Based upon His triumphant death, these blood-bought worshipers continue to cry out to God, "You have made them to be a kingdom and priests to our God; and they will reign upon the earth" (verse 10). By this worship hymn, these glorified saints understand that all for whom Christ died are brought into His kingdom. None for whom He died will fail to be made heavenly citizens. They are made to be a "kingdom," that is, a community of believers under the sovereignty of their enthroned King. Furthermore, they are made to be "priests," servants who have access to the throne of God. They will "reign upon the earth." This is a precursor to Revelation 20 and the thousand-year reign of Christ upon the earth. All who have been redeemed by Christ will ultimately reign with Him.

However, John yet sees more, "Then I looked, and I heard the voice of many angels from around the throne and the living creatures and the elders; and the number of them was myriads of myriads" (verse 11). Literally, myriad means ten thousand, which is the highest number in the Greek language. "Myriads of myriads" —please note, each number is in the plural—equates to ten thousands times ten thousands. This translates into millions upon millions and billions upon billions in this worshiping scene. Right now, each local church is but a small portion of all believers of all ages who worship Christ. But one day, all believers throughout history will join with the angelic hosts in worshiping this sovereign Savior, who has purchased their salvation.

We also discover what is being sung. "Worthy is the Lamb that was slain to receive power and riches and wisdom and might and honor and glory and blessing" (verse 12). The catalyst in worship is the redeeming death of Christ and the increased recognition of His supreme "power and riches and wisdom and might" to save. Because of this recognition, He is to be given "honor and glory and blessing." This thunderous praise is directed exclusively and entirely to the Lamb that was slain before the foundation of the world, to Jesus who alone is worthy.

Verse 13 states that "every created thing which is in heaven, on the earth, under the earth, on the sea, and all things in them, I heard saying, 'to Him who sits on the throne,'" referring to God the Father, and to "the Lamb," a reference to God the Son. They are to receive "blessing and honor and glory and dominion forever and ever." Please note the co-equality of the Father and the Son. Both are equally praised here. This anticipates what the apostle Paul writes in Philippians 2:10–11, where the entire created order—every knee, every mouth—will find itself, whether lost or saved, in this scene around the throne. Though not all people will be saved, nevertheless, all will sing this anthem to God. In the end, God will receive His due. But specifically, redeemed saints will never cease in singing this anthem of praise. They will never stop singing this hymn in the very presence of the Father and the Son, who is the sovereign Savior, the very center of heaven and Controller of human history. As Colossians 1:18 says, Jesus Christ must "have the place of preeminence in all things." Nowhere is this more true than in this heavenly scene.

Finally, "And the four living creatures kept saying, 'Amen.' And the elders fell down and worshiped" (verse 14). There is no end to the praise being offered to the Father and His Son. This adoration is described with an eternal present tense. The four living creatures are the four guardian angels, who are endlessly exclaiming "Amen." The elders, who represent all the redeemed of all the ages, continually "fell down" before the throne, overwhelmed by His sovereign grace. This word "worship" means "to kiss toward." The idea is to prostrate oneself before another of far greater worth and superiority in order to pay homage. This worship expresses to Christ the affection, love, devotion, allegiance and loyalty due to Him because He is infinitely superior. The elders kept falling down again and again and again, ascribing honor and glory and power and blessing to the Lamb upon the throne.

All Glory To Him

As Jesus is currently receiving worship like this in heaven, should we not do the same, now, in this present world? Let us be constantly reminded of the matchless glory and majestic sovereignty of the Lord Jesus Christ. He is the Lion of the tribe of Judah and the Lamb of God who takes away the sin of His people throughout the world. By virtue of His redeeming death, we belong exclusively to the Lord Jesus Christ. This Lion-Lamb owns us because He bought us.

For this very reason, we cannot give Him too much worship. We cannot fall down before Him too often. We cannot adore Him enough. We cannot ascribe to Him too much honor. We cannot say too often how worthy He is to be the object of our affection and the chief reason as to why we live. We cannot express to Him our praise and gratitude with enough depth of feeling, height of emotion, and intentionality of purpose.

May we presently join in this song of adoration with the saints around the throne in heaven. May we never be lukewarm in our worship of our sovereign Savior. May we never be among those who have left their first love. To the contrary, may we be those who have fervent hearts, devoted lives, and obedient wills for the Lord Jesus Christ.

2

Total Depravity
A BIBLICAL AND THEOLOGICAL EXAMINATION

Mark DeVine

The term "total depravity" did not become a fixture of the common theological lexicon until the seventeenth century. An internecine squabble among Dutch Calvinists eventually produced the celebrated acrostic, TULIP. This handy popularized acrostic summarizes the five so-called heads of doctrine articulated at the Synod of Dort. Each of the five points was meant to refute assertions fellow Dutch Reformed brethren had set forth in their Remonstrance of 1610. The death of Jacobus Arminius in 1609 had cleared the way for a family feud free from the potentially complicating presence of either Arminius or his own self-proclaimed favorite biblical exegete, John Calvin, who had died forty-five years earlier. The most alternately endearing and inflammatory product of that feud remains—the TULIP. In it the T=Total Depravity, U=Unconditional Election, L=Limited Atonement, I=Irresistible Grace and P=Perseverance of the Saints.

Dort bears the stamp of early 17th century protestant scholasticism, but the core concern identified by the "T" recalls a subject of recurrent importance reaching back to the exegetical labors and theological clashes of the great reformers Martin Luther and John Calvin, namely, the question of human capacity for God after the Fall. Luther had his Erasmus and both Luther and Calvin had Osiander to argue with on such matters.

But this core concern reaches on back to the Middle Ages with the likes of Abelard and Gottschalk and on back to the early church and the great *Doctor Gratiae*, the Doctor of Grace himself, Augustine of Hippo, who refuted the teaching of the British monk Pelagius. But the contro-

16

versy goes back even further, into Biblical times to the Apostle Paul and his hypothetical interlocutor of Romans 9 ("Why then does He still find fault? For who can resist His will?") and even to Jesus Christ himself who said to and of his followers, "Without me you can do nothing."—and on back perhaps, though not so obviously, to the Garden of Eden itself. We shall revisit this matter of the Garden in due course.

Human capacity for God after the Fall was certainly a theme that captured seventeenth century Dortrecht, the Netherlands. Is the fallen human being able to obey God's commands or exercise saving faith? Yes or no? If not, can he prepare himself for either or at least receive the power to do so and then exercise that power or not according to his free will? This subject of humanity's ability vis-à-vis God periodically agitates the mind of the church and, even when interest in it wanes and fades, it settles just below the surface in seminars and sermons and prayers and wherever the commands of God are taken seriously or the call for repentance and faith is issued.

Blind, Bound, and Dead

Across the centuries, exploration of the consequences of humanity's fall into sin by the global church has produced impressive historic consensus, especially in Western Christianity. The church in the West insists that the consequences of humanity's fall into sin are, in a word, devastating. Given the picture that emerges from the Holy Scripture of sinful humanity, this consensus should not surprise us.

A mere 17 verses into the 2nd chapter of the Bible one confronts the warning of God to humanity's first parents that transgression shall not go unpunished: "on the day you eat from it [the forbidden fruit] you will certainly die." They did eat, and they did die, and, excepting only Enoch, so has every human being born into this world since. "Just as sin entered into the world through one man, and death through sin, in this way death spread to all men, because all sinned" (Romans 5:12). The mortality that characterizes us all goes beyond the looming inevitability of our physical demise. A spiritual death has befallen us as well, resulting in the macabre specter of a planet inhabited by a kind of walking dead: "... you were dead in trespasses and sins in which you previously walked, according to this worldly age" (Ephesians 2:1–3).

Dire divine assessment of fallen humanity's condition spans both Old and New Testaments and evokes a sense of profound futility, hopelessness, even despair: "The Lord saw that man's wickedness was widespread on the earth and that every scheme his mind thought of was nothing but evil all the time" (Genesis 6:5). The apostle Paul could cite the Psalms' tragic and foreboding depiction of the human race as relevant for his own contemporaries:

> There is no one righteous, not even one;
> There is no one who understands,
> there is no one who seeks God.
> All have turned away,
> together they have become useless;
> there is no one who does good,
> there is not even one.
> Their throat is an open grave;
> they deceive with their tongues.
> Vipers' venom is under their lips.
> Their mouth is full of cursing and bitterness.
> Their feet are swift to shed blood;
> ruin and wretchedness are in their paths,
> and the path of peace they have not known.
> There is no fear of God before their eyes (Romans 3:10–18).

As devastating a picture as this passage paints, it represents only the tip of the iceberg where Scripture's dreadful assessment of fallen humanity is concerned. It is as though the condition of sinful humanity is so dark and so multidimensional that only a ransacking of negative language can hope to approach the appalling reality it describes. In the wake of Adam's sin, humanity finds itself spiritually blind, bound, and dead. "Everyone who commits sin is a slave to sin" (John 8:34). The saving work of Jesus Christ delivers from slavery to sin (Romans 6:15–23). Even believers need the eyes of their hearts enlightened (Ephesians 1:18). Human wickedness reaches back not only to the beginning of time but to the beginning of each human life. "Indeed I was guilty when I was born; I was sinful when my mother conceived me" (Psalm 51: 5). After birth, we all, each without exception, seize the opportunity to confirm that we are our disobedient father Adam's progeny: "The wicked are estranged from the womb; they go astray from birth speaking lies" (Psalm 58:3). Augustine dismissed mirages of moral purity attaching to newborns. Of infants, he observed that their innocence is in their limbs, not their wills.[1] If they could rise from that crib and strangle you, they just might!

God blames us for our fall into sin, issues a verdict of guilty against us and directs His wrath toward us, giving us over to a reprobate mind, spiritually suicidal passions, and inevitable idolatry (Romans 1:18–32). Whoever seeks a self-esteem boost should steer clear of most of the Bible and

---

[1] Augustine, *Confessions*, Book I, 11 (New York, NY: Airmont, 1969), 12.

especially Romans 1–3, a passage designed metaphorically to beat us down in our own estimation and shut us up. It would seem that the proper posture requisite to right relationship with God always includes a profound humiliation and docility born of confrontation with our sin and God's own righteous verdict against us "so that every mouth may be shut and the whole world may become subject to God's judgment" (Romans 3:19).

So human depravity concerns human guilt and the spiritually binding, blinding, and deadening consequences of sin. This language highlights an array of incapacities resulting from human rebellion against the only true God. Sinners typically make no effort to do the will of God because they do not want to— "You are of your father the Devil, and you want to carry out your father's desires" (John 8:44). Should a sinner desire to do God's will, weakness prevents him: "For the desire to do what is good is with me, but there is no ability to do it" (Romans 7:18).

The language in the Bible and in the church regarding human evil and sin and the consequences of sin is truly remarkable for its darkness and profundity. Holy Scripture has convinced the church that sin and its consequences are pernicious and devastating beyond exhaustive comprehension. We are confronted, in the words of the apostle Paul, with the "mystery of iniquity" (2 Thessalonians 2:7), an assessment echoed three centuries later for Augustine and a generation of young scholars captivated by the ever elusive quest for answers to the question, *unde mallum?*—whence evil?

All God's Children Love Depravity

Where human depravity is concerned, significant overlap of language and sentiment is observable not only between Arminians and Calvinists but within much of Western Christianity as a whole, especially since Augustine (354–430). The inertia, the default posture, the reflexive instinct in the West is toward strong recognition of human depravity and clear acknowledgement of the necessity of divine grace for salvation. With the sinner's conversion in view, Article Three of the Arminian Remonstrance reads,

> … that man has not saving grace of himself, nor of the energy of his free will, inasmuch as he, in the state of apostasy and sin, can of and by himself neither think, will, nor do anything that is truly good (such as Faith eminently is).[2]

[2] Philip Schaff, *The Creeds of Christendom*, 3 vols. (Grand Rapids, MI: Baker Books, 1931), 3:546.

With the post-conversion continuance of the Christian life in view, Article Four acknowledges that

> the regenerate man himself, without prevenient or assisting, awakening, following and co-operative grace, can neither think, will, nor do good, nor withstand any temptations to evil; so that all good deeds or movements, that can be conceived, must be ascribed to the grace of God in Christ.[3]

Consider even the *Catechism of the Catholic Church* where the fall of Adam results in the universal propagation of a human nature "wounded in the natural powers proper to it; subject to ignorance, suffering, and the dominion of death; and inclined to sin—an inclination to evil that is called 'concupiscence.'"[4] For Roman Catholics, justification, associated with conversion, requires the grace of God and the enablement of the Holy Spirit: "The grace of the Holy Spirit has the power to justify us, that is to cleanse us from our sins and to communicate to us 'the righteousness of God through faith in Jesus Christ.'" Likewise sanctification: "The grace of Christ is the gratuitous gift that God makes to us of his own life, infused by the Holy Spirit into our soul to heal it of sin and to sanctify it."[5] We shall see that how words such as "infused" are employed offers clues to the real crux of disagreement between Dort and the Remonstrance, not only on the nature of human depravity but on the nature of the redeemed life God purposes for His children.

Notwithstanding the substantive and continuing division within the Western Church precisely on the doctrines of justification and sanctification, significant continuities remain. Thanks especially to Augustine's controversy with Pelagius, the whole church in the West evidences a certain compulsion to speak strongly of human depravity and of the necessity of grace for conversion and Holy Spirit-enablement for the Christian life.

The "I" Interprets the "T"

Along the fault line of polarization over humanity's post-lapsarian capacity for God, one side refuses to settle for the common language and substantive continuities we have identified. They may sing Charles Wesley's hymns with sincerity and gusto, but, for them, no Arminian construal of humanity's incapacity toward God ever fully suffices. Indeed, voices

---

[3] Schaff, *The Creeds of Christendom*, 3:547.

[4] *Catechism of the Catholic Chruch*, Second Edition, (Vatican City: Libreria Editice Vaticana,1994) , 102.

[5] Ibid., 481, 484.

with similar aims emerge from a discernible theological stream that runs
at least from Paul of Romans 9 and Ephesians 2 through Augustine, Luther, Calvin, Dort and Edwards. That shared aim centers on the denial that
even a shred of credit accrues to a single converted sinner for the salvation
they enjoy. Just this concern underlies the famous wording of Westminster:
"a natural man... is not able, by his own strength, to convert himself, or to
prepare himself thereunto."[6] Baptists far more Calvinistic in their views
than Paige Patterson can affirm without qualification most of the content
of his chapter, "Total Depravity" in *Whosoever Will*, but they also insist on
saying more.[7]

The crux of disagreement between Dort and the Remonstrance remains largely hidden when the "T" alone is in view. Quick inspection of
the five heads of doctrine promulgated at Dort immediately reveals that
the popularized acrostic TULIP has the consideration of topics out of order. The sequencing of subjects enshrined in the familiar acrostic was determined by un-theological considerations, namely that tulips are spectacularly native to the Netherlands. The tulip is the unofficial national flower
there. But, as we shall see, order matters here.

Dort itself treated the five points in this order: ULTIP, and according
to this language: (1) Of Divine Predestination, (2) Of the Death of Christ,
and the redemption of Men thereby, (3 & 4), Of the Corruption of Man,
his Conversion to God, and the Manner thereof, and finally (5) Of the
Perseverance of the Saints.[8] How striking and illuminating that only the
last two points of the acrostic reflect the order followed at the Synod itself
and only the last point faithfully reflects the language used at Dort.

It is significant that Dort identifies the "T" (total depravity/total inability) and the "I" (irresistible grace/effectual calling) as distinct doctrines
but also, unlike the other three doctrines, treats these two together. Dort
recognizes that the "T" and the "I" inform and illumine each other in crucial ways. The nature and extent of the incapacitation of sinful man is informed and illumined by the nature of his conversion and the manner
thereof, and *vice versa*.

Decisive in Dort's understanding of depravity is the Synod's comprehension of "the manner" of the sinner's conversion. Arminians and Calvinists both affirm that saving faith is a divine gift that has its source in the
grace of God alone. But Dort identifies two very different, indeed diver-

---

[6] *Westminster Confession*, Chapter IX, "Of Effectual Calling," par. III.

[7] Paige Patterson, "Total Depravity," in *Whosoever Will: A Biblical-Theological critique of five-Point Calvinism*, ed. David L. Allen and Steve W. Lemke (Nash-vile, TN: B&H, 2010), 29–44.

[8] Schaff, *The Creeds of Christendom*, 3:581–597.

gent and finally incompatible ways of understanding the gift character of faith. Note the words of Dort:

> Faith is… to be considered as the gift of God, not on account of its being offered by God to man, to be accepted or rejected at his pleasure, but because it is in reality conferred, breathed, and infused into him; nor even because God bestows the power or ability to believe, and then expects that man should, by the exercise of his own free will, consent to the terms of salvation, and actually believe in Christ; but because he works in man both to will and to do [Php. 2:13], and indeed all things in all, produces both the will to believe and the act of believing also.[9]

Two crucial distinctions are pressed: first is the distinction between an offered faith and a conferred or bestowed faith and second, between a faith that might or might not be exercised and one that God ensures will be. Such distinctions make the doctrine of effectual calling or irresistible grace the pivotal point of the TULIP. Where one comes down here reveals where one's true sympathies lie, and predicts where one will take refuge in the category of mystery. Now let us pursue the reasoning of Dort a little further.

After insisting on faith as a conferred or bestowed gift, Dort then anticipates one of the chief Arminian objections to this language that touches both on the matter of human depravity or inability and upon the character and manner of the sinner's confession. The objection is that the will of a sinner thus converted is abolished or overridden such that he is no longer recognizable as a responsible human being. He has become God's puppet. Dort denies that its insistence upon the effectual calling of sinners through the bestowal of saving faith must lead to such a result:

> … [A]s man by the fall did not cease to be a creature endowed with understanding and will, nor did sin, which pervaded the whole race of mankind, deprive him of the human nature, but brought upon him depravity and spiritual death; so also this grace of regeneration does not treat men as senseless stocks and blocks, nor take away their will and its properties, neither does violence thereto; but spiritually quickens, heals, corrects, and at the same time sweetly and powerfully bends it, that where carnal rebellion and resistance formerly prevailed, a ready and sincere spiritual obedience begins to reign; in which the true and spiritual restoration and freedom of our will consist.[10]

---

[9] Ibid., 3:591.
[10] Ibid., 3:591–592.

Dort acknowledges mystery in the conversion of the sinner—"The manner of this operation cannot be fully comprehended by believers in this life."[11] But the mystery emerges precisely because of two truths about which the Synod is not in doubt, but of which it is confident where the regeneration of sinners is concerned:

> [Regeneration] is evidentially a supernatural work, most powerful, and at the same time most delightful, astonishing, mysterious, and ineffable; not inferior in efficacy to creation or the resurrection from the dead, as the Scripture inspired by the author of this work declares; so that all in whose hearts God works in this marvelous manner are certainly, infallibly, and effectually regenerated, and do actually believe. Whereupon the will thus renewed is not only actuated and influenced by God, but, in consequence of this influence, becomes itself active. Wherefore, also man is himself rightly said to believe and repent, by virtue of the grace received.[12]

Divergent reading of Holy Scripture by Arminians and Calvinists centers less on how they understand the consequences of the Fall and more on what constitutes deliverance from those consequences once God begins to direct His saving activity toward a spiritually blind, bound, and dead sinner. For the Arminian, that saving activity involves much that the Calvinist also affirms: enlightening, regenerating, wooing, and enabling. But, for the Arminian, the sinner *must be capable* of successfully thwarting the saving activity of God *against the will of God*.

Accordingly, Arminian thinking sometimes treats saving faith itself or the latent capacity for faith as an offered gift which the sinner accepts or not according to his own free will. Once this potential faith is in the possession of the yet unconverted sinner, he may exercise it or not according to his own will when the gospel is proclaimed. It is interesting to note that, in the Arminian vision, the sinner gets his way in the end but God may not!

The Arminian Holy-of-Holies

This right-of-refusal vis-à-vis God's saving overtures is inviolable for the Arminian. It is the Arminian holy-of-holies. What the Arminian can and cannot say about human depravity traces back to this point. If a potentially distortive systematizing animates the Calvinist mind where sovereign grace is concerned, the Arminian counterpart resides here, in the right-of-refusal. Curious new steps in the order of salvation appear because of it. Note the argument of longtime Southern Baptist New Testament scholar

[11] Ibid., 590.
[12] Ibid.

Frank Stagg. Commenting on Ephesians 2:8 and Philippians 1:29 he contends, "in one sense, faith is God's gift, yet it must be a gift *received*."[13] Faith is offered, not bestowed, and must be received or not according to the free will of the sinner. Subsequently, Jesus Christ, clothed with His gospel, is offered and either accepted or rejected according to the sinner's free-will decision to exercise his newly received capacity for faith or not.

The whole scene is quite complicated. Why is this so? Arminian comprehension of the depravity of sinners typically, and appropriately, finds itself compelled to address matters related to the conversion of sinners. After impressive acknowledgement of the sinners' incapacity before God and the utter need for the grace of God for salvation, including especially the work of the Holy Spirit, an attenuation of the sinner's incapacity is also insisted upon together with a limitation of what God either can or is willing to do to save a sinner. Thus, in Paige Patterson's chapter on Total Depravity:

> Humans are totally depraved. They cannot help themselves. That is what depravity means. Humans are in sin that has come from their father Adam, and now it has been visited upon them. They are helpless and hopeless in that sin ...

Before we consider the end of this sentence, let us note two things: (1) what Patterson has so far asserted accords perfectly with Calvinist and Augustinian reading of Holy Scripture. It is important to remember that Arminianism is not Pelagianism. It is a reform movement within the Reformed branch of the magisterial Reformation of the 16th century. (2) Unlike the Calvinist, for the Arminian (and for the Pelagian too we should note) obligation implies ability. Thus, what God requires of human beings, human beings can perform. Now we continue with Patterson: "they are helpless and hopeless in their sin, *but they can still cry out to God*. All the people on the face of the earth can cry out to God."[14]

Then at the end of Patterson's chapter, as he explores "the manner of the sinner's conversion," he commends Robert Picirilli's own protection of the inviolability of human free-will through a tinkering with the order of salvation: "By definition, pre-regenerating grace is that work of the Holy Spirit that 'opens the heart' of the unregenerate (to use the words of Acts 16:14) to the truth of the gospel and enables them to respond positively in faith."[15]

---

[13] Emphasis mine. Frank Stagg, *New Testament Theology* (Nashville, TN: Broadman Press, 1962), 120.

[14] Emphasis mine. Patterson, "Total Depravity," 43.

[15] Patterson, "Total Depravity," 43.

Why this consistent attenuation of the effects of the fall so that sinners, however blind, bound, and dead they might be, can, nonetheless, effectively "cry out to God"? Why the fierce protection of the sinner's right-of-refusal even after the reception of the gift of faith, even under the saving onslaught of God the Holy Spirit? What is at stake for the Arminian? The Calvinist insists that God, according to His will, wisdom, timing, and use of means "sees to it" that those He means to convert and save are converted and saved. Why does such a view so threaten the Arminian? Why does the sinner's right-of-refusal function as the Arminian holy-of-holies?

The Inviolable Will

Partly the answer is that, for the Arminian, divine determination of the human will destroys moral responsibility, undermines necessary incentives to moral striving, vitiates justice, and compromises true relationship. That obligation implies ability means that God cannot require the impossible of man and where the right-of-refusal is lost, no real relationship is possible. After all, responsibility requires ability to respond, and to respond either positively or negatively, right?

For the Calvinist the answer is no. Obligation to respond remains even after ability to respond has been lost through willful fall into sin. That human beings, through willful rebellion against God, bring such moral and spiritual damage upon themselves that they can no longer respond does not require or result in a "lowering of the bar" by God. We cannot provide what God demands and it is our fault that this is so. Our guilt not only remains but is heightened. Such recognition that neither guilt nor responsibility requires ability in the sinner allows the Calvinist to embrace all the devastating Biblical characterizations of the effects of the fall with full seriousness. Refusal to do so sends the Arminian into an array of exegetical contortions and backflips in order to explain how "blind," "bound," and "dead" mean something somewhat different, somewhat less, indeed decisively less at the crucial point, than a straightforward reading of "blind," "bound," and "dead" would suggest.

But what about true relationship where God determines the wills of sinners in saving conversion? In the Arminian mind, only two realities seem possible: either libertarian free will obtains, especially at the point of conversion, or we are all puppets on a string. By libertarian free will I mean that where a decision or choice is made, its opposite might have been made. Thus, either sinners are capable of successfully and finally thwarting God's saving designs or we are all robots.

Given these limited alternatives, the Arminian construal of the conversion of sinners must protect libertarian free-will. The specter of a ro-

botic Christianity demands it. The necessity of the work of the Holy Spirit
in conversion is maintained but in a carefully proscribed manner. God the
Holy Spirit restores lost libertarian free will, thus making conversion possible but by no means ensuring such an outcome. For the Arminian, the
Holy Spirit does not convert sinners as such, but begins a process that
might or might not culminate in conversion by enabling the human will
to function in a libertarian way when the gospel is offered. God's grace,
strictly speaking, does not convert sinners, but rather makes conversion
possible by both enabling the will, overcoming the spiritually disabling effects of depravity, and wooing the sinner with the promises of the gospel.
But, since the Arminian holy-of -holies, libertarian free will, the right-of-
refusal, must be protected, God the Holy Spirit must not "see to it" that the
sinner repents or believes.

For the Arminian salvation depends upon the will of God and the
grace of God and upon the active work of the Holy Spirit to convert inasmuch as without such divine provision, depraved sinners would remain
spiritually bankrupt and without hope. But clearly, salvation now depends
also, and in a sense, ultimately, not upon God's will in the matter but upon
the sinner's will. For the Arminian, the consequences of sin, though dire,
do not prevent the sinner from determining his own will (he can cry out
to God if he wants) and the work of the Holy Spirit restores self-deter-
mination of will to repent and believe in response to the gospel of Jesus
Christ. Thus, the conversion of the sinner does not ultimately depend upon
God alone (monergism) because God, for the Arminian, always does His
part and His part does not include determination of the wills of sinners.
The sinner can and must determine his own will. Conversion of sinners
requires a divine and a human determining (synergism).

Human depravity, under the apparently universal saving activity of
God, does not result in utter dependence of the sinner upon God for salvation but retains the power (yes power provided by God) to have the last
word in the matter of his own salvation due to the sacrosanct prerogative to determine and exercise one's own will, a prerogative established,
maintained, and kept inviolate by God Himself in order to maintain (1)
the sinner's responsibility (2) legitimate divine justice (3) true relationship
between Himself and human beings and (4) necessary incentives to moral
striving.

Determination of the Will

It will be good now to highlight a major cause of misunderstanding,
failure to communicate, and talking past one another that often characterizes discussion between Arminians and Calvinists. It centers on consider-

ation of the human will. Once the Arminian successfully establishes that human beings have functioning wills, he believes much of the argument with the Calvinist is concluded in his own favor. Establishing that human beings, before and after the fall, as well as before and after conversion possess a functioning will, is a slam dunk and the Arminian is greatly encouraged and emboldened by this fact. Every instance of a human being exercising his will whether recorded in the Bible, occurring in history, or achieved in the Arminian's own life stands as conclusive, incontrovertible proof that human beings have functioning wills. Thus, human beings are capable, before and after the Fall, before and after conversion, of exercising their wills and choosing one available option rather than another in the whole range of human possibility.

But the question of whether human beings have a will, while very significant, nevertheless begs the crucial question at issue where human depravity and effectual calling are concerned. Though he was not the first to recognize this Arminian blind spot and misunderstanding, Jonathan Edwards, more thoroughly than anyone else, identified and clarified this subject in his 1754 essay *On the Freedom of the Will.*[16] There Edwards frames the question not "can man will or choose?" but "how does it come about that man wills or chooses this or that?" These are related but distinguishable and quite different questions. One may, according to Edwards, acknowledge human ability to choose according to one's will or desire between an array of options without addressing the question of how it comes about that one wills and therefore chooses this rather than that. For the Arminian this answer is settled from the outset; while the human will may respond to and be affected by any number of influences, including the enlightening, illuminating, wooing, and enabling activity of the Holy Spirit, ultimately, "the chooser" himself determines his will, determines his desire, and chooses accordingly.

The critical point at issue is not whether human beings have functioning wills but whether human beings can determine their own wills. The answer, from Edwards is "no," they cannot determine their own wills. By this he means that human beings (even before the Fall!) cannot determine their own wills. Another way of stating this seems especially powerful—wills do not have wills! To say that a will determines itself is a nonsensical

---

[16] Jonathan Edwards, "A Careful and Strict Enquiry into the Modern Prevailing Notions of the Freedom of the Will, Which Is Supposed to Be Essential to Moral Agency, virtue and vice, Reward and Punishment, Praise and Blame (1954)," in *A Jonathan Edwards Reader*, John E. Smith, Harry S. Stout, and Kenneth P. Minkema eds. (New Haven, CT: Yale University Press, 1995), 192–222.

tautology. The will chooses according to its preference or desire which it cannot give itself but rather finds itself determined by.

In a certain sense, this point seems provable on a very mundane level. Think of a person, an experience, or a particular food that you dislike or even despise. Well just determine your own will to love such a person, experience, or food. Just do it! We are not talking here about gritting our teeth and going through the motions. We are talking about the kind of genuine exercise of the will that comes from the heart, as it were; a will that truly and non-coercively (a word Arminians love!) desires and pursues what it once did not. Truly, from the heart, pursue time, quality and quantity, with that jerk who grates on your nerves at work. Gobble down those once obnoxious turnips. Sell your condo in Tampa, head north and fight for the privilege to shovel that snow in a 15-below wind-chill. Just do it! Determine your own will.

Much that must characterize the will in the exercise of faith or repentance and faith is affirmed by both Arminian and Calvinist, especially at the point of conversion—it must be free, not-coerced. It must be, in a word "willing." Yet for the Arminian, who admits he will likely, if not inevitably, fail to determine his own will in the mundane matters we have mentioned, is somehow confident that in the deepest most mysterious and most urgent matters of the Spirit, he can and does successfully do so.

That God regularly and unapologetically does determine the wills of whomever He wills need not seek confirmation in common human experience. Holy Scripture makes this plain. "I will place My Spirit within you and cause you to follow My statutes and carefully observe My ordinances" (Ezekiel 36:27). Likewise God hardens Pharaoh's heart so that he won't let His people go, thus determining his will (Exodus 4:21; 7:4, 5). How spectacularly, bluntly, and unapologetically the Bible reports divine intervention into and determination of human wills!

Meandering Mystery

Knowledge, not ignorance, typically provokes warranted Christian confession of mystery. Thus knowledge that Jesus Christ is fully divine and fully human compels confession of the *mystery* of the Incarnation. Such confession insists upon what it knows while acknowledging the inexhaustible and wondrous reality with which it is confronted. Likewise, knowledge of one God in three eternal persons, Father, Son and Holy Spirit, compels confession of the *mystery* of the Trinity. These are the two great, ancient, and foundational *mysteries* of the Christian faith. Each is compelled by confrontation with and the gaining of genuine knowledge of the Living God.

A similar confession of mystery arises where one acknowledges that God determines the will of those He savingly converts to Himself. How can it be that God "sees to it" that a sinner repents and believes the gospel, yet he, the sinner, truly does the repenting and the believing; God does not do it for him. The Calvinist acknowledges mystery here but insists both upon what the Arminian cannot (that God determines the will) and that the will, thus determined, acts freely. Indeed, for the Calvinist, it is only in repentance and faith and obedience that the will acts with true freedom! Thus, Dort explicitly states of the saving conversion of the sinner—he truly believes.

The Arminian takes refuge in mystery where divine sovereignty in the matter of salvation is concerned or, to put it more pointedly, where acknowledgement of sovereign grace seems obvious or when confronted by predestination or election in Holy Scripture. But, take note, little mystery intrudes upon or clouds Arminian clarity and certainty where the Arminian holy-of-holies is concerned. Arminians are certain that sinners retain the right-of-refusal where the conversion of sinners is concerned. Little mystery attaches to the Arminian insistence upon libertarian free will. My own contention is that while straightforward reading of sovereign grace, predestination, and election texts underlies Augustinian and Calvinistic sifting of certainty, doubt, and mystery, an alien norm animates Arminian protection of libertarian free will. Where in Scripture do we learn of this inviolable right-of-refusal, this libertarian free will? Could it be that Augustine himself, by refuting Pelagius on Pelagius' own terms, legitimized content and usage attaching to the little phrase "free will" that really has no place in a biblical view of reality? It is a question worth exploring.

Abandoning the Holy of Holies

A chief feature of my argument is to identify the Arminian holy-of-holies and show how determinative this conviction is to ones understanding of human depravity. Yet, wonder of wonders, the whole Western church, including Arminians of every degree and stripe within it, eventually abandons it. On their own, those who believed that the justice of God, human virtue, and true relationship depended on libertarian free will and the right-of-refusal find that they can do without it. For Baptists who reject effectual calling but assert perseverance of the saints, abandonment comes, at least in some degree, at the point of conversion. For thoroughgoing Arminians who believe in the possibility of apostasy after conversion, abandonment of the right-of-refusal comes in the next life. Even Roman Catholics give it up once a soul springs from Purgatory and traverses the threshold at the Pearly Gates.

Such abandonment of the right-of-refusal accords with Augustine's tracing of the changing possibilities concerning human sin and the human will. Augustine identifies four states according to his famous "*posses*." For Adam and Eve in the Garden before the Fall it was *posse non peccare* (possible not to sin); after the Fall, *non posse non peccare* (not possible not to sin); post-conversion, once again, *posse non peccare* (possible not to sin); and finally, in the new heaven and the new earth, *non posse peccare* (not possible to sin).[17]

The whole, historic, global church somehow manages eventually to affirm the "keeping" power of God; clearly a divine limitation of the human right-of-refusal. For the Baptist who affirms perseverance, apparently God's keeping of the convert does not undermine justice or turn believers into robots. Why not? Eventually the Roman Catholic and the Methodist are happy for God to "see to it" that no one successfully thwarts God's will and jumps out of heaven.

What happened? Why was God's determination of the human will so abhorrent before but not now? For the Calvinist, the language that applies to God's effectual calling largely transfers to the doctrine of perseverance; the language of enlightenment, enablement, and persuasion.

For consistent Arminians, the same dangers that arise where effectual calling is concerned emerge for just the same reasons with respect to perseverance of the saints. In response to Baptist J. R. Graves, the great 19th century Methodist debater, Jacob Ditzler articulated as much:

> [The doctrine of perseverance] destroys all free agency and responsibility. It assumes that after conversion men are perfectly passive in God's hand—have no free will, no choice, no action—are machines.
>
> … It is not good for the moral and intellectual universe that man be deprived of the value, pleasure, and dignity of choice—of free agency. In it alone is there such a type of intellectual and moral dignity and grandeur, and such capacity for happiness and bliss as is pleasing to God, and compatible with his wisdom. The qualification for real mental and moral happiness is freedom of choice.[18]

Once such freedom of choice is undermined, says Ditzler, believers may "lull to repose, ease, carelessness, presumption and ruin."[19] Where the

---

[17] Augustine, "On Rebuke and Grace," in *The Nicene and Post-Nicene Fathers*, Series 1, vol. 5 (Grand Rapids, MI: Eerdmans, 1983), 484–486. Hereafter, NPNF.

[18] J.R. Graves and Jacob Ditzler, *The Graves-Ditzler: or Great Carrollton Debate* (Memphis, TN: The Southern Baptist Publication Society, 1876), 1143.

[19] The *Graves-Ditzler*, 1118.

Bible and theological truth is concerned, it is never legitimate to argue backwards, as Ditzler does, casting aspersion upon a reading of Scripture or an ostensibly biblical doctrine from supposed effects. Be that as it may, let us remember, in the Arminian mind, either libertarian free-will obtains or we are all robots. But is this really so? While the doctrines of effectual calling and perseverance and depravity rightly call forth confession of mystery, it is important not to exaggerate the mystery involved where divine determination of the human will is in view.

Faithful, loving, godly parents do everything in their power to influence, to determine the wills of their children to choose what is good and spurn what is evil. Such parents view this attempt to determine the wills of their children as an essential dimension of their God-given responsibility. When they are successful they do not imagine that they have violated their children's psyches or selfhood. When their children's wills are successfully influenced, neither the parents nor anyone else supposes that somehow the children are not themselves willing and choosing and acting or that they are the puppets of their parents. So it is when God successfully influences and so determines the wills of those He saves through repentance and faith. "Ah!" the Arminian, observes, "but children often successfully thwart the loving overtures of their parents to influence their wills." This is true. But God is much better at this than human parents!

Law and Gospel

Deeper theological concerns become apparent when we consider the Arminian understanding of what actually occurs in the conversion of depraved sinners. They envision some sort of enablement of the sinner that does not inevitably result in conversion but rather in a potential for conversion. Sinners are not awakened to saving faith, but to its possibility. They are not actually made alive in Christ Jesus (Ephesians 2:5) but made spiritually alive in some sort of middle space between their previous state of, let us call it Augustinian or Calvinistic depravity, and actual incorporation into Christ. This middle space is not neutral; in it God exerts persuasive power. God woos the sinner. But the outcome or result of this life in the middle space is ambiguous. Arminians seem to affirm a divine empowerment, a Holy Spirit enablement, a pre-regenerative divine activity that involves a *transfer* of power to the sinner. This power passes into the possession of the sinner inasmuch as the sinner determines whether it accomplishes its intended purpose, namely his conversion, or not. Such a scheme is wrongheaded at more than one level.

First of all, Holy Spirit empowerment must be distinguished sharply from other sorts of empowerment by, for example, exercise or amphetamines or even a course on positive thinking. Each of these may serve as true sources of empowerment in which, indeed, power or energy or capability is transferred to the person, comes into their possession, and thus, under their control for use according to their will. Not so Holy Spirit empowerment. The Holy Spirit is God. The Holy Spirit is the third Person of the divine Trinity. To speak of having the Holy Spirit can be misleading. To have God in any sense implies no control over or use of God but rather something rather opposite, a belonging to Him! God's Spirit-enabled presence within believers involves no surrender of divine power or sovereignty whatsoever. God the Holy Spirit empowers the doing of the will of God, not its mere possibility and certainly not its thwarting!

Secondly, the Arminian construal of conversion threatens a lapse into a works system, a lapse back into law. It opens up a ground for boasting in which what has made the converted sinner different from his unconverted brother (1 Corinthians 4:7) is not the gift of God but rather his own proper and superior acceptance and use of a divine gift his brother squandered.[20] As Luther saw so well, once faith is made into a work, it is no longer the faith that saves, that lives from its object, that cleaves to Christ and credits Christ alone for its own cleaving, that no longer desires a righteousness of its own. Faith now becomes the new work required of sinful man.

The insinuation of such thinking into the believing psyche smuggles a law system into the life of the church—a "going back under law" akin to that which Paul resisted tooth and nail in his Epistle to the Galatians. The foolishness of the Galatians emerged not in their understanding of conversion, of how their life in Jesus Christ "began," indeed, the apostle is very clear, "you began well." Paul uses their having begun well to bring a devastating critique against how they are attempting to continue with Christ. "After beginning with the Spirit, are you now going to be made complete by the flesh?"(Galatians 3:1–3). "The flesh" in Galatians can be understood essentially as the attempt to use works of Law like a ladder to climb up to God. The result ironically is not freedom but slavery. What Arminians defend and call freedom, Paul calls slavery.

---

[20] In 1 Corinthians 4:7 διακρίνω can mean "make superior" or "give an advantage," rather than merely "make different." This stronger sense certainly fits the context of 1 Corinthians 4 where the issue of merit and boasting are in view. It is also difficult to see how the sense of the passage can be comprehended unless the idea of a bestowed as opposed to an offered gift is envisioned.

Garden Variety Depravity

The life bestowed upon and enjoyed by Adam and Eve was character-ized fundamentally by God's permission not prohibition. On the surface, Eve' first words to the serpent's inquiry appear praiseworthy—"We may eat the fruit of the trees of the garden" (Genesis 3:2). Still, humanity was confronted with one divine prohibition: "you must not eat from the tree of the knowledge of good and evil" (Genesis 2:17). Punishment of such eat-ing would be death. In stark contrast there stood the tree of life among the many trees from which our first parents could freely partake. No doubt we are meant to view these trees as representative of God's fundamental will for human life.[21] The tree of life points to the relationship between creature and Creator which God desires and blesses. Conversely, the prohibited tree of knowledge of good and evil, indicates, in some basic way, the human life God opposes and punishes.

Yet, must it not strike us as odd that "the knowledge of good and evil," should be associated with transgression and rebellion against God? Some view creation of humanity in the image of God as highlighting, among other things, the unique position of man as a responsible chooser between good and evil options. In such a case, what could be more helpful, indeed, necessary to humanity's fulfillment of God's will and of his own human nature than the possession of the knowledge of good and evil? Karl Barth's question, one raised periodically but rather infrequently in the history of exegesis, is a valid one:

> It is surprising that in the Christian Church more offense is not taken at the fact—or have we simply read it away—that in Gen. 3 the desire of man for a knowledge of good and evil is represented as an evil desire, indeed the one evil desire which is so characteristic and fatal for the whole race...[22]

What is the explanation? One clue lies in the serpent's suggestion that if Eve should eat of the forbidden fruit, she would become "*like* God, knowing good and evil" (Genesis 3:5). Eve was also attracted to the tree because it was "good for food," and was "delightful to look at" (Genesis 3:6). However, it was the allurement of the tree's power "to make one wise" to which the serpent appealed and on which the Lord God focused: "man has become like one of Us, knowing good and evil" (Genesis 3:22).

---

[21] See Dietrich Bonhoeffer, *Ethics*, trans. N.H. Smith (New York, NY: Mac-millan Publishing co., 1949), 17–20.

[22] Karl Barth, *Church Dogmatics*, (Edinburgh: T&T Clark, 1956), 4:447–449.

Adam and Eve's lapse into sin involved the gaining of a special kind of knowledge, a knowledge appropriate to God alone. It follows that the previous bliss of Eden was characterized by a certain human ignorance wherein Creator and creature occupied their ordained spheres in relation to this distinctive knowledge. Just as loss of innocence implies the gaining of knowledge, so humanity's fall from innocence implies the loss of a distinctive and an apparently salutary ignorance. Note that the partaking of the fruit did indeed result in increased knowledge, namely of nakedness. Yet Adam and Eve were not able to handle this knowledge, they were not able to make holy use of it. Instead they immediately found God's creation less than good. As Chrysostom would have it, they "conceived thoughts above [their] dignity."[23]

J. L. Dagg speaks with the historic church when he points to "the happiness Adam and Eve enjoyed, while their innocence remained."[24] Charles Hodge, in discussing the conditions of Eden, also noted that the innocence of infancy is "sometimes expressed by saying that a child cannot tell its right hand from its left; sometimes by saying that he cannot discern between the evil and the good" (Deuteronomy 1:39; Isaiah 7:16).[25]

Evidently there is a knowledge of good and evil which properly belongs only to God. When our first parents tried to lay hold of such knowledge they were reprimanded because they sought to be "like God." The contrast between the sin of our first parents and the descent of the eternal Son of God in the Incarnation is fascinating. For Christ, who was already divine, to seek to be like God would not be counted as robbery" (Philippians 2:4). For Adam and Eve however, the grasping of the fruit did indeed constitute attempted robbery, a snatching by the creature at that which belongs exclusively to the Creator.

But what is the connection between "the knowledge of good and evil" and "being like God?" Augustine suggests that openness to the serpent's enticement indicates that man had already begun "to live for himself... it was this that made him listen with pleasure to the words, 'ye shall be as gods'."[26] The link between "the knowledge of good and evil" and "being like God" involves the divine omniscience and self-sufficiency.

God is not dependent upon anything outside himself in order to live and be in perfection as the Lord of Glory. "Being Lord of heaven and

---

[23] John Chrysostom, NPNF.1.9. 413. See also, Chrysostom, NPNF.1.10.126.

[24] John L. Dagg, *Manual of Theology and Church Order* (Harrisonburgh, VA: Gano Books, 1982), 143.

[25] Charles Hodge, *Systematic Theology* (Grand Rapids, MI: Eerdmans, 1977), 2:126.

[26] Augustine, *The City of God*, NPNF.1.2.273.

earth" God is not "served by human hands, as though he needed anything" (Acts 17:24–25) since he himself gives to all men life and breath and everything." God minus the world is still God. The affirmation of God's independence, while true, risks misunderstanding.

The early church attempted to comprehend God's self-sufficiency not through the negative term "independence," but through the positive idea of His "aseity." This word means literally, "from oneself." It was used to confess that God lives, exists, and has His being wholly from His own intrinsic sufficiency. Barth connects God's aseity to humanity's tragic fall:

> ... [Adam] saw and took and ate, in the conviction that by taking up his own attitude to the commandment of God, he was understanding God better than God understood Himself, in the intoxicating certainty that by asserting his autonomy he was seeing and doing the real will of God. The error of man concerning himself, his self-alienation, is that he thinks he can love and choose and will and assert and maintain and exalt himself—*sese propter seipsum*—in his being in himself, his self-hood, and that in doing so he will be truly man. Whether this takes place in pride or in modesty, either way man misses his true being. For neither as an individual nor in society was he created to be placed alone, to be self-controlling and self-sufficient, to be self-centered, and to rotate around himself. Like every other creature he was created for the glory of God and only in that way for his own salvation. The aseity which he ascribes to himself is proper only to God.[27]

Humanity's fall into sin results in a condition that must be described in terms of spiritual blindness and deadness and in which the will is enslaved, not free. Arminians and Calvinists can walk hand in hand pretty far down this road and speak much the same language and mean much the same things by that language. But we need to ask whether the Arminian insistence that the work of the Holy Spirit frees the will to *either* repent and believe *or* refuse to do so does not evidence a deeper misunderstanding of the nature of depravity itself. Does not the nature of the transgression that leads to the Fall of humanity involve a grasping at something very close to what the Arminian considers essential to true righteousness, virtue and holiness, namely, a human being living from himself, like God?

Does not the gospel of Jesus Christ promise much more and indeed, something different than a restoration of Eden? Does it not promise a rescue into a loving, wise, and effectual divine determination of the human will which necessarily belongs to Gods "keeping power"?

---

[27] Barth, *Church Dogmatics*, IV, 1, 421.

Forever Children

The union of believers with their Lord establishes them in an ongoing, divinely intended dependence upon Jesus Christ who is their life.[28] The Holy Spirit reveals these things to believers and empowers them to enjoy, in grateful responsive obedience, their liberty as joint heirs of the eternal Son of God. As such they are forever made the adopted children of the Heavenly Father to whom the Spirit cries on their behalf "Abba." The Spirit enables these children to lay hold in their earthly existence of that which has already been purchased for them and is now kept in heaven for those "who by God's power are guarded through faith for a salvation ready to be revealed in the last days" (1 Peter 1:5).

The sure sign, the guarantee of divine sonship and thus of believer's qualification as heirs of God and joint heirs of Christ is the indwelling of the Spirit who empowers faith (Galatians 3:1–5; 4: 4–7). Just as God required faith of Adam and Eve and calls for faith in believers today, so in heaven beyond, perfect faith shall prevail—not the "evidence of things not seen" dimension of faith, but the trust dimension (*fiducia*) that became so pivotal for Luther's theology. The core of the righteousness God requires and produces has never been the power to again and again choose evil over good, but the power and disposition to lean upon everlasting arms, safe and secure from all alarms. The Lord taught His disciples to pray "lead us not into temptation but deliver us from the evil one." And when this same Lord answers the prayer that His kingdom come and that His will be done, so will all knowledge of evil be done away forever and perfect faith prevail.

Sin has spiritually crippled every human being, exposing and deepening our utter dependence upon God for salvation and everything good, including faith. But, *nota bene*, sin did not create our reliance upon God for everything good including the determination of our wills. Grace was not a fallback position once works did not fly. We were created for reliance upon God's power from the beginning. As earthly parents, it is right for us to encourage our children's maturity into adult independence. But with respect to God, independence is the lie, independence is the sin. Before God we are commanded and invited to mature into dependence! Because in Him and from creation, we are and are meant to remain forever children!

---

[28] God providentially "[raises His children] to a more close and constant dependence for their support upon Himself...." *The Westminster Confession*, Chapter 5, "Of Providence," par. V.

3

Unconditional Election
A BIBLICAL AND GOD-GLORIFYING DOCTRINE

Andrew M. Davis

For from him and through him and to him are all things. To him be the glory forever! Amen (Romans 11:36).

With these stirring words, the Apostle Paul concludes the clearest and most exacting doctrinal exposition of the gospel of Jesus Christ found in the Bible. For eleven chapters, Paul has been explaining the gospel, *the power of God for the salvation of everyone who believes* (Romans 1:16). At the end of this spectacular exposition, Paul bursts forth in the most exalted praise of Almighty God, ascribing to Him magnificent wisdom and inscrutable judgments, celebrating the independence of God from all human counsel and the impossibility of putting God in the position of a debtor (Romans 11:33–35). Paul then speaks the words printed above, revealing the divine origin of all things, the fact that all things continue to exist only at God's will, the fact that all things will, in the end, return unto God. Paul's soaring conclusion ascribes to God the glory forever. Amen!

But for what should God be glorified? In context, we must answer that, to God alone should be the glory for every aspect of human salvation. As a matter of fact, we may go so far as to say that nothing in all the universe glorifies God so much as His sovereign action of saving sinners from their sins through the substitutionary death of Jesus Christ. Such a God-centered salvation has glorified Him for millennia, and will glorify Him for eternity. Forever and ever, the Redeemed will study afresh God's saving work through Jesus Christ on their behalf, and they will burst forth again and again, saying, "To God alone, and to no created being, be the glory for our salvation!"

God is jealous for this glory; it is rightfully His, and He will share it with no other. God acts out on this zeal for His own glory many times in Redemptive History. He told Gideon, "You have too many men for me to deliver Midian into their hands." (Judges 7:2) To send the overwhelming majority of warriors home before a battle violates all human reason. But God is very clear about His motives: "In order that Israel may not boast against me that her own strength has saved her..." After the victory was won, God wanted the glory to go to Him alone. He well knew the devilish pride in the heart of man, how prone we are to boast about our own achievements, attributes, possessions, intentions, and choices.

Many passages of Scripture proclaim God's zeal for His own glory and His special desire that no human may boast before Him for *any aspect whatsoever:*

- I am the LORD; that is my name! I will not give my glory to another or my praise to idols (Isaiah 42:8).

- For my own sake, for my own sake, I do this. How can I let myself be defamed? I will not yield my glory to another (Isaiah 48:11).

- Where, then, is boasting? It is excluded (Romans 3:27).

- For it is by grace you have been saved, through faith—and this not from yourselves, it is the gift of God—not by works, so that no one can boast (Ephesians 2:8–9).

- May I never boast except in the cross of our Lord Jesus Christ, through which the world has been crucified to me, and I to the world (Galatians 6:14).

One passage in particular that zeroes in on God's zeal for His own glory in human salvation is 1 Corinthians 1:26–31:

Brothers, think of what you were when you were called. Not many of you were wise by human standards; not many were influential; not many were of noble birth. But God chose the foolish things of the world to shame the wise; God chose the weak things of the world to shame the strong. He chose the lowly things of this world and the despised things—and the things that are not—to nullify the things that are, so that no one may boast before him. It is because of him that you are in Christ Jesus, who has become for us wisdom from God—that is, our righteousness, holiness and redemption. Therefore, as it is written: "Let him who boasts boast in the Lord."

In this amazing paragraph, the Apostle Paul instructs the Corinthian church on the doctrine of election, and specifically what He was seeking in whom He chose to be Christians. According to Paul, God specifically chose certain kinds of people (the "foolish", the weak, the lowly, the despised) far more than others (the wise, the influential, those of noble birth, the strong). This choosing on God's part was to humble the arrogance of man, so that people would realize that it is only because of God that any of us are Christians—"It is because of *him* (i.e. God) that you are in Christ Jesus." It was specifically "so that no one would boast before him." Rather, when we are rightly instructed in the motives of God in selecting whom He wills, we will be completely stripped of our pride and boast only in the Lord. Amazingly, this passage indicates that the election of God even extends to the way a specific local church (e.g. the one at Corinth) is made up—what specific people are its members. God specifically chose the rejects of Corinthian society so that the Christians themselves would be humbled as He saves them and brings them to glory! God's ways are surely not our ways.

This brings us very readily to the topic at hand: the doctrine of unconditional election for salvation. It is the purpose of this chapter to define, unfold, and root in scripture this vital doctrine. It is also our purpose here to defend this doctrine from attacks on it that would seek to undermine its potency. Our goal is that God alone would be glorified in this present world for what He did before the foundation of the world: to choose His elect for salvation from every tribe and nation and people and language, not because of anything He foresaw in them, but simply because of His purpose in grace.

It is also my purpose in this chapter to respond to Richard Land's chapter entitled "Congruent Election: Understanding Salvation from an 'Eternal Now' Perspective," which appears in the volume *Whosoever Wills: A Biblical-Theological Critique of Five-Point Calvinism.*[1] In that article, Land articulates an angle on election that he argues is new and connects both with as much scripture as possible (and not merely certain proof texts) and with the theological tradition in which he was raised. I will seek to show that (1) Land's position is not new at all, but rather the old Arminian view of election based on foreseen faith which has been around for centuries; (2) Land's position does not sufficiently grapple with relevant scriptures on unconditional election, and is actually not based on much exegesis at all;

---

[1] Richard Land, "Congruent Election: Understanding Election from an 'Eternal Now' Perspective," in *Whosoever Will: A Biblical-Theological Critique of Five-Point Calvinism*, ed. David L. Allen and Steven W. Lemke (Nashville, TN: B&H, 2010), 45–59.

(3) While historical traditions are not decisive in this theological debate, church history is helpful for resolving theological questions only when giving us specific insights into relevant Scriptures.

Election Asserted in Scripture

Does the Bible teach the doctrine of election at all? There would be nothing to debate concerning the ground of our election if the Bible did not teach it. But the doctrine of election is so abundantly manifested in Scripture that Land is right in asserting, "I do not believe you can put yourself under the authority of Scripture and not believe in election."[2]

The Bible speaks of election in more than one sense. First, there is the election of Israel as God's special people, chosen out of all the nations of the earth for unique privileges and service to God. God spoke to Israel through Moses saying, "For you are a people holy to the LORD your God. The LORD your God has chosen you out of all the peoples on the face of the earth to be his people, his treasured possession" (Deuteronomy 7:6). Second, there is the election of individuals to a special office or calling. David spoke of God having chosen him to be king over Israel, and of God having chosen Solomon out of all his sons to succeed him as king (1 Chronicles 28:4–5). So also God chose Moses to lead Israel out of Egypt (Exodus 3), Jeremiah to be a prophet (Jeremiah 1:5), and the Twelve to be Apostles of Jesus Christ (John 6:70). Third, there is the election of individual people to be children of God and heirs of salvation in Jesus Christ. It is this third election that concerns us. It is attested to in many places in Scripture:

- [God] chose us in him before the foundation of the world, that we should be holy and blameless before him. In love he predestined us for adoption as sons through Jesus Christ, according to the purpose of his will, to the praise of his glorious grace... (Ephesians 1:4–6).

- If you belonged to the world, it would love you as its own. As it is, you do not belong to the world, but I have chosen you out of the world (John 15:19).

- For we know, brothers loved by God, that he has chosen you (1 Thessalonians 1:4).

- So too, at the present time there is a remnant chosen by grace (Romans 11:5).

[2] Ibid., 51.

- And if those days had not been cut short, no human being would be saved. But for the sake of the elect those days will be cut short (Matthew 24:22).

These verses alone suffice to demonstrate that election for salvation is biblical.

Unconditional Election Defined

The term "unconditional election" is not the most helpful from a Calvinist point of view. It implies that God's election of some people for eternal life is an irrational process that is not rooted in anything that God Himself could define. It implies, really, that God Himself doesn't know why He elects this person and not that person. The fact is that God has a purpose for everything He does, including electing mostly people who are not wise, influential, or of noble birth, electing mostly people who are foolish, weak, and despised in the eyes of the world so that He can shame the powerful, rich, and arrogant of this world (see 1 Corinthians 1:26–28, James 2:5). So also God chooses to elect a multitude of people greater than anyone can count from every tribe, language, people and nation for His own purposes as well. (Revelation 7:9) So "unconditional election" should better be called "sovereign election," for God has His sovereign purposes in who is elected and who is not.

We may define election as follows: Election is the sovereign act of God before the foundation of the earth by which he chooses a certain number of people to be the special objects of his grace resulting in their eternal salvation, not based on any foreseen merit or faith on their part but simply because of His good pleasure.

Understanding Congruent Election

Over against this view of sovereign election is Land's "congruent election," a recent version of the standard Arminian election based on foreseen faith. The word "congruent" means "being in agreement," "harmonious," "conforming to the circumstances or requirements of a situation."[3] Land's desire is to craft an understanding of election that harmonizes with as many relevant passages of scripture as possible, both those that assert God's absolute sovereignty in salvation, and those that assert human responsibility or (as he would understand it) the freedom of the human

[3] Merriam-Webster definition.

will to make ultimate choices in the spiritual realm. He rejects any system which seems based on a handful of proof-texts and does not seek (as he is doing) to harmonize with as many passages as possible. The following is a well-written declaration to which I myself can heartily assent: "We must seek a conceptual understanding of each doctrine of the faith, including election, that allows us to preach on every passage of Scripture without contradiction, confusion, or hesitancy, and without ignoring some 'problem' passages in favor of others more easily harmonized with our particular doctrinal model."[4]

Land also seems to mean by "congruent" an election which is harmonious to God's foreknowledge of each person individually: "The key to a new and more comprehensive understanding of salvation election is a deeper and more complete understanding of God's relation to and experience of 'time.'"[5] Land argues that, because God is uniquely eternal, He has therefore always experienced the totality of time (all human history—past, present, and future), everything before time even began (eternity past), and all that will occur after time has ended (eternity future). Because of God's omniscience and eternity, He was able to look down through the corridors of time before the foundation of the world and know fully what each person would do. Land goes beyond mere foreknowledge as simply knowing ahead of time what will happen. He asserts a deeper, relational kind of knowledge with each person before they even existed: "From God's perspective, there has never been a single moment when God has not had the totality of His experience (their acceptance and after, or their rejection and after) with each and every human being as part of His 'present' (i.e. eternal) experience and knowledge."[6]

Any Christian will readily assent to this. But what Land does is to connect this to predestination based on Romans 8:29–30, which states, "For those God foreknew he also predestined to be conformed to the likeness of his Son, that he might be the firstborn among many brothers. And those he predestined, he also called; those he called, he also justified; those he justified, he also glorified." Land goes on to assert that, if foreknowledge in Romans 8:29 means "pre-experience with," then all the pieces of the biblical puzzle fit together in a "congruent" way: both those verses which emphasize God's sovereignty and those which emphasize human responsibility. Because God has always had personal knowledge of what people will do (both the elect and the non-elect), He is able to make His election based on their faith and response to Him and to the gospel.

[4] Land, "Congruent Election," 51.
[5] Ibid., 55.
[6] Ibid., 56.

That Land is teaching that their election is actually *based on* the faith and response to the gospel of the elect is clearest in two statements. In the first, Land is tracing out his own conversion experience and spiritual life after that. Land writes: "God's experience of my response to, and relationship with, Him has always *caused Him* to deal differently with me than He does with a person with whom God's eternal life experience has been rebellion and rejection."[7] This shows that Land believes his election by God was God's *response* to his faith, and was caused by it. Similarly, at the end of his article, Land asserts "Additionally, salvation election, though close to Calvin's unconditional election, indeed differs, since it is *based on* God's eternal (present) experience with each human being."[8]

This is the "congruent election" Land is arguing for. Fundamental to this is libertarian free will, the ability every human being has to make for him/herself a final, determinative decision about Christ and the gospel. Land asserts that the Calvinistic doctrine of unconditional election goes hand in hand with the idea of an "irresistible call," and of a sovereign reprobation which means the elect *must* be saved, and the reprobate *can't* be saved. Land zeroes in on this doctrine and states that "congruent election" means that the elect merely "will" be saved and the non-elect merely "won't." And Land says very tellingly, "I, for one, see a big difference between 'must' and 'will,' and an even bigger difference between 'won't' and 'can't.'"[9]

Congruent Election a New Name for an Old Doctrine

Land posits "congruent election" as a new insight which, it seems, he hopes will be a basis for unity among Baptists on the issue of election. As we noted above, Land speaks of "a new and more comprehensive understanding of salvation election." The term "congruent election" is, as far as I can tell, a new one. But the basic concept—election based on God's foreknowledge of human choices—is not new at all. Land cites C. S. Lewis's term, the "Eternal Now," as the basis for God's election of future believers. But actually, Jacob Arminius spoke of God's mysterious foreknowledge of the future decisions of free will beings as based on the "infinite Now of eternity which embraces all time."[10] So this concept is not new at all.

---

[7] Ibid., 58–9. (Italics added for emphasis)

[8] Ibid., 59. (Italics added for emphasis)

[9] Ibid., 59.

[10] *The Works of Jacob Arminius*, trans. James Nichols and William Nichols (Grand Rapids, MI: Baker Book House, 1986), 3:65. Arminius went on at length about how difficult it was for him to reconcile God's exhaustive foreknowledge

Certainly, the Arminian theologians called the "Remonstrants" who drew up their five articles in 1610 embraced this same understanding of election based on foreknowledge of faith. In 1612, the Counter-Remonstrants wrote in the *Schriftelicke Conferentie*, "The reason why God has resolved to elect some people and not others is only his pleasure and sheer grace, and not because he has foreseen that one will believe in Christ and the others will not, and that consequently faith is not a cause or condition preceding the election to salvation, but a fruit proceeding from and following the election to salvation. Therefore, it is contrary to God's word if it is taught that the foreseen faith is to some degree a cause of election."[11] John Owen, when writing his careful work *A Display of Arminianism* in 1642 and summarizing his opponents' assertions on election, put their views this way: "As we are justified by faith, so we are not elected but by faith."[12] Remonstrant Nicholas Grevinchoven (1593–1632), in a tract written against Puritan William Ames, said that faith is not merely a necessary condition in him that is to be elect, but a cause moving the will of God to elect the one who has it.[13] So we can see that "congruent election" is really a new name for a very old concept. As a result, church history can help us understand its assertions and make a good reply.

God's Omniscience and Sovereignty

Land's whole concept of "congruent election" rests upon this one concept, that election is based on God's foreknowledge, which Land connects with God's omniscience. There is no doubt that God knows all things that can possibly be known, including all future events. Actually, God's ability to predict the future is one of the unique glories He claims for Himself, and He claims it so strongly that it becomes clear that God alone can foretell the future. In Isaiah 40–49, God carries on His controversy with the

with genuine freedom of human decisions, and asked his debating partner, Francis Junius for help in this mystery: "But how shall the causes be complete of those actions which depend on the liberty of the will, which also, at the very moment when it chose this, was free not to choose it, or to choose another course in preference to that? Wherefore, if ever you have sufficient leisure, I wish that your reverence would treat it thoroughly in your own accurate manner, both this and whatever else relates to that question."

[11] Cited in Edwin Rabbe, ed., *Hugo Grotius: Ordinum Hollandiae ac Westfrisiae Pietas* (1613), in vol. LXVI of *Studies in the History of Christian Thought*, ed. Heiko A. Oberman (New York, NY: E. J. Brill, 1995), 291.

[12] John Owen, "A Display of Arminianism," in *The Works of John Owen*, vol. 10 (Carlisle, PA: Banner of Truth, 1993), 67.

[13] Ibid., 61.

idols that Israel has been worshiping. At two key moments, He declares that He alone can foretell the future:

> Bring in your idols to tell us what is going to happen. Tell us what the former things were, so that we may consider them and know their final outcome. *Or declare to us the things to come, tell us what the future holds, so we may know that you are gods* (Isaiah 41:22–23).

> Remember the former things, those of long ago; I am God, and there is no other; I am God, and there is none like me. *I make known the end from the beginning, from ancient times, what is still to come.* I say: My purpose will stand, and I will do all that I please (Isaiah 46:9–10).

This second quote from Isaiah makes it plain why God alone can know the future: because He alone can ordain events and see to it that they come to pass. It is not merely because God is so observant or so incisive in His knowledge of the world and all of its creatures (including man) that He is able to predict the future. Rather, God knows the future ahead of time because He in His sovereign reign decrees what must certainly come to pass: "I say, 'My purpose will stand, and I will do all that I please.'" This is a clear statement of God's absolute sovereign rule over the universe, and especially over the events of human history.

The reason no created being can predict the future apart from the revelation of God is that God may well overrule that person's intentions or plans. The Book of Proverbs abundantly testifies to this:

- Many are the plans in a man's heart, but it is the LORD's purpose that prevails (Proverbs 19:21).

- To man belong the plans of the heart, but from the LORD comes the reply of the tongue (Proverbs 16:1).

- In his heart a man plans his course, but the LORD determines his steps (Proverbs 16:9).

In Isaiah 7, when two nations make an elaborate plan to invade Judah, topple the Davidic king, and put a puppet on the throne, God's sovereignty overruled their plans: Yet this is what the Sovereign LORD says: "It will not take place, it will not happen…" (Isaiah 7:7). And that was the end of that! So it is with every plan by a created being: it is subject to the overruling will of God.

Therefore, God's foreknowledge is intimately tied to His sovereign rule, and His eternal decrees are the expression of His pleasure. It is not merely that God knows what will come before it happens. It is rather that

God has ordained everything according to the counsel of His will. Ephesians 1:11 makes this abundantly plain as well, linking our final inheritance to God's sovereign plan: "In him we have obtained an inheritance, having been predestined according to the purpose of him who works all things according to the counsel of his will" (Ephesians 1:11).

Land's "congruent election" makes God the responder rather than the initiator, a student rather than a teacher. God studies human hearts rather than transforming them. Before the foundation of the world, God looks down through the corridors of time—the events of which God ordains in every respect according to Isaiah 49:10, Proverbs 19:21, and Ephesians 1:11. Based on this survey through the corridors of time, God "discovers" people who have this independent "faith" which He then rewards with election. This is not the scriptural picture of God's sovereign control over history.

The Role of History in Settling this Issue

Land spends a good deal of time discussing the history of the Baptist movement relative to this doctrinal debate. In a section of his article entitled "Southern Baptist Beginnings: The Birth of a Theological Tradition," Land traces out the interweaving, by his perspective, of Calvinist and Arminian threads that together make up the tapestry of the Southern Baptist heritage. The key quote in this survey came from John Leland, a Separate Baptist circuit-riding preacher and evangelist. In 1791, Leland said that, when it comes to harmonizing "the eternal purposes of God" and "the freedom of the human will," the best possible preaching is "the doctrine of sovereign grace in the salvation of souls, mixed with a little of what is called Arminianism."[14] Land goes on to show that "the majority view" among Southern Baptists has been the "Sandy Creek" Arminian emphasis on human freedom as the melody, and the "Charleston" Calvinistic emphasis on divine sovereignty as the harmony. With moving prose, Land finishes this section saying that this mixture, harmonizing the best of both traditions was his personal heritage, as he says "the air I breathed, the water I drank, and the food I ate as my soul and spirit were fed and nurtured in our Southern Baptist Zion."[15]

In response, I would simply say that, when it comes to resolving a doctrinal issue, the only light church history can shed is by displaying sound or unsound exegesis of relevant scriptural texts, and by exposing the tendencies of human hearts to receive or reject that exegesis. Simply put, church

[14] Quoted in Land, "Congruent Election," 46.
[15] Ibid., 51.

history must expound the scriptures and the human heart or it has nothing to say in resolving a doctrinal issue. It doesn't matter much if 51% of Southern Baptists think this or that about Romans 9:11. What matters is the proper interpretation of that and other relevant passages. Church history can give us proper interpretation since exegetes wrote down their arguments. Church history can also show how people accepted or resisted those arguments. True Baptists are children of the Reformation who stand with Martin Luther saying, "Unless I am convinced by Scripture and plain reason—I do not accept the authority of popes and councils, for they have often contradicted each other—my conscience is captive to the word of God." To the Scriptures alone we must ultimately appeal. "What does the Scripture say?" (Romans 4:3).

The Key Scripture on Election: Romans 9–11

I do not believe that individual election, done before the foundation of the world, was based on anything God foresaw in the elect, but simply based on His own sovereign pleasure. I do not believe we can harmonize "sovereign grace in the salvation of souls" with "a little of what is called Arminianism." Before the foundation of the world, God elected humans based either on His grace alone or on something in the elect that sets them apart from the non-elect. There cannot be two steering wheels in a car, neither can God and man both be the "ultimate cause" of election. And I make these assertions primarily because of key passages of Scripture in Romans 9–11.

It is not possible to make a responsible assertion on the ultimate cause of election (either the sovereign grace of God or the foreseen faith of man) without supporting it with a careful exegesis of Romans 9–11, and especially Romans 9:10–18 and Romans 11:5–8. Though a comprehensive exposition of these passages is beyond the scope of this chapter, it is essential for us to make some comments based on these verses that will help shed light on the issue of election for salvation.

The Election of Romans 9:11–13 is for Individual Salvation

To begin with, we must refute the concept that this section is not addressing election for individual salvation. The common Arminian approach is to assert that Romans 9 is dealing with the election of Israel as a nation to be God's "chosen people," with all of the rights and privileges connected with that status. Land's article asserts this is the issue of Romans 9–11, and that Calvinists have misunderstood Paul's intention. He says that Calvinists have wrongly confused and mingled the election of

Israel corporately (what he calls the Abrahamic election) and the election of individuals to salvation (what he calls salvation election). He then cites H. A. Ironside's amazing statement:

> There is no question here of predestination to Heaven or reprobation to hell; in fact, eternal issues do not really come in throughout this chapter, although, of course, they naturally follow as the result of the use or abuse of God-given privileges. But we are not told here or anywhere else, that before children are born it is God's purpose to send one to heaven and another to hell.... The passage has entirely to do with privilege here on earth.[16]

This is almost mind-boggling! Eternal issues certainly come in right from the start in Romans 9:

> I am speaking the truth in Christ—I am not lying; my conscience bears me witness in the Holy Spirit—that I have great sorrow and unceasing anguish in my heart. For I could wish that I myself were accursed and cut off from Christ for the sake of my brothers, my kinsmen according to the flesh (Romans 9:1–3).

Is it really possible that Paul is expressing this kind of grief, a grief that seems to rack his very being and pour forth from his soul, because of the Jews' privileges "here on earth?" What is Paul willing to be cut off from Christ to achieve? A greater enjoyment of earthly privileges for the Jews? Is it not because he knows that, if the Jews do not repent of their obstinacy and embrace Christ by faith, they will be lost for all eternity? And doesn't Romans 9:27 clearly reveal that Paul is speaking of individual salvation? For it says, "Isaiah cries out concerning Israel: 'Though the number of the Israelites be like the sand by the sea, only the remnant will be saved.'" Saved from what? Paul was clearly speaking of the same spiritual salvation he's been writing about throughout Romans—salvation from God's wrath (Romans 1:16, 5:9). In the very next chapter, Paul says "If you confess with your mouth, 'Jesus is Lord,' and believe in your heart that God raised Him from the dead, you will be saved" (Romans 10:9), and again, "Everyone who calls on the name of the Lord will be saved" (Romans 10:13). No one imagines that "saved" in Romans 10:9, 13 means some retaining of earthly spiritual privilege for Israel. Clearly the issue in Romans 9 is the same throughout Romans, the salvation of individual sinners before a just and holy God.

Therefore, H. A. Ironside's quote cannot be accepted as a valid interpretation of Romans 9–11. Rather, what Paul is bitterly grieving over is

---

[16] Ibid., 54–55.

the fact that the rejection of Christ by so many *individual* Jews will result in their *individual* damnation. Yet we should not imagine that Paul has no concern for the Jews as a national entity. Not at all, for their shared heritage as a nation has given them a certain identity in the world, and Paul is speaking of them as "Israel" at one level. They are "Israelites" (Romans 9:4), "descended from Israel" (Romans 9:6), the nation of Israel about whom Isaiah prophesied (Romans 9:27–28), "Jews" from whom some elect were called (Romans 9:24), "Israel" who fruitlessly pursued a law of righteousness (Romans 9:31), "Zion" in which the stone of stumbling (Christ) was laid (Romans 9:33), the Israel that heard the gospel plainly preached (Romans 10:18–19), the "Israel" who is the disobedient and obstinate people to whom God holds out His hands all day long (Romans 10:21). As a matter of fact, the central focus of Romans 11 as a whole is to prove that God is not done with the physical descendants of Abraham. Since Paul himself is a Jew, and since in every generation a remnant of Jews is retained by God's sovereign election (more on that in a moment), it can be deduced that God has not rejected the nation as a whole, but will continue to work in them. Paul uses the analogy of a cultivated olive tree from which natural branches were stripped (unbelieving Jews) and into which unnatural branches were grafted (believing Gentiles). The cultivated olive tree represents the heritage of the nation of Israel—both physical and spiritual—from which all believers (Jew and Gentile alike) draw nourishing sap.

Paul reaches the crescendo of his addressing the problem of the Jews when he reveals a "mystery"—a truth that could never be known except by revelation from the Spirit of God: "A partial hardening has come upon Israel, until the fullness of the Gentiles has come in. And in this way all Israel will be saved, as it is written, 'The Deliverer will come from Zion, he will banish ungodliness from Jacob'" (Romans 11:25–26). This is a stunning conclusion to the drama: at some point in the future, the physical descendants of Abraham—the Jews—who are alive at that time will turn *en masse* to Christ and embrace Him as Savior by the sovereign power of God. The hardening in part will be removed, and they ("all Israel") will be "saved" by faith in Christ. So Paul most certainly *does* have the nation of Israel in mind the whole time. But his overwhelming grief is caused by obstinately unbelieving individual Jews along the way who will be condemned for all eternity because they refused salvation in Christ and died in their unbelief.

For Land or H. A. Ironside or any other interpreter to miss this individual aspect of Romans 9 is harmful and misleading to others. Paul most certainly *is* speaking of the election of individuals for salvation in Romans 9. The "great sorrow and unceasing anguish" of his heart concerns what he knows will happen to countless individual Jews who die in unbelief: they will be cursed and cut off from Christ for all eternity, condemned to suffer an eternal torment under the just wrath of God. And Paul's emotional reaction to this is the same as Christ's when He wept over Jerusalem (Luke 19:41), and when He lamented their spiritual stubbornness in refusing to come to Him (Matthew 23:37).

Paul's Primary Concern: The Success of God's Word

But significantly, Paul's primary concern is not the salvation or damnation of individual Jews. Rather, it is that the lostness of these Jews will mislead people into thinking somehow that God's word had failed: "It is not as though God's word had failed" (Romans 9:6). Paul's concern is the same as Moses' when he interceded with God on behalf of Israel during the Golden Calf incident. God threatened to wipe Israel out and make of Moses a great nation. Moses prayed that God would not do it, because then the Egyptians would hear of it and assume that God was not able to bring Israel into the Promised Land (Exodus 32:4–11). In the same way, after the ten spies spread a malicious report concerning the Promised Land and the people rebelled and spoke of stoning Moses and going back to Egypt, God again threatened to wipe out the nation of Israel and make of Moses a great nation. Moses again pleaded with God in the same vein: "If you put these people to death all at one time, the nations who have heard this report about you will say, 'The LORD was not able to bring these people into the land he promised them on oath; so he slaughtered them in the desert.' Now may the Lord's strength be displayed, just as you have declared" (Numbers 14:15–17).

Just as Moses twice interceded with God based on concern for God's own glory, God's own reputation as a mighty God whose intentions can never fail, so Paul is concerned that the whole world know that the rejection of Christ by the vast majority of the Jews is absolutely no reflection whatsoever on God. God's word has *not* failed! Why? "Because not all who are descended from Israel are Israel" (Romans 9:6). There is a subset of the physical descendants of Abraham who are also spiritual children of Abraham as well. The true "Israel" are the elect, chosen from before the foundation of the world. The doctrine of election shows that God never fails to achieve His saving purposes in any single individual case. God will most certainly save all the elect, and not a single one will be lost.

Individual Election Proves God's Word Has Not Failed

To support this assertion, in verses 7–13, Paul brings forth two examples from the history of the Jewish nation: first, the case of Isaac and

Ishmael; and second, the case of Jacob and Esau. In quoting the statement, "it is in Isaac that your offspring will be reckoned," Paul is bringing forth the plain example of two biological sons of Abraham, Ishmael and Isaac, of whom one is chosen—Isaac—and one is rejected—Ishmael. So, being a physical descendent of Abraham is not enough to be chosen by God. Perhaps, however, one of the Jews might object, "Paul, that's an unfair example! They had different mothers—one a slave woman, the other was Abraham's true wife!" Paul then brings forth the clincher: Jacob and Esau. These twins were conceived in the same act of marital intercourse (that is the literal translation of verse 10), and grew inside one mother, Rebecca. Now comes the powerful assertion, "Before the twins were born or had done anything good or bad, in order that God's purpose in election might stand, not by works but by him who calls, she was told, 'The older will serve the younger.' Just as it is written, 'Jacob I loved, but Esau I hated.'" (vs. 11–13).

Romans 9:11–13 is the Mortal Wound for Conditional Election

These words really ought to be the death knell of election based on anything foreseen in any human being. Land asserts that Calvinists are making a critical mistake when they confuse national election with individual election. Frankly, the shoe is on the other foot. Paul's quote concerning Jacob and Esau is from Malachi 1, and if one goes back and reads the quote in its original context, the Prophet Malachi goes on to speak of "Edom" in verse 4. As a result of that, the individual experiences of two patriarchs—Jacob and Esau—can be forgotten, swept up in the unfolding of two national histories: that of the Jews and that of the Edomites. But Paul is arguing first and foremost about the plight of individual *people* who are personally rejecting Christ, as I've already shown above. He does so *secondarily* in light of the purposes of God for the whole nation (the Olive Tree of Israel) as I have also shown above. But Jacob was a real man, who displayed faith. Esau was a real man who clearly did not. As a matter of fact, Esau is the quintessential example of the worldly unbeliever who sells his birthright for a bowl of stew and thus clearly had no interest whatsoever in the promises made to Abraham (see Hebrews 12:16). Thus I believe Ironside and Land are both confusing the individual cases of Jacob and Esau—the elect and the reprobate—with the fate of their respective nations in Malachi 1. Paul is speaking about individuals in Romans 9, thus he has "great sorrow and unceasing anguish in his heart."

And, in Romans 9:11–13, Paul is asserting that God's word has not failed in light of Jews rejecting Christ, because biological descent from Abraham does not guarantee personal salvation, and because God's pur-

poses extend to individual salvation. The reason why God chose Jacob and
rejected Esau before they were born or had done anything good or bad
was so that His purpose in election might stand, not by works but by Him
who calls. God clearly wants His election to be based on Himself, not on
anything in man. Notice that "God's purpose in election" is the reason why
election happens before the twins were born. What could this be? The
Greek word "purpose" is πρόθεσις, a very significant word in the Pauline
vocabulary. This is the same word used in Romans 8:28: "And we know
that in all things God works for the good of those who love him, who have
been called according to his *purpose*." God's purpose is His intention by
which He calls the elect to be His possession. The same word also shows
up in Ephesians 1:11: "In him we have obtained an inheritance, having
been predestined according to the *purpose* of him who works all things
according to the counsel of his will." So also in 2 Timothy 1:9, this same
word is used of the actions of God "who saved us and called us to a holy
calling, not because of our works but because of his own *purpose* and grace,
which he gave us in Christ Jesus before the ages began." So the purpose
of God is His plan, His intention, His design, concerning individual salvation—given us before the ages began, by which He predestined us and
called us. Romans 9:11 describes this purpose as the "according to election
purpose," or the purpose of God which accords with election.

Putting the whole thing together, God elected us before the ages began, before any of us had done anything good or bad, so that His purpose
in this kind of election might stand. The Arminian view of election based
on foreseen merit or foreseen faith does not even enter into it. The timing
is everything! If God's purpose in election was to uphold and focus on
human faith by which the elect and the reprobate are distinguished, His
timing (before the foundation of the world) makes no sense. That becomes
even clearer when Paul writes, "not by works but by Him who calls…" The
contrast is *not* as it is with justification, "not by works but by faith" (see
Romans 3:27–28, 9:32). The contrast is "works" vs. "Him," or more simply
"man" vs. "God." God is set against anything in the twins, good or bad, as
the root cause of election. This is His "purpose according to election": to
leave the human side entirely out of the equation when it comes to election. For this very reason, Paul writes a moment later, "So then it depends
not on human will or exertion, but on God, who has mercy" (Romans
9:16).

The Doctrine of Reprobation is Included

Notice also this is where the doctrine of reprobation is clearly taught
as well. Paul is not just addressing God's eternal purpose in electing Ja-

cob, but His eternal purpose in rejecting Esau. I believe this doctrine is so repugnant to the natural sensibilities of the human heart that rejection of unconditional election probably starts here. It seems most people don't struggle over God unconditionally electing people to go to heaven; it's that He doesn't unconditionally elect everyone and therefore unconditionally reprobates some for hell. "I could never believe in a God who could choose people to go to hell apart from anything they say or do!" A prime example of this was John Wesley's angry sermon against predestination called "Free Grace," which he preached in Bristol in 1739. Wesley's logic linking unconditional election with reprobation is clear and accurate:

> You still believe that, in consequence of the unchangeable, irresistible decree of God, the greater part of mankind abide in death, without any possibility of redemption; inasmuch as none can save them but God, and he will not save them. You believe that he hath absolutely decreed not to save them; and what is this but decreeing to damn them? It is, in effect, neither more nor less; it comes to the same thing; for if you are dead, and altogether unable to make yourself alive, then if God has absolutely decreed he will make only others alive and not you, he hath absolutely decreed your everlasting death. You are absolutely consigned to damnation.... Call it therefore by whatever name you please, 'election, preterition, predestination, or reprobation,' it comes in the end to the same thing. The sense of all is plainly this—by virtue of an eternal, unchangeable, irresistible decree of God, one part of mankind are infallibly saved, and the rest infallibly damned.[17]

Wesley's emotional reaction to this doctrine was unmistakable:

> It is a doctrine full of blasphemy.... Such blasphemy this, as one would think might make the ears of a Christian to tingle! ... This is the blasphemy clearly contained in *the horrible decree* of predestination! And here I fix my foot. On this I join issue with every assertor of it. You represent God as worse than the devil; more false, more cruel, more unjust. But you say you will prove it by Scripture! Hold! What will you prove by Scripture? That God is worse than the devil? It cannot be. Whatever that Scripture proves, it cannot prove this; whatever be its true meaning, it cannot mean this. Do you ask, 'What is its true meaning then?' If I say, 'I know not,' you have gained nothing; for there are many Scriptures the true sense whereof [neither] you nor I shall know till death is swallowed up in victory.[18]

---

[17] Quoted in Arnold Dallimore, *George Whitefield*, vol. 1 (Banner of Truth: Carlisle, PA, 1979), 310.

[18] Ibid., 311.

Here is a typical Arminian approach to the topic of reprobation: great emotion, skillful rhetoric, theological/philosophical pre-commitments, and no sound exegesis of "problem passages." Undoubtedly, Wesley is responding to those who would seek to hold his feet to the fire and give a careful, verse by verse exposition of Romans 9, the clearest text in Scripture on reprobation. He merely says, "I don't know what that text means, but I know it *can't* mean that!" Land is seeking a doctrinal understanding of election "congruent" with all the Scriptures, and "not just with certain proof texts."[19] Well, here is the challenge for an Arminian theologian: deal honestly and carefully, verse by verse, with Romans 9. Don't sidestep it, as Wesley did, saying merely "I don't know what it means, but I know it *can't* mean reprobation!"

Romans 9 lays down a two-fold track of unconditional election and reprobation that run side by side. The two cannot be separated, as Wesley clearly and accurately saw. The entire chapter is addressing the grievous question of the almost universal Jewish rejection of Christ, so the issue of reprobation is foremost in his mind.

Romans 9–11 follows Paul's general trend in the whole epistle of raising objections against his own doctrine and answering them. At the end of Romans 8, Paul has been celebrating the absolute security of the believer in Christ because of God's sovereign power in salvation. He is basing our security on the sovereign acts of God the Father in foreknowing, predestining, calling, justifying and glorifying the elect (Romans 8:28–30). He argues that, since God has given us the greatest possible gift already—the gift of His only begotten Son on the cross—everything else in all creation that would achieve our final salvation will also be given, since it is a lesser gift (Romans 8:32). He asserts that, because of Christ's death and intercession for us at the right hand of God, no accusation against us can succeed (Romans 8:33–34). Therefore, nothing in all creation can separate us from the love of God in Christ Jesus our Lord; our final salvation in Him is absolutely guaranteed (Romans 8:37–39).

But if this is so, someone may argue, why did this same God lose the Jews? Weren't they also God's people? And aren't they almost universally rejecting Christ? So if God couldn't hold onto His first "chosen people," why should we Christians think God will be able to hold onto us? The fundamental question Paul is seeking to answer is stated more or less in Romans 9:6: "Has God's word failed?" If God was intending to work final salvation for the Jews, and if faith in Christ is essential to that salvation, and if the overwhelming majority of Jews are rejecting Christ, hasn't God's word concerning the Jews failed?

[19] Land, "Congruent Election," 46.

By asserting the twin doctrines of election and reprobation, Paul proves that God's word hasn't failed because His purpose is being carried out both in Jacob and Esau, both in the elect and the reprobate. This is clearly asserted in adding the words "or bad," when he says "before the twins were born or had done anything good or bad, in order that God's purpose in election might stand..." Just as election for salvation was not based on anything God foresaw in the elect, so also reprobation was not based on anything bad God foresaw in the reprobate. This is the plain meaning of the verse. Jacob's good works did not get him elected, neither did Esau's bad works get him rejected. Rather God's purpose in election comes before any of them. God is everything, not man.

Paul tackles at that very point the rising of a sense of injustice in God's sovereign election: "What shall we say then? Is there injustice on God's part? By no means!" (Romans 9:14) The Arminian view of election based on foreseen faith would not cause such a reaction. But Paul knew that the doctrine he was teaching—of unconditional election based solely on the sovereignty of God—would cause the sense of outrage that Wesley articulated centuries later. So he proves that God is not unjust at all in sovereign election: "For he says to Moses, 'I will have mercy on whom I have mercy, and I will have compassion on whom I have compassion.' So then it depends not on human will or exertion, but on God, who has mercy" (Romans 9:15–16). Human salvation is not for us a matter of justice but a matter of mercy. If God gave us justice, we would all be eternally lost. God does not owe mercy to any sinner. So, by shifting his language significantly (is God *unjust?*, no God is *merciful* as He wills), Paul shows how unconditional election to salvation is not a matter of justice but of mercy, and that mercy is given as a measure of God's sovereign freedom: "I will have mercy on whom I will have mercy." Here truly is free will in human salvation: God's free will! God has the freedom to be generous or not, to be merciful or not, to be gracious or not. No one will be in hell unjustly. No one will be in heaven except by mercy. And none of this ultimately depends on human will or effort at all.

Paul then brings in the case of Pharaoh, and the sovereign hardening of Pharaoh's heart:

> For the Scripture says to Pharaoh, "For this very purpose I have raised you up, that I might show my power in you, and that my name might be proclaimed in all the earth." So then he has mercy on whomever he wills, and he hardens whomever he wills (Romans 9:17–18).

This well-known passage clinches the argument concerning the sovereignty of God both in salvation and reprobation. Land's view does not in any significant way allow for the actions of God in hardening the hearts of the reprobate, which is clearly taught here. The Arminian view consistently asserts that, in order to maintain a genuine test for the human race, God must never interfere with human free will. But if that is so, then what of verse 18: "He has mercy on whomever he wills, and he hardens whomever he wills"? What is this "hardening?" And it will not do to try to point out that Pharaoh hardened his heart first, and then afterward, God hardened it. First of all, it isn't even true. Before Moses even entered Pharaoh's court and commands, "Thus says the Lord, 'Let my people go!'", God had told Moses He would harden Pharaoh's heart (Exodus 4:21). And the first time that the hardness of Pharaoh's heart was mentioned, it does not say either way whether God hardened it or Pharaoh, just that "Pharaoh's heart was hardened" but then adding the significant words, "as the Lord had said" (Exodus 7:13). So, God was fulfilling His promise to harden Pharaoh's heart. When in Exodus 8:15, it says Pharaoh hardened his heart, it again adds the words "as the Lord had said," implying that even Pharaoh hardening his own heart was part of God's hardening it. So it is not accurate to say that Pharaoh hardened his own heart with God remaining perfectly neutral, then after a number of times, finally God hardened his heart. The text in Exodus does not bear this out.

But from the Arminian point of view, it really doesn't matter. Because simply the fact that God would harden a human heart in some way removes their freedom and prevents them from making a free will decision uninfluenced by God. The true Arminian viewpoint has no room whatsoever for any action on God's part of hardening a human heart. Perhaps that's why Land only wants "a little" of what is called Arminianism. The doctrine of congruent election does not adequately make room for God's hardening of the reprobates, as Romans 9:18 clearly says He does.

In fairness, Land says that God does "deal differently with... a person with whom God's eternal life experience has been rebellion and rejection."[20] But this view makes little sense to me. Does part of this "dealing differently" involve hardening that person's heart? And if so, isn't that a cause for at least their continued life of "rebellion and rejection?" Congruent election does not properly address the division of the human race into two different categories based on what God is doing in them: "God has mercy on whom he wills to have mercy, and God hardens those whom he wills to harden" (Romans 9:18).

[20] Ibid., 59.

Romans 11:5–8 Teaches Unconditional Individual Election

Finally, in Romans 11:5–8, Paul speaks of the elect Jews within the larger context of an elect nation of Israel. In Romans 11, Paul is showing that, just as it is wrong to assume that being a Jew makes salvation guaranteed, so it is also wrong to assume that being a Jew now makes salvation impossible. He raises the question, "Did God reject his people?" (Romans 11:1), and answers "By no means! I am an Israelite myself, a descendent of Abraham, of the tribe of Benjamin" (v. 2). Then he asserts, "God did not reject his people, whom he foreknew" (v. 3). Just as in the time of Elijah, when he thought he was the only believer left in Israel, God always has a "remnant, chosen by grace" (v. 5). And this sovereign grace of God is the point of everything. If the remnant is chosen by grace, it cannot be based on works, for if it were, grace would no longer be grace (v. 6). God's grace is clearly held in direct contrast to human works. Now Land may argue that it is not held in contrast to faith, and faith is not a work. But the flow of the argument here is not celebrating human faith but God's sovereign electing grace by which a remnant is preserved in Israel. The conclusion can only fit in the context of the Calvinistic understanding of Romans 9–11: "What then? What Israel sought so earnestly it did not obtain, but the elect did. The others were hardened, as it is written: 'God gave them a spirit of stupor, eyes so that they could not see and ears so that they could not hear, to this very day.'" Here a clear distinction is made between the elect that are receiving personal salvation, and the whole nation of Israel which did not. Thus Ironside's strange assertion that this passage is speaking of national privileges and not of individual salvation must breathe its last. It is completely untenable. Neither does the Arminian view of election harmonize with God giving to Israel a spirit of stupor, eyes that are blind and ears that cannot hear.

Therefore, the plainest handling of Romans 9–11 verse by verse leaves no room for election based on foreseen faith or foreseen merit of any kind. Rather it addresses the problem of so many of Israel's people rejecting Christ, saying that many of them are reprobates whom God is hardening and blinding so that they will not believe; and also that some are elect who are only acting like reprobates, but will someday be returned to the Olive Tree and grafted in again by faith (Romans 11:23). In that way, God's word has not failed at all (Romans 9:6). God's plan according to election is right on schedule and He will accomplish all that He pleases.

Further Arguments Against Election Based on Foreseen Faith

Having gone through Romans 9–11 and rejected "congruent election" or any election based on foreseen faith, I would like to give some further arguments against this basic approach.

(1) Election based on foreseen faith robs God of His glory as sovereign King of the universe.

In this view, God the Creator has surrendered control of the universe to the creature, and He has done so in the most vital matter of God's glory and man's humility: human salvation from sin. God is the responder, man the initiator, though man did not even exist at the time of his election. God is pictured as the student of the human heart, rather than the Potter shaping the clay of the human heart. God looks down through the corridors of time and looks upon man, studying him, analyzing his heart, and "discovering" in man faith, and based on that faith, choosing man. It's as though God is learning His universe, exploring it, like Lewis and Clark exploring the North American continent, seeking to find the origin of the great Mississippi River. But everywhere in Scripture, God is not pictured as the responder but the initiator, and especially so in human salvation. Romans 11:36 says "For from Him and through Him and to Him are all things." So also God testifies to His glory as the Divine Initiator through Isaiah the prophet, especially in dealing with humans who do not even acknowledge Him. In Isaiah 45, God claims the glory over Cyrus the Great more than a century before he was born, speaking of the king of a Persian Empire that didn't even exist when Isaiah wrote. God claims the glory of summoning Cyrus by name, though Cyrus did not acknowledge Him (Isaiah 45:4). In effect God is saying, "I know your name, but you don't know mine." God proclaims Himself as the One who bestowed on Cyrus a "title of honor" (Isaiah 45:4), giving him "treasures of darkness, riches stored in secret places" (Isaiah 45:3). God says He does so because He is the Lord and there is no other, so that, "from the rising of the sun to the place of its setting men may know there is none besides me." God says, "I form the light and create darkness, I bring prosperity and create disaster. I the Lord do all these things" (Isaiah 45:7). Significantly, God claims absolute sovereignty over human salvation, likening it to His creation and providential care over the earth itself: "You heavens above, rain down righteousness; let the clouds shower it down. Let the earth open wide, let salvation spring up, let righteousness grow with it; I, the LORD, have created it" (Isaiah 45:8). God is plainly as much the Creator of human righteousness and salvation as He is the Creator of rain. Therefore, God pronounces a woe on all human beings who quarrel with their Maker, who forget that they are merely potsherds among the potsherds on the ground (Isaiah 45:9). The Apostle Paul, following the powerful train of thought in this awesome chapter quoted these very words in Romans 9: "Does the clay say to the potter, 'What are you making?' Does your work say, 'He has no hands'?" God is the One who created mankind upon the earth to begin with (Isaiah 45:12) and His elect are the work of His hands. He formed them for His own glory, shapes them, gives them faith, calls them out of the darkness of Satan's kingdom into the light of God's Son (Colossians 1:13). To make God the student of the human heart rather than its Creator is to strip Him of His glory. To make God the responder to human faith rather than the Creator of it is to unseat Him from His throne. To make God the discoverer of anything good in His universe rather than the creator of it is to take the words of sovereign initiative from His mouth and the breath of sovereign sustenance from His lips. It is to make man ultimate rather than God, and at the exact point where God claims the greatest glory: the rescue of powerless sinners from the grip of sin and death.

(2) Election based on foreseen faith gives man ground for boasting.

God has crafted a salvation specifically designed to strip man of boasting. God knows well that the root of both Satan's fall and of man's fall is pride, vaunting soaring self-worship which seeks to seize the throne from its rightful Owner. So God has crafted a salvation designed from beginning to end that strips man of any power to boast over Him. From unconditional election before the foundation of the world, through the humiliating death of Christ in our place on the cross, through His sovereign grace in regenerating a spiritually dead sinner (Ephesians 2:1–4), through justification by faith alone by which we are given the free gifts of perfect righteousness in Christ and complete forgiveness of sins, through God's sanctifying work in our justified souls making us gradually more and more like Christ by His Spirit, through His unilateral work in glorifying us finally both in soul and in body, in everything God strips man of His power to boast over Him. As we've seen above, multiple verses declare this to be one of God's greatest goals. However, two in particular link justification by faith alone as stripping man of his ability to boast. In Romans 3:27, Paul says "Then what becomes of our boasting? It is excluded. By what kind of law? By a law of works? No, but by the law of faith." So also, Ephesians 2:8–9 says, "For it is by grace you have been saved through faith, and this not from yourselves, it is the gift of God, not by works so that no one can boast." In other words, God chose faith as the means of our justification specifically because it would strip us of our ability to boast. There is something essentially passive and humble about faith. Faith receives. To then claim that faith is the fundamental cause of our election before the foundation of the world gives man a grounds for boasting on the basis of faith! God wants to save us in such a way that no one can boast before Him. Sovereign, unconditional election strips us of our ability to boast, as we've seen above in 1 Corinthians 1:26–31.

(3) Election based on foreseen faith severs the Scriptural connection between grace and faith.

Scripture consistently presents faith as a gift of God's grace, not the cause of it. The clearest testimony of this is in Ephesians 2:8–9, just cited above. The passage teaches that God, desiring to save us in such a way that we will be stripped of our ability to boast, acts out of grace alone. Grace is the sovereign determination in the heart of God on the basis of Christ's work on the cross to do infinite good to sinners who deserve infinite wrath. From that grace, that determination in the heart of God comes "every good and perfect gift" (James 1:17) necessary for our salvation, including faith. So grace produces faith, rather than faith producing grace. Paul severs the tie that is fundamental to the Arminian view, that faith is something originating from the heart of man. Paul says we are saved "by grace through faith, and *this is not of yourselves, it is the gift of God.*" The Greek grammar is rather simple—"this is not" τοῦτο οὐκ ἐξ ὑμῶν (i.e. originating from yourselves). The word "this" can either refer directly to faith, or to the larger work of salvation generally. In either case, a faith that originates from a sinner's heart and rises up as the grounds for a differentiation by God from one sinner to the next is specifically excluded. Rather, God gives faith as a free gift of grace, then justifies the sinner on the basis of it. Ephesians 2:9 is a heat-seeking missile heading directly for the heart of the doctrine of election based on foreseen faith. For such a view relies on the conception of faith as something resident in the heart of man which he then uses to lift himself up out of the common muck of human rebellion so that Christ can save him. But if faith is not from ourselves but is a specific gift of God to the elect, then all boasting is excluded.

(4) Election based on foreseen faith reverses the fundamental order of cause and effect.

The view against which I am arguing relies on the supernatural ability of God to foresee the future, which any bible-believing person should readily grant. But the real issue is God's education of the human race about salvation. God is the ultimate teacher of salvation, and He is educating us both on His own glory and our native wretchedness. So the Scripture is given to teach us both topics. And the order of salvation is vital to that. It is true that God stands uniquely and regally outside of time, and can step into time however He chooses. It is true that past, present, and future are all equally "now" to God. But that is not the point of the order of salvation. If our election is based on foreseen faith, then that makes faith the cause and our election the effect. But everywhere in Scripture as in experience, cause must *precede* effect or it cannot be *seen* to be the effect; it will not be *understood* to be the effect by the onlooking audience. Since God wanted to be clear about the cause of our election being nothing in man, but only in Himself, He chose us in Christ before the foundation of the world (Ephesians 1:4). The reason for the timing was our education; He Himself could have done it any time and in no way been confused. But we (obviously!) get confused easily. So He made it very clear that there was nothing in us at all by choosing us before the foundation of the world: "Before the twins were born, or had done anything good or bad, in order that God's purpose in election might stand, not by works but by Him who calls…" (Romans 9:11). As John Owen put it, "Now, from hence it would undoubtedly follow that no good thing in us can be the cause of our election, for every cause must in order precede its effect; but all things whereof we by any means are partakers, inasmuch as they are ours are temporary, and so cannot be the cause of that which is eternal."[21]

To develop this more completely, let us first acknowledge that sequencing is important to God's redemptive plan. In Revelation 22:13, Jesus says "I am the Alpha and the Omega, the First and the Last, the Beginning and the End." In three different ways, Jesus is relating the importance of sequencing: alpha is the first letter of the Greek alphabet, and omega is the last; the "first" must precede the "last" and the "beginning" must precede the "end." So it was that Christ Himself was born "in the fullness of time" (Galatians 4:4). God has a very clearly worked out the order of history, with the goal being His own maximum glory in human salvation.

Sequencing is important practically within that plan as well. Take Jesus' miracles as an example. Jesus had been asleep in the back of the boat during a terrible storm on the Sea of Galilee. His disciples, veteran fishermen on that very sea knew they were in dire trouble: the wind was whipping the sea up into a frenzy and water was cascading into the boat; soon they would be inundated and would drown. Suppose they were just about to wake Jesus when suddenly, the storm died down. The wind abated and the waves grew increasingly calmer. The disciples breathed a sigh of relief and decided to let Jesus finish His nap. Suppose an hour later He awoke,

---

[21] Owen, "Arminianism," 55.

stood up, stretched out His hands over the now quiet sea and said "Peace, be still!" Would the disciples have responded, "Truly this man is the Son of God!"? Though God, existing outside of time could have stilled the storm through Jesus *after* the storm had ended, such a sequencing would be incomprehensible to us. It would have been no evidence whatsoever to our minds that Jesus was a miracle-worker. This is the case for all of His miracles: He speaks, the demon leaves; He prays, the loaves and fish are multiplied; He says "Throw your nets on the other side of the boat" and the great catch of fish is hauled in. If the order is reversed, the point is lost. God speaks, then the effect happens. God says "Let there be light" and there is light. Sequencing is everything. Cause *must* precede effect or we will not understand it to have been God's action.

So it was when the royal official went to ask Jesus to come heal his son in John 4. Jesus said "You may go. Your son will live." The man took Jesus at his word and left. As the man was on the way home, his servants met him with the wonderful news that his son was healed. The man inquired as to when it was that the fever left him. He was told that the fever left him yesterday at the seventh hour. "Then the father realized that this was the exact time at which Jesus had said to him, 'Your son will live.' So he and all his household believed" (John 4:53). The timing was crucial. If the fever had left the boy an hour after the man had left to see Jesus, long before he'd even spoken to the Lord, there would have been no clear cause and effect. There would have been, in the man's eyes, no miracle. That is precisely why he asked when exactly the boy was healed. Though God lives outside of time, we do not. Cause must precede effect or we will not understand God's work properly.

Paul actually makes this point powerfully concerning the doctrines of the gospel. In Romans 4, he is addressing the question of justification by faith alone. He is specifically arguing against the idea that justification is grounded on any action by the sinner who is being justified. For any Jewish reader of the epistle, a special concern would be obedience to the Laws of Moses generally and circumcision specifically. Paul reasons conclusively that it is impossible for circumcision to be the cause of justification because of the *sequence* of events in Redemptive History. Because justification came *before* circumcision, then it is clear to anyone that circumcision cannot possibly be the cause of justification; circumcision cannot possibly even be necessary for justification, since Abraham was uncircumcised when he was justified by faith: "Is this blessedness (i.e. total forgiveness of sins) only for the circumcised, or also for the uncircumcised? We have been saying that Abraham's faith was credited to him as righteousness. Under what circumstances was it credited? Was it after he was circumcised, or before? It was not after, but before!" (Romans 4:9–10) Paul reasons from this plainly that neither circumcision nor uncircumcision is relevant whatsoever to justification: "And [Abraham] received the sign of circumcision, a seal of the righteousness that he had by faith while he was still uncircumcised. So then, he is the father of all who believe but have not been circumcised, in order that righteousness might be credited to them. And he is also the father of the circumcised who not only are circumcised but who also walk in the footsteps of the faith that our father Abraham had before he was circumcised" (Romans 4:11–12). Sequencing is everything to the onlooking human audience. God in His omniscience could have had Abraham circumcised first, then justified later, and still denied any causal connection. But we humans would have been deeply confused; Paul could not have made the argument he did in Romans 4:9–10, and the Jews would have had every reason to believe that circumcision is required for justification: cause precedes effect!

The exact same kind of argument (one based on sequencing, and that cause must precede effect) is made in Galatians 3 concerning obedience to the Law of Moses not being the cause of Abraham's blessedness. Again, in Galatians, Paul is arguing against the legalistic Judaizers who would seek to show that people must obey the Law of Moses in order to receive the promises of inheritance given to Abraham. Paul shows that obedience to the Law cannot possibly be the cause of inheritance, because the promises were made 430 years before the Law: "What I mean is this: The law, introduced 430 years later, does not set aside the covenant previously established by God and thus do away with the promise. For if the inheritance depends on the law, then it no longer depends on a promise; but God in his grace gave it to Abraham through a promise" (Galatians 3:17–18).

The sequencing is everything in election as well, as we see plainly in Romans 9:11: "Before the twins were born, or had done anything good or bad, in order that God's purpose in election might stand, not by works but by Him who calls..." God clearly explains 1) that He chose Jacob and not Esau, 2) that He did so before they were born or had done anything *good or bad*, 3) that He did so "in order that God's purpose in election might stand," 4) and that that purpose was "not by works but by Him who calls." Putting it simply on this issue of cause and effect, it seems that God specifically chose to do His election before the foundation of the world (Ephesians 1:4) to prove to the human race that election is absolutely not dependent on anything in the human being at all. That is the doctrine of "unconditional election." It is just as Paul says a few verses later, "It does not therefore depend on the one who wills or the one who runs but on God who has mercy." (Romans 9:16)

"Congruent election," or any view of election that makes God's mere prescience the energy of election, makes human faith the cause of election.

The creature controls the purpose of the Creator, and an effect, faith, gives rise to its cause, election. And the least that can be said about that is that it is staggeringly confusing for God to have done so. It is at least as confusing as if God had circumcised Abraham right before justifying him, and then telling us that his circumcision had nothing to do with his justification. It is at least as confusing as if Jesus had been asleep in the boat during the raging of the storm, continued sleeping after the storm had suddenly abated, awoken, and said "Peace, be still" to the now still waves, and told his disciples that He had stilled the storm. Cause precedes effect.

(5) Election based on foreseen faith is nowhere asserted in Scripture.

The burden of proof is on those who assert that election is based on foreseen faith to make their case from Scripture. Land does not actually cite any passages which make this link, because there are none. Having searched every New Testament use of the Greek words translated "elect" (ἐκλεκτός), "election" (ἐκλογή), or "to choose" (ἐκλέγομαι), whenever it refers to God's elect people, chosen for salvation, there is not a single verse that shows that that election is based on foreseen faith or anything foreseen in the elect whatsoever. Certainly Romans 8:29 links predestination with God's foreknowledge, but the verse does not mention faith at all. As a matter of fact, it is necessary to twist the grammar of Romans 8:29 to make it say that God foreknows this or that about the elect. The verse says that God foreknows people, not certain things about people: "For those whom God foreknew, He predestined to be conformed to the image of His Son, that He might be the firstborn among many brothers." The verse makes no assertion whatsoever about foreseen faith, or anything specific that may be foreseen about them. This leads readily to the next two objections: that such a view misunderstands "foreknowledge" in Romans 8:29, and that such a view neglects the Scriptural evidence that election is the cause of faith, not faith the cause of election.

(6) Election based on foreseen faith fails to understand foreknowledge properly.

As has just been noted, the only verse which might be cited to support this concept of "congruent election" or election based on something foreseen in the individuals is Romans 8:29: "For those whom God foreknew, He predestined to be conformed to the image of His Son, that He might be the firstborn among many brothers." The Greek verb translated "foreknew" in that verse (προγινώσκω) does not necessarily imply knowledge *about* something, although it certainly could have that meaning. The real issue in Romans 8:29 is the grammar which makes it obvious that it is *people* specifically that God foreknows. The direct object of the verb is the relative pronoun οὓς ("those", meaning "those people whom…"). This brings a deeper sense of how it is that God knows people, and not just things about people. As Land has made it plain from faithful theological reasoning, God does indeed know everything there is to know about every person who has ever lived or ever will live. This is the doctrine of God's omniscience, and frankly in that sense the "foreknowledge" of God is merely a subset of His omniscience. Thus we make a needed distinction between God knowing about people and God knowing *people*. The clearest verse showing a distinction between God knowing (or not knowing) people and knowing things about them is Matthew 7:23, in which the Lord Jesus Christ in His role as sovereign Judge of all the earth will say to people, "I never knew you. Away from me, you evildoers." Obviously, Jesus knows "every careless word" they have spoken (Matthew 12:36). He certainly knows that they are "evildoers." In what sense, then, can He make the assertion, "I never knew you"? It must be, then, that there is a deeper way that God "knows" His chosen people—that of a covenant commitment best symbolized by marriage. From the very beginning of marriage, the sexual union between a husband and wife has been euphemized by the verb, "to know." In Genesis 4:1 and again in Genesis 4:25, the text says that "Adam knew his wife" and she conceived and gave birth. In Luke 1, Mary queried the angel concerning the news that she would bear a son, "How can this be, seeing I know not a man?" (Luke 1:34, KJV) It is not that Mary had never met a man, or that there were no men in her village. She certainly "knew about" Joseph, her betrothed. But she had never had the covenant union of marriage with a man usually necessary for the conception of a child. Similarly, in Matthew 1, it says that Joseph obeyed the angel's command and took Mary home as his wife; but he "knew her not" (Matthew 1:25, KJV) until after Jesus was born. Again, this cannot mean that he had no factual knowledge of her or that he knew nothing of her personality. Rather it is speaking of the sexual consummation of their marriage covenant. And since marriage is the most powerful picture of the covenantal union between Christ and His bride, the church, it seems much more likely that this is the same kind of covenantal "knowledge" that Paul has in mind in Romans 8:29. Many scholars have found a similar type of knowledge in Amos 3:2, in which God says to Israel, "You only have I known of all the families of the earth." It is clear that God has intimate knowledge of all the actions and motives of every single family and nation on the face of the earth. But Amos 3:2 is speaking of God's special covenant knowledge of Israel as His chosen people.

Furthermore, at the climax of Moses' powerful intercession with God for His people Israel, Moses asks God to continue to go with Israel and separate them from all the other people on the face of the earth. God grants to Moses this request saying, "This very thing that you have spoken I will do, for you have found favor in my sight, and *I know you by name.*" Again, by this statement, God is not saying that He has more information about Moses than He does about anyone else, but rather that Moses is one of God's elect, chosen by name, in an intimate covenant relationship with Him. Similarly, Jesus, the Good Shepherd, says *"I know my own and my own know me"* (John 10:14). and "My sheep hear my voice, and *I know them,* and they follow me" (John 10:27). And the Apostle Paul, after bringing up the painful topic of the gangrenous effect of false teaching in destroying the faith of some, says, "But God's firm foundation stands, bearing this seal: 'The Lord knows those who are his'" (2 Timothy 2:19). I believe that Romans 8:29 says that God has been "knowing" His chosen people intimately by His grace from before the foundation of the world.

Now it is not impossible that "foreknow" in Romans 8:29 can mean "to have special knowledge about" the elect. But this deeper, richer understanding of God's "knowledge" of His people is far more likely. And since Romans 8:29 is the only verse that *seems* to teach election based on foreknown faith, it is enough for us here merely to cast such a heavy doubt on such an understanding as to reveal how tenuous the entire construction is. That leaves the far more positive teaching of election as unconditional (Romans 9 and 11—see below) and of election as the cause of faith (see the next objection.)

(7) Election based on foreseen faith contradicts Scripture's testimony that election is the ground of faith.

Quite the contrary from the assertion that faith is the cause of election, several Scriptures assert that the opposite is true: election is the cause of faith. When the sovereign God set His electing love on His people before the foundation of the world, it was His purpose to give them every grace necessary to bring them to full perfection in Christ. The initial experience each sinner has with the saving love of God is faith in the gospel of Jesus Christ. This justifying faith is a gift of God which He determined before the foundation of the world to give them.

The verses to which I am referring come in two categories: 1) those that teach that election is the ground of the faith of Christians; 2) those that teach that not being elect is the ground of not believing. In the first category, we find Acts 13:48: "When the Gentiles heard this, they were glad and honored the word of the Lord; and *all who were appointed for eternal life believed.*" The verb translated "appointed" (τάσσω) has the basic meaning of to "place or station a person or thing in a fixed spot", and secondarily to "order, fix, determine, or appoint", frequently by an authority figure who has power to establish someone in an office or position (Luke 7:8, Romans 13:1), or to set a certain day for something to happen (Acts 28:23). In Acts 13, the verb is a passive participle in the perfect tense, denoting an action that took place in the past but is relevant for the present. God is the agent, and He ordained or appointed these people for eternal life before the foundation of the world, and as a result of that, they believed the gospel that Paul and Barnabas preached that day. Election is the cause of faith, not the other way around. Note also that God ordained that these people should have eternal life, not merely that they should believe. Just as God chose us in Christ before the foundation of the world to be holy and blameless in His sight (i.e. perfect in heaven, Ephesians 1:4), so also here in Acts 13:48 it is clear that God ordains people not merely to begin the Christian journey of salvation but also to finish it. Faith is merely a means to an end.

Another such verse is James 2:5: "Listen, my dear brothers: Has not God chosen those who are poor in the eyes of the world to be rich in faith and to inherit the kingdom he promised those who love him?" Again, the order of this verse is election first, faith next. The grammar of this sentence makes it plain that the choosing of God results in their faith. It is true that the KJV omits the words "to be" which shows the cause-effect connection: "Hath not God chosen the poor of this world rich in faith, and heirs of the kingdom…" However, every other major English translation inserts the understood words "to be," thus making election the ground of faith. The reason for this is that the grammar links the phrases "rich in faith" AND "heirs of the kingdom." And while an Arminian understanding of election may have God choosing people because they are "rich in faith," it would never embrace the idea of God choosing people because they are "heirs of the kingdom." Everyone understands the status of being "heirs of the kingdom" as an effect of saving faith, not a cause of it. Therefore, James 2:5 clearly gives us this chain of events logically: God elects people, resulting in faith, resulting in an inherited kingdom.

Another verse in this category is 2 Thessalonians 2:13: "But we ought always to thank God for you, brothers loved by the Lord, because from the beginning God chose you to be saved through the sanctifying work of the Spirit and through belief in the truth." In context, the Apostle Paul has been speaking of people who will believe the powerful delusion Satan will craft in the final days, because they have not believed the truth but have delighted in wickedness (2 Thessalonians 2:12). By contrast, Paul encourages the Thessalonian Christians, giving thanks to God for them. His reasons are based on God's election of them "from the beginning" (which in other such verses in Paul means clearly from the beginning of the world—see

2 Timothy 1:9). God elected them to be saved, finally and completely, not merely to begin the salvation journey. And God also appointed the means for their salvation: the sanctifying work of the Spirit and belief (faith) in the truth. Thus election precedes faith and is the ground of it. God elected them for final salvation, and therefore He elects that they will have faith. Election is the cause of faith, not the other way around.

The final passage in this category linking faith and election comes at the end of one of the most poignant chapters on election in the Bible, John 6. After the feeding of the five thousand, a crowd gathers around Jesus the next day for more food. Jesus then teaches them the deeper lessons of faith in Him as the "bread of life who came down from heaven for the life of the world." As the conflict with His adversaries increases, Jesus uses more and more incendiary language to winnow out the false disciples from the true. He tells them that they have to eat His flesh and drink His blood to have eternal life. After this statement many of His disciples turned back and no longer desired to follow Him. Jesus turned to the Twelve, and asked them directly, "You do not want to leave too, do you?" Peter answered for them all, saying "Lord, to whom shall we go? You have the words of eternal life. We believe and know that you are the Holy One of God." This is a strong assertion of saving faith. Jesus then roots their saving faith in His election of them: "Have I not chosen you, the Twelve?" In other words, in Jesus' mind, their faith was based on His prior election. He also makes a distinction between the true and false among the Apostles, saying "one of you is a devil." In other words, Judas was not one of His sheep, so his future apostasy would not violate the sovereign purposes of God in salvation. Judas never was one of Christ's true sheep, therefore he never had genuine faith. But the point remains: election is the ground of all true saving faith.

The second category of verses are those which show that the reason people do not believe is that they are not elected. This is actually the doctrine of reprobation at work, in which it is asserted that, by passing over people and not electing them, God is ensuring that they will not believe, because faith is a direct work of sovereign grace in the hearts of previously spiritually dead people. The clearest of these verses are found in Jesus' statements in the Gospel of John toward His enemies: "The miracles I do in my Father's name speak for me, but you do not believe because you are not my sheep" (John 10:25–26). Note the order carefully: the reason Jesus' enemies do not believe in Jesus is that they are not "His sheep." Jesus' sheep are the elect, a love gift from the Father to the Son. Jesus speaks of them in John 17:6: "I have revealed you to those whom you gave me out of the world. They were yours; you gave them to me and they have obeyed your word." But in John 10:26 Christ says plainly to His unbelieving enemies that they are not His sheep, and that is the reason why they do not believe.

The expected order is reversed: you are not my sheep because you do not believe. This is the Arminian doctrine, the doctrine of "congruent election." Based on faith, you are chosen. But in John 10:26, it is based on not being elected, you do not believe.

Even more poignantly is this powerful assertion by Jesus in John 6:

> Then Jesus declared, "I am the bread of life. He who comes to me will never go hungry, and he who believes in me will never be thirsty. But as I told you, you have seen me and still you do not believe. All that the Father gives me will come to me, and whoever comes to me I will never drive away. For I have come down from heaven not to do my will but to do the will of him who sent me. And this is the will of him who sent me, that I shall lose none of all that he has given me, but raise them up at the last day. For my Father's will is that everyone who looks to the Son and believes in him shall have eternal life, and I will raise him up at the last day" (John 6:35–40).

Jesus begins by giving the free invitation of the gospel in verse 35: Jesus is the bread of life. Anyone who comes to Him and feeds will have eternal life. To "come to Jesus" is the same as to believe in Him in verse 35. But He then speaks directly to His unbelieving enemies who had seen Him and His miracles and still did not believe. Next, in verse 37, Jesus addresses the universal truths of God's sovereignty in salvation: All that the Father gives Me (i.e. the elect, "given" from the Father to the Son before the creation of the world) will come to Me (i.e. believe in me.) This is absolutely vital for the issue we are studying. The word "all" in this verse means "every single individual elect person." Not a single elect person will fail to come to Christ. Jesus will die for their sins, and not a single one of the elect will be lost, but He will raise them up at the last day. Jesus then speaks of the freeness of the gospel: "everyone who looks to the Son and believes in Him shall have eternal life," and they will most certainly be resurrected by Christ's power on the last day. But in the context, speaking to His unbelieving enemies, Jesus is saying that only the elect will "look to the Son and believe in Him." Jesus makes this even more plain in verse 44: "No one can come to me unless the Father who sent me draws him, and I will raise him up at the last day." That is as much to say, "If you are not elect, you can never come to me." Just as in verse 37, He is saying, "If you are elect, you cannot ultimately refuse to come to me." Throughout John 6, Jesus is repeatedly speaking of the elect and their faith in Him. But He is doing so to enemies who do not believe in Him. He roots their unbelief plainly in their non-election, as He roots the faith and coming to Him of the elect in their election.

Therefore, in this section we have seen clearly the Scripture's plain assertion: eternal election is the ground of all saving faith. It is because of election that all true Christians believe. Congruent election fails doubly: it reverses the order with no scriptural basis whatsoever, and it ignores this powerful scriptural assertion.

(8) Election based on foreseen faith finds good in man apart from sovereign regeneration.

One of the flaws of congruent election or any basically Arminian view of election is that it finds intrinsic good in sinners prior to God's sovereign working in them. And it does so despite the fact that scripture makes such universally dark statements about sinners prior to regeneration. Romans 3:10–12, "There is no one righteous, not even one; there is no one who understands, no one who seeks God. All have turned away, they have together become worthless. There is no one who does good, not even one." Romans 4:5 says God justifies "the wicked." Romans 5:6 says we were "powerless," Romans 5:10 says we were "enemies," Romans 6:17 says we were "slaves to sin," and Romans 7:9 says that when God's commands came we died. Romans 8:7 says the mind of the flesh (i.e. the unregenerate mind) is hostile to God, and that it does not submit to God's law, indeed it *cannot*. Romans 8:8 says those who are "in the flesh cannot please God." This is the natural state of the human being.

No passage sums up our native wretchedness apart from God's saving grace as poignantly as Ephesians 2:1–3:

> As for you, you were dead in your transgressions and sins, in which you used to live when you followed the ways of this world and of the ruler of the kingdom of the air, the spirit who is now at work in those who are disobedient. All of us also lived among them at one time, gratifying the cravings of our sinful nature and following its desires and thoughts. Like the rest, we were by nature objects of wrath.

A simple question then haunts the Arminian view of election based on foreseen faith: what exactly is it that God looks down through the corridors of time and sees in an unregenerate person? Spiritually, we were a putrifying mass of rebellion, enslaved in Satan's dark kingdom, creatures of instinct, living by the five senses and not by faith. Congruent election implies that God, before the foundation of the world, has an experience of such a person suddenly coming to his senses and believing in Christ, thus triggering all the graces that God pours down on that soul to save him. But saving faith itself is a grace from God (Ephesians 2:8–9). It does not exist apart from God's direct, sovereign action on the soul. So also repentance is a gift of God (Acts 11:18, 2 Timothy 2:25). God finds nothing good in the soul of a sinner that He didn't put there, for "every good and perfect gift is from above, coming down from the Father of the heavenly lights, who does not change like shifting shadows" (James 1:17). And again, "What do you have that you did not receive?" (1 Corinthians 4:7)

The Arminian view of foreseen faith implies either that faith is an independent act of the human soul which in the end differentiates the elect from the non-elect, or that faith is equally given to every single person, but that only some people use their faith. But this also runs contrary to scripture. For it posits a dormant saving faith that exists but is not used, which is nowhere attested to in scripture. And it neglects the clear testimony of 2 Thessalonians 3:2 "And pray that we may be delivered from wicked and evil men, for *not everyone has faith.*"

I believe that faith is the "eyesight of the soul," by which invisible light of spiritual truth floods into our souls. I believe, at regeneration, God speaks a creative word of spiritual light in our hearts through the proclamation of the gospel of Jesus Christ. In 2 Corinthians 4:6, Paul likens it to God's original creation in language similar to Genesis 1:3: "For God, who said, 'Let light shine out of darkness,' made his light shine in our hearts to give us the light of the knowledge of the glory of God in the face of Christ." At regeneration, God speaks into the empty darkness of the human soul, saying "Let there be light," the light of the knowledge of the glory of God in the face of Christ. At that moment, God also opens up a "light receptor" in the soul (eyesight) by which the glory of God in Christ can be perceived. This is faith, the eyesight of the soul. The light of Christ then floods into the soul, and the soul believes in Jesus. Justification immediately follows—justification by faith alone, apart from works of the law. The soul "sees" Jesus as glorious and sufficient as Savior, and cries out for salvation. Thus regeneration is very much like Jesus' healing of the man born blind in John 9. No sinner has the power to heal his own sight. Neither can we, as an act of our will, believe in Jesus. That must come as an act of sovereign grace.

So what exactly is it that God saw in the elect before the foundation of the world? By His timeless omniscience, He saw everything—preconversion, postconversion but pre-death, and post-death. Land is right about that. But He also saw us before our regeneration as wicked, wretched sinners in Adam, unbelievers, who will only be hardened if He does not work in our hearts by His sovereign grace. He elects some of such people as trophies of His grace and mercy, and does in them, for them, by them, and through them whatever He deems necessary to save all His elect in Christ and raise them up in glory on the final day.

(9) Election based on foreseen faith reverses who elects whom.

The doctrine of election speaks very plainly that it is God who chooses us in Christ at the moment that we were decidedly *not* choosing Him. I do not deny that, as a consequence of His choosing us, we also choose Him. But to Him alone belongs the glory of the first step. Jesus' statement to His Twelve stands for all time over the question of election: "You did not choose me, but I chose you and appointed you to go and bear fruit—fruit that will last." (John 15:16) Jesus is not saying that they made no choice; rather He is saying that His choice of them was made when they had not yet chosen Him. It is similar to the statement made in 1 John 4:10: "This is love: not that we loved God, but that he loved us and sent his Son as an atoning sacrifice for our sins." This verse is not asserting that we don't now love God, but rather that God loved us first. And perhaps we can go further; God's love for us is the ground and cause of our love for God. So also God's election of us before the foundation of the world is the ground of our choosing to follow Christ by faith at a certain time in history. But the Arminian or congruent election advocate reverses the order: it makes God's election of us follow our election of God logically.

(10) Election based on foreseen faith makes the ultimate difference between someone in heaven and someone in hell something in man and not something in God.

Simply put, in the final analysis, the difference between the two views of election comes down to this: what is the difference between a person who ends up in heaven and someone who ends up in hell. In the Arminian view, the ultimate difference must be seen to be something in the heart of the human: it must be a mixture of grace plus human ability. In the biblical view, the ultimate difference is clearly in the will of God, therefore it is only by grace alone. Speaking of the elect, Ephesians 1:5–6 says God "destined us ... according to the purpose of his will, to the praise of his glorious grace." Salvation in the New Testament is consistently presented as something originating entirely in the will of God, by His free choice.

(11) Election based on foreseen faith makes God's election a matter of justice, compulsion, and reward, not sovereign freedom.

The Arminian view of faith makes God go on a scavenger hunt of all human hearts before the foundation of the world. And, as we discussed in Argument eight (8) above, such a view sees faith as something independently active in the human heart, something that God did not work by His sovereign grace or power. Thus whenever God identifies this independent, man-originated faith, God is compelled by something outside Himself to elect that person to eternal life. This makes election a reward of human merit, and something compelling on the Sovereign God. John Owen cites an Arminian scholar named Grevinchovius as saying faith is "a cause moving the will of God to elect him that hath it, as the will of the judge is moved to bestow a reward on him who according to the law hath deserved it." Yet salvation is constantly presented in Scripture as a free gift of grace, given totally contrary to what we deserved. Romans 4:4–5, arguing for justification by free grace not by human merit, says, "Now when a man works, his wages are not credited to him as a gift, but as an obligation. However, to the man who does not work but trusts God who justifies the wicked, his faith is credited as righteousness." God can never be seen to owe man anything, for "Who has ever given to God that God should repay him? For from him and through him and to him are all things" (Romans 11:35–36).

(12) Election based on foreseen faith strips people of true freedom of choice.

It is often asserted that the doctrine of unconditional election and predestination strips man of all freedom of choice. The fact is that the shoe is actually on the other foot: given the actual status of man as created in the image of God, true human freedom only flourishes in the context of God's sovereign choices. God certainly created man with the ability to make real choices that have real consequences, and the biblical doctrine of God's complete sovereignty in salvation never vitiates man as a responsible agent in His sight. However, the doctrine of election based on foreseen faith makes both God and man subservient to another "force" or "drive" in the universe which neither can ultimately control. Wayne Grudem does an excellent job of developing this point:

> If God can look into the future and see that person A *will* come to faith in Christ, and that person B *will not* come to faith in Christ, then those facts are already *fixed*, they are already *determined*. If we assume that God's knowledge of the future is *true* (which it must be), then it is absolutely certain that person A will believe and person B will not. There is no way that their lives could turn out any differently than this. Therefore, it is fair to say that their destinies are still *determined*, for they could not be otherwise. But *by what* are these destinies determined? If they are determined by God himself, then we no longer have election based ultimately on foreknowledge of faith, but rather on God's sovereign will. But if these destinies are not determined by God, then who or what determines them? Certainly no Christian would say that there is some powerful being other than God controlling people's destinies. Therefore, it seems that the only other possible solution is to say they are determined by some

impersonal force, some kind of fate, operative in the universe, making things turn out as they do. But what kind of benefit is this? We have then sacrificed election in love by a personal God for a kind of determinism by an impersonal force, and God is no longer to be given the ultimate credit for our salvation.[22]

(13) Election based on foreseen faith renders evangelistic prayer meaningless.

Without a doubt, the relationship between prayer and God's eternal plan is an infinite mystery, and neither side on the debate over election can claim a full understanding of it. However, there are some special problems for the advocates of "congruent election" or election based on foreseen faith. In this view, God's sovereign action of working saving faith specifically in the hearts of the elect alone is denied. In order to maintain freedom of the human will and an equal opportunity for all to be saved, such a view must assert that God does not interfere in the inner workings of the human heart, but allows the heart to do whatever it wills. Specifically, God will not "work faith" in the heart of a lost person. The human heart is like a "holy of holies" into which God is not permitted to venture, lest He defile human freedom.

So, if God cannot or will not interfere in the inner workings of the human heart to bring about faith, what exactly are we asking Him to do when we pray for a lost person? The Apostle Paul prayed for lost Israelites in Romans 10:1: "Brothers, my heart's desire and prayer to God for the Israelites is that they may be saved." But in the Arminian view of election, saving faith is the one thing God will not give to a human heart: that's up to the heart to do for itself. If you answer, saying "I am asking God to increase His external persuasions on the sovereign human heart so that faith is more likely to rise up," if God really wants all people to be saved, why isn't He doing that "increased external persuasion" anyway, apart from your prayers?

But if we accept the sovereignty of God over every single step of human salvation, then evangelistic prayers for lost people are completely appropriate, powerfully effective in the hearts of the elect. And we should pray for things God has already decided to do, ordained to do, wills to do, and has predestined will be done. As a matter of fact, these are the only things we should be desiring to pray for: "May your will be done on earth as it is in heaven" (Matthew 6:10). In John 17:11–12 Jesus prays for all the elect to be one, and that none of them will be lost. This is the very thing

---

[22] Wayne Grudem, *Systematic Theology* (Grand Rapids, MI: Zondervan, 1994), 679.

Jesus has already told us God has ordained and absolutely will happen (cf. John 6:39). Certainly there is mystery in the Calvinistic understanding of prayer and the eternally predestined purposes of God, but at least it is biblically demonstrable in Jesus' life and reasonable based on the overall understanding of a sovereign God active in the human heart. But the Arminian view of election makes evangelistic prayer meaningless.

The Benefits of Embracing Unconditional Election

There are many significant benefits that come from embracing the biblical doctrine of unconditional election. The more we meditate on each of these, the richer the doctrine will be in our hearts and lives.

(1) God Gets the Full Glory for Human Salvation

If we accept the doctrine of unconditional election, then we understand that God deserves full praise and glory for every aspect of human salvation. We can live "for the praise of His glorious grace" (Ephesians 1:6), and know that our salvation was God's work for us and in us from beginning to end. We can marvel at the intricacies and infinite mysteries of God's election of us before the foundation of the world, and we can give Him the full glory for every step of His sovereign plan.

(2) The Human Heart is Humbled

The doctrine of unconditional election has a powerful humbling effect on the human heart. We can realize that there was nothing in us whatsoever that moved God to choose us. We were fashioned out of the "same lump of clay" as all the reprobates, and the fact that the sovereign Potter made of us a vessel for glory is completely humbling.

(3) Security

The doctrine of unconditional election means that salvation is from the Lord from beginning to end. It stands outside of time and is rooted entirely in grace. Election is the sovereign determination of God to save us and bring us to perfection in Christ. The gift of faith is a necessary step in that salvation process, and therefore the God who gave us faith to begin with will sustain it every moment until the end of our lives. Our salvation is completely secure since it was neither initiated nor sustained by us. Any other view of salvation introduces a human element that makes the whole chain weak, for a chain is only as strong as its weakest link. If faith is a human work from the beginning, it will be a human work every day of that person's life. No security can exist in this. But since God initiated the faith, so also God will sustain it, specifically in answer to the prayers of Christ, the Great High Priest. Hebrews 7:25 says Jesus ever lives to intercede for us. Romans 8:34 says Jesus is at the right hand of God and is interceding for us. The night before Jesus' death, He said to Peter, "Simon, Simon, Satan has asked to sift you as wheat. But I have prayed for you, Simon, that your faith may not fail. And when you have turned back, strengthen your brothers. (Luke 22:31–32) Jesus' theology of the origin, danger, sustenance, and final triumph of faith is plain: God the Father gave Simon his faith, Satan is attacking it, God the Father strengthens it, and it will not fail. The Arminian view of faith has no room for this kind of intercession. Our salvation is totally secure, because He who began this good work in sovereign election before the foundation of the world will carry it on to completion on the final day.

(4) God-centered Confidence in Evangelistic and Missionary Endeavors.

The doctrine of unconditional election enables the evangelist and missionary to set out boldly for the advance of the gospel of Jesus Christ, because he knows that God has chosen His elect from before the foundation of the world and they will most certainly believe. So the Apostle Paul says, "Therefore, I endure everything for the sake of the elect, that they too may obtain the salvation that is in Christ Jesus, with eternal glory" (2 Timothy 2:10). The doctrine of unconditional election makes the faith of the elect a guaranteed thing because it is a God-given thing. The man-centered view of election makes faith man's work, and puts the burden both on the evangelist in his methods and the lost in their hearing to generate the saving faith which is the whole goal of such outreach. It makes the evangelist tempted to feel intimidation at the daunting prospect of seeking to reach a lost person in an unreached people group, or overweening pride at success, or despair at failure. Such is the man-centered fruit that is the inevitable result of a man-centered view of election. But an evangelist or missionary that goes forth in the name of sovereign grace can do so with a completely humble confidence in God that the mission will be successful under God's eternal purposes.

4

Jesus Saves, No Asterisk Needed
WHY PREACHING THE GOSPEL AS GOOD NEWS REQUIRES DEFINITE ATONEMENT

David Schrock

There is a billboard that I have seen. Perhaps you have seen it too, or one just like it? In two words it pronounces the heart of the gospel: "Jesus Saves!" As far as I can tell, the sign did not include an asterisk on the end of the word, as if to say "Jesus saves, but check the fine print." Rather, in unqualified language it proclaims the beautiful truth that the life, death, and resurrection of the Lord Jesus Christ accomplishes salvation—no asterisk needed.

I write this chapter with the prayer that pastors and parishioners alike might embrace the doctrine of definite atonement and proclaim the gospel with greater confidence, trusting in, praying for, and working with the Lord who died to save a people for his own possession. Despite what many think in our day, a careful understanding of definite atonement does not diminish the gospel. Just the reverse. Definite atonement "undergirds" the preaching of God's Word.[1] How? By esteeming the undiluted success of what Christ accomplished on the cross. At the same time, it protects the work of Christ from hyper-subjective (per)versions of the cross that run

---

[1] Roger Nicole, "Covenant, Universal Call, and Definite Atonement," in *Creator, Redeemer, Consummator: A Festschrift for Meredith G. Kline*, eds. Howard Griffith and John R. Muether (Eugene, OR: Wipf & Stock, 2000), 199.

amok today, posing serious risk to the objective work of Christ's atoning death.[2]

Therefore, the modest goal of this chapter is not to supply an exhaustive argument for definite atonement, so much as it intends to prove one point: Those who preach the gospel of Jesus Christ as the power unto salvation (Romans 1:16) must embrace and declare a cross which actually saves, and the only view that will support such preaching *in the long run* is definite atonement.[3] All other "egalitarian" views (e.g. Arminian, Amyraldian, Molinist, and modified Calvinist) fail because they articulate a view of Christ's atonement that is indefinite, the effectiveness of which depends on a self-generated response of the sinner or on an additional and purposefully effectual work of God. The word "egalitarian" will be used for all views other than definite atonement, for they assume that in Christ's death equal provision was made both for those that would at some point believe as well as those that never would be brought to belief. There is nothing in the atonement itself that distinguishes the one from the other. These views may present a cross that objectively saves but they do so borrowing the theological capital of definite atonement.[4]

To show this biblical-theological reality, this chapter will proceed in three steps. First, we will examine the plain texts of Scripture which support God's particularity and efficacy in the atonement. Second, two biblical-theological arguments will be advanced. From Christ's priesthood and the New Covenant, we will see how Christ's death is both particular and unassailably effective. Third, the universality of the cross will be affirmed

---

[2] Michael Horton, *For Calvinism* (Grand Rapids: Zondervan, 2011), 87–89. Cf. Graeme Goldsworthy, *Gospel-Centered Hermeneutics: Foundations and Principles of Evangelical Biblical Interpretation* (Downers Grove, IL: IVP Academic, 2006), esp. 167–180.

[3] David Allen states, "Anything that operates to undermine the centrality, universality, and necessity of preaching is wrong." David Allen, "The Atonement," in *Whosoever Will: A Biblical-Theological Critique of Five-Point Calvinism* (Nashville, TN: B&H Academic, 2010), 98. I could not agree more. In the same vein, any doctrine that limits the power of the cross to save should also be rejected and revised by the light of Scripture.

[4] Let me clarify what I am not arguing: *Definite atonement is not the gospel.* Someone can deny definite atonement and still proclaim the gospel. What definite atonement does is to protect the saving message of penal substitution from ineffectual moral versions of the cross (e.g. moral example, moral influence, moral government). For a full consideration of definite atonement's ministerial benefits, see Tom Barnes, *Atonement Matters: A Call to Declare the Biblical View of the Atonement* (Webster, NY: Evangelical, 2008), 259–85.

and carefully articulated. In this final section, we will address the "universal significance of particular atonement."[5]

Christ's Death is Particular

Textual proof for definite atonement begins with the straightforward statements that Christ died for a particular people. For instance, Matthew 1:21 states that Christ was born in order to die for "his people." Titus 2:14 also states that Christ "gave himself for *us* to redeem *us* from all lawlessness and to purify for himself *a people for his own possession* who are zealous for good works." New Testament writers regularly speak in the first person plural ('we,' 'us,' 'our') to delimit the work of Christ's death to the people of God.[6] In this case, Paul goes further. He explicitly speaks of a people "redeemed" and "purified" by His death, for His own purposes. There is not a hint of ambiguity here. As the greater paschal lamb, Christ's blood effectively purifies a people from sin so that they can serve the Lord with good works (cf. Hebrews 9:14).[7]

Similarly, Acts 20:28 declares that Jesus shed His blood for "the church," and Ephesians 5:25–27 charges husbands to love their wives as Christ loved the church and gave Himself uniquely for her. Paul's typology in Ephesians is important. Scripture regularly portrays God's love for His people in marital terms (Isaiah 61:10–62:5; Matthew 22:1–14; Revelation 19:6–9; 22:1–3). However, against egalitarians who indiscriminately universalize God's variegated love, Christ loves His bride in a way that He does not love the merchants of Babylon who prostitute themselves with the Great Harlot (Revelation 17–19). If He loved the serpent's seed the way He loves His bride, Christ would not only dishonor His beloved and the suffering she experienced at the expense of her enemies; He would dishonor His own sacrifice by which He cleanses her. It stands to reason that Jesus' particular love for His bride takes the initiative to purify His beloved and protect her from her enemies.[8]

---

[5] Herman Bavinck, *Reformed Dogmatics: Sin and Salvation in Christ*, Vol. 3 (Grand Rapids, MI: Baker Academic, 2006), 470–75.

[6] Cf. Romans 5:8–9; 1 Corinthians 15:3; 2 Corinthians 5:18–19; Galatians 1:3–4; 3:13; Titus 3:5–6; 1 Peter 2:24; 3:18.

[7] Cf. George Smeaton, *The Apostles' Doctrine of the Atonement* (T&T Clark, 1870; reprint: Grand Rapids, MI: Zondervan, 1957), 326–31.

[8] Cf. D. A. Carson, *The Difficult Doctrine of the Love of God* (Wheaton, IL: Crossway, 2000), 16–21.

Going further, Romans 8 explains that Christ died for the "elect" (v. 34), and that for all who are His, He will withhold nothing.[9] In Hebrews, Jesus is described as "the mediator of a new covenant" who dies for the "called" (9:15). Likewise, Hebrews 10 records that Christ's death defeated His enemies (v. 13) and "perfected for all time *those who were being sanctified*" (v. 14).[10] Added to these explicit texts are those instances where Christ offers Himself as a ransom for "many" (Matthew 20:28; cf. Matthew 26:28; Romans 5:19).[11] Drawing on Isaiah 53, Matthew and Paul speak of Christ's death fulfilling the role of the servant, whose death ushers in the everlasting covenant that will extend to all the "eschatological people of God" (Isaiah 54–55).[12]

To this first argument, many egalitarians cry 'foul!' For instance, David Allen calls it a "negative inference fallacy." He cites R. L. Dabney to say, "the proof of a proposition does not disprove its converse." Allen adds, "One cannot infer a negative (Christ did *not* die for group A) from a bare positive statement (Christ did die for group B)."[13] His point would be

---

[9] John Murray, *Redemption Accomplished and Applied* (Grand Rapids, MI: Eerdmans, 1955), 65–69.

[10] Defending believer's baptism, Fred Malone explains how God in Christ "establishes the New Covenant and guarantees its success through the work of an effectual Mediator, a particular redemption for all in the covenant by His substitutionary sacrifice, and an effectual calling of all members of that covenant." Fred Malone, *The Baptism of Disciples Alone* (Cape Coral, FL: Founders, 2003), 81. His argument for believer's baptism has important crossover application for definite atonement (77–95).

[11] Tom Wells, *A Price for a People*, 70–75, 146–51.

[12] D. A. Carson, *Matthew*, The Expositor's Bible Commentary (Grand Rapids, MI: Zondervan, 1984), 8:433. Tom Barnes argues for the particular and effectual nature of the atonement from Isaiah 52:13–53:12. Barnes, *Atonement Matters*, 38–50.

[13] Allen, "The Atonement," in *Whosoever Will: A Biblical-Theological Critique of Five-Point Calvinism* (Nashville, TN: B&H Academic, 2010), 93. In context, R. L. Dabney critiques "ultra-Calvinists" who deny God's loving nature towards all humanity. R. L. Dabney, *Systematic Theology* (1871; reprint: Carlisle, PA: Banner of Truth, 1985), 533. While he affirms that "Christ died for all sinners in some sense" (527), he also argues for the particular efficacy of the atonement. Dabney states, "There is no passage in the Bible which asserts an intention to apply redemption to any others than the elect" (527), and since "Christ's design in His vicarious work was to effectuate exactly what it does effectuate" (528), it must be concluded that Dabney argues for a limited atonement with "temporal" (read: non-salvific) effects (529). Allen's quotation implies that Dabney supports his egalitarian view, but such is not the case. Allen makes definite atonement appear to be a matter of logical gymnastics, but in fact, Dabney and his Reformed breth-

well-taken, if these "bare positive statements" were all there was.[14] However, these texts are but visible geysers forced to the surface by the power of God's plan to save a particular people. As we will see below, the fountainhead of these verses is God's covenantal relationship with His particular people.[15] Additionally, there are a number of passages in John's gospel that confirm the plain statements of particular redemption. As J. Ramsay Michael observes, "Most references to Jesus' death in John's gospel have to do with its benefits *for believers*, of Jesus' own disciples, and are thus

ren pay very careful attention to the whole counsel of Scripture in order to affirm the particular saving and particular non-saving effects of the cross of Christ. Cf. Greg Wills, "Whosoever Will: A Review Essay," in *The Journal for Baptist Theology and Ministry* 7.1 (Spring 2010), 15–18.

Unfortunately, this is but one example where David Allen misrepresents those who defend definite atonement. Confusing matters, he puts defenders and opponents of particular redemption in the same list and concludes, "All were Calvinists, and all did not teach limited atonement" (Allen, "The Atonement," 67). He explains himself in a footnote, "The point here is that they did not teach 'limited atonement' in the sense of a limited imputation of sin to Christ, as Owen taught, and as most modern 'five-point' Calvinists think. Rather, they held a form of universal atonement" (67, fn. 16).

Allen prides himself on defeating limited atonement without quoting a single Arminian or Non-Calvinist (66), but in truth, he misrepresents what is at issue and what definite atonement is asserting. Greg Wills challenges Allen's semantic sleight of hand saying, "Allen is right that most Calvinist preachers have held that Christ died for all persons in some sense. Calvin believed this. So did Edwards and Hodge and Boyce and Dabney. His death for all was such that any person, even Judas, if he should repent and believe the sacrificial death was universal in that it made all men salvable, contingent on their repentance and faith in Christ. But Allen is incorrect to argue that such a position is not limited atonement, for these same theologians affirmed that the atonement was in important respects particular to the elect…. What distinguishes Calvinists from Arminians on this point is that Calvinists hold that Christ died in a fundamental sense particularly for the elect. He intended that his propitiatory sacrifice, which was sufficient for the sins of the world, should be effective for the elect alone. The key difference relates to the question of intent, not to the question of its universal sufficiency" (Wills, "Whosoever Will: A Review Essay," 16–17). Unfortunately, Allen misses this, thus skewing his data.

[14] Peterson and Williams distinguish between weak and strong Calvinist arguments. Allen critiques the weaker argument, without giving heed to the rest of the biblical evidence. Robert A. Peterson and Michael D. Williams, *Why I Am Not an Arminian* (Downers Grove, IL: InterVarsity, 2004), 202–07.

[15] J. Ramsay Michael, *The Doctrine of the Atonement as Taught by Christ Himself* (T&T Clark, 1871; reprint: Grand Rapids, MI: Zondervan, 1953), 69. See also his appendix in the same volume (436–41).

fully consistent with 'particular redemption' as the early English Baptists understood it."[16]

Easily overlooked, John's "given" nomenclature is a technical expression that is undervalued by many egalitarians.[17] Three times, Jesus uses "given me" (*dedōkas moi*) to speak of Jesus' mission (5:36; 12:49; 18:11), but elsewhere it speaks of the particular group of people He has received from the Father (6:37, 39; 17:7, 9, 11, 12, 22, 24). This particular language lends strong support for definite atonement.

In John 6, after feeding the multitudes and giving an unrestricted, universal invitation for all to come to Him (vv. 35–36), Jesus says, "*All that the Father gives me* will come to me, and whoever comes to me I will never cast out. For I have come down from heaven, not to do my own will but the will of him who sent me. And this is the will of him who sent me, that I should lose nothing of *all that he has given me*, but raise it up on the last day" (vv. 37–39). Jesus' words perfectly mesh the universal invitation with God's particular salvation, and the determining factor is not man's will, but God's (vv. 44, 65; cf. Matthew 11:25–27).[18] In this context, salvation belongs to a particular group, those given from the Father to the Son.

John 17 concurs. In his high priestly prayer, Jesus uses the expression repeatedly. In verses 6–8, Jesus states that He gave "the words that [the Father] gave him" to the people the Father "gave [him] out of the world." Apparently, God gave Jesus a message and a people, thus the success of Christ's mission was to deliver that message to them. Next, verse 9 articulates that Jesus' intercession is limited: "I am praying for them." Who is "them"? The text does not leave us to guess. Speaking to the Father, He intercedes, "I am not praying for the world but for those whom you have given me, for they are yours." Because Jesus does not intercede for the world, neither will He die for the world.[19]

---

[16] "Atonement in John's Gospel and Epistles," in *The Glory of the Atonement: Biblical, Theological, and Practical Perspectives*, eds. Charles E. Hill and Frank A. James, III (Downers Grove, IL: InterVarsity, 2004), 109.

[17] For instance, in his study on "Soteriology in the Gospel of John" (*The Grace of God, The Will of Man*, ed. Clark Pinnock [Grand Rapids, MI: Zondervan, 1989]), Grant Osborne questions the doctrine of perseverance and makes no mention of the extent of the atonement in Jesus' prayer, even though he considers the 'given ones' (255).

[18] John L. Dagg, *Manual of Theology* (Harrisonburg, VA: Gano Books, 1982), 324–31.

[19] Cf. John Owen, *The Death of Death in the Death of Christ* (Carlisle, PA: Banner of Truth, 1959), 70–88, 170–72; William Symington, *On the Atonement and Intercession of Christ* (Pittsburgh: United Presbyterian Board of Publication, 1864), *passim*; Hugh Martin, *The Atonement: In Its Relation to the Covenant, the*

Still, many egalitarians disagree. Lightner protests, "It is assumed by those who insist Christ died only for the elect that because He did not pray for the nonelect, He did not die for them. This assumption is not only unwarranted logically, but it is also unscriptural. Limited redemptionists assume Christ did not die for everyone because He did not pray for everyone; and then they argue backwards."[20] Lightner represents egalitarians when he abstracts Christ's sacrifice from its priestly context.

The problem with Lightner's denial of the priestly argument is twofold. Canonically, it misunderstands Christ's priestly office, in which He fulfills all of His ministry. Jesus prays, sacrifices, teaches, and guards the ones whom the Father has given Him (see below). Even more, Lightner's charge of being 'unscriptural' is ironic because he takes no time to examine the office in type or fulfillment. As with most egalitarians, he cites texts describing Christ's sacrifice without relating them to biblical typology outlined in antecedent Scripture. By contrast, those who make priestly arguments for Christ's definite atonement do better justice to the whole counsel of Scripture than those who simply collate texts and cobble together a modified version of Christ's atonement and intercession.

In the text itself, verse 19 states that Jesus intends to die for the ones given Him by the Father.[21] Lightner overlooks the fact that in Christ's priestly prayer, He limits not only His intercession but also His crucifixion. Having prayed for God to reveal Himself to them, to protect them from the evil one, and to sanctify them in truth (vv. 10–18), Jesus prays, "And for their sake I consecrate myself, that they may be sanctified in truth." From the context of the prayer (the night before Jesus death) and from the other usages of "consecrate" in John's gospel (10:36), it is evident that the idea of consecration concerns the mission of Jesus, which is clearly His death, burial, and resurrection.[22] Jesus prays *and* dies for His own.

In between John 6 and John 17, John uses three other terms to describe those for whom Christ died. In John 10, Jesus calls Himself the good shepherd (v. 11). Contrasting Himself with the evil one who kills, steals, and destroys (v. 10) and the hireling who abandons the flock (v. 12), Jesus says in verses 14–15, "I am the good shepherd. I know my own and

Priesthood, the Intercession of Our Lord (London, 1870; reprint, Greenville, SC: Reformed Academic Press, 1976), 49–168.

[20] Robert P. Lightner, *The Death Christ Died: A Biblical Case for Unlimited Atonement*, Rev. Ed. (Grand Rapids, MI: Kregel, 1998), 102–103.

[21] John Owen, *The Death of Death*, 98.

[22] George R. Beasley-Murray, *John*, 2nd Ed. WBC (Nashville, TN: Thomas Nelson, 2000), 301; D. A. Carson, John, PNTC (Grand Rapids, MI: Eerdmans, 1991), 567.

my own know me, just as the Father knows me and I know the Father; and I lay down my life for the sheep."[23] Jesus refers to His sheep as His "own," which in light of John 6:37–39 and John 17, it is most likely that He is referring to the covenant people given to Him by the Father in eternity past.[24]

We see something similar in John 11. There, John quotes Caiaphas's words to show how Jesus' death would bring salvation to Jew and Gentile, alike. Verses 50–53 record, "He did not say this of his own accord, but being high priest that year he prophesied that Jesus would die for the nation, and not for the nation only, but also to gather into one the children of God who are scattered abroad." Running parallel to John 10:14–16, John denotes the particular nature of Christ's death ("for the nation"), and its universal expansion ("also to gather… the children of God who are scattered abroad"). Still, the universalizing of this text is particular. John does not say that Christ died to gather all people without exception; he says that Jesus died for the nation Israel and for the *children of God* scattered around the world. As Baptist scholar J. Ramsay Michaels states, "the 'wider circle' never embraces the whole world," but only the sheep not of this fold (10:16), the children of God scattered (11:53), and the world who will believe the message of the apostles (17:21, 23).[25]

Two other passages speak of Jesus' particular redemption. In John 13:1, after explaining that many in Israel would not believe because God has "blinded their eyes and hardened their hearts" (12:40), Jesus steps up to wash the feet of His disciples. Yet, before detailing the event, John states that Jesus "loved his own who were in the world." These "loved ones" are set in contrast to Judas, who in verse 2 is presented as a seed of the serpent.[26] Thus, while there is in John a universal love for all the world (3:16), this does not mean that God's saving love extends to all people. Jesus "loved his own" and He died for His own. John 15 confirms this. Speaking of His particular love, Jesus says, "Greater love has no one than this, that someone lay down his life for his friends" (v. 13). Clearly, from this statement, the recipients of Christ's atoning love are not all people without exception, but His friends.

[23] Significantly, John 10:16 moves from the particularity of Christ's atoning death to the cosmic reality that there are other sheep "not of this fold" (i.e., not of Israel). Once again, in John there is united a particular atonement with a universal invitation (cf. Revelation 5:9–10).

[24] John Calvin, *Commentary on the Gospel According to John*, trans. William Pringle (Grand Rapids, MI: Baker, 2001), 3:406–08.

[25] J. Ramsay Michael, "Atonement in John's Gospel and Epistles," 109.

[26] Cf. James Haldane, *The Doctrine of Atonement* (1847; reprint, Choteau, MT: Old Paths Gospel Press, n.d.), esp., 95–101.

Christ's Death is Efficacious

The New Testament uses language that speaks of Christ's atonement in certain and efficacious terms.[27] As John Owen observes, "The death and blood-shedding of Jesus Christ hath wrought, and doth effectually procure, for all those that are concerned in it, eternal redemption, consisting in grace here and glory after."[28] Making his case, Owen shows how the apostolic witness uniformly understood Christ's death securing reconciliation (Romans 5:10; 2 Corinthians 5:18–19; Ephesians 2:14–16), justification (Romans 3:23–25; Galatians 3:13; Hebrews 9:12; 1 Peter 2:24), sanctification (Ephesians 5:25–27; Hebrews 1:3; 9:14; 13:12; 1 John 1:7), adoption (Galatians 4:4–5), and glorification (Ephesians 1:14; Hebrews 9:15).[29] Owen is not alone. The Reformed tradition has always argued for the efficacy of Christ's atonement on the basis of Scriptural testimony.

For instance, George Smeaton shows in his two volumes on the cross that the fruits of Christ's work are always effective.[30] Expositing every New Testament text on Christ's death, Smeaton returned again and again to this singular idea: Christ's death was "causally connected" to its effects. Christ's death delivered from death (John 3:16),[31] sought out and effected salvation (Luke 19:10),[32] effected liberation (Matthew 20:28),[33] delivered

---

[27] Tom Wells, *A Price for a People*, 15–33; Roger Nicole, "The Atonement—Part 1" in *Reclaiming the Gospel and Reforming Churches: The Southern Baptist Founders Conference 1982–2002* (Cape Coral, FL: Founders, 2003), 55–61.

[28] John Owen, *The Death of Death*, 47.

[29] Following Robert Lightner (*The Death Christ Died*, 2nd Ed., 45–46), Kenneth Keathley provides a helpful taxonomy of these three positions in *Salvation and Sovereignty: A Molinist Approach* (Nashville, TN: B&H Academic, 2010), 193–97. The efficacy of Christ's death is a major difference between Wesleyan-Armininians who believe Jesus obtained salvation for all, modified Calvinists who teach that Jesus *provided* salvation for all and *applied* it to some, and historic Calvinists who declare that Christ *secured* salvation for His elect.

[30] George Smeaton, *The Doctrine of the Atonement as Taught by Christ Himself*, 2nd Ed. (Edinburgh: T&T Clark, 1871; reprint, Grand Rapids, MI: Zondervan, 1953); idem., *The Apostle's Doctrine of the Atonement* (Edinburgh: T&T Clark, 1870; reprint, Grand Rapids, MI: Zondervan, 1957).

[31] George Smeaton, *The Doctrine of the Atonement as Taught by Christ Himself*, 50.

[32] Ibid., 117.

[33] Ibid.,194. Smeaton goes on to explain from the Old Testament that the term "ransom" is always effectual (195–97) and that even the use of prepositions in the New Testament are never "vague, indefinite, [or] indeterminate." (199).

from divine wrath (Matthew 20:28),[34] pardoned sins (Luke 22:19–20),[35] sanctified the believer (John 17:19),[36] and insured the gift of spiritual life (John 6:51–57).[37] Save the progress of time, the effects of Christ's atonement are "direct and immediate."[38] The cross procures all that is necessary for salvation, and as God ordains the steps of people and nations, He will perfectly apply all that Christ has done by the Spirit of Christ.[39]

When defending definite atonement, Smeaton draws on Romans 5 to show how Christ's atonement causes its intended effect for those who are in covenantal union with Him. In a text that on the surface lends more support for universalism than universal atonement, he shows how the two covenant heads, Adam and Christ, represent their respective races.

> Now this of itself decides on the extent of the atonement. No one doubts that the extent of the fall is coincident with its obvious and manifest effects. If a causal connection obtains between one man's disobedience and the sin, judgment, and death in which the world is now involved, a causal connection obtains, too, between the second man's obedience and the benefits in which all Christians participate. If the fall was pregnant with

[34] "The sacerdotal offering of Christ's life as the culmination of His obedience is further represented as the ransom; and it has a direct or causal connection with present and future deliverance from divine wrath" (Ibid., 205). Not only does Christ's death make ransom presently possible, it secures it for the future.

[35] Ibid., 218, 221, 386, 391.

[36] Ibid., 252.

[37] Reflecting on "the connection between the vicarious sacrifice of Christ and the communication of spiritual life," Smeaton declares, John 6:51–57 "plainly announces that the atonement stands in causal connection with life. The crucified flesh of the Lord, is represented as possessing a life-giving influence, and constituting the new and sole fountain from which life can be derived." Ibid., 271. Accordingly, the extent of Christ's death is coterminous with the extent of those who receive life (cf. Romans 5:18; 6:1–11).

[38] Smeaton, *The Apostle's Doctrine of the Atonement*, 21–25. Definite atonement is not ignorant of the time between crucifixion and application; it merely asserts that what Christ began in the flesh, He will finish in the Spirit. For how else could He truly exclaim, "It is finished" (John 19:30)!

[39] While the personal and subjective work of the Spirit is needed to apply the benefits to every elect child of God, it is Jesus in His role as covenantal mediator who sends the Spirit to do so. The Spirit does not come on His own, nor is He sent by the Father "and *not* the Son." The *filioque* clause, which the Western Church has historically affirmed, says the exact opposite. The Father 'and the Son' are responsible for sending the Spirit, and their work is coordinated (John 14:16, 26; 16:7–15). In obedience to the Father, the Son sends the Spirit to apply all the benefits that He procured on the cross. Cf. Robert Letham, *The Work of Christ*, 237–38; Michael Horton, *For Calvinism*, 93–95.

consequences which cannot be gainsaid, ramify so widely that they are everywhere apparent, the atonement of Christ in like manner produces and will continue to produce results which are as real, and shall ramify as widely, through time and through eternity.[40]

Smeaton's argument is not easily defeated. Just as Adam sinned and caused all of his biological posterity to die, so Christ obeyed and caused all of His spiritual posterity to live (Romans 5:19; cf. Hebrews 2:13). For Smeaton, "the atonement cannot be understood without the idea of a conjunction between Christ and His people," and conversely, this head-body, Christ-church, Shepherd-sheep unity necessitates definite atonement, one that makes vicarious sacrifice the very center of Christ's atoning work.[41] Scripture gives no room for a merely provisional atonement. Rather, the language of Scripture speaks of Christ dying "for" or "in the place of" another.[42] Known as "penal substitution," Christ became the sin-bearing, wrath-removing substitute for His covenant people.[43] As the view goes, Christ did not substitute Himself for an abstract and undefined something, nor does His atoning sacrifice merely have a subjective effect on the sinner. According to the Scriptures, Jesus paid a price for a people,[44] meaning that "Christ's substitution... [was] a definite, one-to-one relationship between him and each individual sinner."[45] Anything less than this "one-to-one" substitution makes the atonement abstract, and worse, ineffective.

---

[40] Smeaton, *The Doctrine of the Atonement as Taught by Christ Himself*, 366.

[41] Ibid., 436–41.

[42] Leon Morris, *The Apostolic Preaching of the Cross*, 3rd Rev. Ed. (Grand Rapids, MI: Eerdmans, 1965), 34–38, 62–64.

[43] This is debated doctrine today. For a defense of penal substitution, see *Pierced for Our Transgressions: Rediscovering the Glory of Penal Substitution* (Wheaton, IL: Crossway, 2007) and *The Glory of the Atonement: Biblical, Theological, and Practical Perspectives*, eds. Charles E. Hill and Frank A. James, III (Downers Grove, IL: InterVarsity, 2004). While many who deny definite atonement uphold penal substitution (Kenneth Keathley, *Salvation and Sovereignty*; David Nelson, "The Design, Nature, and Extent of the Atonement," in *Calvinism: A Southern Baptist Dialogue*, eds. E. Ray Clendenen and Brad J. Waggoner [Nashville: B&H Academic, 2008], 115–138), it is important to remember that Christ's penal substitution is consistent with definite atonement in ways that Arminian and Amyraldian views are not (Robert Peterson and Michael Williams, *Why I Am Not a Armininian*, 198–202; J. K. Grider, "Arminianism," in *Evangelical Dictionary of Theology*, 2nd Ed., ed. Walter Elwell (Grand Rapids, MI: Baker, 2001), 97–98.

[44] Tom Wells, *A Price for a People* (Carlisle, PA: Banner of Truth, 1992), esp., 12–50.

[45] J. I. Packer, "What Did the Cross Achieve? The Logic of Penal Substitution," in *In My Place Condemned He Stood* (Wheaton, IL: Crossway, 2007), 36.

Historically, those who have defended penal substitution have usually embraced definite atonement.[46] While John Owen's trilemma is relevant at this juncture,[47] the reason why penal substitution requires definite atonement is not a logical syllogism; it is a conclusion based on the plain mean-

---

[46] As Cunningham stated more than a century ago, "[T]he nature of the atonement settles or determines the question of its extent." William Cunningham, *Historical Theology* (1862; reprint: Carlisle, PA: Banner of Truth, 1960), 2:349. In his *Historical Theology*, Cunningham shows how the universalists of his day defined substitution in abstract terms and never addressed the covenantal and personal exchange that the apostles regularly describe. Taking on flesh and blood, Christ gives Himself for the seed of Abraham (Hebrews 2:14–19). He does not die merely to relax the law, remove barriers, or make man salvable. *Historical Theology*, 2:348–60. Cf. William G. T. Shedd, *Dogmatic Theology*, ed. Alan W. Gomes (New York, NY: Charles Scribner's Sons, 1889–94; reprint: Phillipsburg, NJ: Presbyterian & Reformed, 2003), 711–20; Tom Wells, *A Price for a People*, 83–89; Robert Letham, *The Work of Christ*, 229–34.

[47] Owen's classic syllogism states, "To which I may add this dilemma to our Universalists: God imposed his wrath due unto, and Christ underwent the pains of hell for, *either all the sins of all men, or all the sins of some men, or some sins of all men*. If the last, some sins of all men, then have all men some sins to answer for, and so shall no man be saved; for if God enter into judgment with us, though it were with all mankind for one sin, no flesh should be justified in his sight: "If the Lord should mark iniquities, who should stand?" (Psalm 130:3).... If the second, that is it which we affirm, that Christ in their stead and room suffered for all the sins of all the elect in the world. If the first, why, then, are not all freed from the punishment of all their sins? You will say, "Because of their unbelief; they will not believe." But this unbelief, is it a sin or not? If not, why should they be punished for it? If it be, then Christ underwent the punishment due to it, or not. If so, then why must that hinder them more than their other sins for which he died from partaking of the fruit of his death? If he did not, then did he not die for all their sins. Let them choose which part they will." Owen, *The Death of Death*, 61–62.

Alan Clifford counters Owen's argument asserting that the problem of unbelief applies to the "supposed believer as it does to unbelievers." Alan Clifford, *Atonement and Justification* (Oxford: Charendon Press, 1990), 112. He charges Owen with following Aristotle more than the apostles, and credits Aristotle's teleology to blinding Owen to multiple intentions in the cross of Christ. If only Owen could have seen that Christ's death achieved multiple intents, then he would not have asserted this crudity of commercial atonement. David Allen cites Clifford with approval. Allen, "The Atonement," 86–87.

Clifford's rebuttal is pastorally-sensitive, but theologically-unconvincing. Cf. Carl R. Trueman, *The Claims of Truth: John Owen's Trinitarian Theology* (Carlisle, PA: Paternoster Press, 1998), esp. 233–40. First, Christ's death procures faith for the elect; it does not, as Clifford phrases it, "remove unbelief" *carte blanche*. God's gift of faith is particular, and for some that means unswerving faith that solidifies churches and bolsters missions (1 Corinthians 12:9a); for others, mustard seed

ing of Scripture.[48] Speaking to a room full of Baptist ministers, Roger Nicole said, "If you analyze the Scriptural language for the nature of the work of Christ, it shows that it is something that is effectual."[49] If Christ *really* gave His life as a ransom for many (Matthew 20:28), if He *really* bore the curse in our place (Galatians 3:13), if He *really* became sin for us (2 Corinthians 5:21); then it must hold that there are some for whom He did not die. Otherwise, how could the ones He ransomed, freed from the curse, and imputed righteousness perish, unless the extent of His propitiation was less than universal. The alternative is to redefine the nature of the atonement, as Robert Letham observes,

> [I]f we wish to maintain that Christ died for all without exception while rejecting universalism, we will have no alternative but to redefine the nature of the atonement. Christ's death will then have secured the salvation of no-one in particular. It will simply be a provisional suffering, dependent for its effect on a believing response by the sinner.... It seems impossible theologically to hold to the penal substitutionary nature of

faith is small and easily discouraged, but it is real, God-given, and over time it bears fruit, even amidst many barren seasons. Clifford does not make this distinction between saving faith that suffers and "total unbelief" (*Atonement and Justification*, 112). Second, Owen's trilemma is speaking of eschatological finalities that cannot be verified or denied by human observation; he speaks from what Scripture reveals, not what is observable in the life of those around him. This does not make assurance impossible; it merely admits that we are finite creatures who depend on revelation, not reason. Third, what Clifford fails to see in his critique of Owen is that the sixteenth century divine was not shaped by Aristotelian logic, but by the texts of Scripture which led him to affirm an inviolable covenant between Christ and the elect. Carl Trueman ably replies to Clifford, when he says, "[Owen's] argument is built upon the notion of the covenant of redemption, which defines Christ's role as Mediator for the elect whom God has given him." Carl Trueman, *The Claims of Truth*, 139. Finally, definite atonement does not stand or fall with John Owen; 'defeating' this man's theology does not mean that one has defeated definite atonement. It is the text of Scripture that must be 'defeated' in order to deny definite atonement.

[48] David Allen accuses John Owen of relying heavily on a scholastic double-payment for sins to defend definite atonement. Allen, "The Atonement," 83–92. However, Greg Wills sets the record straight, "[Owen] relied not so much on the double-payment argument as on the Bible's teaching that Christ's death secured actual ransom, reconciliation, and satisfaction," (Greg Wills, "Whosoever Will: A Review Essay," 16).

[49] Roger Nicole, "The Atonement—Part 2," in *Reclaiming the Gospel and Reforming Churches*, ed. Thomas K. Ascol (Cape Coral, FL: Founders Press, 2003), 73.

the atonement and at the same time maintain that Christ died provision-
ally for all without exception.[50]

For these textual reasons, many who at first mocked and rejected 'limited' atonement have been convinced that "Jesus Saves" without qualification.

Priestly Argument for Particular and Effective Atonement

Scripture gives us inspired texts and inspired types. J. I. Packer calls
the latter "models." In his work on penal substitution, Packer lists three
different kinds of models—"'control models' given in Scripture (God, Son
of God, kingdom of God, [etc]),""dogmatic models that the church crys-
tallized out to define and defend the faith (homoousion, Trinity, nature,
hypostatic union, [etc])," and "interpretive models lying between Scripture
and defined dogma... (penal substitution, verbal inspiration, divinization,
[etc])."[51]

If we follow Packer's modular taxonomy, I would propose that Calvinistic and egalitarian versions of the cross both fall under the banner of
"interpretive models," whereas the priesthood of Christ would be classified
as a "control model." If those classifications are acceptable, then it should
follow that the control model should have priority and interpretive control
over the interpretive model. Or to say it materially, whatever the Bible
teaches about Christ's priesthood will determine the nature and extent
of Christ's atonement. Accordingly, as it will be demonstrated through
an examination of priestly typology in Scripture, definite atonement finds
overwhelming support in the particular and efficacious priesthood of Jesus
Christ.

In contrast to egalitarians who rarely consider the priesthood of
Christ,[52] defenders of definite atonement have regularly appealed to this

---

[50] Robert Letham, *The Work of Christ*, 230.

[51] J. I. Packer, "What Did The Cross Achieve? The Logic of Penal Substitution," in *In My Place Condemned He Stood* (Wheaton, IL: Crossway, 2007), 63.

[52] A noticeable lacuna among egalitarians is their treatment of Christ's priesthood. One is hard-pressed to find from egalitarians a sustained effort to explain
the extent of Christ's atonement in light of His priestly office. Instead, egalitarians usually interpret individual texts without consideration for their epochal
context and the covenant Christ mediates as a priest. The result for egalitarians
is a "text-based" view of the atonement that on first glance appears to find much
biblical support for their general atonement; however, when the "all" and "world"
passages are read in their epochal context, and when Christ's priestly office is
rightly considered, a particular and efficacious view of the atonement results.

biblical-theological office. The power of the argument is found in its comprehensive view of Scripture and the unity of the person and work of Christ.[53] Moreover, there is nothing that Christ did before, during, or after the cross in which He was not serving as a priest. Thus, attention to Christ's priestly office will supply great light on Christ's atoning work.

Concerning the priestly office, O. Palmer Robertson writes, "Under the provisions of the old covenant, the high priest of Israel never offered sacrifices for people indiscriminately. The priestly sacrifices were always offered for specific sinners."[54] What is true in the type is true of the antitype, and it is unmistakable that the high priest represents a particular people.[55] To prove this, we will consider four lines of evidence: (1) The priestly garments which define who the priest represents, (2) the location of the atonement, (3) the sacrifice itself, and (4) the relationship between intercession and atonement.

The Garments

The garments worn by the priest show a clear relationship with the covenant people of Israel (Exodus 28:15–30; 39:8–21). Engraved on his ephod are the names of the twelve tribes of Israel, thus indicating his particular service for these peoples and not others. "Priestly office and priestly garb are inextricably related."[56] In this regard, the priestly attire 'visualizes'

One possible exception is Norman Douty who states, "We maintain that Christ is a divinely provided priest for all mankind" Douty, *Did Christ Die Only for the Elect?* 33. If universalism is true, then this statement is fine. However, if Christ is a universal priest, and some of the ones who he represents are lost, then we must ask: "How is He any better than the priests of the Mosaic Covenant?" For the sake of universal offer, Douty continues, "Any member of Adam's race may have Him as his priest if he will" (33). There is no dispute that Christ's priesthood extends to the nations in a way that the Levitical priesthood never did. "Whosoever will may come," but does that mean Christ is really the priest of all mankind? This section will aim to answer these questions and prove from the canon that as priest, He serves a particular people drawn from all over the world.

[53] William Cunningham, *Historical Theology*, 2:238; John Stott, *The Cross of Christ* (Downers Grove, IL: InterVarsity, 1986), 149–63.

[54] O. Palmer Robertson, "Definite Atonement," in *After Darkness Light: Distinctives of Reformed Theology* (Phillipsburg, NJ: P&R, 2003), 98.

[55] Cf. Stephen Wellum, "The New Covenant Work of Christ: Priesthood, Atonement, and Intercession," in *From Heaven He Came and Sought Her: Definite Atonement in Biblical, Historical, Theological, and Pastoral Persepctive*, eds. Jonathan Gibson and David Gibson (Wheaton, IL: Crossway, forthcoming).

[56] Carol Meyers, *Exodus*, New Cambridge Bible Commentary (New York, NY: Cambridge University Press, 2005), 240.

the particular nature of the atonement.[57] It does so in this way: From head to foot, the priest is to wear the holy attire designed and decorated to teach Israel and later generations what the priest is doing as he enters into the holy of holies.[58]

In fact, this notion of personal relationship between priest and people has been forcefully argued by Hugh Martin as evidence against indefinite atonement. Unpacking Hebrews 5:1, a passage which relates the OT priesthood to Christ, Martin argues that the office of the priest "rests on personal relation," and this relation is not abstract. Rather, the priest represents "individual men, particular persons."[59] Speaking of the Levitical priests, he says,

> The priests of Levi were chosen *for*, or in lieu of, the first-born [Num 3]; and they were ordained *for* [Lev 8–9], or in room and on behalf of men, even for the Israel of God collectively and individually. They acted for individuals; and besides such action, they had no priestly action whatsoever, no official duty to discharge. The introduction of a 'general reference' into the theory of their office is an absurdity.[60]

When one thinks of the extent of the atonement, priestly garments may not be the first thing that comes to mind, but indeed, they are incredibly instructional. They anticipate Christ's particular priesthood.[61]

Location

The location of the sacrifice reinforces the particularity of the atonement. In Exodus, God saves His people from Egypt and brings them to Mount Sinai where He gives Moses a vision of the tabernacle that will serve as the meeting place between YHWH and Israel (25:40). The tabernacle will become central in all that Israel does. While in the wilderness, God's tent dwelt in the center of camp (Numbers 2:2); when Israel entered the land, God set His name in a particular place (Deuteronomy 12;

[57] For instance, speaking of the priest in his vestments, Alec Motyer writes, "[H]e is the visual display of the Lord's 'judgment,' his opinion regarding his people" J. A. Motyer, *The Message of Exodus*, The Bible Speaks Today, ed. J.A. Motyer (Downers Grove, IL: InterVarsity Press, 2005), 279.

[58] David Williams, *The Office of Christ and Its Expression in the Church: Prophet, Priest, King* (Lewiston, NY: Mellen Biblical Press, 1997) 35, 40.

[59] Hugh Martin, *The Atonement*, 58. Martin ties this particular relationship to the definite nature of the atonement.

[60] Ibid., 65.

[61] Cf. Patrick Fairbairn, *The Typology of Scripture: Two Volumes in One* (Grand Rapids, MI: Zondervan, 1956), 2:248–49.

2 Samuel 5), where Israel gathered to worship and the priests made atonement (Leviticus 16, 23). Anticipating the exile, Solomon instructed future generations to pray towards the holy city (1 Kings 8). The location shows the particularity of God, and how God meets with His particular people in a particular place (cf. Genesis 28:10ff).[62]

Yet, the location indicates something else. The atonement is not simply applied to individuals. That is, it is primarily objective, not subjective.[63] Typologically then, in the system outlined in the Pentateuch, the blood is applied to the altar, so that God Himself is propitiated. This Godward orientation does not simply remove an undefined legal barrier for the individual; even under the old covenant, the atonement effectively opens the way into the very dwelling place of God. While the offices of prophet and king are towards men, Christ's priestly work is "directly and immediately towards God."[64] The significance of this orientation is the fact that the priest's work is done in God's abode.

In the Old Covenant, this would be the earthly tabernacle or temple, but in the New Covenant, the author of Hebrews makes it clear that Jesus applied His sacrificial blood to the true altar in heavenly places (Hebrews 9:23–28). Thus, the law does not make sin or sins the immediate object of reconciliation, rather the high priest reconciles the Lord to all those whom he represents as priestly mediator of a new covenant.[65] In this way, Christ is not making a mere provision for the salvation of all men, by somehow qualifying all men for salvation, if only they will believe. This is the position of Norman Douty, who says that Christ died "for every sort of sin ever committed by human kind" and thus He suffered for every person without distinction. He continues, "He could not suffer for the sins of the elect without suffering for those of the non-elect, because both companies have sinned the same sins."[66] The trouble with his view is that Christ died for people, not for faceless sins. As Bavinck has stated, sin is "not a substance" to be expunged, rather it is covenantal breach against a holy God that must be reconciled.[67]

[62] For New Testament Christians, the importance of geography is easily overlooked. For Jesus states in John 4 that worship no longer includes geographical proximity. However, the reason for this is not that location is unimportant; rather, it is because Jesus Himself is the true temple (John 1:14; 2:18–22) and in the New Covenant we come to Him. Cf. Paul M. Hoskins, *That Scripture Might Be Fulfilled: Typology and the Death of Christ* (USA: Xulon Press, 2009), esp. 116–36.

[63] Cf. Hugh Martin, *The Atonement*, 69–71.

[64] Hugh Martin, *The Atonement*, 59.

[65] John Owen, *The Priesthood of Christ*, 211.

[66] Douty, *Did Christ Die Only for the Elect?* 30–31.

[67] Bavinck, *Reformed Dogmatics*, 3:137.

Consequently, when Christ assumed the priestly role, He did not wear the Decalogue on his vestments, but the names of all those saints given to Him by the Father. Of course, the fulfillment of this bearing of the names is not that Christ had served as priest merely for persons as persons, but for the sins of those persons in particular. He suffered for their sins; he died for their sins. Jesus did not die just for David as a person, but for the sins committed by David. Jesus did not die for the sin of adultery in general, but for the specific adultery of David in all its specifically aggravating circumstances. Contra Douty, the sins of each person have their own context and peculiar circumstances and aggravations calling for greater or lesser punishment; his theory, therefore that Jesus just died for the sin of adultery in general does not meet the requirements of biblical justice. No. Christ is effecting propitiation before God as He applies his blood to the altar in heaven reconciling a God whose wrath goes out against each sin committed by those people whom Christ is representing. Consequently, temple typology rejects general atonement.

Sacrifices[68]

"The principle duty and work of the priests under the law was to offer sacrifices,"[69] and as it has been argued thus far, obedient priests represented a specific people in a specific place. They served Israel, and no one else.[70] In fact, there is reason to believe that the priestly office not only advocated for Israel, but it also acted adversely to anyone who might pollute God's dwelling place (Exodus 32:25–29; Numbers 25:10–18; Deuteronomy 33:8–11; 2 Chronicles 26:16–20). In this way, their atoning work foreshadowed Christ's penal substitution and their violent defense of God's dwelling place foreshadows Christ's victory over His enemies—angelic and human (Psalm 110:1, 5–7; cf. Colossians 2:13–15; Hebrews 2: 14–15; Revelation 19:11–21).

Such particularity resulted in YHWH restricting his dwelling and revelation to Israel (Psalm 132:13–18; 147:19–20), as well as the appointment of priests to the people of Israel. This is a very basic point, but one that is often overlooked. David Williams drives the point home,

---

[68] In *Atonement Matters*, Tom Barnes supplies a full biblical theology on the sacrifices and the way they are always particular and efficacious (45–126).

[69] John Owen, *The Priesthood of Christ: Its Necessity and Nature* (Ross-shire: Christian Heritage, 2010), 212.

[70] Cf. Tremper Longman III, *Immanuel in Our Place, The Gospel According to the Old Testament* (Phillipsburg, NJ: P&R, 2001), 139–150.

Indeed, the sacrificial system, although it encompassed those who had identified with Israel by sojourning in their midst, obviously did not apply to those outside the covenant. The covenant was therefore essential to the relationship with God; ... It is perhaps interesting that the word used in Numbers 15:30 to indicate separation from the community is the same one involved in making (cutting) a covenant, a normal word for severing (as in 1 Sam 24:4 or Is 8:15). The covenant involved separation from other nations, so it was appropriate that breaking it involved expulsion back to them.[71]

This covenantal separation prepares the way to examine the particular function of the sacrifices in Israel's temple cult. While sacrifices are seen before the exodus (cf. Genesis 22),[72] Exodus 12–13 permanently inserts sacrifice into Israel's annual calendar. Moreover, the other sacrifices detailed in Leviticus, which complement and explain the purifying work of the first Passover (Leviticus 1–7, 16–17; Deuteronomy 16), form a unified system that provided atonement for Israel until the greater Lamb would come to take away sin once and for all.[73] Collectively, these different offerings explain what Christ did on the cross, and when the question of extent/intent is applied to them, it becomes evident that they are harbingers of a particular redemption. For instance, in Exodus 12, Moses records, "no foreigner shall eat of [the Passover], but every slave that is bought for money may eat of it after you have circumcised him" (v. 43–44).[74] Likewise, in Leviticus 16, the priest offers the sacrifice with the names of Israel etched on his body (v. 4); he sacrifices the animal that comes from the congregation (v. 5) and he kills the goat that is "for the people" (v. 15). Clearly, the Passover and Day of Atonement are only shared with those in the covenantal community. There is nothing universal or general in these sacrifices which typify Christ (1 Corinthians 5:7).

As Williams posits above, the purpose of the Passover was to separate the people of Israel from the nation of Egypt. Paul Hoskins agrees: "As was the case with the earlier plagues (8:22–23), the Passover sacrifice indicates a separation between God's people and Pharaoh's people."[75] It is not that the Passover was made for Israel *and* Egypt and only Israel partook. Rath-

[71] David Williams, *The Office of Christ and Its Expression in the Church*, 14.

[72] See Derek Tidball, *The Message of the Cross* (Downers Grove, IL: InterVarsity Press, 2001), 36–50.

[73] Cf. Robert L. Reymond, *The Lamb of God: The Bible Unfolding Revelation of Sacrifice* (Ross-shire: Mentor, 2006); William Symington, *On the Atonement and Intercession of Jesus Christ*, 93–116.

[74] J. A. Motyer, *The Message of Exodus*, 132–37.

[75] Hoskins, *That Scripture Might Be Fulfilled*, 93.

er, God's intended purpose was to redeem Israel and destroy Egypt (Exodus 9:15–17; 10:1–2; cf. Romans 9:17–18). Psalm 136 records God's *hesed* as a lovingkindness that saved Israel and slaughtered the nations (cf. Isaiah 43:3–4). In the historical narrative of Exodus, this is seen when Pharaoh and his army are destroyed in the waters of judgment (Exodus 14), and then YHWH is praised for being a victorious warrior (Exodus 15:3).

At this point, egalitarians may suppose that if the Levitical priest represented elect and non-elect in Israel, he will represent and redeem ("die for") all people without distinction in the New Covenant, as well. However, this confuses the matter in two ways: First, in the OT, the high priest does not represent spiritual Israel, but Israel according to the flesh. Therefore, his atoning work is according to the flesh, not the Spirit. This is why a greater sacrifice is needed (Hebrews 10:4). When egalitarians read categories of elect and non-elect back into the OT priesthood, they confuse the matter by conflating Christ's spiritual headship with Israel's ethnic constitution. Second, Christ is the mediator of a better covenant and will effectively save His covenant people in a way that the Old Covenant priests never could. We will address this in the next section.

Hebrews reinforces the particular efficacy of the priest's sacrifice. Moving from types in the Old Testament to texts in the New, Hebrews 9:11–12 makes clear that the New Covenant is mediated by a better priest, is accomplished in a "more perfect tent, not made with hands," and is ratified by Christ's superior blood. The result is the security of an "eternal redemption." Christ's work on the cross did not simply make a provision for the sins of the world, it secured an eternal redemption for all those in covenant with him (cf. 13:20–21). Therefore, we must assert with Scripture that the New Covenant is not dependent on human obedience, even the "obedience of faith" (Romans 1:5; 16:26). It is dependent upon Christ, and Christ alone.

Likewise, Hebrews 10 indicates that Christ came to fulfill God's law (vv. 5–7), do the will of His father (v. 9a), and "do away with the first in order to establish the second" (v. 9b). While taking on flesh and blood, Christ's obedience is not for all humanity, it is for His particular people, "those who are being sanctified" (10:14). These are the ones who are described earlier in Hebrews as "brothers" (2:12), "children of God" (2:13), and "the offspring of Abraham" (2:16). These familial terms are not generic but specific,[76] describing the covenant relationship Jesus initiated with

---

[76] "Jesus Christ became a man. Why? Hebrews does *not* suggest that it was in order to be like all other men. No, it was a family matter—not primarily the human family, but the family of the redeemed… children, Abraham's descendents, brothers and the people [of God]." Tom Wells, *A People for a Price*, 63.

those he would represent as priest (5:1).[77]

Intercession

Another indispensible piece to this priestly argument is the unified nature of Christ's intercession and atonement. While many have seen this connection, none have expounded it more thoroughly than William Symington. In his 300-page work on Christ's atonement and intercession he states, "Intercession and atonement are correlates, not merely in nature, but in extent. For whomsoever and for whatsoever he has procured blood, does he plead before the throne of God. This is the leading principle which may serve to guide us in the observations we have to offer on this department of our subject." While running the risk of a circular argument between atonement and intercession, Symington does not rely on deductive reasoning alone. He points to the Bible. He quotes Paul's words in Romans 8:34 that Jesus "maketh intercession *for us*," he refers to Hebrews 7:25, denoting how the ones for whom Christ "liveth to make intercession" are not the general masses but "them only who, as he says in the clause immediately going before, *come unto God by Christ*." Further, he appeals to 1 John 2:1, a passage often cited for the universal language of verse 2. He states, "To the same purpose is the testimony of John—'If any man sin we have an advocate with the Father,' speaking in his own name and that of the christian [*sic*] brethren to whom his epistle is addressed."[78] For Symington, these texts affirm Christ's particular intercession.[79] "It is utterly absurd and pernicious, as well as unscriptural, to suppose that [Jesus] makes intercession for those who live and die in unbelief, who continue to disown his mediatory office, and to place reliance on other grounds of salvation than his infinite merits."[80] Tying his theological conclusions back to the Levitical types, he observes,

> Unless a sacrifice had been previously offered on the brazen altar, he could not enter within the veil, at least his entering could serve no pur-

---

[77] For a thorough discussion between the relationship of the priest to his covenant people, see Geerhardus Vos, "The Priesthood of Christ in Hebrews," in *Redemptive History and Biblical Interpretation*, ed. Richard Gaffin (Phillipsburg, NJ: P&R, 1980), esp. 133–43.

[78] Symington, *On the Atonement and Intercession of Jesus Christ*, 269. All three quotes are Symington's.

[79] Ibid., 194.

[80] Ibid., 269–70. Since Scripture positively affirms his particular intercession and actually denies his intercession for all in general, it must be that Christ's atonement is particular and efficacious.

pose whatsoever; the blood of the burnt-offering had to be carried by him into the holy place and sprinkled upon the mercy-seat. The one was as much a part of his priestly function as the other; and if the latter prefigured Christ [i. e. the appearance and application of the blood] in any part of his sacerdotal service, so also did the former [i. e. the vicarious sacrifice]; *to separate them is to put asunder what God has joined together.*[81]

Not only does Jesus pray for a particular people, the individual petitions are also specific. Describing Jesus' prayer life, Symington writes that it is not "in the mass that the Saviour makes intercession." Rather, "he prays for *each* by himself."[82] No two cases are the same and thus the theanthropic priest prays with the infinite power of the word become flesh. Like the persons He creates and the words He speaks, each utterance has definite content and efficacious power.[83]

In addition to Scriptural testimony and the specificity of His prayers, Symington argues that Christ's intercession envelopes His atonement. Before, during, and after His crucifixion, Jesus prays for His people. Against egalitarians who conceive of atonement in chronological fashion—the atonement first and later application—Christ's earthly life is filled with specific prayers (Matthew 26:36–46; Luke 22:31–32; Luke 23:34; Hebrews 5:7). What Symington proves is that Christ's intercession is a part of His atonement, not a separate entity. Thus, it is impossible for Christ's atonement to come to the non-elect in any real way, because it would have to come with prayer, and if with prayer then with power and efficacy (Hebrews 5:7). But since, all concede a limit to the application, it must be that as Christ went to the cross praying only for the elect, He was only dying for them too.

Altogether, Symington proves from the Scriptures that there is no category for someone who is bought with the blood of Christ but not saved. Such a proposition ignores the way Scripture speaks of Jesus' priestly office, which is always effective and always unifies intercession and atonement. Such a denial of this work, or the suggestion that this atonement and intercession have alternative objects, defames His sacerdotal office. Therefore, if we are to understand anything of Christ's atonement, we must see it in the light of Scripture's teaching on the priesthood. Any argument that makes a case for general atonement that ignores the contours of Scripture regard-

---

[81] Ibid., 112.

[82] Ibid., 272.

[83] As Vanhoozer has more recently stated, Christ's words are always "penetrative" and thus effective. Kevin Vanhoozer, *Remythologizing Theology: Divine Action, Passion, and Authorship*, Cambridge Studies in Christian Doctrine 18 (New York: Cambridge University Press), 361–66.

ing Christ's priestly work and His covenantal blood, ought to be dismissed outright. Jesus' speech-acts can only be rightly understood in the biblical framework, one where His priestly mediation secures an eternal salvation for all who are a part of his eternal covenant (Hebrews 9:12; 13:20–21).

The Covenantal Nature of the Atonement

New Covenant Theology In Baptist History

It is not surprising that Covenant Theology has appealed to the covenants to expound their doctrinal views. What may be more unknown is the fact that many Baptists have appealed to the New Covenant to explain their understanding of the cross.[84] For instance, R. B. C. Howell, writes,

> [God's] purposes are made apparent by all that is revealed to us in relation to the Covenant of Redemption. When He sent forth His Son into the world, He announced Him as "The Messenger of the Covenant" (Malachi 3:1). "The blood of the cross," He designates as "The blood of the Covenant," and "The blood of the everlasting Covenant" (Colossians 1:20; Hebrews 10:29; 13:20; Zechariah 9:11)... *It is evident, therefore, that from that far-off eternity in which He dwelt, God never contemplated our universe, but in connection with a Mediator.*[85]

Historically-speaking, many Baptists who looked to the New Covenant for defending believer's baptism also depended on the New Covenant to understand the extent of the atonement.[86] Another historic Baptist is little-regarded Howard Malcolm. A nineteenth-century pastor, missionary, and college president, Malcolm delivered a lecture to the Boston Baptist Association in 1832 strongly defending the particular extent and unfailing efficacy of the atonement.[87] In his discourse, Malcolm looked to the New Covenant as indubitably securing salvation for all those who were in

---

[84] For instance, Fred Malone in *The Baptism of Disciples Alone* lists Basil Manly, Sr., William B. Johnson, James P. Boyce, P.H. Mell, R.B.C. Howell, John L. Dagg, and C.H. Spurgeon as Baptists who affirmed "covenant theology" (xxix–xxxiii).

[85] Robert Boyte Crawford Howell, "The Cross," in *The Cross and the Covenants* (1854; reprint: Harrisonburg, VA: Sprinkle Press, 1994), 3. Emphasis mine.

[86] Cf. Thomas J. Nettles, *By His Grace and For His Glory: A Historical, Theological and Practical Study of the Doctrines of Grace in Baptist Life*, (Cape Coral, FL: Founders, 2006).

[87] Howard Malcolm, *The Extent and Efficacy of the Atonement* (University Press, 1840; reprint: LaVergne, TN, 2010).

Christ. He quotes a handful of Scriptures that attest to the union between Christ "as a common head representing the elect," and he writes, "What he promised in the covenant, he promised on their behalf, and what he received, he received on their behalf... This federal union certainly places part of the human family in a different situation from the rest; Christ being the covenant head of a part, and not of the whole."[88] Malcolm points to Jesus' "exquisite and forcible parable" in John 10 about the sheep that Jesus calls and propitiates, and he says,

> If the Saviour had no more connection with these than with the rest of mankind, the whole parable becomes absurd and false. All the passages which speak of our dying, rising, living, &c., in and with Christ, become nugatory. In short, to maintain a general atonement, the entire doctrine of the federal union between Christ and his people must be abandoned. And by those who maintain such an atonement, generally, it is abandoned![89]

Malcolm is a good example of a missions-minded Baptist who affirmed definite atonement, not because some creed told him to but because a thorough reading of the text pressed him to see the effectiveness of the New Covenant. To such a reading we now turn.

New Covenant Theology In the Bible

As the cross relates to the covenants of the Bible, it is clear that the crucifixion and resurrection of Jesus Christ is the climax of redemptive history (Luke 24:44–49). And as the Bible indicates, it was a covenantal event. For instance, Luke records how Jesus made the Jewish Passover meal a New Covenant commemoration of His death (22:14–23). Speaking specifically about his blood, Jesus states, "This cup that is poured out for you is the new covenant in my blood" (cf. 1 Corinthians 11:25). In this brief but poignant statement, the New Testament reader is informed that the Lord's Supper is a covenantal meal. Jesus death was and is a covenantal death.

Then, in the epistles and especially in Hebrews, the blessings of the new covenant begin to be delineated. In this sermonic epistle, Christ's death is explained with cultic imagery from the Old Covenant (e. g. priesthood, tabernacle, sacrifice). More to the point, Hebrews stresses the efficacy of the New Covenant ratified by Christ's death.[90] For instance, He-

---

[88] Malcolm, *The Extent and Efficacy*, 63–64.

[89] Ibid., 65.

[90] For an elongated treatment on this subject, see Barry Joslin, *Hebrews, Christ, and the Law: The Theology of the Mosaic Law in Hebrews 7:1–10:18* (Eugene, OR: Wipf & Stock, 2009), 173–223.

brews 9:15–22 sets the death of Christ in covenantal context.[91] In verses 15–17, the author of Hebrews refers to Christ's death three times. In verse 15, he says that Christ's death "redeems them [the called] from the transgressions committed under the first covenant." Significantly, those who are redeemed, "them" in verse 15a, are specifically addressed as those "who are called" (v. 15b). With this language, there is a textual restriction on the extent of the atonement, and a direct covenantal link between the called and the death of Christ. His blessings are reserved for them,[92] and thus the cross "ensures the full effectiveness of the covenant and its promises."[93] Debate arises over the meaning of the term *diatheke* in verses 16–17, but permitting the surrounding context to speak (vv. 15, 18),[94] it seems appropriate for Christ's death to end the first covenant for the "called" and inaugurate a "new covenant" for the same recipients (cf. Ephesians 2:14–16). However, this reading also limits Christ's atoning benefits to those who are in covenant with Him—the non-elect remain outside Christ and under the judgment of God.

Further, in verse 18, the author's general discussion of death moves to the graphic description of Christ's blood. Comparing Christ's blood to the blood that ratified the covenant made at Sinai, he writes, "Therefore not even the first covenant was inaugurated without blood" (v. 18). He assumes that all covenants are inaugurated with blood, and he launches into a full discussion of the way in which the Old Covenant was ratified by blood, and then how Christ's blood supersedes it (vv. 19–25). What is important to note is the way that the covenantal context of the cross demands application of the blood.

In order, verse 19 says that Moses took the blood and applied it to the book of covenant and the people themselves. There does not appear to be a difference between the blood shed and the blood applied: the extent of the oblation and application are the same. Likewise, verse 21 indicates that

[91] William Lane, *Hebrews 9–13*, Word Biblical Commentary (Nashville, TN: Thomas Nelson, 1991), 241.

[92] This recalls Howard Malcolm's statement: "This federal union certainly places part of the human family in a different situation from the rest; Christ being the covenant head of a part, and not of the whole." Malcolm, *The Extent and Efficacy*, 63–64.

[93] Philip E. Hughes, *A Commentary on the Epistles to the Hebrews* (Grand Rapids, MI: Eerdmans, 1977), 368.

[94] For a defense of reading *diatheke* as "covenant" not "testament," see William Lane, *Hebrews 9–13*, 231; O. Palmer Robertson, *The Christ of the Covenants* (Phillipsburg, NJ: P&R, 1980), 138–44; Peter T. O'Brien, *The Letter to the Hebrews*, Pillar New Testament Commentary (Grand Rapids, MI: Eerdmans, 2010), 328–32.

Moses also took the blood and applied it to the tent and all the vessels. The same blood that was shed and applied to the people corresponds to the blood that was applied to the dwelling place of God. Then, he concludes as he moves to discuss the application of Christ's blood, "without the shedding of blood there is no forgiveness of sin" (9:22). The underlying meaning is that blood forgives sin. Finally, Hebrews 9:23–24 says that Jesus' blood didn't just purify a copy of the heavenly tabernacle as the offerings under the Old Covenant did; He actually entered heaven and sat down at the right hand of God as the perfect Lamb of God. So then, there exists in heaven a perfect Mediator, the Son of God, with blood-scarred hands and feet, whose final sacrifice will forever plead the innocence of God's covenant people.

Therefore, in Hebrews, atonement and application are not bifurcated, as they are in the egalitarian view. Rather, because of the covenantal nature of Christ's blood, *they are always conjoined*. Citing the extensive study of W. G. Johnsson, William Lane explains,

> *Aphesis* is a comprehensive term covering both the 'subjective' and 'objective' benefits of Christ's blood. Thus v 23 proceeds to direct attention to the purgation of heavenly things. The juxtaposing of *katharizein*, "to purge," with *aphesis* in v 22 and the resumption of *katharizein* in v 23 shows that the meanings of these two words are closely connected. In this context, *aphesis* signals a definitive putting away of defilement or a decisive purgation.[95]

What is the end result? Christ's atonement did not simply make forgiveness possible; it decisively effected forgiveness and cleansing.

The Newness of the New Covenant

Therefore, based on this covenantal reading of the cross in Hebrews and the rest of the New Testament, it is not too much to say that all Scripture anticipates the New Covenant inaugurated by the blood of Christ (John 5:39; cf. Luke 24:27, 44–46), and that this covenantal reading does not permit a universal atonement. Why? Because the New Covenant is doing something completely new.[96] Applying the newness of the New Covenant to the atonement, Sam Waldron intimates,

---

[95] Lane, *Hebrews 9–13*, 246–47. Cf. W.G. Johnsson, "Defilement and Purgation in the Book of Hebrews," (PhD diss., Vanderbilt University, 1973), 324–29.

[96] For a defense of the newness of the New Covenant, see Peter Gentry and Stephen Wellum, *Kingdom Through Covenant* (Wheaton, IL: Crossway, 2012).

The context of the atonement demands particular redemption. The covenant is the context of Christ's work. Christ's blood is covenantal blood. The covenant in view is explicitly and repeatedly identified as the New Covenant, which is one of the most frequently, stated truths of the New Testament (Matt 26:28; Mark 14:24; Luke 22:20; 1 Cor 11:25; Eph 2:12–13; Heb 10:29; 13:20). Jesus' blood redeems and atones only in connection with this new covenant. Only by ratifying the new covenant and, thus, securing its saving benefits does Christ's death save.[97]

Those who oppose particular redemption pay little attention to the covenantal structures of the Bible, and thus universalize the covenantal blessing of forgiveness, making it conditional upon faith.[98] Urging union with Christ as the fundamental difference, some argue against Christ's death purchasing faith;[99] others argue that faith precedes regeneration.[100] The problem with this is two-fold. First, regeneration is a New Covenant blessing (Ezekiel 36:26–27). The "new birth" depends on the initiative of the Spirit sent by Christ (John 3:1–8); it is not a response to an individual's antecedent faith.[101] Second, making application of Christ's universal atonement dependent upon faith strips from Christ the honor of finishing and applying the covenant to each person individually. It, in effect, makes Him a mediator of the old order. Yet, a clear exposition of Jeremiah 31 and Ezekiel 36 shows that the effective cause of regeneration is the promised Spirit that circumcises the heart. Faith, then, is a fruit of regeneration by the Spirit (Galatians 5:23), not an *a la carte* gift of grace. To say it another way, faith and repentance are covenantal blessings (Zechariah 12:10), gifts procured and applied by the mediator of a better covenant. In short, the New Covenant itself states that forgiveness is given to all who are in covenant with God (Jeremiah 31:34). Definite atonement asserts that this

---

[97] Sam Waldron, "The Biblical Confirmation of Particular Redemption," in *Calvinism: A Southern Baptist Dialogue*, eds. E. Ray Clendenen and Brad J. Waggoner (Nashville, TN: B&H Academic, 2008), 147.

[98] An interesting confirmation of this assertion is found in Gary Schultz's dissertation, where he states, "four-point Calvinism has persisted as a viable option within evangelical theology due primarily to the work of the Dispensational movement and Baptists." "A Biblical and Theological Defense of a Multi-Intentioned View of the Extent of the Atonement" (PhD diss., The Southern Baptist Theological Seminary, 2008), 91.

[99] Douty, *Did Christ Die Only for the Elect?*, 58–60.

[100] Steve W. Lemke, "A Biblical and Theological Critique of Irresistable Grace," in *Whosoever Will*, esp. 134–40.

[101] See Matthew Barrett, "Reclaiming Monergism: The Case for Sovereign Grace in Effectual Calling and Regeneration," (PhD diss., The Southern Baptist Theological Seminary, 2011). Also, see chapter 5 of this book.

covenantal blessing is purchased and applied to all the elect for whom Christ died.

The problem that many egalitarians face is that they believe Christ purchased full forgiveness for everyone (Ephesians 1:7), but they do so without considering the stipulations of the New Covenant. Such universal expansion retains the "limited" effectiveness of the Old Covenant. Egalitarians fail to see the decisive discontinuity between Israel's failed covenant and Jesus' certain covenant, and thus they have an under-realized eschatology of the New Covenant. While Baptists chide their Presbyterian brothers for failing to see the newness of the new covenant when it comes to matters of ecclesiology, most Baptistic egalitarians do the same thing when they hold to a universal atonement where only some are finally saved. Highlighting this problem in relationship to baptism, Bruce Ware writes,

> This new covenant is 'not like' the old covenant, precisely in that God's people 'broke' the old covenant, while this new covenant, by implication, will not be broken. That is, God will not fail to make all of those in the new covenant faithful covenant partners... *There is no category for unbelieving covenant members.* All new covenant participants will be covenant keepers, will know and embrace the law intrinsically, and will know the Lord and be his spiritual people. The two categories of the people of God under the old covenant, then, gives way to one solitary category under the new.[102]

Conjoined with a monergistic view of salvation, such a view of the New Covenant necessitates a particular and definite atonement. By contrast, the egalitarian kerygma states: Jesus died to make possible a new covenant relationship with every single person on earth, but now it depends on you to believe and receive His benefits. While the gospel demands response, it is not surprising that this *quid pro quo* theology results in manufactured decisions and manipulative appeals to come to faith. It misses the power and effectiveness of the New Covenant, where all who are joined to Christ in His death will receive the blessings of this better covenant. For those whom the Savior died, He truly saved![103]

---

[102] Bruce Ware, "The Believer's Baptism View," in *Baptism: Three Views*, ed. David F. Wright (Downers Grove, IL: IVP Academic, 2009), 19–50. Cf. Stephen J. Wellum, "Baptism and the Relationship Between the Covenants," in *Believer's Baptism: Sign of the New Covenant in Christ*, ed. Thomas R. Schreiner and Shawn D. Wright, New American Commentary Studies in Bible & Theology 2 (Nashville, TN: B&H Academic, 2007), 97–161.

[103] Sam Waldron, "The Biblical Confirmation of Particular Redemption," in *Calvinism: A Southern Baptist Dialogue*, eds. E. Ray Clendenen and Brad J. Waggoner (Nashville, TN: B&H Academic, 2008), 147.

A final word on the uniqueness of the New Covenant: Under the Old Covenant, myriads of "redeemed" Israelites died in the wilderness (Psalm 95), but now in the New Covenant, Christ has purchased redemption, justification (and faith), sanctification, and glorification for His particular people.[104] The glory of the cross and beauty of the gospel is that it once and for all saves sinners. It does not make salvation merely possible; it actually accomplishes the salvation of those lost sheep that the shepherd goes out to rescue. This is the power of the gospel that beckons us to proclaim "Jesus Saves!" And it prepares the way for us to consider the cosmic effects of definite atonement.

The Universal Impact of Definite Atonement

Commenting on the universal benefit of Christ's work in the world, Blaise Pascal said, "Without Jesus Christ the world would not exist, for it would necessarily be destroyed or be a hell."[105] To this statement, the strictest Calvinist can agree (Ephesians 1:10; Colossians 1:20). While definite atonement is often criticized for being too narrow in its effects, few if any in the Reformed tradition have ever denied the universal impact of the atonement of Christ's death.

For example, in defending particular redemption, R. B. Kuiper articulates a "Scriptural Universalism" that included aspects of common grace, a universal offer of the atonement, and an eschatological salvation of the world when Christ ushers in the new heavens and new earth.[106] Similarly, Herman Bavinck saw Christ's death effects a new creation in individuals (2 Corinthians 5:17) and in the world at large (Revelation 21–22), while proffering temporary benefits to those outside of Christ.[107] He records, "[Christ] gives to unbelievers many benefits: the call of the gospel, the warning to repent, historical faith, a virtuous life, a variety of gifts and powers, offices and ministries within the church, such as, for example, even the office of an apostle in the case of Judas."[108] Reformed Baptists have also argued for the universal impact of Christ's death. Southern Baptist President (1851–58), R. B. C. Howell observes how Christ's death blesses the world physically, socially, morally, intellectually, and politically. Howell

---

[104] Gary Long, *Definite Atonement*, 45–68.

[105] Quoted by Herman Bavinck, *Reformed Dogmatics*, 3:471.

[106] R. B. Kuiper, *For Whom Did Christ Die? A Study of the Divine Design of the Atonement* (Grand Rapids: Eerdmans 1959; reprint: Eugene, OR: Wipf & Stock, 2003), 78–103.

[107] Bavinck, *Reformed Dogmatics*, 3:470–75.

[108] Ibid., 3:471.

states, "Everywhere its power is plainly seen, refining, and elevating, and ennobling, even those who reject its sanctifying grace."[109]

Accordingly, those who claim that Calvinists limit the effects of Christ's death to only a select group of people speak imprecisely. It is more correct to say that definite atonement holds to *particular, personal salvation* (Ephesians 2:8–9) and *particular, cosmic regeneration* (cf. Matthew 19:28). In the space we have left, we will look at three of those particular universals—namely the universal love of God, the universal language of Scripture, and the universal offer of the gospel. If God is the Creator of the entire universe, as Scripture clearly asserts, it is imperative to see how definite atonement affirms and preserves God's universal intentions in the world, even as it elucidates God's particular plans. To that end, we now turn.

The Universal Love of God

"God is love." No one argues this point. Explaining what it means is another story. Arguing against definite atonement, David Allen equates God's love with his universal will to save all people.[110] Dave Hunt, like Allen, makes God's love a philosophical maxim that if God loves at all, He must love everyone as much as He can—meaning that He must die for everyone without exception.[111] Challenging J. I. Packer's statement that God loves all in some ways and some in all ways, Hunt asks, "What love is this?" He argues, "Love cannot stop short of giving all it possibly could to those who are loved."[112] In other words, for egalitarians there is no place in the mind or heart of God for distinctive loves. However, is that really how Scripture speaks? Egalitarians contend that the differentiating factor in God's love rests in man's freedom alone: Man, not God, limits God's love.[113] However, careful attention to Scripture shows that God's love is variegated.

[109] Howell, "The Cross," 52.

[110] Allen, "The Atonement," 94–96.

[111] Dave Hunt, *What Love Is This? Calvinism's Misrepresentation of God* (Bend, OR: The Berean Call, 2006); idem., *Debating Calvinism: Five Points, Two Views* (Sisters, OR: Multnomah, 2004), 255–65.

[112] Hunt, *What Love Is This?* 395. Dabney's illustration of a man who has sufficient resources in his pocket to help a beggar, but is pledged to give his money to another is a helpful *human analogy* for recognizing that God's love cannot be simply defined as maximally profuse in all cases; God's love is also superintended by wisdom and divine design. R. L. Dabney, *Systematic Theology*, 530.

[113] "God loves all, desires the salvation of all, and genuinely strives to convince wicked men to repent and accept His offer of salvation. Then why are not all saved? Clearly, ... though all are drawn, some willingly repent and believe while others refuse." Hunt, *What Love is This?*, 146.

For instance, as it concerns the love of God, the Bible uses a number of concepts and terms to portray God's love. He is good (Psalm 119:68), merciful and gracious (Psalm 103:8–14), generous (Matthew 5:44–45; Acts 14:16–17), patient (2 Peter 3:9), compassionate (2 Corinthians 1:3), and most significantly, He is covenantally faithful to His own (Jer 31:3; John 13:1).[114] Stressing the complexity of God's love, these character descriptions are often coupled with darker descriptions. In Exodus 34:6–7, YHWH's four-fold love is followed by a sobering warning that He "will by no means clear the guilty." If God loves all maximally, what does it mean that He also intends to bring justice upon their sin? In Psalm 136, YHWH is praised for His steadfast love, even as the Psalmist describes His violent defeat of enemy neighbors (vv. 10–22). Apparently, God's love for Israel came at the expense of God's enemies. Did God love Midian with the same love that He did Israel? If not, why not? Was Israel more righteous? Not according to Scripture (Deuteronomy 7:7–9; Ezekiel 20). God set His love on Israel for His namesake, and saved them not because of their response, but because of His sovereign choice (cf. Malachi 1:2; Romans 9:6–23). Likewise, in a section of Romans where Paul wrestles with God's mysterious decision to choose some and pass over others, he notes "the kindness *and* severity of God" (Romans 11:22). The point here is simply that many who advocate a universal love of God do so apart from the categories of biblical theology.[115] For them, God's love trumps all other attributes and what results is a movement away from biblical truth towards universal conceptions of the atonement.[116]

By contrast a biblical theology of God's love makes Scriptural distinctions. The Father's love for the Son is not the same as His love for creation, yet both are love. Though brief, D. A. Carson's treatment of this subject is most helpful.[117] He lists five ways Scripture speaks of God's love, and he yet cautions against dividing the simple love God. He concludes that if any one of these "loves" is used to define the others, distortions result. So, in the case of egalitarians there is a tendency to make God's unconditional love *too unconditional*. At the same moment, hyper-Calvinists go terribly wrong when they see God's love through the lens of election alone. To say that

---

[114] Frame subsumes God's varying "loves" under the category of goodness. He shows how God's love provides temporal goods to all people and eternal salvation to the elect. John Frame, *The Doctrine of God* (Phillipsburg, NJ: P&R, 2002), 402–45.

[115] Carson, *The Difficult Doctrine of the Love of God*, 9.

[116] At the greatest extreme, God's undifferentiated love results in a theology much like that of Rob Bell, *Love Wins: A Book About Heaven, Hell, and the Fate of Every Person Who Ever Lived* (New York: HarperOne, 2001).

[117] D. A. Carson, *The Difficult Doctrine of the Love of God*, esp. 9–24.

God loves the elect and hates the reprobate *without qualification* is a gross misrepresentation of God. Both reductions of God's love are wrong, and both need to be contested.[118]

Returning to Packer's maxim—God loves all in some ways and some in all ways—the church needs to affirm both according to the propositions and proportions given in Scripture.[119] As Creator, God gladly preserves the earth, fills it with good things and gives common grace to *all without exception*.[120] At the same time, God's redemptive love is given only to His bride (Ephesians 1:3–6; 5:25–33). Christ gives His life for His bride, and as a perfectly faithful husband, He reserves His secret love for those who are in covenant with Him (Psalm 25:14). Like the lover in Song of Songs, He first marries His bride, and then loves her with unbridled passion. Order is important. In contrast to egalitarians who argue for God's maximal love to all people, He does not stain His garments with those who prostitute themselves with the Great Harlot (Revelation 18). Rather, Christ's blood purchases, purifies, and pleads the case of His beloved—those whom He loves with an everlasting love (Jeremiah 31:3).

Christian, do you wonder why you are saved today? It is not because of some insipid universal love; it is because in His grace, God set His love on you before the foundation of the world. He sent His Son adorned as a priest with your name written on His breast, so that His blood could cover your sins. Those who have believed on Christ know this personal, covenantal love. Their faith by which they gain entrance into all the spiritual blessings of the fullness of salvation arises because they have been loved beforehand in a predestining love (Ephesians 1:4-7). While this love is not discerned until you come to faith in Christ. (Galatians 2:20) every aspect of God's saving action toward us comes on the basis of a discriminating love for the elect. Love precedes and prompts our predestination to adoption (Ephesians 1:4, 5), love prompts the giving of the Spirit to regenerate and raise the dead in sins to new spiritual life (Ephesians 2:4) and love appointed the Father's beloved Son to bear the iniquities of the elect in His own body, and thus to bear their wrath to achieve their redemption

---

[118] A similar error occurs when we over-simplify the will of God. See John Piper's excellent appendix in *The Pleasures of God: Meditations on God's Delight in Being God* (Sisters, OR: Multnomah, 2000), 313–40, for a Bible-rich discussion of God's two wills.

[119] "The Love of God: Universal and Particular" in *Still Sovereign: Contemporary Perspectives on Election, Foreknowledge, and Grace*, eds. Thomas R. Schreiner and Bruce A. Ware (Grand Rapids, MI: Baker, 2000), 283.

[120] Incidentally, these promises are also covenantal, given in accordance with God's renewed covenant with Noah (Genesis 8:22ff). Cf. Bavinck, *Reformed Dogmatics*, 3:218.

(Romans 5:8; 1 John 4:10). He loved us with an effectual active, purposeful love that initiated and completed the salvation of those so loved.

Christ is a pure lover. He does not throw the pearls of His sacrificial love at those from whom He does not expect, yes even engender, a return of love. He pursues them effectually to be His bride, a bride that purifies herself through repentance and mortification of sin. Those that in this way are brought to the condition of repentance and faith can experience the fullness of His love (Ephesians 3:14–21). This is far different from saying that God loves all, unconditionally, without exception. Maybe today, you are reading this but don't know Christ: Let all the kindnesses that God has given you—your gifts, joys, family, children, your very own life—and the promise of everlasting love lead you to repentance (Romans 2:4); trust in His Son and then you can experience the personal love of which Paul speaks.

The Universal Language of Scripture

On the surface, universal atonement makes great sense to Bible readers because they are most familiar with passages like John 3:16, Hebrews 2:9, and 2 Peter 3:9, all of which use universal language to describe Christ's death and God's desire to save mankind. However, a closer reading of Scripture shows that there is more going on in these texts than at first meets the eye. To help explain how the universal language of the New Testament supports definite atonement for people from all nations, we will consider two items: (1) the nature of the language itself, and (2) the historical context of the apostles who are positioned at the intersection of the Old and New Covenants.

First, it is not unusual for universal terms to speak of restricted populations.[121] Generally speaking, all (*pas*) and world (*kosmos*) are rarely exhaustive. More often they are used generically, as in Matthew 3: "Jerusalem and *all* Judea and *all* the region about the Jordan" went out to hear John the Baptist (v. 5). To say that Matthew meant all without exception breaks the constraints of language. When preachers or theologians make statements that "*all means all!*" they turn up the volume, but dim the lights.[122] Meaning

---

[121] Tom Wells, *A Price for a People* (Carlisle, PA: Banner of Truth, 1992), 117–19.

[122] Steve Lemke makes such a statement in his argument against irresistible grace, and cites three lexicons to prove his point ("A Biblical and Theological Critique of Irresistible Grace," in *Whosoever Will*, 123). Ironically, he quotes only one of BDAG's five definitions for *pas*. Closer examination of that lexicon shows how *pas* can be used in a number of ways. As is always the case, contextual usage is determinative.

is found "at the level of the sentence" (illocution), not in bare words (locutions).[123] This attention to the text of Scripture is what makes the work of John Owen so strong. He exposits countless texts to determine the author's intended meaning. While few will agree with *all* his exegetical conclusions,[124] his method is far more sound than those who hang their doctrine on isolated locutions suspended in mid-air.[125]

Outspoken Calvinists are not alone in this appeal to language. Moses Stuart, who is not a "five-pointer," writes concerning the universal language of Hebrews 2:9.

> *Hyper pantos* means, *all men without distinction*, i. e. both Jew and Gentile. The same view is often given of the death of Christ. See John 3:14–17; 4:42; 12:32; 1 John 2:2; 4:14; 1 Tim 2:3–4; Tit 2:11; 2 Pet 3:7. Compare Rom 3:29, 30; 10:11–3. In all these and like cases, the words *all*, and *all men*, evidently mean, Jew and Gentile. They are opposed to the Jewish idea, that the Messiah was connected appropriately and exclusively with the Jews, and that the blessings of the kingdom were appropriately and exclusively with the Jews, ... The sacred writers mean to declare, by such expressions, that Christ died really and truly as well, and as much, for the Gentiles as for the Jews.[126]

Significantly, Stuart not only interprets the words of Hebrews 2:9 as a distributive (all without distinction), he principalizes his interpretation saying, "the considerate interpreter, who understands the nature of this idiom, will never think of seeking, in expressions of this kind, proof of the final salvation of *every individual* of the human race."[127] Robert Candlish agrees. He avers that those who advocate a universal atonement satisfy themselves with "accumulat[ing] 'alls' and 'everys,' taken indiscriminately

---

[123] Kevin J. Vanhoozer, *Is There A Meaning in This Text?: The Bible, The Reader, and the Morality of Literary Knowledge* (Grand Rapids, MI: Zondervan, 1998), 310–14. Cf. William Cunningham, *Historical Theology*, 2:340–41.

[124] For instance, many Calvinists would agree with David Allen's critique of Owen's interpretation of John 3:16. Allen, "The Atonement," 78–81. However, disproving Owen's exegesis of one passage, important as it is, does not prove universal atonement.

[125] Introducing his section on the universal texts Owen appeals for patient hermeneutics and a rejection of the hasty triumphalism that so many egalitarians in his day and ours possess when they point to the "bare word" (all or world), believing they have proven themselves. Owen, *The Death of Death*, 190–204.

[126] Moses Stuart, *A Commentary on the Epistle to the Hebrews* (London: H. Fisher, R. Fisher, and P. Jackson, 1834), 304.

[127] Ibid. Cf. A. A. Hodge, *The Atonement* (Philadelphia: Presbyterian Board of Publication, 1867), 423–27.

out of the Bible, ... without regard to context, or connection, or analogy."[128] Thus, as we draw theological implications from a 'plain reading' of Scripture, we must do so in accord with the context in which the word is used.

Second, the New Testament's historical setting gives a better explanation for the use of "all" and "world" than does an egalitarian atonement. This is easily missed by twenty-first century Christians,[129] but in truth the New Testament records a major shift in God's covenantal relations with the world.[130] For two thousand years, God's dealing with mankind was generally restricted to the sons of Abraham. They alone possessed the law, the covenants, and the promises (Psalm 147:19–20; Romans 9:4–5). Written into the law itself was the command to separate from unclean Gentiles (Deuteronomy 23:3). Moreover, during second temple Judaism, faithful Jews sought to recapture God's favor through strict adherence to the law. In this context, is it any wonder that the Jesus (and later his apostles) needed to use universal terms to spur on nationalistic Jews to embrace their Gentile brothers?[131]

Consider the first four chapters of John. In chapter 1, John the Baptist who "was sent to announce a new order of things, widely different, in point of extent, from the levitical economy,"[132] exclaims, "Behold, the lamb of God who takes away the sin of the world" (1:29). This is the first of many places in John's gospel, where the son of thunder argues for the expansion of salvation unto the world. Speaking about the word *kosmos* in John, James Haldane writes, "While the term *world* includes men of all nations, Jews and Gentiles, it particularly refers to the latter. The Jews connected the privileges which they expected under the Messiah's reign with the judgments of God upon the Gentiles; but the Lord informed Nicodemus that the Son of God had come, not for the condemnation, but for the salvation, of men of all nations, whether Jew or Gentiles."[133]

---

[128] Robert Smith Candlish, *The Cross of Christ, The Call of God, Saving Faith: An Inquiry into the Completeness and Extent of the Atonement* (Edinburg: John Johnstone, 1845), xii.

[129] R. B. Kuiper, *For Whom Did Christ Die? A Study of the Divine Design of the Atonement* (Grand Rapids: Eerdmans, 1959; reprint: Eugene, OR: Wipf & Stock, n.d.), 30–34.

[130] "This administration is so opposite to that dispensation which was restrained to one people and family, who were God's peculiar people, and all the rest of the world excluded, that it gives occasion to many general expressions in the Scripture." Owen, *The Death of Death*, 186. Cf. Bavinck, *Reformed Dogmatics*, 3:465.

[131] Symington, *On the Atonement and Intercession of Jesus Christ*, 215; Kuiper, *For Who Did Christ Die?*, 30–34.

[132] Symington, *On the Atonement and Intercession of Jesus Christ*, 220.

[133] Haldane, *The Doctrine of the Atonement*, 155.

Another example is found in the wedding in Cana of Galilee,[134] Jesus enacts a parable to show the brokenness of the Old Covenant, and the larger blessings of the New Covenant.[135] Then, in the Jerusalem temple, Jesus excoriates the merchants who exclude Gentile worshipers from the house of the Lord.[136] Following this flow of thought, John prepares the way for statements in John 3:16 and John 4:42, that Jesus is coming for the world. In the former, Jesus' words come after a lengthy discussion with Nicodemus, where Jesus instructs the teacher of the law that salvation comes by the Spirit, not the flesh. John 3:16 explains God's intention to save Jew and Gentile alike; whereas Jews like Nicodemus presumed upon their favored status, Jesus is stating that God is giving His son for the world— Jews *and* Gentiles.[137] In light of its context, and other uses, the notion of a salvific expansion from Jews to the whole world must be right. Moreover, when John calls Jesus the "Savior of the World" (4:42), the exact phrase comes out of the mouth of a Samaritan, the people John himself wanted to destroy (Luke 9:51–56).[138]

Moving from John's gospel to his epistle, we see something similar. While there are differing Reformed interpretations of 1 John 2:2, it seems best to take his language as "ethnological."[139] Letting Scripture interpret Scripture, John's epistle addresses his audience as "little children" (*teknia* in 2:1, 12, 13c, 18, 28; 3:1–2; cf. John 11:52), and then proceeds to remind them of the fact that Christ died as "the propitiation for our sins," and "not for ours only but also" for the sins of the whole world.[140] Based on such conceptual resonance (children of God), and linguistic similarity in the

---

[134] On the theological significance of Jesus' outreach to the Gentiles in Galilee, see O. Palmer Robertson, *Understanding the Land of the Bible: A Biblical-Theological Guide* (Phillipsburg, NJ: P&R, 1996), 33–37.

[135] D. A. Carson, *The Gospel According to John*, Pillar New Testament Commentary (Grand Rapids, MI: Eerdmans, 1991), 172; Anthony Selvaggion, *The Seven Signs: Seeing the Glory of Christ in the Gospel of John* (Grand Rapids, MI: Reformation Heritage, 2010), 20. Cf. Gary Burge, *John*, NIVAC (Grand Rapids, MI: Zondervan, 1995), 90.

[136] Commenting on the exclusive practices of the Jews, Carson writes, "[B]y setting up in the court of the Gentiles, they have excluded Gentiles who might have come to pray, and have turned the temple into a 'nationalist stronghold'" (*John*, 179). If Carson's observation is right, then Jesus' anger stems from Israel's failure to be a light unto the nations (cf. Isaiah 49:1–7). This missionary failure, which would later infect the early church, gives another reason why John uses cosmic language to universalize the work of Christ.

[137] Haldane, *The Doctrine of the Atonement*, 155–56.

[138] Symington, *On the Atonement and Intercession of Jesus Christ*, 221.

[139] Long, *Definite Atonement*, 106–19.

[140] Cf. For a balanced treatment of 1 John 2 in relation to John 11 see Robert

construction of the contrast (*monon all kai*, John 11:52 and 1 John 2:2), there is great reason to believe that John is broadening the one sacrifice of Christ from Jews to people of all races.[141] As Long concludes, "John wants to make it clear to his readers in this verse (as well as John 3:16) that the Old Testament particularism in relation to the nations of Israel is now past, so he uses the universal term 'whole world.'"[142] These of whom John speaks are not all people without exception, but all those scattered children who will be taken from (*ek*) every tribe, language, people, and nation (Revelation 5:9).

While this chastened universalizing finds repeated use in the New Testament, every passage must be judged according the content and context that the statement is made. Space does not permit consideration of other 'universal texts' (e.g. 1 Timothy 2:4–6; 4:10; Titus 2:11; 2 Peter 3:9), but based on the work of others, it is believed that similar conclusions would be found in these New Testament texts.[143]

The Universal Offer of the Gospel

To understand the particular and universal design of the atonement, academic and armchair theologians must give attention to the whole counsel of Scripture, and they must understand not only *what* the Bible says, but *when* it says it.[144] Matthew 10:5–6 records, "Go nowhere among the Gentiles and enter no town of the Samaritans, but go rather to the lost sheep of the house of Israel. And proclaim as you go, saying 'The kingdom of heaven is at hand.'" It seems that Jesus Himself—while not in error—was reticent to help the woman from Canaan (15:21–28).

W. Yarbrough's, *1–3 John*, BECNT (Grand Rapids, MI: Baker Academic, 2008), 77–81.

[141] "There is not one 'propitiation' for us and another for the rest of the world, but Jesus (*kai autos*) is the only sacrifice, and the only way of salvation for all. The point is not that Jesus died for everyone indiscriminately so that everyone in the world is in principle forgiven, but that all those forgiven are forgiven on the basis of Christ's sacrifice and in no other way." Ramsay, "Atonement in John's Gospel and Epistles," 117.

[142] Long, *Definite Atonement*, 118.

[143] Cf. John Owen, *The Death of Death*, 204–56; William Symington, *On the Atonement and Intercession of Jesus Christ*, 214–34; and George Smeaton's two volumes on the atonement: *The Doctrine of the Atonement as Taught by Christ Himself* and *The Apostles' Doctrine of the Atonement*. Smeaton supplies a careful, exegetical reading of every passage in the New Testament that speaks about Christ's death.

[144] This is what Lints and others have called the "epochal horizon." Richard Lints, *The Fabric of Theology: A Prolegomenon to Evangelical Theology* (Grand Rapids, MI: Eerdmans, 1993), 300–03.

Accordingly, the universal expansion of the church's mission awaited Christ's glorification and the outpouring of the Spirit (Luke 24:44–49).[145] Thus, at Pentecost people "from every nation from under heaven" experienced the gospel in their own language (Acts 2:5ff). Filled with power, God's witnesses were finally able to take the message of salvation to the ends of the earth (Acts 1:8).[146] Hence, the offer of the gospel was made indiscriminately to all without exception.

With this background in place, we can now understand Jesus' Great Commission. Raised from the dead, Jesus has received authority over heaven and earth (Matthew 28:18). The nations are His (Psalm 2), and He has authority to call all men to Himself. Thus, the last thing that Matthew records is Jesus' royal command to make disciples of all the nations (28:19–20). This unlimited command has caused many to question a "limited" atonement. Even those who affirm definite atonement admit the challenge of God's particular sovereign will and His universal call.[147] While not denying the challenge, let me suggest five considerations to help reconcile a definite atonement with a universal offer of salvation.

First, Jesus makes universal invitations in the very same context where He affirms God's particular choice of some and rejection of others. For example, in Matthew 11, Jesus gives praise to God for hiding Himself from "the wise and understanding" and revealing Himself to "little children" (vv. 25–27). In this revealing prayer, Jesus exposes God's intention to save and condemn. Then, in verse 28, He turns around and declares: "Come to me, all who are weary and heavy laden, and I will give you rest." Likewise, in John 6, Jesus gives a universal appeal for all to come and partake of the bread of life (v. 35), but in the next verse He begins to explain why not all will come. Unbelief prevents many from coming to the light (cf. John 3:19–21), but those who are given to the Son by the Father from before the foundation of the world will come: "All that the Father gives me will come to me, and whoever comes to me I will never cast out" (v. 37). Further clarification comes in verses 44 and 65, where Jesus explains how people will believe—God the Father will draw them with the powerful working of the Spirit. Last, John 10:16 speaks of the way that the gospel must draw in sheep from other folds, and yet there are few more Calvinistic verses

---

[145] Haldane, *The Doctrine of the Atonement*, 155–56.

[146] For the way Acts 1:8 fulfills the eschatological promise of God's ministry to "all the nations" (cf. Isaiah 32:1; 49:1–7; Ezekiel 39:29; Joel 2:28–29), see I. Howard Marshall, "Acts," in *Commentary on the New Testament Use of the Old Testament*, eds. G. K. Beale and D. A. Carson (Grand Rapids, MI: Baker Academic, 2007), 528.

[147] Cf. William Cunningham, *Historical Theology*, 2:343–48; Kuiper, *For Whom Did Christ Die?* 84–95.

than John 10:26 which states that many will not believe because they are not of His flock. Belief depends on 'sheepiness,' not the reverse.[148]

Second, not all men hear the message. If the egalitarian view of the cross is correct, it raises the problem of the man on the island.[149] Did Jesus really die and make complete provision for the sins of all men, and then neglect to send His Spirit to give them the news? In Ancient Israel, the priests not only atoned for sin, they were sent out to teach Israel how to walk in holiness (Leviticus 10:11). What kind of priest procures atonement and fails to communicate the message? It is better to trust the character of God, and believe His word that says that from before the foundation of the world He predestined His elect in Christ to reach final salvation (Ephesians 1:3–6), and then to observe that as the sovereign Lord of history, He marked out the time and places of all people (Acts 17:26), and brought the message to all His sheep (John 10:16).[150]

Third, the command is the thing. As was evidenced in Matthew 10:5–6, there was a period of Jesus' ministry when the proclamation of the gospel was restricted. Likewise, as long as the Old Covenant stood, the promises of the gospel were generally restricted to Israel. In the law, Israel was primarily called to holiness and separation from the other nations. If holy warfare indicates anything, it shows that cross-cultural missions was not the main focus in Old Testament Israel. Acts 14:16 confirms this sobering reality: God "allowed all the nations [minus Israel] to walk in their own ways." There are exceptions (e. g. Rahab, Ruth, Uriah the Hittite, etc), but these only prove the rule. Acts 14:17 states that God evidenced Himself to the nations before the advent of Christ through the witness of common grace—harvest seasons and familial gladness—not gospel proclamation. While the infinite merits of Christ's death procured salvation for believing Jews in Israel (Hebrews 11), for nearly two thousand years a universal offer of the gospel was non-existent. What changed all this was the sending of the Spirit and the command of Christ. When Christ died on the cross, he inaugurated a new, Spiritual covenant, one where His Spirit would be poured out on all flesh—not all without exception, but on people from all nations (Acts 2:5, 17). Accordingly, a universal offer of the gospel was now

---

[148] See Matthew Barrett, "The Scriptural Affirmation of Monergism," in chapter 5 of this book.

[149] Russell Moore, "The Man on the Island: Facing the Truth About those who Never Hear the Gospel" [on-line], accessed 15 January 2012, http://www.russellmoore.com/documents/russellmoore/The_Man_on_the_Island.pdf; Internet.

[150] On the scandalous particularism of the gospel, see Cornelius Van Til, *Common Grace and the Gospel* (Phillipsburg, NJ: Presbyterian & Reformed, 1974), 100–101.

needed, because there were sheep in other folds for whom Christ died (John 10:16). As A. A. Hodge pointed out a century ago, our evangelism mandate comes not from our perception of the cross, but simply from the royal commission of our king.[151]

Fourth, the gospel offer is multi-intentional. Not only does the gospel save, it also judges. A double-edged sword, the gospel liberates people from their bondage to sin, death, Satan, and hell, but it also brings judgment on those unwilling to repent and believe. It proclaims penal substitution and *Christus Victor.*[152] This is why Isaiah can say that the Word of God never returns void (55:10–11). As with the parables (Matthews 13:10–17), the gospel opens eyes and closes them. With the medium of the general call, God's voice speaks to His sheep, so that all who have ears to hear may believe and be saved. However, the non-elect may also hear the same message, and to them the beauty of the cross is folly or ugliness. It has a hardening effect, which is a truth that is beyond our full comprehension but which is eminently biblical (Romans 9:18–23). Thus, as with the prophets of old, preachers are sent out to proclaim the gospel, and God in His hidden wisdom brings about the effects of the Word.[153]

Many egalitarians, especially modified Calvinists who adhere to unconditional election, believe that they have protected God from the charge of unfairness by advocating a universal atonement. But the real problem remains, just in a different place. The doctrine of unconditional election is the real source of contention for people who want to charge God with unfairness.[154] Ironically, by rejecting particular redemption, but maintaining a Reformed view of election, God's 'selection process' looks even more arbitrary. The Son dies for the salvation of all, but the Father and the Spirit respectively elect and regenerate some. How is that fair? How is that just? Clearly, if the doctrine of election stands biblically, there is no real apologetic benefit to making the cross of Christ universally atoning. Modified Calvinists are too optimistic that their view of Christ's general atonement will help remove the offense of God's particular election.

Fifth, egalitarians who demand a universal atonement make grace a thing to be picked up and received, instead of a message to be heard and believed. As one example, consider the words of modified Calvinist James

---

[151] A. A. Hodge, *The Atonement*, 418–23.

[152] Henri Blocher, "Agnus Victor," in *What Does it Mean to Be Saved?: Broadening Evangelical Horizons of Salvation*, ed. John G. Stackhouse (Grand Rapids, MI: Baker Academic, 2002), 67–94.

[153] Michael Horton, *Covenant and Salvation: Union with Christ* (Louisville, KY: Westminster John Knox, 2007), 216–242.

[154] See Andy Davis, "Unconditional Election: A Biblical and God-Glorifying Doctrine," in chapter 3 of this book.

Richards, "To us, no maxim appears more certain *than that a salvation of-fered implies a salvation provided*; for God will not tantalize his creatures by tendering them with that which is not in his hand to bestow."[155] What is Richards saying? Apparently, he conceives of the gospel as something material that the evangelist can offer to the recipient. However, that is not how the "good news" is presented in Scripture. God speaks the world into existence. He says "light" and there is light! In 2 Corinthians 4:6, Paul uses this imagery from Genesis 1:3 to explain salvation: "For God, who said, 'Let light shine out of darkness,' has shone in our hearts to give the light of the knowledge of the glory of God in the face of Christ." Shortly after this verse, Paul states that the believer is a new creation in Christ (5:17). What is Paul saying? The gospel is not a thing, it is a message about the man Jesus Christ. And when it is proclaimed, it effects what it demands. This is what Paul means when he says "Our gospel came to you not only in word, but also in power and in the Holy Spirit and with full conviction" (1 Thessalonians 1:5). The good news is not simply information about Jesus, it is the power of God in verbal form to cause dead men to rise (John 11:38–44).

Ironically, many who critique the commercial view of the atonement, have a very commercial, even substantive view of grace. Unless there is something material to present, it cannot be genuine.[156] Yet, is not the word of God sufficient? If God offers salvation to any who meet the condition of faith and repentance, is He not able to provide an eternal redemption? Unlike Catholics who assert the reconstitution of Jesus' body and blood in their mass, Protestants believe God's Word does the work. God creates life by His Word (Ezekiel 37). The gospel is that Word. Therefore, we stand on the rock of His gospel promises, proclaiming "Jesus Saves" to all who will listen, believing that His Word is infinitely sufficient to raise the dead to life.

Altogether, definite atonement preaches the gospel better than the egalitarian view because it always calls unrepentant sinners to account for their sin against God *before* it offers them covenantal blessings. "It pro-

---

[155] James Richards, *Lectures on Mental Philosophy and Theology* (New York: N. W. Dodd, 1846), 322; quoted by Robert Lightner, *The Death Christ Died*, 114–15.

[156] Arguing materially, Roger Nicole gives a helpful analogy from the world of sales. He argues that no one charges Sears and Roebuck with an unethical sales tactic when they promise 300,000 people in the Sunday paper a washer at a certain price. Who would expect that Sears actually has 300,000 washers—one for every newspaper insert? Rather, they simply expect that if they respond to the advertisement, they can own a new washer by days end. By extension, he contends that God's universal offer is by no means unethical, when the offer extends beyond the elect who will believe it. Nicole, "Covenant, Universal Call, and Definite Atonement," 197–98.

vides a real rather than hypothetical salvation as that which is offered. It does not expect the fulfillment of an unrealizable condition on the part of the sinner as a prerequisite for salvation."[157] Whereas general atonement promises actual forgiveness for all humanity before it once again condemns unbelievers to hell; definite atonement is more clear and more certain. John Piper's hypothetical discussion between a "five-pointer" and an unbeliever illustrates this. He converses,

> *Evangelist*: If I assured you before you believe that your sins were cancelled and your freedom from God's wrath was obtained, I would mislead you. Imagine if I said to you, Jesus certainly obtained your deliverance from God's wrath and certainly covered all your sins. Now believe that. What would you say?
>
> *Unbeliever:* I'd say, great. Now what if I don't believe? Then I'm still saved, right? Since my sins were certainly covered. It's done.
>
> *Evangelist*: Yes, that's probably what you would say, and you'd be wrong. Because I would have misled you. The good news that Jesus has for you before you believe on him is not that your sins are certainly cancelled. The good news is that Jesus really propitiated the wrath of God, and really covered the sins of his people. It is finished. And that is what I offer you. It's free. It's full. It's complete. It's glorious. And his absolute promise to you is this: It's yours if you will receive him. Believe on the Lord Jesus Christ, and you will be saved.[158]

Thus, the message we proclaim is not simply a sentimental invitation for whosoever may come;[159] we proclaim with royal and divine authority: "Jesus is Lord. Believe on Him and you will be saved. Reject Him and you will perish." The message of the gospel is always effective because it is a message of salvation *and* judgment. It addresses sinners and calls them to faith and repentance. Any and all who come to Him confessing sin and seeking salvation will be granted life, because after all Jesus died to effect salvation for all those whom the Father draws by the Spirit (John 6:35ff).

---

[157] Roger Nicole, "Covenant, Universal Call, and Definite Atonement," 199.

[158] John Piper, "A Five-Pointer Shares the Gospel" [on-line], accessed 15 January 2012, http://www.desiringgod.org/blog/posts/a-five-pointer-shares-the-gospel; Internet. See his elongated conversation online.

[159] Horton, *For Calvinism*, 89.

Conclusion

In *Oh, Brother Where Art Thou*, there is an infamous character named George "Baby Face" Nelson who shouts as he robs the local bank: "Jesus Saves, but George Nelson withdraws!" With as much gusto but far more godliness, I am afraid that many pulpiteers have preached the gospel like George Nelson. They gladly proclaim the power of the cross and the message that Jesus saves, but they unintentionally commit 'federal' offense when they withdraw the sure message of salvation from an account that is not their own.

Thankfully, many who malign definite atonement preach a message of abundant grace and a cross that really saves. I simply pray that those who love the gospel of Christ crucified in the place of hell-bound sinners will test the arguments in this book to see that Christ's death did not merely make salvation possible; it effected salvation for all the lost sheep scattered throughout the world.

May we who love the Shepherd be willing to risk our lives for His sheep. May we seek to understand and appreciate the doctrine of definite atonement, not so that we can win a debate, but so that we can have greater confidence to go to the people for whom Christ died, people who today do not have street signs proclaiming the gospel to them, many who do not even know His name. Christ has died for these men, women, and children from every tongue, tribe, language, and nation. We must go to them proclaiming without an asterisk: Yesu Anaokoa. Isus Štedi. İsa indirim. Jesus Saves!

5

The Scriptural Affirmation Of Monergism

Matthew M. Barrett

The Calvinism-Arminianism debate oscillates around several controversial issues, usually surrounding the acronymn TULIP. [1] And yet, as
B. B. Warfield said long ago, it is irresistible grace, the "I" in TULIP (or as
Warfield called it, effectual calling and monergistic regeneration), that is
the very "hinge of the Calvinistic soteriology." Monergism, says Warfield,
is the "hall-mark" of Calvinism. [2] Therefore, in a real sense, the Calvinism-
Arminianism debate comes down to this essential issue: Does God act
alone effectually to call and regenerate the dead and passive sinner from
death to new life, causing the sinner to respond in faith and repentance
(i.e., monergism)? Or, as the Arminian must have it, is man active, coop-
erating with or resisting God's grace, so that the efficacy of divine grace is
dependent upon the will of man (i.e., synergism)? For some, such a debate
may appear insignificant. To the contrary, God's glory hangs in the bal-

---

[1] This chapter is a brief treatment of the topic. For a full defense of monergism as well as a full critique of synergism see my forthcoming book on the
subject with P&R (some content in this chapter is taken from the forthcoming
book published by P&R Publishing Co., P O Box 817, Phillipsburg, N.J. 08865
www.prpbooks.com). Also, see Matthew Barrett, "Reclaiming Monergism: The
Case for Sovereign Grace in Effectual Calling and Regeneration," (PhD diss.,
The Southern Baptist Theological Seminary, 2011). Here I interact with far more
secondary literature on the issue.

[2] Benjamin Breckinridge Warfield, *Calvin and Calvinism*, vol. 5 of *The Works
of Benjamin B. Warfield* (Grand Rapids, MI: Baker, 2003), 359.

ance. If God's work in calling and regenerating the sinner is conditioned upon man's will, then God cannot receive *all* of the glory in salvation. But if God works alone, effectually to call and regenerate dead sinners, then He does receive *all* of the glory in our salvation. Therefore, this chapter will seek to demonstrate not only that the overwhelming testimony of Scripture is in support of monergism, but that only monergism can do justice to the glory of God in salvation.

Total Depravity and the Bondage of the Will

In order to understand effectual calling and regeneration, it is first essential to recognize the desperate state of fallen man. Since Mark DeVine has devoted his entire chapter to total depravity, I will only repeat what he has argued at length, namely, that sin has corrupted *every* aspect of man (hence, *total* depravity). Sin has invaded man's deepest recesses, including the human will. The consequence is obvious: every man's will is in bondage and slavery to sin and he can in no way initiate or cooperate with divine grace.[3] The biblical testimony is unanimous, man is dead in his sin and no aspect of man escapes sin's grip (e.g., Ephesians 2:1–3; Romans 3:10–18; 6:15–23; John 8:34; Psalm 58:3). Contrary to Steve Lemke, man is not wallowing in the waters in need of God to throw him a life preserver, leaving it up to the drowning victim to choose whether or not he will grab hold of it.[4] Not at all. Man is dead, lifeless, rotting away at the bottom of the ocean. He does not need a life preserver, but a resurrection! He is like Lazarus, dead in the tomb. He stinketh. What Lazarus needed was the resurrection words of Jesus, "Lazarus, come out" (John 11:43). As we will shortly discover, this is exactly how Scripture speaks of man's special calling and regeneration. Man was dead in sin, but God made him alive in Christ Jesus.

The Gospel Call

God is a gracious God. While man deserves to be left in his sin, condemned and sentenced to hell for all eternity, God sends forth His gospel

---

[3] The trap that many fall into at this point is in thinking that if man is enslaved to sin, he must have no real responsibility in the matter. Quite the contrary, while every man is indeed in bondage to sin and the devil, nevertheless, it is a willful bondage. In short, the sinner *loves* sin. This is what he most desires.

[4] Steve W. Lemke, "A Biblical and Theological Critique of Irresistible Grace," in *Whosoever Will: A Biblical-Theological Critique of Five-Point Calvinism*, ed. David L. Allen and Steve W. Lemke (Nashville, TN: B&H, 2010), 160.

to the ends of the earth. The "gospel call" is the "offering of salvation in Christ to people, together with an invitation to accept Christ in repentance and faith, in order that they may receive the forgiveness of sins and eternal life."[5] The first truth to understand about the gospel call is that it is an invitation for everyone who hears the gospel. Hence, sometimes the gospel call is labeled the *general* or *universal* call, meaning that the gospel is preached indiscriminately to people of any age, race, or nation. Consider Isaiah 45:22, "Turn to me and be saved, all the ends of the earth! For I am God, and there is no other." Here the Lord invites sinners to turn to Yahweh so that they might find salvation. Isaiah again teaches a call to all people in 55:1, "Come, everyone who thirsts, come to the waters; and he who has no money, come, buy and eat! Come, buy wine and milk without money and without price." Here again we see an invitation to everyone to come to Yahweh empty handed to receive true spiritual salvation. Jesus will use this same language in the New Testament when He says to the woman at the well that He has living water which He gives as a gift from God (John 4:10). Jesus promises that the living water that He gives becomes a spring welling up to eternal life (John 4:14), so that one never thirsts again (4:13). Likewise, Jesus uses the imagery of Isaiah when He says, "I am the bread of life" (John 6:35, 48, 51) and invites sinners to come and eat of his flesh that they may live (John 6:54–56). Such an invitation is consistent with the words of Joel 2:32a, "And it shall come to pass that everyone who calls on the name of the LORD shall be saved."

In the New Testament, the general call to all people is specifically referenced to Jesus, the Christ, who is God with us (Matthew 1:23; Isaiah 7:14). Like Yahweh in the Old Testament, Jesus is the source of salvation and redemption and it is through him and him alone that eternal life can be found (John 14:6; Acts 4:12; Romans 10:10–12). Therefore, Jesus says in Matthew 11:28, "Come to me, all who labor and are heavy laden, and I will give you rest." Jesus calls all people to come to him, to trust in him, and to believe in him (cf. Matthew 10:32–33; Luke 12:8; 16:24–26; Mark 8:34–35; Luke 9:23–24). Likewise, John 7:37 states, "On the last day of the feast, the great day, Jesus stood up and cried out, 'If anyone thirsts, let him come to me and drink'" (cf. John 4:13). And again Jesus proclaims, "Truly, truly, I say to you, if anyone keeps my word, he will never see death" (John 8:51). Such a promise is consistent with John 3:16, "For God so loved the world, that he gave his only Son, that whoever believes in him should not perish but have eternal life" (cf. John 6:40; 11:26; 12:46). Such invitations parallel Revelation 22:17, "The Spirit and the Bride say, 'Come.' And let

---

[5] Anthony Hoekema, *Saved by Grace* (Grand Rapids, MI: Eerdmans, 1989), 68.

the one who hears say, 'Come.' And let the one who is thirsty come; let the one who desires take the water of life without price."

The parables of Jesus also describe a gospel call. For example, Matthew 22:1–14 and Luke 14:16–24, which are meant to illustrate the kingdom of heaven, both describe instances where somebody in the parable (Matthew: a king; Luke: a certain man) invites guests to his banquet and then sends out his servant(s), telling his guests to come. Similarly, God sends out the message of his Son, inviting people everywhere to come and enter into the kingdom. This is also the purpose of the great commission in Matthew 28:19–20 where Jesus commands his disciples, "Go therefore and make disciples of all nations, baptizing them in the name of the Father and of the Son and of the Holy Spirit, teaching them to observe all that I have commanded you. And behold, I am with you always, to the end of the age." The words of Jesus here demonstrate that the gospel is to be preached to all, without hesitation or reservation. We do not know who will believe and who will not. We do not know who the elect are. We are to preach the gospel to all, desiring to see all come to repentance and faith.

Furthermore, many times the invitation of the gospel call takes on the form of a command. Consider the words of Jesus in Matthew 4:17, "From that time Jesus began to preach, saying, '*Repent*, for the kingdom of heaven is at hand.'" Likewise, Paul says in Acts 17:30, "The times of ignorance God overlooked, but now he *commands* all people everywhere to repent, because he has fixed a day on which he will judge the world in righteousness by a man whom he has appointed; and of this he has given assurance to all by raising him from the dead" (emphasis added). Here again we see that God commands people everywhere to repent of their sins for a day of judgment is coming. What is important to note at this point is that these commands demonstrate that it is man's duty to repent and believe. In other words, regardless of whether or not man has the spiritual ability to repent and trust in Christ (which, as DeVine demonstrated, the sinner does not), nevertheless, it is still man's duty to do so. Therefore, the indiscriminate preaching of the gospel is necessary.

Besides the gospels, the epistles also present a gospel call to all people. Using the language of Joel 2:32, Peter proclaims in Acts 2:21, "And it shall come to pass that everyone who calls upon the name of the Lord shall be saved" (cf. Romans 10:13). Such a promise is not only for Jews but for Gentiles also as exemplified in Peter's words to the household of Cornelius in Acts 10. The promise of life is held out to those who trust in Christ, "And he commanded us to preach to the people and to testify that he [Jesus] is the one appointed by God to be judge of the living and the dead. To him all the prophets bear witness that *everyone who believes in him receives forgiveness of sins through his name*" (Acts 10:42–43; emphasis added). Similarly, the apostle Paul, explaining how salvation has come to the Gentiles, also holds out the promise of the gospel in Romans 9:33, as he quotes from Isaiah 28:16, "Behold, I am laying in Zion a stone of stumbling, and a rock of offense; and *whoever believes in him will not be put to shame*" (emphasis added; cf. Romans 10:11–13; 1 Peter 2:6). Therefore, John rightly asserts in 1 John 4:15, "Whoever confesses that Jesus is the Son of God, God abides in him, and he in God."

As seen in the passages above, God offers the gospel *freely* to both Jew and Gentile, promising salvation if they believe. Such an offer is consistent with God's desire to see sinners repent and be saved. As Peter states, the Lord is patient towards sinners, "not wishing that any should perish, but that all should reach repentance" (2 Peter 2:9). Likewise, Paul tells Timothy that God our Savior "desires all people to be saved and to come to the knowledge of the truth" (1 Timothy 2:4). Such passages as these reflect God's will of disposition (not His decretive will) in which He not only offers salvation but desires that lost sinners repent and be saved.[6] Many other passages could be considered (Ezekiel 18:23; 33:11; Matthew 23:37; Luke 13:34; 2 Corinthians 5:20; 1 Timothy 2:3–4; 2 Peter 3:9), but the point is clear: God desires that all people be saved, a desire which is manifested in His indiscriminate offer of the gospel to all people.

Therefore, the preaching of the gospel to all people comes out of a *real, genuine desire* to see all people repent and be saved (Numbers 23:19; Psalm 81:13–16; Proverbs 1:24; Isaiah 1:18–20; Ezekiel 18:23, 32; 33:11; Matthew 21:37; 2 Timothy 2:13). The gospel call is a *bona fide* calling that is seriously given. Arminians like Lemke often object that this cannot be the case in light of the Calvinist belief that God chooses to only give His effectual grace to His elect. God's gospel offer would be "disingenuous" and "cynical."[7] However, there is no inconsistency for several reasons. (1) Such an offer is not superfluous because it is the gospel call which is the *very means* by which God converts sinners. (2) God never makes a promise in the gospel offer that He does not keep. God promises that eternal life will be granted on the condition of faith. However, God never promises that He will bestow faith on everyone. (3) The gospel call is seriously meant regardless of the fact that man cannot fulfill it. It is objected that since sinners do not have the ability to believe (due to depravity), a gospel call cannot be genuinely offered. Lemke takes this objection so far as to say

---

[6] Space does not permit a defense of God's will of disposition and decretive will, but see John Piper, "Are There Two Wills in God?" in *Still Sovereign: Contemporary Perspectives on Election, Foreknowledge, and Grace*, ed. Thomas R. Schreiner and Bruce A. Ware (Grand Rapids, MI: Baker, 2000), 107–32.

[7] Lemke, "A Biblical and Theological Critique of Irresistible Grace," 120.

God would be deceptive to make such an offer that He knows man cannot fulfill. However, as Wilhelmus à Brakel states, the "fact that man is not able to repent and believe is not God's fault, but man is to be blamed."[8] God will not lower the conditions of the gospel (faith and repentance) because man, by his own depravity, cannot fulfill them. Moreover, God is not obligated to bestow his grace on anyone. Man is a sinner, deserving only judgment, and for God to fulfill the gospel condition on anyone's behalf is sheer grace. (4) The well-meant offer is just as problematic (if not more problematic!) for the Arminian. In the Arminian view, God offers salvation to those whom He already knows will not believe. What distinguishes the Reformed is that they, as Bavinck states, have the "courage to say that the outcome corresponds to God's will and purpose."[9] As it turns out, it is the Arminian who has the real problem of a *well-meant* offer of the gospel.

It is unfortunate that Arminians like Lemke accuse Calvinists of not truly affirming the well-meant offer of the gospel. Perhaps this is because hyper-Calvinists are wrongly used as representatives instead of Calvinists.[10] However, Calvinists throughout history have embraced and taught the well-meant offer right along side of the effectual call, as is obvious in the Canons of Dort (see V.5 and III–IV.8). Scripture teaches both of these truths and we must let Scripture be our authority on this matter. As eighteenth-century Baptist Andrew Fuller recognized, the same Bible teaches that God desires all who hear the gospel to be saved and that God has only predestined and effectually called some to salvation.[11] If we give way to the grumblings of our finite minds, we will conclude that both cannot be true. But to do so, is to rationalize away what Scripture teaches in one of two directions:

(1) To say that God wants all who hear the gospel to be saved; that therefore he gives to all who hear sufficient grace to be saved if they so desire; this grace, is, however, always resistible; many do resist and thus frustrate God's design. This is the Arminian solution, which leaves us with a God who is not sovereign, and which thus denies a truth clearly taught in Scripture. (2) The other type of rational solution is that of...

[8] Wilhelmus à Brakel, *The Christian's Reasonable Service*, ed. Joel R. Beeke, trans. Bartel Elshout (Grand Rapids, MI: Reformation Heritage, 1993), 2:207 (cf. 2:208).

[9] Herman Bavinck, *Reformed Dogmatics*, ed. John Bolt, trans. John Vriend (Grand Rapids, MI: 2008), 4:37.

[10] Lemke, "A Biblical and Theological Critique of Irresistible Grace," 143–44. Also, see Kenneth Keathley, *Salvation and Sovereignty: A Molinist Approach* (Nashville, TN: B&H, 2010), 49–50.

[11] Andrew Fuller, *The Complete Works of Reverend Andrew Fuller*, ed. Joseph Belcher (Harrisonburg, VA: Sprinkle, 1988), 2:379.

Hyper-Calvinists: Since the Bible teaches election and reprobation, it simply cannot be true that God desires the salvation of all to whom the gospel comes. Therefore we must say that God desires the salvation only of the elect among the hearers of the gospel. This kind of solution may seem to satisfy our minds, but it completely fails to do justice to Scripture passages like Ezekiel 33:11, Matthew 23:37, 2 Corinthians 5:20, and 2 Peter 3:9.[12]

The Arminian way of rationalizing this biblical tension between God's sovereignty and the well-meant offer of the gospel fails. But notice, both the Arminian and the hyper-Calvinist have the same objection, namely, if man is unable to repent and believe then a well-meant offer cannot be genuine. The Arminian responds that man must therefore have ability (whether it be natural to him or enabled by prevenient grace), while the hyper-Calvinist responds by affirming inability but concludes that there can then be no well-meant offer of the gospel. Scripture does not permit us to go in either direction. Arminians may not like the tension between these truths but the reality is, this is a *biblical* tension, which, as Fuller argued, is perfectly consisitent.[13]

Finally, it must be observed that unlike the effectual call, the gospel call can be successfully resisted by sinners. All those whom God has not elected will and do resist the gospel call and consequently further their condemnation before a holy God. Old Testament passages everywhere affirm that many in Israel rejected Yahweh (Proverbs 1:23–25; Hosea 11:1–2; Psalm 78:10; 81:11–13; 95:7–8; Isaiah 5:4; 65:12; 66:4; Jeremiah 17:23; 7:13, 16; 35:17; 32:33). In these passages it is clear that not all in Israel were truly Israel. Stated otherwise, not all who belonged to the exterior nation of Israel were inwardly, spiritually regenerated by the Spirit. Rather, many in Israel rejected Yahweh as Lord over them and instead followed the idolatry of the nations.[14] Though Yahweh called out to them to repent and turn to him, they refused. Such resistance to God's gospel call comes to its climax in the New Testament as many of the Jews reject Jesus Christ himself, the Son of God. One passage that makes such resistance especially evident is Acts 7 where Stephen is martyred for his faith in Christ. Stephen gives a biblical theology of God's redemptive purpose through Israel and when he comes to the end he reminds the Jews putting him on trial that they have

---

[12] Hoekema, *Saved by Grace*, 79.

[13] Fuller, *Works*, 2:381. Fuller utilized Jonathan Edwards to resolve the tension that exists, particularly his distinction between natural and moral inability and ability.

[14] John Frame, The Doctrine of God (Phillipsburg, NJ: P & R, 2002), 317–334.

failed to understand what the Scriptures have said concerning the "coming of the Righteous One" (7:52). Stephen accuses them of being just like their fathers who persecuted the prophets. "You stiff-necked people, uncircumcised in heart and ears, you always resist the Holy Spirit. As your fathers did, so do you" (Acts 7:51; cf. Hebrews 3:8–13). Stephen's statement is telling because not only does he state that the Jews persecuting him are stiffnecked, uncircumcised, and resisting the Spirit, but so were their fathers, failing to heed the message of the prophets who proclaimed of the gospel to come through Christ (Deuteronomy 32:9; Jeremiah 6:10; 9:26; Ezekiel 44:7–9; Malachi 3:7). Indeed, the martyrdom of Stephen by men who resisted God's Holy Spirit sits within the shadow of the crucifixion, where evil men, who had resisted the ministry of Jesus for years (Luke 7:30; Mark 6:5–6; John 6:63; Matthew 22:3), rejecting his invitations to receive eternal life, finally put Jesus to death on a cross (Luke 23:1–49). Therefore, Jesus can cry out, "O Jerusalem, Jerusalem, the city that kills the prophets and stones those who are sent to it! How often would I have gathered your children together as a hen gathers her brood under her wings, and you would not!" (Matthew 23:37; cf. Luke 13:34).

The resistibility of the gospel call is important to reiterate because often it is assumed that Calvinists deny the resistibility of grace. However, Calvinists affirm that God's grace *in the gospel call* can be resisted. It is *when God so chooses effectually to call His elect* that such a calling cannot be finally resisted for God's purposes in saving His elect must come to fruition. The difference here is in God's intention and design. As John Owen says, "Where any work of grace is not effectual, God never intended it should be so, nor did put forth that power of grace which was necessary to make it so."[15]

The Effectual Call

When the gospel call is heard, why is it that some believe while others do not? For the Arminian, while God may enable and initiate grace, ultimately the decision is man's as to whether he will or will not believe. As we shall now see, such a reason for belief and unbelief is contrary to Scripture, which teaches that the only reason anyone believes is because God sovereignly chooses effectually to call His elect. Arminians reject such a statement because it implies that God, not man, is in control of salvation, irresistibly and effectually drawing those whom He has determined

---

[15] John Owen, *A Discourse Concerning the Holy Spirit*, in *The Works of John Owen* (Edinburgh: Banner of Truth, 2000), 3:318.

to save. For the Arminian, God cannot in any way determine who will and will not believe in the gospel. While God's (prevenient) grace is *necessary* to bring the sinner to Christ, it is not *sufficient* to bring about faith and repentance, for the will of man must act to do so. However, as I have demonstrated elsewhere, this is a clear breach of God's sovereignty in calling His elect to Himself.[16] Scripture teaches that when the gospel call goes out to all people, God secretly, irresistibly, and effectually calls His elect and only His elect through this gospel to new life, faith and repentance. As John Dagg observes, the grace in effectual calling is not only *necessary* but also *sufficient* to bring about repentance and faith.[17] The reason for transformation is not to be found in man's will but in God's effectual grace.

Effectual Calling in the New Testament Epistles

The doctrine of effectual calling can be found in Scripture at every turn (Romans 1:6–7; 8:30; 11:29; 1 Corinthians 1:2, 9, 24, 26; 7:18; 2 Thessalonians 2:13–14; Hebrews 3:1–2; 2 Peter 1:10). When Paul refers to calling he is not referring to a gospel call which is a mere invitation that can be resisted, but rather is referring to that calling which is effective, performing and fulfilling exactly that which it was sent to do.[18] Consider Paul's words in Romans 8:28–30,

> And we know that for those who love God all things work together for good, for those who are called according to his purpose [τοῖς κατὰ πρόθεσιν κλητοῖς οὖσιν]. For those whom he foreknew he also predestined to be conformed to the image of his Son, in order that he might be the firstborn among many brothers. And those whom he predestined he also called [οὓς δὲ προώρισεν, τούτους καὶ ἐκάλεσεν], and those whom he called he also justified, and those whom he justified he also glorified.

Paul states in verse 30 that those who have been predestined have also been called and those whom God called he also justified. As Douglas Moo

---

[16] In this chapter I do not present a critique of synergism and prevenient grace. For such a critique see Barrett, "Reclaiming Monergism," chapter 6.

[17] John L. Dagg, *Manual of Theology* (South Carolina: Southern Baptist Publication Society, 1857; reprint, Harrisonburg, VA: Gano Books, 1990), 332. Also, see Greg Welty, "Election and Calling: A Biblical Theological Study," in *Calvinism: A Southern Baptist Dialogue*, ed. E. Ray Clendenen and Brad J. Waggoner (Nashville, TN: B&H, 2008), 234–35.

[18] Thomas R. Schreiner, *Paul: Apostle of God's Glory in Christ* (Downers Grove, IL: InterVarsity, 2001), 241.

notes, there is an "exact correspondence" between those predestined and those called, made evident by the demonstrative pronoun "these" [*toutous*]. "This leaves little room for the suggestion that the links in this chain are not firmly attached to one another, as if some who were 'foreknown' and 'predestined' would not be 'called,' 'justified,' and 'glorified.'"[19] The links in the chain are unbreakable. The link we want to pay special attention to is the verb "he called" which, "denotes God's effectual summoning into relationship with him."[20] Those predestined are the same ones who are called and likewise those called are the same ones as those justified, etc. The calling proceeds necessarily from God's eternal election. Furthermore, Paul must be referring to a calling other than the gospel call because in the gospel call it is not true that all those called are justified. Indeed, with the gospel call many disbelieve and are never justified. Paul does not say that out of all those whom He calls some are justified and then glorified. No, Paul is clear: those He calls are indeed justified and also glorified. Therefore, since many reject the gospel call and are not justified let alone glorified, Paul must be referring to a calling which unfailingly and immutably leads to and results in justification. It is this effectual call which is grounded in predestination and results in justification and glorification (cf. 1 Corinthians 1:9; Hebrews 9:12, 15; Ephesians 4:4; 1 Thessalonians 2:12).

Moreover, Paul cannot have in mind here the gospel call because those who are "called" are promised that not only will all things work for good, but they will be glorified (8:30), demonstrating that calling produces perseverance. Paul in verse 28 shows that the called he has in mind are only those who love God. These are "called according to his purpose," predestined, and promised that all things work together for good. Now it is true that the gospel call is also a call that is "according to his purpose" but it is not true that the gospel call only consists of those who love God and those for whom all things work for good. Therefore, Paul is referring to a call that works.

Furthermore, notice the implications Romans 8:28–30 has for the *ordo salutis*. All those who are called are then justified. Paul states in Romans 5:1 that justification is by faith. Two points must be made. First, since not all have faith once again we see that Paul does not have in mind all people but only the elect. Second, since it is calling which comes before justification and since justification is by faith, it follows that for Paul it is calling which produces faith. We are safe to conclude, therefore, that calling precedes faith in the *ordo salutis*.

---

[19] Douglas J. Moo, *The Epistle to the Romans*, NICNT (1996), 535.
[20] Ibid.

Paul's reference to the effectual call in Romans 8:30 is also referenced elsewhere in Romans as well. When Paul opens Romans he addresses his readers as those "who are called to belong to Jesus Christ" (1:6) and to those in Rome who are loved by God and "called to be saints" (1:7). The call here is again the effectual call as it belongs only to those who are saints and those who belong to Jesus Christ. Paul mentions the effectual call in Romans 9 when he labels those whom God has predestined "vessels of mercy" (as opposed to the reprobate who are "vessels of wrath prepared for destruction" in verse 22), "even us whom he has called," including both Jews and Gentiles (9:23–24). The called ones in Romans 9 are not a reference to all those who hear the gospel but only to those whom God "has prepared beforehand for glory" (9:23).

Paul's use of the effectual call is also apparent in his first letter to the Corinthians. Paul begins his letter by identifying himself as one who has been "called by the will of God to be an apostle of Christ Jesus" (1:1). Paul then identifies believers as those "called to be saints together with all those who in every place call upon the name of our Lord Jesus Christ" (1:2). Paul gives thanks to God for the Corinthian believers "because of the grace of God that was given you in Christ Jesus" (1:4), a grace which enriched them in all speech and knowledge. This same God who gave them grace, Paul says in 1:8, also "will sustain you to the end, guiltless in the day of our Lord Jesus Christ." God's preservation of his elect, Paul says, shows that God is faithful. "God is faithful, by whom you were called into the fellowship of his Son, Jesus Christ our Lord" (1:9). Paul cannot be referring in 1:9 to a general, gospel call which can be rejected but must instead be referring to an effectual call where all those whom God calls experience fellowship with Christ, something that cannot be said of those who reject the general gospel call. The call Paul addresses here is one that brings the elect into union with Christ, a fellowship reserved only for those whom the Father has chosen. Paul's use of "call" to refer to the effectual call in 1:9 is similar to his use of "call" in Romans 1:7; 9:23–24; 1 Corinthians 1:26; Galatians 1:15; and Ephesians 4:1, 4.

Paul continues to speak of an effectual call in 1 Corinthians 1:18–31.

> For the word of the cross is folly to those who are perishing, but to us who are being saved it is the power of God. For it is written, "I will destroy the wisdom of the wise, and the discernment of the discerning I will thwart." Where is the one who is wise? Where is the scribe? Where is the debater of this age? Has not God made foolish the wisdom of the world? For since, in the wisdom of God, the world did not know God through wisdom, it pleased God through the folly of what we preach to save those who believe. For Jews demand signs and Greeks seek wisdom, but we preach Christ crucified, a stumbling block to Jews and folly to Gentiles,

but to those who are called, both Jews and Greeks, Christ the power of God and the wisdom of God. For the foolishness of God is wiser than men, and the weakness of God is stronger than men. *For consider your calling*, brothers: not many of you were wise according to worldly standards, not many were powerful, not many were of noble birth. But God chose what is foolish in the world to shame the wise; God chose what is weak in the world to shame the strong; God chose what is low and despised in the world, even things that are not, to bring to nothing things that are, so that no human being might boast in the presence of God. And because of him you are in Christ Jesus, who became to us wisdom from God, righteousness and sanctification and redemption, so that, as it is written, "Let the one who boasts, boast in the Lord."

The gospel Paul preached (the word of the cross) is both the power and wisdom of God to those who are saved (1:18, 21, 24; cf. Romans 1:16) and at the same time is a gospel which is foolishness to those who disbelieve and perish (1:18, 23, 25). Notice, there is no change in the gospel. The gospel remains the same. However, some hear this gospel and see it as folly while others hear this gospel and see it as the power of life. Paul's words here are similar to 2 Corinthians 2:15–16 where the gospel is a fragrance of Christ. To those being saved it is an aroma of eternal life, but to those perishing it is an aroma of eternal death (2:15–16). Ware helpfully observes, "The gospel, or aroma, is the same! The difference is in those smelling the fragrance and not in the fragrance itself."[21] So if it is not the gospel then what is it that accounts for the fact that some reject the gospel and see it as folly while others, who hear the same message of Christ crucified, accept the gospel as life? The answer is found in 1 Corinthians 1:23–24, "but we preach Christ crucified, a stumbling block to Jews and folly to Gentiles, *but to those who are called*, both Jews and Greeks, Christ the power of God and the wisdom of God." This specific group ("the called ones") is in contrast to the larger group of Jews and Greeks whom Paul says received the message of Christ crucified and saw it as a stumbling block (Jews) and as folly (Gentiles). On the other hand, to the "called ones" Christ is the power and wisdom of God. Such a contrast precludes any idea that Paul is only referring to a general gospel call.[22] Ware explains, "It makes no sense to contrast Jews and Greeks generally with those Jews and Greeks who are called (as 1:23–24 does) if the difference between believing Jews and Greeks and disbelieving Jews and Greeks is in their respective choices only."[23] To the

---

[21] Bruce A. Ware, "Effectual Calling and Grace," in *Still Sovereign: Contemporary Perspectives on Election, Foreknowledge, and Grace*, eds. Thomas R. Schreiner & Bruce A. Ware (Grand Rapids, MI: Baker, 2000), 220n.32.

[22] Schreiner, *Paul*, 241.

[23] Ware, "Effectual Calling and Grace," 222.

contrary, the contrast "is made between those called from disbelieving Jews and Greeks and, by implication, those not called, making up the general class of Jews and Greeks who regard the gospel as weakness and folly."[24] Therefore, any Arminian attempt to read into these verses prevenient grace is in vain. If Paul has in mind merely a general call, one is unable to then explain why some believe and others do not. But if we understand that Paul is comparing those who reject Christ with those whom God calls to Christ effectually then the contrast makes perfect sense and the reason for belief as opposed to unbelief can be identified in the call of God, not in any wisdom of man.

Moreover, Paul must have in mind a calling that is irresistible because those identified as "the called" believe as a result of being called. In contrast to those who are not "the called" and therefore can only see the cross as folly, those who are identified as "the called" (both Jews and Greeks) consequently see Christ as the power and wisdom of God. Being called inevitably results in submitting to the lordship of Christ.[25] Furthermore, verses 26–31 rule out an Arminian interpretation which would view the success of God's call as that which is based on the free will of the sinner. Paul explains that those called are not chosen because of anything in them, their own wisdom or power for example. How could this be when God purposefully chose those who were weak, lowly, and despised, so that "no human being might boast in the presence of God" (1:29)? If it were the case, as the Arminian believes, that certain Jews and Gentiles were regenerated because they themselves believed and if it were the case that certain Jews and Gentiles were elected and chosen because of what they themselves did to believe, then Paul could not exclude all boasting. Man would then have something to boast about "in the presence of God" (1:29). Rather, it is "because of him you are in Christ Jesus" and therefore if anyone is to boast he is to "boast in the Lord" (1:31). All human boasting is excluded and all glory belongs to God!

Paul's other letters also exemplify the effectual call. In Galatians 1:15 Paul says that God not only set me apart before birth but also "called me by his grace" and "was pleased to reveal his Son to me, in order that I might preach him among the Gentiles" (Galatians 1:15–16; cf. 5:13; Jeremiah 1:5). Here Paul shows the Galatians that God elected him before he was born by his good pleasure and then at the proper time called him by his grace. As Ridderbos notes, the divine but gracious determinism in this passage is unavoidable.[26] The calling Paul has in mind refers to the Da-

---

[24] Ibid.

[25] Leon Morris, *1 Corinthians*, TNTC (2008), 52.

[26] Herman N. Ridderbos, *The Epistle of Paul to the Churches of Galatia*, NICNT (1953), 63.

mascus road, where God called Paul to himself by revealing his Son to him by "immediate intervention." "The film was, so to speak, removed from his eyes."[27] Similarly, Paul exhorts the Ephesians,

> I therefore, a prisoner for the Lord, urge you to walk in a manner worthy of the calling to which you have been called, with all humility and gentleness, with patience, bearing with one another in love, eager to maintain the unity of the Spirit in the bond of peace. There is one body and one Spirit—just as you were called to the one hope that belongs to your call— one Lord, one faith, one baptism, one God and Father of all, who is over all and through all and in all (Ephesians 4:1–6).

Call or calling, which "arises out of the gracious, saving purpose of God," is used four times in this passage, reminding the Ephesians that because they have been called by God, their life should be one of faith, hope, unity, and peace. Thielman detects that here "God has called Paul's readers to be part of his people not because of anything they have done but as a free gift."[28] Likewise, Paul writes to the Colossians, "And let the peace of Christ rule in your hearts, to which indeed you were called in one body. And be thankful" (Colossians 3:15). Again, believers have been effectually called into one body characterized by the peace of Christ. Moo highlights the sovereignty of God in such a calling, "*You were called* picks up the language of election that Paul used in v. 12— 'God's chosen people.' Paul frequently uses the verb 'call' (*kaleō*) to denote God's gracious and powerful summons to human beings, by which they are transferred from the realm of sin and death into the realm of righteousness and life."[29] The same can be said for other Pauline passages: "God has called us in peace" (1 Corinthians 7:15), "you were called to freedom" (Galatians 5:13), "you were called in one hope" (Ephesians 4:4), "God did not call us to uncleanness but for holiness" (1 Thessalonians 4:7), and "God has saved us and called us to a holy life" (2 Timothy 1:9).

Likewise to Timothy Paul writes, "Fight the good fight of the faith. Take hold of the eternal life to which you were called and about which you made the good confession in the presence of many witnesses" (1 Timothy 6:12). Calling here is a summons to salvation (in the passive voice; cf. Galatians 5:13; Ephesians 4:1, 4). In his second letter to Timothy Paul charges Timothy not to be ashamed of the gospel nor of the Lord Jesus

[27] Thomas R. Schreiner, *Galatians*, BECNT (2010), 101.

[28] Frank Thielman, *Ephesians*, BECNT (2010), 252.

[29] See Romans 8:30; 9:24; 1 Corinthians 1:9; 7:15–24; Galatians 1:6; 5:8, 13; Ephesians 4:1, 4; 1 Thessalonians 2:12; 4:7; 5:24; 2 Thessalonians 2:14; 1 Timothy 6:12; 2 Timothy 1:9. Douglas J. Moo, *The Letters to the Colossians and to Philemon*, PNTC (2008), 284.

Christ "who saved us and called us to a holy calling, not because of our works but because of His own purpose and grace, which He gave us in Christ Jesus before the ages began" (2 Timothy 1:9). Again, calling here is not deemed successful due to anything in us ("not because of our works"), but purely because of God's "own purpose and grace," which Paul says is rooted in the eternal act ("before the ages began") of election ("he gave us in Christ Jesus").[30] Like election, calling is not based on anything in us (not even faith), but purely on God's good purpose and grace. Paul in 2 Timothy 1:9 sounds much like he does in Romans 8:28 where calling is said to be "according to his purpose" and Romans 9:11–12 where God's choice of Jacob over Esau is prior to them doing anything good or bad so that election would not be on the basis of works but "because of him who calls." Here we see in Paul both an unconditional election and an unconditional call, both of which are inseparable and accomplished apart from man's will to believe.

Not only Paul, but Peter also writes of an effectual call for the elect. According to Peter, Christians are those whom God has caused to be born again to a living hope (1 Peter 1:3). Therefore, Christians are not to be "conformed to the passions of your former ignorance, but as he who called you is holy, you also be holy in all your conduct" (1 Peter 1:14–15). "Calling" does not refer to a mere invitation but rather refers to God's omnipotence in infallibly transferring His elect from darkness to light.[31] Peter mentions the effectual call in 1 Peter 2:9–10 as well, "But you are a chosen race, a royal priesthood, a holy nation, a people for his own possession, that you may proclaim the excellencies of him who called you out of darkness into his marvelous light. Once you were not a people, but now you are God's people; once you had not received mercy, but now you have received mercy." Christ is credited with calling his elect ("chosen race," cf. Isaiah 43:3, 20–21; "a people for his own possession," cf. Exodus 19:5; Hosea 2:23–25) out of darkness (depravity and bondage to sin) and into the marvelous light of salvation. This "chosen and precious" people of God (2:4) were once dead in their trespasses and sins but Christ, through his calling, rescued them from the domain of darkness to experience new life. There is no possibility of a general, gospel call here since the called are referred to as God's "chosen people." The monergistic nature of this calling is apparent in how Peter's language parallels Genesis 1:3–5 where God simply speaks and light appears in the midst of darkness. Paul does the same in 2 Corinthians 4:6 where God shines directly into the heart of his elect, giving them a saving knowledge of Christ. In other words, just as God's word

---

[30] William D. Mounce, *Pastoral Epistles*, WBC, vol. 46 (2000), 482.

[31] Thomas R. Schreiner, *1, 2 Peter, Jude*, NAC, vol. 37 (2003), 80.

creates light, so also does it create faith. Consequently, calling is *performative*, bringing about the reality God intended.[32]

The effectual call is again emphasized by Peter in 2:21, "For to this you have been called, because Christ also suffered for you, leaving you an example, so that you might follow in his steps." Peter is affirming an effectual call that results in faith. Those called follow in the steps of Christ. In other words, just as calling is given and appointed by God so also is suffering. Those called to Christ will suffer as Christ suffered and in this way they will receive eternal life. Indeed, Peter takes the example of Christ's suffering so seriously that he can say that believers have been called not to repay evil for evil but instead have been called to bless those who have insulted and injured them, that they may obtain a blessing (1 Peter 3:9).

The effectual call is so important to Peter that he closes his first letter saying, "And after you have suffered a little while, the God of all grace, who has called you to his eternal glory in Christ, will himself restore, confirm, strengthen, and establish you" (1 Peter 5:10). Earlier we saw how election and effectual calling were inseparable and now we see how effectual calling and perseverance are indivisible. As Schreiner writes, "Here it should simply be said (see esp. 2:9) that 'calling' refers to God's effective work by which he inducts believers into a saving relationship with himself. That the calling is to salvation is clear since believers are called to God's 'eternal glory.'"[33] The fact that Peter is referring to a calling that is salvific is not only manifested by his reference to "eternal glory" but also by the phrase "in Christ." Schreiner comments,

> ... the words 'in Christ' be understood as modifying the entire clause, 'eternal glory' or 'called.' ... Peter thereby emphasized that God's saving calling is effectual in and through Christ. The theme of calling to glory reminds the readers that endtime salvation is sure, for God himself is the one who initiated and secured their salvation. As the rest of the verse will demonstrate, God will certainly complete what he has inaugurated. Their calling to glory is not questionable but sure.[34]

For Peter, effectual calling is a doctrine that not only stems from our unconditional election but also unites us to Christ and guarantees our perseverance unto glory.

Peter again uses language to refer to the effectual call in his second letter. Peter opens by saying, "His divine power has granted to us all things that pertain to life and godliness, through the knowledge of him who

[32] Ibid., 116.
[33] Ibid., 244.
[34] Ibid., 244–45.

called us to his own glory and excellence, by which he has granted to us his precious and very great promises, so that through them you may become partakers of the divine nature, having escaped from the corruption that is in the world because of sinful desire" (2 Peter 1:3–5). Is this calling a mere gospel call and invitation for all people? Not at all. As English readers we often assume that calling always means that an offer has been made, one to be resisted or accepted. But for Peter, calling is no mere offer. To the contrary, God's call is effective, bringing the dead to life and creating faith where there was only unbelief (e.g., 1 Peter 1:15; 2:9, 21; 3:9; 5:10).

Peter also says in 2 Peter 1:10, "Therefore, brothers, be all the more diligent to make your calling and election sure, for if you practice these qualities you will never fall." Notice, calling is identified alongside of election so much so that we could translate them as one— "elective call."[35] Election and calling here are inseparably linked together, precluding the possibility of a general, gospel call. The combination of election and calling by Peter "highlights God's grace," namely, that "he is the one who saves."[36] Moreover, grammatically, as Hoekema observes, "There is only one definite article (*tēn*) before the two nouns, *klēsin* (calling) and *eklogēn* (election). This means that these two are treated as one unit and are to be thought of as such: not your calling as somehow separate from our election, but your calling and election together." Hoekema is building off of A. T. Robertson who says, "Sometimes groups more or less distinct are treated as one for the purpose in hand, and hence use only one article. Cf. ... 2 Peter 1:10."[37] Hoekema and Robertson are grammatically on target which leads to only one conclusion: the unity of calling and election in 2 Peter 1:10 demands that an effectual call is in view. Additionally, what would be the point in telling somebody to confirm his gospel call? This seems senseless once someone has heard the gospel proclaimed. But if the effectual call is in view, a calling that is salvific, the admonition makes perfect sense: make sure you are elected and effectually called. And in verses 5–7 Peter explains how one can do this, namely, by adding to your faith goodness, knowledge, self-control, etc. In short, if one is elected and effectually called, he will be able to observe the fruit of the Spirit taking root in his own life.

Not only do Paul and Peter emphasize the effectual call, but Jude in the opening verse of his letter says, "Jude, a servant of Jesus Christ and brother of James, To those who are called, beloved in God the Father and

---

[35] Ibid., 304.

[36] Ibid.

[37] Hoekema, *Saved by Grace*, 85–86. A. T. Robertson, *Grammar of the Greek New Testament in the Light of Historical Research* (Nashville, TN: Broadman, 1934), 787.

kept for Jesus Christ: May mercy, peace, and love be multiplied to you" (1:1–2). Calling here cannot be the general gospel call to all because Jude identifies the called as those who are beloved in God the Father and kept for Jesus Christ, characteristics not true of all those who receive the gospel call. It is not the case that everyone who receives the gospel call is kept by Christ and loved by the Father in a saving way.

John also uses the effectual call when he writes in Revelation 17:14, "They will make war on the Lamb, and the Lamb will conquer them, for he is Lord of lords and King of kings, and those with him are called and chosen and faithful." Like Jude 1, John identifies those called as those who are with the Lamb who is Christ. Those "called and chosen and faithful" represent the "vindication of the persecuted saints" (cf. Daniel 7:21; Revelation 6:9–11; 12:11; 13:10–17).[38] Also, similar to 2 Peter 1:10, here once again we see calling and election spoken of together. Those with the Lamb "are called and chosen." It is not true of everyone who hears the general, gospel call that they are both called and chosen, found to be faithful to the Lamb.[39]

Jesus Taught the Effectual Call

One of the most important passages on effectual calling is John 6:35–64. In the context of the passage (John 6:22–34), Jesus is interacting with the Jews who did not believe in him (6:36). How can it be the case that some see the signs of Jesus and believe while others, seeing the very same signs, disbelieve? Both have the same knowledge before them and yet some trust in Christ while others hate Him. What is the cause of this difference? What is to account for belief and unbelief? Jesus gives an answer in John 6:37–40.

All that the Father gives me will come to me, and whoever comes to me I will never cast out. For I have come down from heaven, not to do my own will but the will of him who sent me. And this is the will of him who sent me, that I should lose nothing of all that he has given me, but raise it up on the last day. For this is the will of my Father, that everyone who looks on the Son and believes in him should have eternal life, and I will raise him up on the last day.

Notice, Jesus does not explain why some believe and others do not by turning to the fact that some choose him while others do not. While He holds out the promise of life to all (6:35–37, 40, 47, 51), He never says

---

[38] G. K. Beale, *The Book of Revelation*, NIGTC (1999), 880.
[39] Also consider Hebrews 9:15.

that everyone is able to believe, as the Arminian assumes. He tells them what will happen if they do believe, namely, they will never go hungry or be thirsty (6:35), they will receive eternal life (6:40, 47), and they will live forever (6:51). However, while Jesus explains the rewards to be received, He never says the reason as to why some accept and others reject is due to free will. Arminians will interject at this point by arguing that the promises themselves must imply that they can turn and believe otherwise Jesus would be disengenous to hold out such promises to them. Why would Jesus hold out eternal life unless they were able to take it by faith? Surely, "ought" implies "can." The command to believe assumes the ability to believe. However, the thrust of Jesus' words in John 6 shatter this Arminian assumption. Notice, Jesus never makes such an inference, as logical as it might seem. In fact, Jesus' words prove quite the opposite. There is much "ought" in John 6, but there is no "can" to be found. To the contrary, Jesus only affirms a "cannot." As Ridderbos states, Jesus "demonstrates the powerlessness of the natural person ('no one') to come to the salvation disclosed in Christ unless the Father who sent him 'draws' that person."[40]

Notice what Jesus says in verse 37, "All that the Father gives me will come to me, and whoever comes to me I will never cast out." Köstenberger astutely recognizes, contra Ben Witherington, that divine predestination is in view.[41] Likewise, Carson makes two observations worthy of consideration. First, the verb "cast out" (ἐκβάλω; cf. John 2:15; 9:34; 10:4; 12:31) "implies the 'casting out' of something or someone already 'in'. The strong litotes in 6:37f., therefore, does not mean 'I will certainly receive the one who comes', but 'I will certainly preserve, keep in, the one who comes'; while the identity of the 'one who comes' is established by the preceding clause."[42] Jesus' promise that He will never "cast out" implies that there is a set number already chosen, already "in" and it is clear that these are only those whom the Father has given to Jesus. Second, Carson observes that the causal *hoti* and telic *hina* in 6:38 "give the reason for this keeping action by Jesus, in terms of the will of the Father, viz. that Jesus should not lose one of those given to him (6.38f.)." In other words, "6.37 argues not only that the ones given to Jesus will inevitably come to him, but that Jesus will keep them individually (*ton erchomenon* as opposed to *pan ho*) once there."[43] To summarize, Jesus is teaching (1) that if one has been given to Him by the Father then coming to Him is inevitable (effectual) and (2) those given

[40] Herman Ridderbos, *The Gospel of John*, trans. John Vriend (Grand Rapids, MI: Eerdmans, 1997), 232.

[41] Andreas J. Köstenberger, *John*, BECNT (2004), 211.

[42] D.A. Carson, *Divine Sovereignty and Human Responsibility: Biblical Perspectives in Tension* (Eugene, OR: Wipf & Stock, 1994), 184.

[43] Ibid.

to Jesus He will unfailingly keep. Carson is perceptive, "Jesus is repudiating any idea that the Father has sent the Son forth on a mission which could fail because of the unbelief of the people."[44]

The implication for those Jews who disbelieve is startling: the Father has not given you to Christ, which is what is needed for you to come to Christ.[45] Or as Carson states, "You have not been given to the Son by the Father for life and therefore you will not have life but will continue in your unbelief."[46] Jesus makes this same point in John 10:26, "But you do not believe because you are not part of my flock." Notice, Jesus does not say, "You are not part of my flock because you do not believe" as the Arminian argues. The Arminian must condition being part of the flock upon man's free will to believe. But Jesus says the exact opposite, thereby dismantling the Arminian's logic. They do not believe because they are not of his flock. And why exactly are they not of his flock? As Jesus states in John 6:37, they are not of his flock because they have not been given to Jesus by the Father. Jesus makes this same point in John 8:47, "Whoever is of God hears the words of God. The reason why you do not hear them is that you are not of God." Again, the Arminian must have it the other way around: the reason why you are not of God is that you do not hear the words of God. But Jesus says the exact opposite: you do not hear because you are not of God. Free will is nowhere the cause of becoming part of God's flock. Rather, it is God's sovereign choice to give certain sheep to his Son that results in belief.

It must also be noted, lest the Arminian object at this point that coming to Christ is not the same as believing in Christ, that Jesus in 6:35–37 equates the two. Coming to Jesus is equivalent to trusting and believing in Jesus. All those who come to Him will not hunger and all those who believe in Him will not thirst. The parallel is obvious: hungering is to thirsting as coming is to believing. But continuing on in the passage we see Jesus reiterate His point again as the Jews are enraged by His words.

> So the Jews grumbled about him, because he said, "I am the bread that came down from heaven." They said, "Is not this Jesus, the son of Joseph,

---

[44] Ibid.

[45] Ridderbos, *John*, 233.

[46] Arminians may try to avoid the logic of Jesus here by saying that Jesus does not say that some are not given to Jesus. Carson responds, "However, if all are given to Jesus, then all will surely come to him, according to this text; and the logically entailed absolute universalism contradicts both the tenor of the fourth Gospel and those explicit passages which make it clear that only some of the world is given to Jesus (cf. 17:9)." Carson, *Divine Sovereignty and Human Responsibility*, 184.

whose father and mother we know? How does he now say, 'I have come down from heaven'?" Jesus answered them, "Do not grumble among yourselves. *No one can come to me unless the Father who sent me draws him. And I will raise him up on the last day.* It is written in the Prophets, 'And they will all be taught by God.' Everyone who has heard and learned from the Father comes to me— not that anyone has seen the Father except he who is from God; he has seen the Father. Truly, truly, I say to you, whoever believes has eternal life. I am the bread of life. Your fathers ate the manna in the wilderness, and they died. This is the bread that comes down from heaven, so that one may eat of it and not die. I am the living bread that came down from heaven. If anyone eats of this bread, he will live forever. And the bread that I will give for the life of the world is my flesh" (John 6:41–51).

Here again we see Jesus explain that it is impossible for anyone to come to him unless the Father has already given them over to him (6:44; cf. 6:65). Stated otherwise, it is absolutely necessary for the Father to give a sinner to Christ if that sinner is to believe. If they are not given to Christ by the Father then they will not believe. Or as Boice and Ryken state, "If they fail to believe, it is because God has withheld that special, efficacious grace that he was under no obligation to bestow."[47] The only reason some come to Christ is because they were already given to the Son by the Father. Such a teaching by Jesus in no way precludes the fact that all "ought" to come to Christ and believe (cf. 6:51). Yet, "ought" does not imply "can" for Jesus is clear that no one "can" come to Him unless they are drawn to Him by the Father.

This brings us to the precise nature of such a drawing of the elect to Christ by the Father in John 6:37, 44 and 65. These three passages read:

All that the Father gives me will come to me, and whoever comes to me I will never cast out (John 6:37).

No one can come to me unless the Father who sent me draws him. And I will raise him up on the last day (John 6:44).

And he said, "This is why I told you that no one can come to me unless it is granted him by the Father" (John 6:65).

Is such a drawing effectual and irresistible? Or, as the Arminian believes, can this drawing be resisted successfully? For the Arminian, while

---

[47] James Montgomery Boice and Philip Graham Ryken, *The Doctrines of Grace: Rediscovering the Evangelical Gospel* (Wheaton, IL: Crossway, 2002), 159. Also, see Carson, *Divine Sovereignty and Human Responsibility*, 166.

God initiates the drawing, unless the drawing is resistible, man's free will is compromised. God must draw but his work only makes salvation possible, not actual. Ultimately, God's drawing must meet man's approval, as man always reserves the right to refuse.

The major problem with the Arminian interpretation of John 6, however, is that Jesus is not talking about a universal drawing of all men to himself. Prevenient grace is nowhere to be found here. Moreover, not only is a universal grace absent but so also is a grace that is resistible and defeatable. To the contrary, Jesus teaches that the grace He is speaking of here is one that is particular to the elect and effectual. Several observations bear this out.

In John 6, especially 6:44, the drawing of the Father necessarily results in a coming to Christ. In other words, contrary to Arminianism, this is not a drawing that merely makes possible a coming to Christ but rather is a drawing that inevitably and irresistibly leads to Christ. Or as Hendriksen says, "The Father does not merely beckon or advise, he *draws!*"[48] All those drawn do in fact believe. As Jesus explains in 6:44, "No one can come to me unless the Father who sent me draws him [ἑλκύσῃ αὐτόν]. And I will raise him up on the last day." Arminians view 6:44 as saying that while it is true that no one can come to Christ unless the Father draws Him, such a drawing can be resisted. However, such an interpretation fails in two ways: (1) It ignores the fact that "no one can come to me" (i.e., inability) and (2) it fails to finish the verse, viz. "I will raise him up on the last day."

Each of these points deserves consideration. First, in John 6 the grammatical language is in support of an irresistible, effectual drawing. The word draw in Greek is *elkō*, which, as Albrecht Oepke explains, means "to compel by irresistible superiority."[49] Though the Arminian rejects such a notion, the word linguistically and lexicographically means "to compel." Therefore, Jesus cannot be saying that the drawing of the Father is a mere wooing or persuasion that can be resisted. Rather, this drawing is an indefectible, invincible, unconquerable, indomitable, insuperable, and unassailable summons. As John Frame explains, the word "summons" captures the efficacy of this call well. "That word summons brings out God's sovereignty. You might be able to refuse an invitation, but you can't refuse a

---

[48] William Hendriksen, *Exposition of the Gospel According to John*, NTC (2002), 1:238.

[49] Albrecht Oepke, "*Elkō*," in *Theological Dictionary of the New Testament*, ed. Gerhard Kittel, ed. and trans. Geoffrey W. Bromiley (Grand Rapids, MI: Eerdmans, 1964), 2:503. J. Ramsey Michaels agrees in *The Gospel of John*, NICNT (2010), 386.

summons. A summons is an offer you cannot refuse."[50] In short, this summons does not fail to accomplish what God intended. *Elkō* is also used in James 2:6 which says, "But you have dishonored the poor man. Are not the rich the ones who oppress you, and the ones who drag [*elkō*] you into court?" And again in Acts 16:19, "But when her owners saw that their hope of gain was gone, they seized Paul and Silas and dragged [*elkō*] them into the marketplace before the rulers." As Sproul observes, to substitute "woo" in the place of drag in these passages would sound ludicrous. "Once forcibly seized, they could not be enticed or wooed. The text clearly indicates they were *compelled* to come before the authorities."[51] In other words, this is not a mere external effort by God to persuade, but is an internal compelling that cannot be thwarted.

Second, the Father's drawing will indeed result in final salvation, the resurrection on the last day, as is evident in John 6:44. Jesus comes down from heaven to do the will of the Father and what is this will but to lose none of all those whom the Father has given to Him but to raise them up on the last day (John 6:39–40). Surely Jesus cannot be referring to a universal call that is resistible for this would mean that Jesus is promising to raise all up on the last day, a promise He has failed to accomplish since so many disbelieve. Moreover, as Carson observes, "The combination of v. 37a and v. 44 prove that this 'drawing' activity of the Father cannot be reduced to what theologians sometimes call 'prevenient grace' dispensed to every individual, for this 'drawing' is selective, or else the negative note in v. 44 is meaningless."[52] In other words, Jesus is referring only to those whom the Father has given Him and these only will Jesus give eternal life and the resurrection to glory. Here we see once again that the Father's giving of the elect to the Son invincibly leads to final salvation. Therefore, the drawing Jesus speaks of must be effectual.[53]

---

[50] John M. Frame, *Salvation Belongs to the Lord* (Phillipsburg, NJ: P & R, 2006), 184.

[51] R. C. Sproul, *What is Reformed Theology?* (Grand Rapids, MI: Baker, 2005), 154.

[52] D.A. Carson, *The Gospel According to John* (Grand Rapids, MI: Eerdmans, 1991), 293.

[53] Nevertheless, Arminian Grant R. Osborne objects. He argues that if the drawing in John 6:44 is effectual and irresistible then universalism is true for Jesus says in John 12:32 that when He is lifted up He will draw all men to Himself. Grant R. Osborne, "Soteriology in the Gospel of John," in *The Grace of God, the Will of Man*, ed. Pinnock, 248–49; idem, "Exegetical Notes on Calvinist Texts," in *Grace Unlimited*, ed. Clark Pinnock (Eugene, OR: Wipf & Stock, 1999), 171, 184–85. However, the drawing in 12:32 does not refer to all people without exception, but to all people without distinction. The context makes this clear as

To summarize our findings we can conclude the following: (1) The Father's drawing precedes any belief on the sinner's part. (2) The reason a sinner believes is because he has been drawn by the Father to Christ, not vice versa. (3) The reason a sinner does *not* believe is because he has not been drawn by the Father to Christ, not vice versa. (4) The Father's drawing is effectual because (a) *elkō* means "to compel by irresistible superiority"[54] and (b) Jesus ensures us that those drawn will be raised up on the last day, something not true of all people who receive the gospel call. Therefore, the drawing does not make belief a possibility but an inevitable reality. (5) The efficacy of the drawing precludes that it is universal. Rather the drawing is particular, limited to the elect.[55]

It is crucial to observe how the narrative ends, namely, with everyone leaving Jesus because such a teaching is so offensive and difficult to understand (John 6:60–65). How Jesus responds is telling. "It is the Spirit who gives life; the flesh is no help at all. The words that I have spoken to you are spirit and life. But there are some of you who do not believe.... This is why I told you that no one can come to me unless it is granted him by the Father" (John 6:63–65). Two observations are relevant. First, Jesus once again emphasizes the inability of the sinner when he says it is "the Spirit who gives life; the flesh is no help at all." Such inability is affirmed again in John 14:17 when Jesus says, "the world *cannot accept him* [the Holy Spirit], because it neither sees him nor knows him." Second, if, as the Arminian believes, all are drawn, why does Jesus stress his point concerning their persistence in unbelief? Jesus shows in John 6:65 that once again their unbelief serves as evidence that they have not been drawn by the Father. But none of this makes sense if Jesus is talking about a universal call that only makes salvation possible. A calling common to all people is *not* offensive and surely would not lead his hearers to be angered, eventually abandoning Jesus. To the contrary, the reason His teaching is so offensive is because He explains their unbelief by appealing to the Father's sovereign choice,

Jews *and* Greeks both come to Jesus. As Carson and Schreiner argue, Jesus has in mind all *types* and *kinds* of people (cf. Joel 2:28ff), not all people without exception. Carson, *John*, 293, 444; idem, *Divine Sovereignty and Human Responsibility*, 185–86; Thomas R. Schreiner, "Does Scripture Teach Prevenient Grace in the Wesleyan Sense?" in *Still Sovereign: Contemporary Perspectives on Election, Foreknowledge, and Grace*, eds. Thomas R. Schreiner & Bruce A. Ware (Grand Rapids, MI: Baker, 2000), 241–42.

[54] Oepke, "*Elkō*," 503.

[55] John Calvin, *Institutes of the Christian Religion*, ed. John T. McNeil, trans. Ford Lewis Battles, LCC, vols. 20–21 (Philadelphia, PA: Westminster, 1960), 3.24.1.

not man's free will.[56] Those not drawn by the Father and selected remain in their unbelief.

Before concluding our discussion, it is necessary to briefly look at three other passages, namely, John 12:37–40, 17:24, and 10:14ff. In John 12:37–40 we see perhaps the most outstanding instance in all of John's gospel where emphasis is placed on divine sovereignty. Though Jesus had accomplished many miraculous signs, still the people did not believe in him (12:37; cf. Deuteronomy 29:2–4). Why exactly did they not believe? John answers,

> Though he had done so many signs before them, they still did not believe in him, so that the word spoken by the prophet Isaiah might be fulfilled: "Lord, who has believed what he heard from us, and to whom has the arm of the Lord been revealed?" Therefore they could not believe. For again Isaiah said, "He has blinded their eyes and hardened their heart, lest they see with their eyes, and understand with their heart, and turn, and I would heal them."

Why is it that those following Jesus, though seeing his signs, did not believe? John, quoting Isaiah 58:1 and then 6:10, says it is because God himself "has blinded their eyes and hardened their heart" so that they won't believe. Köstenberger comments, "This kind of reasoning places human unbelief ultimately within the sphere of God's sovereignty, and more specifically his (positive or negative) elective purposes. While not rendering people free from responsibility, their unbelief is ultimately shown to be grounded not in human choice but in divine hardening."[57] God has not only granted some faith, but he has hardened others, making sure they do not repent. Stated otherwise, while man's own sinfulness may be the proximate cause of his unbelief, God is the *ultimate* cause of unbelief for it is he who hardens the heart (cf. Exodus 4:21; 7:3; 9:12; 10:1, 20; 27; 11:10; 14:4, 17; Deuteronomy 2:30; Joshua 11:20; 2 Chronicles 36:13; Isaiah 63:17; Romans 9:18; 11:7, 25).[58] As Paul says in Romans 9:18, "So then he has mercy on whomever he wills, and he hardens whomever he wills." While the Arminian may detest such a claim, John saw such a hardening of the heart by God a fulfillment of Isaiah's prophecy, again demonstrating that divine determinism is in view.

In John 17 Jesus gives his "high priestly prayer" in which he asks his Father to "give eternal life to all whom you have given him [the Son]"

---

[56] Carson, *Divine Sovereignty and Human Responsibility*, 186.

[57] Andreas J. Köstenberger, *A Theology of John's Gospel and Letters* (Grand Rapids, MI: Zondervan, 2009), 459–60. Also, see Michaels, *John*, 710.

[58] Bavinck, *Reformed Dogmatics*, 4:41–42.

(17:2). Jesus goes on to say that He has manifested the Father's name to "the people whom you gave me out of the world" (17:6). The predestinarian tone of Jesus' words comes to light even further when he then says, "Yours they were, and you gave them to me, and they have kept your word" (17:6). Most commentators agree that Jesus is referring to his disciples, as is evident in 17:9 where Jesus states, "I am not praying for the world but for those whom you have given me, for they are yours." Here we see that not all are chosen but only some are chosen to be given to the Son. Notice, the "giving" of these disciples to the Son is not merely for service but for salvation. Jesus is not merely praying for their earthly ministry but is praying for the safe keeping of their very souls. This is evident in the fact that the language used here ("you have given me") parallels the language used in John 6:36–65. The salvific nature is also obvious in Jesus asking the Father to sanctify them in the truth (17:17, 19). Moreover, Jesus is acting as their mediator and high priest, praying on their behalf, holding them up before the throne of the Father as those whom He successfully kept (see 17:12, "While I was with them, I kept them in your name, which you have given me"). Christ is the faithful Son who keeps all those entrusted to him by the Father. Jesus, however, does not stop with his disciples, but continues to pray for the elect who will believe after he has been glorified. "I do not ask for these only, but also for those who will believe in me through their word" (17:20). Jesus is praying *with certainty* for the elect who have not yet believed but one day will![59] Those who have not yet heard the message of the disciples, but will soon enough, are already given to Jesus by the Father. Both the particularity and the determinism in this passage are inescapable. The particularity is present in that Jesus is not praying for all the world but only those whom will believe. The efficacy or determinism is present in that Jesus prays for those who *will* believe. Jesus is praying for the elect who have not yet heard the gospel and believed but nonetheless *will certainly do so* since Jesus Himself intercedes on their behalf. Though the faith of these future believers is not yet a reality, the Father has guaranteed it in giving them to the Son and the Son has verified it by praying on their behalf to the Father. Here again we see that belonging to Christ or being given to Christ by the Father is what determines whether or not one will believe.

John 17 shares many similarities with John 10. In John 10:14–18 Jesus says that He is the good shepherd who knows His own sheep and lays down His life for His sheep. Here Jesus is speaking of those Jews who believe in Jesus because they have been given to Him by the Father. However, Jesus also says that He has "other sheep that are not of this fold" and

---

[59] Carson, *Divine Sovereignty and Human Responsibility*, 187.

he "must bring them also" and they will listen to His voice (10:16). Jesus is now referring to the Gentiles who would one day believe.[60] For them also Jesus lays down His life because they are His sheep as well (10:17). But notice, as we saw was the case in John 17, Jesus is guaranteeing that certain Gentiles will in fact believe. How can He make such a guarantee? Jesus can make such a promise *because* the Father has given these sheep to His Son, as becomes plain in John 10:24–29.

> So the Jews gathered around him and said to him, "How long will you keep us in suspense? If you are the Christ, tell us plainly." Jesus answered them, "I told you, and you do not believe. The works that I do in my Father's name bear witness about me, but you do not believe because you are not part of my flock. My sheep hear my voice, and I know them, and they follow me. I give them eternal life, and they will never perish, and no one will snatch them out of my hand. My Father, who has given them to me, is greater than all, and no one is able to snatch them out of the Father's hand. I and the Father are one."

Once again we see that the Father has sheep that He gives to the Son. The reason some do not believe is that the Father has not given them to the Son.[61] The reason others believe and the reason others *will believe in the future* (Gentiles included; cf. 10:16) is that the Father has given them to the Son.

Monergistic Regeneration

A discussion of regeneration flows naturally from effectual calling. Those whom God effectually calls to Himself are made alive (Ephesians 2:1, 5; Colossians 2:13; Romans 8:7–8). The actual word "regeneration" (*palingenesia*) is only used in Matthew 19:28 and Titus 3:5 and only the latter uses the word in the narrow sense, namely, as referring to the first instance of new life. Regeneration in this narrow sense is affirmed throughout Scripture, for even if the word itself is not used, the idea is prevalent (John 1:12–13; 3:3–8; Galatians 6:15; Ephesians 2:5–6, 10; 4:22–24; Colossians 2:11–14; Titus 3:5; James 1:18; 1 Peter 1:3–5; 1 John 2:29; 3:9; 4:7; 5:1, 4). That said, it is appropriate to precisely define regeneration in this narrow sense. I provide the following definition:

> Regeneration is the work of the Holy Spirit to unite the elect sinner to Christ by breathing new life into that dead and depraved

---

[60] Ibid., 190.
[61] Ibid.; Carson, *John*, 393.

sinner so as to raise him from spiritual death to spiritual life, removing his heart of stone and giving him a heart of flesh, so that he is washed, born from above and now able to repent and trust in Christ as a new creation.[62] Moreover, regeneration is the act of God alone and therefore it is monergistic in nature, accomplished by the sovereign act of the Spirit apart from and unconditioned upon man's will to believe. In short, man's faith does not cause regeneration but regeneration causes man's faith.

While space does not permit us to explore the many facets of what regeneration is and is not, in what remains we will zero in on one facet of regeneration, namely, its monergistic nature.[63]

The Circumcision and Gift of a New Heart

In Deuteronomy 30 Israel faces and anticipates the reality of coming exile and judgment for disobedience. However, inspired by God, Moses foretells of a time to come when Israel will experience restoration, redemption, genuine repentance, and new spiritual life rather than judgment and condemnation. Included in such a future restoration is liberation from the slavery of sin. However, liberation from bondage to sin only comes through the circumcision of the heart. In Deuteronomy 30:6 we read, "And the Lord your God will circumcise your heart and the heart of your offspring, so that you will love the Lord your God with all your heart and with all your soul, that you may live" (Deuteronomy 30:6). Eugene Merrill is correct to state that circumcision of the heart here refers to the "radical work of regeneration."[64] If the circumcision of the heart refers to regeneration (cf. Romans 2:25–27) then to what purpose does Yahweh promise to circumcise the heart? Yahweh circumcises the heart "so that" they will love the Lord. The Lord does not circumcise their hearts "because" they acted in repentance and faith by loving the Lord. Rather, it is Yahweh's sovereign act of circumcising the heart that causes the sinner to love Him. Therefore, Yahweh's promise of renewal and restoration is characterized by a sovereign act upon the uncircumcised heart of his elect. Nowhere in

[62] My definition is similar to Hoekema, *Saved by Grace*, 94; John Murray, *Redemption Accomplished and Applied* (Grand Rapids, MI: Eerdmans, 1955), 96; Berkhof, *Systematic Theology*, 469.

[63] For such a study see Barrett, "Reclaiming Monergism," chapter 4.

[64] Eugene H. Merrill, *Deuteronomy*, NAC, vol. 4 (1994), 388. Also, see Mark A. Snoeberger, "The Logical Priority of Regeneration to Saving Faith in a Theological *Ordo Salutis*," *DBSJ* 7 (2002): 70.

Deuteronomy 30:6 do we see any indication that Yahweh's sovereign act of circumcising the heart is conditioned upon the will of man to believe. Rather, it is quite the opposite. Yahweh must first circumcise the heart so that the sinner can exercise a will that believes. In Deuteronomy 29:2–4 Moses summons all of Israel and says, "You have seen all that the LORD did before your eyes in the land of Egypt, to Pharaoh and to all his servants and to all his land, the great trials that your eyes saw, the signs, and those great wonders. But to this day the LORD has not given you a heart to understand or eyes to see or ears to hear." Why is it that those in Israel, who saw the many miracles God performed in saving them from Pharaoh, did not believe? Verse 4 gives the answer, "To this day the LORD has not given you a heart to understand or eyes to see or ears to hear." It is remarkable how much Deuteronomy 29 parallels John 10:26. As Israel saw the miracles and failed to hear and see spiritually so also did the Jews in the gospels see the miracles of Jesus and fail to hear and see spiritually. But again, notice the reason Jesus gives as to why they do not believe, "The works that I do in my Father's name bear witness about me, but you do not believe because you are not part of my flock" (John 10:25–26). Like Deuteronomy 29:2–4, the reason they do not see or hear is because God did not give them "a heart to understand or eyes to see or ears to hear." It is not man's choice or will which determines whether he will spiritually have a heart to hear and see but it is God's sovereign choice to give the sinner a heart to hear and see that is the cause and reason for belief.

The concept of a new heart is also illustrated by the prophet Jeremiah, "But this is the covenant that I will make with the house of Israel after those days, declares the Lord: I will put my law within them, and I will write it on their hearts. And I will be their God and they shall be my people" (Jeremiah 31:33; cf. Hebrews 8:10; 10:16). Similarly the Lord says in Jeremiah 32:39–40, "I will give them one heart and one way, that they may fear me forever, for their own good and the good of their children after them. I will make with them an everlasting covenant, that I will not turn away from doing good to them. And I will put the fear of me in their hearts, that they may not turn from me." Unlike Deuteronomy 30:6, in Jeremiah the phrase "circumcise your heart," the heart being "the organ of understanding and will," is not used. Nevertheless, the phrase is used in Jeremiah 4:4 and the concept is present in 30:6 and 32:39–40 for the text does speak of the Lord writing His law on their hearts (in contrast to writing his law on tablets of stone), giving His people one heart, and putting the fear of the Lord in their hearts. Like Deuteronomy, in Jeremiah regeneration is in view. Notice, it is only when God writes His law within, on the heart, and places within a fear of Himself that the sinner can follow after Him. Hamilton states, "Circumcision of the heart does seem to result in the *ability* to love God and live (Deuteronomy 30:6). The spiritual circumcision (circumcised heart and ears) *enables* people to incline to Yahweh."[65] Hamilton points to Jeremiah 6:10 where Yahweh asks, "Who shall I speak to or warn that they might listen? Behold, their ear is uncircumcised, and they are *not able* to pay attention. Behold, the word of Yahweh has become a reproach to them; they do not delight in it." He concludes, "An 'uncircumcised ear' indicates an *inability* to interest oneself in the word of Yahweh."[66] Therefore, Paul can say in Romans 2:29 that what saves is not a mere external, physical circumcision, but an inward, spiritual circumcision that is "by the Spirit, not by the letter." Consequently, "His praise is not from man but from God." Only when God circumcises the heart does a new ability to believe result.

The concept of a circumcised heart in Deuteronomy 30:6 and a new heart in Jeremiah 31:33 is also taught by the prophet Ezekiel. Yahweh again promises a day to come when His people will experience restoration and renewal.

> And I will give them one heart, and a new spirit I will put within them. I will remove the heart of stone from their flesh and give them a heart of flesh, that they may walk in my statutes and keep my rules and obey them. And they shall be my people, and I will be their God. But as for those whose heart goes after their detestable things and their abominations, I will bring their deeds upon their own heads, declares the Lord GOD" (Ezekiel 11:19–21).

> And I will give you a new heart, and a new spirit I will put within you. And I will remove the heart of stone from your flesh and give you a heart of flesh. And I will put my Spirit within you, and cause you to walk in my statutes and be careful to obey my rules (Ezekiel 36:26–27).

Yahweh explains that in order for a sinner to walk in His statutes, keep His rules, and obey His law, He must first remove the dead, cold, lifeless heart of stone and replace it with a heart that is alive, namely, a heart of flesh. Yahweh does not give the sinner a heart of flesh because the sinner obeys but rather the sinner obeys *because* Yahweh surgically implants a heart of flesh. Such an order is indicated at the beginning of 11:20. Yahweh removes the heart of stone and gives them a heart of flesh "that they

---

[65] James M. Hamilton, Jr., *God's Indwelling Presence: The Holy Spirit in the Old and New Testaments*, NAC Studies in Bible and Theology, (Nashville, TN: B&H, 2006), 47.

[66] Ibid.

may" obey (11:21; 36:27).[67] The same causal order is even more apparent in Ezekiel 36 where Yahweh states that He will "cause you to walk in my statutes and be careful to obey my rules" (36:27). Once again, God does not put a new heart and spirit within in reaction to or because of the sinner's faith, but it is God's sovereign act of implanting a new heart, a new spirit, that causes the sinner to turn in faith and obedience.

As in Ezekiel 11:19–21 and 36:26–27 we again see imagery of God taking that which is dead and making it alive in Ezekiel 37. The Lord takes bones that are dead, dry, and sitting in a heap and breathes new life into them. As 37:5 says, "Thus says the Lord GOD to these bones: Behold, I will cause breath to enter you, and you shall live." The Lord prophecies that he will "lay sinews" upon these dead, dry bones and "will cause flesh to come upon you, and cover you with skin, and put breath in you, and you shall live, and you shall know that I am the LORD" (37:6). When Ezekiel begins to prophecy to these dead bones as he was commanded, suddenly the bones rattle and come to life, enveloped with flesh. At the command of the Lord breath comes from the four winds and suddenly "they lived and stood on their feet" (37:10). The Lord interprets for Ezekiel exactly what has happened. The bones represent the whole house of Israel, without hope, spiritually dead, cut off (37:11). However, the breath of the Lord resurrecting these bones is the restoration to new life. When the Lord breathes new spiritual life into His people, the result is that they know that He is the Lord (37:13–14). God's act to breath new life is not conditioned upon the will of the dead. Dead, dry bones are lifeless (cf. Jer 34:17–20) until God breathes new life into them (flesh, senews).

Though the passages so far present a picture of God's monergistic work in regeneration, Arminians will object that the exact opposite is taught in Deuteronomy 10:16, Ezekiel 18:31, and Jeremiah 4:4 where it is the unregenerate sinner who is supposed to circumcise his own heart. As Deuteronomy 10:16 says, "Circumcise therefore the foreskin of your heart, and be no longer stubborn." Likewise, Ezekiel 18:31 says, "Cast away from you all the transgressions that you have committed, and make yourselves a new heart and a new spirit! Why will you die, O house of Israel?" And again Jeremiah 4:4 reads, "Circumcise yourselves to the LORD; remove the foreskin of your hearts, O men of Judah and inhabitants of Jerusalem; lest my wrath go forth like fire, and burn with none to quench it, because of the evil of your deeds." On the surface, these passages could be interpreted to say that the sinner has the ability in and of himself to change his heart.

---

[67] The language used here is so blatantly "causal" in nature that Block says it highlights "divine coercion." Daniel I. Block, *The Book of Ezekiel, Chapters 25–48*, NICOT (1998), 356.

However, it is essential to notice that though Yahweh commands the sinner to circumcise his heart, He never says the sinner is able to do so. The Arminian objects that a command implies ability ("ought implies can"), but as demonstrated already this is a faulty assumption that not only reads into the text but contradicts a multitude of other texts which explicitly say man cannot in any way turn towards God. But we do not even have to turn to other books of the Bible to discover the inability of man. For example, take the apparent tension between Deuteronomy 30:6 and 10:16. In Deuteronomy 30:6 it is the Lord, Yahweh, who must circumcise the heart, a miracle performed by God so that His people would have the ability to love and obey Him. Merrill makes a keen observation,

> This is an obvious reference to the demand of the Shema (Deut 6:4–5), adherence to which was at the very core of the covenant commitment. *This impossible standard* was always understood as the ideal of covenant behavior, *one to be sought but never fully achieved* (c.f. Matt 22:40; Mark 12:33). Here, however, Moses did not command or even exhort his audience to obedience. He promised it as a natural by-product of the renewal of the heart. People can love God with all their heart *only after the heart itself has been radically changed to a Godward direction*.[68]

Notice how Merrill states that Deuteronomy 30:6 is a reference to the Shema and therefore it is an "impossible standard" not because the law is flawed but because man is depraved. Therefore, the command in Deuteronomy 10:16 is also one that is impossible to achieve. Yet, when Moses gives the command in Deuteronomy 10:16 and in 30:6 he reveals that it is not man who fulfills this command but Yahweh Himself. What is impossible for man is made possible by God's sovereign grace. Consequently, as Merrill observes, it is "only after the heart itself has been radically changed to a Godward direction" that sinners can love God with all their heart.

The same can be said of the apparent tension between Jeremiah 4:4 and 31:33/32:39–40. Notice, in 31:33 Yahweh says He will write His law on their hearts. Longman observes that this expression "intends to contrast with the Ten Commandments that were written on tablets of stone."[69] Longman's reference to the Law makes sense when one considers the command of Jeremiah 4:4. The people are to be in conformity with God's commands and therefore they are commanded to circumcise the foreskin of their hearts. And yet, as already seen, it is impossible for them to obey the command because of their slavery to sin. Jeremiah makes such a point in 17:9–10 where the heart is said to be "deceitful above all things" and

---

[68] Merrill, *Deuteronomy*, 389. Emphasis added.
[69] Tremper Longman III, *Jeremiah, Lamentations*, NIBC (2008), 211.

desperately sick."Therefore, the command given in Jeremiah 4:4 is fulfilled in 31:33 and 32:39–40. As Dearman observes, God promises in Jeremiah 24:7 to give sinners a "new heart" which assumes "the fatal fallibility of the 'old' one!"[70] Therefore, it is presupposed "that Israel must make a radical commitment to God but also that God's people will be unable to fulfill that commitment unless He acts decisively to renew and transform them."[71] Dearman insightfully concludes that the command in Jeremiah 4:3–4 "does not assume that a mere act of the will on their part will make everything restored."[72] The law written on their heart is something they were commanded to do but could not do. Therefore, in fulfillment of his own command, Yahweh himself must write it on their heart. Augustine's prayer then is most appropriate, "Give what you command, and command what you will."[73]

Jesus Teaches the New Birth

One of the most well known and important texts on the new birth or regeneration is the encounter Jesus has with Nicodemus in John 3:3–8. Nicodemus begins the dialogue by stating, "Rabbi, we know that you are a teacher come from God, for no one can do these signs that you do unless God is with him" (3:2). It may appear that Jesus avoids answering the assertion made by Nicodemus when He responds, "Truly truly, I say to you, unless one is born again he cannot see the kingdom of God" (3:3). However, Jesus is simply getting to the heart of the matter, directing his attention to how it is one can know God in a saving way. Nicodemus seems to ask his question wanting an answer, namely, who are you Jesus? The answer Jesus gives shows that the only way one can truly know who God is (and therefore who Jesus is) is by being born again. In other words, Nicodemus will never believe Jesus is from God (let alone that Jesus is the Son of God) unless he first receives the new birth from the Spirit. Therefore, rather than Jesus telling Nicodemus "yes, I am from God" He responds by saying that unless one is born by the Spirit he will never understand who Jesus is in a saving way. As Morris and Carson note, it is not by human reasoning but by spiritual rebirth that one comes to understand Jesus.[74]

---

[70] J. Andrew Dearman, *Jeremiah and Lamentations*, NIVAC (2002), 85.

[71] Ibid.

[72] Ibid.

[73] Augustine, *The Confessions, in The Works of Saint Augustine* I/1, ed. John E. Rotelle, trans. Maria Boulding, (New York, NY: New City, 1997), 10.29, 40.

[74] Leon Morris, *The Gospel According to John*, NICNT (1971), 189; Carson, *John*, 187–88. The way Jesus answers Nicodemus has huge implications for how

The phrase "born again" (γεννηθῇ ἄνωθεν) can also be rendered "born from above."[75] Either translation seems to be textually possible in Greek and conveys the message Jesus is communicating. To render the phrase "from above" indicates where this new birth comes from. The second birth is not one of the earth or of the flesh but rather is one that must come from heaven. Nicodemus took the phrase as "born again" or born a second time, as evidenced in how he is perplexed, wondering how a man can enter a second time into his mother's womb (3:4). Therefore, translating the phrase "born again" is appropriate though "born from above" seems to demonstrate the point that Nicodemus misses, namely, this is not a second natural birth but rather a supernatural birth which must be accomplished by God and God alone.

Jesus is insistent that if Nicodemus is not born again he will not enter the kingdom of God.[76] In theological language, Jesus is teaching the necessity of the new birth. The necessity of this new birth leads Jesus to also explain in 3:5–6 exactly what it means to be born again. "Truly, truly, I say to you, unless one is born of water and the Spirit, he cannot enter the kingdom of God. That which is born of the flesh is flesh, and that which is born of the Spirit is spirit." Jesus says that the birth He speaks of is not one of flesh but of the Spirit (v.6). If one is born of the Spirit he is spirit. John's use of flesh (*sarx*) here is not the same as Paul's use of flesh where flesh refers to the sinful, enslaved nature. Rather, John is referring to flesh as physical flesh. In other words, the contrast is not between sinful flesh and spiritual new life but is between physical birth and spiritual birth or new life. Hence, Nicodemus misunderstands the words of Jesus as referring to physical birth. Jesus must clarify for Nicodemus: I am not talking about an earthly birth of human flesh, but of a spiritual birth from above.

Furthermore, this second birth is of "water and the Spirit" (3:5). There has been considerable debate over what Jesus means by "water." The best interpretation of "water" is one that identifies "water" symbolically, as that which cleanses the believer. Water is used to represent the spiritual washing that must take place for one to be regenerated. Such an association of water with cleansing is supported in the OT. As already seen, Yahweh promises in Ezekiel 36:25–27, "I will sprinkle clean water on you, and you shall be clean from all your uncleannesses, and from all your idols I will cleanse you. And I will give you a new heart, and a new spirit I will put

we understand the order of salvation. Unless one is first born again he cannot know Jesus in a saving way, he cannot believe in Jesus in a saving way.

[75] Literally top to bottom. See Köstenberger, *John*, 123.

[76] Notice, in 3:3 Jesus says unless a man is born again he cannot "see" the kingdom of God, while in 3:5 Jesus answers that a man cannot "enter" the kingdom of God. Seeing and entering are therefore synonymous.

within you. And I will remove the heart of stone from your flesh and give you a heart of flesh. And I will put my Spirit within you, and cause you to walk in my statutes and be careful to obey my rules" (cf. Exodus 30:20–21; 40:12; Leviticus 14:8–9; 15:5–27; Numbers 19; 2 Kings 5:10; Psalm 51:2–3; Isaiah 1:16; 32:15–20; 44:3–5; Jeremiah 33:8; Ezekiel 11:10–20; 39:29; Zechariah 13:1; 14:8; Joel 2:28). Water then is co-ordinate with Spirit demonstrating, as in Ezekiel 36, the cleansing, purifying nature of the Spirit in regeneration. Such a washing or cleansing is at the very essence of what it means to be born by the Spirit.[77]

Additionally, Jesus places emphasis (as will the rest of the New Testament writers) on the role of the Spirit in new birth. He who is "born of the Spirit is spirit" (3:6). In other words, those whom the Holy Spirit regenerates are made spiritual. "Spirit" here must refer to the Holy Spirit (3:8; cf. John 1:13; 1 John 2:29; 3:9; 4:7; 5:1, 4, 18), demonstrating that it is a birth of "divine and supernatural character."[78] Such an emphasis on the Spirit does not begin in the New Testament but rather in the promises of the OT. In the context of redemptive history, Yahweh had covenanted with His chosen people Israel. However, unlike Yahweh, Israel was unfaithful, disobeying the law He put in place (Exodus 20), going after the gods of the surrounding nations (Judges 2:11–15). While all of Israel was God's covenant people, not all within Israel believed. As Paul states, not all Israel is Israel (Romans 9:6). Therefore, God made a new covenant in which He promised to give His people a new heart and a new spirit so that all of His people will walk in His ways. Unlike the old covenant, in the new covenant Yahweh will regenerate *all* of those whom He covenants with so that all of them will keep His statutes and rules and obey Him (Ezekiel 11:20). Yahweh declares that He will put His law within them and will write it on their hearts (Jeremiah 31:33). He will circumcise their heart so that they will love the Lord with all of their heart and soul and live (Deuteronomy 30:6; cf. Colossians 2:11–14). He will give them one heart and put "a new spirit" within them, removing their heart of stone and giving them a heart of flesh (Ezekiel 11:19–20). Moreover, He will sprinkle clean water, cleansing His people from all their uncleanness, causing them to turn from idols and follow the true and living God (Ezekiel 36:25).

Before moving into John 3:7–8, it is essential to observe that the language of "birth" in John 3:3–7 precludes the possibility of synergism. The

---

[77] Sinclair Ferguson, *The Holy Spirit, Contours of Christian Theology* (Downers Grove, IL: InterVarsity, 1996), 122. Also, see Thomas R. Schreiner, *New Testament Theology: Magnifying God in Christ* (Grand Rapids, MI: Baker, 2008), 462–63; Köstenberger, *John*, 123–24.

[78] Murray, *Redemption Accomplished and Applied*, 98.

miracle of human birth is a unilateral activity. There is nothing the infant does to be born. The infant does not birth itself. Nor is it the case that birth is conditioned upon the infants will to accept it or not. Likewise, the same is true with spiritual birth. Man is dead in his sins and spiritually in bondage to sin. His only hope is the new birth and yet such a birth is a unilateral, monergistic act of God. Man plays no role whatsoever in the spiritual birthing event. Rather, God acts alone to awaken new life, as demonstrated in the use of the *passive voice* which tells the reader that the recipient of this new birth is absolutely inactive. Carson writes, "Jesus' reply is not framed in terms of what Nicodemus must do to see the kingdom, but in terms of what must happen to him. The point is made both by the nature of the demanded transformation (a man neither begets nor bears himself) and by the passive mood of the verb."[79] Edwin Palmer explains the birth metaphor,

> In birth a baby is completely helpless. He does not make himself. He is made. He is born. There is complete passivity on his part. Obviously a baby could not have said to his parents before he was born, "I determine that I shall now be born." And so it is in the case of a spiritual birth. That which is not yet born cannot say, "I will to be born." That which is dead spiritually cannot say, "I will to live." And that which has not yet been created can never say, "I will to be created." These are manifest impossibilities. Rather, as in the case of a baby, or creation yet to be, or a dead man, spiritual birth, creation, or life comes wholly at the discretion of the Holy Spirit. It is he who does the deciding, and not man. Man is entirely passive. The Holy Spirit is entirely sovereign, regenerating exactly whom he wills. Consequently, John could say that the children of God are "born not of natural descent, nor of human decision or a husband's will, but born of God" (John 1:13).[80]

In John 3:3–7 there is not a hint of indication that the new birth has anything to do with the human will. To the contrary, Jesus is emphasizing, through the image of birth, the passivity and inability of the sinner and the autonomy of God in creating new life. As Packer states, "Infants do not induce, or cooperate in, their own procreation and birth; no more can those who are 'dead in trespasses and sins' prompt the quickening operation of God's Spirit within them (see Ephesians 2:1–10)."[81] This same principle of

---

[79] Carson, *Divine Sovereignty and Human Responsibility*, 80.

[80] Edwin H. Palmer, *The Person and Ministry of the Holy Spirit: The Traditional Calvinistic Perspective* (Grand Rapids, MI: Baker, 1974), 82–83.

[81] J. I. Packer, "Regeneration," in *Evangelical Dictionary of Theology* (Grand Rapids, MI: Baker, 2001), 925.

monergism is again taught by Jesus as He further explains the role of the Spirit in John 3:7–8.

In John 3:7–8 Jesus turns to the sovereignty of the Spirit in regeneration. Already Jesus has indicated that one must be born of water and Spirit (John 3:5), demonstrating that the new birth is effected by the power of the Spirit. Two points demonstrate the sovereignty of the Spirit. First, in 3:1–8 the new birth is described in the passive voice and it is justified to conclude that here we see examples of the divine passive being used. Hamilton explains that "this new birth is not something that people do to or for themselves. Each time the verb *gennaō* appears in John 3:3–8 it is passive (3:3, 4 [2x], 5, 6 [2x], 7, 8). John 1:13 ('born of God') provides clear warrant for seeing these as divine passives. God causes people to experience the new birth from above by the Spirit."[82] Hamilton continues, "The need for new birth is connected to another clear feature in this passage: the stress on human inability to experience God's kingdom apart from this new birth. The word *dunamai* appears five times in 3:2–5 and again in v.9. The new birth is brought about by God, and without it people are unable to see/ enter the kingdom of God."[83] In summary, the sovereignty of the Spirit is demonstrated by both the presence of the divine passive and the emphasis Jesus places on human inability.

Second, the sovereignty of the Spirit is manifested in how Jesus compares the Spirit to the wind. Jesus states, "Do not marvel that I said to you, 'You [*plural*] must be born again.' The wind [*spirit*] blows where it wishes, and you hear its sound, but you do not know where it comes from or where it goes. So it is with everyone who is born of the Spirit." In the Greek the word for Spirit (πνεῦμα) is also wind and likewise the word for wind is also spirit. Jesus is drawing a clear parallel here between wind and Spirit (as made obvious by 3:8), so that when He speaks of one He is speaking of the other.[84] He is comparing the effects of the wind to the effects of the Spirit. It is very important to note that the phrase the "wind blows where it wishes" conveys the sovereignty of the Spirit. The Spirit is not controlled by the human will but works as God pleases to bring about new life. Therefore, a regeneration dependent upon man's will to believe or a regeneration where God and man cooperate is ruled out by this text. The Spirit's role in the new birth is sovereign because, like the wind, He works apart from human control (John 3:8; cf. John 7:37–38).

To conclude John 3, it needs to be said that to reject what Jesus is teaching in these verses about man's passivity and God's sovereignty is no

---

[82] Hamilton, *God's Indwelling Presence*, 130.
[83] Ibid.
[84] Ridderbos, *John*, 129.

light matter. Therefore, to conclude that man in some way cooperates with God in regeneration (synergism) or that man's will (*liberum arbitrium*) in the act of faith is the cause of regeneration, so that conversion causally precedes regeneration, is an assault on the sovereignty of the Holy Spirit and furthermore denies the proper meaning of the biblical imageries used of the Spirit's work in regeneration. John Murray appropriately warns of the seriousness of interpreting Jesus wrongly here:

> It has often been said that we are passive in regeneration. This is a true and proper statement. For it is simply the precipitate of what our Lord has taught us here. We may not like it. We may recoil against it. It may not fit into our way of thinking and it may not accord with the time-worn expressions which are the coin of our evangelism. But if we recoil against it, we do well to remember that this recoil is recoil against Christ. And what shall we answer when we appear before him whose truth we rejected and with whose gospel we tampered? But blessed be God that the gospel of Christ is one of sovereign, efficacious, irresistible regeneration. If it were not the case that in regeneration we are passive, the subjects of an action of which God alone is the agent, there would be no gospel at all. For unless God by sovereign, operative grace had turned our enmity to love and our disbelief to faith we would never yield the response of faith and love.[85]

The New Birth in John's Epistles

Just as the gospel of John teaches that the grace that regenerates is monergistic, preceding man's faith, so also in John's first epistle is the same truth evident. Consider the following, with special attention to the grammatical construction:

> If you know that he is righteous, you may be sure that everyone who practices righteousness *has been* born of him (1 John 2:29).

> No one born of God makes a practice of sinning, for God's seed abides in him, and he cannot keep on sinning because he *has been* born of God (1 John 3:9).

> Beloved, let us love one another, for love is from God, and whoever loves *has been* born of God and knows God (1 John 4:7).

> Everyone who believes that Jesus is the Christ *has been* born of God, and everyone who loves the Father loves whoever has been born of him (1 John 5:1).

---

[85] Murray, *Redemption Accomplished and Applied*, 99.

For everyone who *has been* born of God overcomes the world. And this is the victory that has overcome the world—our faith. Who is it that overcomes the world except the one who believes that Jesus is the Son of God (1 John 5:4)?

We know that everyone who *has been* born of God does not keep on sinning, but he who was born of God protects him and the evil one does not touch him (1 John 5:18).

The grammar in each of these passages is absolutely essential. Beginning with 1 John 5:1, which Piper calls "the clearest text in the New Testament on the relationship between faith and the new birth,"[86] the Greek reads, Πᾶς ὁ πιστεύων ὅτι Ἰησοῦς ἐστιν ὁ Χριστὸς ἐκ τοῦ θεοῦ γεγέννηται, καὶ πᾶς ὁ ἀγαπῶν τὸν γεννήσαντα ἀγαπᾷ [καὶ] τὸν γεγεννημένον ἐξ αὐτοῦ. Notice, "believes" (πιστεύων) in the phrase "Everyone who believes" (or "Everyone believing") is a present active participle in the nominative case, indicating ongoing faith. In contrast, when John says all those believing "*have been* born of him," "have been born" (θεοῦ γεγέννηται) is a perfect passive indicative, meaning that it is an action that has already taken place in the past (it is completed) and has ongoing effects in the present. As Daniel Wallace explains, the perfect speaks "of an event accomplished in the past (in the indicative mood, that is) with results existing afterwards-the perfect speaking of results existing in the present."[87] In 1 John 5:1, the action in the perfect passive indicative (regeneration) precedes and causes the action in the present active participle (faith). The result is clear: God's act of regeneration precedes belief.

As seen above, the use of the perfect in 1 John 5:1 can also be found in 1 John 2:29, 3:9, 4:7, and 5:4. In 1 John 2:29 the Greek reads, ἐὰν εἰδῆτε ὅτι δίκαιός ἐστιν, γινώσκετε ὅτι καὶ πᾶς ὁ ποιῶν τὴν δικαιοσύνην ἐξ αὐτοῦ γεγέννηται. Those who are doing righteousness *have been born of God* (γεγέννηται). The grammar here is parallel to 1 John 5:1. The phrase "*have been* born of him" is a perfect passive indicative (from γεννάω, to beget or bring forth), while the phrase "everyone who practices righteousness" (πᾶς ὁ ποιῶν τὴν δικαιοσύνην) is a present active participle. Again, the perfect here refers to the new birth, an act that has been completed in the past and has continuing results in the present. Practicing righteous (present tense) is what results from the new birth. Or as Stott says, "A person's righteousness is thus the evidence of his new birth, not the cause

---

[86] Piper, *Finally Alive* (Scotland: Christian Focus, 2009), 118; also see 138–39.

[87] Daniel B. Wallace, *Greek Grammar: Beyond the Basics, An Exegetical Syntax of the New Testament* (Grand Rapids, MI: Zondervan, 1996), 572–73.

or condition of it."[88] To interpret 2:29 as if regeneration came after faith would mean that one's own righteousness would precede regeneration. This interpretation would evidently teach works-righteousness.[89]

It must be observed that Arminians find themselves in a number of contradictions at this point. For example, concerning 1 John 2:29 I. Howard Marshall agrees that practicing righteousness is the result of the new birth not the other way around. "What John is trying to stress is that doing what is right is the consequence of spiritual birth; hence if a person does what is right, this is a sign of spiritual birth." And again, "True righteousness (the kind shown by Jesus) is possible only on the basis of spiritual birth."[90] When Marshall comes to 1 John 5:1 he begins as he did in 2:29 by saying, "Faith is thus a sign of the new birth, just as love (4:7) and doing what is right (2:29; 3:9) are also indications that a person has been born of God."[91] Marshall sounds like a Calvinist. It is obvious even to Marshall that in 2:29, 3:9, and 4:7 doing righteousness, avoiding sin, and loving are all the result of the new birth. One would then expect Marshall to say the same about 1 John 5:1. After all, 5:1 has the same grammatical structure as 2:29, 3:9, and 4:7. Moreover, Marshall begins his commentary on 5:1 in this direction when he says "Faith is thus a sign of the new birth," just like love and doing righteousness. However, Marshall immediately qualifies such a statement by saying,

> At the same time, however, faith is a condition of the new birth: "to all who received him, to those who believed in his name, he gave the right to become children of God" (Jn. 1:12). Here, however, John is not trying to show how a person experiences the new birth; his aim is rather to indicate the evidence which shows that a person stands in the continuing relationship of a child to God his Father: that evidence is that he holds to the true faith about Jesus.[92]

Marshall's logic seems to contradict itself. He begins by saying that faith is a sign of the new birth but then he says faith is a condition of the new birth. It is clear that for Marshall, saying faith is a sign of the new birth is not the same as saying that faith is caused by the new birth and only the result of the new birth. For Marshall, regeneration cannot occur without man having faith first. Consequent to regeneration, faith contin-

---

[88] John R. W. Stott, *Letters of John*, TNTC, 19 (1998), 122.

[89] Ware, "Divine Election to Salvation," 19.

[90] I. Howard Marshall, *The Epistles of John*, NICNT (Grand Rapids, MI: Eerdmans, 1978), 169.

[91] Ibid., 226.

[92] Ibid.

ues and so Marshall can simultaneously say faith is the condition of the new birth and yet faith is the sign of the new birth as shown in 1 John 5:1. Two responses are in order. First, Marshall would never apply his exegesis of 5:1 to 2:29 ("everyone who practices righteousness has been born of him"). Why not? Because it would imply works righteousness! If Marshall were to be consistent he would have to apply the same hermeneutic to 2:29 that he does in 5:1 and it would sound like this:

> "Righteousness is thus a sign of the new birth, just as love (4:7) and do-ing what is right (3:9f) are also indications that a person has been born of God. At the same time, however, righteousness is a condition of the new birth..."

Notice how closely this parallels his comment on 5:1,

> Faith is thus a sign of the new birth, just as love (4:7) and doing what is right (2:29; 3:9ff) are also indications that a person has been born of God. At the same time, however, faith is a condition of the new birth..."[93]

It is astonishing that it can be so obvious to Marshall that in 2:29 righ-teousness could never be the condition of regeneration, but in 5:1, a verse with the same grammatical structure, faith can be the condition of regen-eration. In the end, Marshall refuses to apply his same method of exegesis in 2:29, 3:9, and 4:7 to 5:1. Why? Evidently, to do so would mean that faith precedes regeneration and is caused by regeneration, a conclusion unac-ceptable to an Arminian like Marshall. Therefore, instead, Marshall has al-lowed his Arminian presuppositions to alter the plain meaning of the text.

Second, Marshall not only is inconsistent in his exegesis but he com-pletely ignores the grammar of the text in 5:1. Marshall's statements in 2:29, 3:9, and 4:7 seem to demonstrate (though he never says it explicitly) that he has knowledge of the fact that a perfect passive is being used in the phrase "have been born of God." However, when Marshall comes to 5:1 he ignores the grammar altogether and actually interprets 5:1 as faith being the condition of regeneration, which is the exact opposite of what the text says grammatically, namely, that regeneration (perfect passive indicative) results in faith (present active participle). This negligence of the grammati-cal structure is poor exegesis on Marshall's part.

Marshall, however, not only misconstrues the meaning of 1 John 5:1, but he does so by jumping over the plain meaning of 5:1 in order to appeal to John 1:12. John 1:12–13 reads, "But to all who did receive him, who be-lieved in his name, he gave the right to become children of God, who were

---

[93] Marshall, *The Epistles of John*, 226.

born, not of blood nor of the will of the flesh nor of the will of man, but of God." It must be observed that such a move gives the reader the impression that Marshall does not want to deal with what 5:1 actually says on its own terms but rather he wants to allow *his* interpretation of John 1:12 to be the key factor in providing an alternative interpretation to 5:1.

Furthermore, Marshall's appeal to John 1:12 is unfounded precisely because John 1:12–13 actually proves the opposite of what Marshall wants it to say. Marshall believes that John 1:12 proves that faith is the condition of regeneration for the text says that all who received Jesus, who believed in him (faith), God gave the right to become children of God. There are several problems with Marshall's interpretation here. First, Marshall assumes that the phrase "become children of God" is synonymous with "new birth." However, Marshall never shows evidence that this is the case. Why should the reader assume that the phrase "become children of God" is synonymous with the new birth? Why not interpret becoming a child of God as the result of the new birth? Why not interpret such a phrase as referring to adoption, which is produced by the new birth? Indeed, for several reasons I would argue that the phrase "become children of God" is referring to adoption, not regeneration. (1) The phrase "children of God" in John 1:12 is also used by Paul in Romans 8:15–16 to refer to adoption, not regeneration. Paul writes, "For you did not receive the spirit of slavery to fall back into fear, but you have received the Spirit of adoption as sons, by whom we cry, 'Abba! Father!' The Spirit himself bears witness with our spirit that we are children of God" (Rom 8:15–16; cf. Eph 1:5). Paul's language of adoption is again reiterated when he says in Galatians 3:26, "For in Christ Jesus you are all sons of God, through faith" (cf. Gal 4:5). As a consequence to believing (John 1:12) or having faith (Gal 3:26), one is adopted into God's family as a son.[94] (2) Adoption, as Snoeberger observes, is emptied of meaning "if the regeneration has already placed the

---

[94] It is also important to keep in mind that while those who believe are adopted by God here and now, adoption is also a future hope and reality, something which cannot also be said of regeneration, which is a one-time event at initiation. Paul states in Romans 8:23 that we who have the firstfruits of the Spirit groan inwardly as "we wait eagerly for adoption as sons, the redemption of our bodies." Schreiner and Caneday comment, "Here adoptions is said to become ours when our bodies are redeemed, that is, on the last day. We conclude, then, that there is an already-but-not-yet dimension to adoption as well. As Christians we are adopted into God's family, yet we will not experience the consummation of our adoption until the day of the resurrection." Surely the same cannot be said of regeneration. Thomas R. Schreiner and Ardel B. Caneday, *The Race Set Before Us: A Biblical Theology of Perseverance and Assurance* (Downers Grove, IL: InterVarsity, 2001), 68.

believer into the family of God and given him all the privileges of heirs."[95] (3) Many scholars agree that the phrase "become children of God" in John 1:12 is a reference to adoption, not regeneration.[96]

Second, in order to argue that the phrase "become children of God" is referring to the new birth or regeneration, one must take a leap that is not warranted by the text and assume the text reads that one becomes a child of God because he believes. However, the text does not make such a causal correlation in 1:12. As Ware explains,

> Notice that John does not say, 'He gave them the right to be children of God because they believed in His name.' Rather, he merely notes that these two things both happen: they are given the right to be children of God, and they believe in his name. What he does not say in verse 12 is that becoming children of God results from their faith.[97]

In fact, causal language does not come into view until verse 13 which actually prohibits the new birth being conditioned on man's free will, bringing us to the third problem.

Third, we cannot ignore verse 13, which reads, "who were born, not of blood nor of the will of the flesh nor of the will of man, but of God." Why does Marshall not quote verse 13? Could it be that verse 13 actually would prohibit his interpretation of verse 12? Verse 13 actually clarifies and qualifies verse 12 stating, "who were born, not of blood nor of the will of the flesh nor of the will of man, but of God." In other words, being born is in no way due to the "will of man." Since the will of man is involved in faith, there is no way that faith could precede being born again.

To conclude verse 13, John makes it clear that the new birth is *not* conditioned upon man's will, but is completely and only the act of God. What accounts for having the right to be children of God and believing in Jesus is having been born of God. Therefore, when Marshall concludes from verse 12 that regeneration is conditioned upon man's faith he does so in direct conflict with the rest of the sentence in verse 13 where John is clear that the new birth is in no way conditioned upon man.[98]

---

[95] Snoeberger, "Regeneration," 77–78.

[96] Snoeberger, "Regeneration," 78; Carson, *John*, 126; Ridderbos, *John*, 45; John Calvin, *The Gospel According to St. John*, trans. T. H. L. Parker (Grand Rapids, MI: Eerdmans, 1959), 1:17; Murray, *Redemption Accomplished and Applied*, 81, 87, 132–34; Hoekema, *Saved by Grace*, 96, 185–87; Wayne Grudem, *Systematic Theology* (Grand Rapids, MI: Zondervan, 1994), 738; Robert L. Reymond, *A New Systematic Theology of the Christian Faith*, 2nd ed. revised (Nashville, TN: Thomas Nelson, 1998), 759.

[97] Ware, "Divine Election to Salvation," 20.

[98] Such an interpretation is also in tension with what we have already seen

The same grammar and logic in 2:29 applies to 1 John 3:9, "No one born of God [Πᾶς ὁ γεγεννημένος ἐκ τοῦ θεοῦ; perfect passive participle] makes a practice of sinning, for God's seed abides in him, and he cannot keep on sinning [οὐ δύναται ἁμαρτάνειν; present active infinitive] because he *has been* born of God [θεοῦ γεγέννηται; perfect passive indicative]." 1 John 3:9 is very similar to 1 John 5:18, "We know that everyone who has been born of God does not keep on sinning, but he who was born of God protects him, and the evil one does not touch him." In 3:9 and 5:18 the sinner would be expected to not make a practice of sinning so that he may be born again, if the Arminian view is affirmed. The text, however, never warrants this. Instead, the believer is not to make a practice of sinning because he has been born of God and consequently "God's seed abides in him." Once again, like 5:1 and 2:29 we see the same grammatical structure. The perfect verb (has been born of God) is what grounds and results in the present active infinitive (makes a practice of sinning). The point then is that it is because one has been born again that he does not make a practice of sinning.

In 1 John 4:7 we also see the priority of the new birth, "Beloved, let us love one another, for love is from God, and whoever loves has been born of God and knows God" (Ἀγαπητοί, ἀγαπῶμεν ἀλλήλους, ὅτι ἡ ἀγάπη ἐκ τοῦ θεοῦ ἐστιν, καὶ πᾶς ὁ ἀγαπῶν ἐκ τοῦ θεοῦ γεγέννηται καὶ γινώσκει τὸν θεόν.). Loving (ὁ ἀγαπῶν; present active participle) is the result of having been born of God (θεοῦ γεγέννηται; perfect passive indicative). Love is from God and until God regenerates the dead heart, the sinner cannot love God or neighbor. Therefore, "Whoever loves has been born of God and knows God" (4:7). As John states in 4:19, "We love because he first loved us." John does not say, "He loves us because we first loved him." Rather, it is God's love that precedes the sinner's and it is God's love which enables and produces the sinner's faith, evidenced in love for God and neighbor. This same truth is affirmed in 5:1 where John states that not only is belief in Jesus the result of being born of God but so also is love for the Father who has sent his only Son. Again, love for the Father and the Son is caused by the new birth. But notice, 1 John 4:7 not only says that regeneration precedes love but it also precedes saving knowledge of God. John states that "whoever loves has been born of God and *knows* God." "Knows" is not referring to pure cognitive, factual data of God's existence and acts in the world. Rather, "knows," like love, is tied to saving faith. To have saving

---

is true in 1 John 5:1. Carson, interpreting John 1:12, states, "The tenses and the context of 1 John 5:1 strongly argue that faith, like love (1 John 4:8) is the evidence of the new birth, not its cause." Carson, *Divine Sovereignty and Human Responsibility*, 182.

faith in God is to know God personally. To know God is to have saving faith in God. Again, it must be concluded that saving knowledge of God is the result of God regenerating the believer, not the other way around.

Finally, 1 John 5:4 is another text that supports the Reformed view. John states, "For everyone who has been born of God [γεγεννημένον ἐκ τοῦ θεοῦ; perfect passive participle] overcomes the world [νικᾷ τὸν κόσμον; present active indicative]. And this is the victory that has over-come the world—our faith." What is John referring to when he says that we overcome the world? John is clear in the very next sentence: "And this is the victory that has overcome the world—our faith." So it is faith that over-comes the world and John goes on to say that such faith that overcomes is faith that "believes that Jesus is the Son of God." Again, saving faith is the result of being born of God. Just as righteousness, rejecting sin, and lov-ing God are the result of being born of God so also is having faith which overcomes the world. To reverse this order, as Arminians so often do, is to teach works-righteousness. How unorthodox it would be to say that being righteous (2:29), resisting sin (3:9), loving God and neighbor (4:7), having saving knowledge of God (4:7 and 5:1), possessing a faith that overcomes the world (5:4), and abstaining from sin (5:18) all result in regeneration. Though Arminians would never say such a thing, their reading of the text (that faith precedes regeneration) inevitably ends up in such a direction. In contrast, it is the Calvinist who is exegeting the text according to its proper grammatical structure. All of these benefits, faith included, come from the fountain of regeneration, not the other way around. The same principle is evident in 1 John 5:18, "We know that everyone who has been born of God [γεγεννημένος ἐκ τοῦ θεοῦ; perfect passive participle] does not keep on sinning [οὐχ ἁμαρτάνει; present active indicative], but he who was born of God protects him, and the evil one does not touch him." The reason one does not keep on sinning (which is surely a faith involved deed) is because one has already been born again. Reymond states, "Though he does not say so in so many words, it is surely appropriate, because of his earlier pattern of speech in 1 John 3:9, to understand him to mean that the cause behind one's not sinning is God's regenerating activity." Therefore, John's "estab-lished pattern of speech would suggest that he intended to say that God's regenerating activity is the *cause* of one's believing that Jesus is the Christ, and conversely that such faith is the effect of that regenerating work."[99]

In summary, these passages teach that regeneration precedes and brings about the believer's faith. Schreiner makes two observations which have been seen,

---

[99] Reymond, *Systematic Theology*, 709.

First, in every instance the verb "born" (gennaô) is in the perfect tense, denoting an action that precedes the human actions of practicing righteousness, avoiding sin, loving, or believing. Second, no evangelical would say that before we are born again we must practice righteousness, for such a view would teach works-righteousness. Nor would we say that first we avoid sinning, and then are born of God, for such a view would suggest that human works cause us to be born of God. Nor would we say that first we show great love for God, and then he causes us to be born again. No, it is clear that practicing righteousness, avoiding sin, and loving are all the consequences or results of the new birth. But if this is the case, then we must interpret 1 John 5:1 in the same way, for the structure of the verse is the same as we find in the texts about practicing righteousness (1 John 2:29), avoiding sin (1 John 3:9), and loving God (1 John 4:7). It follows, then, that 1 John 5:1 teaches that first God grants us new life and then we believe Jesus is the Christ.[100]

To conclude, these texts in 1 John not only support the Calvinists position regarding the *ordo salutis* but equally exclude the Arminian position.

Brought Forth by God's Will

James also has much to say concerning regeneration. Speaking of what God has done in and to the believer, James states, "Of his own will he brought us forth by the word of truth, that we should be a kind of firstfruits of his creatures." It is important to note two things in this passage. First, "brought us forth" (ἀπεκύησεν) refers to regeneration, as it is a metaphor for spiritual rebirth. As seen with John 3, just as a baby is brought forth or birthed from the womb, so the sinner is brought forth or birthed by the power of God. The phrase "Father of lights" refers to God as creator and giver of all good gifts to men, but the point is that it is this same Father who brought forth the heavenly lights who also, by his will and the power of his Word, brings forth sinners from spiritual death to new life.[101] Similar to creation, James saw his hearers who were trusting in Christ as the firstfruits of the harvest to come.

Second, God brought us forth of "his own will" (βουληθεὶς). The emphatic "his" highlights both the gracious benevolence of God in begetting new life to sinners and the omnipotence of God in doing so by "his own will."[102] James' language here is very similar to Peter's when he says that

[100] Thomas R. Schreiner, "Does Regeneration Necessarily Precede Conversion?" available from http://www.9marks.org/ejournal/does-regeneration-necessarily-precede-conversion; accessed 6 July 2008; Internet.

[101] Dan McCartney, *James*, BECNT (2009), 110.

[102] James B. Adamson, *The Epistle of James*, NICNT (1976), 75–76.

according to God's mercy "he has caused us to be born again" (1 Peter 1:3). James also shares similarities with John who states that those who believe are born not of the will of man but of God (John 1:12–13). It is not man's will or man's cooperation with God's will that effects this new birth. Rather, it is by God's own will that He brings us forth. As Peter Toon states, "James is teaching what John taught: God takes the initiative and causes new life to begin in the soul."[103] Again, no mention is made of man's cooperation with God's grace nor is there any hint by James that God's work of bringing us forth is conditioned upon man's will to believe. To the contrary, James places all of the emphasis on God. It is God's will, not man's, which brings the sinner into new life in order that he should be the firstfruits of God's creatures. Therefore, it is "by His doing you are in Christ Jesus" (1 Corinthians 1:30).

Caused to be Born Again

Peter also places emphasis on God's sovereignty in the new birth.

> Blessed be the God and Father of our Lord Jesus Christ! *According to his great mercy, he has caused us to be born again* [ἀναγεννήσας] to a living hope through the resurrection of Jesus Christ from the dead, to an inheritance that is imperishable, undefiled, and unfading, kept in heaven for you, who by God's power are being guarded through faith for a salvation ready to be revealed in the last time (1 Peter 1:3–5; emphasis added).

Peter uses the language of causation to describe God's merciful yet powerful act of new birth. Several observations are necessary. First, the reason Peter gives as to why God is to be praised is that in his great mercy God caused us to be born again. Peter will use the language of spiritual begetting again in 1 Peter 1:23 where he says that they "have been born again, not of perishable seed but of imperishable, through the living and abiding word of God." Here Peter shows that God the Father takes the initiative in producing spiritual children by his Word. Second, Peter says that this new birth is according to God's great mercy. By definition mercy precludes any possibility of human works or contribution. Believers prior to the new birth are dead in sin and only deserving of God's judgment and wrath. However, as will be seen in Ephesians 2:4–5, God granted mercy to those who have rebelled against him. Third, the image of birth is used and as with John 3:5–6, so also in 1 Peter 1:3–5 such an image precludes any

---

[103] Peter Toon, *Born Again: A Biblical and Theological Study of Regeneration* (Grand Rapids, MI: Baker, 1987), 40.

human contribution. As Schreiner states, "The focus therefore is on God's initiative in producing new life. No one takes any credit for being born. It is something that happens to us."[104] Schreiner's point is demonstrated when Peter states that out of this great mercy God *caused* us to be born again. God causes, creates, brings about, and produces the new birth not on the basis of anything we have done but purely on the basis of his great mercy.

Made Alive with Christ

While Jesus and Peter explain regeneration through the imagery of birth, Paul explains regeneration through the imagery of resurrection from the dead. As Hoekema states, for Paul "regeneration is the fruit of the Spirit's purifying and renewing activity, that it is equivalent to making dead persons alive, that it takes place in union with Christ, and that it means that we now become part of God's wondrous new creation."[105] Paul speaks of God making dead persons alive in Ephesians 2 where he writes,

> And you were dead in the trespasses and sins in which you once walked, following the course of this world, following the prince of the power of the air, the spirit that is now at work in the sons of disobedience— among whom we all once lived in the passions of our flesh, carrying out the desires of the body and the mind, and were by nature children of wrath, like the rest of mankind. But God, being rich in mercy, because of the great love with which he loved us, even when we were dead in our trespasses, made us alive [συνεζωοποίησεν] together with Christ—by grace you have been saved— and raised us up with him and seated us with him in the heavenly places in Christ Jesus, so that in the coming ages he might show the immeasurable riches of his grace in kindness toward us in Christ Jesus (Ephesians 2:1–7).

In Ephesians 2 we see a powerful picture of what takes place in regeneration. The sinner is dead but God makes him alive. The sinner is in the grave but God resurrects him from the dead. Notice, contrary to Arminianism, there is no contingency here or intermediate stage where God begins to make a sinner alive but whether or not God can finally do so is dependent upon the sinner's decision. Rather, the transition is immediate, instantaneous, and unilateral as the sinner is at one moment dead and the next moment alive (Ephesians 2:10). The situation is comparable with the resurrection of Christ. Christ was dead but God in great power resurrected

---

[104] Schreiner, *1, 2 Peter, Jude*, 61.
[105] Hoekema, *Saved by Grace*, 99.

Him bodily from the grave (Ephesians 1:19–20).[106] Or consider Lazarus who was dead, rotting in the tomb for days, and suddenly, at the command of Christ, he is resurrected and walks out of the tomb alive (John 11).[107] Reymond concludes, "The conclusion cannot be avoided that God's regenerating work must causally precede a man's faith response to God's summons to faith."[108]

Moreover, the sinner who is "made alive" has a situation not only comparable to Christ but the new life he receives is actually found in and with Christ. Paul states that God made us alive *together with Christ* and seated us up with Christ in the heavenly places (2:6), so that in the coming ages we would know the immeasurable riches of his grace in kindness toward us *in Christ Jesus* (2:7). Peter O'Brien explains,

> Paul's readers have come to life with Christ, who was dead and rose again; their new life, then, is a sharing in the new life which he received when he rose from the dead. It is only in union with him that death is vanquished and new life, an integral part of God's new creation, received. Because the believer's previous condition has been spoken of as a state of death (vv. 1, 5), there is no direct reference to Christ's death or to the believer's participation in it. Instead, the sharp contrast between our former condition outside of Christ and being made alive with him is presented.[109]

It is necessary, therefore, to identify being made alive with the resurrection of Christ. As Ferguson states, "Regeneration is causally rooted in the resurrection of Christ (1 Pet. 1:3). Like produces like; our regeneration is the fruit of Christ's resurrection."[110] It is Christ's resurrection which is the very basis of the sinner's coming to life with Christ, as is further demonstrated in 2:6 where the sinner is raised up and seated in Christ. Our spiritual resurrection to new life is made explicit by what Paul contrasts it to, namely, deadness in trespasses and sins and bondage to the world ("following the course of this world," 2:2), Satan ("following the prince of the power of the air," 2:2), and the flesh ("once lived in the passions of our flesh, carrying out the desires of the body and the mind," 2:3). Like the rest of mankind we were "by nature children of wrath" (2:3). Therefore, being made alive, as O'Brien states, implies not only forgiveness but "liberation from these tyrannical forces."[111] Paul's words here in Ephesians 2 closely

---

[106] Thielman, *Ephesians*, 134.

[107] Boettner, *The Reformed Doctrine of Predestination*, 166.

[108] Reymond, *Systematic Theology*, 709.

[109] Peter T. O'Brien, *The Letter to the Ephesians*, PNTC (1999), 167.

[110] Ferguson, *Holy Spirit*, 119.

[111] O'Brien, *The Letter to the Ephesians*, 167.

parallel his words in Colossians, "And you, who were dead in your trespasses and the uncircumcision of your flesh, God made alive together with him, having forgiven us all our trespasses" (2:13; cf. Romans 6:11).

Finally, Paul also states that being made alive together with Christ is by grace ("by grace you have been saved"). O'Brien comments, "He draws attention to a mighty rescue which arose out of God's gracious initiative, which had already been accomplished in Christ, and which has abiding consequences for them: *it is by grace you have been saved*."[112] As seen throughout Paul's epistles, grace stands opposed to merit or any contribution on the part of man (Ephesians 2:8–10). Grace is God's favor towards sinners in spite of what they deserve (Romans 3:21–26; 4:4; 5:15). The word "save" ("by grace you have been saved") can and is many times used to refer to an eschatological reality, the deliverance from God's wrath and final judgment. Thielman observes that in some passages Paul can "describe it [saved] as an ongoing event in the present (1 Cor. 1:18; 15:2; 2 Cor. 2:15) and say, 'Now is the day of salvation' (2 Cor. 6:2; cf. Isa. 39:8; Best 1998:602)." But Paul "normally refers to it as something believers will experience in the future, presumably at the final day (1 Thess. 2:16; 1 Cor. 3:15; 5:5; 10:33; Rom. 5:9–10; 9:27; 10:9; 11:26)."[113] However, as O'Brien explains, the case differs in Ephesians 2 for "saved" refers specifically to what "has already been accomplished and experienced." It describes a "rescue from death, wrath, and bondage and a transfer into the new dominion with its manifold blessings. The periphrastic perfect construction draws attention to the resulting state of salvation."[114] Paul is referring to salvation as something that is "emphatically present for believers" even though the "use of the perfect tense in Eph. 2:5, 8 for salvation is unusual."[115] Paul does draw our attention to the future eschatological consequences of this salvation in verse 7 (being seated with Christ in the coming age). However, in verses 5–6 Paul shows that being saved by grace means that God making us alive together with Christ is also by grace. Therefore, being made alive or regenerated is neither an act that is accomplished by man's works-righteousness nor an act conditioned upon man's willful cooperation. Rather, being made alive is *by grace and by grace alone*, meaning that it is purely by God's initiative, prerogative, and power that the sinner is resurrected from spiritual death.[116] Therefore, it will not do to say with the Arminian that God's grace is a gift to be accepted or resisted. Yes, God's

---

[112] Ibid., 168.
[113] Thielman, *Ephesians*, 135.
[114] O'Brien, *The Letter to the Ephesians*, 169.
[115] Thielman, *Ephesians*, 135.
[116] Schreiner, *Paul*, 246.

grace is a gift, but more than that it is a powerful gift that actually and effectually accomplishes new life as God intends.

Another passage of Scripture which is a powerful example of monergistic regeneration is Colossians 2:11–14 where Paul writes to the Colossians,

> In him [Christ] also you were circumcised with a circumcision made without [human] hands, by putting off the body of the flesh by the circumcision of Christ, having been buried with him in baptism, in which you were also raised with him through faith in the powerful working of God, who raised him from the dead. And you, who were dead in your trespasses and the uncircumcision of your flesh, God made alive [συνεζωοποίησεν] together with him, having forgiven us all our trespasses, by canceling the record of debt that stood against us with its legal demands. This he set aside, nailing it to the cross.

In verse 11 Paul presents the metaphor of circumcision, a clear reference to the Old Testament where Moses and the prophets Jeremiah and Ezekiel call for a "circumcision of the heart" (Deuteronomy 10:16; 30:6; Jeremiah 4:4; Ezekiel 44:7; cf. Romans 2:17). As Moo states, "Paul takes up this concept, claiming that it is the circumcision of the heart, performed by the Spirit—not physical circumcision as such—that marks a person as belonging to the people of God (Rom. 2:28–29). It is this nonphysical circumcision that Paul has in mind here, as the qualification 'not performed by human hands' suggests."[117] The contrast is not a circumcision by human hands but a circumcision by the Spirit on the heart as that which is needed for a person to experience new life in Christ.

As already noted in our commentary on Deuteronomy and Jeremiah, the metaphor of circumcision itself communicates the monergistic work of God. Spiritual circumcision is an act performed upon the recipient by God, apart from the sinner's cooperation. God and God alone circumcises the heart and then and only then can the sinner trust in Christ. As a result of being circumcised spiritually, "No longer are we dominated by those 'powers' of the old era, sin, death, and the flesh; we are now ruled by righteousness, life, grace, and the Spirit (see esp. Rom. 5:12–8:17; 12:1–2; Gal. 1:4; 5:14–6:2)."[118] It is only when spiritual circumcision takes place that the sinner is set free from the flesh. As Paul states in verse 12, we have been "raised with him through faith in the powerful working of God, who raised him from the dead." Paul transitions from the metaphor of circumcision to the metaphor of resurrection. Notice the parallel Paul makes in

---

[117] Moo, *The Letters to the Colossians and to Philemon*, 197.
[118] Ibid., 201.

verses 12–13 between God raising Christ from the dead and God spiritually raising the sinner from the dead. Paul calls this act the "powerful work of God" and rightly so for just as God takes a dead corpse and brings it to life so also does He take a dead soul and breathes new spiritual life into it. As O'Brien notes, the giving of this new life is an "act of pure grace" and is in no way conditioned on man.[119]

The Washing of Regeneration

Paul's words in Colossians show many similarities to his words in Titus,

> For we ourselves were once foolish, disobedient, led astray, slaves to various passions and pleasures, passing our days in malice and envy, hated by others and hating one another. But when the goodness and loving kindness of God our Savior appeared, he saved us, not because of works done by us in righteousness, but according to his own mercy, by the washing of regeneration [λουτροῦ παλιγγενεσίας] and renewal of the Holy Spirit, whom he poured out on us richly through Jesus Christ our Savior, so that being justified by his grace we might become heirs according to the hope of eternal life (Titus 3:3–7).

Like Ephesians 2 and Colossians 2, Paul begins in Titus 3 with man's depravity and slavery to sin, once again emphasizing man's deadness to sin and spiritual inability. Prior to the washing of regeneration man was a slave to evil desires (cf. Titus 2:12; 1 Timothy 6:9), spending his time in malice, envy, and hatred. However, out of his love and goodness "God our Savior" saved us. How exactly did He save us? Not by our own works of righteousness but purely according to His "own mercy." Therefore, according to Paul, salvation is unconditional. Such mercy is made effective by the power of the Holy Spirit who washes the sinner clean as Paul says "by the washing of regeneration [λουτροῦ παλιγγενεσίας] and renewal of the Holy Spirit" (3:5; cf. 2:14; 3:4–5). The very purpose of Christ's redeeming work is for the Spirit to purify a people unto God.

Two observations can be made. First, Paul's two prepositional phrases provide the basis for God's redemption of sinners, the first of which dismisses any "contribution on our part" and the second of which is an "equally strong affirmation that salvation is solely based on God's mercy."[120] Therefore, works-righteousness or works plus faith is clearly eliminated by Paul (Romans 3:21–28; 4:2–6; 9:11; Galatians 2:16; Ephesians

---

[119] Peter T. O'Brien, *Colossians, Philemon*, WBC, vol. 44 (1982), 123.
[120] George W. Knight III, *The Pastoral Epistles*, NIGTC (1992), 340.

2:8–9; Philippians 3:9; 2 Timothy 1:9; cf. Exodus 34:6–7; Psalm 78:38; 86:15). Second, one does not escape the unconditionality of this passage by arguing that while one is saved by faith alone, not works, one must co-operate with God's grace in order to receive the washing of regeneration. This is the Arminian argument and it still contradicts the point Paul is making, namely, that man can contribute absolutely nothing whatsoever to God's work, including the washing of regeneration. To the contrary, man is passive in the washing of regeneration. Such a point is further proven by the language Paul uses for regeneration. Paul refers to regeneration as a "washing" which is accomplished by the Spirit who renews. Paul's language here parallels 1 Corinthians 6:11, where Paul, much like Titus 3:3–7, begins with a long list of the types of depravity the believer once walked in, but then says such were some of you, "But you were washed, you were sanctified, you were justified in the name of the Lord Jesus Christ and by the Spirit of our God." Notice, not only does Paul use the same metaphor of being "washed" to refer to the change and inner renewal or cleansing that must take place, but he once again ties the washing of regeneration to the agency of the Spirit. Paul's union of regeneration and Spirit both in Titus 3:3–7 and 1 Corinthians 6:11 utilizes the New Testament language of Ezekiel 36:25–27 (also used by Jesus in John 3:5), "I will sprinkle clean water on you, and you shall be clean from all your uncleannesses, and from all your idols I will cleanse you" (36:25). God, through Ezekiel, goes on to say in 36:26–27 that He will give them a new heart, putting His Spirit within, and cause them to walk in His ways. As Towner recognizes, the Spirit-enabled doing of the law in Ezekiel cannot be far from Paul's mind in Titus 3.[121] Paul, like Ezekiel, is emphasizing the power of the Spirit to wash or regenerate the sinner, causing him to walk in obedience and new life.

As already demonstrated, Ezekiel 36 and John 3 both attribute to the Spirit the sovereign work of regeneration, which is always monergistic. Paul is no different. As demonstrated already in Ephesians 2:5 and Colossians 2:11–14 so also in Titus 3, Paul connects the washing of regeneration with the Spirit who blows wherever He wills, quickening sinners from death to new life. The difference in Titus 3 is that the metaphor has changed slightly from regeneration as birth (John 3:5) or the resurrection from death to new life (Ephesians 2:5; Colossians 2:13) or circumcision (Colossians 2:14–15), to the washing of the dirty and stained sinner. Yet, though the metaphor shifts, the message remains the same.

---

[121] Philip H. Towner, *The Letters to Timothy and Titus*, NICNT (2006), 774.

Let Light Shine out of Darkness

Another passage which serves to complement what has been seen so far is 2 Corinthians 4:3–6 where we read that God has shone in the hearts of sinners "to give the light of the knowledge of the glory of God in the face of Jesus Christ." Here we see an example of the revealing of the Son to those who are veiled and blinded. However, it is not a mere revelation that takes place but the knowledge Paul speaks of is actually a "light" that pierces into the heart and like creation brings into existence a heart that has been radically changed. To understand this miracle we need to look at the entire passage,

> And even if our gospel is veiled, it is veiled only to those who are perishing. In their case the god of this world has blinded the minds of the unbelievers, to keep them from seeing the light of the gospel of the glory of Christ, who is the image of God. For what we proclaim is not ourselves, but Jesus Christ as Lord, with ourselves as your servants for Jesus' sake. For God, who said, "Let light shine out of darkness," has shone in our hearts to give the light of the knowledge of the glory of God in the face of Jesus Christ (2 Corinthians 4:3–6).

The unbeliever is veiled to the truth of the gospel, blinded by the god of the world so that he cannot see "the light" of the gospel of the glory of Christ. As one who is blind, the sinner is in darkness, unable to see, and without the spiritual light that comes from beholding Christ in faith.

Notice, it is not the case here that man is blinded and veiled but not to the extent that he cannot see or come to the light of Christ (i.e., Semi-Pelagianism). Schreiner explains, "Unbelievers are not portrayed as neutral, having ability to pursue or reject God. Rather, they are held in captivity under the devil's power, prevented by him from seeing the glory of Christ."[122] Nor is it the case that man was blinded and veiled but God provided a prevenient grace so that every man can, if he wills to, cooperate and come to the light (classic Arminianism). Neither of these options is present in the text. To the contrary, God acts in a direct, unilateral, unconditional, monergistic manner, creating sight where there was *only* blindness. As Paul says in verse 6, "For God, who said, 'Let light shine out of darkness,' has shone in our hearts to give the light of the knowledge of the glory of God in the face of Jesus Christ." Hafemann explains that "this shining in the heart most naturally refers to God's work of changing the moral disposition and spiritual condition of his people."[123] Paul is referring to Genesis

---

[122] Schreiner, *Paul*, 138.
[123] Scott J. Hafemann, *2 Corinthians*, NIVAC (2000), 180.

1:3 where God creates light when "darkness was over the face of the deep" (Genesis 1:2). Though darkness hovered over the face of the deep so also did the Spirit, hovering over the face of the waters (Genesis 1:2b), so that at the very word light would be created. As Genesis 1:3–4 states, "And God said, 'Let there be light,' and there was light. And God saw that the light was good. And God separated the light from the darkness." Paul, speaking from personal experience, uses this language and miraculous event to describe, in parallel fashion, what takes place when God transforms a sinner. Just as God calls light into being where there is only darkness, so also God calls spiritual light (the light of the glory of his own Son) into being where there is only spiritual darkness. The language of calling light out of darkness resembles the biblical language of regeneration as an act that brings about a new creation (2 Corinthians 5:17; Galatians 6:15). Frame explains, "Similarly with new creation. Creation is 'out of nothing,' as we saw. Before creation, there was nothing. Nothing can't produce anything. Reality all comes by the creative act of God. The same is true of resurrection. Before resurrection there is death. Death can't produce life. Only God can. So, in the new birth we are passive."[124] Such a divine fiat is not the light of prevenient grace as the Arminian would have it because (1) the light shines directly into the heart and (2) immediately moves the sinner from darkness to light (salvation) without any conditionality or cooperation. The state described here is not an "intermediate state" where man has been enlightened by prevenient grace but now it is up to him to believe resulting in final regeneration. To the contrary, Paul says that man is in darkness and when God shines light into the heart it is the light of the knowledge of the glory of God in the face of Jesus Christ. In other words, the light results in a saving knowledge of Christ in the very heart of man, something that is not true of all people everywhere who receive prevenient grace.

Struck Down by Grace and an Opened Heart

Most passages on regeneration are didactic in nature. However, there are other passages on regeneration that occur within the biblical narrative. Two passages in particular can be found in the book of Acts. Arminians often complain and object to the Calvinist doctrine of monergism because such a view of grace does not respect man's libertarian freedom to choose (or refuse) to believe but works in a way that irresistibly overpowers man. Essentially, the Arminian has compromised the power and efficacy of God's grace for the sake of man's free will. However, there is perhaps no text which demonstrates how erroneous the Arminian view is than

---

[124] Frame, *Salvation Belongs to the Lord*, 186.

Acts 9:3–19. Luke tells us in Acts 8 of Saul, a Hebrew of Hebrews and as to the law, a Pharisee (Philippians 3:5), who was ravaging the church of Jesus Christ, persecuting believers of the Way. Saul was "breathing threats and murder against the disciples of the Lord" (9:1) and after going to the high priest Saul received permission to arrest those in Damascus who belonged to the Way and bring them back to Jerusalem (9:2). But as he went on his way, Christ himself struck Saul down with light from heaven, blinding him. Suddenly a voice said to him, "Saul, Saul, why are you persecuting me?" And he said, "Who are you, Lord?" And the voice said, "I am Jesus, whom you are persecuting. But rise and enter the city, and you will be told what you are to do." Saul was instantly changed. One moment he was persecuting Christians, the next he was a Christian! Why is it that Saul changed from a murderer of God's people and hater of Christ to a man who suddenly believed in the very Christ he was persecuting? If Arminianism is to be consistent, it would have to say that ultimately it was Saul's will to believe that resulted in a changed heart. However, Luke's explanation of what took place on the Damascus road is the exact opposite. Paul was struck down by the Lord himself and the light of Christ pierced the very center of Saul's being, asking him why he continued to persecute those who belonged to the living Savior. Such an encounter with the resurrected Christ turned Saul's heart of stone into a heart of flesh.

Moreover, Luke goes on to explain that the Lord appeared to Ananias in a dream telling him to go to Saul. Ananias, naturally afraid, reminds the Lord that this is the man that has done much evil to the saints in Jerusalem (Acts 9:13–14). Notice how the Lord responds, "Go, for he is a chosen instrument of mine to carry my name before the Gentiles and kings and the children of Israel. For I will show him how much he must suffer for the sake of my name" (Acts 9:15–16). Saul, prior to the Damascus road, was already chosen by God. In other words, just as we saw was the case in Acts 13:48, so also in Acts 9 is it the case that it is God's sovereign choice that resulted in Saul's regeneration to new life. Saul was determined by God to believe and when it came time God violently struck Saul down and radically changed his understanding of Christ.

Finally, lest one conclude that effectual grace in Paul's conversion was unique, one should take heed of the fact that Paul saw his effectual calling and regeneration to be paradigmatic for all believers in Christ (Galatians 1:15–16; 1 Timothy 1:16).[125] Before Paul was born God determined to call him at the proper time (Galatians 1:15). When that time came God effectively revealed his Son to him. In other words, the sovereign grace seen in

[125] Schreiner, *Paul*, 241–42.

Paul's calling and regeneration were only a foretaste of the work God was about to do in other elect sinners as well.

A second passage which also reveals the monergistic nature of regeneration is Acts 16:13–15 where Paul, Silas, and Timothy are traveling, encouraging the churches. Suddenly, Paul receives a vision at night where a man of Macedonia was calling him to Macedonia (Acts 16:9). Paul concluded that God had called them to preach the gospel to those in Macedonia who needed help (16:10). One Sabbath, they went to speak to the women by the riverside. One of these women was named Lydia and the "Lord opened her heart to pay attention to what was said by Paul." Lydia was then baptized along with her household. Why is it that Lydia believed and was baptized? Answer: The Lord opened her heart. Again, the order in the text is telling. The Lord does not open Lydia's heart because she believed, as the Arminian view must have it. Rather, the text says the exact opposite: Lydia believed the gospel message because the Lord opened her heart. Once again, Lydia is a clear example of the Lord's monergistic way of opening a sinner's heart to believe.

Conclusion

It has been a common practice among evangelical traditions in the past to say "you must be born again" in such a way that it is equivalent to the command to repent and trust in Christ.[126] However, as Ferguson explains, these evangelicals wrongly assume that the new birth "is something we must do." "But in the New Testament new birth is something God gives. The point of the metaphor lies in the fact that the new birth is *not* something we can do."[127] As seen above, the new birth is not a work conditioned on our will, but rather any spiritual activity by our will is conditioned upon God's sovereign decision to grant us new life by the Spirit.

A Common Objection to Regeneration Preceding Conversion

This chapter has argued from a variety of biblical texts that God's special call is effectual, regeneration is monergistic, and therefore it follows that effectual calling and regeneration precede conversion (faith and repentance) in the *ordo salutis*. As The Baptist Faith and Message states,

---

[126] Billy Graham, *How To Be Born Again* (Waco, TX: Word, 1977), 150, 152, 158, 168. Also, see idem, *The World Aflame* (Minneapolis: Billy Graham Evangelistic Association, 1967), 134.

[127] Sinclair Ferguson, *The Christian Life: A Doctrinal Introduction* (Edinburgh: Banner of Truth, 1981), 49.

regeneration "is a change of heart wrought by the Holy Spirit through conviction of sin, *to which the sinner responds* in repentance toward God and faith in the Lord Jesus Christ" (article IV; emphasis added). While much more could be said in making the case for monergism—for example, consider the many passages demonstrating that faith and repentance are *effectual* gifts from God (Acts 13:48; Ephesians 2:8–10; Philippians 1:29–30; 2 Peter 1:1; 2 Timothy 2:24–26; Acts 5:31; 11:18;)—it is essential to answer a popular objection, namely, that there are texts in Scripture that justify conversion preceding regeneration.

Lemke and Keathley have argued that regeneration is conditioned upon man's will in conversion. Their Arminian argumentation appeals to three types of passages which, in their view, are determinative for the priority of conversion to regeneration.[128]

1. If one believes then he will receive "eternal life" (John 3:16, 36; 5:24; 6:54, 57; 11:25; 20:31).

2. If one believes then he will receive the Holy Spirit (John 7:38–39; Acts 2:38; Galatians 3:13; 4:6; Ephesians 1:13).

3. If one believes then he will be "saved" (Mark 16:16; Acts 16:31; Romans 1:16; 10:9–10; 1 Corinthians 1:21).

Receiving eternal life, receiving the Spirit, and being "saved" are all equated with regeneration. Therefore, it is argued that since these texts say belief results in eternal life, receiving the Spirit, and being "saved," it must follow that faith precedes regeneration. But are Arminians like Lemke and Keathley correctly interpreting these passages? Upon closer examination, the answer must be no.[129]

Eternal Life

First, there are several passages where believing results in receiving "eternal life." For example, in John 3:14–15 Jesus says that as the Son of Man he must be lifted up, so that whoever believes in Him may have "eternal life." Lemke and Keathley take "eternal life" to mean "regeneration."

---

[128] Lemke, "A Biblical and Theological Critique of Irresistible Grace," 134–40; Keathley, *Salvation and Sovereignty*, 119–23.

[129] In Barrett, "Reclaiming Monergism," chapter 7, I apply a similar critique to the modified view of Millard J. Erickson, *Christian Theology*, 2nd ed. (Grand Rapids, MI: Baker, 2004), 941ff; Gordon R. Lewis and Bruce A. Demarest, *Integrative Theology* (Grand Rapids, MI: Zondervan, 1994), 3:57ff.

Therefore, regeneration (eternal life) follows belief. Lemke and Keathley make the same argument with other passages as well (John 3:16, 36; 5:24; 6:54, 57; 11:25; 20:31). However, equating "eternal life" with regeneration is a case of eisegesis. Jesus is not describing the order of conversion and regeneration, but rather He is comparing "perishing" with living eternally in the age to come as a consequence of faith in Christ here and now. Commenting on John 3:15, Leon Morris defines Jesus' use of eternal life as follows:

> The word rendered "eternal" (always used in this Gospel of life) basically means "pertaining to an age". The Jews divided time into the present age and the age to come, but the adjective referred to life in the coming age, not the present one. "Eternal life" thus means "the life proper to the age to come". It is an eschatological conception (cf. 6:40, 54).[130]

Eternal life is an eschatological concept. Jesus demonstrates this when He says in Mark 10:30 that it is "in the age to come" that one receives "eternal life." As Schreiner and Caneday argue, the phrase "eternal life" is not only a present reality but an eschatological reality and "by definition is life of the age to come."[131] In Scripture, eternal life is said not only to be received in the present (John 5:24; 6:47, 54; 1 John 5:11–13) but to be received in the future (Mark 10:17, 29–30; Romans 2:6–7; Galatians 6:8; 1 Timothy 6:19; Titus 1:2; 3:7; James 1:12; Revelation 2:10). In other words, unlike regeneration, which is a one time instantaneous act that occurs at initiation, eternal life is an eschatological hope that pervades into the present but ultimately is received in the life to come. Therefore, Lemke and Keathley are simply in error to interpret eternal life as specifically referring to the act of regeneration.

Moreover, as Snoeberger observes, in many of these passages cited, life is said not only to follow belief but justification (Titus 3:7), sanctification (Romans 6:22), perseverance (Romans 2:7; Jude 21), and even physical death (2 Corinthians 5:4). "With this in view, the 'life' described in these passages cannot mean regeneration."[132] The point is made clear when one examines other passages (which Lemke and Keathley never mention) that use the phrase eternal life to refer to a gift to be received in the age to come (Mark 10:17, 29–30; Romans 2:6–7, 23; Galatians 6:8; 1 Timothy 6:19; Titus 1:2; 3:7; James 1:12; Revelation 2:10). Notice how peculiar it sounds if we equate eternal life in these passages with regeneration. For example,

---

[130] Morris, *John*, 227. Also see Frank Thielman, *Theology of the New Testament* (Grand Rapids, MI: Zondervan, 2005), 172.

[131] Schreiner and Caneday, *The Race Set Before Us*, 65, 66–67.

[132] Snoeberger, "The Logical Priority of Regeneration," 64.

Jesus, responding to the rich young ruler would state, "Truly, I say to you, there is no one who has left house or brothers... for my sake and for the gospel, who will not receive a hundredfold now in this time... and in the age to come *regeneration* (eternal life)" (Mark 10:29–30). Likewise, Paul would state, "He will render to each one according to his works: to those who by patience in well-doing seek for glory and honor and immortality, he will give *regeneration* (eternal life)" (Romans 2:6–7). Notice, if Lemke and Keathley are right in equating regeneration with eternal life then in Romans 2:6–7 one must do works to be regenerated. The same would apply in passages like James 1:12 and Revelation 2:10. Surely Lemke and Keathley do not want to affirm works-righteousness, but their logic, if applied consistently, inevitably leads to this.

Finally, the flaw in equating regeneration with eternal life is most evident in Titus 3:5–7, "he saved us, not because of works done by us in righteousness, but according to his own mercy, by the washing of regeneration and renewal of the Holy Spirit, whom he poured out on us richly through Jesus Christ our Savior, so that being justified by his grace we might become heirs according to the hope of eternal life." How can regeneration be equated with eternal life when in Titus 3:5 it is regeneration that is said to lead to the hope of eternal life? As Snoeberger writes, "Paul states unequivocally that regeneration must occur in order that (ἵνα) eternal life may result. It is obvious that this 'life' is not regeneration, but the eschatological experience of 'life that truly is life' (1 Tim 6:19)."[133]

Holy Spirit

Second, Lemke and Keathley also enlist a number of passages that make receiving the Holy Spirit contingent upon man's initial faith (John 7:38–39; Acts 2:38; Galatians 3:13; 4:6; Ephesians 1:13). Like eternal life, the reception of the Spirit in these passages is equated with regeneration so that belief must precede regeneration. Consider Acts 2:38 where Peter says, "Repent and be baptized every one of you in the name of Jesus Christ for the forgiveness of your sins, and you will receive the gift of the Holy Spirit." The gift of the Holy Spirit, it is argued, refers to regeneration, and repentance must come first before such a gift can be received. Or consider what Jesus says in John 7:38, "Whoever believes in me, as the Scripture has said, 'Out of his heart will flow rivers of living water.'" John interprets, "Now this he said about the Spirit, whom those who believed in him were to receive, for as yet the Spirit had not been given, because Jesus was not yet glorified" (7:39). Lemke and Keathley conclude from passages like

[133] Ibid., 76–77.

these that belief is the condition for the reception of the Spirit, which they believe is referring to regeneration.

However, like we saw with "eternal life," such an argument is reductionistic for two reasons. (1) No reason or explanation is given as to why one should equate the reception of the Spirit with regeneration. Why not interpret the reception of the Spirit as *the result* of regeneration? Or why should it refer to regeneration at all? Why not to conversion, adoption, justification, indwelling, or union with Christ? Or why not interpret eternal life as distinct from all of them? (2) To the contrary, these passages are best interpreted as meaning that one receives the indwelling of the Spirit at conversion. As James Hamilton has demonstrated at great length, regeneration and indwelling by the Spirit are not to be equated nor are they identical but are distinct events.[134] If they are not distinct then it is very difficult to make sense out of John 7:38–39, "Whoever believes in me, as the Scripture has said, 'Out of his heart will flow rivers of living water.' Now this he said about the Spirit, *whom those who believed in him were to receive, for as yet the Spirit had not been given*, because Jesus was not yet glorified" (emphasis added). Working his way through John's gospel Hamilton explains,

> The Gospel of John has been clear to this point that no one is able to come to Jesus unless the Father draws him (6:44, 65), and that 'everyone who does sin is a slave to sin' (8:34). If the disciples can love Jesus and keep His commandments, it is because they have been drawn to Jesus by the Father and freed from sin by the Son (8:36). Many assume that enabling an individual to believe is equivalent to an individual's reception of the indwelling Spirit [See the stress on ability and inability in John 3:1–12. A form of the word "can" or "able" [δύναμαι] occurs six times there.] But John 7:39 speaks of people who had been enabled to believe in Jesus but had not yet received the Spirit. Similarly in this passage the disciples are assumed to be able to love and obey Jesus before they receive the Spirit. The grammatical connection between John 14:15 and 16 demonstrates the need to recognize that regeneration and indwelling are separate ministries of the Spirit. The disciples are able to love Jesus because they have been regenerated, though they are yet to receive the Spirit. If regeneration and indwelling are not separated, this text becomes very difficult to interpret because of its grammar.[135]

[134] Hamilton, *God's Indwelling Presence*, 127–59.

[135] "Jesus tells the disciples in John 14:15–17 that the Spirit will be given to those who love Him. Their ability to love Jesus comes from the enabling new birth by the Spirit (John 3:3–8). This regeneration then manifests itself in love for Jesus, which results in obedience. Thus John 14:15–17 fits with John 7:39, where those who have believed (i.e., those who have been born again) are described as those who are about to receive the Spirit." Ibid., 75.

A permanent reception or indwelling of the Spirit by all of God's covenant people is a reality of the new covenant. In the old covenant God's presence indwelt the temple (1 Kings 8:10–11) and tabernacle (Exodus 40:34–38), while in the new covenant God indwells not only Jesus who tabernacles among his people (John 1:14, 51), but his Spirit comes and indwells every believer (John 14:17, 23). Rightly, new covenant followers of Christ are called temples of the Holy Spirit (1 Corinthians 6:19), in whom God's Spirit dwells (1 Corinthians 3:16), something not said of old covenant believers. Therefore, while a sinner is regenerated by the Spirit regardless of where he is on the redemptive-historical timeline, being permanently indwelt by the Spirit is only a reality after the glorification of Jesus.[136] Consequently, while regeneration and indwelling are both works of the Spirit, they are not the same but distinct.

For Lemke and Keathley John 7:39 becomes not only difficult but impossible to interpret since they insist on making regeneration synonymous with reception of the Spirit or indwelling. However, if regeneration and indwelling (or the reception of the Spirit) are synonymous as Lemke and Keathley seem to think, then how could believers in the old covenant be regenerate since, as Jesus states in John 7:39, the Spirit had not yet been given? Given the view of Lemke and Keathley, it seems they would have to conclude, if we follow their logic that regeneration and receiving the Spirit are the same, that old covenant believers could not have been regenerate on the basis of John 7:39. Surely we would not want to say that the Spirit did not regenerate old covenant believers. To the contrary, if we distinguish between regeneration and indwelling (on the basis of passages like John 7:39), then there is no problem. While the Spirit regenerated elect sinners in the old covenant, a *permanent* indwelling of *all* believers with the Spirit awaits the new covenant just as Jesus says. For example, in John 3:5, as Hamilton shows, Jesus "speaks not of the Spirit *inhabiting* the one who is born again, but *causing the new birth.*"[137] This interpretation is also consistent with John 7:39 where it does not say "the Spirit was not yet causing the new birth, but that He was about to be received by those who had *believed* in Jesus."[138] Moreover, in John 7:39 it is clear that the permanent reception of the Spirit will not be experienced until after the crucifixion, but in John 3:5 Jesus does expect Nicodemus to understand the experience of the new birth, implying it was a reality in the old covenant.[139] Therefore, Hamilton concludes,

[136] Ibid., 143.
[137] Ibid., 132.
[138] Ibid.
[139] Ibid., 134.

If John 3:6 is speaking of regeneration and not indwelling, then the door is open to an inward enablement by the Spirit (which the Old Testament calls 'circumcision of the heart') prior to the cross. Since John 7:39 refers to believers who are yet to receive the Spirit, it would seem that prior to Jesus' glorification people could be enabled, i.e., regenerated, though they were not indwelt.[140]

Throughout the old covenant we see many examples (Noah, Abraham, David, etc.) of sinners spiritually circumcised and regenerated (Psalm 87; 119:25; Isaiah 55:3; Nehemiah 9:20, 30). As VanGemeren states, "The saints were those who were circumcised of heart, or 'regenerate.'"[141] Therefore, while "the New Testament explicitly states that the reception of the indwelling Spirit could not take place prior to the glorification of Jesus (John 7:39), it does not say that regeneration could not take place."[142]

Regrettably, Lemke and Keathley fail to address John 7:39 at all as well as the larger issue of the textual evidence throughout both the Old and New Testaments which demonstrates that regeneration and indwelling are not the same. Moreover, since regeneration precedes conversion in the *ordo salutis* and since, after Jesus is glorified, it is *at conversion* that the sinner is indwelt by the Spirit (John 7:38–39; Acts 2:38; Galatians 3:13; 4:6; Ephesians 1:13), the passages where belief is said to bring about reception of the Spirit present no problem for the Calvinist.[143] Notice, in all of the texts that Lemke and Keathley put forward (John 7:38–39; Acts 2:38; Galatians 3:13; 4:6; Ephesians 1:13), the Spirit is said to be received upon *faith*. None of these texts say anything about regeneration or new birth, which precedes and causes faith. What they do mention is an indwelling by the Spirit at conversion, which is not the same as regeneration but something that is the *result* and *product* of regeneration. In essence, Lemke and Keathley fail to pay attention to the redemptive-historical timeline of

---

[140] Ibid., 135.

[141] Willem A. VanGemeren, *The Progress of Redemption* (Grand Rapids, MI: Baker, 1988), 167.

[142] Hamilton, *God's Indwelling Presence*, 141.

[143] One could make the objection that after Jesus is glorified believers receive the Spirit at conversion. Granted, this is true. As Hamilton states, "The heart of the person is circumcised, and the ability to believe is created. The indwelling of the Holy Spirit, however, only accompanies the Spirit's life-giving work after the glorification of Jesus. After the glorification of Jesus, regeneration and indwelling can be seen as concurrent, though they remain distinct ministries of the Spirit." Ibid., 143. However, almost all theologians recognize that there is a difference between regeneration and conversion (faith and repentance). Therefore, even if we say that after Jesus is glorified indwelling occurs at conversion, still it has not been shown that conversion or indwelling precedes regeneration.

Scripture and consequently they fall short of distinguishing, as Scripture does, between regeneration by the Spirit and indwelling by the Spirit.

Saved

Third, Lemke and Keathley enlist a host of passages which say that if one believes he will be "saved" (Mark 16:16; Acts 16:31; Romans 1:16; 10:9–10; 1 Corinthians 1:21). To take one example, Lemke and Keathley appeal to Acts 16:31 where Paul and Silas say, "Believe in the Lord Jesus, and you will be saved, you and your household." Apparently "saved" (σωθήσῃ) in this passage refers to regeneration. Therefore, it is only after the sinner believes that he is saved (regenerated). However, such an interpretation of "you will be saved" is reductionistic since there is no contextual reason to read "saved" in such a narrow manner. Paul and Silas use the word "saved" in a general sense, not specifically referring to the inward act of regeneration but to salvation holistically.

Like the passages on "eternal life" and the "Holy Spirit" so also here we see "saved" erroneously equated with regeneration. Again, why should one interpret saved in such a narrow manner? Why not interpret saved as referring to adoption or justification? Or why not interpret saved in a much broader sense as referring to the sinner's escape from hell and wrath in the age to come? Or, better yet, why not interpret saved as a distinct metaphor in and of itself?[144] To interpret saved as synonymous with regeneration is seen to be fallacious when one looks at how other passages would then have to be interpreted. Consider Matthew 27:42, where Jesus is on the cross and his accusers say, "He regenerated (saved) others; he cannot regenerate (save) himself." Clearly, such an interpretation is unwarranted. And again, 1 Corinthians 3:15 would say, "If anyone's work is burned up, he will suffer loss, though he himself will be regenerated (saved), but only as through fire." According to Lemke's and Keathley's understanding, Paul would be teaching that one is actually regenerated on the last day. The same point is made when we consider 1 Peter 1:4–5 where Peter says God has caused us to be born again to a living hope and "an inheritance that is imperishable, undefiled, and unfading, kept in heaven for you, who by God's power are being guarded through faith for a regeneration (salvation) ready to be revealed in the last time." Again, if Lemke, and Keathley are right that "salvation" refers to regeneration then Peter would be saying that we are regenerated twice (born again and again), first in 1:3 at initiation and again in 1:5 in the "last time." To the contrary, "salvation" in 1 Peter 1:4–5 is used to refer to an inheritance we will one day receive in the "last

---

[144] Schreiner and Caneday, *The Race Set Before Us*, 46–86.

time." Or consider Philippians 2:12b–13, "Work out your own regeneration (salvation) with fear and trembling, for it is God who works in you,
both to will and to work for his good pleasure." If "salvation" is to be equated with regeneration then Paul would be instructing the Philippians that
they must work out their own regeneration. But the meaning of "salvation"
in Scripture is very different. Silva explains,

> It is conceded by all parties in the discussion that the term *salvation*
> (or its cognate verb) need *not be restricted, as it normally is in contempo-*
> *rary evangelical language, to the initial act of conversion* ("Have you been
> saved?") or to the status of being in a right relationship with God ("Are
> you saved?").... But the biblical concept of salvation is not thus restricted
> to justification; more commonly what is in view includes God's redemp-
> tive work *in its totality.* Thus, while in a very important sense we have al-
> ready been saved (Eph. 2:5, 8; Titus 3:5), in another sense we are yet to be
> saved (Rom. 5:9–10; 1 Cor. 3:15; 5:5; 2 Tim. 4:18). Calvin rightly claims
> "that salvation is taken to mean the entire course of our calling, and that
> this term includes all things by which God accomplishes that perfection,
> to which He has determined us by His free election."[145]

While salvation can refer to the past (Ephesians 2:5, 8; Titus 3:5; two
passages we already saw support monergism), many passages, including
Philippians 2:12, refer to salvation in its totality or as a reality yet to come
(Romans 5:9–10; 1 Corinthians 3:15; 5:5; 2 Timothy 4:18). Such a point
is made by Schreiner as well who observes that the language of salvation or
deliverance is "fundamentally eschatological." Consider texts like Romans
2:3, 5:9, and 5:10 where one is said to be saved from God's wrath and
saved by his life. Each of these texts uses the future tense "constraining us
as readers to think about future deliverance."[146] Therefore, these texts show
us that salvation is not ours now but it is a "future gift, a hope that we will
be spared from God's wrath on the day of the Lord."[147] Schreiner helpfully
explains,

> When Paul speaks of the gospel 'which results in salvation' (Rom 1:16),
> he has in mind eschatological salvation that will be our possession in
> the coming age. Similarly, the salvation that belongs to those who con-
> fess Jesus as Lord and believe on him in their hearts (Rom 10:9–10; cf.
> Rom 10:13) is fundamentally eschatological. The future tenses refer to
> the coming age.... The eschatological character of salvation is strikingly

---

[145] Emphasis added. Moisés Silva, *Philippians*, 2nd ed., BECNT (2005), 121.
[146] Schreiner, *Paul*, 225. For an extensive treatment of "salvation," see Schreiner and Caneday, *The Race Set Before Us*, 46–86.
[147] Ibid., 225–26.

confirmed in Romans 13:11, where salvation is said "to be nearer than when we first believed." Paul does not speak here of salvation as something obtained at the moment we first believed but as a gift to be given at the last day.[148]

While salvation is fundamentally eschatological, it does have reference to both the past and the present. It would be incorrect, in other words, to restrict salvation to the eschaton since some texts do indeed speak of salvation in the past tense. Take Ephesians 2:5, 8 where Paul says "by grace you have been saved" or Colossians 1:13 where God "rescued us from the authority of darkness and transferred us into the kingdom of his Son." Likewise 2 Timothy 2:9 says He saved us and again in Titus 3:5 Paul writes that God saved us through the washing of regeneration and the renewal from the Holy Spirit. Paul again says in Romans 8:24, "For in hope we have been saved." All of these are in the past tense. However, as Schreiner argues, these "past-tense statements do not cancel out the eschatological dimension of salvation."[149] Rather,

> Paul most commonly assigns salvation to the future, but he can speak of salvation as past since the age to come has invaded this present evil age. The past dimension of salvation, therefore, should be understood within the eschatological framework of Paul's theology. And Romans 8:24 helps us understand that the reality of salvation in the past does not mean that salvation is now complete. Believers still hope for the future realization of their salvation for they have not yet received the full inheritance. Once we grasp the eschatological tension between the future and the present, it is understandable that Paul also describes salvation as an ongoing process in the present. Through the gospel "you are being saved" (1 Cor 15:2); and the eschatological tension of Paul's view is preserved in that such salvation will only be realized through perseverance. In 1 Corinthians 1:18 the gospel's power has seized "those who are being saved" (cf. 2 Cor 2:15). Indeed, the gospel is the reason for their salvation.[150]

Schreiner's point is well taken. "Salvation" is fundamentally a future reality, but it has broken into the past and the present (already not yet). As Sproul states, "We have been saved, are being saved, and shall be saved. There is a past, present, and future dimension to salvation."[151] Therefore, "salvation" is a soteriological category that is *broad*, covering not only the

---

[148] Ibid., 226.

[149] Ibid., 228.

[150] Ibid., 228.

[151] "Our salvation began in eternity, is realized in time, looks forward to heaven." Sproul, *What is Reformed Theology?*, 198.

past and present but the future, and therefore it is erroneous for Arminians like Lemke and Keathley to define "salvation" so narrowly as referring to the one, instantaneous event of regeneration at initiation.[152] It is obvious that Arminians who appeal to such passages have succumbed to a reductionistic interpretation by equating "saved" with "regeneration."[153]

Conclusion: Monergism Preserves God's Glory

What is the dividing line between the Calvinist and Arminian? James M. Boice and Philip Ryken explain it best,

> Having a high view of God means something more than giving glory to God, however; it means giving glory to God *alone*. This is the difference between Calvinism and Arminianism. While the former declares that God alone saves sinners, the latter gives the impression that God enables sinners to have some part in saving themselves. "Calvinism presents salvation as the work of the triune God—election by the Father, redemption in the Son, calling by the Spirit. Furthermore, each of these saving acts is directed toward the elect, thereby infallibly securing their salvation. By contrast, Arminianism views salvation as something that God makes possible but that man makes actual. This is because the saving acts of God are directed toward *different* persons: the Son's redemption is for humanity in general; the Spirit's calling is only for those who hear the gospel; narrower still, the Father's election is only for those who believe the gospel. Yet in none of these cases (redemption, calling, or election) does God *actually* secure the salvation of even one single sinner! The inevitable result is that rather than depending exclusively on divine grace, salvation depends partly on a human response. So although Arminianism is willing to give God the glory, when it comes to salvation, it is unwilling to give him *all* the glory. It divides the glory between heaven and

---

[152] "If 'being saved' … is sometimes viewed as an eschatological event, it cannote reduced to mean 'being regenerated.' Instead, the Scripture-writers seem to use the verb broadly, as a generic or 'package' term." Snoeberger, "The Logical Priority of Regeneration to Saving Faith," 60.

[153] One could possibly object that even though "saved," reception of the "Holy Spirit," and "eternal life" are broadly defined, nevertheless, regeneration is included within such a broad definition and therefore would still come subsequent to belief. However, Snoeberger demonstrates that just because "saved," or reception of the "Spirit," or "life" follow faith "it does not follow that every single aspect" of "saved," "life," or reception of the "Spirit," must follow faith. In other words, while some aspects of "salvation" or "life" may follow faith it is also the case that other aspects precede faith. Snoeberger, "The Logical Priority of Regeneration to Saving Faith," 61, 65.

earth, for if what ultimately makes the difference between being saved and being lost is man's ability to choose God, then to just that extent God is robbed of his glory. Yet God himself has said, "I will not yield my glory to another" (Isa. 48:11).[154]

God's glory is wrapped up in the biblical doctrines of effectual calling and monergistic regeneration and it is only compromised should it unravel at the expense of man's autonomy. Only monergism can do justice to both the biblical text and the insistence of God that He will give His glory to no other (Isaiah 42:8; 48:11; Romans 3:27; Ephesians 2:8–9; 1 Corinthians 1:26–31).

[154] Boice and Ryken, *The Doctrines of Grace*, 34–35.

6

Promises of Preservation
And Exhortations to Perseverance

Thomas R. Schreiner

In the Scriptures we find promises that God will preserve His people to the end. Believers are assured that they will never lose their salvation; they will never apostatize and fall away. At the same time we find threats and warnings that admonish believers in the strongest possible terms about the danger of falling away. Believers are warned that if they forsake Christ and the gospel they will be cursed and experience final judgment. I will argue in this chapter that both of these statements are true, and that they do not contradict one other. My thesis in short is as follows: the elect will certainly be preserved by God and hence will not fall away, and the warnings are the means by which the elect persevere to the end. God's grace guarantees not only initial belief but also perseverance to the end.

Promises of Preservation

Assurance that believers will be preserved to the end pervades the biblical witness. I will introduce texts from Luke, 1 Peter, Jude, John's Gospel, and the Pauline letters to support this claim in order to demonstrate that this theme is not an isolated one.[1]

In Luke 22:31–32 Jesus makes an astonishing statement to Simon Peter. Jesus informs Peter that Satan wanted "to sift you like wheat" (22:31),[2]

[1] Other texts could be presented, but space limitations preclude such.
[2] All scriptural citations in this chapter are from the HCSB unless noted otherwise.

and the result of the sifting would be that Peter is found to be chaff. It is akin to what Peter says in his first letter. "Your adversary the devil prowls around like a roaring lion, seeking someone to devour" (1 Peter 5:8 ESV). The devil delights in devouring faith and bringing people to end-time destruction, and his goal was to quench Peter's faith so that Peter ended up in the same state as Judas: damned by God.

Jesus responds with one of the most astonishing statements in the Gospels. "But I have prayed for you that your faith may not fail" (Luke 22:32). Satan wanted Peter to belong to him, but Jesus prayed that it would be otherwise. He prayed that Peter's faith would "not fail" (μὴ ἐκλίπη), which is another way of saying, that it would last and persevere. There is no hint in the narrative that Jesus' prayer might be unsuccessful. Instead, Jesus' prayer guarantees that Peter's faith will persist until the end. The text makes this clear, for Jesus goes on to say to Peter, "and you, when you have turned back, strengthen your brothers" (22:32). Jesus promises that Peter's faith, which temporarily failed when he denied Jesus, will not ultimately and finally be extinguished. He will repent and return. Jesus does not say "if" Peter returns but "when" (ποτε) he returns, certifying that Peter's faith will survive. But Peter's perseverance can't be attributed to his own strength but to Jesus' intercession for him.[3] Ultimately, Peter's perseverance and the perseverance of all believers is God's work.

After considering Jesus' words to Peter, it is fitting to reflect on Peter's own words regarding God's work in keeping believers. What Peter says about the subject is in a context which features the sovereignty of God in salvation. God foreknows, elects, and causes to be born again those who will be saved on the last day (1 Peter 1:1–3). It is quite remarkable that some uphold the preservation of the saints but deny unconditional election, for they are inseparable for Peter, being joined together in the same context. God's work in sustaining faith until the end is communicated in 1 Peter 1:5, "You are being protected by God's power through faith for a salvation that is ready to be revealed in the last time." Eschatological salvation is received not because of human strength but by virtue of the power of God.

---

[3] Berkouwer rightly remarks, "If anything is certain, it is this, that according to the Scriptures God's grace does not stop short at the limits of human freedom of choice. Whoever claims this is bound to see faith and grace as two mutually exclusive and mutually limiting elements in salvation, and he is bound to emerge with a doctrine of grace that is synergistic in principle." G. C. Berkouwer, *Faith and Perseverance*, trans. R. D. Knudsen (Grand Rapids, MI: Eerdmans, 1958), 90–91.

But isn't final salvation unsure since it is only obtained through human faith? And human faith may fail according to some. Certainly people must continue to believe to be saved; there is no perseverance without faith. But the text is more profound than simply saying: God does His part (He protects us) and we do our part (we believe). We can put it more sharply. How does God protect believers in any significant sense if He doesn't preserve their faith? God's protection doesn't mean believers are spared from physical suffering, for 1 Peter teaches clearly that believers will suffer for their faith. God's protection, then, must mean that God will protect believers from sin. And all sin stems from lack of faith and trust in God. As Romans 14:23 says, "For whatever does not proceed from faith is sin" (ESV). Hence, God must protect Christians by granting them the strength to believe until the end. As Ernest Best says, "The reference to God's power" is "unnecessary and provides no assurance to the believer since what he doubts is his own power to cling to God in trial."[4] Hence, Best rightly argues that the verse teaches that God grants faith to believers. This fits with what we saw in Luke 22:31–32, where Peter's faith does not fail because Jesus prayed for him. First Peter 1:5 teaches, then, that God protects believers by preserving their faith until the day Jesus Christ is revealed.

The letter of Jude warns of the judgment that will be inflicted on those who live ungodly lives and deny the lordship of Jesus Christ. Jude underscores the importance of perseverance. Nevertheless, at the same time he highlights God's keeping and sustaining grace. Believers have been effectually "called" (κλητοῖς) by God and are "kept (τετηρημένοις) by Jesus Christ." The danger from false teachers who propound an antinomian lifestyle must not be overlooked. But Jude doesn't want his readers to be paralyzed with fear. Jesus Christ will keep and preserve them. The book concludes famously with the benediction and v. 24. "Now to Him who is able to protect you from stumbling and to make you stand in the presence of His glory, blameless and with great joy." The word "stumbling" (ἀπταίστους) does not mean here that God is able to keep believers from sinning. In light of Jude's entire message it means that God is able to keep believers from apostasy, from falling away from the faith.[5] This interpretation is verified by the words "make you stand in the presence of His glory." Those who are kept from stumbling stand in God's presence on the final day, having come through the storms of life without losing their faith. Furthermore, Jude doesn't merely mean here that God can keep believers

---

[4] Ernest Best, *1 Peter* (NCB; Grand Rapids, MI: Eerdmans, 1971), 77.
[5] Rightly Richard J. Bauckham, *Jude, 2 Peter* (WBC; Waco, TX: Word, 1983), 122; Douglas J. Moo, 2 Peter, Jude (NIVAC; Grand Rapids, MI: Zondervan, 1996), 300.

from apostasy but He might not do so. Instead, the Lord guarantees that He will preserve them from falling away.[6]

Several texts in John's Gospel emphasize that the Lord will keep His own. In chapter 6 effectual calling is emphasized. Everyone given by the Father to the Son will come to Jesus as the bread of life and believe (John 6:37, 65). Indeed, no one is even able to come to the Son unless the Father compellingly draws him (6:44). John ties effectual calling here to theme of preservation. We see once again that the strands of Reformed soteriology are inextricably bound together. There is no biblical warrant for believing in the preservation of the saints if one denies effectual calling.

The keeping of those who have been drawn to Jesus and are given to Jesus by the Father is conveyed by John 6:39. "This is the will of Him who sent Me: that I should lose none of those He has given Me but should raise them up on the last day." Jesus came to earth to carry out the Father's will (6:38), and the will of the Father is explicitly set forth in v. 39. Jesus will not lose even a single person given to Him by the Father. All of those who are effectually called and only those who are effectually called will be preserved to the end. They are promised that they will enjoy the future resurrection of life, demonstrating that they will be preserved until the eschaton. Indeed, the promise of final resurrection is a regular refrain in the text (John 6:40, 44, 54), certifying that believers will triumph over death and sin, that they will enjoy eschatological life in the age to come.

John 17, in addressing God's keeping and guarding of believers, is remarkably similar to John 6. The Son has granted eternal life to those whom God has given to Him (John 17:2). God's name was revealed to those given by the Father to the Son, and as a result they have kept God's word (17:6). Jesus does not pray for all without exception but only for those given to Him by the Father (17:9), asking that they be preserved from apostasy. Jesus prays for their preservation (17:11), emphasizing that He kept them from straying during His ministry so that not a single one of those truly chosen was lost (17:12). Jesus pleads with the Father to protect them from the evil one so that they will be spared from apostasy in the future as well (17:15; cf. Matthew 6:13), praying that they would be sanctified in the truth (17:17, 19). Doubtless the prayer of Jesus will be answered affirmatively, so that those given by the Father to the Son will be guarded from apostasy.

One of the most famous texts on preservation is found in John 10. Once again it is woven together with other strands of Reformed soteriology. The theme of definite atonement emerges, for Jesus gives His life

---

[6] So Augustine in *James, 1–2 Peter, 1–3 John, Jude* (ACCS; Downers Grove, IL: InterVarsity, 2000), 259.

particularly for His sheep (John 10:11). We also see effectual calling, for Jesus will effectually bring others into His flock (10:16). Indeed, the fundamental reason Jesus' opponents do not believe is "because you are not My sheep" (10:26). It is certainly good biblical theology to say people are not Jesus' sheep because they do not believe. But that is *not* what John teaches in John 10:26. Those who believe do so because they are among those chosen by Jesus. Jesus' sheep "hear [His] voice" and follow the good shepherd (10:27).

The irrevocability of salvation is clear from John 10:28, "I give them eternal life, and they will never perish, and no one will snatch them out of my hand" (ESV). Jesus, as the good shepherd, has given eternal life to His sheep. They enjoy the life of the age to come while living in this present evil age. The nature of eternal life is unpacked in the next clause. Those who have such life "will never perish." The word "perish" (ἀπόλωνται) is a common word in the NT for eschatological judgment. The reception of eternal life cancels out any possibility that those who enjoy it will perish at the final judgment. The security of believers is underscored by the promise that no one will be able to snatch them out of the hand of Jesus or the Father (10:28–29). To posit the notion that believers could choose to jump out of the hand of Jesus or the Father is alien to the text before us. Those who are Jesus' sheep, those who are brought by Jesus into His fold, will never wander from the fold.

Promises of preservation are pervasive in the Pauline letters, and we will look at a few of them here. Pride of place belongs perhaps to Philippians 1:6, "And I am sure of this, that he who began a good work in you will bring it to completion at the day of Jesus Christ" (ESV). The good work begun was the work of salvation, and that saving initial work was performed by God Himself. Paul assures the Philippians that the God who began the good work in them will finish what He started. The saving work will not fail half-way but will be carried out to completion. The inseparable connection between initial and final salvation must be noted here. Since final salvation does not depend ultimately upon the free will of human beings, the same must be said of the initial work of coming to faith. In both cases human beings do choose to believe or keep believing, but the power to believe and the credit for believing stems from and belongs to God.

Romans 8:28–39 functions as the most sustained and powerful text on preservation in Paul. We see again that the strands of Pauline soteriology must not be disentangled from one another. In Romans 8:29–30 we find what William Perkins called "The Golden Chain." Those whom God foreknew, predestined, called, and justified will be glorified. Every link in the chain is forged by God. He set His covenant affection (foreknew) upon those who were His,[7] predestined them to salvation, called them effectually to Himself through the gospel (cf. 2 Thessalonians 2:14), and justified them by faith. Paul's aim here is to assure believers that they will certainly be glorified since they have experienced all of these other saving blessings. The future glorification of believers does not depend fundamentally or finally on the will of believers, for glorification is a divine work.[8] Since God is the One who foreknows, predestines, calls, and justifies, He is the One who will certainly glorify. There is no suggestion here that some of those who are foreknown might drop out and fail to reach glorification. The text provides minimal comfort if apostasy from the faith is possible, for when believers think about the future, knowing their own fickle hearts which are prone to wander, they worry about falling away.

It is also apparent in Romans 8 that, biblically speaking, it makes no sense to uphold the promise of final glorification, while denying unconditional election. Those who are glorified are also identified as those upon whom God set His covenant affection before history began, whom He predetermined would be saved, and whom He called effectually by His grace. The Arminian position is the only consistent alternative biblically and theologically. If one gets in by free will, then one can opt out through free will. But of course the text teaches no such thing. God's sovereign election turned our hearts towards Christ and that same grace will keep us until we are glorified. The keeping grace of God is celebrated in Romans 8:35–39. Nothing will sever believers from Christ's love. Paul contemplates the circumstances in life that would provoke apostasy: stresses, persecution, starvation, demons, future fears, and present sorrows. But nothing in all of creation (including the will of believers, for that is part of creation) will ever separate believers from the love of Christ. The love of Christ which first wooed and won believers will keep them until the end.

In 1 Corinthians 1:7 Paul looks ahead to the day when Christ Jesus will be revealed in all His glory. This leads him to reflect on a promise for the believers in Corinth. The believers are promised that Christ "will also confirm you until the end, blameless in the day of our Lord Jesus Christ" (1 Corinthians 1:8).[9] Paul reaffirms God's preserving grace in a confessional statement. "God is faithful, by whom you were called into the fellowship of his Son, Jesus Christ our Lord" (1 Corinthians 1:9). Since the affirmation

[7] See S. M. Baugh, "The Meaning of Foreknowledge," in *Still Sovereign: Contemporary Perspectives on Election, Foreknowledge, and Grace*, ed. Thomas R. Schreiner and Bruce A. Ware (Grand Rapids, MI: Baker, 2000), 183–200.

[8] Contrary to Marshall who thinks the chain can be broken and that believers may apostatize. I. Howard Marshall, *Kept by the Power of God: A Study of Perseverance and Falling Away* (Minneapolis, MN: Bethany Fellowship, 1969), 103.

[9] My translation.

of God's faithfulness follows immediately upon the promise that God will keep believers to the end, Paul teaches that God is faithful in the sense that He will preserve believers until the day of Christ. Again, we see the link between God's efficacious call to salvation and the promise of final salvation. The God who called believers into fellowship will never let them go.

Paul often uses the phrase "God is faithful" to assure believers that God will sustain their faith until the end. For instance, in 1 Corinthians 10:1–12 the believers at Corinth are warned about the danger of apostasy with examples from OT Israel. They are admonished to beware for the one who thinks "he stands" must "take heed lest he fall" (1 Corinthians 10:12 ESV). This incredibly strong warning about apostasy does not rule out assurance of salvation. For Paul comforts them with the promise, "No temptation has overtaken you except what is common to humanity. God is faithful, and He will not allow you to be tempted beyond what you are able, but with the temptation He will also provide a way of escape so that you are able to bear it" (1 Corinthians 10:13). All of the "God is faithful" texts in Paul address the issue of final salvation. The promise does not focus in context, then, on sin in general. What is promised in v. 13 is the strength to resist apostasy. God will protect believers so that they will never depart from the Lord.

Paul prays in 1 Thessalonians 5:23 for final sanctification for the Thessalonians, asking that they be preserved blameless until the day Christ comes. Being kept blameless doesn't mean that they would be sinless. He asks God to preserve them from final apostasy. Apparently, Paul's prayer is one of the means that God will use to fulfill His purposes, for he immediately adds in 1 Thessalonians 5:24 that, "He who calls you is faithful, who also will do it." The God who initially and powerfully called believers to salvation is faithful to His promises. He will certainly fulfill Paul's petition offered in 5:23 and keep the Thessalonians from departing from the Lord. Two common themes in the Scriptures are found here. First, we see the importance of means in biblical theology. God promises to keep His people but He uses means to keep them from falling away from God. Hence, prayer is not beside the point in God's preservation of His people but an essential means by which they are kept. Second, the indissoluble connection between effectual calling and final salvation is again enunciated. The Thessalonians did not become believers by virtue of their own strength but because God called them (cf. also 1 Thessalonians 1:4; 2:12; 4:7; 2 Thessalonians 2:13–14). And the God who brought them to Himself will also keep them. Free will was not ultimate in their initial salvation, nor is it in their final salvation.

Paul also reminds the Thessalonians of the Lord's faithfulness in 2 Thessalonians 3:3. "But the Lord is faithful; He will strengthen and guard

you from the evil one." What is remarkable about this promise is that it
resonates with the words of the Lord's prayer. "And do not bring us into
temptation, but deliver us from the evil one" (Matthew 6:13). The petition in the Lord's prayer, as is the case with the prayer in 1 Thessalonians
5:23, relates to apostasy.[10] Jesus exhorts His disciples to pray that they will
not enter into and fall into temptation, where they are delivered into the
hands of the devil and renounce their faith. The text in 2 Thessalonians
3:3 contemplates another dimension of God's saving and preserving work.
Using words that are very similar to what we find in the Lord's prayer,
Paul assures the believers that "the Lord is faithful." He is faithful in that
He will strengthen and establish believers so that they will be guarded and
protected from the devil. They will not fall into his clutches and fall away,
but will instead enjoy final salvation. We see again that prayer is one of the
means by which God's promises are realized. Paul is not uncertain about
whether believers will finally be saved. He is confident of their final salvation since the Lord is faithful.

In 2 Timothy 2:12 Paul warns believers, "If we deny him; He will also
deny us." This saying echoes the words of Jesus who said, "Whoever denies
Me before men, I will also deny him before My Father in heaven" (Matthew 10:33). Here we find a remarkable warning addressed to believers. If
they ultimately and finally deny Jesus, they will be denied by Jesus in the
eschaton on the day of final judgment. But there is sin which is not apostasy, for 2 Timothy 2:13 asserts, "If we are faithless, He remains faithful,
for He cannot deny Himself." This text could be interpreted to restate 2
Timothy 2:12 in which case it would mean that those who do not exercise
faith until the end will be judged by the God who remains faithful to Himself. Such an interpretation is certainly possible and does not contradict
anything in Pauline theology. Nevertheless, it is unlikely that Paul has such
a meaning in view here. In every other instance the "God is faithful" texts
in Paul assure believers that they will be guarded until the end, and thus it
is doubtful that this verse should be interpreted differently. Furthermore,
the form of the saying diverges from what we saw in the previous verses.
Paul could have easily followed the pattern of the previous sayings and
said something like, "If we are faithless, he will judge us." The variance
from the pattern suggests that a distinct point is made here. Faithlessness
here is not the same thing as denying Jesus. The sin that marks the lives
of believers must be distinguished from apostasy. If someone denies the
Lord, his fate is final judgment. Nonetheless, there is sin which is not in

[10] So Donald A. Hagner, *Matthew 1–13* (WBC; Dallas, TX: Word, 1993),
151.

the same category as apostasy, for it is not permanent loss of faith.[11] God remains faithful to His own, and will not deny Hemself by withdrawing His promise to save them.

We have seen that there is ample and convincing evidence that those who truly know God will never fall away. The God who elected and called believers will keep them to the end. Their faith will persist because God is faithful, and He will complete the good work that He has started.

Exhortations to Perseverance

God will keep His own until the end, and yet such a promise does not cancel out the need for exhortations to persevere until the end. Indeed, we have already seen in some of the texts above that the promises of preservation sit cheek by jowl with prayers and exhortations to persevere, indicating that the two were viewed as complementary. Berkouwer rightly says, "For what is striking about the Scriptures is that the passages concerning the steadfastness of God's faithfulness and the passages with admonitions are inseparable. We do not encounter a single passage that would allow anyone to take the immutability of the grace of God in Christ for granted."[12] In biblical theology strong affirmations of assurance did not preclude equally strong warnings, suggesting that the warnings are not contrary to but supportive of assurance in the faith. Keathley mistakenly says that I believe promises of preservation are "subordinate to the warning passages."[13] I would argue instead that the two passages stand in correlation. Furthermore, the promises of preservation indicate that believers will certainly heed the warnings. So, if anything, Keathley has it backwards. Keathley also misunderstands what Caneday and I mean by "conceivable" (181). It doesn't mean that we think damnation is possible for believers. It means that believers think about what would happen if they were to apostatize, and reflecting on the danger always keeps believers from apostasy.

---

[11] Rightly George W. Knight III, *Commentary on the Pastoral Epistles* (NIGTC; Grand Rapids, MI: Eerdmans, 1992), 407. Contrary to Hodges who thinks one can lose one's faith altogether and still be saved. Zane Hodges, *Absolutely Free! A Biblical Response to Lordship Salvation* (Grand Rapids, MI: Zondervan, 1989), 107.

[12] Berkouwer, *Faith and Perseverance*, 97.

[13] See Kenneth D. Keathley, "Perseverance and Assurance of the Saints," in *Whosoever Will: A Biblical-Theological Critique of Five-Point Calvinism. Reflections from the John 3:16 Conference*, ed. David L. Allen and Steve W. Lemke (Nashville, TN: Broadman & Holman, 2010), 173. The same chapter published in *Whosoever Will* is found in Kenneth D. Keathley, *Salvation and Sovereignty: A Molinist Approach* (Nashville, TN: Broadman & Holman, 2010), 164–190.

I would suggest that Keathley doesn't understand our position because he can't imagine threats being genuine without apostasy being truly possible. But I would argue that the situation is similar to Jesus' temptation. Jesus' temptation was genuine, but Jesus could not sin.

Many texts can be adduced in the NT which teach that works are necessary for eternal life. Keathley worries that I may teach salvation by works.[14] It is hard to respond to his charge since he makes his comments without doing exegesis of the relevant texts. Furthermore, both Caneday and I make it clear that works are not the *basis* of salvation. Keathley seems in this regard to be similar to Free Grace advocates, who think that any appeal to the necessity of works amounts to works-righteousness. Caneday and I make it clear that works are not the *ground* of righteousness, but we show in text after text that works are *necessary* for final salvation. Simply calling that "works-salvation" without doing the hard work of exegesis does not pass muster. Keathley asserts that "Perserverance cannot be understood in terms of good works and great efforts without having the result of dismantling the Reformation" (185). Now I know what he is worried about, and I share the same concern. But again, Keathley makes assertions about the role of works without any exegesis. We must beware of overreading the necessity of works, as Keathley rightly cautions (187). Certainly works are not the basis for eternal life, but they are the necessary fruit of faith. For instance, in Matthew 7:15–20 Jesus warns His disciples about false prophets. They are identified and discerned by their fruit. In the context of Matthew 5–7 it is clear that fruit refers particularly to the moral character of the false prophets. Jesus' words function as an implicit warning to His disciples. They must not follow the path of those who proclaim the word of the Lord but behave in morally dissolute ways.

The next paragraph in Matthew pursues a similar theme (Matthew 7:21–23). Jesus declares that "many" who prophesied in His name, cast out demons, and performed miracles do not belong to Him. Their ministry may be remarkable and astonishing, but their authenticity is measured by their obedience. They will be rejected on the day of judgment because they failed to do the Father's will. Jesus will drive them away because they are lawbreakers. Only those who build on the rock will survive the storm of the final judgment (Matthew 7:24–27). And what does it mean to build on the rock? It means that one hears and keeps the words of Jesus (Matthew 7:24, 26). Those who fail to act upon and to obey Jesus' words will be destroyed. The "narrow gate" in the context of Matthew (7:13–14), therefore, focuses on obedience. Only those who obey Jesus will receive a final reward, and those who spurn His word will be judged.

[14] Keathley, "Perseverance and Assurance of the Saints," 166, 182–83.

One of my goals is to show that warnings and exhortations pervade the New Testament. It is not an isolated theme! We have already seen that the theme in Matthew (7:13–27; 10:32–33), and many other texts in Matthew (and Mark and Luke for that matter) could be cited. But I turn to a couple of texts from Johannine literature. One of the most famous texts in John's Gospel has to do with Jesus being the vine and His disciples the branches (John 15). Jesus' disciples can't do anything unless they draw their strength and nourishment from Jesus as the vine. If they remain connected to the vine, they will bear fruit and flourish. But in 15:6 Jesus warns the disciples, "If anyone does not remain in Me, he is thrown aside like a branch and he withers. They gather them, throw them into the fire, and they are burned." Certainly this text should be understood as a warning and admonition for the disciples. Moreover, this text is not simply speaking about rewards. Jesus threatens the branches themselves with destruction. Branches that do not remain in Jesus will be "thrown aside." They will dry up and wither and then be cast into the fire where they will be burned. Nothing is said about their "fruit" being burned. The branches themselves will be consigned to the flames. Jesus warns His disciples in a most bracing way. If they do not continue in Him, they will face the fires of hell.

An equally strong warning is found in 2 John 7–9. "Many deceivers have gone out into the world; they do not confess the coming of Jesus Christ in the flesh. This is the deceiver and the antichrist. Watch yourselves so you don't lose what we have worked for, but that you may receive a full reward. Anyone who does not remain in Christ's teaching but goes beyond it, does not have God. The one who remains in that teaching, this one has both the Father and the Son." John warns his readers about false teachers who deny the incarnation, who reject the idea that Jesus is the Christ in the flesh. They are deceivers and antichrists. The readers are admonished to be on guard so that they do not accede to such teaching. They must not "lose" what they "have worked for" but "receive a full reward." The wording here may lead some to the conclusion that John thinks of rewards distinct from salvation, especially since he uses the language of "losing" one's reward. Actually, however, the context is clear. *The reward is salvation.* And yes, John warns them about not losing it. I will explain shortly why this does not contradict the notion that believers cannot and will not fall away. That the reward is salvation is apparent from 2 John 9. For those who end up agreeing with the false teachers and reject that Jesus is the Christ in the flesh do "not have God." It could scarcely be clearer. Only those who adhere to orthodox Christology have "both the Father and the Son" (2 John 9). To sum up, the reward in view clearly relates here to eternal life. Believers are warned to be watchful. They must not stray from the teaching about the Christ. If they do, they will not be saved.

I will not linger here over the teaching of 1 John, but John emphasizes in the letter that assurance of eternal life belongs to those who keep God's commands (2:3–6, 28; 3:4–10, 24; 5:2–3), those who love fellow believers (2:7–11; 3:11–18, 23; 4:7–21; 5:2–3) and those who confess that Jesus is the Christ come in the flesh (2:22–24; 3:23; 4:2–3; 5:1, 5–6).[15] Those who claim new life in Christ, while pursuing a life of sin or while indulging in hatred and resentment or who have an unorthodox Christology, have no assurance that they truly belong to God (cf. 5:13).

The necessity of perseverance is also underscored in Revelation. Only those who conquer and overcome will experience eternal life.[16] Only those who conquer until the end will "eat from the tree of life, which is in God's paradise" (2:7). Each of the seven letters have a refrain which emphasizes that believers must conquer and persevere to the end to enter the new creation (2:7, 11, 17, 26; 3:5, 12, 21). Nor is there any doubt that eternal life is at stake. John is not merely talking about rewards. For those who overcome will enter, as we saw, "paradise" (2:7). Or, as 2:11 says they "will never be harmed by the second death." The "second death" is defined as "the lake of fire" (20:14), and hence there is no doubt that believers must conquer and persevere to the end to receive eternal life. And the other texts calling upon believers to conquer sound out the same theme. Those who don't overcome won't eat the manna of the kingdom and will not have the stone required to enter in (2:17). Only those who overcome will exercise authority over the nations (2:26), sitting with Jesus on His throne (3:21). Overcomers will be part of God's new temple in the new creation (3:12). Those who conquer will be clothed in white garments and their names will never be erased from the book of life, and Jesus will confess their name before God and angels (3:5). The verse echoes Jesus' words that those who acknowledge Him before others will be acknowledged by Jesus on the last day (Matthew 10:32). The inheritance is given to those who overcome, and those who fail to conquer and fall prey to sin will find that their destination is the lake of fire (Revelation 21:7–8).

We see similar exhortations in Pauline literature. Colossians 1:21–23 is a good example. "Once you were alienated and hostile in your minds because of your evil actions. But now He has reconciled you by His physical body through His death, to present you holy, faultless, and blameless before Him—if indeed you remain grounded and steadfast in the faith

---

[15] See Christopher David Bass, *That You May Know: Assurance of Salvation in 1 John* (NAC; Nashville, TN: Broadman & Holman, 2008); D. A. Carson, "Johannine Perspectives on the Doctrine of Assurance," *Explorations* 10 (1996): 59–97.

[16] See Richard Bauckham, *The Theology of the Book of Revelation* (Cambridge: Cambridge University Press, 1993), 14.

and are not shifted away from the hope of the gospel that you heard." We see here the typical contrast between "then" and "now" in Pauline letters. Before the Colossians were saved, they were estranged from God by virtue of the evil in their lives. Now, however, they are reconciled to God through the atoning work of Christ by which they will be presented before God on the last day as holy. Paul introduces a condition regarding this end time presentation. The words "if indeed" (εἴ γε) are righty translated here, and there is no warrant for translating them as "since."[17] Paul says that believers will be presented as blameless before God on the last day if they persevere until the end. They must "continue (ἐπιμένετε) in the faith" (ESV) and not depart from the hope of the gospel. If they do depart, they will not be blameless before God but guilty.

I have argued above that all those who belong to the Lord will be preserved until the end by the grace of God. Some take the truth of God's sustaining grace and argue that it is unbiblical to posit any conditions regarding final salvation. Apparently they are more Pauline than Paul! For it is an exegetical fact that can't be denied that Paul has a condition here. Theological statements which claim there are no conditions for final salvation gloss over texts like these. It is more accurate to say that final salvation will not be obtained without persevering to the end, and God will grant us the grace to persevere. Such a promise does not nullify the force of the condition as I will argue below.

In Romans 11:17–24 Paul uses the analogy of the olive tree which represents the people of God. Even though the Jews were the people of the promise, many of them have been cut off as branches from the olive tree. Paul is not addressing here Jews who became Christians and later apostatized. He refers to ethnic Jews who were part of the people of the promise. When many of them heard the gospel, however, they refused to believe its message. With the coming of the Christ and His death and resurrection a new era in salvation history has dawned. The new people of God is constituted from those who belong to Jesus, from those who are "in" Him.

---

[17] Against S. Lewis Johnson, Jr., "Studies in the Epistle to the Colossians: IV. From Enmity to Amity," *Bibliotheca Sacra* 119 (1962): 147. For more convincing analyses of conditions, see James L. Boyer in the *Grace Theological Journal*, "First Class Conditions: What Do They Mean?" 2 (1981): 75–114; idem, "Second Class Conditions in New Testament Greek," 3 (1982): 81–88; idem, "Third (and Fourth) Class Conditions," 3 (1982): 163–175; idem, "Other Conditional Elements in New Testament Greek," 4 (1983): 173–188; cf. also Daniel B. Wallace, *Greek Grammar Beyond the Basics: An Exegetical Syntax of the New Testament* (Grand Rapids: Zondervan, 1996), 679–712. See also Thomas R. Schreiner & Ardel B. Caneday, *The Race Set Before Us: A Biblical Theology of Perseverance and Assurance* (Downers Grove, IL: InterVarsity, 2001), 192–93.

The era when Israel was God's theocratic people has ceased. The church of Jesus Christ now constitutes the people of God, and Jews who put their trust in Jesus are members of the church. Hence, Jews who do not trust in Jesus are severed from the olive tree. I am not saying that such Jews actually committed apostasy, for they were members of the theocratic people but were not actually saved. Here we must observe the difference between the people of God in the old covenant and the new covenant.

Paul addresses Gentile Christians at this juncture. They "stand by faith" and thus must beware of pride (Romans 11:20). Indeed, they must "fear" (φοβοῦ). What should they fear? Paul warns them that if the "natural branches" (Jews who did not believe) were not spared, then Gentiles who cease believing will not be spared either (Romans 11:21). It must be observed again how some scholars write or talk about assurance in the abstract, and they seem to have no room for fear in their theology of assurance. But again they clearly depart from the very words Paul uses. How easy it is to formulate theology apart from the biblical text! Now I don't think the fear here is a paralyzing fear where believers are struck by abject fear and terror. This is a fear that leads to action, or more accurately, it spurs one to faith. There is a healthy fear of throwing away one's participation in Christ that provokes one to cling to Him.

Gentile believers are clearly warned about falling away from Christ in Romans 11:22. "Therefore, consider God's kindness and severity: severity toward those who have fallen but God's kindness toward you—if you remain in His kindness. Otherwise you too will be cut off." Believers must be grateful for God's saving kindness and goodness which they have experienced in Christ. On the other hand, God's severity is meted out on those who fall away from Him. Gentile believers are admonished to continue in God's kindness. For if they depart from it, they will be "cut off" just as the Jewish branches were lopped off. Paul could scarcely be clearer. Believers must heed the Pauline warning and persevere in order to be saved.

We see a similar warning in Galatians 5:2–4. The Galatians were tempted to receive circumcision, the initiation rite for Judaism, to secure entrance into the people of God. According to Paul, such a gambit represents another gospel and warrants an eschatological anathema (Galatians 1:8–9). There is no compromise: one either clings to the work of Christ on the cross (Galatians 1:4; 2:21; 3:1, 13; 4:4–5; 5:11; 6:14) or one trusts in circumcision and the law for salvation (Galatians 2:16; 3:2, 5, 10–12, 18; 4:21; 5:18). Hence, Paul says, "Look: I, Paul, say to you that if you accept circumcision, Christ will be of no advantage to you" (Galatians 5:2 ESV). What Paul means here is that there will be no *saving* advantage for his readers if they submit to circumcision. They can't have both Christ and circumcision; they can't have both the cross and the law. Salvation comes from either one or the other. The decision to be circumcised is not a light matter, for one's final destiny is at stake.

Paul continues the argument in Galatians 5:3. Those who rely on circumcision for salvation are required to keep the entire law in order to be saved. Of course, such a task is impossible, showing that salvation only comes through Christ. Hence, Paul threatens them again in Galatians 5:4, "You who are trying to be justified by the law are alienated from Christ; you have fallen from grace." The aorist verbs here "alienated" (κατηργήθητε) and "fallen" (ἐξεπέσατε) do not designate past time. Studies on verbal aspect have taught us that it is a mistake to think that the aorist tense designates past time. Context is decisive in determining the significance of the tense used. Paul probably uses aorists here to impress upon readers the finality and seriousness of accepting circumcision, but he is not reflecting on a decision the readers have already made.[18] They have not been circumcised yet! He warns them, then, in no uncertain terms that the acceptance of circumcision means that they will be estranged from Christ and that they will fall from grace. We can think of the words of Jesus here. If we deny Jesus, He will deny us. And trusting in circumcision for salvation is a concrete way of denying Jesus.

I hope the many warning passages (and there are many more!) noted here indicate that such warnings are pervasive in the NT. The letter to the Hebrews is a sermon with one main point (Hebrews 13:22), and the main point is: don't fall away. The letter is punctuated with warnings (2:1–4; 3:12–4:11; 5:11–6:12; 10:26–39; 12:25–29).[19] Scot McKnight rightly says that the warnings should be interpreted synoptically. In other words, the warning passages should not be isolated from one another.[20] They mutually cast light on one another. Hence, we should not interpret the warning text in Hebrews 6 as if it were distinct from the warnings elsewhere in the letter.

The first warning admonishes the readers not to "drift away" (Hebrews 2:1) or to "neglect such a great salvation" (2:3). Those who do drift away

---

[18] Lightfoot takes the aorists as gnomic. J. B. Lightfoot, *The Epistle of St. Paul to the Galatians with Introduction, Notes and Dissertations* (reprint; Grand Rapids, MI: Zondervan, 1957), 204.

[19] It is not imperative for the point being made here to delineate precisely where the warning texts begin and end. Scholars disagree on the specific parameters of the warning passages. But my point is merely that warnings pervade the letters however one identifies them.

[20] Scot McKnight, "The Warning Passages of Hebrews: A Formal Analysis and Theological Conclusions," *Trinity Journal* 13 (1992): 21–59. McKnight argues that believers can abandon the salvation they once had. I will indicate at the conclusion of the essay why I differ from this assessment.

will not "escape" (2:3). Against Keathley it is quite unnatural to interpret this statement to say, "genuine belief will not turn back."[21] Such a statement is true theologically and is taught in other texts, but it doesn't match the wording of this text. Note how Keathley turns the warning into a declaration. What we have here is a matter of simple grammar. Keathley turns the "if" statements into a declaration, but in doing so he overturns the actual wording of the text. The punishment for those who neglect their salvation is greater than the punishment inflicted on OT Israel for its transgressions (2:2–3), suggesting that final judgment is in view. As we shall see, it is likely, given the other warning texts, that drifting and neglecting here refer to apostasy. The first warning, however, is not completely clear in terms of the sin or consequence and must be discerned by subsequent texts.

The second warning text is much clearer (3:12–4:11). The believers are warned about apostasy, about departing (ἀποστῆναι) from the living God (3:12). They must beware of falling into the same sins as the wilderness generation: unbelief and disobedience (3:12, 18, 19; 4:2, 3, 6, 11). They must not harden their hearts as Israel did (3:8, 13, 15; 4:7). We can be quite sure that apostasy is the issue at hand, for those who harden their hearts and disbelieve and disobey will not enter God's rest (3:11, 18; 4:1, 3, 5, 6, 8, 9, 10, 11). God's rest designates the final rest, and hence stands for the heavenly inheritance that awaits believers. In other words, those who do not heed the warnings will be excluded from the heavenly rest. To put it in theological terms; they will not go to heaven but to hell. The warning here assists us in reading the other warnings in Hebrews, for it is quite unlikely that in some warning texts the readers are admonished about losing rewards and in others they are warned about final judgment. Each of the warnings makes the same point, but the author creatively uses different language so he can engage the readers' minds with different images and pictures of what will happen to them if they fall away.

The third warning text in Hebrews (5:11–6:12) is certainly the most famous. Since all the other warning texts in Hebrews address Christians, as is evident by the use of second person plural ("you") and first person plural ("we," "us") pronouns, it is unlikely that the author addresses a distinct group in chapter 6.[22] They are described as "enlightened" (φωτισθέντας), and the same term is used to designate the Hebrews' response to suffering when they first became believers in 10:32. The readers also "tasted the heavenly gift" (6:4) and "tasted God's word and the powers of the coming

---

[21] Keathley, "Perseverance and Assurance of the Saints," 186.

[22] In defense of the view that they were "almost Christians," see John Owen, *Hebrews: The Epistle of Warning* (Grand Rapids: Kregel, 1953), 96–98. This work is an abridgement by M. J. Tyron of John Owen's *Exposition of the Epistle to the Hebrews* originally published in eight volumes. Roger Nicole, "Some Com-

age" (6:5). Scholars differ on defining "the heavenly gift," but it probably denotes salvation. The "word" refers to the gospel which was proclaimed, and "the powers of the coming age" the fulfillment of salvation history with the death and resurrection of Christ. The key question for our purposes is whether the readers' experience of these blessings was saving or partial. Did they just "sip" these blessings or did they ingest them fully? In other words, does the word "taste" signify something short of salvation or salvation itself? The only other use of the word "taste" (γεύομαι) in Hebrews refers to Jesus tasting death for others (2:8). Clearly, Jesus did not merely "sip" death; He experienced it fully. The only evidence we have from Hebrews suggests, therefore, that the readers truly experienced salvation, the gospel, and the powers of the coming age.

The readers were also "partakers of the Holy Spirit" (6:4). Some understand this to refer to experiences with the Spirit short of salvation. But the word "partakers" (μετόχους) suggests the contrary. Elsewhere in Hebrews the word is used of companions (1:9), of those who share a heavenly calling (3:1), of those who share in Christ (3:14), and of legitimate children who receive discipline (12:8). The verb "share" (μετέχω) indicates that Jesus partook of flesh and blood like all other human beings (2:14), of partaking of milk (5:13), and of the tribe to which one belongs (7:13). In every case the word is used of a real and genuine sharing and partaking. In no instance does the term denote an incomplete or partial sharing. The most natural way to take the phrase is that the readers truly shared in the Holy Spirit. And the Holy Spirit *is the sign* that one is a believer. Those who don't have the Spirit don't belong to God (Romans 8:9). When Paul wanted to persuade the Galatians that they were already Christians and didn't need to be circumcised, he reminded them that they received the Spirit when they believed (Galatians 3:1–5). Similarly, at the Apostolic Council Peter argued that circumcision was unnecessary by reminding those present that Cornelius and his friends received the Spirit without submitting to the rite (Acts 15:7–11). What it means to be a Christian is to receive God's Spirit (1 Corinthians 2:16). It seems likely, therefore, that the author addresses his readers as Christians.

ments on Hebrews 6:4–6 and the Doctrine of the Perseverance of God with the Saints," in *Current Issues in Biblical and Patristic Interpretation: Studies in Honor of Merrill C. Tenney Presented by His Former Students*, ed. Gerald F. Hawthorne (Grand Rapids, MI: Eerdmans, 1975), 355–364; Wayne Grudem, "Perseverance of the Saints: A Case Study of Hebrews 6:4–6 and the Other Warning Passages in Hebrews," in *Still Sovereign: Contemporary Perspectives on Election, Foreknowledge, and Grace*, ed. Thomas R. Schreiner and Bruce A. Ware (Grand Rapids, MI: Baker, 2000), 133–182.

And he warns them in 6:6 about falling away (παραπεσόντας). What he writes here should not be read as a declaration. He is not saying that they have fallen away. He warns them, as he does in every other warning passage, against falling away.[23] In other words, he admonishes them not to commit apostasy, not to depart from the faith. That apostasy is in mind is suggested by the terms he uses, for they would be crucifying Jesus again and "holding him up to contempt" (6:6). The language used indicates that they would be spurning Christ's death by relapsing, communicating that His death was in vain. The consequences of apostasy, as we saw in 3:12–4:11, is clearly damnation. They can't repent again (6:4), and their final end is cursing and burning (6:8). Some want to say that the illustration in 6:7–8 is about rewards, but it is not the *fruit* that is burned but the *ground*, and the ground stands for the person.[24] The warning in Hebrews 5:11–6:12 is addressed to believers, admonishing them to hang on until the end so that they would not be damned forever.

The warning in 10:26–31 fits with what was just said about 5:11–6:12. The danger is apostasy, for the readers are admonished about sinning deliberately (10:26). This matches sinning defiantly in the OT for which there was no forgiveness (cf. Num. 15:30). And Hebrews is saying precisely the same thing, for when one sins willfully, when one turns his back on the Lord, "there no longer remains a sacrifice for sins" (10:26). What the author says here makes perfect sense. If a person repudiates Christ and tramples Him under foot (10:29), then he can't avail himself of His sacrifice. And if they are cut off from His sacrifice, then they are headed for destruction. They will face God's vengeance on the last day (10:30). They will face the "terrifying" prospect of falling "into the hands of the living God" (10:31). Now if that isn't the final judgment, it is hard to know what it is. It scarcely sounds like a passage that says one will lose rewards! Clearly, the sin is apostasy, for the readers are warned about profaning "the blood of the covenant" and insulting "the Spirit of grace" (10:29). Profanation means that one treats Christ's blood as unclean, and the word for "insult" (ἐνυβρίσας) is incredibly strong. The author warns the readers: do not forsake Christ. For if you do, there is no hope for forgiveness and the only prospect is certain judgment. The "reward" that is promised for those who endure is eternal life (10:35). Those who "shrink back" from Christ will face destruction (ἀπώλειαν), but those who persevere in faith will "preserve

---

[23] See my discussion of this issue. Thomas R. Schreiner, *Run to Win the Prize: Perseverance in the New Testament* (Wheaton, IL: Crossway, 2010), 41, n. 24.

[24] Some attempt to restrict what the author says to rewards. E.g., Michael Eaton, *No Condemnation: A New Theology of Assurance* (Downers Grove, IL: InterVarsity, 1995), 216–17.

their souls" (περιποίησιν ψυχῆς, 10:39 ESV). The word for "destruction" here is a typical NT word for what happens at the final judgment, and hence the author contrasts salvation with damnation.

In 12:25 the author returns to the word "escape," recalling 2:3, and framing the warning texts so that the first and last admonition strike a similar note. Again, he emphasizes that the punishment under the new covenant will be more severe than it was under the old (12:25–26). The judgment on Israel on earth functions as a type of a heavenly judgment, which is even more severe. The danger is eschatological ruin since "our God is a consuming fire" (12:29).

The warnings in Hebrews and in the remainder of the New Testament are severe and bracing. Readers are exhorted not to depart from Jesus, for if they do so they will face eschatological judgment. Good works are not just optional but necessary to receive eternal life. Perseverance is clearly a condition for receiving the final blessing. Do the warnings work against the promise of preservation? I will argue that they do not, but another observation should be made at this point. It is better to keep the tension between the warnings and the promises than it is to dismiss either.[25] If none of our explanations work, we must not deny what the biblical text teaches. At the end of the day, we can't fully explain the Trinity or the person of Christ, but we don't deny either the threeness or oneness of God. We affirm both. In the same way, even if we can't fully understand how Jesus can be fully God and fully man, we accept both and teach both. I think we can go farther than simply saying we have a mystery here, but it is better to say what we have here is a mystery instead of dismissing either God's promises or threats, for the wisdom of God is wiser than human thought.

Warnings as Means

Many think the warning passages dampen assurance. Surely there is no warrant or basis of assurance for those giving themselves to evil. The scriptural writers do not furnish assurance if a person is abandoning the Lord. Those forsaking God should not be confident but should be shaken

---

[25] This is the solution proposed by Gerald L. Borchert, *Assurance and Warning* (Nashville: Broadman, 1987). Keathley suggests that I reject Carson's compatibilism ("Perseverance and Assurance of the Saints,"177). But I don't mention Carson or compatibilism in the article, and Keathley actually misunderstands my point. I was only saying that we should not opt for mystery too quickly, for there are certainly mysteries in theology. I was not and am not rejecting mystery or compatibilism in principle. In addition, I don't think Borchert and Carson say precisely the same thing about the warning texts, but that is a discussion for another place or another time.

out of their apathy. On the other hand, the intention of the warnings is actually to provide assurance for those who respond to the admonitions in faith and obedience. For the warnings are one of the means God uses to keep His own. Salvation is not obtained apart from heeding the warnings but by means of attending to them.

My contention is that the warnings are always effective in the lives of the elect. Hence, no one who is elect will ever face damnation, for the elect invariably apply the warnings to themselves and thereby escape destruction. God's grace secures perseverance in the life of His own.[26] Nor can one say: "Since I am elect, I can ignore the warnings and admonitions in scripture." For election is proved and demonstrated by one's perseverance. One confirms one's call and election by doing the will of God (cf. 2 Peter 1:5–11).

Is it false and artificial to say that the warnings are always effective in the lives of the elect? The answer is no. We know from scripture that all the elect will believe since they have been chosen before the foundation of the world (Ephesians 1:4). Still, they must repent and believe to be saved. Their election does not exclude the need to exercise faith. The call to persevere works in precisely the same way. All the elect will persevere, but the promise of preservation does not cancel out admonitions, nor does it contradict the notion that faith alone saves. What we learn from this is that the elect will certainly heed the warnings, and hence the warnings, just like initial faith and repentance, become one of the means by which the elect make it to the end.

Two examples from the Scriptures demonstrate that warnings are one of the means used to secure the promises. The first text from Acts 27 illustrates the principle, for the text speaks of physical rather than spiritual preservation. An angel appears to Paul during the raging storm on the Mediterranean which threatened the lives of everyone on board, promising him that God would preserve the life of everyone sailing with him (27:24). And Paul is confident that it will turn out exactly as God said, that every

---

[26] Berkouwer insightfully remarks on the subject. "We will never be able to understand these words if we see the divine preservation and our preservation of ourselves as mutually exclusive or as in a synthetic cooperation. Preserving ourselves is not an independent thing that is added paradoxically to the divine preservation. God's preservation and our self-preservation do not stand in mere coordination, but in a marvellous way they *are* in correlation. One can formulate it best in this way: *our* preservation of ourselves is entirely oriented to *God's* preservation of us" (*Faith and Perseverance*, 104). He also claims, "Preserving ourselves does not imply that we contribute our part and that God contributes His. Our preserving is oriented to His, and it is included in it. Faith can never say, and will never say, 'This is our part'" (105).

single person will survive the storm at sea. And what God promises comes to pass. Every one of the 276 passengers made it to the island of Malta. After giving the assurance that everyone would live, however, Paul also issued a strong warning.

The sailors tried to escape the ship in the little boat, "pretending that they were going to put out anchors from the bow" (27:30). When Paul saw this he declared, "Unless these men stay in the ship, you cannot be saved" (27:31). Apparently the skill of the sailors was needed to guide the ship during the storm. But why does Paul threaten the centurion and soldiers with loss of life since he had already received a promise that all would live? Isn't the warning beside the point given the assurance that all would survive? The answer is that the warning is the means God used to secure the promise. The promise did not become a reality apart from the warning but through it. As Berkouwer says,

> The doctrine of the perseverance of the saints can never become an *a priori* guarantee in the life of believers which would enable them to get along without admonitions and warnings. Because of the nature of the relation between faith and perseverance, the whole gospel must abound with admonition. It has to speak thus, because perseverance is not something that is merely handed down to us, but it is something that comes to realization only *in the path of faith.* Therefore the most earnest and alarming admonitions cannot in themselves be taken as evidence against the doctrine of perseverance.
>
> To think of admonition and perseverance as opposites, as contradictories, is possible only if we misunderstand the nature of perseverance and treat it in isolation from its correlation with faith. For the correct understanding of the correlation between faith and perseverance, it is precisely these admonitions that are significant, and they enable us to understand better the nature of perseverance.[27]

God promises to save the elect, but the warnings are one of the means God uses to keep them until the end.

Another illustration comes from the eschatological discourse in Mark 13. The end time distress is sketched in by Mark. Some believers will be put to death (13:12), but "the one who endures to the end will be saved" (13:13). The salvation here must be spiritual, for 13:12 states that some will be slain, and hence there is no promise that the elect will be saved from physical death. The same principle applies to 13:20. The tribulation will be so intense that "no human would be saved" (13:20) unless the Lord had shortened the days. "But for the sake of the elect, whom he chose, he

---

[27] Berkouwer, *Faith and Perseverance*, 110–111.

shortened the days" (13:20). Again spiritual salvation is intended, and Jesus startles the readers with the intensity of the suffering that is coming, for it will be so bad that even the elect would apostatize unless the Lord intervened and shortened the time of suffering. But the elect cannot and will not apostatize. As 13:22 says, "False christs and false prophets will arise and perform signs and wonders, to lead astray, if possible, the elect." Even the elect would put their hopes in false messiahs, if it were possible, given the impressiveness of the signs they will perform. But God preserves His own, and the elect will not be duped by the wizardry of messianic pretenders. The promises are sure. It is impossible for the elect to fall away!

The assurance granted by the readers in Mark 13 does not eliminate the need for warnings. Indeed, the warnings are incredibly strong. Believers must not put their faith in false christs and false prophets (13:21). The admonition is crucial, for surely anyone who believes in a false christ instead of the true Christ will not receive eternal life on the last day. Hence, believers must "be on guard" (13:23). They must "Be on guard" and "keep awake" (13:33) and "stay awake" (13:35). Indeed, the text ends with the warning again: "Stay awake" (13:37). Only those who stay awake will obtain eternal life. But why do the readers need warnings about falling prey to false christs since they are assured that as the elect they will believe? Apparently Mark did not think warnings and promises contradicted one another! The warnings accord with and serve the promise. The warnings are one of the means by which the promise of final salvation is realized.

What About Those Who Lapse?

It could be objected that the case made here does not succeed since some of those who hear the warnings indeed fall away. Doesn't that mean that some of the elect actually lose their salvation?[28] Or, doesn't it suggest that warnings and promises aren't compatible after all? When we look at the Scriptures carefully, however, we see that those who fall away did not belong to the elect. They prove that they were not truly part of the people of God by falling away.

The false teachers in 1 John illustrate the point made here. These teachers were part of the church and gave every indication that they were believers. Subsequently they departed from the community and apparently established a rival fellowship. What should we make of them? Have they lost

---

[28] So Dale Moody, *The Word of Truth: A Summary of Christian Doctrine Based on Biblical Revelation* (Grand Rapids, MI: Eerdmans, 1981). See especially 337–365. Cf. also idem, *Apostasy: A Study in the Epistle to the Hebrews and in Baptist History* (Greenville, SC: Smyth & Helwys, 1991).

their salvation? Were they members of the elect that did not persevere to
the end? John comments, "They went out from us, but they did not belong
to us; for if they had belonged to us, they would have remained with us.
However, they went out so that it might be made clear that none of them
belongs to us" (1 John 2:19). The departure of these people demonstrates
that they never truly belonged to God and to the church. If they were truly
believers, they would have persevered and remained in the faith. Their departure proves their inauthenticity. John doesn't teach that they abandoned
a salvation they once had. He indicates that they did not genuinely have it
in the first place. Moody dissents from this reading, saying that the verse
should be translated they "went out from us because they were no longer
of us."[29] But he wrongly inserts the word "no longer" in the text, for John
doesn't say they were "no longer" part of us, but they were never part of
God's people, and their inauthenticity is proved by their defection.[30]

Another text that teaches this truth is Matthew 7:21–23. Jesus warns
His readers that not everyone who invokes Him as Lord will enter the
kingdom of heaven. Only those who do the Father's will shall receive the
inheritance. There will be many who prophesy, exorcise demons, and do
miracles who will be excluded from the kingdom. Jesus will send them
away as "lawbreakers." But note what Jesus says. He doesn't say that they
were once saved and then lost it. He says, "I never knew you" (7:23). They
were never part of the people of God. They only appeared to belong to
Jesus. When we look back retrospectively at those who fall away, it will be
apparent that they were not truly regenerate.

Biblical writers recognized that there were some within the church
who were not truly believers. Paul writes in 1 Corinthians 11:19 that
"There must, indeed, be factions among you, so that those who are approved may be recognized among you." The word "approved" (δόκιμοι) signifies those who are truly saved in the church, and Paul implies that there
are "unapproved" (ἀδόκιμοι) people in the church. The word "unapproved"
(ἀδόκιμοι) in Paul always refers to unbelievers (cf. 2 Corinthians 13:5, 6,
7; 2 Timothy 3:8; Titus 1:16). Those who apostatize were not elected to
salvation; they are the "unapproved," who never belonged to God from the
beginning.

The last example comes from 2 Timothy. Hymenaeus and Philetus
were teaching false doctrine, persuading some of their deviant ideas. Hence,

---

[29] Moody, *The Word of Truth*, 357.

[30] Such texts do not contradict the view that we have warnings to believers
in Hebrews. What we find in Hebrews is a *prospective* text which warns believers,
while what we see in 1 John and in the other texts discussed below are *retrospective*
texts which consider those who have lapsed.

"the faith of some" was being overturned (2 Timothy 2:18). Did those who sided with Hymenaeus and Philetus lose their salvation?[31] It could appear that way to the untutored eye. But Paul explains why such a conclusion is off-center, for "the Lord knows those who are his" (2 Timothy 2:19). Paul draws here on Numbers 16:5 where Korah and his compatriots rebelled against Moses and Aaron. Korah and his friends appeared to belong to the people of God, but their actions demonstrated that they were not truly "His." So too, those whose faith was overturned did not truly belong to God. They only appeared to be believers.

To sum up, those who fall away, as is evident from a number of texts, were not genuine believers. They gave every appearance of being believers, but they were not genuinely a part of the people of God. Those who persevere to the end show by their perseverance that they were truly elect, and those who fail to persevere demonstrate that they were never chosen by God.

Conclusion

The doctrines of preservation and perseverance are not contradictory but complementary. Or to put it another way, they are correlated. Those who persevere until the end do so because of God's preserving and sustaining grace. All of those whom God has foreknown and elected will certainly be glorified. Not a single person who has been chosen by God to be saved will be lost. God will certainly keep those in whom He has begun His good work of salvation. At the same time, the Scriptures warn and admonish believers of the necessity of persevering to the end, threatening them with eternal punishment if they do not continue in the grace of God. I have argued that such warnings do not contradict the promises of preservation. On the contrary, the warnings are the means by which the promise of final salvation is obtained.

End-time salvation is not secured apart from the warnings but *through* them. Hence, God uses the admonitions and warnings in scriptures as one of the means to keep His elect from falling away. Of course, there are some who appear to be genuine believers who fall away. Scripture informs us, however, that they were never truly part of the people of God. Jesus never "knew" them as His own. They were never part of Christ's flock. They show by their departure that they did not truly belong to the church of Jesus Christ.

---

[31] So Moody, *The Word of Truth*, 352.

7

The Compatibility of Determinism And Human Freedom

Bruce A. Ware

In his chapter, "Reflections on Determinism and Human Freedom,"[1] Jeremy Evans opens by asserting that the problem related to human free will and the nature of salvation is "not the compatibility of divine sovereignty and human freedom,"[2] since he claims to uphold the "comprehensive sovereignty"[3] of God along with his own commitment to libertarian freedom.[4] Rather, the problem is "whether we can make sense of the idea that human freedom and causal determinism are compatible."[5] A few pages later Evans states the main purpose of his chapter:

> This chapter aims to provide some thoughts on why endorsing a strong Calvinist view of human freedom is unnecessary even when taking the problem of sin seriously. Again, I affirm the comprehensive sovereignty of God, which is compatible with human freedom, and deny the claim that *determinism* is compatible with human freedom.[6]

---

[1] Jeremy A. Evans, "Reflections on Determinism and Human Freedom," in David L. Allen and Steve W. Lemke, eds., *Whosoever Will: A Biblical-Theological Critique of Five-Point Calvinism* (Nashville, TN, B&H: 2010) 253–274.

[2] Ibid., 253.

[3] Ibid., 255.

[4] Ibid., 253–254

[5] Ibid., 253.

[6] Ibid., 255–256 (italics in original).

My chapter aims to show, contrary to Evans, that determinism and human freedom are compatible in that 1) their compatibility is necessary in order to account for Scripture's own depictions of God's dealings with free human beings, and 2) careful reflection and reasoning based on this biblical teaching undergirds what we see in Scripture, viz., that determinism and human freedom are compatible. We will consider first, then, (some, limited) evidence from Scripture that demonstrates the compatibility of determinism and free and responsible human choosing. Second, we will consider a select number of philosophical issues that relate to and flow out of this biblical teaching, showing that these serve to buttress and undergird what a careful reading of Scripture has already taught us, viz., that determinism and human freedom are compatible. The conclusion I hope to commend, then, is that the best and most faithful reading of the Bible, along with careful reflections from reason, combine to demonstrate that determinism and human freedom are compatible.

The Compatibility of Determinism and Human Freedom Demonstrated from Select Passages of Scripture

Why would any thoughtful Christian hold the position that determinism is compatible with human freedom? The answer that some biblically minded Christians have given is this: determinism and human freedom are compatible at least insofar as the Bible demonstrates that *God's determination* of what people do is compatible with their carrying out those determined actions with *genuine human freedom and responsibility*. Passage after passage of Scripture[7] leads to the conclusion that appeal either to God's determined will alone, or to human free choosing on its own, is inadequate in accounting for many actions that occur in the Scriptures. These passages demonstrate that one must appeal *both* to God's determined will along with human free choice(s) in order to give a full and accurate accounting of just what happened. But if this is the case—i.e., if one must appeal both to God's determined action along with human free action to explain why some event took place—then it is clear that these two together are real and really involved in what takes place; hence, they are compatible. Consider

[7] One should bear in mind that even if only one passage of Scripture, rightly and best understood, indicates that God's determined will that some certain action take place, and human free and responsible choosing to carry out that divinely determined action also takes place, then determinism and human freedom are compatible. That is, either they're compatible or they're not; if even one passage indicates that they are compatible, then they are compatible. But the reality we face in Scripture is that many such "compatibilist" texts are present, though in the space this article affords, we'll look only at four of these.

with me just a very small sampling of what we might call some clear compatibilist texts.

Exodus 3:21–22

First, early in the Book of Exodus, we learn some of God's plans for how He would deliver His people Israel from Egypt. Among the many ways God worked to make this happen is this remarkable detail: God said to Moses, "And I will give this people [Israel] favor in the sight of the Egyptians; and when you go, you shall not go empty, but each woman shall ask of her neighbor, and any woman who lives in her house, for silver and gold jewelry, and for clothing. You shall put them on your sons and on your daughters. So you shall plunder the Egyptians" (Exodus 3:21–22). It appears, then, that God was able to determine something to happen that required for its fulfillment people acting freely in doing what they most wanted to do. This event is not merely accounted for by appeal to God's foreknowledge. That is, God does not tell Moses merely that He knows that before Israel leaves, when the Israelite women ask their Egyptian neighbors for their gold, silver, and clothing that they will give these items to the Israelites. No, there is more than merely this. God tells Moses, "I will give this people favor in the sight of the Egyptians," indicating that God causes something to happen within the Egyptians that leads them to make the choice to give of their wealth to the Israelites before they leave. So, it is not that God merely foreknows what the Egyptians will do, but God determines ("I will give this people favor") what the Egyptians will do. And yet, there is every reason to think that when the Egyptians give the Israelites of their wealth, as God has determined that they do, that the Egyptians did so freely. That is, they did exactly what they most wanted to do, while they also carried out what God determined that they do. It is apparent, then, that we have a case here of the compatibility of divine determinism and human freedom.

Allow me to press this point just a bit further. If you asked the question, "Why did the Israelites leave Egypt with silver, gold, and fine clothing from the Egyptians?" you have to give two (not one) answers to be complete. It won't do merely to say, "The Egyptian women chose to give the Israelite women of their wealth," or conversely, "God caused the Egyptian women to look with favor on the Israelite women so that when asked, the Egyptian women gave of their wealth." Here's the point: Both answers are true, but each is a partial truth. You have to give *both answers together* for the full accounting of what takes place, according to this text. Well, if it is the case that "the Egyptian women chose to give of their wealth" and "God caused the Egyptian women to give of their wealth" are both necessary accountings of the same event, and both true of the same event, then the two statements are compatible. But be clear on this: the first statement is one of the human freedom expressed by those Egyptian women, and the second statement is one of the determination of God to bring something to pass through these Egyptian women that He predicted He would do; hence, human freedom (of the Egyptian women giving of their wealth) and divine determination (God causing them to favor the Israelites) are compatible.

Isaiah 10:5–15

Second, God brought punishment upon the northern kingdom of Israel and the southern kingdom of Judah through the military conquests of foreign nations. He raised up the Assyrians against Israel who took Samaria, its capital city, captive in 722 B.C. And He raised up the Babylonians against Judah who took Jerusalem, its capital city, captive in 586 B.C. That it was *God* who brought about these actions of punishment is clear from innumerable passages, and that *free peoples* and nations carried out the military campaigns is also clear. God raised them up and used them to accomplish His determined will, yet they did what they most wanted when they pillaged Samaria and Jerusalem, respectively. God's determination and human freedom, again, must be seen as compatible.

One passage in particular highlights just how astonishing this compatibility is. In Isaiah 10, we read:

> Ah, Assyria, the rod of my anger; the staff in their hands is my fury! Against a godless nation I send him, and against the people of my wrath I command him, to take spoil and seize plunder, and to tread them down like the mire of the streets. But he does not so intend, and his heart does not so think; but it is in his heart to destroy, and to cut off nations not a few; for he says: "Are not my commanders all kings? Is not Calno like Carchemish? Is not Hamath like Arpad? Is not Samaria like Damascus? As my hand has reached to the kingdoms of the idols, whose carved images were greater than those of Jerusalem and Samaria, shall I not do to Jerusalem and her idols as I have done to Samaria and her images?" When the Lord has finished all his work on Mount Zion and on Jerusalem, he will punish the speech of the arrogant heart of the king of Assyria and the boastful look in his eyes. For he says: "By the strength of my hand I have done it, and by my wisdom, for I have understanding; I remove the boundaries of peoples, and plunder their treasures; like a bull I bring down those who sit on thrones. My hand has found like a nest the wealth of the peoples; and as one gathers eggs that have been forsaken, so I have gathered all the earth; and there was none that moved a wing or opened the mouth or chirped." Shall the axe boast over him who hews

with it, or the saw magnify itself against him who wields it? As if a rod should wield him who lifts it, or as if a staff should lift him who is not wood! (Isaiah 10:5–15, ESV).

Notice two features of this account that are crucial to our understanding of God and His work in the world. 1) Consider first who the primary actor is who brings destruction on the people of Israel and Judah. Clearly, it is not Assyria, who is merely the "axe" and "saw" (10:15) whom God uses to bring about His work. No, the primary actor is God himself who devises and carries out this destruction of His own people through the instrumentality of the pagan nation of Assyria. That God is the primary actor is stressed in 10:5 where Assyria is the "rod of my [i.e., God's] anger," in 10:6 where God is said to "send" and "command" Assyria to do exactly what they do, in 10:12 where we read of the time when "the Lord has finished all His work on Mount Zion and on Jerusalem," referring to God's work of punishment being completed through this pagan army, and in 10:15 where God is the subject who hews with the axe [Assyria] and wields the saw [Assyria], so that the boasting for what occurs should be attributed to the One who hews and wields, not to the mere instruments He uses.

2) Notice second the responsibility Assyria bears before God for the actions that they carry out, actions which fulfill the very determined will of God Himself. Verse 12 gets to the heart of this where we read, "When the Lord has finished all his work on Mount Zion and on Jerusalem, he will punish the speech of the arrogant heart of the king of Assyria and the boastful look in his eyes" (10:12). In other words, despite the fact that Assyria was fulfilling exactly what God ordained they do, and despite the fact that they were God's own instrument (His rod, and axe, and saw) in carrying out God's determined will of judgment against His people, they nonetheless are held accountable for the arrogance of their heart and their lofty pride that led them to think that their superiority gave them the right to destroy what they viewed as the weak and despicable people of Israel.

So, here we have it: God has determined precisely what the Assyrians carry out, and yet God judges the Assyrians for the haughtiness of their hearts in doing what God determined they do. Because they did what they most wanted, with hearts and minds that conceived of their actions in ways that they chose, they acted freely. But clearly also God determined that they do exactly what they did, so much so that when their work of destruction is over, God will declare, "*the Lord* has finished *all his work* on Mount Zion and on Jerusalem" (10:12, italics added). That is, they did exactly what they most wanted to do while they also carried out what God determined that they do. Clearly, then, we have a case here of the compatibility of divine determinism and human freedom.

Before we leave this text, notice again that *two answers* are needed to the question: "Who brought this devastation upon the people of Israel?" One answer, "The Assyrians did, out of the haughtiness of their own hearts," is true. But another answer, "God did, by His determination to use Assyria as His instrument of judgment" also is true. In fact, either answer without the other is incomplete and misrepresents what this passage says really took place. But if both are true, and if both are necessary to give a full account of the destruction of Israel, then it is clear that the two answers together are compatible. The free and responsible actions of the Assyrians, as shown by their arrogant hearts conceiving and carrying out exactly what they most wanted to do, is fully compatible with God's determination to raise up Assyria, commanding and sending them to do exactly what God willed that they do. Divine determination and human freedom, then, are compatible.

Isaiah 44:28–45:4; Ezra 1:1

Third, Cyrus, king of the Medo-Persians, issued a decree that enabled the Israelite exiles in Babylon to return to Jerusalem in 538 B.C. to begin the process of rebuilding the temple. And of course, God predicted through the Prophet Jeremiah that He (God) would be the one who would bring them back to the land. In Jeremiah 24:6, God declared, "I will set my eyes on them [Israel] for good, and I will bring them back to this land. I will build them up, and not tear them down; I will plant them, and not uproot them." And in Jeremiah 29:10, He promises, "When seventy years are completed for Babylon, I will visit you [Israel], and I will fulfill to you my promise and bring you back to this place." But the human instrument God used to make this happen was Cyrus. Interestingly, though, evidently Cyrus was unaware that he was being used of the Lord to bring about the fulfillment of this promise even as he issued his decree for the Israelites to return. Isaiah tells us that God chose Cyrus as His instrument, to fulfill His promise to Israel:

> [It is the LORD] who says of Cyrus, "He is my shepherd, and he shall fulfill all my purpose"; saying of Jerusalem, "She shall be built," and of the temple, "Your foundation shall be laid." Thus says the LORD to his anointed, to Cyrus, whose right hand I have grasped, to subdue nations before him and to loose the belts of kings, to open doors before him that gates may not be closed: "I will go before you and level the exalted places, I will break in pieces the doors of bronze and cut through the bars of iron, I will give you the treasures of darkness and the hoards in secret places, that you may know that it is I, the LORD, the God of Israel, who call you by your name. For the sake of my servant Jacob, and Israel my chosen, I

call you by your name, I name you, though you do not know me" (Isaiah 44:28–45:4, ESV).

Cyrus is described as God's "shepherd" (44:28), God's "anointed" (45:1), who will fulfill all of God's own purposes (44:28). So, God granted to Cyrus military victories enabling him to ascend to a position of world domination (45:1–3). Yet in all of this, even though Cyrus is blessed by God, anointed by God, and called by God to carry out God's will for His people Israel, Cyrus doesn't even know this God of Israel (Isaiah 45:4—"though you do not know me"), whose will he is carrying out.

To add to this, when the fulfillment of God's promise commences and Cyrus does issue the decree by which Israel returns to the land, God moves Cyrus to do what he does. The Book of Ezra opens with these words, "In the first year of Cyrus king of Persia, that the word of the LORD by the mouth of Jeremiah might be fulfilled, the LORD stirred up the spirit of Cyrus king of Persia, so that he made a proclamation throughout all his kingdom and also put it in writing" (Ezra 1:1). We have again, here, an example of the compatibility of divine determinism and human freedom. Certainly God foreknew what He predicted, viz., that Cyrus would proclaim a decree by which the exiled Israelites would return to Jerusalem to rebuild its temple. But clearly what these passages describe involves more than mere foreknowledge. God works in a multitude of ways to bring to pass exactly what He has determined: He works to name Cyrus, to raise him up as king of the newly ascending nation of Persia, He gives military successes to Cyrus, He moves his heart to assist the Jews in exile, and He stirred him up to write the proclamation he did. These are not matters merely of divine foreknowledge; these are matters of divine determination. And yet, would we want to deny that Cyrus acted freely? Certainly, he did what he most wanted as he assembled his military for various campaigns. He did what he most wanted as he made the proclamation for Israel to return. He did what he most wanted when he promised safe passage to the exiles as they made the long and dangerous journey back to Jerusalem. That is, Cyrus did exactly what he most wanted to do, while he also carried out what God determined that he do. It appears, then, that we have a case here of the compatibility of divine determinism and human freedom.

Notice again that two answers are needed in explaining the return of the Jewish exiles to Jerusalem. Is it adequate to say merely that the Israelites returned because Cyrus proclaimed a decree promising them safety and supplies to travel to Jerusalem and rebuild the temple? Or is it adequate to say merely that God brought the exiled people of Israel back from Babylon to Jerusalem through the decree of Cyrus just as He promised and determined He would do? Each answer is true. But each answer, though true, is partial. Each is a necessary part of the full answer, but neither is sufficient in itself. A full accounting of why the exiles of Israel returned from Babylon to their homeland involves both answers. Both are true, and both are necessary elements of the full answer; hence, both answers are compatible as they together give the full reason for the Israelites return from exile. But the first answer appeals to the free decisions Cyrus made in choosing to send the exiles back to Jerusalem. And the second answer appeals to the determination of God to bring His people back from Babylon 70 years after they were deported, and to do so through the instrumentality of Cyrus, king of Persia. Well, if both answers are true, and if both answers are necessary for a full accounting of the events recorded in Scripture, and furthermore, if the first answer involves free human agency while the second answer involves divine determination, then it follows that free human agency and divine determination are compatible.

Acts 2:23; 4:27–28

Fourth, consider the words of Peter explaining how it was that Jesus, the Christ, was put on the cross. In two places early in the Book of Acts, he states:

> this Jesus, delivered up according to the definite plan and foreknowledge of God, you crucified and killed by the hands of lawless men (Acts 2:23, ESV).

> ... for truly in this city there were gathered together against your holy servant Jesus, whom you anointed, both Herod and Pontius Pilate, along with the Gentiles and the peoples of Israel, to do whatever your hand and your plan had predestined to take place (Acts 4:27–28, ESV).

We've landed now at the central action carried out in all of human and cosmic history. The death of Christ on the cross is the single most important event to happen in all of the created order. So, it seems important that we have a clear understanding from Scripture just how it is that Jesus ended up on that cross. As we can see from the passages quoted, Peter gives us two, not just one, answers, both of which are necessary for a full accounting, and only together are they sufficient to explain who put Jesus on the cross.

One answer to the question of who put Jesus on the cross, of course, is this, "Wicked people put Him there." That they are wicked is explicitly indicated in 2:23 where Peter says that Jesus was "crucified and killed by the hands of lawless men," and it is implied by mentioning Herod, Pilate, Gentiles and Jews, all of whom said and did various expressions of hatred and evil in their giving up of Christ to be crucified. But another answer is also given by Peter: "God put Jesus on the cross according to His long-standing plan and purpose, and He did so through the agency of the wicked people who plotted and carried out His crucifixion." Both statements by Peter stress that God acted according to the plan He already had in place of putting His Son on the cross, but the claim recorded in 4:27–28 says in addition that this plan was carried out precisely through and not apart from the very wicked acts of Herod, Pilate, Gentiles and Jews. So once again we see that two answers are needed to account for why Jesus was put on the cross. Wicked men put Him there, and God put Him there through the plans, words and deeds of these wicked men. Since both answers are true, and both are necessary for a full accounting of what took place, it follows that these two answers are compatible.

But what do these two answers involve? The first answer, that wicked people put Jesus on the cross, clearly involves the plans and actions of free moral agents. How could they be charged with being "lawless" were they not free in what they did? They are held responsible for their choices and actions, and hence all that they did was done by them freely. But the second answer, that God put Jesus on the cross according to this eternal plan and through the agency of wicked men, involves God's determination of what He would do, a determination carried out precisely through and not apart from free moral agents. So here we have it: The free and responsible actions of the wicked men who schemed and nailed Jesus to the cross, as shown by their jealous and vengeful hearts conceiving and carrying out exactly what they most wanted to do, is fully compatible with God's determination to put His Son on the cross, working through everything ("to do whatever your hand and your plan had predestined to take place"—Acts 4:28) they did to bring to pass exactly what God had willed from eternity past must take place. Divine determination and human freedom, then, are compatible.

Reasoned Reflections from the Teachings of these Compatibilist Texts

Oh so many more texts could be advanced in support of the claim that the Bible demonstrates that *God's determination* of what people do is compatible with their carrying out those determined actions with genuine *human freedom and responsibility*. But these will suffice to show that a faithful reading of such texts requires the conclusion that we do indeed see compatibilism displayed in Scripture. Having seen some of the specific texts, I wish now to make some more general observations and reasoned inferences from the teachings of these compatibilist texts of Scripture.

First, to avoid this compatibilist conclusion, someone might challenge one or both of its central claims. One could challenge, on the one hand, whether or not the human agents involved really could act freely after God had determined to bring to pass the very things that they chose to do. Or, on the other hand, one could challenge whether God actually had determined what would take place through those very human agents.

Regarding the first option, to go this route is sobering when one begins to take a fuller accounting of all of the compatibilist texts there are in the Bible! Will this become the norm in solving this problem, i.e., that if God has determined something, then the people who carry out what God determined did not act freely? I think one will find soon that this will not work well in trying to avoid compatibilism. Too many passages, including ones we've seen here, make clear that God determines what someone does, and yet they are held responsible for their actions. Recall the Assyrians who carry out precisely what God raised them up and called them to do, and yet when they have finished their brutal work (better: when God's ordained work of judgment through them is done), God judges them for the arrogance that led them to carry out what He determined that they carry out. Recall the wicked men who put Christ on the cross. Are we to conclude that since they carried out exactly what God ordained ("to do whatever your hand and your plan had predestined to take place"—Acts 4:28), that they did not act freely and responsibly? No, everything about these compatibilist texts indicates that both of these realities are simultaneously true: 1) God planned and determined what would take place in such a way that His determination included the very people through whom it would take place, and 2) moral agents marked by genuine freedom[8] and responsibility for their actions carried out exactly what they most wanted to do, and in this they were free as they carried out what God determined they do.

And what of the second option, of denying that there is real divine determination here. Recall a point made earlier: Since God declares in advance not merely what will take place (as though He were relying only on His exhaustive foreknowledge), but He declares in advance what He will do to make it take place including determining those through whom it will take place ("I will give this people favor"—Exodus 3:21; "I send him [Assyria] … I command him [Assyria]"—Isaiah 10:6; "He [Cyrus] is my shepherd, and he shall fulfill all my purpose"—Isaiah 44:28; "delivered up according to the definite plan and foreknowledge of God"—Acts 2:23; "to do whatever your hand and your plan had predestined to take place"—Acts 4:28), the conclusion that God determined their actions is simply unavoidable. So here we have it, genuine human freedom and divine determina-

---

[8] I'll return below to just what this freedom is.

tion are both simultaneously true of what took place, and only with both together are they sufficient in giving a full accounting of what took place; hence, divine determination and human freedom are compatible.

Second, an important distinction needs to be made. We dare not reduce the description of compatibilism being made here to a claim of what might be called a "co-agency of (mere) collaboration." By co-agency of collaboration (or collaborative co-agency) I have in mind a situation where two or more parties both work in carrying out some task, and both together are required to accomplish the task, yet each acts independent from any determining influence from/on the other even as they work together. As an example of such collaborative co-agency, consider this scenario: Sally's car is stuck in the snow and she cannot get it free. Sam and Fred, driving past, see her distress and stop. Sam gets out and pushes Sally's car as Sally tries again to move it forward, but it remains stuck. Fred gets out and joins Sam in pushing, and now the car is loosed so Sally is able to drive free. In such a case, while it is true that Sam and Fred collaborated (lit: they co-labored) in pushing Sally's car, and both Sam's and Fred's actions must be taken together to account for freeing the car, it is not the case that Fred determined Sam's actions or that Sam determined Fred's actions. Each person acted independently of any determining influence by the other, even though it is only as they acted together in collaboration that we can account fully for the task being accomplished.

Such mere collaborative co-agency is not sufficient, though, to explain the many compatibilist texts of Scripture. It is not merely the case, for example, that the Assyrians engaged in warfare against Israel, while God, acting independent of Assyria's activities and with no determining influence over Assyria's actions, works to use these actions as a fitting judgment on His disobedient people. Put differently, it is not the case that God saw what the Assyrians were plotting and thought to Himself, "Well, isn't this convenient! Since the Assyrians are planning on destroying Israel (and of course, I have nothing to do with the plans they are making or whether/how they carry them out), I can collaborate with them and use their actions as a means of bringing My judgment upon My people." Such a notion misses entirely one of the elements central to the compatibilist texts of Scripture. It is not merely that God acts, and human moral agents act, and it is only as one considers both actions together that one can account for what took place. Rather, although compatibilism involves co-agency, to be sure, it is not merely a co-agency of collaboration. Rather, the co-agency of compatibilism (or compatibilist co-agency) necessarily involves the two elements of *determination* and *freedom*. Compatibilist co-agency understands 1) God as agent determining what, when, and how something will take place along with determining those free agents through whom

His plan and work will be accomplished, in conjunction with 2) free moral agents who make their decisions in keeping with their own natures and their highest desires, all the while choosing to do precisely what God has determined that they do.

To make sure the importance of this distinction is clear, consider again how we answer the question, "Who put Christ on the cross?" A biblically faithful response will involve two answers, as we saw above: 1) wicked men put Christ on the cross, and 2) God put Christ on the cross. Thus far our two answers, though correct as far as they go, lack a precision and specificity that Acts 2:23 and 4:27–28 would want to include. As our answers stand now, they could be interpreted as expressive merely of a co-agency of collaboration, i.e., it is both true that certain human moral agents and God the Father did their own respective parts which, together, accounts for putting Christ on the cross. While true as far as this goes, what is lacking here is the determinative connection between the agency of the wicked men and their actions, and the agency of God who planned, purposed and predestined exactly what took place through these wicked men and their actions. So, for a fully faithful account of these texts, and to provide a more careful and precise biblical response, here is how the co-agency of compatibilism would reply to the question of who put Christ on the cross: 1) wicked men acted out of the hatred and jealousy of their own natures, devising and doing what they most wanted, with the aim and result of putting Christ on the cross, and 2) God determined that His Son would die an atoning death on a cross, and to bring this to pass He planned and predestined what wicked men would carry this out along with all of the actions they would do to accomplish this, such that as they acted freely in putting Christ on the cross they fulfilled precisely what God determined they do. This, then, is the co-agency of compatibilism that we find in so many passages of Scripture. Given the biblical testimony that the determination of God is compatible with free human choices and actions that carry out the pre-determined will of God, we accept, then, these truths as demanded by a faithful and careful reading of Scripture.

Before leaving the distinction between collaborative and compatibilist co-agency, it should be observed that there is an element couched within the co-agency of compatibilism that needs to be brought out into the open—a feature that is implicit in what we've just seen that we need now to make explicit. While the co-agency of compatibilism truly is a form of co-agency, it does not mean that each of the actions has equal priority or equal ultimacy in what takes place. This (equal priority and equal ultimacy of the two actions) may be the case, and often is, with the co-agency of collaboration, but it never is the case with compatibilist co-agency. To see this, consider again the question, "Who put Christ on the cross?" As observed above, we need two answers (not just one), expressing the co-agency involved: "Wicked men did," and "God did." But, that one of these answers has priority over the other, that one has an ultimacy that the other lacks, must also be seen. Consider this: Do both of these answers stand in equal causal relation to each other, or does one of these two answers give rise to and account for the other? While it is true that the answers "Wicked men did" and "God did" both are needed to answer, "Who put Christ on the cross?" it is also clear that one of these answers has priority over the other, that only one has an ultimacy that the other lacks. The choices of wicked men to put Christ on the cross took place *because of* the prior and ultimate determination of God to put His Son on the cross by the hands of these godless men. So, while both answers are needed for a full accounting of what took place, the co-agency of compatibilism is evident here precisely in that one of those answers, and not the other, stands as the ultimate answer, the one that has priority and primacy in relation to the other. *Because* God determined long ago to put His Son on the cross by the hands of these godless men in the ways they did, therefore these men chose and acted as they did, out of their natures freely, while fulfilling what God had determined that they do.

Third, the kind of human freedom at work in compatibilism needs to be explicated more clearly. Thus far, I have purposely avoided giving an explicit definition to "freedom" or "free will" because I wanted the compatibilist texts of Scripture to demonstrate that somehow, in some way, it must be the case that determinism and human freedom are compatible. That is, if Scripture is allowed simply to be read and understood for what it says, it seems clear in many, many texts that two things have to be accepted as true: 1) God has determined what human agents carry out, and 2) those human agents who carry out what God has determined are held responsible for their actions. But, if these human agents are morally responsible before God for what they do, they should best be understood as free in doing what they do, despite the fact that they are carrying out what God determined they do. So, while we may not yet understand the sense in which they are free and morally responsible for their actions when they carry out what God has determined they do, nonetheless we need to see and accept that somehow, in some way, because they are morally responsible, they must be seen as genuinely free.

Why allow Scripture first to demonstrate the compatibility between determinism and some sense of human freedom before defining what that freedom is? This is exactly where many discussions of whether determinism and human freedom are compatible go astray from the very outset, in that they begin with a definition of "freedom" that is, of necessity, *incompatible* with determinism. So, the text is never allowed to correct this assessment, because the text cannot be examined without this incompatibilist definition of freedom already in mind and already established. So instead here, we have seen from looking at texts of Scripture that determinism and freedom *are* compatible, and we were not forced to deny what is evident in these texts by imposing a definition of freedom that would have ruled out from the get go their compatibility—which compatibility is required from a fair and honest reading of those texts.

What is the understanding of freedom often assumed that of necessity rules out and denies compatibilism, and what understanding of freedom best accords with the compatibilism seen in these texts? We'll take these in order.

1) The sense of freedom often asserted from the outset, and one that surely is incompatible with determinism, is often called "libertarian freedom." The libertarian notion of freedom asserts the supposed "power of contrary choice," viz., that an agent is free in making a choice if and only if, at the moment he makes that choice, he could have chosen contrary to what in fact he did choose. David Basinger, a libertarian himself, writes that proponents of libertarian freedom hold that "given the conditions preceding any voluntary decision, more than one decision must be possible—the person making the decision must be in a position to choose differently."[9] Or again, libertarians hold the view that "some human actions are chosen and performed by the agent without there being any sufficient condition or cause of the action prior to the action itself."[10] By "sufficient condition or cause," Hasker is claiming that none of the factors or conditions present when a choice is made, nor any set of those factors or conditions, will necessitate *just this choice and not another*. In other words, libertarian freedom asserts, then, that when making a libertarianly free choice, at the exact moment of choosing with all things being just what they are at that moment, none of the conditions true then, nor any set of those conditions, requires the agent to make just one choice, but rather given those exact conditions, he could choose one thing or something to the contrary.

Although this view of freedom is widely held and even wildly popular in some circles, it is highly questionable whether the libertarian notion of freedom is coherent. I have argued elsewhere[11] that though the libertarian notion of freedom has an intuitive appeal and initial sense of reasonable-

[9] David Basinger, *The Case for Freewill Theism: A Philosophical Assessment* (Downers Grove, IL: InterVarsity, 1996), 26.

[10] William Hasker, *Metaphysics: Constructing a Worldview* (Downers Grove, IL: InterVarsity, 1983), 32, quoted in Evans, "Reflections on Determinism and Human Freedom," 253.

[11] See my *God's Greater Glory: The Exalted God of Scripture and the Christian Faith* (Wheaton, IL: Crossway, 2004) 61–95, esp. 85–88.

ness, that on examination it proves to fail altogether to account for why persons do what they do. In summary, here's the problem: if at the moment that an agent chooses A, with all the conditions being just what they are when the choice is made, he could instead have chosen –A or B, then it follows that any reason or set of reasons the agent would give for why he chose A would be the *identical reason or set of reasons* for why instead the agent might instead have chosen –A or B. But if the reason(s) for A are identical to those for –A or B, then there is no answer to the question, "Why did the agent choose A *instead of* –A or B?" or "Why might the agent have chosen –A or B *instead of* A?" If the reasons are identical for why the agent might choose A, on the one hand, or –A or B, on the other hand, then there is no explanation at all for why the agent chose just what he did. Hence, this view of freedom fails altogether to explain why we do what we do, and since it cannot give a causal explanation for effects (choices) that take place, it proves to be incoherent as a conception of human volition.

Despite this major problem with libertarian freedom, it remains the prevailing view of freedom among many, including many Christians. I won't speculate here just why this may be the case, but I will turn now to this central point: all parties agree—both libertarians and non-libertarians—that if the kind of freedom we have is libertarian freedom, then we must conclude that determinism is flatly incompatible with human freedom. Here's why: If God has determined that a human agent do A, then it must be the case that he will do A. But if he must do A and he cannot do –A or B, then he is not (libertarianly) free. Or from the other direction: If an agent possesses libertarian freedom and so has the power of contrary choice, then when he does A, it must be the case that he could have done instead –A or B, and hence it cannot be the case that he was determined to do just A, or –A, or B. Libertarian freedom, then, by its very nature as defined by its advocates, stands completely contrary to compatibilism. Yes, some things can be determined, but if they are, they cannot be carried out (libertarianly) freely. Or some things can be carried out (libertarianly) freely, but if they are, they cannot have been determined. Every human choice and action is either (libertarianly) free, or determined, but it cannot be both.

In light of this, it does seem disingenuous, then, for Jeremy Evans, an advocate of libertarian freedom, to affirm, as quoted earlier, "the comprehensive sovereignty of God, which is compatible with human freedom."[12] Does not the word "comprehensive" in the phrase "comprehensive sovereignty" mean that it includes everything? But is it not the case that for

---

[12] Evans, "Reflections on Determinism and Human Freedom," 255–256.

any and all libertarianly free actions done by moral creatures, that God does not and cannot exert any control over just what happens? Isn't this at the heart of the solution to the problem of evil as libertarians conceive it—that God should not be held accountable for evil done by His moral creatures, since they brought about the evil that they did with libertarian freedom such that God could not prevent (without destroying their libertarian freedom) them from doing it? And just imagine for a moment how many morally free creatures there are in the world at any given time and how many free choices and actions these moral creatures make every moment, every hour, every day—*none of which God can control.* And yet to call God's sovereignty "comprehensive" seems to stretch its definition beyond any reasonable limit. Better yet, it would seem to me, would be to simply tell the truth—Evans' view is one in which God sovereignly made a choice to restrict the extent of His own sovereignty when He chose to create creatures with libertarian freedom. To the extent that they make their choices and carry out their actions with this libertarian freedom (which accounts for a huge percentage of what takes place in human history!), God does not and cannot sovereignly control what they do. To be sure, He can attempt to influence, and He can respond, but one thing He cannot do is ensure that what He wants to take place (or not take place) will happen (or not happen) if libertarianly free creatures are responsible for what is done. Well, then, it seems that libertarian freedom is not only incompatible with determinism, it also is incompatible with the comprehensive sovereignty of God, despite protestations to the contrary.

In light of the biblical study above, though, we have seen that the Bible demonstrates over and again human choices and actions for which those human agents are held morally responsible while it also is the case that what they choose and do fulfills exactly what God had determined. We have seen, that is, that compatibilism is demonstrated from Scripture, that divine determination and human morally free choice and action both happen together. Yet, if libertarian freedom, by definition, is contrary to compatibilism and cannot account, then, for what we see demonstrated in Scripture, it behooves us to consider another understanding of human freedom—one that both accounts for why we do what we do as free human agents, and one that accords with the compatibilism that Scripture demonstrates.

2) Another sense of human freedom, and one that is compatible with divine determinism while also accounting for why we choose and act as we do, is sometimes called, "freedom of inclination."[13] According to this view of freedom, an agent is free in making a choice if and only if, at the

[13] For further discussion, please see my *God's Greater Glory*, esp. 78–84.

moment he makes that choice, he is not constrained or coerced in his choosing but rather chooses according to his *deepest* desire, his *strongest* inclination, or according to what he most wants. Of course, since the agent chooses according to his deepest desire or strongest inclination, it makes no sense to imagine that his freedom consists in his ability to do otherwise—right? If his deepest desire and strongest inclination is to choose A, then what sense does it make to say that he might, instead, have chosen –A or B? Why would he choose contrary to his *deepest* desire or *strongest* inclination? What sense does that make? For to choose –A or B would be to choose against what may be thought to be his highest desire, but if he really did that, then his choice of –A or B would actually be the choice that he desired most! The simple way to understand freedom of inclination is this: as morally free agents, we always choose and do what we most want. That is, when all of the various factors that go into our choosing have weighed in, as it were, our minds eventually settle on the one thing that we desire the most. Our freedom, then, is seen in just this: we think and consider and plan and muse, but in the end, we make a choice—a choice that represents our deepest desire, our strongest inclination, or more simply, what we most want.

Now, it should be clear that we may have, and often do have, competing desires as we endeavor to "make up our minds." Consider the dieter (my apologies to some readers for this illustration). He may desire the chocolate cake, and the berry pie, and strawberry shortcake, and he may also desire to stay on his diet and refuse them all. Clearly, he has competing desires. Yet, it is also clear that he will make one (and only one) choice. After thinking, and musing, and listening to other's comments, and considering his prior commitments, etc., he will eventually do the one thing that he most wants. Let's say that his diet has been going well, and he is with people who have encouraged him in the gains (losses!) he's seen, and he chooses to refrain. There can be no doubt but that he had other desires strongly at work in him. But it is also just as sure that he acted according to only one of those desires, the desire that prevailed in his own mind and heart as he considered all of the factors. His freedom, then, was seen in his ability to choose and act according to his strongest inclination, not in some supposed power of contrary choice.

How, then, is freedom of inclination compatible with divine determinism? To the extent that God is able to know all of the factors that go into our minds formulating the strongest inclinations for our choices, He also is in a position to influence those factors and by that, He can ensure what strongest inclination will actually come to pass in our minds and hearts. Something like this must have happened with the Egyptian women who gave their silver, gold, and fine clothing to the Israelites—right? As you recall, God said, "I will give this people [Israel] favor in the sight of the Egyptians" (Exodus 3:21) indicating some work in them that would incline their hearts to want, as their strongest inclination, to do what otherwise one would never expect them to do, viz., give of their wealth to the Israelites. Something like this must have taken place in God's work with the Assyrians. God not only controlled many factors that resulted in their military successes and ascendency over other nations, but He also knew that through these military triumphs Assyria would grow haughty and so would develop a highest inclination to destroy the Israelites. At least we know this—the Bible does not indicate merely that God knew that Assyria would destroy Israel, but the Bible indicates that God raised up Assyria, commissioned Assyria, to do just what they did. This requires some means God used in the hearts and minds of these Assyrians to assure that what they most wanted—what became, over time, their deepest desire and strongest inclination—was exactly what God determined that they do. Yet, because they did exactly what they most wanted, they are held morally responsible for their actions, even though what they did actually fulfilled the prior determination of God.

And of course, in order for God to bring about some of His determined ends, He must grant to us altogether new inclinations (the "new hearts" of Ezekiel 36:26), since none of our inclinations, by our old natures, would ever choose to do what God has called us to do. Here is the marvel and the miracle of God's gracious effectual calling and the new birth. Whereas before we were born again, our highest inclinations were always, in one form or another, to turn from God and reject the gospel of Christ (e.g., Romans 8:6–8; 1 Corinthians 1:18–25), now, by His work of grace and the renewing work of the Spirit, God brings about in His elect a new heart that manifests a new strongest inclination and deepest desire to turn from sin to the very Christ we formerly despised. The opening of our blind eyes (2 Corinthians 4:4–6) is the very work of God to grant us desires for Him and longings for Christ we did not have before.

So we see, then, that because our freedom is a freedom of inclination, and because the sovereign God is able to influence those factors that give rise to our highest inclinations—either mildly through monitoring factors that affect our inclinations, or more radically through giving us altogether new inclinations through new minds and new hearts—we are able to affirm together that God is able to determine what free creatures carry out. There is no conflict in this assertion, and most importantly, it is an assertion based squarely on the teaching of God's Word.

Conclusion

There is much, much more that could be said at this point, but not all can be done or said in one article or chapter. What we have been able to see, though, is remarkable biblical testimony of the fact that *God's determination* of what people do is compatible in Scripture with their carrying out those determined actions with genuine *human freedom and responsibility*. How remarkably clear Scripture is, if we but let it speak for itself. Yes, both divine determination of free actions, and the genuine freedom and moral accountability of those actions, go together in the teaching of Scripture, and so they must go together in the theology of our minds and hearts.

We are not in a position, then, where we need to choose one over the other. If God determines something to take place, and this only occurs as human agents bring those determined actions to pass, we do not have to conclude that they could not have been free. Or if we see moral human actions that bring moral accountability for what was done, we do not have to reject God's determinative influence in what took place. Rather, as we see over and again throughout the Bible, God is able to determine the events of history, and the actions of innumerable moral creatures. But, while this is true, these actions also take place as His moral creatures choose and act according to their deepest desires and strongest inclinations, thus acting in genuine freedom and moral accountability, yet all the while they are carrying out exactly and precisely what God, long ago, planned and determined that they do. That both are true is crystal clear in the Bible, if passages are allowed to be read and understood for what they say. Since both divine determination and moral freedom and responsibility are taught in Scripture, and since both, then, are true and compatible, may we, with humility, make and fulfill this pledge: What therefore God hath joined together, let no man put asunder. For the glory of God, and to the end of understanding better who we are before this Sovereign, may this be so.

8

God's Sovereignty Over Evil

Stephen J. Wellum

The relationship of God to sin and evil—what is famously known as "the problem of evil"—is one of the most difficult problems in all theology. Non-Christians often appeal to the problem of evil, especially in its logical or philosophical form, as a crucial reason for not believing in the existence of God, thus placing Christians in a defensive posture which necessitates some kind of apologetic answer. In its logical form, it is a serious challenge to the Christian faith since it seeks to demonstrate the internal inconsistency of our theological beliefs. Often dubbed by many as the "Achilles' heel" of theology, it attempts to argue that it is illogical to affirm simultaneously belief in the God of the Bible who is sovereign, omnipotent, and perfectly good and the existence of evil in the world. For if a good God exists and He is all-powerful to prevent evil, then why is there all the suffering and evil in the world? (which, sadly, is not difficult to document). Regardless of whether we are talking about *moral* evil, i.e., the sin of rational creatures, or *natural* evil, i.e., anything that brings suffering or difficulty into the lives of people such as earthquakes, floods, and diseases, how can there be evil in the world, if the Christian God exists?

The problem of evil, however, is not just an issue that non-Christians raise and which rightly requires a full-blown biblical-theological answer; it is also a problem for Christians, in at least two ways. First, it is a problem in regard to our daily lives, questions, and struggles, what has been labeled the "emotional or religious problem of evil." Christians too, live in a fallen world ravaged by sin, and even though we may not question in exactly the same way as the non-Christian how God and evil can exist simultaneously, we often wrestle with the relationship of God's sovereignty to evil and wonder why specific evils happen to us and others. We often cry with the people of God in Scripture, "Why?" and "How long O Lord?" and if not careful, we may even question and doubt God's rule over the world and other truths about Him. It is certainly the case that all of us, if we live long enough, will not escape some form of suffering in our lives. It is for this reason that Christians too wrestle with the problem of evil and it is also why, if possible, we must think through the issue biblically and theologically in order to place ourselves in a better position to respond to suffering and evil in a proper and godly way.

Second, the problem of evil is a problem for Christians in the sense that *within* Christian theology, given differing conceptions of divine sovereignty, human freedom, and God's providential rule over the world, there is an ongoing debate as to which theological viewpoint is more *biblical* in its theologizing about the relationship of God to evil. In terms of this latter debate, within evangelical theology (including Southern Baptist life), broadly speaking, lie the theological positions of Arminianism and Calvinism. Both viewpoints have much in common and both are considered within the boundaries of orthodox theology, yet given their different construal of divine providence they sharply disagree on how we ought to think of God's sovereignty over evil. On the one hand, Calvinists often contend that the Arminian solution to the problem of evil—famously known as "the free will defense"—incorporates a libertarian view of human freedom which leads to a reduction of divine sovereignty and is thus inconsistent with the biblical data and less than an adequate answer theologically and practically. On the other hand, most Arminians charge Calvinists with so (over)emphasizing divine sovereignty that the *logical* entailment is that God must be viewed as ultimately responsible for evil and that human freedom is an illusion—obviously conclusions which Scripture does not endorse and, it must be added, which no responsible Calvinist affirms.

A recent example of this specific charge against Calvinism is the essay by Bruce Little, "Evil and God's Sovereignty."[1] In Little's discussion of the problem of evil he states that his aim is not to give his solution to the problem, even though it is quite evident in his essay that he aligns with the "free will defense." Instead, he states that his purpose is to examine "answers given by those in the theological tradition called Calvinism"[2] in

---

[1] Bruce A. Little, "Evil and God's Sovereignty," in David L. Allen and Steve W. Lemke, eds., *Whosoever Will: A Biblical-Theological Critique of Five-Point Calvinism* (Nashville, TN: B&H, 2010), 275–298. Cf. Roger E. Olson, *Against Calvinism* (Grand Rapids, MI: Zondervan, 2011), 83–101, who makes a similar charge.

[2] Little, "Evil and God's Sovereignty," 276.

order to discover how Calvinists discuss the problem and thus evaluate, at least on this point, the merit of Calvinism as a theological position. Eventually, at the end of his investigation, Little concludes that Calvinism, *if* it is logically self-consistent, requires the unbiblical belief that "God is morally responsible for evil."[3] It is for this reason that Little rejects the merits of Calvinism and opts for a view which he does not disclose other than to say it is neither Calvinist nor Arminian, whatever that position is![4]

Even though this charge against Calvinism is fairly common, it is a serious one which requires some kind of response. Is it the case that those who believe in a high view of divine sovereignty must *logically* conclude that God is morally responsible for evil, as Little and others in the Arminian tradition contend? If so, then clearly Calvinism is out of step with Scripture, but no responsible Calvinist would agree with such a conclusion. So how should Calvinists respond to such an indictment? What does Scripture teach in regard to the relationship between God's sovereignty and evil and what kind of response can we give to the problem of evil raised by non-Christians and even wrestled with by Christians?

The purpose of this chapter is to outline briefly a basic Calvinist response to these questions. Given the constraints of a single chapter, the sheer complexity and difficulty of the topic (which is certainly an understatement!), and the desire not merely to be polemical but to present a positive biblical-theological case for how we ought to think through the relationship between God's sovereignty over evil and its implications for our lives, I will proceed in four steps: (1) I will discuss two methodological issues which are important in the overall treatment of the issue; (2) I will summarize the sweep of biblical data which must be considered if one wants to do justice to the God, sin, and evil relationship in Scripture; (3) In light of the biblical data, I will lay out how I, as a Calvinist, would respond to the challenge raised by the problem of evil in a biblically faithful and logically consistent way; (4) I will conclude with some biblical-theological reflections of a more practical nature on the subject of a sovereign God and the problem of evil.

Methodological Issues in the Discussion

In attempting to answer the question: What does the Bible teach on the relationship of God's sovereignty over evil? we are *doing* theology. The discipline of theology, at its heart, seeks to apply all of Scripture to all of life, which minimally involves correctly interpreting the whole Bible on its

[3] Ibid., 297.
[4] See ibid., 277.

own terms and drawing proper conclusions which are consistent with the entire canonical presentation.[5] Theology best fits under the rubric of "faith seeking understanding." Starting with Scripture, grounded in its own self-attestation, we learn "to think God's thoughts after Him." We let Scripture speak for itself as God's plan progressively is disclosed to us across the warp and woof of redemptive history.[6] As we read Scripture we discover on the basis of God's own self-revelation through human authors, for example, who He is, how He governs the world, the nature of His providential activity, who we are, what our problem is, and how all of God's purposes have come to fulfillment in our Lord Jesus Christ. We learn to bring our thoughts captive to Christ and answer our questions in light of Scripture and not the other way around.

This may sound basic and straightforward, but unfortunately it is not always consistently followed, especially when we compare how various people actually do theology. So before I turn to the biblical data regarding God's sovereignty over evil, I will first underscore two implications of this understanding of theology for our discussion of the problem of evil.

Sola Scriptura

This wonderful reformation phrase should never be used as a mere slogan; two important points are entailed by it. First, at its heart, *sola scriptura* reminds us that Scripture alone is our final authority and epistemological warrant for all of our theological proposals. Thus, when we begin to ask such questions as: What is meant by God's sovereignty? How are we to think of the relationship between God's sovereignty, human freedom, and evil? *Sola scriptura* demands that we find our answers first and foremost in Scripture. This is not to deny that we all come to Scripture with pre-conceived ideas in a whole host of areas including our indebtedness to historical theology. It is no doubt the case that we approach Scripture with various understandings of the nature of divine sovereignty, human freedom, and so on, but *sola scriptura* entails that Scripture is able to, and it must correct our pre-understandings. Thus, how we understand the nature and scope of God's sovereign rule in the world must come from Scripture and not from what we think it is. How we understand the nature of human freedom must also be derived from Scripture as we think through how

[5] For this understanding of theology, see John M. Frame, *The Doctrine of the Knowledge of God* (Phillipsburg, NJ: P&R, 1987), 76.
[6] I have developed these points at length in Peter J. Gentry and Stephen J. Wellum, *Kingdom through Covenant: A Biblical-Theological Understanding of the Covenants* (Wheaton, IL: Crossway, 2012), chapters 1–3.

Scripture presents our human choices in relationship to God's sovereign rule and action in the world, and so on. In fact, as I will argue below, Scripture teaches a number of truths about divine sovereignty, human freedom, and the reality of evil, and it is the theologian's task to make sure that in his theologizing *all* of these biblical truths are maintained simultaneously *and* precisely in the way that Scripture presents them. Given *sola scriptura* I have no right to pick and choose certain biblical truths or privilege one set of truths over another. I must let Scripture unpack the God-evil relationship on its own terms, and even if tension arises between the data, my reason must never re-interpret or eliminate the data simply because I do not grasp how it all fits together or it seems illogical to me.[7]

Second, *sola scriptura* entails that Scripture serves as the standard/criterion by which we evaluate the use of extrabiblical concepts and terms. As theology *applies* Scripture to all areas of life, including the question of God's relationship to evil, theology does more than merely repeat Scripture. Inevitably and correctly, as theology moves from "canon to concept" it often employs the use of extrabiblical terminology for at least two reasons.[8] First, it does so *constructively* in order to make sense of the biblical data, to clear up confusion, and to demonstrate that God's unified revelation is coherent and non-contradictory. Second, it does so *apologetically* in order to defend the faith against its critics, especially those who contend that Scripture is logically incoherent—a crucial charge leveled against us by the logical problem of evil. So, for example, words and concepts such as the "Trinity," "hypostatic union," "*communicatio idiomatum*," are all extrabiblical, yet they are legitimate because they faithfully and accurately explicate and elucidate the biblical data both in terms of the constructive and apologetic task of theology. But it is crucial to note: the criterion by which these terms/concepts are judged appropriate is Scripture.[9]

In the problem of evil discussion this point is especially pertinent in how we define what is meant by human freedom.[10] As I will argue below,

---

[7] For a discussion of this use of reason in theology, see Wayne Grudem, *Systematic Theology* (Grand Rapids, MI: Zondervan, 1994), 34–35; and for how we must avoid reductionism in our theological conclusions, see D. A. Carson, *How Long O Lord? Reflections on Suffering and Evil* (Grand Rapids, MI: Baker, 1990), 220–27.

[8] The term from "canon to concept" comes from Kevin Vanhoozer's work in discussing theological method and hermeneutics. See e.g., Kevin J. Vanhoozer, *The Drama of Doctrine: A Canonical-Linguistic Approach to Christian Theology* (Louisville, KY: Westminster John Knox, 2005).

[9] See the discussion of this point in Kevin J. Vanhoozer, *Remythologizing Theology: Divine Action, Passion, and Authorship* (Cambridge: Cambridge University Press, 2010), 408.

[10] For a more complete discussion of this point see chapter 7 by Bruce Ware.

Scripture presents humans as free, i.e., we make choices, we do what we want to do, and we are held responsible by God for our choices. However, nowhere does Scripture give us a precise definition of human freedom. The biblical data on the nature of human freedom is underdetermined. So as we begin to theologize and move from "canon to concept" it is legitimate to wrestle with the nature of "freedom" and even employ extrabiblical categories/definitions to help clarify what is meant by the concept, yet we must reject concepts of freedom which undermine or lead us to re-define or eliminate biblical teaching. Not all definitions of "freedom" are equal; in the end they must be judged by Scripture in terms of their consistency with the biblical teaching.

In the current theological/philosophical discussion, there are two basic views of human freedom which are primarily discussed and adopted—libertarian free will and compatibilistic freedom. The most basic sense of libertarian freedom is that a person's act is free if it is not causally determined. For libertarians this does not mean that our actions are random or arbitrary. Reasons or causes may play upon the will as one chooses, but none of them is *sufficient* to incline the will decisively in one direction or another. Thus, a person could always have chosen otherwise than he did.[11] On the other hand, the most basic sense of compatibilism is that human actions are causally determined, yet free. In other words, a compatibilist view of freedom perceives the human will as decisively and *sufficiently* inclined toward one option as opposed to another, yet it is still free as long as the following requirements are met: "(1) The immediate cause of the action is a desire, wish, or intention internal to the agent, (2) no external event or circumstances compels the action to be performed, and (3) the agent could have acted differently if he had chosen to."[12] If these three conditions are

---

[11] David Basinger, "Middle Knowledge and Classical Christian Thought," *Religious Studies* 22 (1986): 416, states it this way: for a person to be free with respect to performing an action he must have it within his power "to choose to perform action A or choose not to perform action A. Both A and not A could actually occur; which will actually occur has not yet been determined." Also see William Hasker, *Metaphysics* (Downers Grove, IL: InterVarsity Press, 1983), 32–44; and Michael Peterson, et al. *Reason and Religious Belief* (New York, NY: Oxford Press, 1991), 59–61.

[12] Peterson, *Reason and Religious Belief*, 59. The third requirement that Peterson, et al. lists is very important—the agent could have acted differently if he had chosen to. Libertarians argue that no one is free who could not have (actually) done otherwise. Compatibilists argue that the meaning of the phrase "could have done otherwise" must be carefully defined. The key issue here is the meaning of *can* or *could*. There are at least seven ways that this expression can be understood. And it is only in one of these ways that the compatibilist can not affirm "could

met, then even though human actions are determined, they may still be considered free.

When one considers these two conceptions of human freedom two points need to be considered: first, most admit that they are both possible views in the sense that there is no logical contradiction in affirming either one; second, they both cannot be true. How, then, does one decide between them? Ultimately, if *sola scriptura* means anything, one must embrace the view which best fits the biblical data, not our pre-conceived notions of what human freedom is or ought to be.

Now it is precisely at this point that the question is often begged in regard to the freedom debate. Many Calvinist critics, including Jeremy Evans and Bruce Little, adopt a libertarian view of human freedom without ever wrestling with whether that view of human freedom is consistent with the Scriptural data. Instead, they *assume* a libertarian view for various reasons external to Scripture, bring that understanding to the biblical data, and then argue that a high view of divine sovereignty is not compatible with it![13] But the problem with this kind of reasoning is that this is precisely the question at issue. No doubt, *if* one adopts a libertarian view, by definition, it will lead to a re-definition and reduction of divine sovereignty but this is precisely what Scripture will not allow! As Bruce Ware admirably demonstrates in chapter 7, Scripture teaches both a high view of divine sovereignty *and* human freedom which necessitates that the view of freedom we adopt must be consistent with this biblical teaching, which in

have done otherwise." However, in the other six ways, it is perfectly appropriate for the compatibilist to affirm that the "agent could have done otherwise" and if being able to do otherwise is the criterion for being free, then a compatibilist can legitimately speak of freedom. On this important point, see John S. Feinberg, "God Ordains All Things," in David Basinger and Randall Basinger, eds., *Predestination and Free Will: Four Views of Divine Sovereignty and Human Freedom* (Downers Grove, IL: InterVarsity Press, 1986), 26–28; cf. John S. Feinberg, *No One Like Him: The Doctrine of God* (Wheaton, IL: Crossway, 2001), 625–676.

[13] On this point see Jeremy A. Evans, "Reflections on Determinism and Human Freedom," in Allen and Lemke, eds. *Whosoever Will*, 253-56; Little, "Evil and God's Sovereignty," 281–94. Little argues that many Calvinists reject the notion of free will by which he means libertarian freedom (281) and then rejects any idea that God can ordain all things since this would be a denial of libertarian freedom (284), which again begs the question. What Little must first wrestle with is the biblical data in regard to the divine sovereignty-human freedom relationship and then after looking at the biblical data choose a view of human freedom which is consistent with that data. Otherwise, Scripture is not functioning as an authority for him; instead he is deciding his metaphysical options, namely the nature of divine sovereignty and human freedom, on a criterion external to Scripture. But what precisely is that? He never tells us, but it is certainly not Scripture.

the current discussion is some form of compatibilism. Even though "compatibilism" is an extrabiblical concept and it does not solve all the freedom questions, it is a better fit with the biblical teaching regarding God's sovereignty and as such, it is the view which ought to be adopted. Libertarian freedom should be rejected since it denies from the outset that God can and does ordain our *free* decisions, something which Ware demonstrates and which I will argue below.[14]

Drawing "Logical" Conclusions from Scripture

A second methodological issue central in the discussion is what it means to be "logical" in our theological conclusions. On both sides charges of inconsistency are made, but more often than not the accusation is leveled against the Calvinist. Bruce Little constantly makes this charge. He argues that Calvinists, who believe that God ordains all things, including evil, must *logically* conclude that God is responsible for evil,[15] that no person can fight against social injustice since it would be an exercise in futility,[16] that we must conclude that God actually needs evil to receive all glory to Himself,[17] and that humans in reality have no free will (of course, free will defined in a libertarian sense without biblical argument).[18]

From the outset, it is important to note that on all these assertions, Calvinists would deny that these conclusions *logically* follow from their belief that God ordains all things including the free actions of His creatures. Obviously this raises the important methodological question of how to demonstrate logical consistency in one's argument, and similar to our discussion above, we must be careful that we do not beg the question in our answer. At the most pedantic level, in order to draw logical conclusions we must first make sure that we have sufficient data to make those conclusions. Our premises must be true, including in our case, a proper understanding of such things as divine sovereignty, human freedom, and the relationship between the two—all of which assumes that we have enough data to draw on in order properly to say what is logical or not. Yet is this

---

[14] This point is strongly emphasized by John M. Frame, "The Problem of Evil," in Christopher W. Morgan and Robert A. Peterson, eds., *Suffering and the Goodness of God* (Wheaton, IL: Crossway, 2008), 148–152; cf. idem., *The Doctrine of God* (Phillipsburg: P&R, 2002), 160–82. For a defense of this assertion, see Carson, *How Long O Lord?*, 199–228; Feinberg, *No One Like Him*, 625–676; Frame, *Doctrine of God*, 21–159.

[15] Little, "Evil and God's Sovereignty," 280, 288, 293, 296–97.

[16] Ibid., 284.

[17] Ibid., 287–292.

[18] Ibid., 294.

not precisely where problems begin to rise since the premises we employ and the knowledge we have must be derived from Scripture? But Scripture, as God's Word, is true, infallible, and inerrant, however it is *not* exhaustive in its teaching and instruction, especially in regard to these matters. All we have to do is read the book of Job and notice that in God's response to Job, He does not give him a detailed answer to all of his questions. In fact, repeatedly God says to Job, your judgment is wrong about me since you simply do not know enough.[19] Or, another famous text that makes this exact point is Deut 29:29: "The secret things belong to the LORD our God, but the things revealed to us and to our children forever...."[20]

It is for this reason that Christian theology has always made the crucial distinction between *archetype* and *ectype* knowledge, related to the Creator-creature distinction at the heart of the entire God-world relationship.[21] *Archetypical* knowledge refers to the perfect knowledge of God, whereby He knows Himself and all things perfectly and comprehensively. He knows His holy character; He knows all propositional truths and possibilities, as well as their logical relations. He knows His plan for every detail of creation and history, as well as the relations between all events and objects. His understanding is infinite and without error.[22] This is why for God there are no mysteries or unknowns. So, for example, it is *not* a mystery to Him *how* He exists as three persons subsisting in one identical divine nature, or *how* He created the universe *ex nihilo*, or *how* His sovereign rule over the world is perfectly compatible with human responsible action.

Yet our knowledge, as creatures is only *ectypical*, i.e., a finite subset of His knowledge, which also includes Scripture. We ought to rejoice that we have true, objective knowledge precisely because our knowledge is a subset of God's perfect knowledge, and God has chosen to disclose Himself to us, both in nature and Scripture. But, in the end, even the knowledge we receive from Scripture, though true and infallible, is still finite and limited. God has simply not revealed everything about Himself and the world to us; what He has revealed is sufficient for us and our salvation, but it is not exhaustive. That is why for us "mysteries" are inevitable; *not* myster-

---

[19] For a further discussion of this point, see Carson, *How Long O Lord?*, 153–78.

[20] Unless otherwise stated, all Scriptural citations will come from the NIV (1984).

[21] For a discussion of the *archetype-ectype* distinction in theology, especially in reference to our knowledge of God, see Richard A. Muller, *Post-Reformation Reformed Dogmatics: The Rise and Development of Reformed Orthodoxy, ca. 1520 to ca. 1725* (4 vols.; Grand Rapids, MI: Baker, 2003), 3:164–70.

[22] See Frame, *Doctrine of God*, 469–512; Feinberg, *No One Like Him*, 299–320, for a discussion of omniscience.

ies in the sense of contradictions, but in terms of unknowns. We, as finite creatures, simply do not know everything, now and for all-eternity. The Creator-creature distinction, and its corollary the *archetype-ectype* distinction, will never be erased even in the new heavens and new earth. What does this point have to do with our discussion? Three points are important to address.[23]

1. In drawing *logical* conclusions, given the fact that we only have *ectypical* knowledge, we must be careful that all of our premises are correctly warranted by Scripture *and* precisely in the manner Scripture presents them. Thus, as noted above, what we mean by divine sovereignty, human freedom, and the relationship between the two, must first be drawn from Scripture and *not* imposed from without, i.e., from extrabiblical concepts that are not warranted by Scripture.

2. Given our *ectypical* knowledge, we should not be surprised when tensions arise between the biblical data, what I am calling "mystery" or better, "unknowns" that God has chosen not to disclose to us (e.g., Deut 29:29). As "faith seeks understanding," namely, as we rationally think through the tensions/mysteries of Scripture, *if* our exegesis is correct, we must learn to live with *biblically* derived tensions/mysteries.[24] So, for example, as I will argue below, when all the biblical data is considered, Scripture teaches that God foreordains all things, including evil, yet His ordination of all things does not remove our human freedom and responsibility, and it does not entail that God is secretly responsible for evil. How do we *know* this? On the grounds that Scripture affirms all of these truths. But someone objects: This does not seem "reasonable" or "logical" to me. *How* can God foreordain all things, including our future free actions, and they still be free? How are we to make sense of such an assertion? My response is this: I am not completely sure, yet we are warranted in believing such propositions because Scripture teaches them; Scripture is my epistemological warrant for knowing what is *logically* possible and impossible. However, I fully admit that the reason why it is difficult to comprehend is due to the fact that the knowledge we have of these kinds of relationships is only a creaturely, *ectypical* knowledge. In the end, on some matters such as these, we simply do not know enough. God has not completely disclosed Himself to us in all of these matters, and even if He had, we would probably still not be able

[23] For an extensive treatment of these points, see James Anderson, *Paradox in Christian Theology* (Eugene, OR: Wipf & Stock, 2007).

[24] It is important to state that not everything in theology is a mystery and we must not appeal to mystery too quickly. It is only after we have done our exegesis of the relevant biblical data and stay true to how Scripture presents the tensions within the biblical data, that we can appeal to mystery on matters that Scripture does not fully address.

to grasp fully all the nuances of the divine sovereignty-human freedom relationship (which is certainly an understatement!). Thus, for the critic to charge that it is *illogical* or *irrational* to assert that God is able to foreordain our free human actions, if Scripture actually teaches such a metaphysical state of affairs, is to assume that he has the kind of knowledge that God only has, which is quite an assumption!

3. Even though "mystery" or "unknowns" are inevitable and thus acceptable in theology, we must reject the existence of contradictions in our theologizing. The warrant for this assertion is rooted in the doctrine of God and especially the reality of God's *archetypical* knowledge. For the triune God of Scripture there are no contradictions since He is the sovereign-personal Lord who plans all things, knows all things, and does so in a way that is consistent with His nature and character. In addition, even though Scripture is not exhaustive, it is *His* Word and thus true and non-contradictory. What this entails is that in our theologizing, we must carefully exegete Scripture with the confidence that all of Scripture fits together as a whole. We let Scripture unpack the God-human freedom-evil relationship on its own terms, making sure we do justice to all the biblical data in a non-contradictory way. As we seek to understand the whole counsel of God as an exercise in "faith seeking understanding," we often have to admit that we come to points we simply do not fully grasp. Yet, because Scripture is God's Word, it is incumbent upon us to show that there is no necessary contradiction in our putting the pieces together, even though we may not be able fully to explain all the "hows" and "whys." In other words, in our theological proposals we must demonstrate that they are true to Scripture, non-contradictory, all the while acknowledging that in some areas which Scripture does not fully explain, we simply do not know *how* all the data fits together.

In other words, in our theologizing we must work hard to understand what the Scripture teaches and stay within the biblical parameters. Scripture needs to speak for itself on its own terms—*sola scriptura*. Furthermore, as the data is put together, it is legitimate to employ terms and concepts that are extrabiblical only if they are consistent with the biblical teaching. It is our job to show that there is no necessary contradiction within our theological conclusions. Ultimately, at the end of the day, the test of whether our theological view is *biblical* is whether it does justice to *all* of Scripture and whether it consistently leads us to affirm and not contradict other areas in our theology that we know to be true, or at least, we are more confident of, once again, rooted in Scripture. With these methodological issues in place, let us now outline the crucial biblical data which is central to how the Bible thinks about God's sovereignty over evil and the challenge of the problem of evil.

The Biblical Data: God, Sin, and Evil

What does the Bible teach about how we should think about the relationship between a sovereign God and the existence of sin and evil? Any answer to this question must consider at least four biblical truths:[25] (1) God is completely sovereign in His providential rule of the universe including His rule of sin and evil so that nothing in His world is done outside of his foreordained plan and/or permission; (2) God is perfectly good, holy, righteous, and just. In no way whatsoever is God to be viewed as responsible for sin and evil nor an accomplice of it; the goodness of God is a non-negotiable; (3) Human creatures (and angelic creatures) are free and morally responsible for their choices and actions—they deliberate, choose, rebel, obey, believe—but their freedom never limits God's sovereign rule over the universe; (4) Sin and evil are real; they are not illusory, nor a mere privation of the good. Let us look at each of these points in turn.

The Sovereignty of God over All Things

God's complete, universal, and efficacious sovereignty is taught throughout Scripture and as such it encompasses everything that happens in the world. In this regard think of a number of texts which, in a *general* or overall way, teach that God is sovereign over all things. For example, the Psalmist can ask: "Why do the nations say, 'Where is their God?'" and the answer is immediate: "Our God is in heaven; *he does whatever pleases him*" (Psalm 115:2–3, emphasis mine), whether that is "in the heavens and on the earth, in the seas and all their depths" (Psalm 135:6). In fact, as the Psalmist continues, God's sovereignty extends over both the natural world and the human world, including within it, human actions and choices (see e.g., Psalm 135:7–12). Nothing, Scripture teaches, occurs outside of God's plan and purposes; nothing is done apart from his will, plan, and permission—a lesson, for example, that king Nebuchadnezzar had to learn firsthand. In his memorable words, Nebuchadnezzar lifts his eyes to heaven after his sanity is restored and he praises the sovereign Lord by confessing, "His dominion is an eternal dominion; his kingdom endures from generation to generation. All the peoples on the earth are regarded as nothing. He does as he pleases with the powers of heaven and the peoples of the earth. No one can hold back his hand or say to him: 'What have you done?'" (Daniel 4:34–35; cf. Psalm 33:10–11). This is the same sentiment

---

[25] My discussion of the biblical data is indebted to Carson, *How Long O Lord?*, 199–228; Frame, *Doctrine of God*, 21–182; Feinberg, *No One Like Him*, 625–796.

that is echoed throughout Isaiah as the nation of Israel is encouraged with the fact that the covenant Lord is on His throne, bringing about His plans and purposes in such a way that no one can or will thwart Him (see Isaiah 14:24–27; 40:1–31). Specifically, in Isaiah 46:8–13 this point is strongly emphasized. God is presented as the One who knows the end from the beginning because it is rooted in His purpose, plan, and will. As v. 10 emphasizes: "I make known the end from the beginning, from ancient times, what is still to come. I say: *My purpose will stand, and I will do all that I please*" (emphasis mine), which includes within it both the natural order and the plans and actions of human beings.

In fact, one of the most sweeping statements of God's complete sovereign rule over the world is Ephesians 1:11. In the larger context of this text, Paul is rejoicing in the triune God of sovereign grace: the Father who has unconditionally chosen a people for salvation in Christ in eternity past according to His grace (Ephesians 1:4–6), the Son who, in history, has accomplished our redemption and who is now bringing "all things in heaven and earth" under His headship and Lordship (Ephesians 1:7–10), and the Spirit, who as the precious seal, deposit, and guarantee of our inheritance, is keeping us to the end as we await the consummation of God's saving plan and purposes in Christ. In the midst of this glorious long sentence, running from vv. 3–14, Paul once again speaks about our predestination in Christ as part and parcel of God's plan—a plan in which God "works out everything in conformity with the purpose of his will" (Ephesians 1:11). This statement is so sweeping that it is difficult to deny that it is teaching the universal and efficacious sovereign rule of God over His universe—a teaching that is found from Genesis to Revelation.[26]

Scripture, however, does not merely make general statements about God's complete, universal, and efficacious sovereignty. In text after text, God's *specific* sovereignty over all creation, including the natural world and the human domain, is stressed. For example, God not only assigns time and places to people so that none of us even live anywhere apart from His sovereign plan, rule, and appointment (Acts 17:26), but even the most mundane natural processes are ascribed to His activity (Genesis 8:22; Job 38–40; Psalm 65:9–11; 104:14; 148:8; Matthew 5:45; 6:26, 30; Acts 14:17). Scripture certainly speaks of the reality of secondary natural

---

[26] For a fine treatment of this text and its implications for understanding God's complete sovereignty, see Feinberg, "God Ordains All Things," 29–32. Feinberg rightly notes that "[t]his verse, then, indicates that what occurs is foreordained by God, and nothing external to God such as the foreseen actions or merits of God's creatures determines his choices. God deliberates, chooses and accomplishes all things on the basis of his purposes" (30).

causes such as the water cycle, but it never views these natural processes as independent of God's providential activity and will. So, as D. A. Carson rightly points out, "The writer of Ecclesiastes knows of the water cycle, but biblical authors prefer to speak of God sending the rain than to say, 'It is raining.'"[27] In Scripture both statements are true: "God sends the rain" and "it is raining" but the latter statement is never independent of the first.

Furthermore, Scripture teaches that God's specific sovereignty is also involved in everyday affairs of life, including our human choices. So, kings come and go (Psalm 33:10–11; Isaiah 45:1–46:13); wombs are closed and opened (Genesis 17:15–22); the hairs of our head are numbered (Matthew 10:29–30); unintentional manslaughter (Exodus 21:13) and family misfortune (Ruth 1:13, 20) are both related to the will of God; and the seemingly chance events of people's lives (Proverbs 16:33), including the random shot of an arrow which wounds Ahab thus fulfilling the word of the Lord (1 Kings 22:1–28, esp. v. 28 and 22:34, 38), are all under the sovereign plan and rule of God. Even in relation to human choices and actions, God is not thwarted since His sovereign plan and purpose prevails (Proverbs 16:9; 21:1, 30–31). We plan our course and we do so freely and responsibly, yet it is the Lord's purpose that prevails as Proverbs 19:21 reminds us: "Many are the plans in a man's heart, but it is the LORD's purpose that prevails." These kinds of statements are taught repeatedly in Scripture. In the OT, God announces ahead of time His purposes and raises up leaders to fulfill that very plan (e.g. Cyrus, Isa 45:1) without a hint that His purposes and promises can ever be thwarted. Or, in the NT, in the case of Peter, Jesus predicts his denial so that Peter does exactly what the Lord says he will do, yet he does it freely and responsibly (Luke 22:34, par.). All of this data leads to the conclusion that God's sovereignty is both *universal* and *efficacious*, i.e., God's decree and plan encompasses everything and it always accomplishes its purpose. John Frame nicely summarizes this kind of data when he writes,

> God never fails to accomplish what he sets out to do. Nothing is too hard for him (Jer. 32:27); nothing seems marvelous to him (Zech. 8:6); with him nothing is impossible (Gen. 18:14; Matt. 19:25; Luke 1:37). His purpose always prevails (Isa. 14:24–27; Job 42:2; Jer. 23:20).... Creatures may oppose him, to be sure, but they cannot prevail (Isa. 46:10; Dan. 4:35). For his own reasons, he has chosen to delay the fulfillment of his intentions for the end of history and to bring about those intentions through a complicated historical sequence of events. In that sequence, his purposes appear sometimes to suffer defeat, sometimes to achieve

---

[27] Carson, *How Long O Lord?*, 202.

victory. But each apparent defeat actually makes his eventual victory all the more glorious.[28]

What about God's sovereignty over evil? No doubt this subject is a bit trickier and one has to tread carefully in order to preserve the complex nuances of biblical teaching, yet Scripture does teach that God is sovereign over evil. However, where this occurs evil is *never* ascribed to God as if He were responsible for it and we are not, but Scripture is clear that sin and evil do not escape God's sovereign sway. For starters, sin and rebellion exist as part of God's foreordained plan. It is difficult to make sense of Revelation 13:8, "…. the Lamb [Jesus the Christ] that was slain from the creation of the world," the typological relationship between Adam and Christ (e.g., Rom 5:14), and Peter's statement in Acts 2:23, "…. This man [Jesus] was handed over to you by God's set purpose and foreknowledge….", without saying that Adam's fall and Christ's cross were part of the foreordained plan of God. In addition, as noted above, God's plan encompasses human decisions and not just good ones; it also includes our sinful choices without rendering us not responsible for our choices (see Genesis 45:5–8; Isaiah 44:28; Luke 22:22; Acts 2:23–24; 4:27–28; 13:27; Revelation 17:17).

In regard to the last observation, read together Joshua 10:8, 40 with 11:20 (cf. Judges 1:4, 7; 4:23; 20:35). As Joshua enters the promised land and he is commanded to wage war and destroy the people of the land, not only does the Lord assure him of success (10:8), which he achieves by his and the people's choices and actions (10:40), but we are also told that God is actively involved in the battles. "For it was the LORD himself who hardened their hearts to wage war against Israel, so that he might destroy them totally, exterminating them without mercy, as the LORD had commanded Moses" (11:20). Yet there is no evidence in the text that the hardening of the people's hearts removed their free and responsible action. Instead, what we have is dual agency: the humans involved choose and act *and* simultaneously God acts. But, it is important to note, as Bruce Ware so ably argues in chapter 7, we should not view this as merely a case of "co-agency of (mere) collaboration."[29] Instead, Scripture teaches that in the very same act, namely, the warfare waged, God has foreordained the event (given His eternal plan and knowledge of all things, including future free actions of His creatures) and acted in it,[30] while simultaneously hu-

---

[28] Frame, "The Problem of Evil," 143.

[29] See Bruce Ware, chapter 7, for this discussion.

[30] Historic Christian theology has always affirmed that divine omniscience includes God's knowledge of all things including the past, present, and future free actions of His creatures, in contrast to views such as open theism. For a defense

man agents are acting in a free and responsible manner. In fact, the same phenomenon is also found before this incident in God's interaction with Pharaoh and his sinful choices through Moses. Prior to Pharaoh hardening his own heart in rebellion against the Lord (Exodus 8:15, 32; 9:34), God says to Moses, "When you return to Egypt, see that you perform before Pharaoh all the wonders I have given you the power to do. But I will harden his heart so that he will not let the people go" (4:21)—a pattern that is emphasized repeatedly in the unfolding narrative (Exodus 7:3; 9:12; 10:20; 14:4, 8)—alongside the emphasis on Pharaoh freely and responsibly hardening his heart. Importantly, Paul also picks up this very point as he discusses dual agency in the unbelief and disobedience of the nation of Israel in their rejection of Jesus the Messiah. The reason that many ethnic Jews have rejected their Messiah is due both to God's choice in election *and* their culpable unbelief (see Romans 9–10).[31]

All of this is to say, Scripture teaches that God's foreordained plan and sovereign actions in history include within it human decisions, even decisions which are sinful choices, without a hint of any reduction of human responsibility for those actions. This is why merely to argue that the *entire* problem of evil is resolved by appealing to the abuse of human free will, as "the free will defense" does, is not a sufficient biblical response, even though it is part of the response. Yet, with that said, it is important to balance this teaching with the second truth which is necessary to maintain if we are going to have a proper understanding of the relationship between God's sovereignty, sin, and evil, namely an unequivocal affirmation of the goodness, holiness, and justice of God.

---

of this point, see Frame, *Doctrine of God*, 469–512; Feinberg, *No One Like Him*, 294–320.

[31] Examples could be multiplied. For example, if Naaman has enjoyed military victory, it is God's doing (2 Kings 5:1). Sinful king Nebuchadnezzar and Cyrus are both God's servants (Jeremiah 25:9; 27:6; 2 Chronicles 36:22ff) whether they are chastening or releasing the covenant people who have rebelled. God himself raises up the Assyrians (Isa 10:5ff), as well as the Babylonians (2 Chronicles 36:17; Habakkuk 1:6). In Job, we see that Satan was given permission to bring harm to Job's possessions and children and though this harm came through secondary agents (Job 1:12, 15, 17, 19), yet Job can see behind it all the hand of the Lord (Job 1:21). But though Job says that the Lord has done this, yet he does not blame God for the evil or say that God has done wrong. In the book of Revelation it is repeatedly made clear that the authority of the dragon and of his beasts is "given" to them (Rev 17:17), which, similar to Job, speaks of the evil one not being able to do anything apart from God's sovereign rule and permission.

The Goodness of God

Despite everything Scripture says about God's sovereignty and His foreordination of all things, including evil, the Bible insists that God is perfectly good. To say that God is good is another way of describing His perfect moral character. God, as the moral standard of the universe, acts in ways that are consistent with Himself. Scripture describes God's goodness as His perfect righteousness, kindness, love, grace, covenant faithfulness, compassion, and much more. One of the defining texts of the OT, which Scripture repeatedly refers to in order to underscore the covenant Lord's goodness, is Exodus 34:6: "The LORD, the LORD, the compassionate and gracious God, slow to anger, abounding in love and faithfulness." This text becomes a bedrock description of God throughout the entire canon which repeatedly teaches that God's ways and works are perfect and just (Deuteronomy 32:4), that God takes no pleasure in sin and evil (Psalm 5:4), in fact His eyes are too pure to even look upon evil (Habakkuk 1:13), and that God is acting to put away sin and evil finally and definitively, which is precisely what He has done in Christ and His cross and resurrection.[32]

It is for this reason that in thinking through the biblical relationship between God and evil, we can never call into question God's sovereignty nor His goodness. As Carson rightly reminds us, in Scripture, "God is *never* presented as an accomplice of evil, or as secretly malicious, or as standing behind evil in exactly the same way that he stands behind good."[33] The goodness of God is a *non-negotiable* in Scripture (see Deuteronomy 32:4; Habakkuk 1:13; 1 John 1:5; Revelation 15:3–4) and this truth has to be stressed simultaneously and equally with the affirmation that God foreordains all things including both good and evil.

No doubt, it is not easy to hold both of these truths together but hold them together we must. As "faith seeks understanding," distinctions and clarifications must be made. For example, Carson makes the helpful distinction that in Scripture God is presented as not standing behind good and evil in exactly the same way, hence the affirmation in theology of the language of "permission" or God's *asymmetrical* relation to good and evil. Yet, even the language of permission and asymmetrical relations must be viewed in light of God's sovereignty, or what Frame calls God's "*efficacious* permission."[34] But "permission" is still a helpful term, as long as it does not

---

[32] For a more detailed treatment of God's goodness, see Frame, *Doctrine of God*, 402–445.

[33] Carson, *How Long O Lord?*, 205.

[34] Frame, "The Problem of Evil," 161.

reduce the biblical teaching regarding divine sovereignty, and as long as it helps drive home the fine nuances that Scripture demands that we make, namely that even though God foreordains all things, including evil, sin and evil are always attributed to the creature and not to God. Sin and evil are always our fault; God is never to blame since He is perfectly good.

The Freedom and Responsibility of Human Creatures

From the opening chapter of the Bible, human beings, who are created in God's image, are presented as free and morally responsible creatures—we significantly choose, rebel, obey, believe, defy, and so on—and we are rightly held accountable for our actions. In fact, human choices (including the rational choices of angelic creatures) are so significant that Adam's rebellious decision to disobey God in space-time history, as the covenant head of the human race, has brought about the entrance of moral sin and evil into the world, which has also led to God's curse upon the earth (Genesis 3:17–19; cf. Romans 5:12–21). Human choice, in other words, is so significant and important that it has personal and cosmic implications! This is why Scripture teaches that moral evil precedes natural evil, and natural evil is a consequence of creaturely sin and rebellion against God (see Genesis 3; Romans 8:19–22). In the end, the Bible is clear that natural evil will cease, through Christ's redemptive work, when on the final day God will remove the curse placed upon the old creation and usher in a new heaven and new earth (Revelation 21–22). Moreover, even after the Fall, and given the disastrous effects of sin on all people, Scripture still treats human beings as responsible for their actions. The Bible does not diminish human responsibility even though humans are sinners by nature and by action (Ephesians 2:1–3). In our fallenness, we freely delight in our sin and willingly stand in opposition to God's rightful rule over us, which Scripture views as our very spiritual depravity and inability (Romans 8:7). As a result, we stand under God's judgment and wrath (Romans 8:1; Ephesians 2:1–3), but we stand under that judgment as responsible creatures.

It is important to note, though, that when Scripture speaks of human freedom and responsibility, it is everywhere presupposed and assumed, yet it is never defined. As already noted, in the current theological discussion, there are two basic views of human freedom that are primarily discussed and adopted—libertarian free will and compatibilistic freedom. Given that these are two possible views in the sense that there is no logical contradiction in affirming either one, how does one decide between them? As discussed above, the answer is: we choose the view of human freedom that best fits the biblical data and does not contradict it. In this regard, if we take seriously the biblical data regarding divine sovereignty, one has to conclude that the best view to adopt is compatibilism, even though it is not perfect in its overall view (which is what you would expect of extrabiblical terms and concepts). Yet, it is a better view than libertarianism given the fact that libertarianism is very difficult, if not impossible, to reconcile with a biblical view of God's sovereignty because, by definition, libertarianism demands that our choices are not determined in advance by God since we always have the freedom to choose otherwise, even contrary to our character and desires. In addition, Scripture never presents the human will as independent of God's plan as libertarianism does, and libertarianism has a difficult time accounting for *why* we choose what we do if nothing sufficiently inclines the will and if we can always do otherwise. Just think of our freedom in the consummated state. In the new creation, we will, thankfully, *not* sin and thus not have the ability to do otherwise, but if libertarianism is true, that would entail that in the final state we would not be free! Furthermore, libertarianism has a difficult time accounting for God's freedom, which is clearly tied to His nature, character, and desires, so that God is the paradigm of freedom par excellence, yet in His choices, specifically related to His moral character, He cannot do otherwise than that which is holy, just, and good.[35]

Instead, it is best to think of human freedom compatibilistically. Not only is this way of viewing human freedom more consistent with divine sovereignty, it also fits better with how Scripture presents our freedom and choices, namely that we speak and act according to our character. As Frame nicely reminds us, human freedom in Scripture is according to our character. He writes, "We follow the deepest desires of our heart. As Jesus emphasizes, a good tree bears good fruit, and a bad tree bears bad fruit (Matthew 7:15–20; Luke 6:43–45). To my knowledge, Scripture never refers to this moral consistency as a kind of freedom, but the concept of heart-act consistency is important in Scripture, and theologians and philosophers have often referred to it as freedom."[36] Frame continues to note that in everyday life, we regularly think of freedom in this way, namely as doing what we want to do. That is why "[w]hen we do not do what we want, we are either acting irrationally or being forced to act against our will by someone or something outside ourselves."[37] Thus, in order to make sense of a biblical view of human freedom in light of God's sovereignty

---

[35] For a full critique of libertarian freedom, see Frame, *Doctrine of God*, 119–159. For a critique of libertarian freedom and Arminian solutions to reconcile divine foreknowledge and human freedom, including middle knowledge, see Feinberg, *No One Like Him*, 625–775.

[36] Frame, "The Problem of Evil," 149.

[37] Ibid.

and the overall teaching of Scripture in other areas, it is best to affirm that human choices are genuine and real in a compatibilistic sense. In this discussion we must not beg the question in regard to the freedom debate, especially since Scripture teaches that human decisions are compatible with divine sovereignty.

The Reality of Sin and Evil

This last truth is also crucial to stress, especially in a pluralistic world comprised of many worldviews which deny the reality of evil. For example, as Douglas Groothuis reminds us, there are many views which "solve" the problem of evil simply by dispensing with evil itself. As he notes, "[t]his route is taken by various forms of pantheism, such as Advaita Vendanta Hinduism, Zen Buddhism, assorted New Age worldviews and mind-science churches such as Christian Science, Religious Science and Unity. Since all is ultimately divine, evil is unreal; it is only a problem of perception, and not a problem of objective reality."[38] In the strongest of terms, Scripture affirms the reality of sin and evil. In fact, sin/evil are so real that the only way to eradicate them is by the Triune God of sovereign grace acting to save, centered in the incarnation of God the Son and His triumphant cross work on our behalf. Scripture has no problem affirming the reality of sin and evil; it even contends in the strongest way possible that humans, especially in our fallen condition, do not take sin/evil seriously enough. This is one of the reasons why we, in our sin, see no need for a Lord and Savior to do what we could never do, namely defeat, destroy, and eradicate sin and evil in the universe and in ourselves.

In addition, when thinking about the reality of evil, it is best not to think in privation categories, even though there is a long history which does so.[39] To think of evil in this way is to think of it as a kind of defect in God's good universe, as the absence of the good rather than the presence of something not good, due to finite creatures lacking a fullness of being. But if we are not careful, a number of implications seem to follow which are all unbiblical notions. First, if pushed to the wall, evil as privation seems to entail that our explanation for human sin and creaturely evil is now a metaphysical explanation, namely, finite creatures lack a fullness of being and thus tend to become less perfect, which, unfortunately, is what has occurred. However, if this is the case, then it seems that "sin" becomes

---

[38] Douglas Groothuis, *Christian Apologetics: A Comprehensive Case for Biblical Faith* (Downers Grove, IL: InterVarsity Press, 2011), 620.

[39] See Frame's helpful discussion of "privation" in "The Problem of Evil," 144–52.

confused with "finitude" and by God's creative act to make finite creatures, sin and evil become a kind of defect in creation itself, rather than a moral rebellion of creatures against God. Second, if this is so, then salvation will look different than Scripture says it is, namely that in order to remove sin and evil, God will have to remove our finitude, which is certainly not a biblical notion. Third, Scripture does not require us to say that evil is nonbeing, or a mere negation of the good. Rather, creatures sin against God and become sinners. Good and evil both exist, even though Scripture certainly speaks of the priority of good over evil in history and the positive value of good in itself, which is not the case with evil. But with that said, given creaturely rebellion, sin and evil are real in God's universe and ultimately part of God's foreordained plan.

An Initial Theological Reflection on the Biblical Data

The above description of the biblical data which summarizes how we should think about the relationship between God's sovereignty, human freedom, and the existence of sin and evil, is hardly exhaustive, but I am convinced that it accurately reflects the biblical teaching. If this is so, then one cannot give a *biblical* solution to the problem of evil without first affirming each of these four truths and doing so *simultaneously*, regardless of the difficulty of doing so. In fact, throughout Scripture these truths are placed side-by-side without qualification or embarrassment. One cannot think of God's eternal plan and the entire God-world relationship without affirming these four truths as foundational to the very fabric of Scripture and God's providential actions in the world. To deny them, to diminish them, or to redefine them, is to present the God-world relationship differently than it is presented in Scripture. Four examples will suffice to demonstrate the side-by-side placement of these truths; examples which are taken from a spectrum of God's diverse relationships with human agents.[40]

The first example is Genesis 50:19–20 which portrays God's sovereign action in the everyday decisions of individuals. After Jacob's death, his sons approach their brother, Joseph, and plead that they become his slaves fearing that Joseph would enact revenge upon them for their previous wicked actions. Joseph's response is that he will do no such thing: "Am I in the place of God?" (v. 19), he asks. Furthermore, he sees in their very actions the plan and purpose of God. In those memorable words he says, "You intended to harm me, but God intended it for good to accomplish what is now being done, the saving of many lives" (v. 20). What is crucial to note

---

[40] Also see Carson, *How Long O Lord?*, 205–212, for a further discussion of these points.

in Joseph's response is how he affirms *simultaneously* that in the sinful actions of his brothers which involved intention, planning, and choice (see the planning and scheming taking place in Genesis 37), God was also intending and acting but for a good purpose. However, God's intention is *not* merely a kind of clean-up operation *ex post facto*. From Genesis to Revelation, the God of the Bible is presented as the one who plans and knows all things, which is taught in the narrative itself. The dreams Joseph received ahead of time outlined the future events to occur. Scripture is teaching that in the very same action, namely the selling of Joseph into slavery, there was double agency: God was sovereignly acting and working out His foreordained plan for good, while human agents were freely and responsibly acting, sadly in this case, in a sinful and evil way, all in accordance with God's plan. Precisely *how* God foreordained the free actions of His creatures in this episode is left unexplained, but Scripture affirms that he did so without diminishing His sovereignty, reducing our free and responsible action, and making Himself responsible for the evil actions of His creatures.

The same truth is taught in our second example, Isaiah 10:5–19, which depicts an illustration of God's sovereign rule over the nations. Given that Bruce Ware has discussed this example in chapter 7, I will only make a few comments that illustrate the point at hand. First, God's sovereignty is strongly underscored in the text. It is God who chooses to use the Assyrians as His agents of judgment; they are completely under His authority and power. They are called "the rod of *my* anger" and "the club of *my* wrath" (v. 5, emphasis mine). The intensive use of the verbs in v. 6 emphasizes God's sovereign initiative and action: "I send..." and "I dispatch...".[41] Interestingly, when God finishes with Assyria, He does not let them off the hook; instead they are brought to judgment for their wicked and evil actions even though those actions were God's foreordained means to execute judgment upon Israel (v. 12)! Just because they are instruments in God's hand, this fact does not remove their human responsibility. Second, human freedom and responsible choices are taught. The Assyrians plan, scheme, boast, and carry out their evil actions against Israel without any idea that they are instruments in God's sovereign hand. There is no evidence in the text that they are acting in any way other than what they desire and intend. Their purpose is not to bring God's judgment upon the nation or ultimate-

---

[41] See J. Alec Motyer, *Isaiah: An Introduction and Commentary*, TOTC (1999), 95. As Motyer introduces this important text he makes the astute comment: "This passage asserts a philosophy of history, how the historical facts arise from hidden supernatural causes, and how the human actors who are the hinges on which history outwardly turns are themselves personal and responsible agents within a sovereignly ordered and exactly tuned moral system."

ly to see good result; instead their purpose is nothing but destruction (vv. 7–11, 13–14). Third, God's actions in salvation and judgment are always good and according to the perfect standard of his nature and character, yet the actions of the Assyrians are wicked through and through, even though their very actions are part of God's plan. As in Genesis 50, God is presented as acting in the very same event, namely the Assyrians waging war against Israel, yet God's action is perfectly good and just, while creaturely action is viewed as wicked and sinful and liable to judgment. *How do all of these truths fit together?* Theology tries to make sense of the data by making careful and necessary distinctions such as: God's *asymmetrical* relationship to good and evil, or God's acting remotely vs. proximately thus preserving dual agency and the reality of secondary agents, or even speaking of God's permission of sin and evil.[42] Yet, Scripture does not say specifically *how* all the data goes together, but it does assume that it does, thus demanding that we hold together *all* of the biblical data simultaneously and that in our theologizing we do not deny or reduce any of the biblical teaching.

The third example involves the most important event of all human history, namely the cross of our Lord Jesus Christ (Acts 2:22–24; 4:23–31). Scripture is forthright that at the heart of God's eternal plan of redemption for this world is the cross work of Christ. Peter proclaims this very point in Acts 2:23 where he argues that the cross is simultaneously part of the foreordained and foreknown plan of God and thus supremely good. Yet at the same time he teaches that those who crucified our Lord are responsible for their actions and they will be brought to judgment—"you, with the help of wicked men, put him to death by nailing him to the cross" (v. 23). In other words, just because the cross is part of God's foreordained plan, those who were part of that very plan to crucify Him, are still responsible for what they did. In a very real sense, they should not have crucified the Lord, even though it was foreordained that they would. Thus, as in the above texts, in the cross, side-by-side, God's eternal plan is accomplished in exact detail *and* that plan includes within it the free and responsible actions of humans. In other words, in the cross, God foreordains the free actions of His creatures as the means by which it takes place. Once again, here is dual agency at work, or better, compatibilism: God plans; His plan includes our free and responsible actions; God's actions are good; and in this case human action is sinful and evil. As in the previous texts, precisely

---

[42] For helpful discussions on how theology has sought to nuance their formulations in order to do justice to the diversity of biblical data, see Carson, *How Long O Lord?*, 212–227; Feinberg, *No One Like Him*, 625–734; Frame, "The Problem of Evil," 157–164; Vanhoozer, *Remythologizing Theology*, 297–386.

how God did this is left unexplained, but nonetheless, Scripture affirms all the biblical truths simultaneously.

The last example is a set of texts pertaining to our salvation, election, and our Christian lives. John 6:37–40 teaches God's election of His people to salvation—"All that the Father gives me will come to me and whoever comes to me I will never drive away" (v. 37). This is part of the biblical data which teaches that God unconditionally chooses a people for Himself before the foundation of the world (cf. Ephesians 1:4–6), rooted and grounded in His sovereign grace and eternal plan. The emphasis of the verse, as Carson rightly notes, is that all those whom the Father has chosen and given to the Son will be kept until the end.[43] Yet, at the same time, v. 40 stresses our human responsibility to believe, even though God has chosen us: "For my Father's will is that everyone who looks to the Son and believes in him shall have eternal life, and I will raise him up at the last day."

The same point is taught in Romans 9–10. As the apostle Paul wrestles with why his fellow countrymen did not believe in their Messiah, two answers are given which are both true. First, they did not believe due to God's sovereign choice of a people for Himself: "not all who are descended from Israel are Israel" (Romans 9:6). In other words, just because one was physically a Jew did not automatically make him part of the people of God salvifically. From eternity past, and worked out on the stage of history, God's election shows itself by some believing and others not. We know that this is what Paul is teaching given how he responds to the potential objections to his teaching (vv. 14, 19, 22), since all of his responses only make sense if we assume unconditional election.[44] Yet, we must immediately add, Paul can also give another reason, *which is equally true*, for the Jews' unbelief, namely that they refused to believe, thus underscoring their free and responsible choice in their rejection of Christ (see Romans 9:30–10:21). *How* can both of these be true simultaneously? No answer is given, but both are taught which necessitates that we affirm both equally as part of the fabric of God's providential rule and reign over this world. No doubt, theology, in the mode of "faith seeking understanding," attempts to nibble at the edges and provide an answer with careful definitions, distinctions, and clarifications. Yet, in the end, a complete answer is not forthcoming given the fact that God has not exhaustively revealed Himself to us. But given that Scripture teaches that God foreordains all things including our free and responsible action, our thinking through the relationship between God's sovereignty, human freedom, and sin and evil must do justice to this biblical teaching.

[43] See Carson, *How Long O Lord?*, 209.

[44] See Thomas R. Schreiner, *Romans*, BECNT (1998), 478–530, for this point.

One last text, Philippians 2:12–13, also teaches God's sovereign action and our responsible choices side-by-side in our sanctification. How does a Christian grow in grace? The apostle Paul answers with a twofold response. First, we grow in grace by our own choices and actions—"continue to work out your salvation with fear and trembling" (v. 12). If we are not growing in holiness and godliness it is ultimately our fault and we will be held responsible for it. Yet, this is not all that is involved in the Christian life. We also grow in grace due to God's sovereign work in us by His Spirit which brings about our transformation—"for it is God who works in you to will and to act according to his good purpose" (v. 13). Without the effective work of the Spirit in rebirth and then in our lives, none of us would be conformed to the image of Christ. However, this point does not entail that we are not active in our sanctification and that we merely need to "let go and let God." Instead the very evidence that the Spirit of God is at work in us is that He makes us active in our sanctification. Once again, divine sovereignty and human responsible action is placed side-by-side without qualification or complete explanation.

With this biblical data in mind, and the exhortation that we must maintain *all* of the four truths simultaneously if *sola scriptura* is going to mean anything for our theological proposals, let us now apply the biblical data to the difficult question of the problem of evil. Let us think through briefly how I, as a Calvinist, respond to this important challenge.[45]

Responding to the Problem of Evil

Two Preliminary Responses

Before I respond specifically to the problem of evil, I begin with two preliminary responses. First, given my understanding of the biblical data, as outlined above, in my response to the problem of evil I must do justice to *all* of the four truths simultaneously. Immediately this entails that some responses and "solutions" to the problem that have been given in the past are automatically eliminated as viable *biblical* solutions. For example, one cannot respond to the problem of evil by calling into question God's sovereignty, power, and knowledge. As Frame rightly notes, "Given what the Bible teaches about God's sovereignty, then, the various attempts to show that God is too weak to prevent evil do not seem promising."[45]

[45] Frame, "The Problem of Evil," 144. Frame gives the example of Harold Kushner, *When Bad Things Happen to Good People* (New York, NY: Schocken, 1981), and also the solution of process theology, such as David Ray Griffin, *God, Power, and Evil* (Philadelphia, PA: Westminster, 1976). I would also add the

Nor, is it enough, as most Arminian theology claims, to think that the entire problem of evil is explained by the abuse of human freedom, hence the so-called, "free will defense." No doubt, given the biblical data, a crucial reason why moral evil exists is certainly due to human (and angelic) rebellion and choice. God created the world good (Genesis 1:26, 31) and nothing which comes from His creative hand is evil. It is only due to Adam's sin, rooted in a space-time historic fall, that moral evil, and then natural evil, result (Genesis 3). Moreover, as noted above, evil is not metaphysically necessary, as if it is part and parcel of God's creation of a world. Instead, evil is the result of creaturely rebellion. God is not the author of evil. He did not directly cause or create evil in the same way He created the universe.[46] Yet, sin and evil are part of God's eternal plan and the entire explanation of it must include this fact. But with that said, it is also not enough, on the Calvinist side, to explain evil in terms of "God's will" without qualification. The biblical data leads to the conclusion that God stands behind good and evil asymmetrically, no matter how difficult it is to wrap our thinking around this data.

All this is to say that in responding to the problem of evil, if we are to do so *biblically*, we must hold *all* of the biblical truths together, which, in the end, entails that *mystery* is inevitable. Our task, then, is not to explain all of the *how's* since that would require an *archetypical* knowledge we do not have. So, how does God foreordain our free human actions? How does God foreordain evil in such a way that He is not responsible and He remains perfectly good, while we, as creatures, are responsible for it? My answer: I am not exactly sure but I know that He does since Scripture teaches it. Our task, then, given that Scripture is true, unified, and finite, yet from Him who knows no mysteries, is to show that there is no necessary contradiction in the biblical data. In this regard, Carson is wise to admit that in our wrestling with the problem of evil we cannot eliminate mystery. He rightly notes that, "[t]he problem looks neater when, say, God is not behind evil in any sense. But quite apart from the fact that the biblical texts will not allow so easy an escape, the result is a totally nonmysterious God."[47] Or, he continues with the helpful observation that, "[a]fter reading some neat theodicies that stress, say, that all suffering is the direct result of

literature of open theism since they operate with an unbiblical understanding of God's sovereignty, power, and knowledge. See, Clark H. Pinnock, et al. *The Openness of God* (Downers Grove, IL: InterVarsity Press, 1994); John Sanders, *The God Who Risks: A Theology of Divine Providence* (2nd ed: Downers Grove, IL: InterVarsity Press, 1997); Gregory A. Boyd, *Satan and the Problem of Evil: Constructing a Trinitarian Warfare Theodicy* (Downers Grove, IL: InterVarsity Press, 2001).

[46] See Groothius, *Christian Apologetics*, 626–27, who makes this point.

[47] Carson, *How Long O Lord?*, 225.

sin, or that free will understood as absolute power to the contrary [libertarian] nicely exculpates God, I wonder if their authors think Job or Habbakuk were twits. Surely they should have seen that there is no mystery to be explained, and simply gone home and enjoyed a good night's sleep."[48] Ultimately, in our response to the problem of evil, we must demonstrate that there is no necessary contradiction between the biblical data but we will not be able to explain the full scope of divine providence.

Second, in responding to "the problem of evil," it is important to stress that there is no *the* problem but a number of *problems* which have to be answered on their own terms. John Feinberg, in his excellent work, *The Many Faces of Evil*, has made this point abundantly clear.[49] In fact, it is helpful to distinguish three different problems of evil: the logical, the evidential, and the emotional or practical problem of evil, all of which require a slightly different answer given the differences between them.

Probably the most famous is the *logical* problem which accuses Christian theology of logical inconsistency in believing the four truths outlined above. I will return to this problem below. The *evidential* problem of evil, which I will not directly address in this chapter due to space constraints, is slightly different from the logical problem. Instead of being a deductive argument, it is inductive based on the observation of the amount of evil in the world. Furthermore, instead of arguing for a necessary contradiction between the biblical data, it argues that given the *amount* and *kinds* of evil in the world, it is *implausible* to think that God exists.[50] Lastly, there is the

[48] Ibid.

[49] See John S. Feinberg, *The Many Faces of Evil: Theological Systems and the Problems of Evil* (Revised and Expanded Edition: Wheaton, IL: Crossway, 2004), 17–30.

[50] For an excellent discussion and response to the evidential problem of evil from within a Calvinist theology, see Feinberg, *The Many Faces of Evil*, 207–391. At its heart, the evidential problem treats theism as a large-scale hypothesis or explanatory theory that implies specific consequences for the way the world should be. Thus, if Christian theism is true, then, it is argued, we should legitimately expect the world to turn out a certain way. My response to this is twofold. First, what you think the world should look like if God exists is very difficult to demonstrate. On what grounds does one know this? Second, the argument assumes that *there is no morally sufficient reason* for God to permit so much evil rather than a lot less. But, as I will argue in my response to the logical problem of evil, this is an unbiblical assumption. Scripture does give us ample grounds to say that God is sovereign, God is good, and that He has a morally sufficient reason for evil existing. If this is so, then arguing from the *fact* of evil (i.e., the logical argument), and from the *amount* and *variety* of evil (i.e., the evidential argument) equally assumes that the critic has grounds for knowing that God does *not* have a morally compelling reason for permitting the existence of evil. But on what grounds? In my view,

emotional or *religious* problem of evil. The questions raised by this problem are *not*: Why is there evil in the world in a general sense? Or, how God can be omnipotent and good and allow evil to exist? Rather, the questions asked are more personal: Why is this specific evil happening to me? Why did God allow my loved one to die? Can I trust Him in the midst of this tragic event? The *emotional* problem is certainly one which may be experienced by Christians. Given that all of us, if we live long enough and Christ does not return prior to our death, will experience suffering and tragedy in our lives, we may even question God's purposes in our lives.

In the end, our response to the *problems* of evil will depend upon the specific nature of the problem addressed, but whatever specific problem of evil we are addressing, we must do so from *within* the biblical data discussed above. Let us now turn specifically to the *logical* and *emotional* problems of evil.

Responding to the Logical Problem of Evil

The logical problem of evil charges Christianity with holding to a logical contradiction between the four biblical truths outlined above. It is a deductive problem; given the truth of the premises, the conclusion necessarily follows. The argument has been stated in numerous places and it takes the following form.

1. God's power means God can prevent any evil, since God can do absolutely anything.

2. God's goodness means He would prevent any evil.

3. But there is evil.

4. So, God *cannot* exist.[51]

How do we respond to this challenge in a way that is both biblically faithful and removes the necessary contradiction? It is important to note that in answering *logical* problems, all that is required is to demonstrate that the conclusion of the argument does not follow from the premises.[52]

---

even though the evidential problem is different from the logical problem, the answer to both of them is similar.

[51] Groothius, *Christian Apologetics*, 629.

[52] Often a distinction is made between a "defense" vs. a "theodicy." For this distinction, see Alvin Plantinga, *God, Freedom, and Evil* (Grand Rapids, MI: Eerdmans, 1974). A defense responds by proposing a possible solution that renders the argument as a *non sequitur*, i.e., the conclusion does not *logically* follow from

How do we do this? By laying out a possible solution or by adding a premise to the argument which is consistent with the biblical data, but which also explains why the conclusion is *not* logically necessary.

Is there such a premise? There is, but before I state it, I need to note a couple of beliefs the logical problem assumes without argument. Groothius does a nice job in describing both of these beliefs: "(1) God can prevent any evil, since God can do absolutely anything, and that (2) there is never a sufficient reason for God to allow evil."[53] But these beliefs, given the overall teaching of Scripture, are highly debatable. For example, in terms of belief (1), as Groothius continues, "[i]t may be that God can only bring about certain goods by letting some evils exist, and that God therefore cannot just do *anything*." In this regard, Groothius discusses the example of God's omnipotence not entailing that He can bring about contradictions, since contradictions are not possible things. In a similar vein, John Feinberg argues in a detailed way that belief (1) is possible only if God contradicts other valuable things He has decided to do, directly contradicts what Scripture reveals about all of His attributes, and/or performs actions which we would desire He not do because they would produce a greater evil than we already have in our world.[54] Whether one agrees, for example, with the entire analysis Feinberg lays out is not the point. Rather, the point is that belief (1) cannot be assumed. The same may be said for belief (2). In fact, to ground belief (2) as true, one would minimally require an *archetypical* knowledge which we do not have. Furthermore, Scripture does give us reasons to believe that God has morally sufficient reasons for allowing evil; minimally, the whole plan of redemption is one of those reasons, even though it is true that Scripture does not give us the entire explanation.

What premise, then, can we add to the argument to demonstrate that there is no necessary contradiction between affirming premises 1–3? Groothius nicely restates the argument with an added premise which is both biblically faithful and which renders the argument a *non sequitur*.

1. God is omnipotent and omniscient.

2. God is omnibenevolent.

3. There is objective evil.

the premises. However, a defense does not answer all the *how* questions; it simply demonstrates that there is no necessary contradiction in maintaining the four biblical truths simultaneously. A theodicy is the more grand attempt of seeking to justify God's ways to us, of demonstrating the goodness of all of His actions. In my discussion I am employing a defense.

[53] Groothius, *Christian Apologetics*, 630.

[54] See Feinberg, *The Many Faces of Evil*, 167–180.

4. For any evil that God allows, God has a morally sufficient reason
   for allowing this evil, even if we do not know what this morally sufficient reason is in some cases.[55]

When the argument is restated in this fashion, it should be evident
that if God has a morally sufficient reason for evil then it does *not* logically
follow that there is an inconsistency between the existence of the God of
Scripture and the existence of evil in the world. To argue that there is *no*
morally sufficient reason would not only have to overturn biblical data at
this point, it would also have to argue a universal negative, which is impossible to do. Thus, with this added premise, the *logical* problem of evil is
resolved in a biblically faithful and logically consistent way.

In spite of this solution, an obvious question remains: What is the
morally sufficient reason? It is important to note that an answer to this
question does not have to be given in order to resolve the problem. All one
needs to demonstrate is that the added premise in question is *possibly* true,
which certainly is the case. Scripture gives us every reason to think that
God's planning and permission of evil, given His perfect goodness, and
in light of our human free actions, is for a morally sufficient reason, even
though we may not know all the ins and outs of the reason. Yet, Christians throughout the ages have sought to say something more about God's
reasons for allowing sin and evil in His universe. To be sure, all of these
possible answers may be helpful but it should be stressed: (1) none of them
is necessary to solve the logical problem of evil; and (2) none of them is a
complete answer given that our knowledge is only *ectypical*. In the end, on
the basis of Scripture, it is enough to affirm that God has a morally sufficient reason for allowing evil, yet none of our answers will be completely
sufficient even though we have ample reasons to trust what God has disclosed about His character and ways in Scripture.

What are some of the morally sufficient reasons that Christians have
proposed? Probably the most famous reason is "human free will" or what
is known as the "free will defense." This solution assumes libertarian freedom and it argues that God has permitted evil for a morally sufficient
reason because in choosing to give humans libertarian free will, it is not
within His power to create a world containing moral good but no moral
evil or guarantee that free creatures never go wrong. As such, it is logically
possible for God and evil to exist simultaneously and for God to have a
reason that would justify Him in permitting evil to exist.[56] However, even

---

[55] Groothius, *Christian Apologetics*, 630.

[56] See Feinberg, *Many Faces of Evil*, 67–122, who argues for the logical consistency of the free will defense.

though this defense is logically consistent, in my view it is not biblically adequate, given our discussion of the biblical data above. Libertarian freedom, by definition, is inconsistent with a strong view of divine sovereignty and on this basis alone it is not an acceptable *biblical* solution. Given that Scripture teaches that God's foreordination and our free human actions are compatible, then the "free will defense" is not an acceptable Calvinist solution to the logical problem of evil.[57] To be sure, human freedom is *part* of the reason—even a crucial reason—God allowed evil, but it cannot be viewed as the only reason.

Are there other reasons that are more faithful to the biblical text? There are and most of them are associated with "the greater-good defense" against the problem of evil. At the heart of these reasons, as Frame nicely states, "is the claim that the presence, or at least the possibility, of evil in the world is good, when seen from a broader perspective."[58] Obviously one has to be careful with these kinds of reasons, since we do not have exhaustive knowledge of God's plan. We must affirm that evil is not logically necessary in God's plan; instead God has planned it for reasons known to Him, and which are all morally sufficient. All we can do is look at how Scripture speaks of the positive uses of evil. So, for example, God uses evil to test His servants (Job; 1 Peter 1:7; James 1:3); to teach them patience and perseverance (James 1:3–4); to judge evildoers now and in the age to come (Deuteronomy 28:15–68; Matthew 25:41–46); to discipline us (Hebrews 12:7–11); to give us greater joy when our present suffering is replaced by the consummated state (1 Peter 4:13); to display God's glory (John 9:3; Romans 9:17), and so on. All of these reasons and many more, underscore the fact that evil is truly abhorred in and of itself, but there are ways that God uses evil, and thus planned evil, to achieve His good purposes. We also know that on the last day, God's justice, holiness, righteousness, and mercy will be clearly displayed so that no one will ever accuse Him of wrong.

In addition, Frame lays out some helpful reminders when thinking of "greater-good" reasons for God planning/permitting evil which must be kept in mind when thinking biblically about the relationship between

---

[57] See Feinberg, *No One Like Him*, 777–796, who makes this point.

[58] Frame, "The Problem of Evil," 152. William Wainright, *Philosophy of Religion*, 2nd ed. (Belmont, CA: Wadsworth, 1999), 75, explains the "greater-good defense" this way: "This defense attempts to show (roughly) that (1) evil... is logically necessary to some good, that (2) this good outweighs the evil, and that (3) there are no alternative goods not involving those evils that would have been better." In other words, all evils serve some justifiable purpose in God's plan. See Groothius, *Christian Apologetics*, 637–46.

God and evil.[59] First, we must define "greater-good" theistically. It is not our pleasure that is the greater-good but God's glory, even though it is true that what brings God glory, in the end, also benefits His people (see Romans 8:28). Second, if we are to evaluate God's actions correctly, we must evaluate them over the full extent of human history. As Frame reminds us, "[t]he Christian claim is not that the world is perfect as it is now; in fact, Scripture denies that it is. But the full goodness of God's plan will be manifest only at the end of redemptive history."[60] For reasons known only to Himself, God has chosen to work out His sovereign purposes over millennia. Evil would not be such a problem if it were resolved in a short period of time. But God has chosen to work patiently over time which prolongs God's consummating work and reminds us that in the long haul God does work out all things, including our suffering, for the good of His people (Romans 8:28) and with Paul, we will be able to say that "our light and momentary troubles are achieving for us an eternal glory that far outweighs them all" (2 Corinthians 4:17). Third, God often surprises us by the ways in which He brings good out of evil. Whether it is in the case of the Patriarchs, Joseph, Job, the nation of Israel, or most significantly in the cross of Christ, we have ample reason to say that God does all things well. With these reasons and many more, the burden of proof is on the objector who needs to show that there is no morally sufficient reason for God allowing evil and bringing good out of it (a universal negative), especially when the entire Scriptural teaching says otherwise.

Responding to the Emotional Problem of Evil

It is important to distinguish the *logical* from the *emotional* or religious problem of evil. In regards to the latter, wrestling with the problem of evil is more often felt than thought. Even Christians who know why sin and evil exist, largely due to creaturely rebellion against God, struggle with suffering, tragedies, and evil in our lives. We cry out from the depths of our heart, "How long O Lord?" and "Why?" In these questions we are not wanting to know how it is logically possible to reconcile God's existence with the existence of evil, instead we want to know why suffering and evil have come into our lives or the lives of others. Our response to these kinds of questions may overlap with the previous response, but mostly it will consistently bring people back to the God of Scripture in all of His glory and splendor. It will seek to remind people of God's great plan of redemption across the storyline of the Bible, and ultimately lead them to Christ

[59] Frame, "The Problem of Evil," 154–57.
[60] Ibid., 155.

and His cross which alone is the ground of our trust, confidence, and hope. For it is in the Gospel that we see how horrendous sin and evil are to God, how they have been defeated in Christ's work, and that the consummated state consists in a new creation where righteousness dwells and God is all in all. In other words, we must respond to this variation of the problem of evil by taking people back to the Gospel and thinking through the Bible's own presentation of the God-human-evil relationship. With this in mind, I want to conclude with five biblical-theological reflections which attempt to capture important points that are essential to remember as we live in a fallen world, under God's sovereignty, and in light of the cross work of our Lord Jesus Christ.[61]

Concluding Biblical-Theological Reflections on the Problem of Evil

First, as an important apologetic point, we must not think that it is only Christian theology which must answer the problem of evil; *every* worldview, Christian and non-Christian alike, must also face it, yet they will do so differently depending upon their view. For example, naturalistic/ atheistic viewpoints must first explain, given their overall view, how they can even *account* for the distinction between good and evil. What is the basis for objective, universal moral standards if, for sake of argument, naturalism is true? Naturalists will often raise the problem of evil against Christianity, but in so doing, they *assume* a clear distinction between good and evil and that objective evil exists, which their own view cannot explain.[62] Thus, in order to get the argument off the ground, naturalists have to borrow parasitically from Christianity which alone can account for the distinction between good and evil, rooted and grounded in God as the standard. In this way, Frame is correct to argue that many non-Christian worldviews, including naturalism, have a "'problem of good.' Without God, there is neither good nor evil."[63] The same could be said about other non-Christian views but my point is simply that everyone has to wrestle with the problem of evil, in light of their own worldview claims.[64] In terms of Christian

[61] For a very helpful and moving discussion of the *emotional* problem of evil, see John S. Feinberg, *Where is God? A Personal Story of Finding God in Grief and Suffering* (Nashville, TN: B&H, 2004); also cf. Morgan and Peterson, eds. *Suffering and the Goodness of God*, 165–237.

[62] See Groothius, *Christian Apologetics*, 617; Frame, "The Problem of Evil," 155, who makes this precise point. Also see C. S. Lewis, *Mere Christianity* (San Francisco, CA: HarperSanFrancisco, 2001), who made this argument famous.

[63] Frame, "The Problem of the Evil," 155.

[64] See Groothius, *Christian Apologetics*, 617–25, who gives further examples

thought, our problem is not *accounting* for the distinction between good and evil. We can make sense of our moral revulsion and condemnation of wicked actions. Our challenge is to make sense of why God plans and permits sin and evil, pain and misery. In answering these questions, as noted above, we are driven back to the Scriptures and entire storyline of the plan of God's work of redemption in Christ.

Second, the Bible's storyline takes seriously the distinction between "creation" and the "fall" and thus the present fallenness and abnormality of this world. A helpful and common way of thinking through the storyline of Scripture is by the grid: creation, fall, redemption, new creation. When thinking about the problem of evil, and specifically the thorny question of the origin of evil and its relationship to God's plan, the distinction between "creation" and the "fall" is utterly essential to maintain. Scripture is clear that God created the universe "good" (Genesis 1:10, 12, 18, 21, 25, 31) and that everything that came from His creative hand was perfectly good. No doubt, as noted above, sin and evil are part of God's foreordained plan, but Scripture never concludes that God is responsible for evil in any way, nor does it conclude that a high view of divine sovereignty entails this conclusion.[65]

Instead, Scripture distinguishes "creation" and "fall" and it roots this distinction in history. Sin entered the world by our creaturely act of rebellion, first in the angelic realm and then in the human world. Sin is not here because it is a metaphysical necessity tied to our finitude, nor is it here because that is just the way things are. Instead, sin is here due to our moral rebellion against God in history and that is why sin and evil are a reality, which Scripture nowhere denies or minimizes. In fact, Scripture takes sin and evil so seriously that the entire plan of redemption is to destroy it and to remove it from God's universe! And, thankfully, because sin and evil are not metaphysically necessary, in removing sin and evil, He does not have to scrap us and start all over again. Instead, God must remove our sin by paying for it in full, and then transform us by the power of the Spirit, thus restoring us to our state of goodness, yet better, now that Christ has

---

of non-Christian worldviews that have a difficult time accounting for the distinction between good and evil, including Buddhism, Hinduism, and other religious viewpoints. I would also argue that even though Islam can claim a standard for good and evil rooted in Allah's will, Islam has a major problem in accounting for the distinction between good and evil. Their view of God is fairly arbitrary and God's will is not rooted in His perfect moral character. In addition, they teach a works righteousness view of salvation which requires that God does not enforce moral standards perfectly and justly. But that is an argument for another day.

[65] Contra Little, "Evil and God's Sovereignty," 284–298.

come.[66] All of this is to say that the God of the Bible stands absolutely opposed to sin and evil. The same Scripture which teaches that God fore-ordains all things, including sin and evil, also teaches that sin and evil are an abnormality, an intrusion and a distortion of this good world, which God alone can remedy by the enfleshment of God's Son, His cross work on our behalf, and the power of the Spirit to make us new creations in Christ. Furthermore, even though it is true that God makes use of evil in order to bring about His good purposes, Scripture does not conclude that evil and sin are thus less than what Scripture says they are. Evil remains evil: totally, radically, and absolutely, and God stands completely against it as the entire storyline of Scripture makes abundantly clear.

Many application points could be drawn from this discussion, especially when we confront the reality of sin, evil, and suffering in this world. However, the main point is that since Eden and this side of the consummation, all of us live in an abnormal and fallen world, and none of us escapes this abnormality. Ultimately, when we suffer it is due to the present condition of this world. This is why all suffering is *not* related to a specific sin, as the book of Job makes abundantly clear. Yes, it is true that some suffering may be due to our sin (e.g. Acts 5; 1 Corinthians 11; cf. Hebrews 12), but it is not always the case. Suffering first and foremost is part of the present condition of this world, now awaiting the consummation, which requires that we have realistic expectations when suffering faces us head on. To be sure, we do not often know why specific suffering comes our way; that is tied to the sovereign plan of God. Yet we do know that we will face sin and evil, and when we do, God is not to blame; all blame is first placed back in Genesis 3, and thereafter with every creature who chooses to act contrary to the good commands and purposes of God.

Third, in God's plan of redemption, God not only demonstrates that He is sovereign over sin and evil, but also that in His sovereignty, holiness, justice, and grace He is rooting out sin and evil in the cross work of Christ, thus demonstrating that He is perfectly good and trustworthy. Scripture teaches that in redemption, God is not indifferent to our suffering and plight. Even though we do not deserve anything from Him but judgment, God has displayed His grace and sovereignly acted to defeat sin and evil. In fact, it is precisely because He is the sovereign and gracious Lord that we can have real hope, help, relief, and comfort since He is able not only to sympathize with us, He is also powerful to save. Is this not what the storyline of Scripture teaches? In the coming of Christ, the promised "age to come" has dawned and in His death and resurrection He has defeated sin, death, and the evil one and won for us our salvation (e.g. Romans

---

[66] See Groothius, *Christian Apologetics*, 625–29, who emphasizes these points.

3:21–25; Colossians 2:13–15; Hebrews 2:14–15; 1 Corinthians 15:56–57; Revelation 5). In so doing, God has demonstrated that He is utterly trustworthy, faithful, and good. We might not know all the mysteries of His ways, including how all the biblical data fits together. Yet, we do know that the truth of God's sovereignty and goodness is beyond question. In our redemption, God is not sitting idly by, without care or concern for His people. In the cross and resurrection we have the greatest demonstration imaginable of God's sovereignty over evil and His willingness to identify with us in order to save us from sin, evil, and death. In our facing suffering there are many questions. But as we think of our sufferings in light of Christ and His cross, we learn how to trust. God Himself has suffered unjust suffering and when we remember this, we learn that God is for us and not against us, that He is completely trustworthy, and that He stands opposed to sin and evil in a far greater way than we can even imagine. After all, what does the incarnation of God's Son, His life, death, and resurrection teach us if not that God hates sin and evil and that He sovereignly acts to destroy it, even though it is part of His foreordained plan (Acts 2:23). Thus, if we can trust God in using evil for good purposes in the cross, we can certainly trust Him in all other events, even though we may not know all the morally sufficient reasons behind those events.[67]

Fourth, given the biblical balance between God's sovereignty over sin and evil, creaturely responsibility for it, and God's goodness and utter determination to defeat and destroy it, we must also fight with all of our might against sin and evil, in line with what God Himself is doing. Interestingly enough, this conclusion is the opposite of Bruce Little. Little contends that a high view of divine sovereignty entails that "Christians should not be engaged in standing against social injustice (that which the Bible calls evil)" since "[i]f God is really sovereign and He ordains evil, it would be impossible for mere humans to stop it, so standing against social injustice would be an exercise in futility."[68] As argued above, this conclusion is simply a *non sequitur* since Scripture teaches both God's sovereignty over evil and His complete opposition to it. In this regard, John 11:33–35 is a very important text. As Jesus approaches the tomb of Lazarus in sovereign power to raise him, He is literally "outraged in spirit, and troubled."[69] Jesus, as God the Son incarnate, is outraged at the death of His friend, and thus sin which has brought death into this world. He is not outraged with

---

[67] For an excellent discussion of how the problem of evil must be viewed in light of the cross, see Henri Blocher, *Evil and the Cross* (trans. David G. Preston: Downers Grove: InterVarsity Press, 1994).

[68] Little, "Evil and God's Sovereignty," 284.

[69] See Carson, *The Gospel According to John*, PNTC (1991), 415.

Himself as the Lord, even though sin, evil, and death are part of God's eternal plan and why He is going to the cross in the first place. Rather, He is outraged by what sin has wrought by creaturely actions, which He has come to defeat and destroy. Jesus in all of His sovereignty stands in complete opposition to sin and evil, and we must do likewise. When moral evil takes place, we do not blame God or respond in a *laissez faire* manner. Rather, we fight sin and evil by proclaiming the Gospel and by God's grace, seeing people made new; by standing for justice and righteousness and punishing evildoers, through the appropriate authorities, for their responsible actions. We never justify sin and wrong actions by appealing to divine sovereignty at the expense of human responsibility, nor do we reduce God's sovereignty in light of human choices. We hold the biblical teaching in tension as we fight with all our might against sin and evil, in line with what God Himself is doing.

Fifth, what about specific suffering in our lives? Often when we go through suffering we wish that God would have allowed us to go through something else. Why do we experience specific suffering? Why do some escape specific tragedies and others do not? There are many points that could be noted, but I conclude with these thoughts. John 21:15–23 reminds us that God calls all of us to different callings in life. When Peter asked about John's future, Jesus never answered him directly but instead said, "Follow me." Our lives are part of God's sovereign plan and most of the time we do not know what the Lord has ordained for our lives. As we live before the Lord, we must maintain simultaneously the biblical data without denying, minimizing, or marginalizing it. For the Christian, we are assured that even in our suffering in this life, which is part of the fallenness of this world order, God never allows us to experience anything we cannot bear by His grace and power (1 Corinthians 10:12–13). Sometimes the suffering we experience is due to persecution for the Lord's name, which we should consider joy (Mark 8:34–38; 2 Timothy 3:12; 1 Peter 4:12–16). Other times it may be due to the discipline of the Lord (Hebrews 12:1ff). Yet in many cases, we experience difficulties related to the abnormality of this world, but not knowing why the specific events beset us. What we are assured of though is this: our God is sovereign and the defeat of sin and evil is accomplished. We live our lives in full conviction that in Christ, we have every assurance that God is sovereign over evil and that until the end, we can live confidently, trusting God's promises and Word.

It is no doubt the case that the relationship of God to sin and evil is one of the most difficult questions in all theology. In this chapter, I have sought to present a positive case of how one Calvinist thinks through the issue in light of the biblical data and in response to the charge of contradiction leveled against us, both from within Christian theology and without. Even though many questions remain, one thing is sure: our sovereign and gracious triune God is worthy of all of our confidence and trust. Solutions to the problem of evil by Arminian theology are not only biblically inadequate for the reasons discussed, but in the end, they rob us of our confidence in our sovereign God who is working out all things in this world for His glory and our good. We only have knowledge of God's plan and actions as creatures, but in light of God's actions in creation and redemption; in light of God's incredible plan of redemption centered in the coming of our Lord Jesus Christ and His incredible triumphant cross work for us; we have every reason to trust what God has said and to live in confident expectation for our sovereign God to consummate what has already begun in Christ in a glorious new heaven and new earth (see Revelation 21–22). While we continue to live between the ages, as we await the second coming of our Lord when this fallen order will finally be put away, may we live as those who trust God's promises no matter what we experience, proclaim Christ as our only hope and salvation, and stand with our great God against sin and evil as we await the end.

9

Calvinism Foundational For Evangelism and Missions

Thomas K. Ascol

The late William R. Estep, distinguished professor of church history at Southwestern Baptist Theological Seminary, once plainly stated what many who share his views but not his courage hesitate to express:

> Calvinism is anti-missionary. The Great Commission is meaningless if every person is programmed for salvation or damnation, for [then] evangelism and missionary effort are exercises in futility.[1]

The soteriology that is associated with the famous Genevan reformer has had to bear this type of accusation since Jesuit apologist, Robert Bellarmine's counter-reformation charge in the late sixteenth century that Protestantism is inherently anti-missionary.[2] Though it is easy to find examples of believers of Calvinistic persuasion whose evangelistic engagement is shameful in its anemia, that task does not become more difficult when one examines the more Arminian regions of evangelicalism.

---

[1] William R. Estep, "Doctrines Lead to 'Dunghill' Prof Warns," *Founders Journal* 29 (Summer 1997): available at www.founders.org/journal/fj29/contents. html (accessed January 12, 2012).

[2] Kenneth J. Stewart, *Ten Myths about Calvinism: Recovering the Breadth of the Reformed Tradition* (Downers Grove, IL: IVP Academic, 2011), 128–29. Other examples of such accusations can be found in Laurence M. Vance, *The Other Side of Calvinism*, rev. ed. (Pensacola, FL: Vance Publications, 1999), 28–35, *passim*; Steve Lemke, "The Future of Southern Baptists as Evangelicals" (paper present-

This fact was documented by Ed Stetzer, Vice President of Research and Ministry Development for LifeWay Christian Resources, when he published a report in 2007 based on research conducted by LifeWay and the North American Mission Board of the Southern Baptist Convention. The report, entitled, *Calvinism and SBC Church Leadership: Key Findings and Evangelistic Implications*, concludes that while research indicates that Southern Baptist church leaders who are "five-point Calvinists" tend to share the gospel slightly more often than their non-Calvinist counterparts, "church growth statistics in terms of annual baptism rates indicates that there is little difference between Calvinist and non-Calvinist led churches."[3] A closer examination of those rates and evangelistic practices indicates that both Calvinists and Arminians within the Southern Baptist Convention (SBC) have much room for growth.[4]

This point is happily being recognized by a growing number of Southern Baptists who do not share the Calvinistic convictions of the contributors in this book. Sometimes, however, the acknowledgment is couched in terms that suggest Calvinism and evangelism do not naturally go together. Statements like, "Even though he is a Calvinist, he believes in evangelism" or "He does not let his Calvinism get in the way of his evangelism," are frequently heard.

I want to argue in this chapter that the relationship between historic Calvinism and biblical evangelism is best understood in terms of "therefore"

---

ed at the Maintaining Baptist Distinctives Conference, Mid-America Baptist Theological Seminary, Cordova, TN, April 2005), available from http://www.nobts.edu/Faculty/ItoR/LemkeSW/Personal/SBCfuture.pdf (accessed January 10, 2012), 12–15; Dave Hunt, *What Love Is This?*, 2nd ed. (Bend, OR: Berean Call, 2004), *passim*; Nelson Price, "Evangelical Calvinism is an Oxymoron," *The Christian Index*, November 23, 2006, available from http://www.christianindex.org/2780.article (accessed January 21, 2008).

[3] Ed Stetzer, *Calvinism and SBC Church Leadership: Key Findings and Evangelistic Implications* (Nashville: LifeWay Research, 2007), available from http://www.edstetzer.com/Calvinism%20and%20Southern%20Baptist%20Church%20Leadership%20presentation.pdf (accessed January 3, 2012), 20.

[4] I do not use "Arminian" in a pejorative fashion but as a historically accurate alternative to the cumbersome "non-Calvinist" appellation. Roger Olsen appropriately advocates this use of the term in his review of David Allen's and Steve Lemke's book, *Whosoever Will: A Biblical-Theological Critique of Five-Point Calvinism* (Nashville, TN: B&H Academic, 2010). In his review, which appears on Southwestern Baptist Theological Seminary's *Baptist Theology* website, Olsen notes that "all of the authors are Arminians in the classical sense." The review is available from http://www.baptisttheology.org/WhosoeverWill.cfm (accessed January 13, 2012).

rather than "nevertheless." Calvinism is, above all else, a biblical theology. Evangelism is a biblical practice. It stands to reason, then, that Calvinism, when understood and applied properly, would undergird and propel evangelism and missions. Both Scripture and Christian history demonstrate that this is indeed the case.[5]

Testimony of Scripture

John MacArthur provocatively declared in a 2007 sermon that "Jesus was a Calvinist." The charges of being irreverent and anachronistic that resulted came from people who obviously missed his point. MacArthur was simply saying—admittedly in a provocative way—that historic Calvinism derives its views from the teachings of Jesus. No self-respecting Calvinist would ever disagree. In fact, in the way that MacArthur meant it, we could go on to say that all of the prophets and apostles were also Calvinists. No anachronism is intended. Rather, the point simply needs to be reestablished (as other chapters in this book have done quite well) that Calvinism owes its convictions to the Word of God, not to a sixteenth century reformer. As Charles Spurgeon stated,

> We only use the term "Calvinism" for shortness. That doctrine which is called "Calvinism" did not spring from Calvin; we believe that it sprang from the great founder of all truth. Perhaps Calvin himself derived it mainly from the writings of Augustine. Augustine obtained his views, without doubt, through the Holy Spirit of God, from diligent study of the writings of Paul, and Paul received them from the Holy Ghost and from Jesus Christ, the great founder of the Christian Church. We use the term then, not because we impute an extraordinary importance to Calvin's having taught these doctrines. We would be just as willing to call them by any other name, if we could find one which would be better understood, and which on the whole would be as consistent with the fact.[6]

---

[5] One reason that dialogue about Calvinism and Arminianism has so often been plagued by misunderstanding is due to imprecision in definition of the terms. Though I recognize that there are good reasons for not limiting the term "Calvinism" to the so-called five-points that have historically been associated with that theology, for the sake of clarity I am largely limiting my focus to those five doctrinal ideas as they relate to evangelism. Because the key doctrines in contention receive full treatment in other chapters, I will not attempt to give a rigorous exegetical defense of them but will clarify and assert them for the purpose of showing how they impel missions and evangelism.

[6] C. H. Spurgeon, *The Early Years* (Edinburgh: The Banner of Truth Trust, 1967), 162.

For the sake of space and to avoid redundancy, this chapter limits its biblical consideration of the doctrines of Calvinism and their bearing on the practice of evangelism to the teachings and practices of Jesus and Paul.

Jesus

Jesus described His mission as coming to "seek and to save the lost" (Luke 19:10). No one would ever question the evangelistic, missionary heart of our Savior. In the midst of His mission—and as a significant part of it—Jesus teaches the absolute sovereignty of God in salvation. Furthermore, there is no incongruity between that doctrine and His teaching on total depravity, unconditional election, particular redemption or the priority of regeneration over faith and His sincere call to people to trust Him as Lord.

Salvation must come through the sovereign grace of God due to the spiritual and moral condition of its objects. Because of the fall, all mankind is by nature enslaved to sin. Jesus said, "Truly, truly I say to you, everyone who commits sin is a slave to sin" (John 8:34). This enslavement extends to all of the faculties belonging to human nature, including the understanding, the affections and the will. The result is that by nature people love darkness rather than the light (John 3:19) and that even their wills have been taken captive by sin.

Jesus was under no delusions about the bondage of the human will to sin. He said to a crowd that followed Him, "No one can come to me unless the Father who sent me draws him" (John 6:44; cf. v. 65). He uses a word of ability, "can" (*dunamai*) to make His point that the natural man does not possess the ability in and of himself to come to Christ for salvation. In the very same setting Jesus explained the availability of salvation to anyone and everyone who believes. "For this is the will of my Father, that everyone who looks on the Son and believes in him should have eternal life, and I will raise him up on the last day" (John 6:40). Just prior to this he exhorted His hearers to labor "for the food that endures to eternal life, which the Son of Man will give to you" (John 6:27) and, when questioned, taught that "work of God" that leads to eternal life is to "believe in him whom he has sent" (John 6:29). Inability in no way negates responsibility.

Consequently, the spiritual inability of people to trust in Christ apart from the regenerating work of the Spirit never hindered Jesus from issuing evangelistic calls. In fact, the most beloved evangelistic words that our Savior ever uttered were spoken immediately after one of the clearest teachings on mankind's spiritual inability. "For God so loved the world that he gave his only Son, that whoever believes in him should not perish but have eternal life" (John 3:16) comes after Jesus explained to Nicodemus that, though he was a teacher of Israel, he remained spiritually helpless without the new birth. "Truly, truly, I say to you, unless one is born again he cannot see the kingdom of God" (John 3:3). And again, "Truly, truly, I say to you, unless one is born of water and the Spirit, he cannot enter the kingdom of God" (John 3:5).

"Seeing" and "entering" are metaphorical descriptions of trusting. They describe the act of believing unto salvation. Jesus tells Nicodemus that such faith is impossible "unless" one is born again. But total depravity is no barrier to evangelism because of the glorious reality of the Holy Spirit's sovereign work of granting new birth. Jesus underscores the helplessness of Nicodemus and the sovereignty of the Spirit whose regenerating work is necessary for saving faith when he says, "Do not marvel that I said to you, 'You must be born again.' The wind blows where it wishes, and you hear its sound but you do not know where it comes from or where it goes. So it is with everyone who is born of the Spirit" (John 3:7–8).

The inability of a lost person to repent and believe the gospel while in an unregenerate state is no barrier to evangelism because of the power of God's Word and Spirit. Jesus said, "It is the Spirit who gives life; the flesh is no help at all. The words that I have spoken to you are spirit and life" (John 6:63). God's Spirit uses His Word to enable a spiritually blind person to see the kingdom and a spiritually dead person to enter the kingdom. The inability of the one who needs to see and enter is overcome by the sovereign work of the Spirit through the ministry of the Word.

We are given a graphic illustration of how this works when Jesus stood before the tomb of His dead friend, Lazarus. He was facing a physically impossible situation as far as human nature and ability are concerned. Yet, He said, "Lazarus, come out" (John 11:43). He commanded him to do what he was unable to do knowing full well that the power of His Word would grant the very ability necessary to comply with what He commanded. This is precisely the position of every Christian evangelist. We speak the Word of Christ to those who cannot see or enter the kingdom, who cannot come to Him in faith unless drawn by the Father—in other words, to those who cannot repent and believe the gospel on their own. Yet, we can extend the call of the gospel with hope and confidence that the Spirit, who sovereignly blows like the wind, can take that Word and grant the ability to comply with the terms of that call.

It is precisely because Calvinists have confidence in the abiding Word of God as the means whereby sinners are born again (1 Peter 1:23) that they are willing to preach the gospel and press its claims on anyone and everyone. There is no need to rely on fleshly methods because what is needed to bring a lost person to salvation is a sovereign work of God. As Jesus said, "the flesh is of no help."

Coupled with this confidence in the Spirit and Word to bring about the new birth is the assurance that the doctrines of election and atonement give, namely, that God will indeed save all of the people He has chosen and for whom Christ has offered up His life as a propitiation. Jesus said, "All that the Father gives me will come to me, and whoever comes to me I will never cast out"(John 6:37). Here we are informed that there are people whom the Father has given to the Son. Furthermore, we are assured that all of those people will come to (believe in) Christ. Finally, this verse teaches that all whom the Father gives to the Son and who (unfailingly) come to the Son will be kept by the Son—they will never be cast out. Our Lord's teaching here guarantees the success of evangelism. There are people who will come to Christ and be saved.

This wonderful assurance that comes from the doctrine of election does not mean that election in and of itself saves. Election is not salvation. It is *to* salvation. Everything necessary for sinners to be made acceptable in the sight of God must also be provided. Jesus does precisely this in His life and death for His people—a relationship that He often describes in terms of a shepherd and His sheep.

In John 10 Jesus drew out this analogy to teach His atoning, exclusive relationship with His people. "I am the good shepherd. The good shepherd lays down his life for the sheep" (John 10:11). "I am the good shepherd. I know my own and my own know me, just as the Father knows me and I know the Father; and I lay down my life for the sheep" (John 10:14–15). Jesus depicts His substitutionary, sacrificial death in terms of laying down His life for the sheep (John 10:17–18). When the Jews questioned His identity, Jesus very bluntly responded with a stark indictment: "you do not believe because you are not part of my flock" (John 10:27). As the good shepherd He tenderly cares for His sheep to the point of dying for them. Then He pointedly excludes His critics not only from His flock but also from the scope and saving benefits of His death by revealing that they are not His sheep.

What comes next understandably confounds Arminians but is no surprise to Calvinists. To those very people who are not part of His flock, and who have accused Him of blasphemy, Jesus responds with a persuasive argument that concludes with a plain admonition. "If I am not doing the works of my Father, then do not believe me; but if I do them, even though you do not believe me, believe the works, that you may know and understand that the Father is in me and I am in the Father" (John 10:37,38). He commands them to believe.

If our omniscient Savior called people whom He knew were not the Father's elect to believe the evidence for His Messiahship, how much more should His finite disciples indiscriminately call people to trust Him? The promise of salvation is to anyone who will believe. The responsibility of Christians is to declare this promise while proclaiming the gospel with arguments and encouragements to our hearers to do just that: trust Christ. We have been sent (John 20:21) and commissioned (Matthew 28:18–20; Mark 16:15) to make disciples through proclaiming the gospel.

The fact that our Sovereign has commanded us to preach the gospel is reason enough to do the work of evangelism. David Allen, however, sees things differently. He writes, "Some Calvinists today are engaged in evangelism for the simple reason that *they do not know who the elect are*, in addition to Christ's missionary commands" and asserts that "this motivation is insufficient."[7] Certainly there are other realities that can and should enter into a Christian's motivation for seeking to win people to Christ. Most notably—and glaringly absent from David Allen's list—is the glory of God that is manifested both in the witnessing and in the salvation of a sinner who is rescued by His grace.

How that fact diminishes the sufficiency of our Lord's command to serve as motivation for His disciples is beyond me and exceeds the bounds of Scripture. Genuine love for Christ necessarily moves toward obedience of His commandments (John 14:15). The Arminian complaint that a Calvinist "cannot look a congregation in the eyes or even a single unbelieving sinner in the eye and say, 'Christ died for your sins,'"[8] is similarly rooted in extra-biblical teaching on evangelism. Nowhere in the Bible do we find such an evangelistic argument employed. Consequently, one is left wondering what canon of authority Allen is employing in his warnings of Calvinism's "problems for evangelism."[9]

---

[7] David L. Allen, "The Atonement: Limited or Universal?" in *Whosoever Will*, 96. Allen criticizes Calvinists in general and Mark Dever in particular for not citing "Christ's death for all men, and God's universal saving will" as motivations for evangelism. Ibid., 97.

[8] Ibid., 97.

[9] Ibid., 96–98. Allen's critique falls flat when evaluated in the light of Scripture. He writes, "Since Christ did not die for the sins of the non-elect and since they do not know who the elect are, it is simply impossible in a preaching or witnessing situation to say to all directly 'Christ died for you.' I do not see how this untenable position can do anything but undermine one's evangelistic zeal since the actual 'saveability' of the listeners may secretly be in question" Ibid., 97–98. If this is the *sine qua non* of evangelistic zeal then why is such language completely absent from Scripture? One searches in vain for any evangelistic conversation in holy writ that includes the appeal, "Christ died for you." Allen's criticism impresses only those whose consciences are bound by something other than the inerrant, infallible and sufficient Word of God.

Paul

Certainly Paul did not evangelize this way. Rather, he proclaimed the saving work of Jesus to Jews and Gentiles alike with the clear understanding that God commands "all people everywhere to repent" (Acts 17:30). The authority of God's revealed will was enough for him to declare it as a universal obligation without any declaration to the Athenians that Jesus had died for the sins of any one of them in particular. Nor were his evangelistic appeals based on some supposed hope that his hearers would be able in and of themselves to repent and believe. Following the theology of his Savior, he writes, "For the mind that is set on the flesh is hostile to God, for it does not submit to God's law; indeed, it cannot. Those who are in the flesh cannot please God" (Romans 8:7,8). With Jesus, Paul teaches that the natural man does not possess the ability to come to Christ for salvation, to obey God's law (which requires faith) or to please God (which faith and repentance do).

There is a consistency to Paul's practice as observed in his evangelistic messages in Acts. In Antioch of Pisidia Paul evangelized in the synagogue by giving a biblical-theological overview of redemptive history (Acts 13:16–25), showing how Jesus was crucified and raised from the dead as the culminating event of that history (Acts 13:26–37). He then concludes with an encouragement to trust Christ for salvation: "Let it be known to you therefore, brothers, that through this man forgiveness of sins is proclaimed to you, and by him everyone who believes is freed from everything from which you could not be freed by the law of Moses" (Acts 13:39). He does not ask them to believe that Jesus died for them specifically. Rather, he explains that in Christ is found forgiveness and this is for "everyone who believes." It is interesting that Luke's record of Paul's and Barnabas' ministry to Jews and Gentiles in that city ends with the notation that "as many as were appointed to eternal life believed" (Acts 13:48).

Those who had been appointed to eternal life are the same ones described by Jesus as having been given to Him by the Father. They are the same ones for whom Jesus exclusively prayed just before He was betrayed and arrested (John 17:6, 9). In Ephesians 1:4–6 Paul included himself and his Christian readers when he described how they came to be recipients of this distinguishing grace of God: "He chose us in him before the foundation of the world, that we should be holy and blameless before him. In love he predestined us for adoption as sons through Jesus Christ, according to the purpose of his will, to the praise of his glorious grace, with which he has blessed us in the Beloved." They were appointed to be saved from eternity through God's sovereign election. When the gospel was proclaimed to them in the power of the Holy Spirit they believed and actually were saved.

This is the way it works in every individual's conversion. The knowledge that God has indeed chosen specific people to be saved who infallibly will be saved by believing the gospel should encourage and motivate us to do the work of evangelism. The doctrine of election, rightly held, dispels discouragement when there seems to be little fruit from our evangelistic efforts. This is exactly the way that God designed it to work and the way we see it working in Paul's own life.

Paul traveled to Corinth after his ministry in Athens. Many of the Jews there rejected his evangelistic efforts. They "opposed and reviled him" (Acts 18:6). Yet, Paul stayed "a year and six months, teaching the Word of God among them" (Acts 18:11). God used the doctrine of election to encourage him to stay. Luke records how this happened. "And the Lord said to Paul one night in a vision, 'Do not be afraid, but go on speaking and do not be silent, for I am with you, and no one will attack you to harm you, for I have many in this city who are my people'" (Acts 18:9,10). They were God's people in terms of election, but not yet converted. They would be converted but only through believing the gospel. Therefore Paul must keep preaching and teaching the Word. He can do so confidently because he knows that God has a people who will believe the gospel and be saved.

In the last New Testament letter Paul wrote, he explains to Timothy how the doctrine of election motivated him to bear up under extreme difficulties, even while in prison. It is because of his preaching of the gospel that he found himself suffering in chains as if he were a criminal. "But," he writes, "The word of God is not bound! Therefore I endure everything for the sake of the elect, that they also may obtain the salvation that is in Christ Jesus with eternal glory" (2 Timothy 2:9,10; cf. 1–8). Paul was willing to endure hardship, deprivation, persecution and even death because he knew that no matter what happened to him, the Word of God would continue to do its work in bringing all of God's elect to salvation through faith in Jesus Christ.

Far from being a discouragement to evangelism, election provides a great motivation to preach the gospel indiscriminately and hopefully because it guarantees that there will be people—people whom God has chosen—who will believe the message and be saved. When understood in light of God's overarching purpose to glorify Himself through the salvation of sinners, the doctrine of election undergirds and fuels passion to see God glorified in saving the most obstinate unbelievers.

This explains the juxtaposition of Paul's expressed burden for the salvation of unconverted Jews and his stark teaching on election in Romans 9–10. Nowhere is the sovereignty of God in election taught more plainly than in Romans 9. The idea that God chooses some and not others to be saved inevitably raises objections that God is unjust and that people, therefore, cannot be held responsible. Paul anticipates and addresses these concerns in his exposition of the doctrine in chapter 9. In response to both objections he appeals to the fundamental reality that God is God and has sovereign prerogatives to do as He will with His creatures. "What shall we say then? Is there injustice on God's part? By no means! For he says to Moses, 'I will have mercy on whom I have mercy, and I will have compassion on whom I have compassion.' So then it depends not on human will or exertion, but on God, who has mercy. For the Scripture says to Pharaoh, 'For this very purpose I have raised you up, that I might show my power in you, and that my name might be proclaimed in all the earth'" (Romans 9:14–17). Since mercy is undeserved it cannot be injustice to withhold it. Paul's second response is even more direct. "You will say to me then, 'Why does he still find fault? For who can resist his will?' But who are you, O man, to answer back to God? Will what is molded say to its molder, 'Why have you made me like this?' Has the potter no right over the clay, to make out of the same lump one vessel for honorable use and another for dishonorable use?" (Romans 9:19–21). The Creator has complete rights over His creation.

Paul does not hesitate to vindicate God's sovereign right to love Jacob and hate Esau because he is unembarrassed by the divine purpose of election (Romans 9:10–13). Neither does he hesitate to bracket his plain teaching on this subject with expressions of his passionate burden that his fellow Jews come to know Christ savingly. Before he launches into his robust teaching on unconditional election he declares the depth of his longing for the salvation of his kinsmen. "I am speaking the truth in Christ—I am not lying; my conscience bears me witness in the Holy Spirit—that I have great sorrow and unceasing anguish in my heart. For I could wish that I myself were accursed and cut off from Christ for the sake of my brothers, my kinsmen according to the flesh" (Romans 9:1–3). Similarly, after his defense of God's sovereign right to choose certain people and not others to receive His mercy, Paul says of the Jews, "Brothers, my heart's desire and prayer to God for them is that they may be saved" (Romans 10:1). Unconditional election does not blunt evangelistic passion.

Paul believed that his fellow Jews could be saved because the promise of the gospel is for anyone and everyone who believes. Election in no way diminishes that. Paul understood this and that is why he could go on to write, "If you confess with your mouth that Jesus is Lord and believe in your heart that God raised him from the dead, you will be saved. For with the heart one believes and is justified, and with the mouth one confesses and is saved. For the Scripture says, 'Everyone who believes in him will not be put to shame.' For there is no distinction between Jew and Greek; for the same Lord is Lord of all, bestowing his riches on all who call on him.

For 'everyone who calls on the name of the Lord will be saved'" (Romans 10:9–13). This is true without regard to election and is to be received by anyone who submits to the authority of Scripture.

Since "faith comes from hearing, and hearing through the word of Christ" (Romans 10:17) it is absolutely essential that those who have the word of Christ declare it to those who need to hear and believe. Anyone who believes that the doctrine of election undermines the necessity or passion for evangelism is not thinking biblically. Consider Paul's logical argument for evangelism and missions: "How then will they call on him in whom they have not believed? And how are they to believe in him of whom they have never heard? And how are they to hear without someone preaching? And how are they to preach unless they are sent? As it is written, 'How beautiful are the feet of those who preach the good news!'" (Romans 10:14,15). The elect will be saved. They will not be saved apart from believing the gospel. Therefore the gospel must be preached throughout the world. And it can be preached confidently, knowing that God has chosen people who will believe and be saved.

Testimony of History

This understanding of God's saving purposes has fueled the work of evangelism and missions throughout Christian history. Among the greatest missionaries and evangelists the world has ever known are those who believed what has historically been denominated as Calvinism. It is hard to understand, then, how anyone who has even a cursory awareness of church history could ever make the charge that Calvinism is a hindrance to evangelism. Yet, such baseless accusations have the staying power of urban legends.

When he was President of Southeastern Baptist Theological Seminary, Paige Patterson made the following statement, including a challenge, to students and faculty.

> Now, I don't care what any Calvinist has to say about it, Calvinism, as a doctrinal commitment, has always had the effect of being a drag, to put it the best way, kindest way, a drag on missions and evangelism. All you have to do is prove me wrong, but you have to do it in some other way than citing Spurgeon, because he's been cited often enough and it is not really impressive to cite Spurgeon and one or two others and say we've proved you wrong. No, look at the whole. Look at what has happened across the centuries. Wherever Calvinism takes a strong root, evangelism begins to suffer and world missions begins to suffer. And it is understandable why. Here is a man who believes that God has created this number of people over here to be saved and, because he believes in

irresistible grace, they're going to get saved no matter what. So what is the necessity of my going to them? Well, in my mind of course I treat it this way: I say, Well, I've got to go to them because God's told me to go to them. So the fact that I'm a Calvinist doesn't make any difference really. God has told me to do it, so I've got to go to them. But let me tell you what. In your heart, if you don't think it's going to make any difference to begin with because what's done is done in eternity past, you ain't going to go. That's just the truth of the matter. Very seldom do people go. The fact that there are some exceptions only underscores the rule.[10]

The breadth of this accusation is hard to understand. Even allowing for hyperbole, however, it is easily disproven. History records more than "some exceptions" to Patterson's charge, even if one disregards (inexplicably) the testimony of Charles Spurgeon. In fact, history demonstrates the exact opposite. Far from being a drag on missionary endeavors, Calvinism has actually been a *catalyst* for them.

John Calvin and the Puritans

John Calvin himself advocated the work of evangelism and so led out in bold evangelistic efforts that Philip Hughes refers to him as the "Director of Missions" and calls Geneva under Calvin's leadership a "school of missions."[11] In his book, *Concerning the Eternal Predestination of God*, Calvin writes, "Since we do not know who belongs to the number of the predestined and who does not, it befits us so to feel as to wish that all be saved. So it will come about that, whoever we come across, we shall study to make him a sharer of peace.... But it will be for God to make it effective in those whom He foreknew and predestined."[12] From Geneva, hundreds of missionaries were sent out across Europe and as far away as South America. Many of them were sent into the very flames of martyrdom.[13]

Under Calvin's tutelage many French refugees in Geneva were trained, examined and commissioned to return to their homeland to preach the

[10] Transcribed from an audio recording of a "Student Forum" at Southeastern Baptist Theological Seminary in Wake Forest, North Carolina, held November 1, 2000.

[11] For documentation and elaboration of this, see the excellent article by Ray Van Neste, "John Calvin on Evangelism and Missions," *Founders Journal* 33 (Summer 1998), 15–21.

[12] John Calvin, *Concerning the Eternal Predestination of God*, trans. J. K. S. Reid (London: James Clarke and Co., Limited, 1961), 138.

[13] For more on Calvin's missionary heart and activity, see Michael Haykin, "Calvin and Missions," *Founders Journal* 75 (Winter 2009), 20–27; Frank James, III, "Calvin the Evangelist," *Founders Journal* 75 (Winter 2009), 3–6.

gospel and plant churches, at the risk of their own lives. Records indicate that in 1555 five churches had been planted in France through this effort. Because of persecution, they were not able to meet openly. After four more years the number of churches grew to more than one hundred. Growth continued so rapidly that "scholars estimate that by 1562 there were more than 2,150 churches established in France with approximately three-million Protestant souls in attendance."[14]

The Puritan movement in the seventeenth century, well-known for its Calvinistic convictions, continued and expanded the evangelistic and missionary zeal of Geneva. In 1879 Alexander Grosart called Richard Baxter "the most successful preacher and winner of souls and nurturer of won souls, that England has ever had."[15] Baxter's *Call to the Unconverted* and *Reformed Pastor* underscore this assessment. His passion for mission work among the Indians of New England made him eager to assist missionary John Eliot in securing a new charter for the Corporation for the Propagation of the Gospel in New England in 1660–62. Baxter's vision for called-out missionary workers, whom he called "unfixed Ambulatory Ministers," helped persuade Eliot to give himself to that work in a full time capacity. Other examples of Calvinistic passion for evangelism and missions can be easily found among Baxter's Puritan contemporaries.[16]

George Whitefield

The great eighteenth-century evangelist, George Whitefield, provides a further example of how the doctrines of grace as explained by Calvinism impels missions and evangelism. He crisscrossed the Atlantic Ocean thirteen times preaching wherever he could gather a crowd not in spite of his doctrinal commitments but, as he put it, because "the doctrines of our election, and free justification in Christ Jesus are daily more and more pressed upon my heart. They fill my soul with a holy fire and afford me great confidence in God my Saviour."[17] Whitefield affirmed in the plainest language his belief in the biblical doctrine of election. He writes, "I believe

---

[14] Frank James, "Calvin the Evangelist," available at www.founders.org/journal/fj75/article1.html (accessed Jan 14, 2012).

[15] Cited in Sidney H. Rooy, *The Theology of Mission in the Puritan Tradition* (Delft: W.D. Meinema, 1965), 148.

[16] Rooy's work gives ample supporting evidence, as does J.I. Packer, in *A Quest for Godliness: The Puritan Vision of the Christian Life* (Wheaton, IL: Crossway, 1990), 291–308.

[17] Cited in Arnold A. Dallimore, *George Whitefield, The Life and Times of the Great Evangelist of the Eighteenth-Century Revival*, vol. 1 (Edinburgh: Banner of Truth, 1970), 407.

the doctrine of reprobation, in this view, that God intends to give saving grace, through Jesus Christ, only to a certain number, and that the rest of mankind, after the fall of Adam, being justly left of God to continue in sin, will at last suffer that eternal death which is its proper wages."[18]

In a widely heralded letter, Whitefield refuted John Wesley's accusation that if unconditional election is true then preaching is in vain. With reasoning that is rooted in the Apostle Paul's understanding of how salvation comes to sinners, he explains,

> O dear Sir, what kind of reasoning—or rather sophistry—is this! Hath not God, who hath appointed salvation for a certain number, appointed also the preaching of the Word as a means to bring them to it? Does anyone hold election in any other sense? And if so, how is preaching needless to them that are elected, when the gospel is designated by God himself to be the power of God unto their eternal salvation? And since we know not who are elect and who reprobate, we are to preach promiscuously to all. For the Word may be useful, even to the non-elect, in restraining them from much wickedness and sin. However, it is enough to excite to the utmost diligence in preaching and hearing, when we consider that by these means, some, even as many as the Lord hath ordained to eternal life, shall certainly be quickened and enabled to believe. And who that attends, especially with reverence and care, can tell but he may be found of that happy number?[19]

Knowledge that God has chosen particular people who will be saved provides much encouragement to stir up "diligence" among both preachers and hearers of the gospel. Though such reasoning may provide insufficient motivation for those of a more Arminian bent, it was more than adequate for the greatest evangelist of the eighteenth century.

William Carey

Many, if not most, of the early Baptist leaders in missions and evangelism have been men of a decidedly Calvinistic persuasion. William Carey is largely regarded to be the "Father of Modern Missions." He was, in the words of Timothy George, "like Bunyan before him and Spurgeon after him… an evangelical Calvinist."[20] Before he ever left England's shores to

---

[18] "A Letter from Mr. Whitefield to the Rev. Mr. John Wesley" available online at www.spurgeon.org/~phil/wesley.htm (accessed January 26, 2012).

[19] Ibid.

[20] Timothy George, *Faithful Witness, the Life and Mission of William Carey* (Birmingham, AL: New Hope, 1991), 57.

take the gospel to India, Carey rejected both Arminianism on the one hand and hyper-Calvinism on the other. He was firmly convinced, however, of historic, evangelical Calvinism. When assessing the lessons that Carey's legacy can teach us today as we seek to make Christ known, George puts at the top of the list, "*The sovereignty of God.*"

> Carey knew that Christian missions was rooted in the gracious, eternal purpose of the Triune God, Father, Son, and Holy Spirit, to call unto Himself a redeemed people out of the fallen race of lost humankind. As a young pastor in England he confronted and overcame the resistance of those Hyper-Calvinistic theologians who used the sovereignty of God as a pretext for their do-nothing attitude toward missions. It was not in spite of, but rather because of, his belief in the greatness of God and His divine purpose in election that Carey was willing "to venture all" to proclaim the gospel in the far corners of the world.[21]

This evaluation is supported by the "Serampore Compact" that Carey and his fellow missionaries drew up on October 7, 1805 as a summary of guiding principles for their work. They agreed that three times each year this compact would be read aloud at each mission station. The first part of that document declares their understanding of God's sovereignty in salvation.

> We are firmly persuaded that Paul might plant and Apollos water, in vain, in any part of the world, did not God give the increase. We are sure that only those ordained to eternal life will believe, and that God alone can add to the church such as shall be saved. Nevertheless we cannot but observe with admiration that Paul, the great champion for the glorious doctrine of free and sovereign grace, was the most conspicuous for his personal zeal in the work of persuading men to be reconciled to God. In this respect he is a noble example for our imitation.[22]

A Calvinistic understanding of God's grace in salvation did not diminish William Carey's commitment to evangelism and missions. Rather, like Paul, his doctrinal convictions undergirded missionary efforts.

Andrew Fuller

While Carey ventured out to the unreached people groups of the world, his friend and fellow pastor, Andrew Fuller, became a leading sup-

---

[21] Ibid., 171.

[22] This document is available from Christian History Institute, Box 540, Worcester, PA 19490.

porter of the work back home.[23] In many respects Fuller was the theologian of the modern missionary movement. His writings, most notably, *The Gospel Worthy of All Acceptation*, demonstrate the harmony between what he held as "strict Calvinism" (in contrast to the "false Calvinism" of hyper-Calvinism) and the necessity and urgency to preach Christ to all people. Citing Paul's arguments in Romans 9–11, Fuller rightly notes that the apostle "believed the doctrine of Divine decrees, or that God 'worketh all things after the counsel of his own will;' but he had no idea of making these things a part of the *rule of duty*; either so as to excuse his countrymen from the sin of unbelief, or himself from using every possible means that might accomplish their salvation."[24] Such is the reasoning that has always informed all evangelical Calvinism. Responsibility to make disciples of the nations derives from what God has clearly revealed to be His will and is in no way diminished by what He has revealed to be His eternal purpose. As Fuller further explains, "election, while it places no bar in the way of any man which would not have been there without it, resolves the salvation of the saved into *mere grace*."[25]

While it is certainly true that the doctrine of God's unconditional election can be abused to justify lack of evangelistic effort it must be recognized that the fault for such inaction is found not in the doctrine itself but in the misuse of it. One of Fuller's repeated emphases about this point is the importance of fashioning our views of this subject "with simplicity" from the teachings of Scripture. "A Christian minister also, if he take his views simply from the Scriptures, will find nothing in this doctrine to hinder the free use of warnings, invitations, and persuasions, either to the converted or to the unconverted.[26]

It is failure at just this point—to submit simply to the teaching of God's Word—that causes some to judge Calvinism inconsistent with zealous evangelism. Nowhere is this made more evident than in the way that some voice their objections to particular redemption. Fuller argues,

> There is no contradiction between this pecularity [sic] of *design* in the death of Christ, and a universal obligation on those who hear the gospel to believe in him, or a universal invitation being addressed to them. If

[23] He was joined in his efforts by John Sutcliffe, John Ryland, Jr. and Samuel Pearce. It was from these men, along with Carey—all of whom were Particular Baptists—that the Baptist Missionary Society emerged in England.

[24] This is from the second edition of *The Gospel Worthy of All Acceptation* in Andrew Fuller, *The Complete Works of Andrew Fuller*, ed. Joseph Belcher, 3 vols., reprint edition (Harrisonberg, VA: Sprinkle Publications, 1988), 2:372.

[25] Fuller, *Works*, 2:753.

[26] Ibid., 2:752–3.

God, through the death of his Son, have promised salvation to all who comply with the gospel; and if there be no natural impossibility as to a compliance, nor any obstruction but that which arises from aversion of heart; exhortations and invitations to believe and be saved are consistent; and our duty, as preachers of the Gospel, is to administer them, without any more regard to particular redemption than to election; both being secret things, which belong to the Lord our God, and which, however they be a rule to him, are none to us.[27]

The reason that some do judge particular redemption to be a hindrance to evangelism stems from an unbiblical understanding of what the message of evangelism actually entails. As noted above, David Allen is representative of many who think that it is essential to say indiscriminately what no evangelist in the New Testament is ever recorded as having said to unbelievers, namely, that "Christ died for your sins." If the Bible required or even exemplified such evangelistic language then the charge that particular redemption undermines evangelism would have some merit. Again, Fuller acknowledges this point in exposing the error of those who make it. "If that which sinners are called upon to believe respected the particular design of Christ to save them, it would then be inconsistent; but they are neither exhorted nor invited to believe any thing but what is revealed, and what will prove true, whether they believe it or not. He that believeth in Jesus Christ must believe in him as he is revealed in the gospel, and that is as the Saviour of *sinners*. It is only *as a sinner*, exposed to the righteous displeasure of God, that he must approach him."[28] Christ is the object of faith that saves. The call of the gospel is "believe in the Lord Jesus and you will be saved," not "believe that Jesus died for your sins in particular and you will be saved."

Adoniram Judson

The torchbearers for Baptist missions on the other side of the Atlantic in the nineteenth century shared their English brothers' commitment to Calvinism. Adoniram Judson, who gave his life to preach Christ to the Burmese, was encouraged and sustained in his hard missionary work by the sovereignty of God in the work of salvation. The only English sermon he ever preached in Burma was on John 10:1–18. In it he argues that because the elect must be called to faith in Christ, Christian pastors must be faithful in going to those who are lost in order to make Christ known.

---

[27] Ibid., 2:374.
[28] Ibid., 2:374.

We come now to consider the main duty of a Christian pastor. First he must call his people. Though enclosed in the Saviour's electing love, they may still be wandering on the dark mountains of sin, and he must go after them; perhaps he must seek them in very remote regions, in the very outskirts of the wilderness of heathenism. And as he cannot at first distinguish them from the rest, who will never listen and be saved, he must lift up his voice to all, without discrimination, and utter, in the hearing of all, that invitation of mercy and love which will penetrate the ears and the hearts of the elect only.[29]

Because we know that Christ has "many people" yet in the world, we must seek them by preaching the gospel, even in hard places, in order that they might be saved.

Judson wrote a liturgy to be used in the Burmese churches in order to help these young bodies get grounded in biblical doctrines and practices. One part of it is called "A Creed, in Twelve Articles; or, A Summary of the Doctrine of the Lord Jesus Christ." In it we find a clear affirmation of the doctrines of grace.

> ART. III. According to the Scriptures, man, at the beginning, was made upright and holy; but listening to the devil, he transgressed the divine commands, and fell from his good estate; in consequence of which, the original pair, with all their posterity, contracted a depraved, sinful nature, and became deserving of hell.
>
> ART. IV. God, originally knowing that mankind would fall and be ruined, did, of his mercy, select some of the race and give them to his Son, to save from sin and hell.
>
> ART. V. The Son of God, according to his engagement to save the elect, was in the fulness of time, conceived by the power of God, in the womb of the virgin Mary, in the country of Judea and land of Israel, and thus uniting the divine and human natures, he was born as man; and being the Saviour Messiah, (Jesus Christ,) he perfectly obeyed the law of God, and then laid down his life for man, in the severest agonies of crucifixion, by which he made an atonement for all who are willing to believe.[30]

The biblical teachings of election and particular atonement, which motivated his own missionary work, were set before new converts to guide them into biblical patterns of worship and life.

---

[29] Francis Wayland, ed. *Memoir of the Life and Labor of the Rev. Adoniram Judson*, D.D., 2 vols. (Boston, MA: Phillips, Sampson, & Co., 1835), 2:490.
[30] Ibid., 2:469.

Judson's last public address to an American audience came July 5, 1846, before a joint gathering of several Baptist congregations in Boston. He had lost his voice and had his prepared message read by Rev. Dr. Sharp. It is entitled, "Obedience to Christ's Last Command a Test of Piety" and is a moving call to heed the Great Commission. The whole basis of his appeal is that those who love Christ must love what He loves and be committed to His purposes. Judson establishes his point in terms of particular redemption and election.

> What is the object on which the heart of the Saviour is set? For what purpose did he leave the bosom of the Father, the throne of eternal glory, to come down to sojourn, and suffer, and die in this fallen, rebellious world? For what purpose does he now sit on the mediatorial throne, and exert the power with which he is invested? To restore the ruins of paradise—to redeem his chosen people from death and hell—to extend and establish his kingdom throughout the habitable globe.[31]

When the heart of a believer is thus captured by this grand design and passion of the Savior then the call to pursue the divinely revealed purpose through missions and evangelism will be seen as privilege and joy.

Luther Rice

Judson's doctrinal and missionary commitments were shared by his colleague, Luther Rice. Originally part of that missionary team which sailed with Judson to India, Rice returned to America in 1813 after being baptized as a believer. His goal in returning was to help raise support for what had become the first Baptist missionaries from America. His biographer, James B. Taylor, said that Rice "was a decided believer in the doctrine of divine sovereignty. God was contemplated as working all things after the counsel of his own will."[32]

Rice was not hesitant to declare his views on the sovereignty of God's grace, or as it is commonly known, Calvinism. In a letter to a friend he wrote concerning this doctrine, "This you are aware is not only an item in my creed, but enters into the very ground-work of the hope of immortality and glory, that has become established in my bosom; and constitutes the basis of the submission and joyfulness found in my religious experience." The sovereignty of God in salvation, as expressed in historic Calvinism,

---

[31] Ibid., 2:519.

[32] James B. Taylor, *Memoir of Rev. Luther Rice, One of the First American Missionaries to the East* (Baltimore, MD: Armstrong and Berry, 1841), 288.

was the foundation of his missionary commitments. He went on to elaborate,

> How absurd it is, therefore, to contend against the doctrine of election, or decrees, or divine sovereignty. Let us not, however, become bitter against those who view this matter in a different light, nor treat them in a supercilious manner; rather let us be gentle towards all men. For who has made us to differ from what we once were? Who has removed the scales from our eyes? Or who has disposed us to embrace the truth?[33]

Conclusion

Both the biblical and historical records demonstrate that those doctrines that are commonly known as Calvinism, far from hindering missions and evangelism, actually fuel such work. Rightly held, these truths have fostered the most unrelenting, persevering, and confident gospel advance in the history of Christianity. Only by ignoring evidence can the charge that Calvinism kills evangelism be given any consideration. The simple, verifiable truth is that the doctrines of total depravity, unconditional election, particular redemption, effectual calling and perseverance of the saints have been held by Bible-believing Christians throughout the history of the church. Some of the most useful evangelists and missionaries the church has produced have owned these doctrines as biblical. Far from being an obstacle that must be overcome in order to comply with the call of our Lord's "Great Commission," this understanding of God's sovereignty in salvation has provided the foundation and motivation for embracing that call.

There is great confidence that comes from knowing that every person whom the Father has given to the Son will unfailingly come to trust Jesus for salvation. Hope and encouragement to keep preaching the gospel is bred by the assurance that Christ will not lose any of those people but will raise them up at the last day. The revelation that His death has not only made salvation possible, but has actually atoned for God's elect and that they will be found in "every tribe and language and people and nation" (Revelation 5:9) compels the heart that has been transformed by sovereign grace to love the nations and to long to see the gospel come to them in power.

These great doctrines of God's Word guarantee the success of our evangelistic efforts. God has a people who will be saved through the preaching of the gospel. He has chosen them. Jesus has died for them. The Spirit will

---

[33] Ibid., 289, 293–94. See also, James B. Taylor, "Luther Rice on God's Sovereignty and Man's Responsibility," *Founders Journal* 9 (Summer 1992), 10–16.

regenerate them through the Word of God. These truths have strengthened God's people to spend and be spent for the sake of Christ throughout
the history of his church. Rightly held, they will have that same impact in
our own day.

Part Two

IO

John Calvin's Understanding Of the Death of Christ

Thomas J. Nettles

The question concerning Calvin's understanding of the extent of the atonement does not determine the legitimacy of definite, thus limited, atonement as opposed to a truly universal, or general, atonement. His view makes neither of these views true or false. That must be decided by Scripture alone. The historical investigation, however, is not irrelevant even in discerning the biblical viewpoint. Knowing what Calvin believed and how he got to that position can be a helpful exercise. His manner of argument and how he synthesized his exegesis of a variety of passages into a coherent, though often complicated, doctrine can open our eyes to ideas that we have not considered before.

The Helpfulness of Historical Theology in General

Realizing that we have entered a flow of discussion far downstream means that we use the documents that constitute historical theology to catch up with the dialogue. We enter it respectfully but with frankness. Where we can detect missteps, we seek to point them out and help provide corrective; where we see the error of our own ways, hopefully we humbly submit; where we see change that is more clearly in a biblical direction, we admire with joy the providence of God and the clarity of Scripture; where we see decline, we look for reformers.

Some thinkers along this pilgrimage of doctrinal discussion embody summaries of the entire discussion to that point much better than others.

One finds immensely more profit in pausing to hear what they say than in any other multitude of reposes along the way. Athanasius consolidated the biblical teaching on the deity of Christ at a strategic time, gathering together the clear affirmations of others before him (particularly Irenaeus and Tertullian) and putting them into a canonical and soteriological framework that, after the death struggle of underdeveloped and heretical ideas, virtually settled orthodoxy on the deity of Christ. Leo I did the same for the unity of Christ's person while maintaining the irreducible integrity of both the divine and the human natures. Augustine of Hippo embodied massive and brilliant consolidation of Trinitarian thought, a Christian understanding of redemptive history as true history, and the relation between human sin, the nature of human choice, and the dependence on grace for salvation. In spite of his brilliant consolidation of the doctrine of grace, his view of justification fell short of a fully biblical view. His understanding of the unilateral and efficacious operation of grace was profound, he saw the death of Christ as the ground of forgiveness of sin, but the biblical model of imputed righteousness eluded him, leaving him with a transformational concept of becoming righteous before God. It still was God's gift by grace but involved the process of internal sanctification.

Reformation thinkers, interpreting the Bible through many of the insights of Augustine, added to this profound sense of racial and personal sin and delight in grace a fully articulated scheme of imputation, including imputation of righteousness. That soteriological breakthrough did not betray Augustine, but complemented his biblical insights sewing up the doctrine of grace with an exegetical gem that gave perfect harmony to the Law/Gospel motif of the two testaments. Luther's own pilgrimage into the doctrine of justification by imputed righteousness took several years and is not clearly in evidence until 1520, even after his 1519 treatise on two kinds of righteousness. Development, therefore, can be a natural progress into greater clarity as one truth serves as an exegetical key to open the door to another.

The Importance of Calvin and the Thesis of this Article

John Calvin was a master of exegesis, theology, evangelical encouragement, and polemics. Allowing his words to enter and influence the discussion always enriches any issue with depth and the need seriously to engage his ideas. Often we find that what he has said states the truth more clearly and boldly and with greater overall coherence than any voice that has preceded him. Most of his mistakes stand so clearly silhouetted against the white light of his truth, and, from our perspective, so egregious and outrageous that we can easily see them and will not be led to repeat them (read, union of church and state and Servetus). His view of baptism catches the unity of Scripture and the unity of the people of God with such forceful clarity, in the view of some of his followers, that they find it compelling and use it as a major component of their formulation of the church and its doctrine; others, equally devoted to the large picture of Calvin's understanding of God, human sin, and gratuitous redemption, find his view of infant sprinkling so counter-intuitive, absolutely unsupported by any specific passage of Scripture and contrary to the regulative principle, and tending to blend the flesh of the Old Covenant with the Spirit of the New, that they cannot unite in church relationships with those that maintain the principle of infant "baptism" and church membership. On the gospel, they unite; on the church, they part.

On the atonement, however, Calvin's formulation brought together historic insights in the Augustinian and Anselmic tradition and the peculiarities of Reformation truth so concisely and clearly that his description of the purpose and overall impact of Christ's death seems unassailably biblical. Christ's death for sinners was an unending source of wonder for Calvin, and also a key to the entire spectrum of his theology. What more can be said than he has said? That is what this article is about. Disagreement has arisen over whether Calvin viewed the atonement as particularly and purposely efficacious for the elect only or whether it gives the same advantage toward salvation for all fallen humanity throughout the world and throughout all ages. Does Calvin view Christ's work of reconciliation as peculiarly designed to manifest saving grace to the elect only or is Christ's death of such a nature that one can make no distinction in the provisions it facilitates for all people?

In the end the evidence seems mixed. It calls for some pretty subtle nuances of interpretation and detailed work in synthesizing many important discussions of Calvin. The thesis of this article is simple: Calvin's discussion of the atonement gives sufficient warrant for his theological progeny to infer that he believed that Christ's atoning work was intrinsically efficacious for the salvation of the elect only. Both the nature of the atonement, in Calvin's extended comments on it, and its connections as the necessary and pivotal mean for God to execute His eternal purpose of redemption give warrant for one to conclude this—limited atonement may be inferred from several pivotal exegetical/doctrinal discussions and is more consistent with his overall theological view than is a general atonement. It is not unwarranted from Calvin's writings to infer that for Calvin Christ's death merited from God all the subsequent blessings that would certainly be given to all for whom Christ purchased them.

Some Limitations of Warrant on a Tricky Investigation

If it could be demonstrated that Calvin's theology does not provide an unambiguous answer to the question of his view of the extent of the atonement, that does not warrant several things. One, as mentioned above, it does not mean that the doctrine of limited atonement itself is wrong or even unimportant. Two, it does not mean that he opposed the doctrine or that it is inconsistent with his overall theological scheme. Three, it does not mean that there are not thick moments in some of his extended biblical and theological reflections, isolated to themselves and extrapolating from them legitimate doctrinal inferences, that would yield a view of a purposefully limited atonement in accord with covenantal redemption—Jesus shed His blood as a seal to the eternal covenant in which the Father gave a specific people to the Son. Four, it does not mean that those passages where Calvin indicates universal effects of the cross-work of Christ are utterly inconsistent with a more isolated intentional effect of the atonement for the elect only. This would especially be the case if he explains his understanding of universal language to mean something other than each and every individual in the world.

A Cogently-Argued Alternative

In his chapter in *Whosoever Will*, Kevin Kennedy has argued that Calvin believed that the atonement rendered possible equal benefits for all mankind universally. He introduced the reader to all the most important literature in this debate, both ancient and modern, from both sides of the question. I recommend that the reader survey his discussion of it. His purpose was to set before the reader some of the "elements in Calvin's writings that are incongruous with a limited atonement." He did not claim to give an utterly exhaustive treatment or to seal the question with absolute certainty, but to give enough information and interpretation "to show how it is not unreasonable to claim that Calvin held to a universal atonement." He argued his thesis cogently, provided some compelling primary source material, and interpreted the material forcefully. His evidence demonstrated that Calvin did believe that Christ's death by its nature could potentially save all the sinners of the world. Kennedy noted an impressive number of passages in which Calvin affirms that the death of Christ was for the "world" and "all sinners." He showed that Calvin universalized the "many" passages of Scripture including Isaiah 53 and Romans 5. Calvin based the free offer of the gospel on that precept of "a universal atonement." Calvin's doctrine of aggravated guilt for any person that would hear the gospel and refuse to appropriate Christ's death as his salvation finds its force in some kind of universal effect of the atonement.[1]

The Power of Substitution in Calvin

The entire Reformed tradition has built its soteriology on Calvin's formulation, while departures from it (e.g., Governmental theories and Moral Influence theories) have resulted in corruptions through other parts of biblical doctrine. Calvin's explanation centers on the necessity of substitution. From that great reality arise satisfaction of the Father's wrath and offended justice from Christ's expiatory and propitiatory work, and thus, reconciliation, redemption, regeneration, sanctification, resurrection, and glorification. None of these latter could exist apart from the reality that Christ bore our sins in His own body on the tree. Calvin's *Institutes of the Christian Religion*, his theological treatises, his commentaries, and his polemical writings are so filled with beautiful comments on the death of Christ and its effects that one quickly grasps this as perhaps more germane to the overall doctrinal system of Calvin than divine sovereignty. Divine sovereignty on the matter of salvation is mediated through Christ's death.

With pristine clarity and immediate biblical authority Calvin stated: "The form of Christ's death also embodies a singular mystery. The cross was accursed, not only in human opinion but by decree of God's law. Hence, when Christ is hanged upon the cross, he makes himself subject to the curse. It had to happen in this way in order that the whole curse—which on account of our sins awaited us, or rather lay upon us—might be lifted from us, while it was transferred to him."[2] In a summary of many of the redemptive blessings intrinsic to Christ's victorious substitutionary death, Calvin exulted, "Hence faith apprehends an acquittal in the condemnation of Christ, a blessing in his curse." That transmutation of curse to blessing gives profitable substance for thought as we "keep sacrifice and cleansing constantly in mind." That contemplation then gives assurance that "Christ is our redemption, ransom, and propitiation," and also serves as a "satisfaction" but also a "laver to wash away our corruption."[3]

---

[1] Kevin Kennedy, "Was Calvin a 'Calvinist," in *Whosoever Will: A Biblical-Theological Critique of Five-Point Calvinism*, ed. David L. Allen and Steve W. Lemke (Nashville, TN: B&H, 2010) 191–212.

[2] John Calvin, *The Institutes of the Christian Religion*, 2 vols., trans. Ford Lewis Battles (Louisville, KY: Westminster John Knox Press, 2006), 1:510. II. xvi. 6. All quotes from the *Institutes* will cite this translation and edition denominated simply as *Institutes* and will include page numbers and the more universal division into book, chapter and paragraph.

[3] Ibid., 511.

His comment on 1 Peter 2:24, "Who his own self bare our sins," in-cludes several of the elements mentioned above as resident in the cross-work of Christ.

> This form of speaking is a fitting one to set forth the efficacy of Christ's death. As under the Law in order to be released from guilt the sinner substituted a victim in his own place, so Christ took on Himself the curse due to our sins, so that He might atone for them before God. He expressly adds, upon the tree, because He could not offer such an expia-tion except on the Cross. Peter therefore well expressed the truth that Christ's death was a sacrifice for the expiation of our sins, for when He was fixed to the Cross and offered Himself as a victim for us, He took on Himself our sin and our punishment. Isaiah, from whom Peter has taken the substance of his doctrine, employs various forms of expression—that He was smitten by God's hand for our sins, that He was wounded for our iniquities, that He was afflicted and broken for our sake, and that the chastisement of our peace was laid on Him (Isa 53:5). Peter's intention has been to set forth the same truth by the words of this verse, namely that we are reconciled to God on this condition, that Christ made Him-self the surety and the guilty one for us before His judgment-seat in order to suffer the punishment due to us.[4]

Similarly Calvin's comments on Galatians 1:4 shows many elements of Christ's obedience unto death including its place in God's sovereign purpose.

> These words, "who gave himself for our sins, are very important. He wanted to tell the Galatians straight out that atonement for sins and per-fect righteousness are not to be sought anywhere but in Christ. For He offered Himself to the Father as a sacrifice. And He was such an offering as we must not try to match with any other satisfactions. So glorious is this redemption that it should ravish us with wonder. Moreover, what Paul here ascribes to Christ is referred elsewhere in Scripture to God the Father. And it is proper to both; for, on the one hand, the Father by his eternal purpose decreed this atonement and in it gave this proof of His love for us that He spared not His only-begotten Son but delivered Him up for us all. And Christ, on the other hand, offered Himself a sacrifice to reconcile us to God. From this it follows that His death is the satisfac-tion for sins.[5]

[4] John Calvin, *Calvin's New Testament Commentaries: Hebrews and I and II Peter*, trans. W. B. Johnson. edd. David W. Torrance and Thomas F. Torrance (Grand Rapids, MI: Eerdmans, 1963), 278. All quotes from Calvin in the New Testament commentaries will be from this series. Book, translator, date, and page will be noted, and after the first citation a short form will be used.

[5] *Galatians*, trans. T. H. L. Parker, 1965, 11.

Christ died so that by His death he might "purchase us to be his own property."[6] Christ has nailed the 'Hand-writing of the law which was contrary to us, to His cross" so that "we are freed from all the curse and guilt of the law."[7] Paul differs in nothing between Galatians and Romans, so Calvin observed. Though in the secret counsel of God, He has loved His elect eternally, He hates us in so far as we are sinners, and with regard to ourselves, we are always enemies "until the death of Christ is interposed to propitiate God." But even in that condition, His eternal counsel prevailed and while we were enemies He gave His only begotten Son; our knowledge and assurance does not come from a secret revelation of the eternal purpose of God but from the way we are brought to regard Christ and His cross and see in it "the beginning of our reconciliation to God, so that we are convinced that it is by the expiation that has been made that God, who before was justly hostile to us, is now propitious to us." Our reception into favor cannot bypass, therefore, the death of Christ. In that event, "the guilt, for which we were otherwise punishable, has been taken away."[8]

Considerations of the Universal in Calvin's View

The affirmations of universal provision in other passages should be filtered through two realities. One, Calvin did receive the formula that Christ's death was sufficient for all but efficient only for the elect. He affirms this in connection with his exegesis of I John 2:2, a passage to be quoted later, and in his polemical treatise *Concerning the Eternal Predestination of God.*[9] This is the same view stated later by the Synod of Dort under the second head of doctrine, articles three through six, and also affirmed by John Owen. Looking at the redemptive work of God from the standpoint of men, all that God provides for the reclaiming of fallen humanity is set before them as theirs if they will but take it. Christ need not do more to procure forgiveness for any person that would go to Him in faith. Such a person would find forgiveness, justification, the presence of the Spirit by faith, and the promise of eternal life for those who do not

---

[6] Ibid. 12.

[7] Ibid. 42.

[8] *Romans*, trans. R. MacKenzie (1973), 110. The comments are on 5:10.

[9] *The Gospel According to John: Part Two 11–21 and The Fist Epistle of John*, trans. T. H. L. Parker (1961), 244. Kevin Kennedy mentions these two instances of Calvin's use of this formula in *Whosoever Will*, 209, and concedes that Calvin approved the formula in these places. His comment, however, is that "Calvin may be inconsistent in this instance." Calvin, as we shall see, is not at all inconsistent but argued strongly for the absolute efficiency of the atonement for the elect.

move away from the hope of the gospel. Should any person on earth go to Christ he will find in Him all the blessings that His death has procured. That the Father has purposed His death only for the elect does not alter Christ's sufficiency for any that would come to Him.

That comment leads to the second factor that must be borne in mind. Calvin always poises his theological discussion delicately between the unilateral necessity of divine grace for any of the blessings of grace to come to sinners on the one hand, and the universal call with a recognition of ultimate human responsibility on the other. Those that do not come to Him are to be blamed for not doing so. Even though only by the secret operations of His electing grace does the Spirit apply any of the benefits, from our standpoint we are to regard every person as a candidate to receive those blessings that Christ has died to procure, and that their refusal is the result of sin, not of non-election *per se*, and constitutes a criminal resistance to the divine benevolence. Calvin treated Romans 5:18 in this light asserting that "Paul makes grace common to all men, not because it in fact extends to all, but because it is offered to all." Thus, grace in its efficacious operation is not a common property as in the concept of prevenient grace taught by Wesleyans, but is common in the setting forth of all its blessings by the preaching of the word and the promise of forgiveness to believers. Calvin goes on, "Although Christ suffered for the sins of the world, and is offered by the goodness of God without distinction to all men, yet not all receive Him."[10] The language is carefully constructed, and Calvin's precise affirmation will become clearer below. One can see that what Christ accomplished through His death, was accomplished for the world, a reality that justifies preaching the Messianic redemption to all nations. The gospel also is offered to all men irrespective of their being Jew or Gentile. Though so openly and freely declared, not all of those to whom the gospel is preached receive Christ.

Calvin always approached the details of responsible human choice as a manifestation of immutable divine pleasure with a perfect confidence in the compatibility of these two. Note his comments on Acts 13:27 where Paul claims that the Jews fulfilled the Scriptures in their killing of Christ.

> Thus we see that it is not only creatures lacking understanding who are under the providence of God, but also the devil and all the ungodly, so that He may execute among them what He has determined in His own mind. Similarly we find in chapters 3:17ff and 4:28, that, when the enemies of Christ were absolutely mad for His destruction, they nevertheless did not get what they wanted, but rather they brought into being by their own efforts what God had determined according to His own purpose.

[10] *Romans*, 118.

Indeed it does a great deal from the commendation of the divine truth, that not only is He powerful enough to fulfil what He has promised, but those, who try to reduce His purposes to nothing, put out their labour in establishing them, albeit against their will. For how could the truth of God not stand, when its greatest enemies are forced to fulfil it? Yet here we need prudence lest we confuse Satan with God. For the Jews are not to be excused because they fulfilled Scripture, because it is their corrupt will that must be considered, and not the outcome, which was not what they expected, no indeed, when it ought to be regarded like a miracle. If their action is looked at in itself, it is completely contrary to God. But just as with wonderful skill God controls movements in the sun and the other planets that are contrary and in conflict with each other, so by His secret influence, He directs the perverse efforts of the ungodly towards a different end than they thought and intended, so that they may do nothing but what He has willed. As far as they are concerned those men indeed act against his will, but the outcome is according to the will of God, in some sort of incomprehensible way. Since this procedure is contrary to nature, it is no wonder if it is not visible to carnal wisdom. Accordingly it must be perceived by the eye of faith, or rather it must be treated with reverence and adoration; but the dogs who carp at it must be rejected along with their petulance.[11]

The Christian, while finally having the glory of God and His will as that which ultimately governs his affection, nevertheless, acts in accordance with the possibility that each and every individual is a candidate for the saving mercy of God. By the same token, any individual may so misuse the truths of the gospel that they render them, as far as our stewardship is concerned, of no effect. Calvin represented this as the danger of the Ephesian elders in Acts 20. From a purely phenomenological standpoint, the potential within every aspect of saving truth can be rendered of no effect by the unfaithfulness of men and their blind refusal to consent to the purpose of God in each part. Faithless ministers not only endanger souls but profane the sacred blood of the Son of God and make "useless the redemption acquired by Him, as far as they are concerned." It is not useless in the infallible purpose of God but "as far as they are concerned;" to the degree that their faithless work is concerned in the matter, it is useless. Such unfaithful ministry is a "hideous and monstrous crime, if by our idleness, not only the death of Christ becomes worthless, but also the fruit of it is destroyed and perishes." In the same passage, however, Calvin reminds the reader that the "church is acquired by God so that we may know that He intends it to remain complete for Himself, because it is right that He have and hold those whom He has redeemed." In the meantime, the "whole human race has

[11] John Calvin, *Acts*, trans. W. G. D. McDonald (1965), 372.

been given over to Satan's possession" until Christ sets us free and "gathers us into the inheritance of the Father."[12] Men left to themselves will obliterate, ignore, pervert, and render vain every overture of divine grace to a fallen race; God, however, by the secret operations of His Spirit following the precise course of His eternal purpose will bring to effect every part of His gracious design and glorify Himself allowing nothing that He has set in motion by His decree to fall short of its perfect design.

We see the same defeat of grace in Calvin's look at 2 Peter 2 when he pointed out that "those who throw over the traces and plunge themselves into every kind of licence are not unjustly said to deny Christ, by whom they were redeemed." That does not mean that Christ's purpose to "have us as a people separated from all the iniquities of the world, devoted to holiness and purity" will fail in any instance.[13]

Interpreting 2 Timothy 2 Calvin recognized that the instances of apostasy from vital doctrine are many and sometimes notable for the conspicuous position of those that fall. This, however, "cannot prevent God from preserving his church to the end." The "salvation of the elect is in God's secret keeping," and whether the number is great or small, they are sealed and will not be harmed. God will allow the reprobate to "depart to their own fate for which they were destined, for the number with which God is satisfied remains untouched."[14] Many have the advantage of true doctrine, the blessings of Christian fellowship, have partaken of the sweetness of a fellowship in which real operations of the Holy Spirit have been abundantly manifest—in short, have been showered with many opportunities for grace—but have still remained apart from Christ or even become more hostile to Christian truth. None of that, however, diminishes the immutable certainty of all the operations of grace for God's elect.

Dealing with Paul's desire for the emasculation of those that were unsettling the Galatians, Calvin noted that from the standpoint of our consideration of men, "God commends to us the salvation of all men without exception, even as Christ suffered for the sins of the whole world."[15] From our viewpoint, every aspect of salvation is an open possibility for every person in the world for the precept is to preach to every creature, to hold forth Christ as the sure atoning sacrifice for every man. Calvin even ends his most rigorous discussion on unconditional particular election with the prayer, "Also that it may please him to grant this grace not only to us, but

---

[12] *Acts* vol. II, trans. John W. Fraser (1973), 184.

[13] *Hebrews and I and II Peter*, 346.

[14] *The Second Epistle of Paul to the Corinthians and the Epistles to Timothy, Titus, and Philemon*, trans. T. A. Smail (1964), [The Epistles to Timothy], 316–17.

[15] *Galatians*, 99.

also to all people and nations."[16] But, as in the case of those that were destroying the church through their pollution of the gospel with the rot of human works, zeal for the glory of God may arise in particular situations to see some individuals as expendable for the glory of God. "Godly minds are sometimes carried beyond the consideration of men to fix their gaze on the glory of God and the Kingdom of Christ. For to the extent that the glory of God is more excellent than the salvation of men, it ought to ravish us to a corresponding love and regard." Those who discern that there is an assault on the glory of God "forget men and the world and would rather that the whole world should perish than that any part of God's glory should be lost."[17] Only the revelation that God Himself has made distinctions among men in accord with His own good pleasure and for His own glory can justify the anathema of an individual that contradicts God's truth. This recognition on the part of Christians that sometimes the horizontal concern for the salvation of each and every individual must give way to more profound vertical concerns comes from the clear knowledge that every aspect of the message that is set forth promiscuously finds root only in those that God distinguishes by sovereign grace.

Biblical warrant for an imprecatory posture toward the hostile and unfaithful, in Calvin's overall view, comes from the way that God Himself operates with apostates. If from terror of persecution some deny Him, it comes not only from weakness but from infidelity and their blindness to glory and sight limited to the allurements of the world. In comments on 2 Timothy 2, Calvin observed that those that deny Christ, He will deny, employing Matthew 10:33 as a supportive text. Our faithlessness, however, can in no way detract from the Son and His glory because He is all sufficient in Himself and stands in no need of our confession. He does not deviate from His own truth; He will not recognize any as His own that deny Him in the hour of crisis. At the same time that "ungodly apostates" may only find false hope from their mistaken confidence in a mutable God, we hold firmly that "our faith is founded on the perpetual and unchangeable truth of Christ so that no human unfaithfulness or apostasy should be able to shake it."[18]

These apostasies of doctrine and character make the possible effect of redemptive grace irrelevant to those that commit them. Though set before them with sincerity, and left to their own will to give a hearty acceptance of proffered gospel advantages, their unexceptionable refusal proves the necessity of effectual grace. In the case of the Galatian heretics, had they really "appreciated this blessing of redemption they would never have fallen

---

[16] *Sermons on Ephesians*, 49.
[17] Galatians, 99.
[18] *The Epistles to Timothy*, 311, 312.

away to alien observance." The one that "knows Christ aright holds Him fast, embraces him with both arms, is completely taken up with Him and desires nothing beyond Him."[19] They acknowledge and feel the "excellence of the Son of God" who "gave Himself as the price of our redemption" whereby the truly called benefit from "atonement, cleansing, satisfaction, and all the fruit that we receive from the death of Christ." It is not enough to regard "Christ as having died for the salvation of the world" for its effectual benefit comes only to the one that claims "the effects and possession of this grace for himself personally."[20] This is the one who does not mix personal works or worth with what Christ has done but finds himself dependent upon and satisfied with Christ alone who suffered to procure a righteousness for us:

> Why should we need to get from elsewhere what we could give ourselves? If the death of Christ is our redemption, then we were captives; if it is payment, then we were debtors; if it is atonement, we were guilty; if it is cleansing, we were unclean. And so, on the other hand he who ascribes his cleansing, pardon, atonement, righteousness or deliverance to works makes void the death of Christ.[21]

They make the death of Christ void, not because they render it fruitless of its original purpose, but because they fail to receive its benefits in that they seek another shelter. A safe haven is not safe for those not in it. The atonement has everything that the whole world needs for salvation. Nothing else can save any individual in the world. No provision other than the death of Christ is made for all people everywhere. In His glory and excellence and in accordance with His authority to plead the merits of His blood for any that come to God through Him, no one in the whole world need think that he is excluded from coming, but "the expiation of Christ, effected by his death, belongs properly to us when we cultivate righteousness in unrightness [sic, misprint for uprightness] of heart" and when, rather than overlooking our sins, we "are turned from iniquity and begin a new life."[22] Since He has become a curse for us, anyone that is under the curse of the law may embrace this cursed One to be freed of his curse. We are to regard every aspect of grace as open to us and we are culpable not to take advantage of it. Where in the whole world is one that Christ by His atoning work is unable to save? While it is true that "remission of sins cannot be separated from repentance, nor can the peace of God be in those

[19] *Galatians*, 11.
[20] Ibid., 11, 44.
[21] Ibid., 44.
[22] *The First Epistle of John*, 239.

consciences where the fear of God does not reign,"[23] nevertheless, no place harbors an individual that has sin beyond the reach of Christ by His atoning work. So Calvin believed.

The Death of Christ a Sure and Special Gift for the Elect

Even so, God limits the effects of it by a covenantal arrangement in which he views some only as beloved for the sake of Christ; for them alone does He allot the full blessings of eternal redemption by placing them in Christ's perfect obedience even unto death so that the fullness of forgiveness and the reward of eternal life is theirs and theirs only. "The Spirit of regeneration is given only to those who are members of Christ."[24] In light of this, one must acknowledge that there is a more involved and deeply coherent theological argument that Calvin employed in his discussion of the work of Christ that must be grasped before one can adopt the conclusion that Calvin did not believe in effectual atonement. Roger Olson's review of *Whosoever Will* points to Calvin's comments on 1 John 2:2 as "the one passage… that seems to affirm limited atonement." This simply is not the case and shows that Olson is unacquainted with some major arguments in the Calvinistic corpus. Olson's unwarranted remark is not Kennedy's fault.

Calvin's discussion of 1 Timothy 2 gives a highly pertinent bridge to this discussion. In this place he quite clearly asserts that Paul does not mean each and every individual by his use of the words "all" and "world." Confronted with the challenge that the phrase, "willeth that all men be saved" contradicts predestination, Calvin turned aside that application of the phrase. Calvin believed that Paul referred to "classes and not of individuals." He applied this idea to further discussion by saying that "the Mediator is not given only to one nation, or to a few men of a particular class, but to all, for the benefit of the sacrifice, by which He has expiated for our sins, applies to all." Christ as mediator does not relate to one nation only but to those that were far off. In putting forth his interpretation, Calvin insisted that the word *all* should "always be referred to classes of men but never to individuals. It is as if he had said 'Not only Jews, but also Greeks, not only people of humble rank but also princes have been redeemed by the death of Christ.'"[25]

Calvin then concluded that pivotal paragraph with a sentence that establishes the context for his uses of "all and "world" when referring to the death of Christ. Having just explained *all*, Calvin closes the paragraph,

[23] Ibid.

[24] *Titus*, 383.

[25] *Epistles to Timothy*, 210.

"Since therefore He intends the benefit of His death to be common to all, those who hold a view that would exclude any from the hope of salvation do Him an injury." We conclude the same meaning when Calvin says one page later, "The Holy Spirit bids us pray for all, because our one Mediator bids all to come to Him, since by His death He has reconciled all to the Father."[26] That all men, that is, both Jew and Gentile, all classes and nations of men, are included in Christ's sacrifice and intercession justified Paul's mission to the Gentiles and calls for the universal proclamation of Christ as the only Savior of the world, freely available for all that will come to Him. By *all* Calvin referred to the New Covenant provision that brought the Messiah to people of every tongue, and tribe, and nation, none of them being omitted—both circumcision and uncircumcision may claim the Messiah as theirs for there is one Mediator between God and Man.

That Christ's death has a particular focus for the certain salvation of the New Covenant people of God comes immediately upon the heels of this explanation. Calvin does not divide Christ's office as mediator to make His death and His intercession asymmetrical, but he argued that "there is a necessary connexion between Christ's sacrificial death and His continual intercession." These two parts of His priestly office operate for the benefit of the same group of people. "The meaning is that once by His death He made expiation for our sins to reconcile us to God, and now, having entered the heavenly sanctuary, He appears in the presence of the Father for our sakes that we may be heard in his name." After taking a few blows at the Roman Catholic system of the intercession of the saints, Calvin distinguished Christ from them by saying that "the intercession by which God's favour is won for us is founded on sacrifice—a thing made clear also by the whole system of the ancient priesthood." Only if one has made an atoning sacrifice is he qualified to intercede, for he has procured the basis of forgiveness for those for whom he intercedes. The saints have done no such thing and therefore have no qualification to intercede.[27]

Calvin sprinkled his holy hostility to the Roman doctrine of the intercession of the saints throughout his corpus of work as he gave the place of exclusive pre-eminence to the intercession of Christ, always built on the certainty of His atoning work. In 1 John 2 Calvin showed a peculiar tenacity about this issue. Since the saved do indeed continue to sin while they are in the process of sanctification, Christ appears before God as our advocate "for the purpose of exercising towards us the power and efficacy of his sacrifice." Bluntly and plainly put, "Christ's intercession is the continual application of His death to our salvation. The reason why God does

[26] Ibid., 211.
[27] Ibid., 212, 213.

not impute our sins to us is because He looks upon Christ the intercessor." Christ's intercession is the proper application of His death, not only in the original forgiveness of sins at the point of our legal union with Christ in justification, but in the continual mercy of Christ in cleansing us from all sin, for the source of our pardon and the "cause of our cleansing" is that "Christ expiated our sins by His blood."[28] No departed saints may provide such an efficacious foundation to their supposed intercession. Theirs would be a mere supplication; Christ comes with the meritorious and sacrificial shedding of His blood on behalf of those for whom He intercedes.

The effect of Christ's expiation in His intercession is the seamless continuation of His favor, begun on the cross, toward those that the Father gave Him. Because of this He is called both our advocate and our propitiation for "he who procures grace for us must be furnished with a sacrifice." Our full comfort lies in this, that not only did Christ die "once to reconcile us to the Father but also continually intercedes for us" for the "fruit of his death is ever fresh and lasting for us, that by his intercession He propitiates God to us and that He sanctifies our prayers by the odour of His sacrifice and helps us by the good-will of His advocacy."[29] If Christ intercedes for us, then He has died for us; if He died for us, then He certainly will intercede for us. Since He has done the greater in dying, He can not fail to do the lesser in interceding.

Calvin's comments on the next phrase in 1 John, "And not for ours only," etc. fits with his comments on 1 Timothy 2. Calvin asked "how the sins of the whole world have been expiated." Some dream that the reprobates and even the devils themselves eventually find salvation through Christ's expiation, a notion that Calvin calls the "dreams of the fanatics" and "a monstrous idea not worth refuting." Some apply the formula that "Christ suffered sufficiently for the whole world but effectively only for the elect.," as an explanation of the text; that was common among the scholastics, and Calvin affirms that the theological proposition is in itself true. That proposition, however, does not apply to this case for the answer is simple. "John's purpose," Calvin states, "was only to make this blessing common to the whole Church." He then clearly states the same principle already used in 1 Timothy, "under the word 'all' he does not include the reprobate, but refers to all who would believe and those who were scattered through various regions of the earth." The language is appropriate for such a use, for by it "the grace of Christ is really made clear when it is declared to be the only salvation of the world."[30] Truly there is no other name.

[28] *The First Epistle of John*, 241
[29] Ibid., 243, 244.
[30] Ibid., 244.

His universal language, therefore, in relation to Christ's atoning work, without exception, finds its meaning in the context of these three things: one, Christ alone is the savior of all who will be saved and there is no other savior; two, it is a linguistic device to express the expansion of the Messiah's saving work beyond the Jews to the whole world, that is, the New Covenant inclusion of the Gentiles, the uncircumcised; three, Calvin explicitly says that Christ's propitiatory work, both in justification and intercession, does not include the reprobate, and thus includes only the elect.

Calvin viewed John 17 in this light. Jesus had power over all men to give eternal life to those that the Father had given Him. There is, therefore, one *all* of those given to Christ within the *all* of those over whom Christ has power. As Calvin noted, Christ has not been placed in command of "the whole world to bestow life indiscriminately." Though the reprobate are given Him along with the elect, "only the elect belong to His own flock, which He guards as a shepherd." The kingdom of Christ extends to all men but "it is saving only to the elect who follow the Shepherd's voice with willing obedience." Others obey Him by the force of His providential decrees until at last He destroys them with the rod of iron. For the elect, however, He sanctifies Himself that they too may be sanctified. The Holy Spirit cleanses us by the holiness of Christ and makes us partakers of His holiness. He is our righteousness by imputation of righteousness and He is our sanctification through inward transformation by which we are renewed to true holiness. "Although this sanctification belongs to the whole life of Christ, it shone brightest in the sacrifice of His death; for then He appeared as the true high Priest who consecrated the Temple, the altar, all the vessels and the people by the power of His Spirit."[31] Not only was His death the source of our justification but as the perfection of His obedience through the things that He suffered it also consummated His holiness and provided both the source and the model for our renewal. As true high priest He consecrated the people by His death, and all that He consecrated shall be holy.

Calvin's first five sermons on Ephesians show conclusively that he saw every benefit of election as made certain by God's viewing us in Christ, and specifically in Christ as having died for us. Since the "only begotten Son is given to us, how should not all the benefits which he has in himself be communicated to us with him and through him?" Calvin asked.[32] In his prayer to close the first sermons, Calvin asked God to "show us that the heritage which has been purchased for us by the blood of his only Son

[31] *John*, 146.
[32] John Calvin, *Sermons on the Epistle to the Ephesians*, trans. Arthur Golding (1577) (Edinburgh: Banner of Truth Trust, 1973), 20).

is ready for us, and that we cannot miss it, seeing that we go to it with true and invincible constancy of faith"[33] We will never have an adequate grasp of the origin of salvation if we refuse to look to God's eternal counsels "by which he has chosen whom he pleased and left the remainder in their confusion and ruin."[34] Because of election, the Spirit enlightens the chosen and draws them to the faith of the gospel. "Faith depends upon God's election, or else we must make St. Paul a liar."[35] When God looks at us, however, He does not see goodness or faith or anything that would commend us to Him, but only the evil that is in us and is obnoxious to His wrath. Calvin asked rhetorically, "Did God, then, have an eye to us when he vouchsafed to love us?" Then he answered, "No! No! for then he would have utterly abhorred us. It is true that in regarding our miseries he had pity and compassion on us to relieve us, but that was because he had already loved us in our Lord Jesus Christ." He had before Him the "pattern and mirror in which to see us, that is to say, he must have first looked on our Lord Jesus Christ before he could choose us and call us."[36] We are His enemies and He is contrary to us and can only love us when He is "willing to cast his eye upon our Lord Jesus Christ and not look at us at all"[37] He wrote of this same dynamic in his discussion of John 17:23, "and lovedst them even as thou lovedst me." Calvin affirmed a perfect congruity between election and reconciliation when he noted that "we are loved in a double sense in Christ. First because the Father chose us in him before the creation of the world (Eph. 1:4). Secondly, because in Him also God has reconciled us to Himself and shown that He is gracious to us (Rom. 5:10)." Then to seal the perfect symmetry between those that are elected and those for whom Christ died, Calvin exclaimed, "See how we are both enemies and friends until atonement has been made for our sins and we are restored to favour with God!." The love that is ours simply in Christ before the foundation of the world becomes ours properly when we are justified and "God is appeased in Christ."[38]

The reason for God's discrimination in election must be consigned only to His will, to His secret purpose, and Paul does so clearly lest the faithful "think that they had faith through their own impulse and free will. I told you earlier that faith is a fruit of election."[39] One may know his election, therefore, not from any specific knowledge of God's secret coun-

[33] Ibid., 21.
[34] Ibid., 23.
[35] Ibid., 28.
[36] Ibid., 33 (on 1:3, 4).
[37] Ibid., 52 (on 1:7–10).
[38] John, 150.
[39] *Sermons of Ephesians*, 44 (on 1:4–6).

sels, but from the fact of his faith in Christ. Calvin says it simply, "How do we know that God has elected us before the creation of the world? By believing in Jesus Christ."[40] Christ is the mirror in which God beholds us to love us and at the same time is the mirror into which we look to know God's favor towards us. If we have faith, we are adopted, and all because He elected us before the creation of the world. Christ is the party to whom "we must resort to be assured that God loves us and acknowledges us as his children, and consequently, that he had adopted us before we knew him and even before the world was created."[41] We continually focus on Christ, for it is certain that God may reprobate whom He pleases and elect whom he pleases, and the only sure token of election is our continual turning to Christ, having His sufficiency engraved on our hearts. "For the gospel may well be preached to all men, even to the reprobate, but for all that, God does not extend to them this special grace of quickening them into life" by which He also extends the mercy of continual repentance "till we are made partakers of the glorious immortality which he has so dearly bought for us."[42]

All of these gifts come to us because Christ "made himself our surety both in body and soul, and answered for us before God's judgment to win absolution for us."[43] Our looking to Christ indicates the entire chain of God's redemptive grace toward us. If we look, we know that we would not do so if we were not regenerated; if that efficacious grace has pointed us to Christ, then we are elect; if we are elect, it is so only because God looked at us through Christ's covenantal agreement to die for us. The reconciling work of Christ thus brings to pass salvation for all, without exception, of those given to Christ to redeem.

God cannot love us in ourselves but must hate us; in love, however, He predestinated us to adoption only because He is "willing to cast his eye upon our Lord Jesus Christ and not look at us at all." His look at Christ shows that "our sins are done away by such payment and satisfaction." God's acceptance of this in Christ is thus the ground of God's electing love of us. "Seeing then it is so," Calvin goes on to say "let us not falter in our groanings, but let us moderate our affections so that we are content that our redemption has been purchased for us in the person of our Lord Jesus Christ, and let us trust in him that he will accomplish for us *the same thing in us and our persons that he has accomplished for us in his own*."[44] All that He accomplished in His own body at the end of His perfectly obedient life

[40] Ibid., 47 (on 1:4–6).
[41] Ibid., 48 (on 1:4–6).
[42] Ibid., 48 (on 1:4–6).
[43] Ibid., 51.
[44] Ibid., 78 (on 1:13, 14, italics mine.)

accrues to the credit of all those on whose account He came and suffered. In that light, Calvin encouraged believers to find assurance that Christ will indeed accomplish what He intended in His redemptive death. "In the same way," Calvin explained, "when [Paul] speaks of the redemption which was purchased for us, to show that if we feel the effect of it in ourselves, so that we are not in any doubt about the things Jesus Christ has done for us, we must not fear that he has suffered in vain."

Calling inevitably flows to the elect as an effect of Christ's death, and thus the death of Christ becomes a foundation of our assurance before God. He would not have called us if Christ had not died for us; and if Christ died for us, then God surely will call us. Calvin continued, "For surely His sufferings would be to no purpose at all towards us, if it did not reach us so that it might result in our profit, and that we might enjoy it. That, therefore, is what is purchased in the person of our Lord Jesus Christ."[45] In that assured result he reiterated what he had earlier affirmed when he encouraged believers, abased in themselves, to be "so renewed in the image of God that it may shine perfectly in us, till we are made partakers of the glorious immortality which he has so dearly bought for us."[46] From calling to glorious immortality the fruit of Christ's death will not be truncated.

Some of these same ideas emerge from his discussion of 2 Corinthians 5:18–21. In his introduction to that discussion Calvin made it clear that the entire context in Paul's mind is related to "the grace of regeneration which God confers specially upon His own elect." He does this as the "Creator of the church by refashioning His people into His own image."[47] Calvin calls this a "remarkably important passage" and thus worthy of an examination of the words virtually one by one. Calvin made the point that in Christ's reconciling work, God the Father also was active carrying out His plan initiated before the foundation of the world. Although He must "regard us with abhorrence" until we are justified by remission of sins, He nevertheless loves us as having been given to Christ before the foundation of the world. "We were loved from before the foundation of the world, but not apart from Christ."[48] He agreed that the love of God was first in order as regards God, but as regards us "His love has its foundation in the sacrifice of Christ." Divine sovereignty unites the two distinct manifestations of love by providing the mediator to reconcile God's sovereign selection with the real condition of human sin. If God is viewed apart from a mediator,

[45] Ibid., 79 (on 1:13, 14).
[46] Ibid., 49 (on 1:4–6).
[47] *Epistles to Timothy*, 76.
[48] Ibid., 78.

"we can only perceive of Him as being angry with us, but when a mediator is interposed between us, we know that He is pacified towards us." Immediately Calvin reminds his reader that "it is also needful for us to know that Christ came forth to us from the fountain of God's free mercy." For those upon whom eternal love has been set in Christ, therefore, Christ came forth to placate the Father's wrath against them as sinners that they may be adopted as children with Christ's sacrifice "the pledge of His receiving them into His favour."[49]

This unbreakable connection of purpose and means dominates Calvin's interpretation of Romans 8:28–39. God's purpose is fundamental to the entire argument, and is stated clearly by Paul at the beginning "so that we may know that the fact that everything happens to the saints for their salvation depends on the free adoption of God as the first cause."[50] God's foreknowledge is not mere prescience of anything "outside himself" concerning the creature as a basis for his action, but is the operation of His good pleasure in marking out those that He purposed to elect. Since those so marked are to be conformed to the image of His Son, the chief trait of their salvation will be manifest through the enduring of a cross of suffering in pursuit of a more glorious purpose than this corrupt world can possibly offer. "Our participation in the cross is so connected with our vocation, justification, and finally our glory, that they cannot in any way be separated."[51] Vocation consists not only of the external call of the word that comes to all that hear preaching but the power of the Spirit by which God gives an inward constraint to his elect. This is the point at which the believer's experience makes contact with the eternal purpose of God and through which he may gain assurance of good standing before God. By this calling, the believer goes to the cross for justification, which is the "unmerited imputation of righteousness," or, as stated again, "having been absolved from the sentence of God."[52] Justification embodies the assurance of the blessing of glorification showing that present troubles create eventual gain and involve no loss. This glorification as yet has been exhibited "only in our Head, yet, because we now perceive in Him the inheritance of eternal life, His glory brings to us such assurance of our own glory, that our hope may justly be compared to a present possession."[53] The blessings from foreknowledge to glorification are all bound up in the pronouncement of judgment on the Son rather than the elect. God is for us, not against us, in all these trials

---

[49] Ibid., 78, 79.
[50] *Romans*, 180.
[51] Ibid., 181.
[52] Ibid., 183, 185.
[53] Ibid., 182.

because He spared not His own Son; and that was precisely for the reason that He might grant His elect all that the Son brings in His substitution-ary death and resurrection with the intercession that follows. The power, and comfort, of calling included in these blessings sees in the cross "the fatherly love of God" in that He did not hesitate "to bestow His Son for our salvation." The argument, Calvin observed, is from the greater to the lesser—"since He had nothing dearer, more precious, or more excellent than His Son, He will neglect nothing which He foresees will be profitable to us." The giving over to death of God's Son naturally means the bestowal of all blessings that are resident within this death; the Father will never fail to bestow what the Son has purchased to those for whom He has pur-chased them. "He will neglect nothing which He foresees will be profitable to us." The called, therefore, must consider "what Christ brings to us with Himself, for as He is a pledge of God's boundless love towards us, so He has not been sent to us void of blessings or empty-handed, but filled with all heavenly treasures, so that those who possess Him may not want any-thing that is necessary for their complete happiness."[54] This same reality constitutes the substance of what Calvin meant, when, in his commentary on Ephesians 1 he called Christ the "material cause, both of eternal elec-tion, and of the love which is now revealed," therefore, the one by whom "the love of God is poured out to us." As seen in his sermons on Ephesians above, God's love to His chosen comes only as He views them through the complete satisfaction of His wrath accomplished by Christ. When he calls Christ the material cause, he refers to Christ's redemptive work in which "we are reconciled to God through Christ" since it is by "His death He has appeased the Father towards us."[55] His absolution and justification of us serves as the foundation for His session at the right side of God where He is "a perpetual advocate and intercessor in the defence of our salvation." If any thing in heaven or earth wanted to condemn us it would render "void the death of Christ" as well as "fight against the incomparable power with which the Father has honoured Him."[56] We must not view Him in a pos-ture of continual intercession as if on knees with imploring hands, but His intercession is the completed reality and the eternal efficacy of "His death and resurrection, which takes the place of eternal intercession, and to have the efficacy of lively prayer for reconciling the Father and making Him ready to listen to us."[57]

---

[54] Ibid., 184.
[55] *Ephesians*,126–28.
[56] *Romans*, 185.
[57] Ibid., 186.

Before the foundation of the world, therefore, the elect from the good
pleasure of God are seen in Christ, and thus chosen and loved in Him,
through His covenanted redemptive work; That work brings all the blessings of grace, including vocation, or effectual calling, by which we obtain
present and vital union with Christ and thus all the treasures of His redemptive death. We are maintained through the crosses of this life by the
perpetual efficacy of His redemption which pleads, as it were, throughout
eternity as the cause of God's being not only propitious toward us but
fatherly, since in Christ we are His sons. Eternal predestination, the death
of Christ, and present intercession are so intertwined in Calvin's view that
one must concede that all and only those included in the first and last are
the objects of the middle. Since the middle is the material cause of the first
and the last, one can hardly concede to a view that makes that cause to be
void of any of its proper effects.

This same order of election proceeding on the basis of a covenanted
atonement summarized Calvin's view of the priestly work of Christ treated
in the *Institutes*. Though in ourselves, our corruptions deserve God's hatred,
He finds in us remnants of His good creation, His own handiwork that He
loves. To restore us, therefore, He must wipe away the enmity by an expiatory sacrifice fully sufficient for the purpose. "Therefore, by His love God
the Father goes before and anticipates our reconciliation in Christ. Indeed,
'because he first loved us', he afterwards reconciles us to himself." Until,
however, Christ actually suffers and dies, there is in us the "unrighteousness that deserves God's indignation." Christ's death constitutes, therefore, the justification of God's love for us before the creation of the world,
and the removal of enmity subsequent to His death [Romans 5:8–10]. Of
whom but the elect is this true? The love that is premundane as well as
post-propitiation "was established and grounded in Christ"[58]

Later Calvin addressed this same dynamic in asking, "How did God
begin to embrace with His favor those whom He had loved before the
creation of the world? Only in that He revealed His love when He was
reconciled to us by Christ's blood." Christ's work is a meritorious work
and thus its effects cannot be denied Him by the Father. Calvin viewed
Christ's obedience as a work by which "Christ truly acquired and merited
grace for us with His Father." All that Christ has gained by His obedience
cannot, with justice, be denied by the Father. Calvin calls such a relationship between merit and reward a "commonplace," something so obvious
and so consistent with all true understanding of the proper cause and effect
relationship between merit and reward, that none that perceive the relationship can deny its truthfulness. If Christ, therefore, "made satisfaction

[58] *The Institutes* 1:506, Book II.xvi.3, 4, 5.

for our sins, if He paid the penalty owed by us, if He appeased God by His obedience—in short, if as a righteous man He suffered for unrighteous men—then He acquired salvation for us by His righteousness, which is tantamount to deserving it." Thus, if we know that "the effect of His shedding of blood is that our sins are not imputed to us," then by necessary consequence "it follows that God's judgment was satisfied by that price." Calvin goes on then to assert the absurdity of Christ's suffering unless it is to effect the salvation of those for whom He paid. "It was superfluous, even absurd, for Christ to be burdened with a curse, unless it was to acquire righteousness for others by paying what they owed." Again, Calvin presents the same idea but includes a larger view by including Christ's death as a part of His entire work of merit, by whom those for whom He performed it must benefit since God cannot deny reward to those that have indeed kept all the demands of the Law. "For if righteousness consists in the observance of the law, who will deny that Christ merited favor for us, when, by taking that burden upon himself, he reconciled us to God as if we had kept the law?"[59]

Conclusion

The reasons that many think Calvin believed in "limited" atonement are abundant and not unclear. God, to summarize Calvin's progressive argument, loves us because He sees us through Christ's covenantal sacrifice; He elects us in that context only; He forgives us [certainly] because of the redeeming death of Christ, a death that is precisely meritorious as culminating the obedience of Christ and must be rewarded with a gift to those for whom He has served as substitute; Christ Himself, in the very presence of God the Father, applies the fruit of His redemptive labors to the very ones for whom He has died to procure this office of Mediator; He sends His Spirit as a seal to keep them until the final manifestation of the redemptive purchase, the "Church itself,"[60] when all that have faith [given because of election, because of love, because of viewing us in Christ's sacrifice] enter eternity for the unending display of His glory.

[59] *The Institutes* 1:528–34, Book II. xvii.1–6.
[60] *Ephesians*, 132.

I I

Sovereign Grace and Evangelism In the Preaching of John Bunyan

Ben Rogers

On August 19, 1688 John Bunyan preached his last sermon. Two days later he contracted a fatal illness trying to reconcile an estranged father and son and died on August 31. His final sermon was an exposition on John 1:13, and in this sermon he preached that God's sovereign grace is the only hope for fallen men. Man, by nature, is "in the dark dungeon of sin, [and] sees nothing of the kingdom of God."[1] So blinded is man by sin that he cannot even see the gospel "before he be brought into a state of regeneration."[2] The sovereign grace of God is needed, therefore, to regenerate sinners and make them willing and able to believe. After preaching on sovereign grace, Bunyan ends his final sermon on a different note—on an evangelistic note. He asks his hearers to "make a strict inquiry whether you be born of God or not? Are you brought out of the dark dungeon of this world into Christ? Have you learned to cry, 'My Father? ... Cannot you be satisfied without you have [*sic*] peace with God? Pray you, consider it, and be serious with yourselves."[3]

In his final sermon Bunyan preached that God was absolutely sovereign in salvation, and he urged sinners to come to Christ for salvation.

---

[1] John Bunyan, *Mr. Bunyan's Last Sermon*, in *The Works of John Bunyan*, ed. George Offor, 3 vols. (Glasgow: W.G. Blackie and Son, 1854: Reprint, Edinburgh and Carlisle, PA: Banner of Truth Trust, 1999), 2:756.
[2] Ibid.
[3] Ibid.

This was nothing new for Bunyan: he had been doing both for the past thirty-three years. In this chapter I will argue that John Bunyan preached that God was absolutely sovereign in salvation, and he invited sinners to come Christ for salvation. He taught that both statements were true and involved no contradiction. In fact, in his preaching he frequently evangelized sinners by preaching sovereign grace.

Since the focus of this chapter is on the preaching of John Bunyan, I will not be discussing sovereign grace and evangelism as it appears in his allegories, autobiography, doctrinal treatises, poetry, and polemical works. The focus of this chapter will be strictly limited to sermonic material. Unfortunately, Bunyan's sermon notes have not survived, and there is only one sermon-length work to be found among his collected works. Nevertheless, given what is known about Puritan preaching in general, and Bunyan's own methods in particular, at least nineteen works in the Bunyan corpus appear to be either expanded sermons or a series of sermons preached on a particular text.[4] Our focus will be limited to the material found in these works.

Sovereign Grace in the Preaching of John Bunyan

Sovereign grace is a prominent theme in Bunyan's preaching. It appears in nearly every published sermon we possess, and it is probably his favorite biblical theme to discuss after justification by faith alone. He taught that sovereign grace is "God's free, sovereign, good pleasure, whereby he acteth in Christ towards his people."[5] In Bunyan's sermons, God's sovereign grace is displayed in a number of ways, but he usually discusses it in connection with three divine acts of sovereign grace: election, effectual calling, and perseverance.

---

[4] Puritan preachers typically divided their sermons into three sections: explanation, doctrine, and uses. In the explanation section the meaning of the sermon text is explained. The doctrine or observation section consists of a series of theological truths stated in propositional form that are either explicitly taught or implied by the sermon text. In the use and application section the preacher attempts to practically apply the text and the doctrines to various categories of hearers. Bunyan follows this pattern, and thus for the purpose of this study I have only consulted works that follow this pattern. *The Holy City; or, the New Jerusalem* (3:395) is the only exception. It was included because Bunyan specifically says that this work represents a series of sermons he preached on Revelation 21:10–27; 22:1–4 while in prison.

[5] John Bunyan, *The Saints Privilege and Profit*, in *Works* 1:644.

Election

Election is one of the most prominent expressions of sovereign grace in Bunyan's preaching. He refers to it as the "Magna Charta" of salvation,[6] the "root" of all mercies,[7] and the ultimate cause of salvation.[8] The most robust definition of election in his sermons can be found in *The Work of Jesus Christ as an Advocate*. He describes election as a sevenfold cord, and lists them as follows:

> (1.) Election is eternal as God himself, and so without variableness or shadow of change, and hence it is called "an eternal purpose," and a "purpose of God" that must stand. (2.) Election is absolute, not conditional; and, therefore, cannot be overthrown by the sin of the man that is wrapt up therein. No works foreseen to be in us was the cause of God's choosing us; no sin in us shall frustrate or make election void. (3.) By the act of election the children are involved, wrapped up, and covered in Christ; he hath chosen us in him; not in ourselves, not in our virtues, no, not for or because of anything, but of his own will. (4.) Election includeth in it a permanent resolution of God to glorify his mercy on the vessels of mercy, thus foreordained to glory. (5.) By the act of electing love, it is concluded that all things whatsoever shall work together for the good of them whose call to God is the fruit of this purpose. (6.) The eternal inheritance is by a covenant of free and unchangeable grace made over to those chosen; and to secure them from the fruit of sin, and from the malice of Satan, it is sealed by this our Advocate's blood, as he is Mediator of this covenant, who also is become surety to God for them; to wit, to see them forthcoming at the great day, and to set them then safe and sound before his Father's face after the judgment is over. (7.) By this choice, purpose, and decree, the elect, the concerned therein, have allotted to them by God, and laid up for them, in Christ, a sufficiency of grace to bring them through all difficulties to glory.[9]

Thus, for John Bunyan, election is eternal, absolute, and unconditional. It is based on neither foreseen faith nor merit.

As the previous quotation suggests, Bunyan believes election to be an act of sovereign grace in which all three Persons of the Trinity are involved. He specifically attributes the choice of some men for salvation to the Father. He writes, "The Father by his grace hath bound up them that shall go to heaven in an eternal decree of election; and here, indeed, is the

---

[6] John Bunyan, *Israel's Hope Encouraged*, in *Works* 1:600
[7] Ibid., 601.
[8] John Bunyan, *Saved By Grace*, in *Works* 1:339.
[9] John Bunyan, *The Work of Jesus Christ as an Advocate*, in *Works* 1:163–64.

beginning of our salvation."[10] But he is quick to point out that the Father saves no man without the work of the Son or the Spirit. He writes, "The Father designs us for heaven, the Son redeems from sin and death, and the Spirit makes us meet for heaven."[11] Election, for Bunyan, is thus an act of sovereign grace in which the Father is the chief actor, but the Son and the Spirit are not excluded.

His preaching on election reveals an awareness that some find this doctrine objectionable. In a sermon on Psalm 130:7, he notes, "We have indeed some professors that take a great pet against that foundation of salvation, that the mercy that is from everlasting has laid."[12] And again, in a sermon on 1 John 2:1, he writes, "I know that there are some that object against this doctrine as false."[13] Bunyan, however, is unmoved. Not only does he believe his doctrine of election to be the Scriptural doctrine of election, he opposes these objectors for two reasons. First, the denial of unconditional election robs Christ of His glory. He writes:

> Since the kingdom, government, and glory of Christ is wrapped up in it, and since the calling, justification, perseverance, and glorification of his elect, which are called his body and fullness, is wrapt up therein, it may not be laid aside nor despised, nor quarreled against by any, without danger of damnation.[14]

And secondly, the denial of unconditional election robs believers of comfort. He believed that the doctrine of election properly understood was a valuable tool in fending off spiritual assaults. And when men object to this comfortable doctrine, they "wrest that weapon out of [their] hand, with which [they] so cudgelleth the enemy."[15]

Effectual Calling

Like unconditional election, effectual calling is another prominent expression of sovereign grace in Bunyan's sermons. He drew a distinction between the outward call of the gospel and the effectual call of the Holy Spirit. The outward call is the proclamation of the gospel to all men and all men are invited to come to Christ for salvation. But the outward call,

---

[10] Bunyan, *Saved by Grace*, 1:143–44.
[11] Ibid., 1:347.
[12] Bunyan, *Israel's Hope Encouraged*, 1:600.
[13] Bunyan, *The Work of Jesus Christ as an Advocate*, 1:164.
[14] Bunyan, *Israel's Hope Encouraged*, 1:600.
[15] Bunyan, *The Work of Jesus Christ as an Advocate*, 1:164.

without the sovereign and saving power of the Spirit attending it, saves no one. Bunyan writes:

> Some men think an invitation, an outward call, a rational discourse, will do; but they are much deceived, there must be a power, and exceeding great and mighty power, attend the Word, or it worketh not effectually to the salvation of the soul. I know these things are enough to leave men without excuse, but yet they are not enough to bring men home to God. Sin has hold of them, they have sold themselves to it; the power of the devil has hold of them, they are his captives at his will; yea, and more than all this, their will is one with sin, and with the devil, to be held captive thereby: and if God gives not contrition, repentance, or a broken heart, for sin, there will not be no not so much as a mind in man to forsake this so horrible a confederacy and plot against his soul.[16]

The outward call of the gospel simply cannot overcome human depravity.

Bunyan is convinced that an act of sovereign grace is necessary to convert sinners due to the Fall and its effects. He believes that Adam passed on a sinful (or fallen) nature to every one of his descendants, and because of this, fallen men are both unwilling and unable to believe the gospel. He compares their spiritual condition to a child in the womb, a prisoner in a dark dungeon, and a corpse in a grave—they see nothing of the Kingdom of God.[17] Man's heart is fenced in and wrapped up on every side by an impenetrable "coat of mail" which shields and fences the heart from all gospel doctrine.[18] In short, man's heart is an "unweldable mountain and a rock," and it must be broken by an act of sovereign grace.[19]

The Holy Spirit is the author of the effectual call and it is the fruit of the Father's electing love. This process begins with spiritual regeneration. Bunyan uses various metaphors to describe this act. At times he describes it as a siege and envisions the Spirit taking the sinners "heart by storm"[20] in order to make "seizure of us."[21] On other occasions he refers to it as being "born of God," or the "new birth," and compares it to "a man being raised out of the grave."[22] Bunyan employs these metaphors to make a theological point: regeneration is a monergistic act in which men are "utterly passive."[23]

---

[16] John Bunyan, *The Acceptable Sacrifice*, in *Works* 1:715.

[17] Bunyan, *Mr. Bunyan's Last Sermon*, 2:756.

[18] Bunyan, *The Acceptable Sacrifice*, 1:703.

[19] John Bunyan, *Christ a Complete Saviour*, in *Works* 1:216.

[20] Bunyan, *The Acceptable Sacrifice*, 1:709.

[21] Bunyan, *Saved by Grace*, 1:346.

[22] Bunyan, *Mr. Bunyan's Last Sermon*, 2:756.

[23] Bunyan, *The Pharisee and the Publican*, in *Works* 2:250.

Bunyan taught that the Spirit works three graces into the hearts of the elect through the effectual call. The first of these is faith. Faith is the fruit, effect, and sign of the new birth, not its cause.[24] In a sermon on Ephesians 2:5 he argues that faith is "not in our own power... but is given by God to those which he saveth, that thereby they may embrace and put on that Christ by whose righteousness they must be saved."[25] In addition to faith, the Spirit also works repentance into the hearts of those He effectually calls to salvation. Bunyan describes it as a grace that is "given" and "implanted." And thirdly, the Spirit also produces hope in the hearts of those He effectually calls. He writes, "By this good Spirit we are made to wait with patience until the redemption of the purchased possession comes."[26]

As was the case with election, Bunyan's preaching reveals an awareness that some find this doctrine objectionable. He refers to such objectors as "free willers": those who deny "to the Holy Ghost the sole work in conversion."[27] And as was the case with election, Bunyan strenuously opposes such objectors. In one sermon he compares them to the Pharisee in Luke 18:10–13 who thanked God for his condition, but was actually praising his own goodness. He writes, "Favour, mercy, grace, and 'God I thank thee,' is in their mouths, but their own strength, sufficiency, free-will, and the like, they are the things they mean, by all such high and glorious expressions."[28] To deny the effectual call robs God of glory.

Perseverance

Along with unconditional election and effectual calling, the perseverance of believers from conversion to glorification is an act of sovereign grace. Bunyan denies that perseverance is the product of human industry and argues that it depends, "not upon human power, but upon him that hath begun a good work in us."[29] Perseverance is a "wonderful thing," a great and glorious act of sovereign grace. He writes:

Christians, were you awake, here would be [a] matter of wonder to you, to see a man assaulted with all the power of hell, and yet come off a conqueror! Is it not a wonder to see a poor creature, who in himself is weaker than the moth, to stand against and overcome all devils, all the world,

[24] John Bunyan, *The Strait Gate*, in *Works* 1:378. See also Bunyan, *The Pharisee and the Publican*, 2:258. See also Bunyan, *The Water of Life*, in *Works* 3:552.

[25] Bunyan, *Saved by Grace*, 1:339.

[26] Ibid., 1:347.

[27] John Bunyan, *The Strait Gate*, in *Works* 1:389.

[28] Bunyan, *The Pharisee and the Publican*, 2:236.

[29] Bunyan, *Saved by Grace*, 1:339.

all his lusts and corruptions? Or if he fall, is it not a wonder to see him, when devils and guilt are upon him, to rise again, stand upon his feet again, walk with God again, and persevere after all this in the faith and holiness of the gospel? He that knows himself, wonders; he that knows temptation, wonders; he that knows what falls and guilt mean, wonders; indeed, perseverance is a wonderful thing, and is managed by the power of God; for he only is able to keep you from falling, and to present you faultless before the presence of his glory with exceeding joy.[30]

In his preaching Bunyan assigns the work of perseverance to both the Spirit and the Son. The Spirit effectually calls and keeps us: "By this good Spirit we keep that good thing, even the seed of God, that at the first by the Word of God was infused into us, and without which we are liable to the worst damnation."[31] However, in preaching on perseverance, he most commonly discusses the perseverance of the saints in connection with the ongoing work of the ascended Christ.[32]

The ascended Christ preserves believers after conversion through His intercessory work as their High Priest.[33] This intercessory work primarily involves four petitions. First, Christ prays for the elect to be brought home to God. Second, He prays that the sins they commit after conversion might be forgiven. Third, He prays that the graces they received at conversion might be maintained and supplied. And fourth, He prays that their persons may be preserved unto His heavenly kingdom.[34]

In addition to His intercessory work, the ascended Christ preserves believers as their Advocate with the Father. Bunyan believes that Christ's

---

[30] Ibid., 1:340.

[31] Ibid., 1:347.

[32] Fans of *The Pilgrim's Progress* will remember the vision of the fire burning against the wall in the House of the Interpreter. Though a man with water continually cast water on the fire to extinguish it, it burned "hotter and higher." The Interpreter says to Christian, "This is Christ, who continually, with the oil of his grace, maintains the work already begun in the heart: by the means of which, notwithstanding what the devil can do, the souls of his people prove gracious still." See John Bunyan, *The Pilgrim's Progress*, in *Works* 3:100.

[33] "To be saved and brought to glory, to be carried through this dangerous world, from my first moving after Christ till I set my foot within the gates of paradise, this is the work of my Mediator, of my high priest and intercessor; it is he that fetches us again when we are run away; it is he that lifteth us up when the devil and sin has thrown us down; it is he that quickenth us when we grow cold; it is he that comforteth us when we despair; it is he that obtains fresh pardon when we have contracted sin; and he that purges our consciences when they are loaded with guilt." See John Bunyan, *Christ a Complete Saviour*, 1:215.

[34] Bunyan, *Christ a Complete Saviour*, 1:203.

intercession covers the daily infirmities and common faults of believers, but heinous sins require the special advocacy of Christ.[35] David's adultery, murder, and hypocrisy is one such example; Peter's denial is another. As an Advocate, Christ pleads for the fallen saint at the bar of God's justice against Satan, the accuser. Though Satan would have the believer damned, the Advocate prevails by presenting his own merits to the Father and the Father's interest in the elect. Thus believers persevere not only because of Christ's intercession, but because of his advocacy as well.

The Pastoral Usefulness of Sovereign Grace

Bunyan obviously believes that sovereign grace is a biblical concept, and thus it naturally appears in his preaching when he believes his sermon texts calls for it. This, however, is not the only reason he discusses these themes in his preaching. His published sermons reveal that he preached on sovereign grace and sovereign grace-related themes for the purpose of achieving a variety of pastoral ends. In the next section, we will see that he uses sovereign grace in the evangelization of certain categories of sinners. In addition to evangelism, he uses sovereign grace to comfort and sanctify the saints.

Bunyan frequently discusses sovereign grace and sovereign grace-related themes in his preaching to comfort believers. Christian life, as Bunyan envisions it, is attended with many difficulties. Believers must contend with indwelling sin and the guilt and doubts that attend it, the malice of Satan and hell, and the rage of persecuting men. And because of these trials, Christians often become dejected and discouraged. The preaching of sovereign grace comforts God's people as they contend with their enemies. For example, in a sermon on Psalm 51:7, he reminds the dejected believer who is broken-hearted over sin, that conviction and contrition for sin is evidence of grace and the fruit of election. He writes, "But see, these are the souls whose welfare is contrived in the heavens. God consulted their salvation, their deliverance, their health, before his Son came down from thence. Doth not therefore this demonstrate, that a broken-hearted man, that a man of a contrite spirit, is of great esteem with God?"[36] And in a sermon on Ephesians 3:18–19, he addresses believers who are afflicted by the sharp-pointed, fiery darts of Satan, "that great and dogged Leviathan."

---

[35] He writes, "Not every cause, but such and such a cause; the cause that is very bad, and by which they are involved, not only in guilt and shame, but also in danger of death and hell."

[36] Bunyan, *The Acceptable Sacrifice*, 1:692.

He writes:

> But now, answerable to the spreading of these sharp-pointed things,
> there is a super-abounding breadth in the sovereign grace of God, the
> which whoso seeth and understandeth, as the Apostle doth pray we
> should, is presently helped: for he seeth that this grace spreadeth itself,
> and is broader than can be, either our mire, or the sharp-pointed things
> that he spreadeth thereupon for our vexation and affliction: "it is broader
> than the sea."[37]

And in a sermon on 2 Timothy 4:6–8, Bunyan comforts persecuted
believers with the sovereignty of God over all things. He writes, "The cup
that God's people in all ages have drank of, even the cup of affliction and
persecution, it is not in the hand of the enemy, but in the hand of God;
and he, not they, poureth out the same. So that they, with all their raging waves, have banks and bounds set to them, by which they are limited
within their range, as the bear is by his chain."[38] In short, though "the devil
will tempt us, sin will assault us, and men will persecute us," they cannot
do it everlastingly. Sovereign grace is everlasting and it should encourage
Israel to hope.[39]

Bunyan believes that the preaching of sovereign grace is sanctifying
as well as comforting. One of the objections he often anticipates when
preaching on sovereign grace is that it leads to moral laxity. Rather than
"tending to looseness and lasciviousness," he argues that "the doctrine of
free grace believed is the most sin-killing doctrine in the world."[40] The
fact that man contributes nothing to his salvation promotes humility and
destroys pride. Furthermore, it promotes love as well. He writes:

> Why should any thing have my heart but God, but Christ? He loves me,
> he loves me with love that passeth knowledge. He loves me, and he shall
> have me: he loves me, and I will love him: his love stripped him of all
> for my sake; Lord let my love strip me of all for thy sake. I am a son of
> love, an object of love, a monument of love, of *free* love, of *distinguishing*
> love, of *peculiar* love, and of love that passeth knowledge: and why should
> not I walk in love? In love to God, in love to men, in holy love, in love
> unfeigned? This is the way to improve the love of God for thy advantage,
> for the subduing of thy passions, and for the sanctifying of thy nature.[41]

---

[37] John Bunyan, *The Saints' Knowledge of Christ's Love*, in *Works* 2:5.

[38] John Bunyan, *Paul's Departure and Crown*, in *Works* 1:726.

[39] Bunyan, *Israel's Hope Encouraged*, 1:600.

[40] Bunyan, *Saved By Grace*, 1:358.

[41] John Bunyan, *The Saints' Knowledge of Christ's Love*, 2:39.

As we have seen, Bunyan uses sovereign grace and sovereign grace-related themes to both comfort and sanctify God's people.[42] And as will be seen below, he also uses it in evangelism, along with other techniques.

Evangelism in the Preaching of John Bunyan

Although he never uses the term "evangelism" in his published sermons, John Bunyan frequently and consistently invites the reader to "come to Christ" or "close with Christ" for salvation. His sermons are filled with evangelistic appeals, but it should be noted that these are the appeals of a Puritan pastor of the seventeenth century. He believed that conversion is neither smooth nor easy.[43] It is a process that normally involves passing through a series of phases or stages before the sinner actually closes with Christ.[44] Thus evangelism, for Bunyan, involved more than simple invitations. It included awakening insensible sinners, humbling the self-righteous, and encouraging fearful doubters. In this section, Bunyan's evangelistic preaching to sinners in each of these stages will be examined.

The Insensible Sinner

Bunyan believes that the conversion process normally begins with the sinner being insensible of his spiritual condition. This sinner is either ignorant or unconcerned about sin, righteousness, and judgment and will remain so unless he is awakened. He is not necessarily openly profane, although Bunyan believes that all openly profane persons are, in fact, insen-

---

[42] For the sake of space I have limited this discussion to these two uses. There are many more that could be mentioned. For example, in *Come and Welcome to Jesus Christ* Bunyan makes the following observation about John 6:37: "Coming to Christ is not by the will, wisdom, or power of man, but by the gift, promise, and drawing of the Father." He then proceeds to list seven uses and applications from this observation. See 1:275–79.

[43] Bunyan said, "Come, come, conversion to God is not so easy and so smooth a thing as some would have men believe it is." See *The Acceptable Sacrifice*, 1:720.

[44] Bunyan's *ordo salutis* can be found in various places throughout his collected works. See *A Map Shewing the Order & Causes of Salvation & Damnation, Saved by Grace* (1:350–354), and *Grace Abounding to the Chief of Sinners*. The conversion of Christian in *The Pilgrim's Progress* also illustrates this. There are a number of good secondary works on this subject as well. See Richard Greaves, *John Bunyan* (Grand Rapids: WM. B. Eerdmans Publishing Company, 1969); Pieter de Vries, *John Bunyan on the Order of Salvation*, trans. C. Van Haaften (New York: Peter Lang, 1994); and David B. Calhoun, *Grace Abounding: The Life, Books & Influence of John Bunyan* (Fearn, Ross-shire: Christian Focus Publications, 2005).

sible sinners. The superstitious, the persecutor, and those whose minds are concerned only with worldly matters all fit his description of an insensible sinner. This kind of unbeliever must be awakened, and Bunyan sought to rouse such hearers by preaching on two awakening subjects.

The first of these is the inevitability of death. Bunyan warns the insensible sinner that death is inevitable and frequently comes unexpectedly. It is the great "feller, the cutter down," that "puts a stop to a further living here, and that which lays a man where judgment finds him."[45] Not only is death the feller, it is "God's sergeant, God's bailiff." He explains:

> He arrests in God's name when he comes, but seldom gives warning before he clappeth us on the shoulder; and when he arrests us, though he may stay a little while, and give us leave to pant, and tumble, and toss ourselves for a while upon a bed of languishing, yet at last he will prick our bladder, and let out our life, and then our soul will be poured upon the ground, yea, into hell, if we are not ready and prepared for the life everlasting.[46]

In addition to the inevitability of death, Bunyan sought to awaken the insensible sinner by preaching on the terrors of hell. Bunyan employed his considerable imaginative powers to describe hell with terrible vividness. In a sermon on Luke 16:19–31, he offers the following similitude:

> Take a man, and tie him to a stake, and with red-hot pinchers, pinch off his flesh by little pieces for two or three years together, and at last, when the poor man cries out for ease and help, the tormentors answer, Nay, 'but besides all this,' you must be handled worse. We will serve you thus these twenty years together, and after that we will fill your mangled body full of scalding lead, or run you through with a red-hot spit; would not this be lamentable? Yet this is but a flea-biting to the sorrow of those that go to hell.[47]

He goes on to say:

> He that goes to hell shall suffer ten thousand times worse torments than these, and yet shall never be quite dead under them. There they shall be ever whining, pining, weeping, mourning, ever tormented without ease; and yet never dissolved into nothing. If the biggest devil in hell might pull thee all to pieces, and rend thee small as dust, and dissolve thee into nothing, thou wouldst count this a mercy. But here thou mayest lie and fry, scorch, and broil, and burn for ever.[48]

[45] Bunyan, *Christ a Complete Saviour*, 1: 220.
[46] Ibid., 1:221.
[47] John Bunyan, *A Few Sighs From Hell*, in *Works* 3:693.
[48] Ibid. 3:694.

Bunyan concludes with the following warning, "Friends, I have only given a very short touch of the torments of hell. O! I am set, I am set, and am not able to utter what my mind conceives of the torments of hell. Yet this let me say to thee, accept of God's mercy through our Lord Jesus Christ, lest thou feel THAT with thy conscience which I cannot express with my tongue."[49]

The Outwardly Reformed

Bunyan believes that those who have been awakened from their spiritual slumber typically have "one spark of enmity still." Rather than coming to Christ for salvation, the awakened sinner turns not to Christ, but to the law for righteousness and attempts an outward reformation. He writes:

> He will either turn from one sin to another, from great ones to little ones, from many to few, or from all to one, and there stop…He will turn from profaneness to the law of Moses, and will dwell as long as God will let him upon his own seeming goodness. And now observe him, he is a great stickler for legal performance; now he will be a good neighbor, he will pay every man his own, will leave off his swearing, the alehouse, his sports, and carnal delights; he will read, pray, talk of Scripture, and be a very busy one in religion, such as it is; now he will please God, and make him amends for all the wrong he hath done him, and will feed him with chapters, and prayers, and promises, and vows, and a great many more such dainty dishes as these, persuading himself that now he must needs be fair for heaven, and thinks beside that he can serveth God as well as any man in England. But all this while he is as ignorant of Christ as the stool he sits on, and no nearer to heaven than was the blind Pharisee; only he has got in a cleaner way to hell than the rest of his neighbors are in.[50]

Those who are outwardly reformed but inwardly unconverted must be humbled and made to despair of their own righteousness and performances. He sought to do this in his sermons by preaching on three humbling topics.

First, he preached the law to humble the outwardly reformed. Bunyan believes that the outwardly reformed fundamentally misunderstand the law. He writes, "It is not granted to the law to be the ministration of light and life, but to be the ministration of death."[51] It requires perfect obedience, and to break it at any one point is to fall under the curse of the whole.

---

[49] Ibid., 3:384.
[50] Bunyan, *Saved By Grace*, 1:351.
[51] Bunyan, *The Pharisee and the Publican*, 2:227.

Thus if the outwardly reformed accurately evaluate their works in light of the law, they would quickly discover that their best works are "imperfect, scanty, and short."[52]

Second, he preached on the righteousness of Christ to humble the outwardly reformed. The only righteousness that would be accepted at the bar of God's justice is the righteousness of Christ. The law requires both perfect obedience and satisfaction for sin. The outwardly reformed can provide neither; Christ can provide both. Bunyan writes, "So then, Christ having brought in that part of obedience for us, which consisteth in a doing of such obediental acts of righteousness which the law commands; he addeth thereto the spilling of his blood, to be the price of our redemption from that cursed death, that by sin we had brought upon our bodies and souls."[53] But in order to partake of this redemption, the outwardly reformed must look for righteousness outside of themselves.

Third, he preached on sovereign grace to humble the outwardly reformed. They mistakenly believe that salvation can be earned by either good deeds or religious duties. And so Bunyan sought to disabuse them of these notions by emphasizing the sovereign character of salvation. For example, in a sermon on the parable of the Pharisee and the publican (Luke 18:10–13), he specifically addresses the outwardly reformed and argues that Christians are not saved because they were better "than the kindreds, tongues, nations, and people of the earth." Their separation from them "was of mere mercy, free grace, goodwill, and distinguishing love: not for, or because of, works of righteousness which any of them have done; no, they were all alike."[54] And in a sermon on Ephesians 2:5, Bunyan poses the question 'Who are they that are to be saved by grace?' He answers, "Not the self-righteous…he saveth not such without he first awaken them to see they have need to be saved by grace."[55] And in a sermon on Acts 24:14–15, Bunyan warns those who have but a "formal or feigned profession" of the "soul-amazing misery" that awaits them that falsely believe they are converted when they are strangers to "election, conversion, and a truly gospel conversation."[56]

The Despairing Sinner

Having been humbled by the law, the insufficiency of his own personal righteousness, and sovereign grace, the outwardly reformed sinner

[52] Ibid., 2:241.
[53] Ibid., 2:247.
[54] Ibid., 2:234.
[55] Bunyan, *Saved By Grace*, 1:347.
[56] John Bunyan, *Of the Resurrection of the Dead*, in *Works* 2:119.

becomes thoroughly convicted and humbled. But rather than coming to Christ for righteousness and salvation, he becomes dejected and despairs. Being unable to find any grace within his soul, he "concludes he doth not belong to God's mercy, nor hath an interest in the blood of Christ, and therefore dares not presume to believe; wherefore, as I said, he sinks in his heart, he dies in his thoughts, he doubts, he despairs, and concludes that he shall never be saved."[57] Bunyan sought to encourage this type of hearer to come to Christ in his preaching by addressing Satan's objections and holding forth the promises of the gospel.

The first objection to the sinner's coming is that he is unworthy of eternal life. Bunyan writes: "This is Satan's master argument; thou art a horrible sinner, a hypocrite, one that has a profane heart, and one that is an utter stranger to a work of grace. I say this is his maul, his club, his master-piece; he doth with this as some do with their most enchanting songs, sings them everywhere."[58] Bunyan answers this objection with the example of the Jerusalem sinner. The Jerusalem sinner was the worst and biggest of all sinners—they were the very killers of Christ. And yet Christ commands that mercy be offered there first. He writes:

> Neither is there, set this aside, another argument like it, to show us the willingness of Christ to save sinners; for, as was said before, all the rest of the signs of Christ's mercifulness might have been limited to sinners that are so and so qualified; but when he says, "Begin at Jerusalem," the line is stretched out to the utmost; no man can imagine beyond it; and it is folly here to pinch and spare, to narrow, and seek to bring it within scanty bounds; for he plainly saith, "Begin at Jerusalem," the biggest sinner is the Jerusalem sinner.[59]

The force of Bunyan's argument is simple: if Christ will forgive and accept Jerusalem sinners, who won't he accept if they come to him aright?

The second satanic objection to coming to Christ for life is that the would-be comer is not elect and therefore should not come. This, Bunyan argues, is a perversion of the doctrine of election. And he speaks rather forcefully to the sinner who makes this objection against himself, saying, "Now thou talkest like a fool, and meddlest with what thou understandest not: no sin, but the sin of final impenitence, can prove a man reprobate; and I am sure thou hast not arrived as yet unto that; therefore thou understandest not what thou sayest, and makest groundless conclusions against

---

[57] Bunyan, *Saved By Grace*, 1:352.
[58] John Bunyan, *The Jerusalem Sinner Saved*, in *Works* 1:96.
[59] Bunyan, *The Jerusalem Sinner Saved*, 1:87.

thyself."[60] Bunyan imagines that his hearer responds with the following: "But I am afraid I am not elect, or chose to salvation, though you called me fool a little before for so fearing." And he responds, this time, more gently, saying:

> Though election is, in order, before calling, as to God, yet the knowledge of calling must go before the belief of my election, as to myself. Wherefore, souls that doubt the truth of their effectual calling, do but plunge themselves into a deeper labyrinth of confusion that concern themselves with their election; I mean, while they labour to know it before they prove their calling. Wherefore, at present, lay the thoughts of thy election by, and ask thyself these questions: Do I see my lost condition? Do I see salvation is nowhere but in Christ? Would I share in this salvation by faith in him? And would I, as was said before, be thoroughly saved, to wit, from the filth as from the guilt? Do I love Christ, his Father, his saints, his words, and ways? This is the way to prove we are elect. Wherefore, sinner, when Satan, or thine own heart, seeks to puzzle thee with election, say thou, I cannot attend to talk of this point now, but stay till I know that I am called of God to the fellowship of his Son, and then I will show you that I am elect, and that my name is written in the book of life.[61]

Third, Bunyan believes that Satan often tries to convince coming sinners that they have committed the unpardonable sin by sinning against the Holy Spirit. To those who have been tempted thus, Bunyan writes, "If thou hast, thou are lost for ever; but yet before it is concluded by thee that thou hast so sinned, know that they that would be saved by Jesus Christ, through faith in his blood, cannot be counted for such."[62] He then offers three proofs of this statement. First, Christ's promise to receive all that come to Him cannot be frustrated. Second, he that has sinned against the Holy Spirit has no heart to come, and can by no means be made willing to come to Christ for life. And third, all this must be done against manifest tokens to prove the contrary, or after the shining of gospel light upon the soul, or some considerable profession of Him as the Messiah, or the Savior of the world.[63]

In addition to answering Satan's objections, Bunyan encourages the despairing sinner to close with Christ by holding out the promises of the gospel in his preaching. Speaking from his own experience, Bunyan says:

[60] Ibid., 1:88.
[61] Ibid., 1:102.
[62] Ibid., 1:102.
[63] Ibid., 1:103.

O how excellent are the Scriptures to thy soul! O how much virtue doest thou see in such a promise, in such an invitation! They are so large as to say, Christ will in no wise cast me out! My crimson sins shall be white as snow! I tell thee, friend, there are some promises that the Lord hath helped me to lay hold of Jesus Christ through and by, that I would not have out of the Bible for as much gold and silver as can lie between York and London piled up to the stars; because through them Christ is pleased by his Spirit to convey comfort to my soul. I say, when the law curses, when the devil tempts, when hell-fire flames in my conscience, my sins with the guilt of them tearing me, then is Christ revealed so sweetly to my poor soul through the promises that all is forced to fly and leave off to accuse my soul.[64]

As an evangelist, John Bunyan sought to move sinners through the *ordo salutis*. The insensible sinner will not come to Christ, so he must be awakened. The outwardly reformed sinner will not look outside of himself for righteousness, so he must be humbled. And the despairing sinner will not close with Christ for fear of rejection, so he must be encouraged. Though it is not uncommon for Bunyan to make indiscriminate evangelistic invitations,[65] he generally tailored his evangelistic preaching to these specific categories of hearers and addressed them accordingly.

Come and Welcome to Jesus Christ

In 1678 John Bunyan published an expanded version of a sermon he preached on John 6:37 entitled *Come and Welcome to Jesus Christ*. It was probably his greatest sermon. At the very least, it was his most popular. It was already in its sixth edition in the year Bunyan died. This work has the distinction of being the best example of Bunyan's preaching on both sovereign grace and evangelism. Throughout this sermon, discussions of sovereign grace and evangelistic invitations abound, often side by side. For Bunyan, a strong emphasis on the absolute sovereignty of God in salvation

---

[64] Bunyan, *A Few Sighs From Hell*, 3:721.

[65] One such example is found at the end of a sermon on Psalm 130:7. After speaking extensively on sovereign grace throughout this sermon, Bunyan addresses sinners in general, saying, "Sinner, doth not all this discourse make thy heart twitter after the mercy that is with God, and after the way that is made by this plenteous redemption? Methinks it should; yea, thou couldst not do otherwise, didst thou but see thy condition: look behind thee, take a view of the path thou hast trodden these many years. Dost thou think that the way that thou are in will lead thee to the straight gate, sinner? Ponder the path of thy feet with the greatest seriousness, thy life lies upon it; what thinkest thou?" See 1:620.

is clearly not incompatible with great evangelistic zeal. In fact, the former should lead to the latter.

Sovereign Grace

All of the expressions of sovereign grace that are found throughout Bunyan's sermons are present in *Come and Welcome to Jesus Christ*. Election is a prominent theme in this sermon. Bunyan opens by explaining that all of those predestined for salvation are the Father's gift to the Son. He writes:

> Those intended as the gift in the text, are those that are given by covenant to the Son; those that in other places are called "the elect," "the chosen," "the sheep," and "the children of promise." These be they that the Father hath given to Christ to keep them; those that Christ hath promised eternal life unto; those to whom he hath given his word, and that he will have with him in his kingdom to behold his glory.[66]

The giving of the elect by the Father to the Son not only teaches the doctrine of election, it also implies the doctrine of reprobation as well. Though Bunyan rarely speaks of reprobation in his sermons, here he argues that the giving of some implies the passing over of others:

> The Father hath not given all men to Christ... he hath, therefore, disposed of some another way. He gives some up to idolatry; he gives some up to uncleanness, to vile affections, and to a reprobate mind. Now these he disposeth of in his anger, for their destruction, that they may reap the fruit of their doings, and be filled with the reward of their own ways.[67]

And after explaining the various phrases of the text, Bunyan makes a series of general observations about the overall meaning and significance of John 6:37. The first of these observations is this: "Coming to Christ is not by the will, wisdom, or power of man, but by the gift, promise, and drawing of the Father."[68] Bunyan is convinced that John 6:37 clearly teaches unconditional election.

Effectual calling is another prominent expression of sovereign grace in this sermon. The Father gives the elect to the Son, and the Son promises to "put forth a sufficiency of all grace as shall effectually perform this

---

[66] John Bunyan, *Come and Welcome to Jesus Christ*, in *Works* 1:243.
[67] Ibid., 1:245.
[68] Ibid., 1:275.

promise."[69] He will do this by making the means of grace effectual for their calling and conversion. He writes, "As was said to the evil spirit that was sent to persuade Ahab to go and fall at Ramoth-Gilead; Go: 'Thou shalt persuade him, and prevail also: go forth and do so.' So will Jesus Christ say to the means that shall be used for the bringing of those to him that the Father hath given him."[70]

Bunyan insists that fallen men are not able to come to Christ. He believes, as we have seen already, that man is dead spiritually and cannot come unless supernaturally drawn. In this sermon he asks the reader, "What power has he that is dead, as every natural man spiritually is, even dead in trespasses and sins? Dead, even as dead to God's New Testament things as he that is in his grave is dead to the things of this world. What power hath he, then, whereby to come to Jesus Christ?"[71] Sinners come to Christ only because all three Persons of the Trinity commit themselves to their conversion. He writes:

> Christ thus engageth to communicate all manner of grace to those thus given to him to make them effectually come to him. "They shall come;" that is, not if they will, but if grace, all grace, if power, wisdom, a new heart, and the Holy Spirit, and all joining together, can make them come. I say, this word, shall come, being absolute, hath no dependence upon our own will, or power, or goodness; but it engageth for us even God himself, Christ himself, and the Spirit himself.[72]

Like election, Bunyan believes John 6:37 clearly teaches effectual calling.

Bunyan also discusses perseverance in this sermon, but not as frequently as election or effectual calling. Perseverance is clearly implied by the text: those who are given by the Father will surely come and not be cast out. And so Bunyan does not address perseverance extensively. He does, however, discuss perseverance in dealing with the absoluteness of the promise of John 6:37. He raises the following objection to the absoluteness of the promise: "how shall they escape all those dangerous and damnable opinions, that, like rocks and quicksands, are in the way in which they go?" He answers:

> The gift of the Father, laid claim by the Son in the text, must needs escape them, and in conclusion come to him. There are a company of *Shall-comes* in the Bible that doth secure them; not but that they may

[69] Ibid., 1:246.
[70] Ibid.
[71] Ibid., 1:275.
[72] Ibid., 1:254.

be assaulted by them; yea, and also for the time entangled and detained
by them from the Bishop of their souls, but these *Shall-comes* will break
those chains and fetters, that those given to Christ are entangled in, and
they shall come, because he hath said they shall come to him.[73]

Toward the end of the sermon he returns again to the subject of perseverance and argues that all comers will be received by Christ because he
is their faithful high priest who ensures both their coming and reception
by his intercession.[74]

Evangelism

In this same sermon, even as he discusses sovereign grace-related
themes like election, reprobation, and the effectual call, Bunyan invites
his reader to come to Christ for salvation. He does this throughout the
sermon in two ways. First, he answers various objections fearful or despairing sinners may have to closing with Christ for salvation. One of the most
common objections fearful sinners raise is that they are so bad that Christ
will refuse them if they come. He says that the word 'in no wise' "cutteth
the throat" of these objections. Bunyan argues:

> But I am a great sinner, sayest thou.
> 'I will in no wise cast out,' says Christ.
> But I am an old sinner, sayest thou.
> 'I will in no wise cast out,' says Christ.
> But I am a hard-hearted sinner, sayest thou.
> 'I will in no wise cast out,' says Christ.
> But I am a backsliding sinner, sayest thou.
> 'I will in no wise cast out,' says Christ.
> But I have served Satan all my days, sayest thou.
> 'I will in no wise cast out,' says Christ.
> But I have sinned against light, sayest thou.
> 'I will in no wise cast out,' says Christ.
> But I have sinned against mercy, sayest thou.
> 'I will in no wise cast out,' says Christ.
> But I have no good thing to bring with me, sayest thou.
> 'I will in no wise cast out,' says Christ.[75]

[73] Ibid., 1:258.
[74] Ibid., 1:290.
[75] Ibid., 1:279–80.

Bunyan argues that the phrase 'in no wise cast out' overcomes any and every objection to coming to Christ based on the sinner's own unworthiness.

Another common objection is that the sinner has waited too late and is now past forgiveness. He responds to this by saying "thou canst never come too late to Jesus Christ, if thou dost come." He continues, "Now is the day of salvation. Now God is upon the mercy-seat; now Christ Jesus sits by, continually pleading the victory of his blood for sinners; and now, even as long as this world lasts, this word of the text shall still be free, and fully fulfilled; And him that cometh to me I will in no wise cast out."[76] And then he pleads with him to come to Christ, saying, "Sinner, the greater the sinner thou art, the greater the need of mercy thou hast, and the more will Christ be glorified thereby. Come then, come and try; come, taste and see how good the Lord is to an undeserving sinner."[77]

Bunyan also addresses those two troubling objections Satan usually makes against coming sinners: they are not elect, and they have committed the unpardonable sin. When Satan objects against the sinners coming to Christ, saying "thou art not elected," Bunyan tells him to answer:

> But I am coming, Satan, I am coming; and that I could not be, but that the Father draws me; and I am coming to such a Lord Jesus, as will in no wise cast me out. Further, Satan, were I not elect, the Father would not draw me, nor would the Son so graciously open his bosom to me. I am persuaded, that not one of the non-elect shall ever be able to say, no, not in the day of judgment, I did sincerely come to Jesus Christ.[78]

And regarding the sin against the Holy Spirit, Bunyan reminds the fearful sinner that God gives neither the grace nor the heart to come to Christ to those who commit the unpardonable sin. The fact that the sinner wants to come to Christ and may be moving in that direction is proof that he has not committed the unpardonable sin.[79]

Bunyan's purpose in these examples is quite clear: there is no reason that every sinner should not come to Christ for salvation. Their badness, their lateness, and the devil's objections should hinder no sinner from coming. To all that come to him, Christ says, "I will in no wise cast out."

In addition to answering objections, Bunyan also invites sinners to come to Christ by encouraging his readers to "boldly venture" upon the promise of this text. Bunyan invites "any him" to come to Christ for salva-

---

[76] Ibid., 1:253.
[77] Ibid.
[78] Ibid., 1:284.
[79] Ibid.

tion. He writes, "Him, any him that cometh, hath sufficient from this word of Christ, to feed himself with the hopes of salvation." He continues:

> Coming sinner, what promise thou findest in the word of Christ, strain it whither thou canst, so thou dost not corrupt it, and his blood and merits will answer all; what the word saith, or any true consequence that is drawn therefrom, that we may boldly venture upon it. Take it then for granted, that thou, whoever thou art, if coming, art intended in these words; neither shall it injure Christ at all, if, as Benhadad's servants served Ahab, thou shalt catch him at his word.[80]

In fact, encourages the hearer to "catch" Christ at His word saying, "Catch him, coming sinner, catch him in his word, surely he will take it kindly, and will not be offended at thee."[81]

John Bunyan finds sovereign grace in nearly every phrase of John 6:37. And yet in those same phrases, he finds justification for inviting sinners, especially fearful or despairing sinners, to come to Christ for salvation. In *Come and Welcome to Jesus Christ* we find one of the most (if not the most) robust discussions of sovereign grace in all of Bunyan's sermons, and we find his evangelistic zeal burning as brightly and as hotly as it does in any of his works.

Conclusion

In this chapter John Bunyan's preaching on sovereign grace and evangelism has been considered. He preached that God is absolutely sovereign in salvation. God unconditionally elects, effectually calls, and infallibly preserves some sinners for salvation. And he preached for the conversion of sinners. He sought to awaken the slumbering, humble the proud, and comfort the despairing so that they might come to Christ and be saved. He even uses sovereign grace to accomplish this great end. Bunyan doesn't attempt to reconcile these ideas because he doesn't believe they need reconciling. He believed that Scriptures teach that God is absolutely sovereign in salvation, and that sinners must repent and come to Christ for salvation. Both statements are true and involve no contradiction.

---

[80] Ibid., 1:263.
[81] Ibid., 1:264.

12

"These Radical Doctrines"
THE SBC AND EVANGELICAL CALVINISM

Jeff Robinson

In November of 1861, the citizens of Georgia did not know what lay in store for them in the coming four years. War had broken out with the North just six months earlier and in those early days the outcome looked hopeful for the Confederacy; the South had scored a key victory at the first battle of Bull Run in Manassas Junction, Virginia, and Confederate strategists were outflanking a federal blockade designed to hem in southern vessels near the coastline by building small, fast ships that could outmaneuver Union boats.[1] Most ministers in the South assured parishioners that God was fighting for the cause of the Confederacy and that victory was inevitable.

On November 15, 1861, Southern Baptist theologian and journalist Henry Holcombe Tucker stepped to the podium at the state capitol in Milledgeville to address the Georgia legislature and delivered a sermon to mark a day of fasting, humiliation and prayer. Like other southern ministers, Tucker was certain the South was fighting a grand cause for which it held a divine mandate; however, he warned Georgians that it was God who would have the first and last word as to the outcome of the war, for His decrees were immutable and His judgments perfect. There was an eternal design for the war: "Let us remember that God is in the war. Let

---

[1] James M. McPherson, *Battle Cry of Freedom: The Civil War Era* (New York, NY: Oxford University, 1988), 221.

us further remember that he has not brought these calamities upon us without a purpose."[2]

What was that purpose? It was at least two-fold, Tucker surmised, but southerners should not make snap judgments in trying to pin down God's secret decrees; God is utterly sovereign and is bringing all things about for His own glory: "Without presuming to know any of the secrets of Infinite wisdom, the Almighty has revealed himself to us sufficiently to warrant us in saying that these afflictions must have been brought upon us either as a punishment for sins that are past, or as a means of making us better in the future, or for both ends."[3]

Tucker's words to the legislature provide an open window into his theology; Tucker was, as were most Southern Baptists of his day, committed to the absolute sovereignty of God in His providential Lordship over all of creation. Belief in such a doctrine was foundational for Tucker's commitment to evangelical Calvinism in its baptistic expression. For Tucker as for all who stood in the stream of historic Reformed orthodoxy, God exercised His gracious, absolute kingship over creation, but also exercised it in the salvation of sinners.[4] To wit, in the spring of 1887, the Baptist newspaper in Maine, *Zion's Advocate*, began fomenting for a union between

[2] Henry Holcombe Tucker, "God in the War: A Sermon Delivered before the Legislature of Georgia, in the Capital at Milledgeville, on Friday, November 15, 1861, Being a Day Set apart for Fasting and Prayer by his Excellency the President of the Confederate States." Sermon delivered to the Legislature of Georgia, 15 November, 1861. Academic Affairs Library, University of North Carolina at Chapel Hill, Chapel Hill, NC.

[3] Ibid.

[4] In this chapter, the author will use the terms "Calvinism," "Reformed theology" and "doctrines of grace" as a general reference to refer to that branch of theology that traces its roots to the Genevan Reformer John Calvin, that was expressed in the teachings of the English and New England Puritans and articulated in confessions of faith such as the Westminster Confession and its Baptist derivative The Second London Confession of 1689. The Reformed tradition is an heir of Augustine in its anthropology and soteriology. While Calvinistic Baptists differed with many in the Reformed tradition on issues such as baptism and ecclesiology, they generally stand within that tradition, with the clear examples being seen in the Particular Baptists of England in the seventeenth century and in America in the eighteenth and nineteenth centuries. Thus, the author is employing these terms to refer to Reformed views, particularly as they relate to the doctrines of providence and salvation by grace alone as encapsulated in the five "solas" of the Reformation: *sola Scriptura, sola gratia, sola fide, solo Christo, soli deo gloria*. From his writings, it is fair to assume that many SBC ministers from the founding of the denomination in 1845 into the 1920s would have affirmed all five pillars of Reformation theology as expressed in the Second London Confession. With re-

Free-Will Baptists and Calvinistic Baptists in New England. Though he considered the *Advocate* a strong Baptist ally in the northern United States, Tucker, who served four different tenures as editor of the *Christian Index* of Georgia, did little to cloak his dissatisfaction at such a notion; unless one of the denominations changed their theology, that is, unless the Free-Will Baptists embraced the doctrines of grace, then the union would amount to an attempt to wed two groups who were unequally yoked. Tucker did not hesitate to call out his fellow editor with regard to what Baptists believed and to demand more information with regard to the theological particulars of such an audacious proposal.

> The Advocate says, among other things, that "they (the Free-Will Baptists) are finding that doctrinally there is nothing now that separates Baptists from Free Baptists." The italics are ours. This implies that there was a time when there was a doctrinal difference, but that a change has taken place, and there is no difference now. Does the Advocate mean by this that we have changed? If not, let the fact be declared. But if the Advocate admits that we have changed, then let him specify whom he means to include under the word we. He may mean to speak of and for the Baptists of Maine only, and he may represent them truly, though we hope not. If he means to include all the Baptists of the United States, then we protest. The Baptists of the South hold to the doctrines of grace just as they have always held them.[5]

For Tucker, who had his finger firmly on the pulse of Southern Baptists as a traveling preacher, theologian, denominational statesman and state newspaper editor, to be a Southern Baptist was to be a Calvinist. Tucker typified Southern Baptist leaders and ministers of his day; he held to a warm-hearted experiential Calvinism that viewed God as the unilateral actor in predestination, election, regeneration and justification, acts that rescued fallen men from the abyss of sin and death. In the late twentieth/early twenty-first centuries, it has become somewhat fashionable among populist leaders of the Southern Baptist Nashville to cry, "What hath Geneva to do with Nashville?" implying that Calvinism is an alien invasion, an illegal immigration across Southern Baptist borders.[6]

gard to the tenets that emerged from the Synod of Dort in 1619 as an abstract of Reformed soteriology, later referred to as the "Five Points of Calvinism," many Southern Baptist ministers would have subscribed to all five points and others would have held to at least four points, disagreeing with others on particular, or limited, atonement.

[5] Henry Holcombe Tucker, "Union, Right and Wrong," *The Christian Index and Southwestern Baptist* (31 March 1887), 8

[6] One particular manifestation of this anti-Calvinism stance is found in *Who-*

So what is the relationship between the soteriology and the sovereign God of John Calvin and the Southern Baptist Convention? This chapter will argue that SBC leaders were, from the denomination's founding in 1845, deeply committed to the doctrines of grace, but departed from them in the 1920s as revivalism, pragmatism and other factors conspired to bring about an eclipse of what the early SBC divines called "These radical doctrines" or "The Old Theology." This chapter will focus in particular on the soteriological commitments of the major figures of the first 80 years of SBC life and will also examine the undeniably Reformed roots of the denomination's major confessions of faith.

The Southern Baptist Convention formally began in 1845 when delegates gathered in Augusta, Georgia, and voted to separate from Northern Baptists. Early Southern Baptist presidents, including founding leader W.B. Johnson, as well as the major writers such as Tucker and Jesse Mercer, along with educators such as P. H. Mell and J. L. Dagg, many of whom were instrumental in the nascent denomination's genesis, all held to a theology of the sovereign grace of God in salvation, which is where this investigation begins.

W B. Johnson and the founding of the SBC

When 293 delegates met in Georgia in May of 1845, they elected William B. Johnson (1782–1862) as the denomination's founding president. Both theologically and pragmatically, he was the quintessential man to fill such a critical role. Johnson was active in the founding of the South Carolina Baptist Convention in 1821 and was the only man present at the founding of both the General Missionary Convention in 1814 and the SBC thirty-one years later. For twenty-eight years he had served as president of the Baptist convention in South Carolina and held the same office in the General Missionary Convention from 1841 to 1845. Like a majority of the SBC's first delegates and early leaders, Johnson held to a Reformed or Calvinistic understanding of salvation. Johnson, along with the early SBC churches and associations, were heirs of the faith as articulated in the 1689 Second London Confession of Faith, the most fulsome and influential confessional expression of Reformed theology in its baptistic expression. Johnson was one of the key leaders among Baptists

soever Will: A Biblical-Theological Critique of Five-Point Calvinism, ed. David L. Allen and Steve W. Lemke (Nashville: B&H Academic, 2010), which is a collection of papers from the John 3:16 Conference held in Woodstock, GA, in November of 2008. Speakers at the conference included many well-known SBC pastors and several professors from various denominational seminaries.

in South Carolina, home of the first Baptist association in the South, the Charleston Association, which was established in 1751 after adopting the Second London Confession of 1689 as its statement of faith. The association maintained the Calvinism of the confession as a statement of belief at least until the end of the nineteenth century.[7]

In November of 1822, Johnson preached a sermon before the Charleston Baptist Association, titled *Love Characteristic of Deity*, a sermon that provides a window into his understanding of salvation. Writes Tom J. Nettles, "The sermon constitutes an accurate and muscular exposition of the doctrine of God's love as illuminating and illuminated by the doctrines of grace."[8] Johnson sets forth God's love as particular and not general, in much the same way a father has affections for all children but possesses a particular and more profound love for his own offspring, and Johnson subjugates every event, including the fall of the angels, to the absolute sovereignty of God.[9] The oft-rejected and highly debated petal of the TULIP is the third one, limited, or particular atonement. But it was not a problem for Johnson; he pointed out in his sermon that Christ did not come merely to make salvation promiscuously available; He came, rather, to accomplish redemption for His elect people: "One great object that Christ had in view, in undertaking the office of Mediator, was actually to redeem and introduce to glory, all believers in his name, all who were his people."[10] Sinners trust in Christ as Lord and Savior only after God has unilaterally regenerated their hearts, Johnson argued, upholding the Calvinistic view of the priority of regeneration: "This recovery (of right standing before God) consists in the renovation of their hearts by the Holy Spirit, the necessity of which is so strongly expressed by our Lord in these terms: 'Except a man be born of water and of the Spirit, he cannot enter the kingdom of God.' This is the first step in their actual recovery. They are then justified freely by an interest in the blood righteousness of their Redeemer, received under the influences of the Spirit by faith in his adorable name."[11]

In the same sermon, Johnson expresses a distinction between moral ability and natural ability in fallen human beings, a distinction at the heart of Jonathan Edwards' case for the enslavement of the human heart to sin in his classic work *The Freedom of the Will*. There is no external compulsion that keeps man from fleeing to Christ, but his spiritual disability lies in the

---

[7] W. B. Johnson, "Love Characteristic of the Deity," in *Southern Baptist Sermons on Sovereignty and Responsibility*, ed. Thomas J. Nettles (Harrisonburg, VA: Gano Books, Sprinkle Publications, 1984), 36–37.

[8] Ibid.

[9] Ibid., 38–39.

[10] Ibid., 61.

[11] Ibid., 62.

lack of a moral motivation to press into God's kingdom.[12] While Johnson held to the bondage of the will, the sovereignty of God in salvation and in God's prerogative in electing a peculiar people to salvation, he also clearly upheld man's responsibility to repent and believe the Gospel and expected evangelism and missions to continue as the irreducible task of the church until Jesus returns. God's particular love for His people alongside the duty of all men everywhere to repent and believe the gospel, run across the landscape of Scripture side-by-side like twin tracks, he asserted. The particular love of God by no means undermines the Christian's necessity to love all men. "This representation of Jehovah's love, explodes, therefore, the idea, which obtains among so many, and which in their view forms a strong objection against the Gospel scheme, vis.: That it is inconsistent to say our salvation is purchased at the price of full atonement, and yet a free pardon is proclaimed to the sinner."[13]

Johnson was the unequivocal leader of the first incarnation of the Southern Baptist Convention. His Calvinistic theology was by no means exceptional among leaders and delegates. He held to precisely the same doctrinal convictions on these issues as that of another major figure in the nascent SBC, Patrick Hues Mell.

Patrick Hues Mell

So influential was Patrick Hues Mell (1814–1888), an entire region surrounding Greensboro, Georgia, was for decades known as "Mell's Kingdom" for his pastoral ministry in the area. Mell was perhaps the quintessential pastor/theologian/denominational statesman. He was first a pastor to God's flock, serving Greensboro Church for ten years, Antioch Church for twenty-eight years, and Bairdstown Church for thirty-three years. Mell's son recalled that his father was above all a preacher of the gospel of Jesus Christ: "His piercing eyes glowed or melted in tender pathos as his mind grasped the glorious truths of the gospel; he held his hearers spellbound many times a full hour, and, if the theme was unusually grand, and far-reaching in its fuller development, he stood for an hour and a half, yet his people never thought he preached long… (he) clothed his ideas in language so plain, so simple, so strong, so beautiful, that the truth was fixed in the minds of his listeners."[14] Mell was a theologian; he served as professor of ancient languages at Mercer College and in 1860 served as vice

---

[12] Ibid., 39.

[13] Ibid., 58.

[14] P. H. Mell, Jr., *Life of Patrick Hues Mell* (Louisville, KY: Baptist Book Concern, 1895), 64–65.

chancellor at the University of Georgia and served as chancellor (office of president today) there over the final ten years of his life. Mell was one of the great denominational statesmen in SBC history. All told, he served as president of the SBC three different terms, serving for one year in 1863, from 1866 to 1871 and 1880 to 1886. He also served for decades as moderator of the Georgia Association and as president of the Georgia Baptist Convention. Mell stands as one of the unquestioned granite cornerstones during the critical early years of the SBC.

And Mell was a Calvinist, whose commitment to the doctrines of grace undergirded his preaching with pathos and vigor, a reality that characterized Southern Baptists and Georgia Baptists of his day. When Baptist preachers avoided the doctrines of grace in their preaching, Mell lamented their neglect with sorrow: "Some have even preached doctrines not consistent with (the doctrines of grace), and some have openly derided and denounced them."[15] Therefore, Mell resolved "to counteract, as far as I was able, the tendencies to Arminianism." One such effort that provides a clear example of his commitment to evangelical Calvinism was his written response to Russell Reneau, a Methodist camp-meeting preacher who publicly challenged the truthfulness of Calvinism. Mell's response is a tour-de-force in defense of the biblical veracity and logical power of the sovereignty of God in salvation. Mell showed the biblical inconsistency of the Arminian view of foreknowledge, arguing that God's knowledge of an event still makes certain that it will come to pass; Arminian attempts at getting God off a perceived hook do not square with Scripture and are unnecessary.

> Now, God's decree is synonymous with God's will. Substitute, therefore, in the extract taken from Calvin, the word 'willed' for the word 'decreed', and the Calvinistic idea of foreknowledge will stand thus: "God therefore foreknows all things that will come to pass, because He has willed that they shall come to pass." Or it may be stated in two propositions, thus: 1st. Nothing can come to pass in time except what God wills shall come to pass; 2nd. God foreknows that certain things will come to pass, because He wills they shall come to pass.[16]

Mell spent much of the remainder of the work exposing the logical fallacies of the Arminian doctrine of foreknowledge as it relates to election and predestination. Later, Mell asserted that implicit in the doctrine

[15] Patrick Hues Mell, "Predestination and the Saints Perseverance, Stated and Defended from the objections of Arminians, in a review of two sermons, published by Rev. Russell Reneau," in *A Southern Baptist Looks at Predestination* (Harrisonburg, VA: Sprinkle Publications, 1995), 6.

[16] Ibid., 53.

of predestination is the even more controversial and pride-slaying truth of reprobation. For Mell, reprobation was not active, but passive; he argued from Romans 9:22–23 that God passes over those who are not among His elect.

> In reference to men, predestination is divided into two parts: first, as it relates to the elect, and second, as it relates to the non-elect. Having decreed to create a world, and to people it with beings who would voluntarily sin against him, he determined from eternity to save some, and to leave others to perish in their sins. 'Willing to show his wrath, and to make his power known,' He 'endured with much longsuffering' these as 'the vessels of wrath fitted to destruction;' and that he might make known the riches of his glory on those as 'the vessels of mercy which he had afore prepared unto glory.' Romans 9:22, 23. 'To carry out his purpose of grace, he chose some to holiness and eternal life, entered for their sake, into the Covenant of Redemption with the Son and the Holy Ghost, appointed his Son as their substitute, to suffer in their stead, and having died to rise again, and appear as their advocate before his throne, appointed all the intermediate means necessary and, by an infallible decree, made their salvation sure. Those, 'whose names are not written in the book of life' (Rev. 20:15), who were 'appointed to wrath' (1 Thess. 5:9), who were 'before of old ordained to condemnation' (Jude 4) who would 'stumble at the word, being disobedient, whereunto also they were appointed' (1 Peter 2:8), he determined to leave in their sins, and to endure them with much longsuffering as vessels of wrath fitted to destruction.'[17]

Basil Manly, Sr.

Another important leader at the foundation of the SBC was Basil Manly, Sr. (1798–1868), an educator, preacher, administrator and denominationalist of whom Tom Nettles wrote, "played a strategic role in the development of the uniqueness of Southern Baptists. No man of his generation possessed greater contextual insights or sympathetic gifts for discerning the needs of Southern Baptists of the South in the mid-nineteenth century."[18] Like Mell, Manly was one of the SBC's premier pastor/

[17] P. H. Mell, "Predestination and the Saints Perseverance Stated and Defended," in Robert B. Selph, *Southern Baptists and the Doctrine of Election* (Harrisonburg, VA: Gano Books, 1988), 54–55.

[18] Thomas J. Nettles, *By His Grace and For His Glory: A Historical, Theological and Practical Study of the Doctrines of Grace in Baptist Life*, Revised and Expanded 20th Anniversary Edition (Cape Coral, FL: Founders Press, 2006), 136. Nettles' study is an expansive and in-depth examination of the history of Reformed Theology in Baptist life. Nettles examines the major figures, institutions and churches

theologians. He served as pastor at Edgefield Court House from 1822 till 1826, then became pastor of one of the South's most prominent Baptist churches, First Baptist Church of Charleston, South Carolina, in 1826 where he remained for twelve years. During his time in Charleston, Manly helped to establish a Baptist newspaper for the South and was among the founders of Furman University. From 1838 to 1855 Manly served as president of the University of Alabama. Alongside Johnson and Mell, Manly was one of the key leaders who established the SBC in 1845 and, when the new denomination was formed, he was elected president of the Domestic Mission Board. Deeply committed to theological education, the elder Manly was instrumental in establishing The Southern Baptist Theological Seminary in 1859 and his son, Basil Manly, Jr., served as one of the founding faculty members.

Manly's commitment to the doctrines of grace is beyond question. Those great truths ring clearly in a sermon Manly preached on April 8, 1849 at Pleasant Grove Church in Fayette County, Alabama. Manly delivered the sermon before leaders of the Tuscaloosa and North River associations in an attempt to reconcile the two parties over the issue of Arminianism. Writes Nettles, "The North River Association, under the leadership of David W. Andrews, had altered its confession of the doctrines of election and effectual calling so that a danger of susceptibility to Arminianism was very real."[19] Exegeting Philippians 2:12–13 ("Work out your own salvation with fear and trembling; for it is God that worketh in you, both to will and to do, of his own pleasure."), Manly argued that fallen man, cast adrift from divine truth, naturally tends toward an Arminian understanding of election and an overemphasis on man's moral duty to repent of his sins and believe in Christ.[20]

> The greatest reason, however, why the Christian family is divided on one or the other side—rejecting one or the other of these great doctrines—is that the doctrine of dependence on the divine being, throws us constantly into the hands, and on the mercy of God. Proud man does not like it; prefers to look at the other side of the subject; becomes blinded, in part, by gazing at one view of the truth alone; and forgets the Maker, in whom he lives, and moves and has his being.[21]

who subscribed to the doctrines of grace from the rise of the Baptist denomination out of English Separatism in the early seventeenth century to the twenty-first century SBC in America.

[19] Thomas J. Nettles, *Southern Baptist Sermons on Sovereignty and Responsibility* (Harrisonburg, VA: Sprinkle Publications, 1995), 8.

[20] Ibid., 20–21.

[21] Ibid., 21–22.

Manly encouraged the North River Association to hold the line on the historic Reformed position on election and avoid attempting to remove the valid biblical tension between God's absolute sovereignty and man's responsibility. "My brethren," he said, "however mysterious and incomprehensible it may be, that God chose a poor sinner like me –freely chose me, loved me, redeemed me, called me, justified me, and will glorify me – I will rejoice in the truth, and thank him for his free grace! O, where is the boasting then? Not at the feet of Jesus; not at the cross. It belongs not to that position."[22]

Basil Manly, Sr., bequeathed both his love for education and his theology of sovereign grace to his son, Basil Manly, Jr., who became one of the founders of the SBC's first seminary, The Southern Baptist Theological Seminary, which opened in Greenville, South Carolina, in 1859.

Establishing a confessional institution:
James Petigru Boyce, Basil Manly, Jr., John Albert Broadus

In his recent examination of The Southern Baptist Theological Seminary's first 150 years of ministry to the churches of the Southern Baptist Convention, Gregory A. Wills demonstrated clearly that the theology of founding President James P. Boyce was that of the seminary and the prevailing theology of the Baptist South. Many Baptists in the South subscribed to all five points of Dort's TULIP, while most held to at least four, hesitating on the most controversial petal, the "L" or limited atonement. Still, Boyce, Southern Seminary, and an overwhelming majority of Baptists in the South held to some form of Calvinism. "The theology that Boyce relied upon was Calvinism," writes Wills. "It was the doctrine of the seminary's Abstract of Principles and the prevailing theology of Baptists in the nineteenth-century South. A significant number rejected the doctrine of 'limited atonement,' and the rest did not make belief in it a condition of fellowship. But the churches and associations generally refused fellowship with pastors or churches that rejected other aspects of Calvinism."[23]

Born in Charleston, South Carolina into a family that was antebellum Southern gentry, Boyce (1827–1888) was educated at Brown University under Francis Wayland and then at Princeton Theological Seminary under the venerable Reformed theologian Charles Hodge. A visionary leader, Boyce first served as editor of the Baptist newspaper in his home state, the *Southern Baptist*, and then became pastor of First Baptist Church of Co-

---

[22] Ibid., 25.
[23] Gregory A. Wills, *Southern Baptist Theological Seminary 1859–2009* (New York, NY: Oxford University Press, 2009), 90–91.

lumbia, South Carolina from 1851 to 1855. From 1855 to 1859 he taught theology at Furman University and his inaugural address, *Three Changes in Theological Institutions*, laid the groundwork for Boyce's most ambitious ministry accomplishment: beginning a theological seminary to train young men in the SBC for ministry. In 1859, Boyce, along with John A. Broadus, Basil Manly, Jr., and William Williams founded The Southern Baptist Theological Seminary in Greenville, South Carolina. One of Boyce's "three changes" as articulated in the address at Furman, was that a theological institution, to be healthy, must necessarily be a confessional institution.[24] As a matter of stewardship before the churches and the denomination, faculty members, Boyce argued, must pledge by signature to teach "in accord with and not contrary to" the school's statement of faith.[25] At Southern Seminary's founding, Boyce commissioned founding faculty member Basil Manly, Jr., to draw up a confession of faith to summarize the new institution's doctrinal commitments. Manly penned *The Abstract of Principles*, a twenty-article summary of the central doctrines of the evangelical faith, a confession that was decidedly Calvinistic in its theological orientation. But this is not surprising, given the fact that Boyce, Manly, Broadus and William Williams all held firmly to the doctrines of grace. The *Abstract*'s theology and confessional bloodlines will be explored in greater scope later in this chapter.

In addition to serving as president and chief fundraiser for the seminary, Boyce also taught systematic theology and used his own work, *Abstract of Systematic Theology* as the textbook. In it, Boyce's exposition of Christian doctrines makes clear, as Tom Nettles writes, "his wide reading, his close reasoning, [and] his passion for Reformed thought."[26] This rings

[24] Timothy George, ed., James Petigru Boyce, *Selected Writings* (Nashville, TN: Broadman, 1989), 53–56. Asserted Boyce: "It seems to me, gentlemen, that you owe this to yourselves, to your professors, and to the denomination at large; to yourselves, because your position as trustees makes you responsible for the doctrinal opinions of your professors, and the whole history of creeds has proved the difficulty without them of convicting errorists of perversions of the Word of God—to your professors, that their doctrinal sentiments may be known and approved by all, that no charges of heresy may be brought against them; that none shall whisper of peculiar notions which they hold, but that in refutation of all charges they may point to this formulary as one which they hold *ex animo*, and teach in its true import—and to the denomination at large, that they may know in what truths the rising ministry are instructed, may exercise full sympathy with the necessities of the institution, and look with confidence and affection to the pastors who come from it."

[25] Ibid.

[26] Tom Nettles, *The Baptists: Key People Involved in Forming a Baptist Identity*, Volume Two: *Beginnings in America* (Ross-shire, Scotland: Mentor, 2005), 261.

clear in Boyce's chapter on the doctrine of election where, after setting forth the Arminian view, one he calls "just the opposite in every respect of the Calvinistic theory," Boyce undertakes a lengthy discourse to prove that six things are true of election.[27] His discussion provides an outline of the Calvinistic doctrine of unconditional election, summarizing it as: "(1) An act of God, and not the result of the choice of the elect; (2) That this choice is one of individuals, and not of classes; (3) That it was made without respect to the action of the persons elected; (4) By the good pleasure of God; (5) According to an eternal purpose; (6) That it is an election to salvation and not to outward privileges."[28] In his systematic theology, Boyce also clearly affirms the total depravity of man, the salvific efficacy of the atonement exclusively for God's elect, the impossibility that God's people can successfully and eternally resist God's effectual grace and perseverance of the saints.

The fall of man, his utter ruin and comprehensive depravity are central themes in Boyce's theology, thus the need for unilateral grace which Boyce places at the heart of his soteriology.[29] Not only does God provide effectual grace in drawing a sinner and regenerating his heart, but he also gives grace throughout the Christian life so that true believers persevere to the end. After examining biblical illustrations of apostasy, Boyce writes of perseverance, "It is objected, however, that while we have instance of some who are rescued from their grievous sins and backslidings, the Scripture also gives examples of others who are left to perish. But the doctrine of God's word is that of the perseverance of believers; of the elect of God; of those called to be saints."[30]

Boyce was by no means alone in his resolute subscription to the doctrines of grace; the other members of the founding faculty held to the same theology of sovereign grace as the seminary's inaugural president. Broadus, for example, famously wrote in Boyce's memoirs, "This is believed by many of us to be really the teaching of the Apostle Paul as elaborated by Augustine, and systematized and defended by Calvin."[31] Similarly, in his *Catechism of Bible Teaching*, Broadus, as Nettles points out, couches his understanding of effectual call in a question-answer exchange treating the relationship of regeneration to faith, placing regeneration before faith in

[27] James P. Boyce, *Abstract of Systematic Theology* (Hanford, CA: den Dulk Christian Foundation, 1980): 348.

[28] Ibid.

[29] Thomas J. Nettles, *James Petigru Boyce: A Southern Baptist Statesman* (Phillipsburg, N.J.: P&R, 2009), 421–23.

[30] Ibid., 437.

[31] John A. Broadus, *Memoir of James Petigru Boyce* (New York, NY: A. C. Armstrong and Son, 1893), 265.

line with the historic Reformed expression of the doctrine: "Does faith come before the new birth?" Answer: "No, it is the new heart that truly repents and believes."[32] In 1891, following a trip to Europe, Broadus wrote a letter to the *Western Recorder* newspaper of Kentucky, ruminating upon his stopover in Geneva and commending the theology upon which Southern Seminary had been built: "The people who sneer at what is called Calvinism might as well sneer at Mount Blanc. We are not in the least bound to defend all of Calvin's opinions or actions, but I do not see how anyone who really understands the Greek of the Apostle Paul or the Latin of Calvin and Turretin can fail to see that these latter did but interpret and formulate substantially what the former teaches."[33]

The Calvinistic commitments of Basil Manly, Jr., will be seen in the section below in Southern's confession of faith, *The Abstract of Principles*, which he wrote. Manly's theological convictions were similar to those of his colleagues, Boyce and Broadus. Perhaps one of the clearest defenders of what Charles Spurgeon called "the Calvinistic system," was a friend and contemporary with Southern Seminary's founders, J. L. Dagg, the SBC's first writing theologian.

John Leadley Dagg

John Leadley Dagg's systematic theology begins its section on particular atonement—a subsection of the book's chapter on the sovereignty of God's grace in salvation—with a clear and unapologetic assertion of the Calvinistic view of the atonement: "The Son of God gave his life to redeem those who were given to him by the Father in the Covenant of Grace. The Scriptures teach that the Son of God, in coming into the world and laying down his life, had the salvation of a peculiar people in view."[34] To prove the doctrine of particular redemption, or what is often called "limited" redemption to account for the "L" in Dort's TULIP, Dagg appends numerous passages of Scripture to his exposition. Like his fellow evangelical Calvinists in the SBC, Dagg fully acknowledged that Scripture calls for a full, "promiscuous," and genuine call to all unconverted people, irrespective of their standing as elect/non-elect, but on the day of Christ's final return, only those whom God chose before the foundation of the world will have their sins covered by the blood of Christ. "Redemption will not be universal in its consummation," he wrote. "For the redeemed will be out of every

---

[32] Nettles, *By His Grace and for His Glory*, 148.

[33] A.T. Robertson, *Life and Letters of John Albert Broadus* (Philadelphia, PA: American Baptist Publication Society, 1909), 396–97.

[34] John Leadley Dagg, *Manual of Theology* (Harrisonburg, VA: Gano Books, Sprinkle Publications, 1990), 324.

kindred, tongue, nation, and people; and therefore cannot include all in any of these divisions of mankind. And redemption cannot have been universal in its purpose; otherwise the purpose will fail to be accomplished, and all, for which the work of redemption was undertaken, will not be effected."[35]

While not as oft-remembered or quoted today as his contemporaries Boyce, Broadus, Charles Hodge or B. B. Warfield, Dagg (1794–1884) was one of the most revered evangelical leaders of nineteenth century America. Dagg overcame extraordinary problems – a limited education, near-blindness, and physical disability – to become a great pastor in Philadelphia and elsewhere and then an educator both in Alabama and as president at Mercer University in the 1840s and 1850s. Dagg's above-quoted systematic theology, first published in 1857, was the first systematic written by a Baptist in America. In the biographical preface to the reprint, Tom Nettles writes, "Dagg's theology has been classified as 'moderate Calvinistic Augustinianism.' Such nomenclature should not leave the impression that the soteriological or theological doctrines of Calvin were rejected or hidden in any way. Properly understood, the phrase paints Dagg as an experiential Calvinist, not simply a scholastic theologian. The most notable structural evidence of Dagg's experientialism is seen in his combination of the truths of duty and grace in an impressive and graphic manner."[36] Dagg himself grounded his own doctrinal roots in the theology of the Puritans—John Bunyan, Richard Baxter, Thomas Boston and John Owen—whom he regularly studied as a young theologian.[37]

Dagg's systematic theology gives lively expression to the doctrines of old Puritanism. For example, his articulation of the doctrine of election breathes the same air of God's absolute sovereignty as Owen, Bunyan, Edwards and other Puritan divines: "The Scriptures clearly teach that God has an elect or chosen people... Whatever may have been our prejudices against the doctrine of election as held and taught by some ministers of religion, it is undeniable, that, in some sense, the doctrine is found in the Bible; and we cannot reject it, without rejecting that inspired book... The Scriptures teach expressly, that God's people are chosen to salvation... The Scriptures plainly teach that election of grace is from eternity."[38]

As a theologian at Mercer, Dagg taught these doctrines to a generation of Southern Baptist pastors, one of whom, like Dagg, became a leading voice in the denomination, but a voice that has largely been silenced in the twenty-first century, H. H. Tucker.

[35] Ibid.

[36] Ibid., np.

[37] John Leadley Dagg, "Autobiography of Rev. John L. Dagg," in *Manual of Theology* (Harrisonburg, VA: Gano Books, Sprinkle Publications, 1990), 20–21.

[38] Ibid., 309–10.

Henry Holcombe Tucker

In his tribute to the aforementioned Tucker in the preface of a 1902 volume of editorials which the Georgia Baptist Convention published, Henry McDonald, Tucker's pastor for many years in Atlanta, called his late parishioner the "Jonathan Edwards of the South." Indeed, Tucker (1819–1889) was Edwardsean in his ability to synthesize theology with crucial worldview-related disciplines such as philosophy, contemporary culture and religious movements of his day.

Born in Warren County Georgia in 1819, Tucker bore the namesake of his grandfather, Henry Holcombe, one of the eminent Baptist pastors in Georgia in the early nineteenth century. Holcombe was one of the founders of the Georgia Baptist Convention. Tucker spent his teen years in Philadelphia and received a classical education, graduating from Columbian College in Washington, D. C. in 1838 and for two years he practiced law in Forsyth, Ga. Theologically, he was mentored and trained by Dagg.

While Tucker was noted as an educator, his work as editor of the *Christian Index* was the means by which he achieved perhaps his greatest notoriety in Georgia and across the Baptist South, a region Tucker tenderly referenced in his editorials as "my Southern Zion." Tucker spent four separate tenures as editor of the *Index* from 1866—just a few months after the close of the Civil War—through 1889. In 1888 Tucker bought the *Index* and operated it until his abrupt death in September of 1889.

While Tucker served as a pastor for a brief time, he viewed himself as a shepherd-editor at the helm of the *Index*, writing often on doctrine and biblical exposition. He sought to teach, rebuke and warn from the editor's chair. Upon his death, one longtime admirer said of Tucker, "the ink that touched his pen turned to light."

A stalwart evangelical Calvinist in the mold of John Dagg, J. P. Boyce, Basil Manly, Jr., P. H. Mell and John Albert Broadus, Tucker wrote prolifically on the doctrines of grace and related topics such as divine providence, examples of which were quoted in the introduction to this chapter. Tucker regularly fed readers of the *Index* on a meaty diet of expositions and analysis of the doctrines of grace. One topic that found its way often into his writings—indeed, the topic that may have earned him the moniker "the Jonathan Edwards of the South"—was the total depravity of fallen man. In an editorial in early 1885, Tucker pointed out that Jesus's words in John 6:44, "No man can come to me except the Father which hath sent me draw him," offended and repelled many who had previously been following Jesus. The doctrine of God's sovereignty in salvation naturally stirred up their rebellious nature, he wrote: "It was the doctrine that they could not bear. They were disgusted; they turned away from him, and never did come back. Up to this point they had received his instructions, but when it came to this, their nature rebelled, they could not endure it, and they abandoned him forever." At the center of Tucker's theology was the belief that sinful man lacked the moral ability to come to God. Most sinners, Tucker asserted, are like the Pharisees; they want to seek God on their terms and in their own time. The New Testament, however, does not speak of salvation as being available at the whims of man, Tucker argued. It must come from a unilateral work of God's sovereign grace.

> What Christ said is the very last thing that human nature will ever admit; it is the great point of differentiation between human wishes and God's plans. It is the gospel distilled down to its last and strongest essence. Jesus the Savior, the inability of men to accept him as a Savior, God the author and finisher. Why cannot men come to Christ? There is no mechanical, no physical impossibility. It is simply because of their own innate wickedness, simply because of their own total depravity. The inability is one for which they are to blame. Is it to be expected that human nature will ever accept such a doctrine as this? No man ever did it and no man ever will—without help; and the help must be strong as the arm of the Almighty. None but he who created man in the first place can so create him over again as to make him the antagonism of his former self.[39]

Tucker has largely been lost to posterity today, but in the late-nineteenth century, he shone as one of the brightest constellations in the Southern Baptist galaxy.[40] Unlike Tucker, B.H. Carroll has not fallen into the dustbin of denominational history.

B.H. Carroll

Benajah Harvey Carroll (1843–1914) has been called the "Colossus of Baptist History" by some historians. Born in Carroll County, Mississippi, Carroll served as a soldier in the Confederate Army during the Civil War and, after his conversion in 1865, was pastor of First Baptist Church of Waco, Texas, for twenty-nine years. During his time as a soldier, Carroll lived as a convinced agnostic, but once he was converted, became one of the SBC's most prominent nineteenth century leaders. He is best known as the founder of Southwestern Baptist Theological Seminary in 1905. The school was first called Baylor Theological Seminary, but was renamed af-

---

[39] Henry Holcombe Tucker, "Disgusted," *The Christian Index and Southwestern Baptist* (12 February 1885), 8.

[40] For a fuller account of Tucker's life, theology and ministry, see C. Jeffrey Robinson, Sr., "The Pastoral Intent of the Writings of Henry Holcombe Tucker," PhD Dissertation, The Southern Baptist Theological Seminary, 2008.

ter moving to its permanent location in Fort Worth, Texas, in 1908. As Nettles points out, Carroll sought to build the seminary on the "rocks of predestination" and adhered "clearly and strongly to traditional Baptist Calvinism."[41]

In his monumental commentary on the English Bible, Carroll links the "golden chain of salvation" in Romans 8 to the believer's eternal security in Christ. God calls, regenerates, justifies, and sanctifies His elect who were chosen before the foundation of the world. Naturally, Carroll argues, since these doctrines apply to the sinner, perseverance is a logical consequence.[42] In linking the doctrines in the golden chain of salvation together, Carroll espouses a Calvinistic understanding of the decrees and purpose of God in election and predestination.

> And then the Spirit's covenant-obligations were to apply [Christ's] work of redemption in calling, convicting, regenerating, sanctifying and raising from the dead the seed promised to the Son, the whole of it showing that the plan of salvation was not an afterthought; that the roots of it in election and predestination are both in eternity before the world was, and the fruits of it are in eternity after the judgment. The believer is asked to consider this chain, test each link, shake it and hear it rattle, connected from eternity to eternity. Every one that God chose in Christ is drawn by the Spirit to Christ. Every one predestinated is called by the Spirit in time, and justified in time and will be glorified when the Lord comes.[43]

This is exceedingly good news, Carroll wrote, for the sinner, once he is acquitted of breaking God's law through Christ's sacrifice, will certainly run the race to the end. He concludes his discussion of Romans 8 with a section on the fifth point of the Calvinistic Tulip, perseverance of the saints. "No charge can be brought against a believer because it is God, the Supreme Judge, who has justified him. Justification is the verdict, or declaration, of the supreme court of heaven that in Christ the sinner is acquitted. This decision is rendered once for all, is inexorable and irreversible. It is registered in the book of life, and in the great judgment day that book will be the test book on the throne of judgment."[44]

In his exposition of Paul's glorious doxological excurses on election in Ephesians 1, Carroll articulates and heartily commends the Calvinistic understanding of election through a rapid-fire set of questions reminiscent of catechetical teaching: "Election—what is it? Abstractly it means choice.

[41] Nettles, *By His Grace and For His Glory*, 176–77.
[42] B.H. Carroll, *An Interpretation of the English Bible*, Vol. 5 (Cape Coral, FL: Founders Press, 2001), 171–73.
[43] Ibid., 172–73.
[44] Ibid., 173.

Concretely there may be an election of a nation, like Israel, for a national or typical purpose, but that is not what he is discussing here. He is discussing the election of individuals, or persons. When did this election take place? Before the world was. As it took place then, and as we were not existing then, in whom did it take place? We were elected in Christ. To what end were we elected? That we should be holy and without blemish in love."[45] As did most Southern Baptists of his day, Carroll obviously delighted in the doctrines of God's sovereign grace in Christ.

A Cloud of Additional Witnesses

The men whose theological commitments have been set forth above represent a small sampling of Southern Baptist leaders of the nineteenth century who clearly espoused Calvinism of either the four or five-point variety. Many other nineteenth century Baptists who either worked in the early SBC or were near forerunners of the denomination, taught, preached and wrote out of a thoroughgoing Calvinistic framework. All of these men were deeply aware of and were often personal friends with men that drifted into true hyper-Calvinism. All of them knew the foundational error that caused that phenomenon and did not over-react by pointing to historic confessional Calvinism as the problem. Instead they continued to assert their absolute dependence on divine mercy both for personal salvation and for any hope of success in the mandate of Christ, in whom all power resides, to go into all the world. These included noteworthy Baptist ministers and leaders such as Jesse Mercer, W. T Brantley, R.B. C. Howell, Luther Rice and Richard Fuller.

Luther Rice, for example, in addition to being the zealous promoter of missions and education among early nineteenth-century Baptists, was particularly noted for his superior and powerful doctrinal preaching. J. B. Taylor, who considered Rice as "one of the most interesting public speakers in our land," noted not only his power and eloquence in preaching but that the content centered on the "more sublime doctrines of our holy religion." Among these were "a lively apprehension of the doctrine of human depravity" initiated by the "fearful and utter ruin" of humanity in Adam's fall. He presented an "exceedingly impressive" picture of the "terribleness of Jehovah's wrath," and a commensurate dependence of the sinner on the "sovereignty of God," especially the "efficacious atonement of Jesus Christ" and the "necessity and power of the Spirit's operation." Taylor also remembered Rice's public prayers which never omitted "the most humiliating confessions of the exceeding sinfulness of sin, while he gloried in the freeness

[45] Carroll, *An Interpretation*, 6:77.

and sovereignty of that grace, which is treasured in Christ Jesus, and which is made effectual unto salvation by the indwelling of the Holy Spirit."[46] Rice's own testimony on this issue is so vitally one with the purpose of this volume that it justifies a lengthy quote.

> How many proofs have we of the truth of what God says: "That he will work, and none shall let it." The conduct of his providence is wonderful; it evinces his sovereignty and his inscrutable wisdom, as well as his boundless benevolence. In one place, we may behold the people deeply anxious about eternal concerns, while the inhabitants of neighboring places are wrapt up in careless, profound stupidity. Here a faithful minister of Christ preaches the gospel with clearness and energy, but apparently without success…; there, the people become anxious, even where the gospel is not preached in purity, or where the minister himself is opposed to an awakening…. What but the glorious sovereignty of Jehovah does all this evince? He will send by the hand of whom he will send. "He will have mercy on whom he will have mercy, and whom he will he hardeneth." He will bless his faithful servant, to whom he has committed only scanty abilities, rather that the man of eminent endowments, lest his hand should be overlooked, and the attention be directed to the creature, instead of the Creator… How absurd it is, therefore to contend against the doctrine of election, or decrees, or divine sovereignty.[47]

Rice went on to remind believers to be gentle with all men for only grace had removed the scales from their eyes to embrace the truth. Otherwise, like many friends and relatives, they too would be, "replying against God, rejecting his mercy, despising his truth, neglecting the Saviour, or stupidly unsolicitous about the welfare of our immortal souls. Oh! To grace how great a debtor."[48]

Mercer (1769–1841), a pastor, educator and journalist maintained a witness exemplary of this virtually unanimous commitment to evangelical Calvinism. Mercer founded Mercer University in Macon, Georgia, and pastored several churches. He also served as editor of *The Christian Index* newspaper in Georgia for many years. In his detailed study of Mercer's theology, Anthony L. Chute observes that the man whom Georgians called "Father Mercer" built his ministry upon a framework of "evangelistic Calvinism." That is to say, Mercer's theology was Calvinism deeply committed to the gospel missionary endeavor.[49] Mercer was a typical Baptist

[46] J. B. Taylor, *Memoir of the Rev. Luther Rice* (Baltimore, MD: Armstrong and Berry, 1840), 267–77.

[47] Ibid., 331–32.

[48] Ibid., 333.

[49] Anthony L. Chute, *A Piety Above Common Standard: Jesse Mercer and Evangelistic Calvinism* (Macon, GA: Mercer University, 2004), x–xi.

of his day in Georgia, Chute argues, because he was a Calvinist: "[Georgia Baptists] began to cooperate with one another through the formation of associations and soon discovered that there were significantly different viewpoints within their fellowship. They thus deemed it necessary to exclude several ministers who persistently promoted Arminian doctrine. They also included a Calvinistic confession of faith to define themselves with more precision."[50] When Southern Baptists have written confessions of faith, they have expressed the doctrines of old.

Unity With "All True Protestants": Confessions in the Reformed Tradition

In 1837, eight years before the birth of the Southern Baptist Convention, the junior editor of *The Christian Index* of Georgia urged "regular Baptists in America" to adopt a confession of faith in what he termed the "Old Tradition." The Baptist confessional tradition, in his view, was a descendant of one of church history's grandest and most famous statements of faith, the *Westminster Confession of Faith*. The editor pointed out that all the great Baptist confessions bore intimate kinship to the Westminster Standards with adjustments to reflect distinctive Baptist doctrines.[51] Before setting forth a model confession—beginning with a statement asserting the authority of Scripture—he argued for reasserting "Our Old Confession of Faith":

> The Baptists as a denomination have always regarded the Bible as being amply sufficient for all the purposes of faith and practice. But knowing that many persons, holding wild and visionary notions upon religious subjects, often use the same language, and say that they too, make the Bible their standard; and knowing that their views and practices, are often misunderstood and often misrepresented, our brethren have felt it important to get up certain briefs, or compends of their faith, so that their adoption of the Bible in general terms, might not seem to be a sort of shield for heterodox opinions, and that there might be a oneness of doctrine and practice among themselves. These summaries of faith have

---

[50] Ibid.

[51] Peculiarly Baptist emphases appeared in the Assembly Confession on the following subjects: the obligation to preach the Gospel in all ages and nations (new Chapter XX); the singing of "Hymns and Spiritual Songs" (added to the Westminster's injunction to sing Psalms XXII); disuse of the term "Sacrament" and of the Presbyterian definition of the sacraments (Chapter XXVII); and provision for lay preaching (Chapter XXVI:11). In addition, the characteristic Baptist emphasis on the Church is made by enlarging Chapter XXVI into nine detailed chapters (Lumpkin, *Baptist Confessions*, 238–239).

generally been taken from the Old Confession, published in England, first in 1643, and subsequently in 1689; adopted by the Philadelphia Association in 1742 and the Charleston in 1767.[52]

Fast forward to 1859 at the founding of The Southern Baptist Theological Seminary when Founding President James P. Boyce commissioned Basil Manly, Jr., to write a statement of faith that would establish clear confessional standards for the theology taught at the seminary. The result was the first confession produced by Southern Baptists, the *Abstract of Principles*, and, as R. Albert Mohler, Jr., the ninth president of the seminary, pointed out in his inaugural convocation address in August of 1993, Manly wrote an abstract of the Second London Confession of 1689. Manly's resultant confession clearly committed the new seminary to the doctrines of grace, doctrines which Boyce had learned from the Princeton divines and shared by Southern Baptists and other evangelical Reformed denominations. More than that, it spoke volumes about the theology of the nascent Southern Baptist Convention; after all, Southern was the first and only seminary established in those pre-Civil war days to serve Southern Baptists. In that opening convocation, which was a call for Southern to return to the confessionalism of Boyce, Mohler told convocation attendees that the seminary's theology stands in the stream of the Second London and Westminster confessions of faith.

> The younger Manly had also enjoyed a Princeton Seminary education... At Princeton, both Manly and Boyce had studied under the imposing figure of Samuel Miller, a stalwart defender of Presbyterian theological and ecclesiastical standards, who argued "The necessity and importance of creeds and confessions appears from the consideration that one great design of establishing a Church in our world was that she might be, in all ages, a depository, a guardian, and a witness of the truth." That same conviction drove Boyce, both Manlys, John A. Broadus, and those who deliberated with them, to propose an *Abstract of Principles* based upon the Second London Confession, which was itself a Baptist revision of the Westminster Confession.[53]

Mohler was merely recovering the confessional vision that Boyce, Broadus and Manly had established 144 years earlier in establishing Southern

---

[52] Jesse Mercer, "Our Old Confession of Faith," *The Georgia Christian Index*, 5 January, 1837, 10.

[53] R. Albert Mohler Jr., "Don't Just Do Something, Stand There," fall convocation address at The Southern Baptist Theological Seminary, available at http://www.albertmohler.com/1993/08/31/dont-just-do-something-stand-there/ accessed on January 15, 2012.

as a confessional institution. In expressing the content that would make up the confession, Boyce established three guidelines for the drafting of the abstract, all three centered upon the doctrines of grace, doctrines which typified the beliefs of Southern Baptists of the nineteenth century:

> The abstract of principles must be: 1. A complete exhibition of the fundamental doctrines of grace, so that in no essential particular should they speak dubiously; 2. They should speak out clearly and distinctly as to the practices universally prevalent among us; 3. Upon no point, upon which the denomination is divided, should the convention, and through it the seminary, take any position.... The doctrines of grace are therefore distinctly brought out in the abstract of principles. No less true is this of Baptist practices.... While, however, it was deemed essential to avow distinctly and unreservedly the sentiments universally prevalent among us, both as to doctrine and practice, it was equally important that upon those questions upon which there was still a difference of opinion among Southern Baptists, the seminary articles should not bind the institution.[54]

When the SBC was born in 1845, leaders concluded that no new confession of faith was needed because most individual churches and associations already had their own confessions, many of which were derivatives of the Second London Confession of 1689. The Abstract's Reformed commitments and kinship to its famous Particular Baptist predecessor is clear throughout. The confession begins with an article on Scripture, establishing the historic Baptist basis for epistemology and, after articles on God and the Trinity, under the heading of "Providence," sets forth the absolute sovereignty of God, a foundational tenet of historic Reformed theology: "God from eternity, decrees or permits all things that come to pass, and perpetually upholds, directs and governs all creatures and all events; yet so as not in any wise to be the author or approver of sin nor to destroy the free will and responsibility of intelligent creatures." The next two articles also follow the Second London Confession precisely in setting forth the doctrines of election and the fall and resultant total depravity of man. Manly's article on election is pithy but clearly establishes the historic Reformed position: "Election is God's eternal choice of some persons unto everlasting life-not because of foreseen merit in them, but of His mere mercy in Christ—in consequence of which choice they are called, justified and glorified."[55] Article eight establishes the classic Reformed priority of

---

[54] James P. Boyce, "The Two Objections to the Seminary, V," *The Christian Index*, 25 June 1874, 2, quoted in Wills, *Southern Baptist Theological Seminary 1859–2009*, 31.

[55] Ibid.

regeneration before faith, which follows two articles later. Manly articulated regeneration as "a change of heart, wrought by the Holy Spirit, who quickeneth the dead in trespasses and sins enlightening their minds spiritually and savingly to understand the Word of God, and renewing their whole nature, so that they love and practice holiness. It is a work of God's free and special grace alone."[56] The language is strikingly similar to that of chapter ten, paragraphs one and two, on effectual calling in the *Second London Confession*, a statement of faith modeled after and on many major doctrines identical to the Westminster standards.

Baptist historian Timothy George correctly argues that the ties between the Westminster standards and Baptist theology via the Second London Confession and its American cousin, the Philadelphia Confession, are undeniable.[57] "Among Baptists in America the theology of Westminster was transmitted through the Philadelphia Confession of Faith," he writes. "Despite a persistent Arminian strain within Baptist life, until the twentieth century most Baptists adhered faithfully to the doctrines of grace as set forth in the Pauline-Augustinian-Reformed theology."[58] Thus, Southern Seminary's confession, and the first confession written by Southern Baptists, was thoroughly Reformed in its theological trajectory. Southern Baptists as a denomination would not have to draw up a confession of faith until Darwinian evolution and related thought reared its head in the early twentieth century. When E. Y. Mullins and others wrote and published the *Baptist Faith & Message* at the 1925 meeting of the SBC, the framers drew heavily on a pithy summary of the doctrines of grace, the *New Hampshire Confession*.

New Hampshire Confession and the BF&M

The *Baptist Faith & Message*, the SBC's confession of faith since its adoption in 1925, is a modified version of the *New Hampshire Confession*.[59]

---

[56] Ibid.

[57] The Philadelphia Association—the first Baptist association on U.S. soil—adopted a confession that was virtually identical to the *Second London Confession* with the addition of articles on hymn-singing and the laying of hands upon baptized believers. Twenty-five years later in 1767, the Charleston Association in South Carolina adopted the *Philadelphia Confession*. Both associations served as major formative influences during their early years in America.

[58] Timothy George, "Baptists and the Westminster Confession," in *The Westminster Confession into the 21st Century: Essays in Remembrance of the 350th Anniversary of the Westminster Assembly*, Volume 1, ed., J. Ligon Duncan (Ross-shire, Scotland: Christian Focus, 2003), 155.

[59] Ten additional sections were added concerning the resurrection, the second

The *Baptist Faith & Message* has undergone two revisions, the first in 1963 at the hands of theological moderates, the last in 2000 by theological conservatives, the latter restoring it to its original conservative theological roots. The *New Hampshire Confession* was published by the Baptist Convention of New Hampshire in 1833 and later recommended to the churches for adoption.[60] A committee initially drew up the eighteen-article statement of faith and it was finalized by John Newton Brown. In 1853, Brown served as editorial secretary of the American Baptist Publication Society. On his own authority, that year, Brown revised the confession and published it in *The Baptist Church Manual*.[61] The rise of free-will Baptists late in the 18th century under the leadership of Benjamin Randall in New Hampshire prompted the convention to write a confession of faith that has been seen by some historians as articulating a milder form of Calvinism.[62]

The *New Hampshire Confession* expresses the fall of man in the third article, setting forth total depravity in vivid terms, with man "being by nature utterly void that that holiness required by the law of God, wholly given to the gratification of the world, of Satan, and of their own sinful passions, therefore under just condemnation to eternal ruin, without defense or excuse."[63] Article four sets forth the remedy, capturing the heart of Reformed soteriology in a crisply worded statement: "The salvation of sinners is wholly of grace."[64] Article seven places regeneration before faith, which appears in article eight and then article nine, "Of God's Purpose of Grace," establishes election as unconditional, an act in which God "graciously regenerates, sanctifies and saves sinners."[65] The articles in the *Baptist Faith & Message* expand on the sinfulness of man and salvation, but adopt the New Hampshire language on election virtually without revision. The *New Hampshire Confession* is much briefer than the *Second London*

coming of Christ, religious liberty, war and peace, education, social service, cooperation, evangelism and missions, stewardship, and the Kingdom of God. Additionally, the wording of Articles 7, 9, and 18 was considerably changed. Articles 12 and 16—Harmony of Law and Gospel and Civil Government, respectively—of the *New Hampshire Confession* were deleted.

[60] William L. Lumpkin, *Baptist Confessions of Faith* (Valley Forge, PA: Judson Press, 1969), 360.

[61] Ibid, 361.

[62] For a refutation of the view that the New Hampshire Confession sought to soften the Calvinistic theology held by a majority of American Baptists in that day, see Thomas J. Nettles, *By His Grace and for His Glory* (Grand Rapids, MI: Baker Books, 1986), 44–45.

[63] Lumpkin, *Baptist Confessions*, 362.

[64] Ibid.

[65] Ibid.

Confession and less expansive on the doctrines of grace than the *Abstract of Principles*, but establishes salvation by God's sovereign grace in an economy of words nonetheless.

Departure and Return

Southern Presbyterian divine James Henley Thornwell wrote that, "Where money is the great want, numbers must be sought; and where an ambition for numbers prevails, doctrinal purity must be sacrificed. The root of evil is the secular spirit of all our ecclesiastical institutions."[66] A drive for numbers among Southern Baptists sits at the heart of the loss of a robust confessional and Reformed theology. But it is certainly not the only factor.

The doctrines of grace held the theological franchise among Southern Baptists well into the twentieth century. The growth of revivalism, the rise of pragmatism as a means of denominational and local church growth and what Timothy George calls "a general theological laxity" all conspired, along with other factors, to set Southern Baptists adrift from their Calvinistic doctrinal roots. As George points out, three major controversial movements in the nineteenth century, Campbellism, Landmarkism and hyper-Calvinism also affected the reception of Reformed theology among Baptists in the South.[67] Campbellism, which rejected the use of creeds and confessions of faith altogether, loosened Southern Baptists' commitment to confessional Reformed theology, George argues, while Landmarkism led Baptists to prize ecclesiological distinctives at the expense of theological commitments, and hyper-Calvinism "took the form of a virulent anti-missionary, anti-evangelistic emphasis" that dried up churches and soured some in the SBC on Calvinism altogether."[68]

In the twentieth century, Reformed theology fell on hard times in the SBC. But in recent years, it is making a comeback, particularly among young Southern Baptist pastors and leaders. And while even the introduction of the doctrines of grace is controversial in some places in the SBC in 2012, there was no controversy over them at the denomination's beginning. Theological rediscovery of roots so fruitful in producing the godly stalwarts of Baptist life in the past should be a joyful experience like the discovery of valuable family gold coins feared lost forever. It certainly should not meet with anger at the discovery, disdain toward those that see their value, or resolute denial that such a family treasure ever existed. "Those coins belong

---

[66] James Henley Thornwell, *The Life and Letters of J. H. Thornwell*, B. M. Palmer, ed. (Edinburgh: Banner of Truth, 1974), 291.

[67] George, "Baptists and the Westminster Confession," 156–57.

[68] Ibid.

to someone else and can do us no good," is a most inappropriate response to the recovery of a valuable past that holds promise to enrich the future.

13

The Glorious Impact of Calvinism Upon Local Baptist Churches

Tom Hicks

Historic Calvinistic Baptists, or Particular Baptists, seamlessly integrated their Calvinism with orthodox Baptist ecclesiology.[1] Malcolm Yarnell, however, has expressed his concern that Calvinism may have a negative impact on the Baptist doctrine of the local church. Yarnell believes that Calvinism might lead to a blurred distinction between the Old and New Testament polities and practices of local churches, to the loss of religious tolerance and liberty, to a mixture of believers and unbelievers in church membership, to aristocratic elitism in church leadership, and to ecclesiological antinomianism that is lax about confessional subscription and church discipline.[2] But nothing about the Calvinist doctrine of salvation interferes with the Baptist doctrine of the church, and the historic picture shows that Calvinism and Calvinistic pastors and missionaries had a glorious impact upon the ecclesiology of local Baptist churches.

While Calvinism is broader than the five heads of the Canons of Dort (popularly termed the five points of Calvinism), consider how the five

---

[1] Early Calvinistic Baptists were called "Particular Baptists" because of their belief in a particular atonement, rather than a general atonement. They held that Christ died for a "particular" people, those whom God had chosen for salvation, and not for each individual in the world who has ever lived.

[2] See Malcolm B. Yarnell III, "The Potential Impact of Calvinist Tendencies upon Local Baptist Churches," in *Whosoever Will: A Biblical and Theological Critique of Five-Point Calvinism*, eds. David L. Allen and Steve W. Lemke (Nashville, TN: B&H, 2010), 213–32.

points of Calvinism are well-integrated with the Baptist doctrine of the local church.[3] Unconditional election and limited atonement imply that there is only one people of God, one universal church in both the Old and New Testaments (Romans 9:6–13; 11:11–24).[4] God's elect people are a single body for whom Christ died, to whom He sends the Holy Spirit, and who share in a common salvation. Historic Calvinists believed that elect of all ages are one universal church (Hebrews 12:23; Colossians 1:18).[5] But they also understood that the local church polity and practices under the

---

[3] The five points of Calvinism include: Total Depravity, Unconditional Election, Limited Atonement, Irresistible Grace, and Perseverance of the Saints. For excellent treatments of the "five points of Calvinism," see Edwin H. Palmer, *The Five Points of Calvinism: A Study Guide*, 3rd ed. (Grand Rapids, MI: Baker, 2010); David N. Steele, Curtis C. Thomas, S. Lance Quinn, *The Five Points of Calvinism: Defined, Defended and Documented*, 2nd ed., updated and expanded (Phillipsburg, NJ: P&R, 2004); Robert B. Selph, *Southern Baptists and the Doctrine of Election* (Harrisonburg, VA: Sprinkle, 1996); for the most extensive discussion of the "five points," see Loraine Boettner, *The Reformed Doctrine of Predestination* (Phillipsburg, NJ: P&R, 1991). For information on how the Calvinistic system extends well beyond the "five points" and is a positive statement of the whole Bible's teaching about theology and all of life, see Kenneth J. Stewart, *Ten Myths About Calvinism: Recovering the Breadth of the Reformed Tradition* (Downers Grove, IL: IVP, 2011), and Joel R. Beeke, *Living for God's Glory: An Introduction to Calvinism* (Lake Mary, FL: Reformation Trust, 2008).

[4] Dispensationalism wrongly teaches that God has two peoples, Israel and the church, and that He has a different program for each. Dispensationalist theologian, Charles Ryrie, notes that the primary *sine qua non* of dispensational theology is that "[a] dispensationalist keeps Israel and the church distinct." Charles C. Ryrie, *Dispensationalism*, rev. and exp. (Chicago, IL: Moody, 2007), 46. Baptist theologian James Leo Garret correctly notes that dispensationalism is an "incursion" into Baptist theology, which only emerged in the last 150 years or so. James Leo Garrett, *Baptist Theology: A Four-Century Study* (Macon, GA: Mercer, 2009), 560–70.

[5] Contrary to Dispensationalism and Landmarkism, the Calvinistic Second London Baptist Confession of 1677/1689 (Chapter 10, Paragraph 1) affirms the existence of the universal church as follows: "The catholic or universal church, which (with respect to internal work of the Spirit, and truth of grace) may be called invisible, consists of the whole number of the elect, that have been, are, or shall be gathered into one, under Christ the head thereof; and is the spouse, the body, the fulness of Him that fills all in all." See William L. Lumpkin, *Baptist Confessions of Faith* (Valley Forge: PA, Judson, 1969), 285. The First London Confession of 1644 (Chapter 33) likewise declares, "That Christ has here on earth a spiritual kingdom, which is the Church, which He has purchased and redeemed to Himself as a particular inheritance, which Church, as it is visible to us, is a company of visible saints." Lumpkin, *Baptist Confessions*, 165.

old covenant were different from those under the new covenant. Christ's historic atonement for His chosen people divides redemptive history into two main parts and results in a distinction between two different church polities in the old and new covenants. Under the old covenant, the church had received promises and prophecies and was required to perform sacrifices and circumcision in a national church structure, but now that Christ has come, the old covenant shadows have been fulfilled and the structure and polity of the local church has changed under its new covenant administration (Ephesians 2:11–21).

The doctrines of total depravity and irresistible grace imply something about the nature of preaching, the composition of the local church, the government of the local church, and liberty of conscience. Consider their impact on preaching. Since God irresistibly calls the elect to salvation through His Word, the preacher is not to tamper with the Word of God or seek to manipulate people into making professions of faith (2 Corinthian 4:1–6), but ought to proclaim the gospel clearly and boldly with love to God and love to men. The preacher may be confident that the elect will respond to faithful preaching (2 Timothy 2:10; 1 Corinthians 1:23–24) because God will irresistibly draw His elect people to salvation in Christ through the clear and faithful proclamation of God's Word.

Irresistible grace is also theologically integrated with the composition of the local church. Local churches should be composed of regenerate members (Roman 1:7; 1 Corinthians 1:2; 1 Peter 1:1–2), and God's irresistible grace produces regeneration and conversion (John 6:45; 1 Peter 2:9–10). The local church should not merely be composed of those who have "made decisions for Christ" or "prayed a sinner's prayer," but of those who have been effectually called from the heart to salvation. Church rolls ought to be composed of those who trust and love Christ and keep His good commandments because their hearts have been transformed by the Holy Spirit.

God's sovereign and irresistible grace is also the basis of congregational government in the local church. Because God irresistibly changes the hearts of all His people, there is no need for a ruling elite or pastoral aristocracy since whole congregations of those whose hearts have been irresistibly drawn to Christ may be trusted to make wise decisions on the most important matters of church life (2 Corinthians 2:6–8). The doctrine of irresistible grace promotes deep humility between pastors and congregations because both know that any wisdom and goodness they have comes from God's grace alone (1 Corinthians 15:10; 4:7) and does not arise naturally from themselves (John 3:27). Irresistible grace promotes patience and perseverance in pastors because it helps them to understand that God alone sanctifies His people in His time and by His appointed means, and that no amount of pastoral authority, administrative savvy, effective programming, or manipulation can speed up God's hand (1 Corinthians 3:5–9). Pastors who understand irresistible grace will faithfully discharge their biblical responsibilities without losing heart, and they will feel free to leave the results of their obedience to God (2 Corinthians 4:1–6). Churches composed of irresistibly drawn believers will also be well-equipped to choose wise pastors and will humbly follow their pastoral leadership, recognizing them as gracious gifts of God (Hebrews 13:7, 17).

Irresistible grace is also tightly tied to liberty of conscience and religious liberty. God alone irresistibly calls human beings to salvation; therefore, they cannot be saved at the point of a gun or through government programs or legislation (John 18:36). Total depravity teaches that human beings do not have the moral freedom to choose Christ (John 6:44; Romans 3:10–12); therefore, government coercion cannot bring men to salvation. So, irresistible grace is the foundation of Calvinistic Baptists' doctrine of liberty of conscience, which teaches that God alone is the Lord of conscience, and the government cannot and must not coerce the human conscience (Acts 5:29). Earthly governments are established by God's sovereign decree and must be obeyed in all things lawful (Romans 13:1), but they do not have the right or power to compel belief in Christ.

The fifth point of Calvinism, the perseverance of the saints, helps to explain church discipline. Perseverance teaches that God not only graciously forgives elect believers and imputes Christ's righteousness to them, but He also graciously makes them more and more holy after the likeness of Christ (2 Thessalonians 2:13), such that they will never completely or finally fall away from Him, but always continue to fight the fight of faith, pressing on into holiness. That means there is no such thing as a Christian who has made a "decision for Christ" but subsequently freely chooses to live a godless life. Rather, when God effectually calls the elect to Christ, He also graciously shapes their wills to produce the fruit of faithful obedience in them (John 15:16; 1 Corinthians 15:10; Philippians 2:12–13). The doctrine of perseverance further shows how church discipline is not a species of legalism. Church discipline is not about requiring people to conform slavishly to God's standards (Romans 8:15); rather, it identifies God's people as those who persevere in obedience because God graciously preserves them (1 Peter 1:5) and causes them to bear fruit (Romans 15:16). While perseverance engages human work, it can only take place due to an act of God's free and unconditional grace that preserves the believer.

The thesis of this chapter is that *Calvinism has had a glorious impact on the polity and practices of local Baptist churches*. Far from tempting Baptists to slide into ecclesiological error, Calvinism has served to support, strengthen, and advance robust Baptist ecclesiology throughout history.

The following chapter will examine several historic Calvinistic Baptist ministers and will demonstrate their commitment to the orthodox Baptist doctrine of the church.

Benjamin Keach (1640–1704)

Consider the ecclesiology of English Particular Baptist pastor, Benjamin Keach. Keach was not only a pastor, he was also arguably the greatest second generation Baptist theologian.[6] He was raised in a poor home and initially trained to be a tailor. He was converted at age fifteen under the preaching of the Anglican Matthew Mead and became energized with an unrelenting zeal for Christ that would characterize him until his dying day. Keach soon showed that he was a gifted Bible teacher and preacher. After he turned eighteen, God called him into pastoral ministry, and he served in that capacity until he died.[7]

Benjamin Keach's Journey into Calvinism

Though Keach began his life in Christ as a General Baptist who believed in free will and a general atonement, his personal study of Scripture and discussions with godly men convinced him to change his opinions and become a Particular Baptist. According to William Cathcart, "at first he was an Arminian about the extent of the atonement and free will, but the reading of the Scriptures and the conversation of those who knew the will of God more perfectly relieved him from both errors."[8] Keach renounced

---

[6] During his ministry, Keach penned over 43 distinct works, including study aids, sermons, allegories, theological treatises, polemical works, and writings on personal piety. He was a relentless defender of the truth, writing in support of justification by faith alone, religious liberty, believer's baptism, congregational hymn singing, the Sunday Sabbath, and against Quakerism and Romanism. Austin Walker rightly notes that Keach "became the foremost theologian of the Particular Baptists and one of their acknowledged leaders." Austin Walker, *The Excellent Benjamin Keach* (Dundas, ON, Canada: Joshua Press, 2004), 29.

[7] For additional biographical information about Benjamin Keach, see Michael A. G. Haykin, *Kiffin, Knollys, Keach: Rediscovering Our English Baptist Heritage* (Leeds: Reformation Today Trust, 1996), 82–103; Thomas J. Nettles, *The Baptists: Key People Involved in Forming a Baptist Identity* (Fearn, Scotland: Mentor, 2005), 1:163–93; James Barry Vaughn, "Benjamin Keach," in *Baptist Theologians*, ed. Timothy George and David Dockery (Nashville, TN: Broadman Press, 1990), 49–76; Austin Walker, *The Excellent Benjamin Keach* (Dundas, Ontario: Joshua Press, 2004).

[8] *The Baptist Encyclopedia* (Philadelphia, PA: Louis H. Everts, 1881), 637–38.

Arminianism and fervently retained Calvinism throughout the remainder of his life.

His change to Calvinistic theology came around the time of his move from the Winslow church to the Southwark church, which met on Tooley Street in London just off the Thames River.[9] When he arrived at Southwark, Keach became good friends with two Particular Baptists: Hanserd Knollys and William Kiffin. Some historians believe these two men were instrumental in his conversion from Arminianism to Calvinism.[10] According to Crosby, Keach became a Calvinist by "consulting both men and books," but Crosby does not tell us which "men" or which "books" influenced him.[11] What is known for sure is that Benjamin Keach began teaching and preaching Calvinistic theology during his ministry at Southwark. The effect of this change on the local church is not absolutely clear, but some say that his preaching split the church. Austin Walker explains, "It is not clear precisely what happened to the congregation [at Southwark] when Keach became a Particular Baptist. It is possible he persuaded the majority of them of the truth he had now come to believe, though Whitley says he split the church."[12] Whatever happened, the historical records demonstrate that the Southwark congregation came to flourish under Keach's ministry. When he first accepted the call to Southwark, the congregation was very small, but as he labored in the ministry, the church grew until

---

[9] There is some disagreement about exactly when Keach became a Calvinist. Tom Nettles represents the majority opinion when he states, "A move to London provided contact with the Particular Baptists, opportunity for study, and brought about his adoption of the Calvinist stance of the Particular Baptists." Thomas J. Nettles, "Benjamin Keach (1640–1704)," in *The British Particular Baptists 1638–1910*, ed. Michael A. G. Haykin (Springfield, MO: Particular Baptist Press, 1998), 1:97. On this view, Keach was a General Baptist when he moved to London, but then converted to Calvinism through study and interactions with the London Particular Baptists. A dissenting perspective holds that Keach became a Calvinist while still pastoring the church at Winslow, and he arrived at Southwark already a Calvinist. David Copeland writes, "Keach probably was a Particular [Baptist] at heart by 1668 when he accepted the Southwark pastorate." David A. Copeland, *Benjamin Keach and the Development of Baptist Traditions in Seventeenth-Century England* (Lewiston, NY: The Edwin Mellen Press, 2001), 34. Though the historical data is inconclusive, I am inclined to agree with the majority opinion.

[10] Walker, *The Excellent Benjamin Keach*, 99–100.

[11] Thomas Crosby, *The History of the English Baptists from the Reformation to the Beginning of the Reign of King George I* (London: n.p, 1740; reprint, Paris: AR, The Baptist Standard Bearer), 4:271.

[12] Walker, *The Excellent Benjamin Keach*, 103.

it needed to move to a larger building at Horse-lie-down, where it came to have nearly one thousand members.[13]

Never mincing words, Keach wrote clearly about his Calvinistic convictions. In *Gospel Mysteries Unveiled or Exposition of the Parables*, published only a few years before he died, Keach commented on Matthew 20:14–16, "Take what belongs to you and go. I choose to give to this last worker as I gave to you. Am I not allowed to do what I choose with what belongs to me? Or do you begrudge my generosity? So, the last will be first and the first last." In commenting on this verse, Keach's strong Calvinism is clearly displayed. "Election is an act of God's sovereignty, or the good pleasure of His will; for which He passed by the fallen angels, and only sets His heart upon, and chooses some of the lost sons of Adam. Election necessarily pre-supposes some chosen, and the rest passed by."[14] He went on to write, "Election is wholly bottomed upon God's sovereign grace, because whatsoever is supposed (by our opponents) to be the condition of it, lies under God's decree to give His Spirit to His elect, to renew them, to sanctify them, and His grace, particularly faith to believe, and strength to persevere."[15] Thus, pastor Keach clearly believed that election is eternal, free, unconditional, and effectual, and that all other saving graces in God's people, including regeneration, faith, and persevering faithfulness, necessarily flow out of God's gracious unconditional election.

Keach was not only a proponent of a Calvinistic doctrine of salvation, but he was also deeply committed to orthodox Baptist ecclesiology. It never occurred to Keach that his Calvinism might be in conflict with his Baptist ecclesiology; rather, he believed the two truths to dovetail in perfect harmony.

The Universal Church and Particular Congregations

Keach believed that God's people compose one universal church, but that they are to be gathered into local churches. He wrote, "In the universal Church are many particular congregations or communities of Christians."[16] He further said, "[T]he universal or invisible church cannot be removed or taken away."[17] Keach taught the existence of both the universal

---

[13] Copeland, *Benjamin Keach*, 59.

[14] Benjamin Keach, *Exposition of the Parables and Express Similitudes of Our Lord and Savior Jesus Christ* (1701; reprint, Grand Rapids, MI: Kregel, 1974), 537.

[15] Ibid., 538.

[16] Benjamin Keach, *Preaching from the Types and Metaphors of the Bible* (Grand Rapids, MI: Kregel, 1972), 687.

[17] Keach, *Exposition of the Parables*, 496.

church and local churches, holding that these truths harmonize with one another, all the while distinguishing between them.

Though Keach believed in a universal church, he also believed that the form of its local expression is markedly different in the Old and New Testaments. He wrote, "The Jews had the kingdom of God with them; but at last it was utterly taken away from them; they lost it, and are without it to this day; they were God's visible church; they had all the legal ordinances and statutes committed to them... [but] its standing was expired, and that could not abide longer (it being a typical church) when the anti-type was come, that ceased."[18] In another place, he explained:

> The Church-State of the Jews, or that under the Old-Testament, quite differs from the Gospel-Church State; the Jewish-Church-Constitution was National, the whole Nation of the Jews; and every individual Person that proceeded from Abraham's Loins, were admitted as Members of that Church under the Law, or in Times of the Old-Testament, and therefore his Infant-Seed were and might be admitted members thereof. But in the Times of the Gospel, the Church is not National, but Congregational. Show us what whole Nation or People, none excepted, were by Christ's Appointment constituted as a Gospel-Church, as the People of Israel or Jewish Nation were... [But] Gospel-Churches... consisted of none but of such who professed Faith and Regeneration... and consisted of no other but such who were called, or did profess faith in Jesus Christ.[19]

Therefore, Keach understood the unity and diversity of the people of God. He taught that there is only one universal church, stretching across all periods of redemptive history, but he also taught that the Jewish church, along with its structure and polity, has now ceased in Christ. Christ came and instituted a new structure and polity for Gospel churches under the new covenant. New covenant church structure, defined by New Testament revelation, is different from and better than old covenant church structure, though there is but one universal church.

Since Keach carefully distinguished between the visible churches of the Old and New Testaments, he avoided the Paedobaptist doctrines of infant baptism and church-state synthesis. He skillfully defended the doctrine of believers baptism and the new covenant separation of church and state in works such as *Pedo-baptism disproved* (1691), *The Rector Rectified and Corrected: or Infant-Baptism unlawful* (1692), and *The ax laid to the root:*

---

[18] Ibid., 496–97.
[19] Benjamin Keach, *The Rector Rectified and Corrected: or Infant-Baptism unlawful* (London: n.p., 1692), 19.

or, One more blow at the foundation of infant baptism and church membership (1693).

He argued for believer's baptism over against paedobaptism in *The ax laid to the root*. Paedobaptists argued for the baptism of infants on the basis of the unity of the covenant of grace. They said that since there is only one covenant of grace in the Old and New Testaments, and since infants were included in the covenant of grace under the Old Testament administration, they must also be included under the New Testament administration. To counter this argument, Keach taught that though there is only one covenant of grace since the fall (Genesis 3:15), the Abrahamic covenant was not the covenant of grace, but instead was a temporary external covenant made with the Jewish church, until Christ, the seed of Abraham, should come from them. Keach said, "That Covenant that was made with, or did of Right belong unto the fleshly Seed of Abraham, as such, even to ungodly Ones, as well as to the godly, was not the Covenant of Grace; but the Covenant or Law of Circumcision, was made with, or did of Right belong unto the Fleshly Seed of Abraham… Therefore the Covenant of Circumcision was not the Covenant of Grace."[20] Because the Abrahamic covenant of circumcision is fulfilled and abrogated in Christ (Hebrews 8:13), Keach argued, there is no biblical warrant to include infants in the Gospel church, nor is there any warrant to apply the new covenant sign of baptism to infants.

Keach also argued for the separation of church and state and religious liberty in the new covenant and against theocracy and religious persecution. In *Distressed Zion Relieved*, he condemned the Roman Catholic Church for confounding principles of the Jewish church with the Gospel church. He declared that "[Rome] has made void the Laws and Constitutions of the Gospel; making the Church National, and forming whole Kingdoms into one Universal Church… You have been guilty of shedding a mighty mass of innocent Blood, by cutting off Millions of Men, Women and Children without cause, and many other unspeakable Enormities have you committed."[21] Keach abhorred the idea of a national church in the New Testament administration. He believed that national churches lead inevitably to the pollution of local church purity and to the persecution of true believers.

Keach's doctrine of unconditional election corresponds to his doctrine of the universal church of all ages. But, his doctrine of a historically realized limited atonement that divides history into two parts corresponds to

---

[20] Benjamin Keach, *The ax laid to the root: or, One more blow at the foundation of infant baptism and church membership* (London: n.p., 1693), 20
[21] Benjamin Keach, *Distressed Zion Relieved* (London: n.p., 1689), 149.

the distinction between type and antitype, between shadow and reality, between the Jewish church and the Gospel church. Thus, Keach, a Calvinistic Baptist pastor-theologian, had a well-developed understanding of how the universal church relates to particular congregations, such that his orthodox Baptist ecclesiology was both preserved and advanced.

The Responsibilities of Pastors and Local Congregations

In *The Glory of a True Church, and Its Discipline Displayed*, Keach described the relationship between pastors and their congregations. Far from advocating any kind of aristocratic elitism among pastors within churches, Keach outlined the biblical responsibilities of pastors and congregations, carefully dividing their mutual obligations and urging deep humility and trust between them.

He listed five areas of pastoral responsibility. First, "[t]he work of a Pastor is to preach the Word of Christ, or to feed the flock, and to administer all the ordinances of the gospel which belong to his sacred office, and to be faithful and laborious therein, studying to show himself approved to God."[22] Second, "[a] pastor is to visit his flock, to know their state, and to watch over them."[23] Third, he should "pray for them at all times, and with them also when sent for and desired, and as opportunity serves; and to sympathize with them in every state and condition, with all love and compassion."[24] Fourth, he ought to be "a good example in conversation, charity, faith and purity"[25] Fifth, a pastor must lead with "impartiality, not preferring the rich above the poor, not lord it over God's heritage, nor assume any greater power than God has given him; but to show a humble and meek spirit, nay to be clothed with humility."[26]

Though a pastor is charged with leading and instructing the congregation, Keach taught that the weightiest decisions in church life are to be made by the congregation, not the pastor. Some of those decisions include choosing whether to call a pastor and what to pay him, deciding which candidates to admit into church membership, and voting to exclude members as an act of church discipline. Keach taught that the congregation is to choose its pastors and support them financially. He said that a pastor is "ordained pastor or elder of that particular church that chose him."[27]

---

[22] Benjamin Keach, *The Glory of a True Church, and Its Discipline Displayed* (London: n.p., 1697), 8–9.
[23] Ibid., 9.
[24] Ibid., 10.
[25] Ibid.
[26] Ibid.
[27] Ibid., 16.

On the question of pastoral pay, Keach said that churches have a "duty to provide a comfortable maintenance for them and their families, suitable to their state and condition."[28]

Regarding admission to church membership, Keach wrote, "The person must give an account of his faith; and of the work of grace upon his soul before the church... when the majority [of the church] are satisfied, and yet one or two persons are not, the church and elder will do well to wait a little time, and endeavor to satisfy such persons, especially if the reasons of their difference seem weighty."[29] The whole church was to hear the testimonies of applicants for membership. After hearing them, the church as a whole was to vote on each candidate.

Regarding church discipline, Keach believed that the decision to excommunicate a sinning member is the responsibility of the church as a whole, not the pastor of the church. He wrote, it "appears to me from Mat. 18. 'If he will not hear the church,' it is not said, 'if he will not hear the elder, or elders.' As also that of the apostle, in directing the church to cast out the incestuous person, he does not give this counsel to the elder or elders of the church, but to the church; so he commands the church to withdraw from every brother that walks disorderly. 'Purge out the old leaven, that you may be a new lump' [1 Corinthians 5:7]."[30]

Thus, Keach was far from advocating any form of pastoral aristocracy, which usurps the responsibilities God has given to the church. He was a congregationalist. He believed that pastors are to lead with strength and authority in their teaching ministry and that the congregation should follow biblical pastoral leadership. But congregations of effectually called, regenerate church members are entrusted with the responsibility of making the weightiest decisions in the church under the leadership of their pastors.

Andrew Fuller (1754–1815)

Andrew Fuller was another English Particular Baptist who had much to say about orthodox Baptist ecclesiology. He was born to Particular Baptist parents in the Fenland village of Wicken in February of 1754 and grew up in the little farming community of Soham, Cambridgeshire, where his family attended a Particular Baptist church.

Fuller said, "My father and mother were Dissenters, of the Calvinistic persuasion, who were in the habit of hearing Mr. [John] Eve, a Baptist minister, who being what is here termed 'high' in his sentiments, or tinged

[28] Ibid., 14.
[29] Ibid., 17–18.
[30] Ibid., 21.

with false Calvinism, had little or nothing to say to the unconverted."[31]
Eve did not make direct appeals to the lost to call them to salvation, but
instead taught that they must look for a warrant to believe within themselves before coming to Christ. In his childhood, Fuller confessed to be a
sinner who lied, cursed, and swore. But, in the midst of all his sin, Fuller's
conscience was often heavily weighed down with feelings of guilt and fear.
When he grew into a youth, he came into contact with Bunyan's *Grace
Abounding to the Chief of Sinners* and *Pilgrim's Progress* along with Ralph
Erskine's *Gospel Sonnets* and *A Gospel Catechism for Young Christians*, which
call on all sinners to come to Christ for free and gracious salvation. Fuller
read these books with tears in his eyes, but his heart never changed, and
he wrongly waited for an internal warrant from God to believe in Christ.
When he finally came to realize that every sinner has an external warrant
to believe in the Word of the Christ, he gratefully wrote:

> I well remember that I felt something attracting in the Savior. I must – I
> will – yes, I will trust my soul – my sinful, lost soul in His hands. If I
> perish, I perish. However, it was, I was determined to cast myself upon
> Christ, thinking peradventure, He would save my soul; and if not, I could
> but be lost. In this way I continued above an hour, weeping and suppli-
> cating mercy for the Savior's sake: (my soul has it still in remembrance,
> and is humbled in me!) and as the eye of the mind was more and more
> fixed upon Him, my guilt and fears were gradually and insensibly re-
> moved. I now found rest for my troubled soul; and I reckon that I should
> have found it sooner, if I had not entertained the notion of my having no
> warrant to come to Christ without some previous qualification.[32]

After Fuller understood that Christ is freely offered to everyone in the
Word of God, he cast himself upon Jesus and finally found rest for his
troubled soul.[33]

---

[31] John Ryland, Jr., *The Life and Death of the Reverend Andrew Fuller* (London:
Button and Son, 1816), 17.

[32] Ibid., 29–30.

[33] For more biographical information on Andrew Fuller, see Ryland, *The
Life and Death of the Reverend Andrew Fuller*; Gilbert S. Laws, *Andrew Fuller:
Pastor, Theologian, Ropeholder* (London: Carey Press, 1942); Thomas J. Nettles,
*By His Grace And For His Glory: A Historical, Theological, and Practical Study of
the Doctrines of Grace in Baptist Life*, rev. and exp. (Cape Coral, FL: Founders,
2006), 55–77; Thomas J. Nettles, "Andrew Fuller" in *The British Particular Bap-
tists 1638–1910*, ed. Michael A. G. Haykin (Springfield, MO: Particular Baptist
Press, 2000), 2:97–141.

Andrew Fuller's "Strict" Calvinism

Though Fuller rightly cast off the High Calvinism of his youth, he never departed the least bit from the orthodox Calvinism of previous generations. Fuller declared, "My change of views on these subjects never abated my zeal for the doctrine of salvation by grace, but in some respects increased it. I never had any predilection for Arminianism, which appeared to me to ascribe the difference between one sinner and another, not to the grace of God, but to the good improvement made of grace given us in common with others."[34] In one correspondence, Mr. Richardson asked Fuller, "And what [is] a strict Calvinist?" Fuller replied, "One that really holds the system of Calvin. I do not believe everything that Calvin taught, nor anything because he taught it; but I reckon strict Calvinism to be my own system."[35]

Fuller made his convictions on the doctrine of unconditional election clear. "The doctrine of free or unconditional election may be clearly demonstrated and proved to be a dictate of right reason. If men be utterly depraved, they lie entirely at the discretion of God either to save or not to save them. If any are saved, it must be by an act of free grace."[36] Thus, Fuller helpfully called Baptists away from High Calvinism, which he did not even regard to be worthy of the name "Calvinism," but he never stopped insisting on strict orthodox Calvinism.[37]

[34] Andrew Fuller, *The Complete Works of the Rev. Andrew Fuller* (1801; reprint, Harrisonburg, VA: Sprinkle, 1988), 1:16.

[35] Ibid., 1:77.

[36] Ibid., 2:675.

[37] Interestingly, High Calvinism's (or Hyper-Calvinism's) fundamental defect has more in common with Arminianism than it does with genuine Calvinism. Both Arminians and Hyper-Calvinists accept the premise that if God issues a commandment, then human beings must have the ability to obey that commandment. Arminians conclude from this that since God commands all to believe, all must be able to believe. Hyper-Calvinists, on the other hand, conclude from this same notion that since the unconverted are not able to believe, God must not command them to believe. Orthodox Calvinists deny the premise that God's commands imply an ability to keep them. True Calvinism asserts that God commands all men everywhere to believe, and insists that all men are responsible to believe, but also says that none is able to believe apart from His irresistible grace. True Calvinism follows Augustine, who prayed, "Give [me] what You command, and command [me to do] what you will." Augustine, "On the Gift of Perseverance," in *Nicene and Post-Nicene Fathers*, eds. Alexander Roberts, James Donaldson, Philip Schaff, and Henry Wace, 1st ser., 14 vols (Peabody, MA: Hendrickson, 1994), 5:547. The notion that divine commands automatically imply that human beings have an ability to obey them is a pillar of Pelagianism.

Against Antinomianism and Lax Ecclesiology

Andrew Fuller is often remembered for his helpful arguments against High Calvinism and for global missions in his important work, *The Gospel Worthy of All Acceptation*. But Fuller also wrote against all forms of antinomianism and in favor of robust Baptist ecclesiology. Though he was a strict Calvinist by his own confession, Fuller was also a strong advocate of pure local Baptist churches, regenerate church membership, and the faithful practice of church discipline.

To show that true Calvinism does not produce a lax spirit in the moral conduct of the believer either within or without the local church, consider Fuller's clear arguments against antinomianism. He wrote:

> First, this doctrine [of antinomianism] directly militates against all those Scriptures which speak in favor of the moral law, and afford us an honorable idea of it; such as the following: — 'O how I love Your law!' — 'The law is holy, and the commandment is holy, just and good.' — I come not to destroy the law, but to fulfill it.' — 'Do we make void the law through faith? God forbid: yea, we establish the law.' — 'I delight in the law of God after the inner man.' — 'I with my mind serve the law of God.' Secondly, this doctrine reflects upon God Himself for having given a law under one dispensation which is at variance with a gospel given under another. Thirdly, it justifies the sinner in the breach of the law. There can be no evil in sin, but in proportion to the goodness of that law of which it is a transgression. Fourthly, it is in direct opposition to the life and death of the Savior. By the former, he obeyed its precepts, by the latter endured its penalty, and by both declared it to be holy, just, and good. Every reflection, therefore, upon the moral law is a reflection upon Christ. Fifthly, it strikes at the root of all personal religion, and opens the flood-gates to iniquity. Those who imbibe this doctrine talk of being sanctified in Christ, in such a manner as to supersede all personal and progressive sanctification in the believer.[38]

Thus, Fuller set himself in opposition to the antinomian spirit, believing it to be contrary to Scripture, the gospel, and growth in grace.

Fuller not only opposed antinomianism at the individual level, but he also opposed antinomianism at the church level. He held that God lovingly prescribed a pattern of doctrine and practice that local churches are required to believe and obey. He advocated strong confessions of faith in local churches, regenerate church membership, and the practice of church discipline. On the necessity of creeds, Fuller wrote:

---

[38] Fuller, *The Complete Works*, 2:661–62.

The man who has no creed has no belief; which is the same thing as being an unbeliever; and he whose belief is not formed into a system has only a few loose, unconnected thoughts, without entering into the harmony and glory of the gospel. Every well-informed and consistent believer, therefore, must have a creed – a system which he supposes to contain the leading principles of Divine revelation.[39]

It is not enough for believers to embrace a collection of doctrines. Rather, they must hold to the coherent system of biblical truth as a whole. Fuller was no doctrinal minimalist, and would not agree with those who taught that an understanding of the basics of the faith was sufficient for healthy Christianity. Instead, he believed that healthy Christians should understand the whole Bible systematically.

Yet Fuller did not content himself to argue for the need for creeds among individual Christians. He further taught that local churches have the right and obligation to draw up and enforce coherent and thorough confessions of faith among their memberships. He argued that it is no infringement upon Christian liberty to require confessional subscription from individual Christians. Fuller explained:

It may be pleaded that the objection does not lie so much against our having creeds or systems as against our imposing them on others as the condition of Christian fellowship. If, indeed, a subscription to articles of faith were required without examination, or enforced by civil penalties, it would be an unwarrantable imposition on the rights of conscience; but if an explicit agreement in what may be deemed fundamental principles be judged essential to fellowship, this is only requiring that a man appear to be a Christian before he can have a right to be treated as such.... If Christ has given both doctrines and precepts, some of which are more immediately addressed to Christians in their social capacity, they must not only possess such a right [to form and enforce creeds], but are under obligation to exercise it.[40]

For Fuller, the fundamental principles of the faith extend beyond the basics of the gospel to include the total system of biblical theology in summary form. Fuller taught that churches should be confessional churches and that their memberships ought to subscribe to confessions that summarize the whole counsel of God.

Fuller not only believed strongly in confessional subscription, but he also believed in regenerate church membership. Local church membership is not to be composed of believers and unbelievers, but of believers only.

[39] Fuller, *The Complete Works*, 3:449.
[40] Ibid., 3:449–50.

Fuller wrote:

> The principles, moreover, on which the Corinthians were forbidden to
> commune with unbelievers in theory, equally forbid our communing
> with unbelievers in practice. There can be no Christian communion in
> the one case, any more than in the other. 'Light and darkness, righteous-
> ness and unrighteousness,' are as impossible to unite here as there; and a
> separation from the world is as impracticable in the latter case as in the
> former.[41]

Fuller was by no means lax in his insistence on regenerate church
membership as the only right form of church order. He did not believe
that unbelievers and believers should be allowed to covenant together in
a local church; rather, he taught that local churches ought to be separate
from the world.

In a letter to Mr. M'Lean, Fuller went on approvingly to describe how
his friend and disciple, William Carey, also a Calvinistic Baptist, came to
an older church, which had become loose in the practice of church discipline. Fuller wrote:

> Carey, for example, when he went to Leicester, found them a very corrupt
> people. The very officers of the church had indulged in drunkenness, and
> the rest were discouraged; and so discipline was wholly neglected. After
> advising with his brethren in the ministry, brother Carey, and the major-
> ity of the church agreed to renew covenant.... – That they would in future
> execute and be subject to a strict and faithful discipline.
>
> This measure had its effect. Almost all their loose characters stood
> out; or, if any signed, they were subject to a close watch in future. By
> these means the church was purged; and Carey, before he went to India,
> saw the good effects of it. A considerable revival in religion ensued, and
> many were added.[42]

Thus, Andrew Fuller, a strict Calvinistic Baptist, opposed antinomianism
in all its forms, including ecclesiological antinomianism, though he also
loved the doctrines of grace. He believed that local churches should adopt
and enforce confessions of faith, or creeds, which contain whole systems
of doctrine. He also believed that local churches should faithfully practice church discipline. Fuller's Calvinism in no way discouraged obedience
to the Scriptures within the local church. Rather, his understanding of
God's irresistible grace and the preserving influence of the Holy Spirit was
wholly consistent with his Baptist confessionalism and practice of church
discipline.

[41] Ibid., 3:472.
[42] Ibid. 3:479.

William Carey (1761–1834)

William Carey, an English Particular Baptist, and the "Father of Modern Missions," built his mission work on warm evangelical Calvinism and Baptist ecclesiology. He went to the mission field because he believed that God powerfully conquers the depraved hearts of stubborn sinners. That truth sustained him through the trials that awaited him in India. Carey believed that church planting is a missionary's primary task. He understood that churches are not established by political power and that they do not grow by infant baptism, but that local churches are founded and expanded only by preaching the gospel of Jesus Christ and God's sovereign salvation of sinners.

Carey was born to Anglican parents, Edmund and Elizabeth Carey, on August 17, 1761 in the town of Paulerspury, England. Because of a skin condition, Carey initially looked for a vocation in which he could work indoors, safely away from the sun. He sought to become a shoemaker's apprentice, which suited both his medical needs and his plodding temperament. While studying his trade, a fellow apprentice, John Warr, called Carey's Anglican convictions into question. They debated the issue between themselves for a time, but Warr eventually convinced Carey to listen to Thomas Chater's preaching. Chater was a dissenting minister, and Warr had hoped that Chater might persuade Carey to leave his Anglican views and become a dissenter himself. Carey did listen to Chater's preaching, which raised more questions and caused Carey to set out to find the truth. According to Samuel Pearce, after carefully studying the question, Carey realized the error of Anglicanism and discovered his own need of conversion. He "exchanged the pharisee's self-righteousness for the publican's meekness, and flung his sorely-felt helplessness upon Christ's grace. In his contrite spirit the Holy One could dwell. In the crucified and risen Redeemer, he found deliverance and peace."[43] After Carey was converted, the Particular Baptist, John Ryland Jr., baptized him.[44]

William Carey's Calvinism

Though he was originally an Arminian, Carey became a Calvinist through the influence of Thomas Skinner, who gave him a copy of *Help*

[43] S. Pearce Carey, *William Carey* (1923; reprint, London: The Carey Press, 1934), 32.

[44] For more biographical information about William Carey, see Timothy George, *Faithful Witness: The Life and Mission of William Carey* (Birmingham, AL: New Hope Press, 1991); Pearce Carey, *William Carey*.

to Zion's Travelers by Robert Hall. Hall's book presented and defended the evangelical Calvinism of Particular Baptists and helped Carey to comprehend and systematize the teachings of Scripture about divine sovereignty and human responsibility in salvation. Carey wrote:

> Mr. Skinner one day made me a present of Mr. Hall's *Help to Zion's Travelers*; in which I found all that arranged and illustrated which I had been so long picking up by scraps. I do not remember ever to have read any book with such raptures as I did that. If it was poison as some then said, it was so sweet to me that I drank it greedily to the bottom of the cup. And, I rejoice to say, that those doctrines are the choice of my heart to this day.[45]

When Carey speaks of "those doctrines," he is referring to the doctrines of grace, that system of theology which exalts the sovereignty of God in the salvation of sinners. Tom Nettles says, "In addition to the Hall volume, Carey began to frequent places of worship where he would hear sermons from respected and trusted ministers."[46] It was through such biblical Calvinistic preaching that he became more and more convinced of Calvinistic theology.

Carey's motivation for global missions was deeply rooted in his Calvinism. He believed that God is great and worthy of worship among all the nations; therefore, Christian missionaries should go to the nations to evangelize the lost and plant churches. He further believed that God promised to save men and women from every tribe and tongue and that God's sovereign promise could not fail because He would certainly bring it to pass by irresistibly and effectually calling the elect of all nations to Himself. Timothy George correctly notes, "While his plan was a call for action based on genuine compassion for the lost, it was grounded in something deeper still; namely, the character of God himself."[47]

Far from having any hyper-Calvinistic tendencies, Carey's Calvinism was much like Andrew Fuller's "strict Calvinism." Carey had learned from Fuller and Fuller from Edwards "that evangelism and Calvinism could be reconciled. There was no contradiction between the universal obligation of all who hear the gospel to believe in Christ and the sovereign decision

---

[45] Eustace Carey, *Memoir of William Carey, D.D.* (Hartford, Canfield, and Robins, 1837), 16.

[46] Nettles, *The Baptists*, 1:283.

[47] Timothy George, "William Carey," in *The British Particular Baptists 1638–1910*, ed. Michael A. G. Haykin (Springfield, MO: Particular Baptist Press, 2000), 2:153.

of God to save those whom he has chosen."[48] All human beings have the "natural ability" to believe in Christ and all are thus responsible to believe in Him. The problem with sinners is not that they lack natural ability, but that they lack the desire to come to Christ for salvation. Therefore, Carey believed in freely inviting and calling all men without exception or distinction to come to Christ for salvation, but he understood that only the elect would respond to that call.

The Mission to India: Calvinism and Local Churches

Carey's strategy for his mission in India was based on both his Calvinistic soteriology and Baptist ecclesiology. His Calvinism furnished him with the strength and discipline to continue plodding in his mission work.[49] He believed that his primary work was to pray, preach, teach, and translate the Bible. He did all these things without any visible evidence of fruitfulness for seven years. Carey wrote:

> I feel as a farmer does about his crop: sometimes I think the seed is springing and thus I hope; a little time blasts all, and my hopes are gone like a cloud. They were only weeds which appeared; or if a little corn sprung up, it quickly dies, being either choked with weeds, or parched up by the sun of persecution. Yet I still hope in God, and will go forth in his strength, and make mention of his righteousness, even of his only.[50]

Carey understood that his role was to be faithful to what God had commanded, and that God's role was to bring about the conversion of sinners. This knowledge strengthened his resolve to continue in the work, while entrusting the outcome to the Lord.

Carey's Baptist convictions also gave shape to his mission work. He did not believe that local churches would be established and grown through political change, but only as the Word and Spirit penetrated human hearts. So, Carey set out, not primarily to influence Indian culture, but to preach the gospel for the salvation of souls and to establish local churches with regenerate memberships. He explained the missionary's strategy from the book of Acts using Paul's missionary journeys as templates for the present.

---

[48] Ibid., 2:151.

[49] For more on Carey's Calvinistic motivation for mission work, see William Travis, "William Carey: The Modern Missions Movement and the Sovereignty of God," in *The Grace of God and the Bondage of the Will*, eds. Thomas R. Schreiner and Bruce A. Ware (Grand Rapids, MI: Baker, 1995), 2:323–36.

[50] George, "William Carey," 2:156.

He wrote:

> Paul and Barnabas, however, went forward; in every city they preached
> the Word of the Lord, entering into the Jewish synagogues and first
> preaching Christ to them, and then to the Gentiles. They were heard
> with great candor and eagerness by some, and rejected by others with ob-
> stinacy and wrath, and cruel persecution.... Having penetrated as far as
> Derbe, they thought proper to return by the way that they came, calling
> at every city where they had sown the good seed, and finding in most, if
> not all these places, some who had embraced the gospel, they exhorted
> and strengthened them in the faith, formed them into a church state, and
> ordained them elders, fasted and prayed with them.[51]

Carey showed that Paul preached the gospel and God provided the
harvest of souls. Paul then gathered these God-given converts into local
churches and set up biblical church polity for them. Carey patterned his
own mission work after Paul's when he went to India. He preached the
Word and trusted God to provide conversions in His time through His
appointed means. When Carey finally did see converts, he baptized them
and assembled them into local churches of regenerate membership with
biblical polity and biblical church discipline.

Carey never confused the church and the state or mingled the kingdom of God with the fallen world, but he did believe that when established
churches are faithful to Christ's commands, they address social concerns.
Timothy George writes:

> [Carey] was deeply disturbed by the horrors of the slave trade and joined
> with other evangelical Christians in calling for the abolition of this evil
> institution.... Although Carey never lost sight of the eternal destiny of
> every person made in the image of God, he was from the beginning also
> concerned with the "this worldly" aspects of the Gospel.[52]

Thus, Carey was a faithful Calvinistic Baptist missionary who understood the priorities of his missionary calling, to preach the gospel for conversions and to establish biblical churches. But he also understood that
Christians are to keep Christ's commandments in this world, effecting
social change, if possible, to the glory of God. Carey was a strict Calvinist
whose Calvinism fueled and strengthened his missionary heart, and he was
a Baptist whose orthodox Baptist ecclesiology provided the structure of his
missionary endeavor.

---

[51] William Carey, *An Enquiry into the Obligations of Christians, to Use Means
for the Conversion of the Heathens* (Leicester: n.p., 1792), 20–21.

[52] George, "William Carey," 2:146.

Conclusion

This chapter has sought to prove that Calvinism and Baptist ecclesiology are not inconsistent but find happy agreement both logically and historically. Benjamin Keach, Andrew Fuller, and William Carey were all shown to be staunch Calvinists who were also convinced Baptists. Many other Calvinistic Baptists could have also been examined. English Baptists, such as John Spilsbury, William Kiffin, Hanserd Knollys, and John Gill, and American Baptists, such as John Clarke, Isaac Backus, John Leland, Oliver Hart, John Gano, Richard Furman, and Shubal Stearns, were all Calvinists and Baptists.

Calvinism has categories sufficient to support the distinction between the Old and New Testament structures of the church, the separation of church and state, religious tolerance and liberty, regenerate church membership, congregationalism, strong confessional subscription, and church discipline. Historic Calvinistic Baptists have written extensively on these subjects and they have practiced them in their own churches. Therefore, far from undermining Baptist ecclesiology, history shows that Calvinism serves to support and advance it.

Index of People and Places

385

Index of Scripture References

CPSIA information can be obtained at www.ICGtesting.com
Printed in the USA
LVOW090229290612

288059LV00001BD/4/P